journey of transformation

Edited by John Ranieri and
Peter Savastano

SETON HALL UNIVERSITY

Kendall Hunt
publishing company

Kendall Hunt
publishing company

www.kendallhunt.com
Send all inquiries to:
4050 Westmark Drive
Dubuque, IA 52004-1840

Printed in the United States of America
10 9 8 7 6 5 4 3

Epigraph

The purpose of education is to show a person how to define himself authentically and spontaneously in relation to his world—not to impose a prefabricated definition of the world, still less an arbitrary definition of the individual himself. The world is made up of the people who are fully alive in it: that is, of the people who can be themselves in it and can enter into a living and fruitful relationship with each other in it. The world is, therefore, more real in proportion as the people in it are able to be more fully and more humanly alive: that is to say, better able to make a lucid and conscious use of their freedom. Basically, this freedom must consist first of all in the capacity to choose their own lives, to find themselves on the deepest possible level. A superficial freedom to wander aimlessly here and there, to taste this or that, to make a choice of distractions (in Pascal's sense) is simply a sham. It claims to be freedom of "choice" when it has evaded the basic task discovering who it is that chooses. It is not free because it is unwilling to face the risk of self-discovery.

The function of a university is, then, first of all to help the student discover himself: to recognize himself, and to identify who it is that chooses.

This description will be recognized at once as unconventional and, in fact, monastic. To put it in even more outrageous terms, the function of the university is to help men and women save their souls and, in so doing, to save their society: from what? From the hell of meaninglessness, of obsession, of complex artifice, of systematic lying, of criminal evasions and neglects, of self-destructive futilities.

Thomas Merton, "Learning to Live" 358–59

Contents

To the Reader vii

Overview. ix

I. *Nostra Aetate*   1

II. Plato   5

The Apology of Socrates 6

The Republic—Allegory of the Cave 22

The Republic—The Myth of Er 25

The Symposium (selections). 30

III. The Hebrew Bible   43

Genesis—The Story of Abraham 53

Genesis—The Story of Joseph 62

Exodus (selections) 73

Ruth. 97

IV. The New Testament   115

The Gospel According to Luke 117

The Acts of the Apostles (selections). 153

V. *The Bhagavad Gita* (selections)   175

VI. St. Augustine   197

The Confessions (selections) 200

VII. Dante Alighieri   233

The Divine Comedy 233

Inferno (selections) 235

Purgatory (selections) 277

Paradise (selections) 290

VIII. Charles Dickens   301

A Christmas Carol 304

IX. Leo Tolstoy   343

The Death of Ivan Ilych 346

X. Pope Benedict XVI   377

God Is Love (selections) 377

XI. Thomas Merton   395

"Learning to Live" 397

To the Reader

What is the best way to live? No question is more important. The readings assembled in this volume each attempt to address it. When reading them you may find that they sometimes offer remarkably similar answers, but in other ways they diverge significantly. In the latter case, you, the reader, are confronted with a challenge—which *is* the best way to live? How are you to decide? Not to decide is not an option, since this is not just any question, but the question about how we are to live. Whatever your goals, plans, dreams—however you go about the day to day business of living, you are already operating with some ideas about how this question is to be answered. Most likely these ideas have their origins in the influences that have shaped you up to this point in your life—family, friends, peers, religious tradition, and the values embodied in American society. Perhaps you have been influenced by things you have read, listened to, or watched. Whatever the sources of ideas, values, and goals that guide your approach to life, the aim of this course is to get you to think about how you live and why. One of the best ways to begin thinking about these questions is to consider what others who have thought deeply about them have said.

Most of the texts found in this reader are considered "classics." But you are not being asked to read them simply because others have judged them to be classics. Rather, the reason why they have been designated classics is because, regardless of their age, these works have shown a remarkable ability to speak to people across the centuries. We read them for their abiding relevance, not because they are old. Bear this in mind as you read. Perhaps this is your first encounter with these texts. If so, you may find at least some of them to be unfamiliar, challenging, or even frustrating to read. In the case of a book such as the Bible, you may have the opposite experience. If you come from a religious tradition that takes the Bible to be the word of God, you may think that you already know what it means.

In any case, regardless of the level of familiarity or unfamiliarity you bring to these texts, it is important to adopt certain intellectual attitudes when reading. The first would be openness. Many of the authors you will be reading come from perspectives other than your own. In order to understand them you will need to make an effort to enter into their perspective.

A second and related attitude you will need is intellectual humility. When confronted with readings that are difficult or unfamiliar you may be tempted to dismiss the ideas encountered as stupid or irrelevant. Resist this temptation. Be open to the possibility that the author you are reading is smarter than you are, has thought more deeply about these things than you have, and is offering a perspective on how to live that needs to be taken seriously. If you are confused, annoyed, or frustrated by a particular reading, it is not a sign that the author is a dope; your reaction might very well indicate that you need to delve more deeply into the text in order to grasp the author's meaning. As a general rule, it is wise to bear in mind that you need to understand an author before you are capable of forming a judgment about what you have read.

A third quality you will need in approaching these readings is an attitude of attentiveness. The selections found in this volume are not meant to be perused superficially. They are meant to be read with care and reflection. They have been carefully selected and edited so that you can get a basic sense of the authors without being overwhelmed with an enormous amount of reading. One of the primary reasons for doing this is so that you will have time to read attentively. Please give the readings the attention they deserve.

Finally, it might be useful to consider why we designate certain courses as "core." At the risk of stating the obvious, it is because "core" means essential, fundamental, basic; and, as noted above, there is no question more important than the question concerning how we are to live. Notice also that the focus here is on fundamental *questions*. The aim of a course such as "Journey of Transformation" is to get you, the reader, to consider certain questions about what makes for a worthwhile life. We trust that, over time, you will work out answers for yourself. This book is written with the conviction that the authors included here can be of some help in that process.

Overview

One of the most appealing features for both students who take CORE 1101: "The Journey of Transformation" and CORE 2101: "Christianity and Culture in Dialogue," and for the professors who teach them, is that these two Signature Courses are often taught through the lens of the particular scholarly discipline of the professor who teaches them. "The Journey of Transformation," the course that you are about to embark upon, is a journey; and hopefully you will be transformed by having taken it, as well as enriched by the disciplinary perspective of your professor for the course. While it may seem both a cliché and trite, this course has the potential to truly transform the way you understand the Catholic tradition intellectually and spiritually, the world in which you live, and, most importantly, your own personal life. This is true both metaphorically and literally.

Over the past 20 years, neuroscience research has demonstrated that what we think and the ideas to which we expose ourselves have a direct impact upon our physical, emotional, and spiritual well-being. Our brains, it seems, are much more malleable than we believed. Therefore, in many ways, we are what we think. Based on the theory of neuroplasticity, which is the technical term for the malleability of the brain, the ideas that you will explore in "The Journey of Transformation" have the potential not only to transform you intellectually and spiritually but also to have positive effects upon the structure of your brain and upon your sense of wellbeing.

The course begins with a reading from *Nostra Aetate,* a document written during the Second Vatican Council. *Nostra Aetate* addresses the relationship between Christianity and Catholic Christianity in particular, and non-Christian religious traditions. We might think of the selection from *Nostra Aetate* as setting the tone for the rest of the course. The aim of this first reading is to highlight what is universally good and true in the non-Christian traditions, most especially in relation to the other two Abrahamic religious traditions, Judaism and Islam, as well as all that is true and good in Hinduism and Buddhism. *Nostra Aetate* also outlines what it is about the Christian Revelation that is unique in relation to these non-Christian traditions.

From there we move on to Plato's *Republic* and particularly to the famous "allegory of the cave." This selection actually has a lot in common with the selection from the *Bhagavad Gita* that you will read a bit later in the semester. Both the "allegory of the cave" in Plato's *Republic* and the selection from the *Gita* stress that there is a stark contrast between how we humans perceive truth from actual Truth. Hopefully, reading both of these texts will inspire you to embark on your own search for a firsthand experience of Truth with a capital "T" and to awaken you from your deluded sense of reality to that which is "really" Real. After reading the *Republic,* you will read Plato's *Apology,* or, more correctly, *The Apology of Socrates,* which tells the story of the trial of Socrates and his death sentence by poisoning. In many ways the

Apology is about what happens when one questions the cherished beliefs of one's society, such as Socrates did. Perhaps here we can think of the transformative effects of living philosophy as a way of life. To do so can often transform one's worldview with such depth and poignancy that it no longer is possible to remain quiet, even though to speak out, as Socrates did, cost him his life. Social change agents are not always appreciated by the societies and cultures that are the targets of such agents.

Christianity shares a common heritage with Judaism and with the ancient Greeks. The Hebrew Scriptures, which Christians commonly refer to as the Old Testament or the First Testament, and the writings of Plato and other Greek philosophers of the time, were foundational to the thinking of the early Fathers of the Church. Therefore, it's fitting after Plato that our next selections are drawn from the Hebrew Bible, specifically from the Books of Genesis, Exodus, and Ruth. Each of these three readings stresses the themes of journey and transformation, respectively. In Genesis we read the story of Abraham being called by God to go forth from his homeland to a new place. In Exodus, the Hebrew people are led by God from enslavement in Egypt to wander in the desert for 40 years, mysteriously led by God in the form of a "pillar of smoke" to the Promised Land where God has promised them they will thrive and flourish. In Ruth, we read about the relationship between Ruth and her mother-in-law Naomi. Despite Naomi's attempts to convince Ruth not to follow her back to Bethlehem, Ruth nevertheless pledges her fidelity to go with Naomi wherever she may go.

From the readings in the Hebrew Scriptures we move on to the selections from the foundational text of Christianity, the New Testament. Specifically, we read Luke's Gospel in which the ultimate transcendent mystery of God's personal love is revealed and embodied in the person and life of Jesus of Nazareth. Having grounded ourselves in the Gospel narrative of Jesus' earthly life as written by Luke, we move on to read selections of Augustine's *Confessions,* thought by some scholars to be one of the first autobiographies and the prototype for that genre up to the present time.

While Augustine does not have a major role in the Eastern or Greek Church, his impact is significant in the Latin or Roman Church where his theology has played, and still plays, an important role in how the Church understands the redemptive role of Jesus' life, death, and resurrection in the economy of salvation. In this sense, reading Augustine's *Confessions* is the model par excellence of and for a journey of transformation. Following Augustine, we are offered selections from Dante's *Divine Comedy,* a poetic masterpiece if ever there was one. Dante takes his readers on a visionary journey through Hell, Purgatory, and Paradise, the invisible worlds of the Christian cosmos. A product of the medieval world with its privileging of allegorical and symbolic approaches to reading texts, the many different levels of meaning that such an approach to reading Dante provides have been a source of spiritual transformation for those who have read him from the time in which he wrote to the present. Perhaps reading Dante's *Divine Comedy* will have a similar transformative effect on you.

While during the course of the semester you will also read selections from other more modern sources to be chosen by your professor, we end "The Journey of Transformation" with a selection from Pope Benedict's *Deus Caritas Est* (God is Love), a contemporary reflection on one of the most important of Christian doctrines, "God is Love." In this encyclical, the transformative effects of God's Love are elucidated by insights Pope Benedict offers his readers about the different forms of human love in relation to God's Love—the transformative effects of God's Love in personal human relationships, including erotic love; the relationship between Christian Charity and political justice; the relationship between the Church and the state; and, the symbiotic relationship of all of the foregoing by which the world can be transfigured and transformed by the power of Love.

Hopefully, through reading and thinking deeply about each of these important selections, as well as by discussing them in class with your professor and with your fellow students, you will gain important insights into what it means to be human, what really matters and is of lasting value in terms of your own life journey, and the riches the Catholic intellectual tradition has to offer to potentially help you grow as a human being and to inspire you to make a valuable contribution to the world in which we live in these first few decades of the 21st century.

Nostra Aetate

Editors' Introduction

It is not an overstatement to say that the Second Vatican Council has had (and continues to have) a greater impact on the Catholic Church than any event since the Protestant Reformation. Vatican Two was an ecumenical council, that is, a meeting of representatives of the entire Church, consisting mainly of the world's Catholic bishops. The Council was called by Pope John XXXIII in January of 1959. One of the main purposes behind Pope John's calling of an ecumenical council was to provide the Church with an opportunity for updating (*aggiornamento* in Italian), especially with regard to the Church's attitude toward the modern world. It would not be accurate, though, to say that Pope John set out to "modernize" the Church. His intention was to draw upon tradition in order to address contemporary questions. In his opening address to the Council, John warned those assembled not to heed the "prophets of gloom" in their midst, who saw only the negative aspects of modern society. The pope was not advocating an uncritical acceptance of everything modern, but he was nudging the Church in the direction of a more open yet critical stance toward modernity. He also made a point of reminding his listeners that while the substance of the Catholic faith was permanent and abiding, the way that faith was expressed could vary in accordance with the needs of the time and place. The Council met from October 9, 1962 to December 8, 1965 in four two to three month sessions. It produced sixteen documents: four major Constitutions, nine Decrees, and three Declarations (including *Nostra Aetate*). The legacy and proper understanding of the Council is still debated, and these debates show little sign of abating any time soon.

One result of the Council's work on which there is near unanimous agreement is that *Nostra Aetate* represented a significant change in the attitude of the Catholic Church toward other religions. It was promulgated on October 28, 1965. The brevity of the declaration belies its importance as a breakthrough in inter-religious dialogue. Nowhere is this change more evident than in the document's treatment of Judaism and the Jewish people. Centuries of negative attitudes toward Judaism were repudiated in the space of one paragraph. The Jewish roots of Christianity are emphasized, the collective charge against the Jewish people for the death of Jesus is rejected, and anti-Semitism is decried. If today's readers of the text take for granted the attitude toward other religions displayed in the document, this may be due in part (at least among Catholics) to the fact that the teaching of Nostra Aetate has been taken to heart over the last five decades. Beginning as it does with the recognition that the quest for meaning is common to all people, *Nostra Aetate* is a fitting text with which to begin a volume that takes this quest to be its central focus.

Declaration on the Relation of the Church to Non-Christian Religions

1. In this age of ours, when men are drawing more closely together and the bonds of friendship between different peoples are being strengthened, the Church examines with greater care the relation which she has to non-Christian religions. Ever aware of her duty to foster unity and charity among individuals, and even among nations, she reflects at the outset on what men have in common and what tends to promote fellowship among them.

All men form but one community. This is so because all stem from the one stock which God created to people the entire earth (cf. Acts 17:26), and also because all share a common destiny, namely God. His providence, evident goodness, and, saving designs extend to all men (cf. Wis. 8:1; Acts 14:17; Rom. 2; 6-7; 1 Tim. 2:4) against the day when the elect are gathered together in the holy city which is illumined by the glory of God, and in whose splendor all peoples will walk (cf. Apoc. 21:23 ff.).

Men look to their different religions for an answer to the unsolved riddles of human existence. The problems that weigh heavily on the hearts of men are the same today as in the ages past. What is man? What is the meaning and purpose of life? What is upright behavior, and what is sinful? Where does suffering originate, and what end does it serve? How can genuine happiness be found? What happens at death? What is judgment? What reward follows death? And finally, what is the ultimate mystery, beyond human explanation, which embraces our entire existence, from which we take our origin and towards which we tend?

2. Throughout history even to the present day, there is found among different peoples a certain awareness of a hidden power, which lies behind the course of nature and the events of human life. At times there is present even a recognition of a supreme being, or still more of

a Father. This awareness and recognition results in a way of life that is imbued with a deep religious sense. The religions which are found in more advanced civilizations endeavor by way of well-defined concepts and exact language to answer these questions. Thus, in Hinduism men explore the divine mystery and express it both in the limitless riches of myth and the accurately defined insights of philosophy. They seek release from the trials of the present life by ascetical practices, profound meditation and recourse to God in confidence and love. Buddhism in its various forms testifies to the essential inadequacy of this changing world. It proposes a way of life by which men can, with confidence and trust, attain a state of perfect liberation and reach supreme illumination either through their own efforts or by the aid of divine help. So, too, other religions which are found throughout the world attempt in their own ways to calm the hearts of men by outlining a program of life covering doctrine, moral precepts and sacred rites.

The Catholic Church rejects nothing of what is true and holy in these religions. She has a high regard for the manner of life and conduct, the precepts and doctrines which, although differing in many ways from her own teaching, nevertheless often reflect a ray of that truth which enlightens all men. Yet she proclaims and is in duty bound to proclaim without fail, Christ who is the way, the truth and the life (Jn. 1:6). In him, in whom God reconciled all things to himself (2 Cor. 5:18-19), men find the fulness of their religious life.

The Church, therefore, urges her sons to enter with prudence and charity into discussion and collaboration with members of other religions. Let Christians, while witnessing to their own faith and way of life, acknowledge, preserve and encourage the spiritual and moral truths found among non-Christians, also their social life and culture.

3. The Church has also a high regard for the Muslims. They worship God, who is one, living and subsistent, merciful and almighty, the Creator of heaven and earth,[1] who has also spoken to men. They strive to submit themselves without reserve to the hidden decrees of God, just as Abraham submitted himself to God's plan, to whose faith Muslims eagerly link their own. Although not acknowledging him as God, they venerate Jesus as a prophet, his virgin Mother they also honor, and even at times devoutly invoke. Further, they await the day of judgment and the reward of God following the resurrection of the dead. For this reason they highly esteem an upright life and worship God, especially by way of prayer, alms-deeds and fasting.

Over the centuries many quarrels and dissensions have arisen between Christians and Muslims. The sacred Council now pleads with all to forget the past, and urges that a sincere effort be made to achieve mutual understanding; for the benefit of all men, let them together preserve and promote peace, liberty, social justice and moral values.

4. Sounding the depths of the mystery which is the Church, this sacred Council remembers the spiritual ties which link the people of the New Covenant to the stock of Abraham.

The Church of Christ acknowledges that in God's plan of salvation the beginning of her faith and election is to be found in the patriarchs, Moses and the prophets. She professes that all Christ's faithful, who as men of faith are sons of Abraham (cf. Gal. 3:7), are included in the same patriarch's call and that the salvation of the Church is mystically prefigured in the exodus of God's chosen people from the land of bondage. On this account the Church cannot forget that she received the revelation of the Old Testament by way of that people with whom God in his inexpressible mercy established the ancient covenant. Nor can she forget that she draws nourishment from that good olive tree onto which the wild olive branches of the Gentiles have been grafted (cf. Rom. 11:17-24). The Church believes that Christ who is our peace has through his cross reconciled Jews and Gentiles and made them one in himself (cf. Eph. 2:14–16).

Likewise, the Church keeps ever before her mind the words of the apostle Paul about his kinsmen: "they are Israelites, and to them belong the sonship, the glory, the covenants, the giving of the law, the worship, and the promises; to them belong the patriarchs, and of their race according to the flesh, is the Christ" (Rom. 9:4–5), the son of the virgin Mary. She is mindful, moreover, that the apostles, the pillars on which the Church stands, are of Jewish descent, as are many of those early disciples who proclaimed the Gospel of Christ to the world.

As holy Scripture testifies, Jerusalem did not recognize God's moment when it came (cf. Lk. 19:42). Jews for the most part did not accept the Gospel; on the contrary, many opposed the spreading of it (cf. Rom. 11:28). Even so, the apostle Paul maintains that the Jews remain very dear to God, for the sake of the patriarchs, since God does not take back the gifts he bestowed or the choice he made.[2] Together with the prophets and that same apostle, the Church awaits the day, known to God alone, when all peoples will call on God with one voice and "serve him shoulder to shoulder" (Soph. 3:9; cf. Is. 66:23; Ps. 65:4; Rom. 11:11–32).

Since Christians and Jews have such a common spiritual heritage, this sacred Council wishes to encourage and further mutual understanding and appreciation. This can be obtained, especially, by way of biblical and theological enquiry and through friendly discussions.

Even though the Jewish authorities and those who followed their lead pressed for the death of Christ (cf. John 19:6), neither all Jews indiscriminately at that time, nor Jews today, can be charged with the crimes committed during his

---

1. Cf. St. Gregory VII, Letter 21 to Anzir (Muir), King of Mauretania (*PL* 148, col. 450 ff.).
2. Cf. Rom. 11:28-29; cf. Dogm. Const. *Lumen Gentium* (*AAS* 57, 1965, 20).

passion. It is true that the Church is the new people of God, yet the Jews should not be spoken of as rejected or accursed as if this followed from holy Scripture. Consequently, all must take care, lest in catechizing or in preaching the Word of God, they teach anything which is not in accord with the truth of the Gospel message or the spirit of Christ.

Indeed, the Church reproves every form of persecution against whomsoever it may be directed. Remembering, then, her common heritage with the Jews and moved not by any political consideration, but solely by the religious motivation of Christian charity, she deplores all hatreds, persecutions, displays of antisemitism leveled at any time or from any source against the Jews.[b]

The Church always held and continues to hold that Christ out of infinite love freely underwent suffering and death because of the sins of all men so that all might attain salvation. It is the duty of the Church, therefore, in her preaching to proclaim the cross of Christ as the sign of God's universal love and the source of all grace.

5. We cannot truly pray to God the Father of all if we treat any people in other than brotherly fashion, for all men are created in God's image. Man's relation to God the Father and man's relation to his fellow-men are so dependent on each other that the Scripture says "he who does not love, does not know God" (1 Jn. 4:8).

There is no basis therefore, either in theory or in practice for any discrimination between individual and individual or between people and people arising either from human dignity or from the rights which flow from it.

Therefore, the Church reproves, as foreign to the mind of Christ, any discrimination against people or any harassment of them on the basis of their race, color, condition in life or religion. Accordingly, following the footsteps of the holy apostles Peter and Paul, the sacred Council earnestly begs the Christian faithful to "conduct themselves well among the Gentiles" (1 Pet. 2:12) and if possible, as far as depends on them, to be at peace with all men (cf. 12:18) and in that way to be true sons of the Father who is in heaven (cf. Mt. 5:45).

---

b See D. 57.

Plato

Editors' Introduction

Nowhere is philosophy as a way of life presented more eloquently and beautifully than in the dialogues of Plato. Central to these dialogues is the figure of Socrates, who was Plato's teacher and mentor. Socrates left no writing of his own, so it is mainly through Plato that we know about the Socratic way of philosophizing. There seems to be general agreement among scholars that of Plato's nearly thirty works, the earlier dialogues probably capture the essence of the historical Socrates more closely than the later dialogues, where Plato begins to use Socrates as a mouthpiece for his own philosophical views.

Plato (427–347 B.C.) was born into an aristocratic family in Athens. To be an adult male citizen of a Greek city-state (*polis*) such as Athens normally meant taking an active part in its civic life. It is clear from many of Plato's dialogues that he took an enormous interest in the relationship between the philosophical life and the world of politics. However, having seen Socrates condemned to death by the citizen-jurors of Athens,

Plato withdrew from active engagement in politics. Instead, he founded a school known as the Academy, whose most famous student was the philosopher Aristotle. Apparently the lure of politics continued to exert a pull on Plato, and in the later part of his life he attempted to put his political philosophy into practice in the Greek city-state of Syracuse (in present day Sicily). These efforts were unsuccessful, and Plato returned to Athens.

Following his teacher Socrates, Plato's approach to philosophy emphasizes the idea of conducting one's life by following one's questions. At least in the early dialogues, Socrates rarely if ever comes to a definite conclusion about the questions he raises. Philosophy, so understood, is literally "love of wisdom," without any implication that wisdom is already possessed by the philosopher. To turn Plato's philosophy into a series of doctrines or answers to philosophical questions is to seriously distort its meaning and purpose. Plato deliberately chose to write in dialogical form, so as to engage his readers in a process of questioning. And from his esteemed teacher he learned that the best place to begin is by questioning oneself.

Apology of Socrates

When reading the Apology, it will quickly become clear that Socrates does not seem to be apologizing for anything (if by "apology" we mean saying we are sorry for having done something wrong). Instead, "apology" as used here is more accurately understood as Socrates' defense of himself at his trial. The dialogue is an account, written by Plato, of one of the most famous trials in history. How much of the dialogue records "what actually happened" and how much is based upon Plato's recollection or imagination is still debated. The main reason to read the Apology is that it is such a wonderful example of what it means to practice philosophy as a way of life. Today it is more common to think of philosophy as an academic discipline, forced on students as part of their university education. But for Socrates, philosophy was fundamentally about how to live. Approach the dialogue with this in mind.

The trial of Socrates (469–399 B.C.) took place in Athens in 399 B.C. The court that tried him was composed of 501 citizen jurors, selected by lot. The decision of the court was based upon a majority vote. It is worth noting that Athens was at the time undergoing a period of political unrest, with the result that the city was agitated and full of tensions. Some of Socrates' friends and allies were in the thick of this crisis, and he may very well have been a victim of the passions unleashed by the conflicts besetting the city. But the dialogue also makes it clear that Socrates had made enemies for himself by his relentless questioning of the beliefs of Athenian society.

The work is divided into three parts. The first part consists of Socrates' actual defense, including his response to the specific charges leveled against him. This section constitutes most of the dialogue. The second part is a short speech given by Socrates after his conviction in which he proposes what he deems to be the most appropriate penalty. The dialogue ends with Socrates' warning to Athens in which he prophesies that his death will not bring about the end of the city's woes. As the dialogue concludes, readers are left wondering whether Socrates' speech to his accusers is much of a defense at all, and what that could mean.

How you, O Athenians, have been affected by my accusers, I cannot tell; but I know that they almost made me forget who I was—so persuasively did they speak; and yet they have hardly uttered a word of truth. But of the many falsehoods told by them, there was one which quite amazed me;—I mean when they said that you should be upon your guard and not allow yourselves to be deceived by the force of my eloquence. To say this, when they were certain to be detected as soon as I opened my lips and proved myself to be anything but a great speaker, did indeed appear to me most shameless—unless by the force of eloquence they mean the force of truth; for if such is their meaning, I admit that I am eloquent. But in how different a way from theirs! Well, as I was saying, they have scarcely spoken the truth at all; but from me you shall hear the whole truth: not, however, delivered after their manner in a set oration duly ornamented with words and phrases. No, by heaven! but I shall use the words and arguments which occur to me at the moment; for I am confident in the justice of my cause (Or, I am certain that I am right in taking this course.): at my time of life I ought not to be appearing before you, O men of Athens, in the character of a juvenile orator—let no one expect it of me. And I must beg of you to grant me a favour:—If I defend myself in my accustomed manner, and you hear me using the words which I have been in the habit of using in the agora, at the tables of the money-changers, or anywhere else, I would ask you not to be surprised, and not to interrupt me on this account. For I am more than seventy years of age, and appearing now for the first time in a court of law, I am quite a stranger to the language of the place; and therefore I would have you regard me as if I were really a stranger, whom you would excuse if he spoke in his native tongue, and after the fashion of his country:—Am I making an unfair request of you? Never mind the manner, which may or may not be good; but think only of the truth of my words, and give heed to that: let the speaker speak truly and the judge decide justly.

And first, I have to reply to the older charges and to my first accusers, and then I will go on to the later ones. For of old I have had many accusers, who have accused me falsely to you during many years; and I am more afraid of them than of Anytus and his associates, who are dangerous, too, in their own way. But far more dangerous are the others, who began when you were children, and took possession of your minds with their falsehoods, telling of one Socrates, a wise man, who speculated about the heaven above, and searched into the earth beneath, and made the worse appear the better cause. The disseminators of this tale are the accusers whom I dread; for their hearers are apt to fancy that such enquirers do not believe in the existence of the gods. And they are many, and their charges against me are of ancient date, and they were made by them in the days when you were more impressible than you are now—in childhood, or it may have been in youth—and the cause when heard went by default, for there was none to answer. And hardest of all, I do not know and cannot tell the names of my accusers; unless in the chance case of a Comic poet. All who from envy and malice have persuaded you—some of them having first convinced themselves—all this class of men are most difficult to deal with; for I cannot have them up here, and cross-examine them, and therefore I must simply fight with shadows in my own defence, and argue when there is no one who answers. I will ask you then to assume with me, as I was saying, that my opponents are of two kinds; one recent, the other ancient: and I hope that you will see the propriety of my answering the latter first, for these accusations you heard long before the others, and much oftener.

Well, then, I must make my defence, and endeavour to clear away in a short time, a slander which has lasted a long time. May I succeed, if to succeed be for my good and yours, or likely to avail me in my cause! The task is not an easy one; I quite understand the nature of it. And so leaving the event with God, in obedience to the law I will now make my defence.

I will begin at the beginning, and ask what is the accusation which has given rise to the slander of me, and in fact has encouraged Meletus to prove this charge against me. Well, what do the slanderers say? They shall be my prosecutors, and I will sum up their words in an affidavit: 'Socrates is an evil-doer, and a curious person, who searches into things under the earth and in heaven, and he makes the worse appear the better cause; and he teaches the aforesaid doctrines to others.' Such is the nature of the accusation: it is just what you have yourselves seen in the comedy of Aristophanes (Aristoph., Clouds.), who has introduced a man whom he calls Socrates, going about and saying that he walks in air, and talking a deal of nonsense concerning matters of which I do not pretend to know either much or little—not that I mean to speak disparagingly of any one who is a student of natural philosophy. I should be very sorry if Meletus could bring so grave a charge against me. But the simple truth is, O Athenians, that I have nothing to do with physical speculations. Very many of those here present are witnesses to the truth of this, and to them I appeal. Speak then, you who have heard me, and tell your neighbours whether any of you have ever known me to hold forth in few words or in many upon such matters . . . You hear their answer. And from what they say of this part of the charge you will be able to judge of the truth of the rest.

As little foundation is there for the report that I am a teacher, and take money; this accusation has no more truth in it than the other. Although, if a man were really able to instruct mankind, to receive money for giving instruction would, in my opinion, be an honour to him. There is Gorgias of Leontium, and Prodicus of Ceos, and

Hippias of Elis, who go the round of the cities, and are able to persuade the young men to leave their own citizens by whom they might be taught for nothing, and come to them whom they not only pay, but are thankful if they may be allowed to pay them. There is at this time a Parian philosopher residing in Athens, of whom I have heard; and I came to hear of him in this way:—I came across a man who has spent a world of money on the Sophists, Callias, the son of Hipponicus, and knowing that he had sons, I asked him: 'Callias,' I said, 'if your two sons were foals or calves, there would be no difficulty in finding some one to put over them; we should hire a trainer of horses, or a farmer probably, who would improve and perfect them in their own proper virtue and excellence; but as they are human beings, whom are you thinking of placing over them? Is there any one who understands human and political virtue? You must have thought about the matter, for you have sons; is there any one?' 'There is,' he said. 'Who is he?' said I; 'and of what country? and what does he charge?' 'Evenus the Parian,' he replied; 'he is the man, and his charge is five minae.' Happy is Evenus, I said to myself, if he really has this wisdom, and teaches at such a moderate charge. Had I the same, I should have been very proud and conceited; but the truth is that I have no knowledge of the kind.

I dare say, Athenians, that some one among you will reply, 'Yes, Socrates, but what is the origin of these accusations which are brought against you; there must have been something strange which you have been doing? All these rumours and this talk about you would never have arisen if you had been like other men: tell us, then, what is the cause of them, for we should be sorry to judge hastily of you.' Now I regard this as a fair challenge, and I will endeavour to explain to you the reason why I am called wise and have such an evil fame. Please to attend then. And although some of you may think that I am joking, I declare that I will tell you the entire truth. Men of Athens, this reputation of mine has come of a certain sort of wisdom which I possess. If you ask me what kind of wisdom, I reply, wisdom such as may perhaps be attained by man, for to that

extent I am inclined to believe that I am wise; whereas the persons of whom I was speaking have a superhuman wisdom which I may fail to describe, because I have it not myself; and he who says that I have, speaks falsely, and is taking away my character. And here, O men of Athens, I must beg you not to interrupt me, even if I seem to say something extravagant. For the word which I will speak is not mine. I will refer you to a witness who is worthy of credit; that witness shall be the God of Delphi—he will tell you about my wisdom, if I have any, and of what sort it is. You must have known Chaerephon; he was early a friend of mine, and also a friend of yours, for he shared in the recent exile of the people, and returned with you. Well, Chaerephon, as you know, was very impetuous in all his doings, and he went to Delphi and boldly asked the oracle to tell him whether—as I was saying, I must beg you not to interrupt—he asked the oracle to tell him whether anyone was wiser than I was, and the Pythian prophetess answered, that there was no man wiser. Chaerephon is dead himself; but his brother, who is in court, will confirm the truth of what I am saying.

Why do I mention this? Because I am going to explain to you why I have such an evil name. When I heard the answer, I said to myself, What can the god mean? and what is the interpretation of his riddle? for I know that I have no wisdom, small or great. What then can he mean when he says that I am the wisest of men? And yet he is a god, and cannot lie; that would be against his nature. After long consideration, I thought of a method of trying the question. I reflected that if I could only find a man wiser than myself, then I might go to the god with a refutation in my hand. I should say to him, 'Here is a man who is wiser than I am; but you said that I was the wisest.' Accordingly I went to one who had the reputation of wisdom, and observed him—his name I need not mention; he was a politician whom I selected for examination—and the result was as follows: When I began to talk with him, I could not help thinking that he was not really wise, although he was thought wise by many, and still wiser by himself; and thereupon I tried to explain to him that he thought himself wise, but was not really wise; and the consequence was that he hated me, and his enmity was shared by several who were present and heard me. So I left him, saying to myself, as I went away: Well, although I do not suppose that either of us knows anything really beautiful and good, I am better off than he is,—for he knows nothing, and thinks that he knows; I neither know nor think that I know. In this latter particular, then, I seem to have slightly the advantage of him. Then I went to another who had still higher pretensions to wisdom, and my conclusion was exactly the same. Whereupon I made another enemy of him, and of many others besides him.

Then I went to one man after another, being not unconscious of the enmity which I provoked, and I lamented and feared this: but necessity was laid upon me,—the word of God, I thought, ought to be considered first. And I said to myself, Go I must to all who appear to know, and find out the meaning of the oracle. And I swear to you, Athenians, by the dog I swear!—for I must tell you the truth—the result of my mission was just this: I found that the men most in repute were all but the most foolish; and that others less esteemed were really wiser and better. I will tell you the tale of my wanderings and of the 'Herculean' labours, as I may call them, which I endured only to find at last the oracle irrefutable. After the politicians, I went to the poets; tragic, dithyrambic, and all sorts. And there, I said to myself, you will be instantly detected; now you will find out that you are more ignorant than they are. Accordingly, I took them some of the most elaborate passages in their own writings, and asked what was the meaning of them—thinking that they would teach me something. Will you believe me? I am almost ashamed to confess the truth, but I must say that there is hardly a person present who would not have talked better about their poetry than they did themselves. Then I knew that not by wisdom do poets write poetry, but by a sort of genius and inspiration; they are like diviners or soothsayers who also say many fine things, but do not understand the meaning of them. The poets appeared

to me to be much in the same case; and I further observed that upon the strength of their poetry they believed themselves to be the wisest of men in other things in which they were not wise. So I departed, conceiving myself to be superior to them for the same reason that I was superior to the politicians.

At last I went to the artisans. I was conscious that I knew nothing at all, as I may say, and I was sure that they knew many fine things; and here I was not mistaken, for they did know many things of which I was ignorant, and in this they certainly were wiser than I was. But I observed that even the good artisans fell into the same error as the poets;—because they were good workmen they thought that they also knew all sorts of high matters, and this defect in them overshadowed their wisdom; and therefore I asked myself on behalf of the oracle, whether I would like to be as I was, neither having their knowledge nor their ignorance, or like them in both; and I made answer to myself and to the oracle that I was better off as I was.

This inquisition has led to my having many enemies of the worst and most dangerous kind, and has given occasion also to many calumnies. And I am called wise, for my hearers always imagine that I myself possess the wisdom which I find wanting in others: but the truth is, O men of Athens, that God only is wise; and by his answer he intends to show that the wisdom of men is worth little or nothing; he is not speaking of Socrates, he is only using my name by way of illustration, as if he said, He, O men, is the wisest, who, like Socrates, knows that his wisdom is in truth worth nothing. And so I go about the world, obedient to the god, and search and make enquiry into the wisdom of any one, whether citizen or stranger, who appears to be wise; and if he is not wise, then in vindication of the oracle I show him that he is not wise; and my occupation quite absorbs me, and I have no time to give either to any public matter of interest or to any concern of my own, but I am in utter poverty by reason of my devotion to the god.

There is another thing:—young men of the richer classes, who have not much to do, come about me of their own accord; they like to hear the pretenders examined, and they often imitate me, and proceed to examine others; there are plenty of persons, as they quickly discover, who think that they know something, but really know little or nothing; and then those who are examined by them instead of being angry with themselves are angry with me: This confounded Socrates, they say; this villainous misleader of youth!—and then if somebody asks them, Why, what evil does he practise or teach? they do not know, and cannot tell; but in order that they may not appear to be at a loss, they repeat the ready-made charges which are used against all philosophers about teaching things up in the clouds and under the earth, and having no gods, and making the worse appear the better cause; for they do not like to confess that their pretence of knowledge has been detected—which is the truth; and as they are numerous and ambitious and energetic, and are drawn up in battle array and have persuasive tongues, they have filled your ears with their loud and inveterate calumnies. And this is the reason why my three accusers, Meletus and Anytus and Lycon, have set upon me; Meletus, who has a quarrel with me on behalf of the poets; Anytus, on behalf of the craftsmen and politicians; Lycon, on behalf of the rhetoricians: and as I said at the beginning, I cannot expect to get rid of such a mass of calumny all in a moment. And this, O men of Athens, is the truth and the whole truth; I have concealed nothing, I have dissembled nothing. And yet, I know that my plainness of speech makes them hate me, and what is their hatred but a proof that I am speaking the truth?—Hence has arisen the prejudice against me; and this is the reason of it, as you will find out either in this or in any future enquiry.

I have said enough in my defence against the first class of my accusers; I turn to the second class. They are headed by Meletus, that good man and true lover of his country, as he calls himself. Against these, too, I must try to make a defence:—Let their affidavit be read: it contains something of this kind: It says that Socrates is a doer of evil, who corrupts the youth; and who does not believe in the gods of the state, but has other new divinities of his own. Such is the charge; and now let us examine the particular counts. He says that I am a doer of evil, and corrupt the youth; but I say, O men of Athens, that Meletus is a doer of evil, in that he pretends to be in earnest when he is only in jest, and is so eager to bring men to trial from a pretended zeal and interest about matters in which he really never had the smallest interest. And the truth of this I will endeavour to prove to you.

Come hither, Meletus, and let me ask a question of you. You think a great deal about the improvement of youth?

Yes, I do.

Tell the judges, then, who is their improver; for you must know, as you have taken the pains to discover their corrupter, and are citing and accusing me before them. Speak, then, and tell the judges who their improver is.—Observe, Meletus, that you are silent, and have nothing to say. But is not this rather disgraceful, and a very considerable proof of what I was saying, that you have no interest in the matter? Speak up, friend, and tell us who their improver is.

The laws.

But that, my good sir, is not my meaning. I want to know who the person is, who, in the first place, knows the laws.

The judges, Socrates, who are present in court.

What, do you mean to say, Meletus, that they are able to instruct and improve youth?

Certainly they are.

What, all of them, or some only and not others?

All of them.

By the goddess Here, that is good news! There are plenty of improvers, then. And what do you say of the audience,—do they improve them?

Yes, they do.

And the senators?

Yes, the senators improve them.

But perhaps the members of the assembly corrupt them?—or do they too improve them?

They improve them.

Then every Athenian improves and elevates them; all with the exception of myself; and I alone am their corrupter? Is that what you affirm?

That is what I stoutly affirm.

I am very unfortunate if you are right. But suppose I ask you a question: How about horses? Does one man do them harm and all the world good? Is not the exact opposite the truth? One man is able to do them good, or at least not many;—the trainer of horses, that is to say, does them good, and others who have to do with them rather injure them? Is not that true, Meletus, of horses, or of any other animals? Most assuredly it is; whether you and Anytus say yes or no. Happy indeed would be the condition of youth if they had one corrupter only, and all the rest of the world were their improvers. But you, Meletus, have sufficiently shown that you never had a thought about the young: your carelessness is seen in your not caring about the very things which you bring against me.

And now, Meletus, I will ask you another question—by Zeus I will: Which is better, to live among bad citizens, or among good ones? Answer, friend, I say; the question is one which may be easily answered. Do not the good do their neighbours good, and the bad do them evil?

Certainly.

And is there anyone who would rather be injured than benefited by those who live with him? Answer, my good friend, the law requires you to answer—does any one like to be injured?

Certainly not.

And when you accuse me of corrupting and deteriorating the youth, do you allege that I corrupt them intentionally or unintentionally?

Intentionally, I say.

But you have just admitted that the good do their neighbours good, and the evil do them evil. Now, is that a truth which your superior wisdom has recognized thus early in life, and am I, at my age, in such darkness and ignorance as not to know that if a man with whom I have to live is corrupted by me, I am very likely to be harmed by him; and yet I corrupt him, and intentionally, too—so you say, although neither I nor any other human being is ever likely to be convinced by you. But either I do not corrupt them, or I corrupt them unintentionally; and on either view of the case you lie. If my offence is unintentional, the law has no cognizance of unintentional offences: you ought to have taken me privately, and warned and admonished me; for if I had been better advised, I should have left off doing what I only did unintentionally—no doubt I should; but you would have nothing to say to me and refused to teach me. And now you bring me up in this court, which is a place not of instruction, but of punishment.

It will be very clear to you, Athenians, as I was saying, that Meletus has no care at all, great or small, about the matter. But still I should like to know, Meletus, in what I am affirmed to corrupt the young. I suppose you mean, as I infer from your indictment, that I teach them not to acknowledge the gods which the state acknowledges, but some other new divinities or spiritual agencies in their stead. These are the lessons by which I corrupt the youth, as you say.

Yes, that I say emphatically.

Then, by the gods, Meletus, of whom we are speaking, tell me and the court, in somewhat plainer terms, what you mean! for I do not as yet understand whether you affirm that I teach other men to acknowledge some gods, and therefore that I do believe in gods, and am not an entire atheist—this you do not lay to my charge,—but only you say that they are not the same gods which the city recognizes—the charge is that they are different gods. Or, do you mean that I am an atheist simply, and a teacher of atheism?

I mean the latter—that you are a complete atheist.

What an extraordinary statement! Why do you think so, Meletus? Do you mean that I do not believe in the godhead of the sun or moon, like other men?

I assure you, judges, that he does not: for he says that the sun is stone, and the moon earth.

Friend Meletus, you think that you are accusing Anaxagoras: and you have but a bad opinion of the judges, if you fancy them illiterate to such a degree as not to know that these doctrines are found in the books of Anaxagoras the Clazomenian, which are full of them. And so, forsooth, the youth are said to be taught them by Socrates, when there are not unfrequently exhibitions of them at the theatre (Probably in allusion to Aristophanes who caricatured, and to Euripides who borrowed the notions of Anaxagoras, as well as to other dramatic poets.); and they might pay their money, and laugh at Socrates if he pretends to father these extraordinary views. And so, Meletus, you really think that I do not believe in any god?

I swear by Zeus that you believe absolutely in none at all.

Nobody will believe you, Meletus, and I am pretty sure that you do not believe yourself. I cannot help thinking, men of Athens, that Meletus is reckless and impudent, and that he has written this indictment in a spirit of mere wantonness and youthful bravado. Has he not compounded a riddle, thinking to try me? He said to himself:—I shall see whether the wise Socrates will discover my facetious contradiction, or whether I shall be able to deceive him and the rest of them. For he certainly does appear to me to contradict himself in the indictment as much as if he said that Socrates is guilty of not believing in the gods, and yet of believing in them—but this is not like a person who is in earnest.

I should like you, O men of Athens, to join me in examining what I conceive to be his inconsistency; and do you, Meletus, answer. And I must remind the audience of my request that they would not make a disturbance if I speak in my accustomed manner:

Did ever man, Meletus, believe in the existence of human things, and not of human beings? . . . I wish, men of Athens, that he would answer, and not be always trying to get up an interruption. Did ever any man believe in horsemanship, and not in horses? or in flute-playing, and not in flute- players? No, my friend; I will answer to you and to the court, as you refuse to answer for yourself. There is no man who ever did. But now please to answer the next question: Can a man believe in spiritual and divine agencies, and not in spirits or demigods?

He cannot.

How lucky I am to have extracted that answer, by the assistance of the court! But then you swear in the indictment that I teach and believe in divine or spiritual agencies (new or old, no matter for that); at any rate, I believe in spiritual agencies,—so you say and swear in the affidavit; and yet if I believe in divine beings, how can I help believing in spirits or demigods;—must I not? To be sure I must; and therefore I may assume that your silence gives consent. Now what are spirits or demigods? Are they not either gods or the sons of gods?

Certainly they are.

But this is what I call the facetious riddle invented by you: the demigods or spirits are gods, and you say first that I do not believe in gods, and then again that I do believe in gods; that is, if I believe in demigods. For if the demigods are the illegitimate sons of gods, whether by the nymphs or by any other mothers, of whom they are said to be the sons—what human being will ever believe that there are no gods if they are the sons of gods? You might as well affirm the existence of mules, and deny that of horses and asses. Such nonsense, Meletus, could only have been intended by you to make trial of me. You have put this into the indictment because you had nothing real of which to accuse me. But no one who has a particle of understanding will ever be convinced by you that the same men can believe in divine and superhuman things, and yet not believe that there are gods and demigods and heroes.

I have said enough in answer to the charge of Meletus: any elaborate defence is unnecessary, but I know only too well how many are the enmities which I have incurred, and this is what will be my destruction if I am destroyed;—not Meletus, nor yet Anytus, but the envy and detraction of the world, which has been the death of many good men, and will probably be the death of many more; there is no danger of my being the last of them.

Some one will say: And are you not ashamed, Socrates, of a course of life which is likely to bring you to an untimely end? To him I may fairly answer: There you are mistaken: a man who is good for anything ought not to calculate the chance of living or dying; he ought only to consider whether in doing anything he is doing right or wrong—acting the part of a good man or of a bad. Whereas, upon your view, the heroes who fell at Troy were not good for much, and the son of Thetis above all, who altogether despised danger in comparison with disgrace; and when he was so eager to slay Hector, his goddess mother said to him, that if he avenged his companion Patroclus, and slew Hector, he would die himself—'Fate,' she said, in these or the like words, 'waits for you next after Hector;' he, receiving this warning, utterly despised danger and death, and instead of fearing them, feared rather to live in dishonour, and not to avenge his friend. 'Let me die forthwith,' he replies, 'and be avenged of my enemy, rather than abide here by the beaked ships, a laughing-stock and a burden of the earth.' Had Achilles any thought of death and danger? For wherever a man's place is, whether the place which he has chosen or that in which he has been placed by a commander, there he ought to remain in the hour of danger; he should not think of death or of anything but of disgrace. And this, O men of Athens, is a true saying.

Strange, indeed, would be my conduct, O men of Athens, if I who, when I was ordered by the generals whom you chose to command me at Potidaea and Amphipolis and Delium, remained where they placed me, like any other man, facing death—if now, when, as I conceive and imagine, God orders me to fulfil the philosopher's mission of searching into myself and other men, I were to desert my post through fear of death, or any other fear; that would indeed be strange, and I might justly be arraigned in court for denying the existence of the gods, if I disobeyed the oracle because I was afraid of death, fancying that I was wise when I was not wise. For the fear of death is indeed the pretence of wisdom, and not real wisdom, being a pretence of knowing the unknown; and no one knows whether death, which men in their fear apprehend to be the greatest evil, may not be the greatest good. Is not this ignorance of a disgraceful sort, the ignorance which is the conceit that a man knows what he does not know? And in this respect only I believe myself to differ from men in general, and may perhaps claim to be wiser than they are:—that whereas I

know but little of the world below, I do not suppose that I know: but I do know that injustice and disobedience to a better, whether God or man, is evil and dishonourable, and I will never fear or avoid a possible good rather than a certain evil. And therefore if you let me go now, and are not convinced by Anytus, who said that since I had been prosecuted I must be put to death; (or if not that I ought never to have been prosecuted at all); and that if I escape now, your sons will all be utterly ruined by listening to my words—if you say to me, Socrates, this time we will not mind Anytus, and you shall be let off, but upon one condition, that you are not to enquire and speculate in this way any more, and that if you are caught doing so again you shall die;—if this was the condition on which you let me go, I should reply: Men of Athens, I honour and love you; but I shall obey God rather than you, and while I have life and strength I shall never cease from the practice and teaching of philosophy, exhorting any one whom I meet and saying to him after my manner: You, my friend,—a citizen of the great and mighty and wise city of Athens,—are you not ashamed of heaping up the greatest amount of money and honour and reputation, and caring so little about wisdom and truth and the greatest improvement of the soul, which you never regard or heed at all? And if the person with whom I am arguing, says: Yes, but I do care; then I do not leave him or let him go at once; but I proceed to interrogate and examine and cross-examine him, and if I think that he has no virtue in him, but only says that he has, I reproach him with undervaluing the greater, and overvaluing the less. And I shall repeat the same words to every one whom I meet, young and old, citizen and alien, but especially to the citizens, inasmuch as they are my brethren. For know that this is the command of God; and I believe that no greater good has ever happened in the state than my service to the God. For I do nothing but go about persuading you all, old and young alike, not to take thought for your persons or your properties, but first and chiefly to care about the greatest improvement of the soul. I tell you that virtue is not given by money, but that from virtue comes money and every other good of man, public as well as private. This is my teaching, and if this is the doctrine which corrupts the youth, I am a mischievous person. But if any one says that this is not my teaching, he is speaking an untruth. Wherefore, O men of Athens, I say to you, do as Anytus bids or not as Anytus bids, and either acquit me or not; but whichever you do, understand that I shall never alter my ways, not even if I have to die many times.

Men of Athens, do not interrupt, but hear me; there was an understanding between us that you should hear me to the end: I have something more to say, at which you may be inclined to cry out; but I believe that to hear me will be good for you, and therefore I beg that you will not cry out. I would have you know, that if you kill such an one as I am, you will injure yourselves more than you will injure me. Nothing will injure me, not Meletus nor yet Anytus—they cannot, for a bad man is not permitted to injure a better than himself. I do not deny that Anytus may, perhaps, kill him, or drive him into exile, or deprive him of civil rights; and he may imagine, and others may imagine, that he is inflicting a great injury upon him: but there I do not agree. For the evil of doing as he is doing—the evil of unjustly taking away the life of another—is greater far.

And now, Athenians, I am not going to argue for my own sake, as you may think, but for yours, that you may not sin against the God by condemning me, who am his gift to you. For if you kill me you will not easily find a successor to me, who, if I may use such a ludicrous figure of speech, am a sort of gadfly, given to the state by God; and the state is a great and noble steed who is tardy in his motions owing to his very size, and requires to be stirred into life. I am that gadfly which God has attached to the state, and all day long and in all places am always fastening upon you, arousing and persuading and reproaching you. You will not easily find another like me, and therefore I would advise you to spare me. I dare say that you may feel out of temper (like a person who is suddenly awakened from sleep), and you think that you might easily strike me dead as Anytus advises, and then you would sleep on

for the remainder of your lives, unless God in his care of you sent you another gadfly. When I say that I am given to you by God, the proof of my mission is this:—if I had been like other men, I should not have neglected all my own concerns or patiently seen the neglect of them during all these years, and have been doing yours, coming to you individually like a father or elder brother, exhorting you to regard virtue; such conduct, I say, would be unlike human nature. If I had gained anything, or if my exhortations had been paid, there would have been some sense in my doing so; but now, as you will perceive, not even the impudence of my accusers dares to say that I have ever exacted or sought pay of any one; of that they have no witness. And I have a sufficient witness to the truth of what I say—my poverty.

Some one may wonder why I go about in private giving advice and busying myself with the concerns of others, but do not venture to come forward in public and advise the state. I will tell you why. You have heard me speak at sundry times and in divers places of an oracle or sign which comes to me, and is the divinity which Meletus ridicules in the indictment. This sign, which is a kind of voice, first began to come to me when I was a child; it always forbids but never commands me to do anything which I am going to do. This is what deters me from being a politician. And rightly, as I think. For I am certain, O men of Athens, that if I had engaged in politics, I should have perished long ago, and done no good either to you or to myself. And do not be offended at my telling you the truth: for the truth is, that no man who goes to war with you or any other multitude, honestly striving against the many lawless and unrighteous deeds which are done in a state, will save his life; he who will fight for the right, if he would live even for a brief space, must have a private station and not a public one.

I can give you convincing evidence of what I say, not words only, but what you value far more—actions. Let me relate to you a passage of my own life which will prove to you that I should never have yielded to injustice from any fear of death, and that 'as I should have refused to yield'

I must have died at once. I will tell you a tale of the courts, not very interesting perhaps, but nevertheless true. The only office of state which I ever held, O men of Athens, was that of senator: the tribe Antiochis, which is my tribe, had the presidency at the trial of the generals who had not taken up the bodies of the slain after the battle of Arginusae; and you proposed to try them in a body, contrary to law, as you all thought afterwards; but at the time I was the only one of the Prytanes who was opposed to the illegality, and I gave my vote against you; and when the orators threatened to impeach and arrest me, and you called and shouted, I made up my mind that I would run the risk, having law and justice with me, rather than take part in your injustice because I feared imprisonment and death. This happened in the days of the democracy. But when the oligarchy of the Thirty was in power, they sent for me and four others into the rotunda, and bade us bring Leon the Salaminian from Salamis, as they wanted to put him to death. This was a specimen of the sort of commands which they were always giving with the view of implicating as many as possible in their crimes; and then I showed, not in word only but in deed, that, if I may be allowed to use such an expression, I cared not a straw for death, and that my great and only care was lest I should do an unrighteous or unholy thing. For the strong arm of that oppressive power did not frighten me into doing wrong; and when we came out of the rotunda the other four went to Salamis and fetched Leon, but I went quietly home. For which I might have lost my life, had not the power of the Thirty shortly afterwards come to an end. And many will witness to my words.

Now do you really imagine that I could have survived all these years, if I had led a public life, supposing that like a good man I had always maintained the right and had made justice, as I ought, the first thing? No indeed, men of Athens, neither I nor any other man. But I have been always the same in all my actions, public as well as private, and never have I yielded any base compliance to those who are slanderously termed my disciples, or to any other. Not that I have any

regular disciples. But if any one likes to come and hear me while I am pursuing my mission, whether he be young or old, he is not excluded. Nor do I converse only with those who pay; but any one, whether he be rich or poor, may ask and answer me and listen to my words; and whether he turns out to be a bad man or a good one, neither result can be justly imputed to me; for I never taught or professed to teach him anything. And if any one says that he has ever learned or heard anything from me in private which all the world has not heard, let me tell you that he is lying.

But I shall be asked, Why do people delight in continually conversing with you? I have told you already, Athenians, the whole truth about this matter: they like to hear the cross-examination of the pretenders to wisdom; there is amusement in it. Now this duty of cross-examining other men has been imposed upon me by God; and has been signified to me by oracles, visions, and in every way in which the will of divine power was ever intimated to any one. This is true, O Athenians, or, if not true, would be soon refuted. If I am or have been corrupting the youth, those of them who are now grown up and have become sensible that I gave them bad advice in the days of their youth should come forward as accusers, and take their revenge; or if they do not like to come themselves, some of their relatives, fathers, brothers, or other kinsmen, should say what evil their families have suffered at my hands. Now is their time. Many of them I see in the court. There is Crito, who is of the same age and of the same deme with myself, and there is Critobulus his son, whom I also see. Then again there is Lysanias of Sphettus, who is the father of Aeschines—he is present; and also there is Antiphon of Cephisus, who is the father of Epigenes; and there are the brothers of several who have associated with me. There is Nicostratus the son of Theosdotides, and the brother of Theodotus (now Theodotus himself is dead, and therefore he, at any rate, will not seek to stop him); and there is Paralus the son of Demodocus, who had a brother Theages; and Adeimantus the son of Ariston, whose brother Plato is present; and Aeantodorus, who is the brother of Apollodorus, whom I also see. I might mention a great many others, some of whom Meletus should have produced as witnesses in the course of his speech; and let him still produce them, if he has forgotten—I will make way for him. And let him say, if he has any testimony of the sort which he can produce. Nay, Athenians, the very opposite is the truth. For all these are ready to witness on behalf of the corrupter, of the injurer of their kindred, as Meletus and Anytus call me; not the corrupted youth only—there might have been a motive for that—but their uncorrupted elder relatives. Why should they too support me with their testimony? Why, indeed, except for the sake of truth and justice, and because they know that I am speaking the truth, and that Meletus is a liar.

Well, Athenians, this and the like of this is all the defence which I have to offer. Yet a word more. Perhaps there may be some one who is offended at me, when he calls to mind how he himself on a similar, or even a less serious occasion, prayed and entreated the judges with many tears, and how he produced his children in court, which was a moving spectacle, together with a host of relations and friends; whereas I, who am probably in danger of my life, will do none of these things. The contrast may occur to his mind, and he may be set against me, and vote in anger because he is displeased at me on this account. Now if there be such a person among you,—mind, I do not say that there is,—to him I may fairly reply: My friend, I am a man, and like other men, a creature of flesh and blood, and not 'of wood or stone,' as Homer says; and I have a family, yes, and sons, O Athenians, three in number, one almost a man, and two others who are still young; and yet I will not bring any of them hither in order to petition you for an acquittal. And why not? Not from any self-assertion or want of respect for you. Whether I am or am not afraid of death is another question, of which I will not now speak. But, having regard to public opinion, I feel that such conduct would be discreditable to myself, and to you, and to the whole state. One who has reached my years, and who has a name for wisdom, ought not to demean himself. Whether this opinion

of me be deserved or not, at any rate the world has decided that Socrates is in some way superior to other men. And if those among you who are said to be superior in wisdom and courage, and any other virtue, demean themselves in this way, how shameful is their conduct! I have seen men of reputation, when they have been condemned, behaving in the strangest manner: they seemed to fancy that they were going to suffer something dreadful if they died, and that they could be immortal if you only allowed them to live; and I think that such are a dishonour to the state, and that any stranger coming in would have said of them that the most eminent men of Athens, to whom the Athenians themselves give honour and command, are no better than women. And I say that these things ought not to be done by those of us who have a reputation; and if they are done, you ought not to permit them; you ought rather to show that you are far more disposed to condemn the man who gets up a doleful scene and makes the city ridiculous, than him who holds his peace.

But, setting aside the question of public opinion, there seems to be something wrong in asking a favour of a judge, and thus procuring an acquittal, instead of informing and convincing him. For his duty is, not to make a present of justice, but to give judgment; and he has sworn that he will judge according to the laws, and not according to his own good pleasure; and we ought not to encourage you, nor should you allow yourselves to be encouraged, in this habit of perjury—there can be no piety in that. Do not then require me to do what I consider dishonourable and impious and wrong, especially now, when I am being tried for impiety on the indictment of Meletus. For if, O men of Athens, by force of persuasion and entreaty I could overpower your oaths, then I should be teaching you to believe that there are no gods, and in defending should simply convict myself of the charge of not believing in them. But that is not so—far otherwise. For I do believe that there are gods, and in a sense higher than that in which any of my accusers believe in them. And to you and to God I commit my cause, to be determined by you as is best for you and me.

● ● ●

(The jurors vote 281 to 220 to find Socrates guilty.) There are many reasons why I am not grieved, O men of Athens, at the vote of condemnation. I expected it, and am only surprised that the votes are so nearly equal; for I had thought that the majority against me would have been far larger; but now, had thirty votes gone over to the other side, I should have been acquitted. And I may say, I think, that I have escaped Meletus. I may say more; for without the assistance of Anytus and Lycon, any one may see that he would not have had a fifth part of the votes, as the law requires, in which case he would have incurred a fine of a thousand drachmae.

And so he proposes death as the penalty. And what shall I propose on my part, O men of Athens? Clearly that which is my due. And what is my due? What return shall be made to the man who has never had the wit to be idle during his whole life; but has been careless of what the many care for—wealth, and family interests, and military offices, and speaking in the assembly, and magistracies, and plots, and parties. Reflecting that I was really too honest a man to be a politician and live, I did not go where I could do no good to you or to myself; but where I could do the greatest good privately to every one of you, thither I went, and sought to persuade every man among you that he must look to himself, and seek virtue and wisdom before he looks to his private interests, and look to the state before he looks to the interests of the state; and that this should be the order which he observes in all his actions. What shall be done to such an one? Doubtless some good thing, O men of Athens, if he has his reward; and the good should be of a kind suitable to him. What would be a reward suitable to a poor man who is your benefactor, and who desires leisure that he may instruct you? There can be no reward so fitting as maintenance in the Prytaneum, O men of Athens, a reward which he deserves far more than the citizen who has won the prize at Olympia in the horse or chariot race, whether the chariots were drawn by two horses or by many. For I am in want, and he has enough; and he only gives you the appearance of happiness, and I give you the reality. And if I am to estimate the penalty fairly, I should say that maintenance in the Prytaneum is the just return.

Perhaps you think that I am braving you in what I am saying now, as in what I said before about the tears and prayers. But this is not so. I speak rather because I am convinced that I never intentionally wronged any one, although I cannot convince you—the time has been too short; if there were a law at Athens, as there is in other cities, that a capital cause should not be decided in one day, then I believe that I should have convinced you. But I cannot in a moment refute great slanders; and, as I am convinced that I never wronged another, I will assuredly not wrong myself. I will not say of myself that I deserve any evil, or propose any penalty. Why should I? because I am afraid of the penalty of death which Meletus proposes? When I do not know whether death is a good or an evil, why should I propose a penalty which would certainly be an evil? Shall I say imprisonment? And why should I live in prison, and be the slave of the magistrates of the year—of the Eleven? Or shall the penalty be a fine, and imprisonment until the fine is paid? There is the same objection. I should have to lie in prison, for money I have none, and cannot pay. And if I say exile (and this may possibly be the penalty which you will affix), I must indeed be blinded by the love of life, if I am so irrational as to expect that when you, who are my own citizens, cannot endure my discourses and words, and have found them so grievous and odious that you will have no more of them, others are likely to endure me. No indeed, men of Athens, that is not very likely. And what a life should I lead, at my age, wandering from city to city, ever changing my place of exile, and always being driven out! For I am quite sure that wherever I go, there, as here, the young men will flock to me; and if I drive them away, their elders will drive me out at their request; and if I let them come, their fathers and friends will drive me out for their sakes.

Some one will say: Yes, Socrates, but cannot you hold your tongue, and then you may go into a foreign city, and no one will interfere with you? Now I have great difficulty in making you understand my answer to this. For if I tell you that to do as you say would be a disobedience to the God, and therefore that I cannot hold my tongue, you will not believe that I am serious; and if I say again that daily to discourse about virtue, and of those other things about which you hear me examining myself and others, is the greatest good of man, and that the unexamined life is not worth living, you are still less likely to believe me. Yet I say what is true, although a thing of which it is hard for me to persuade you. Also, I have never been accustomed to think that I deserve to suffer any harm. Had I money I might have estimated the offence at what I was able to pay, and not have been much the worse. But I have none, and therefore I must ask you to proportion the fine to my means. Well, perhaps I could afford a mina, and therefore I propose that penalty: Plato, Crito, Critobulus, and Apollodorus, my friends here, bid me say thirty minae, and they will be the sureties. Let thirty minae be the penalty; for which sum they will be ample security to you.

● ● ●

(The jurors vote to condemn Socrates to death.) Not much time will be gained, O Athenians, in return for the evil name which you will get from the detractors of the city, who will say that you killed Socrates, a wise man; for they will call me wise, even although I am not wise, when they want to reproach you. If you had waited a little while, your desire would have been fulfilled in the course of nature. For I am far advanced in years, as you may perceive, and not far from death. I am speaking now not to all of you, but only to those who have condemned me to death. And I have another thing to say to them: you think that I was convicted because I had no words of the sort which would have procured my acquittal—I mean, if I had thought fit to leave nothing undone or unsaid. Not so; the deficiency which led to my conviction was not of words—certainly not. But I had not the boldness or impudence or inclination to address you as you would have liked me to do, weeping and wailing and lamenting, and saying and doing many things which you have been accustomed to hear from others, and which, as I maintain, are unworthy of me. I thought at the time that I ought not to do anything common or mean when in danger: nor do I now repent of the style of my defence; I would rather die having spoken after my manner, than speak in your manner and live. For neither in war nor yet at law ought I or any man to use every way of escaping death. Often in battle there can be no doubt that if a man will throw away his arms, and fall on his knees before his pursuers, he may escape death; and in other dangers there are other ways of escaping death, if a man is willing to say and do anything. The difficulty, my friends, is not to avoid death, but to avoid unrighteousness; for that runs faster than death. I am old and move slowly, and the slower runner has overtaken me, and my accusers are keen and quick, and the faster runner, who is unrighteousness, has overtaken them. And now I depart hence condemned by you to suffer the penalty of death,—they too go their ways condemned by the truth to suffer the penalty of villainy and wrong; and I must abide by my award—let them abide by theirs. I suppose that these things may be regarded as fated,—and I think that they are well.

And now, O men who have condemned me, I would fain prophesy to you; for I am about to die, and in the hour of death men are gifted with prophetic power. And I prophesy to you who are my murderers, that immediately after my departure punishment far heavier than you have inflicted on me will surely await you. Me you have killed because you wanted to escape the accuser, and not to give an account of your lives. But that will not be as you suppose: far otherwise. For I say that there will be more accusers of you than there are now; accusers whom hitherto I have restrained: and as they are younger they will be more inconsiderate with you, and you will be more offended at them. If you think that by killing men you can prevent some one from censuring your evil lives, you are mistaken; that is not a way of escape which is either possible or honourable; the easiest and the noblest way is not to be disabling others, but to be improving yourselves. This is the prophecy which I utter before my departure to the judges who have condemned me.

Friends, who would have acquitted me, I would like also to talk with you about the thing which has come to pass, while the magistrates are busy, and before I go to the place at which I must die. Stay then a little, for we may as well talk with one another while there is time. You are my friends, and I should like to show you the meaning of this event which has happened to me. O my judges—for you I may truly call judges—I should like to tell you of a wonderful circumstance. Hitherto the divine faculty of which the internal oracle is the source has constantly been in the habit of opposing me even about trifles, if I was going to make a slip or error in any matter; and now as you see there has come upon me that which may be thought, and is generally believed to be, the last and worst evil. But the oracle made no sign of opposition, either when I was leaving my house in the morning, or when I was on my way to the court, or while I was speaking, at anything which I was going to say; and yet I have often been stopped in the middle of a speech, but now in nothing I either said or did touching the matter in hand has the oracle opposed me. What do I take to be the explanation of this silence? I will tell you. It is an intimation that what has happened to me is a good, and that those of us who think that death is an evil are in error. For the customary sign would surely have opposed me had I been going to evil and not to good.

Let us reflect in another way, and we shall see that there is great reason to hope that death is a good; for one of two things—either death is a state of nothingness and utter unconsciousness, or, as men say, there is a change and migration of the soul from this world to another. Now if you suppose that there is no consciousness, but a sleep like the sleep of him who is undisturbed even by dreams, death will be an unspeakable gain. For if a person were to select the night in which his sleep was undisturbed even by dreams, and were to compare with this the other days and nights of his life, and then were to tell us how many days and nights he had passed in the course of his life better and more pleasantly than this one, I think that any man, I will not say a private man, but even the great king will not find

many such days or nights, when compared with the others. Now if death be of such a nature, I say that to die is gain; for eternity is then only a single night. But if death is the journey to another place, and there, as men say, all the dead abide, what good, O my friends and judges, can be greater than this? If indeed when the pilgrim arrives in the world below, he is delivered from the professors of justice in this world, and finds the true judges who are said to give judgment there, Minos and Rhadamanthus and Aeacus and Triptolemus, and other sons of God who were righteous in their own life, that pilgrimage will be worth making. What would not a man give if he might converse with Orpheus and Musaeus and Hesiod and Homer? Nay, if this be true, let me die again and again. I myself, too, shall have a wonderful interest in there meeting and conversing with Palamedes, and Ajax the son of Telamon, and any other ancient hero who has suffered death through an unjust judgment; and there will be no small pleasure, as I think, in comparing my own sufferings with theirs. Above all, I shall then be able to continue my search into true and false knowledge; as in this world, so also in the next; and I shall find out who is wise, and who pretends to be wise, and is not. What would not a man give, O judges, to be able to examine the leader of the great Trojan expedition; or Odysseus or Sisyphus, or numberless others, men and women too! What infinite delight would there be in conversing with them and asking them questions! In another world they do not put a man to death for asking questions: assuredly not. For besides being happier than we are, they will be immortal, if what is said is true.

Wherefore, O judges, be of good cheer about death, and know of a certainty, that no evil can happen to a good man, either in life or after death. He and his are not neglected by the gods; nor has my own approaching end happened by mere chance. But I see clearly that the time had arrived when it was better for me to die and be released from trouble; wherefore the oracle gave no sign. For which reason, also, I am not angry with my condemners, or with my accusers; they have done me no harm, although they did not mean to do me any good; and for this I may gently blame them.

Still I have a favour to ask of them. When my sons are grown up, I would ask you, O my friends, to punish them; and I would have you trouble them, as I have troubled you, if they seem to care about riches, or anything, more than about virtue; or if they pretend to be something when they are really nothing,—then reprove them, as I have reproved you, for not caring about that for which they ought to care, and thinking that they are something when they are really nothing. And if you do this, both I and my sons will have received justice at your hands.

The hour of departure has arrived, and we go our ways—I to die, and you to live. Which is better God only knows.

The Republic

Plato's *Republic* (written around 380 B.C.) is generally considered one of the greatest (if not the greatest) of his dialogues. While *The Apology* is an early dialogue, *The Republic* comes from Plato's middle period. What this means (among other things) is that although the figure of Socrates as Plato actually recalled him is still very much in evidence, Plato is also beginning to expound his own philosophy by placing it in the mouth of his teacher.

The overarching theme of *The Republic* is the nature of justice. In the course of considering this question, a good part of the work is taken up discussing the relationship between justice as manifest in the soul and justice as embodied in the city-state (polis). Socrates poses the issue in a provocative way by asking his friends (and us) why someone should be just in a world where justice does not always pay, and where the unjust seem to prosper. In the view of Socrates (and Plato), a city or state will be just when the souls of those who comprise it are properly ordered, and when the proper ordering of the soul is reflected in the proper ordering of the state. At the same time, Socrates also underlines the fact that it is difficult if not impossible for a person to possess a just (that is, properly balanced) soul in a city-state that is itself disordered. On this point it is crucial to bear in mind that, for the Greeks, human beings are social and political by nature. There is no such thing for them as an "individual" apart from the community. So if the community is unjust it will have a terrible effect on the souls of its members.

We need to be very careful here about what it is that Plato is doing in the dialogue. There is a common misperception that he was designing an "ideal state" or utopia. This mistaken notion needs to be strongly qualified if not thrown out completely. Why? Because for Plato, the "city founded in speech" by Socrates has a greater degree of reality than the corrupt polis in which he lived. For Plato, what we tend to refer to as "the real world" is actually a world of appearances in which opinion (rather than true knowledge) reigns. In his view most people live most of their lives without knowledge of the true nature of reality. Plato depicts this situation in the allegory of the Cave. Those few persons fortunate enough to escape from the cave and to gain knowledge of what is truly real are the philosophers, the "lovers of wisdom." If these philosophers were to rule, the city-state could be healthy and just.

But what are the chances of this happening? *The Republic* ends on an ambivalent note (as do so many of Plato's dialogues). On one hand, Socrates confesses to his young friend Adeimantos that it is unlikely that the city he has described will ever come to pass in this world. But that is not cause for despair. As Socrates reminds Adeimantos, "It matters nothing whether it exists anywhere or shall exist; for he (the philosopher) would practice the principles of this city only, no other." In other words, whether the city exists or not on earth, those who are wise and just will lead their lives in accordance with its principles, regardless of the cost. In this way we are brought back to the question with which *The Republic* began: whether it is worthwhile to be just in a world that is so often unjust. The dialogue ends with Socrates reminding his audience that even if justice is not to be realized in this world, it will count for a great deal in the afterlife. In the myth of Er he describes the eternal consequences that follow from the pursuit of justice and injustice. Socrates concludes by exhorting his hearers that the myth "would save us, if we would be guided by it."

Allegory of the Cave

Socrates. Glaucon.

Socrates. And now, I said, let me show in a figure how far our nature is enlightened or unenlightened: Behold human beings living in an underground den, which has a mouth open towards the light and reaching all along the den; here they have been from their childhood, and have their legs and necks chained so that they cannot move, and can only see before them, being prevented by the chains from turning round their heads. Above and behind them a fire is blazing at a distance, and between the fire and the prisoners there is a raised way; and you will see, if you look, a low wall built along the way, like the screen which marionette players have in front of them, over which they show the puppets.

I see.

And do you see, I said, men passing along the wall, carrying all sorts of vessels, and statues[1] and figures of animals made of wood and stone and various materials, which appear over the wall? Some of them are talking, others silent.

You have shown me a strange image, and they are strange prisoners.

Like ourselves, I replied; and they see only their own shadows, or the shadows of one another, which the fire throws on the opposite wall of the cave?

True, he said; how could they see anything but the shadows if they were never allowed to move their heads?

And of the objects which are being carried in like manner they would only see the shadows?

Yes, he said.

And if they were able to converse with one another, would they not suppose that they were naming what was actually before them?

Very true.

And suppose further that the prison had an echo which came from the other side, would they not be sure to fancy when one of the passers-by spoke that the voice which they heard came from the passing shadow?

No question, he replied.

To them, I said, the truth would be literally nothing but the shadows of the images.

That is certain.

And now look again, and see what will naturally follow if the prisoners are released and disabused of their error. At first, when any one of them is liberated and compelled suddenly to stand up and turn his neck round and walk and look towards the light, he will suffer sharp pains; the glare will distress him, and he will be unable to see the realities of which in his former state he had seen the shadows; and then conceive some one saying to him that what he saw before was an illusion, but that now, when he is approaching nearer to being and his eye is turned towards more real existence, he has a clearer vision,—what will be his reply? And you may further imagine that his instructor is pointing to the objects as they pass and requiring him to name them,—will he not be perplexed? Will he not fancy that the shadows which he formerly saw are truer than the objects which are now shown to him?

Far truer.

And if he is compelled to look straight at the light, will he not have a pain in his eyes which will make him turn away to take refuge in the objects of vision which he can see, and which he will conceive to be in reality clearer than the things which are now being shown to him?

True, he said.

And suppose once more, that he is reluctantly dragged up a steep and rugged ascent, and held fast until he is forced into the presence of the sun himself, is he not likely to be pained and irritated ? When he approaches the light his eyes will be dazzled, and he will not be able to see anything at all of what are now called realities.

---

1. Thus the prisoners see only shadows cast by images of real things,—not even shadows cast by real things themselves.

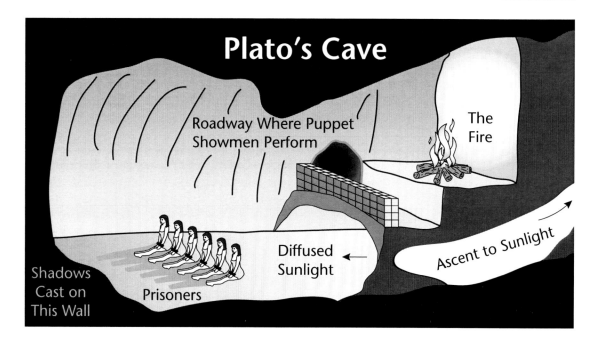

Plato's Cave

Roadway Where Puppet Showmen Perform

The Fire

Shadows Cast on This Wall

Prisoners

Diffused Sunlight

Ascent to Sunlight

Not all in a moment, he said.

He will require to grow accustomed to the sight of the upper world. And first he will see the shadows best, next the reflections of men and other objects in the water, and then the objects themselves; then he will gaze upon the light of the moon and the stars and the spangled heaven; and he will see the sky and the stars by night better than the sun or the light of the sun by day?

Certainly.

Last of all he will be able to see the sun, and not mere reflections of him in the water, but he will see him in his own proper place, and not in another; and he will contemplate him as he is.

Certainly.

He will then proceed to argue that this is he who gives the season and the years, and is the guardian of all that is in the visible world, and in a certain way the cause of all things which he and his fellows have been accustomed to behold?

Clearly, he said, he would first see the sun and then reason about him.

And when he remembered his old habitation, and the wisdom of the den and his fellow-prisoners, do you not suppose that he would felicitate himself on the change, and pity them?

Certainly, he would.

And if they were in the habit of conferring honors among themselves on those who were quickest to observe the passing shadows and to remark which of them went before, and which followed after, and which were together; and who were therefore best able to draw conclusions as to the future, do you think that he would care for such honors and glories, or envy the possessors of them ? Would he not say with Homer, "Better to be the poor servant of a poor master," and to endure anything, rather than think as they do and live after their manner.

Yes, he said, I think that he would rather suffer anything than entertain these false notions and live in this miserable manner.

Imagine once more, I said, such an one coming suddenly out of the sun to be replaced in his old situation; would he not be certain to have his eyes full of darkness?

To be sure, he said.

And if there were a contest, and he had to compete in measuring the shadows with the prisoners who had never moved out of the den, while his sight was still weak, and before his eyes had become steady (and the time which would be needed to acquire this new habit of sight might be very considerable), would he not be ridiculous? Men would say of him that up he went and down he came without his eyes; and that it was better not even to think of ascending; and if any one tried to loose another and lead him up to the light, let them only catch the offender and they would put him to death.

No question, he said.

This entire allegory, I said, you may now append, dear Glaucon, to the previous argument; the prisonhouse is the world of sight, the light of the fire is the sun, and you will not misapprehend me if you interpret the journey upwards to be the ascent of the soul into the intellectual world according to my poor belief, which, at your desire, I have expressed—whether rightly or wrongly God knows. But, whether true or false, my opinion is that in the world of knowledge the idea of good appears last of all, and is seen only with an effort; and, when seen, is also inferred to be the universal author of all things beautiful and right—parent of light and of the lord of light in this visible world, and the immediate source of reason and truth in the intellectual; and that this is the power upon which he who would act rationally either in public or private life must have his eye fixed.

I agree, he said, as far as I am able to understand you.

Moreover, I said, you must not wonder that those who attain to this beatific vision are unwilling to descend to human affairs; for their souls are ever hastening into the upper world where they desire to dwell; which desire of theirs is very natural, if our allegory may be trusted.

Yes, very natural.

And is there anything surprising in one who passes from divine contemplations to the evil state of man, misbehaving himself in a ridiculous manner; if, while his eyes are blinking and before he has become accustomed to the surrounding darkness, he is compelled to fight in courts of law, or in other places, about the images or shadows of images of justice, and is endeavoring to meet the conceptions of those who have never yet seen absolute justice?

Anything but surprising, he replied.

Any one who has common sense will remember that the bewilderments of the eyes are of two kinds, and arise from two causes, either from coming out of the light or from going into the light, which is true of the mind's eye, quite as much as of the bodily eye; and he who remembers this when he sees any one whose vision is perplexed and weak, will not be too ready to laugh; he will first ask whether that soul of man has come out of the brighter life, and is unable to see because unaccustomed to the dark, or having turned from darkness to the day is dazzled by excess of light. And he will count the one happy in his condition and state of being, and he will pity the other; or, if he have a mind to laugh at the soul which comes from below into the light, there will be more reason in this than in the laugh which greets him who returns from above out of the light into the den.

That, he said, is a very just distinction.

But then, if I am right, certain professors of education must be wrong when they say that they can put a knowledge into the soul which was not there before, like sight into blind eyes.

They undoubtedly say this, he replied.

Whereas, our argument shows that the power and capacity of learning exists in the soul already; and that just as the eye was unable to turn from darkness to light without the whole body, so too the instrument of knowledge can only by the movement of the whole soul be turned from the world of becoming into that of being, and learn by degrees to endure the sight of being, and of the brightest and best of being, or in other words, of the good.

Very true.

And must there not be some art which will effect conversion in the easiest and quickest manner; not implanting the faculty of sight, for that exists already, but has been turned in the wrong direction, and is looking away from the truth?

Yes, he said, such an art may be presumed.

And whereas the other so-called virtues of the soul seem to be akin to bodily qualities, for even when they are not originally innate they can be implanted later by habit and exercise, the virtue of wisdom more than anything else contains a divine element which always remains, and by this conversion is rendered useful and profitable; or on the other hand, hurtful and useless. Did you never observe the narrow intelligence flashing from the keen eye of a clever rogue—how eager he is, how clearly his paltry soul sees the way to his end; he is the reverse of blind, but his keen eyesight is forced into the service of evil, and he is mischievous in proportion to his cleverness?

Very true, he said.

But what if there had been a circumcision of such natures in the days of their youth; and they had been severed from those sensual pleasures, such as eating and drinking, which, like leaden weights, were attached to them at their birth,[2] and which drag them down and turn the vision of their souls upon the things that are below—if, I say, they had been released from these impediments and turned in the opposite direction, the very same faculty in them would have seen the truth as keenly as they see what their eyes are turned to now.

Very likely.

Yes, I said; and there is another thing which is likely, or rather a necessary inference from what has preceded,—that neither the uneducated and uninformed of the truth, nor yet those who never make an end of their education, will be able ministers of State; not the former, because they have no single aim of duty which is the rule of all their actions, private as well as public; nor the latter, because they will not act at all except upon compulsion, fancying that they are already dwelling apart in the islands of the blest.

Very true, he replied.

Then, I said, the business of us who are the founders of the State will be to compel the best minds to attain that knowledge which we have already shown to be the greatest of all—they must continue to ascend until they arrive at the good; but when they have ascended and seen enough we must not allow them to do as they do now.

What do you mean?

I mean that they remain in the upper world; but this must not be allowed; they must be made to descend again among the prisoners in the den, and partake of their labors and honors, whether they are worth having or not.

But is not this unjust? he said; ought we to give them a worse life, when they might have a better?

You have again forgotten, my friend, I said, the intention of the legislator, who did not aim at making any one class in the State happy above the rest; the happiness was to be in the whole State, and he held the citizens together by persuasion and necessity, making them benefactors of the State, and therefore benefactors of one another; to this end he created them, not to please themselves, but to be his instruments in binding up the State.

The Myth of Er

Well, I said, I will tell you a tale; not one of the tales which Odysseus tells to the hero Alcinous, yet this too is a tale of a hero, Er the son of Armenius, a Pamphylian by birth. He was slain in battle, and ten days afterwards, when the bodies of the dead were taken up already in a state of corruption, his body was found unaffected by decay, and carried away home to be buried. And on the twelfth day, as he was lying on the funeral pile, he returned to life and told them what he had seen in the other world. He said that when his soul left the body he went on a journey with a great company, and that they came to a mysterious place at which there were two openings in the earth; they were near together, and over against them were two

---

2. Plato means: "If the son should be freed from the tendencies to the world of change (the world of 'becoming') which have become attached to the soul by the pleasures of eating and drinking, and hold it down like leaden weights," etc.

other openings in the heaven above. In the intermediate space there were judges seated, who commanded the just, after they had given judgment on them and had bound their sentences in front of them, to ascend by the heavenly way on the right hand; and in like manner the unjust were bidden by them to descend by the lower way on the left hand; these also bore the symbols of their deeds, but fastened on their backs. He drew near, and they told him that he was to be the messenger who would carry the report of the other world to men, and they bade him hear and see all that was to be heard and seen in that place. Then he beheld and saw on one side the souls departing at either opening of heaven and earth when sentence had been given on them; and at the two other openings other souls, some ascending out of the earth dusty and worn with travel, some descending out of heaven clean and bright. And arriving ever and anon they seemed to have come from a long journey, and they went forth with gladness into the meadow, where they encamped as at a festival; and those who knew one another embraced and conversed, the souls which came from earth curiously enquiring about the things above, and the souls which came from heaven about the things beneath. And they told one another of what had happened by the way, those from below weeping and sorrowing at the remembrance of the things which they had endured and seen in their journey beneath the earth (now the journey lasted a thousand years), while those from above were describing heavenly delights and visions of inconceivable beauty. The story, Glaucon, would take too long to tell; but the sum was this:—He said that for every wrong which they had done to any one they suffered tenfold; or once in a hundred years—such being reckoned to be the length of man's life, and the penalty being thus paid ten times in a thousand years. If, for example, there were any who had been the cause of many deaths, or had betrayed or enslaved cities or armies, or been guilty of any other evil behaviour, for each and all of their offences they received punishment ten times over, and the rewards of beneficence and justice and holiness were in the same proportion. I need

hardly repeat what he said concerning young children dying almost as soon as they were born. Of piety and impiety to gods and parents, and of murderers, there were retributions other and greater far which he described. He mentioned that he was present when one of the spirits asked another, 'Where is Ardiaeus the Great?' (Now this Ardiaeus lived a thousand years before the time of Er: he had been the tyrant of some city of Pamphylia, and had murdered his aged father and his elder brother, and was said to have committed many other abominable crimes.) The answer of the other spirit was: 'He comes not hither and will never come. And this,' said he, 'was one of the dreadful sights which we ourselves witnessed. We were at the mouth of the cavern, and, having completed all our experiences, were about to reascend, when of a sudden Ardiaeus appeared and several others, most of whom were tyrants; and there were also besides the tyrants private individuals who had been great criminals: they were just, as they fancied, about to return into the upper world, but the mouth, instead of admitting them, gave a roar, whenever any of these incurable sinners or some one who had not been sufficiently punished tried to ascend; and then wild men of fiery aspect, who were standing by and heard the sound, seized and carried them off; and Ardiaeus and others they bound head and foot and hand, and threw them down and flayed them with scourges, and dragged them along the road at the side, carding them on thorns like wool, and declaring to the passers-by what were their crimes, and that they were being taken away to be cast into hell.' And of all the many terrors which they had endured, he said that there was none like the terror which each of them felt at that moment, lest they should hear the voice; and when there was silence, one by one they ascended with exceeding joy. These, said Er, were the penalties and retributions, and there were blessings as great.

Now when the spirits which were in the meadow had tarried seven days, on the eighth they were obliged to proceed on their journey, and, on the fourth day after, he said that they came to a place where they could see from above a line of light, straight as a column, extending right through the whole heaven and through the earth, in colour resembling the rainbow, only brighter and purer; another day's journey brought them to the place, and there, in the midst of the light, they saw the ends of the chains of heaven let down from above: for this light is the belt of heaven, and holds together the circle of the universe, like the under-girders of a trireme. From these ends is extended the spindle of Necessity, on which all the revolutions turn. The shaft and hook of this spindle are made of steel, and the whorl is made partly of steel and also partly of other materials. Now the whorl is in form like the whorl used on earth; and the description of it implied that there is one large hollow whorl which is quite scooped out, and into this is fitted another lesser one, and another, and another, and four others, making eight in all, like vessels which fit into one another; the whorls show their edges on the upper side, and on their lower side all together form one continuous whorl. This is pierced by the spindle, which is driven home through the centre of the eighth. The first and outermost whorl has the rim broadest, and the seven inner whorls are narrower, in the following proportions—the sixth is next to the first in size, the fourth next to the sixth; then comes the eighth; the seventh is fifth, the fifth is sixth, the third is seventh, last and eighth comes the second. The largest (or fixed stars) is spangled, and the seventh (or sun) is brightest; the eighth (or moon) coloured by the reflected light of the seventh; the second and fifth (Saturn and Mercury) are in colour like one another, and yellower than the preceding; the third (Venus) has the whitest light; the fourth (Mars) is reddish; the sixth (Jupiter) is in whiteness second. Now the whole spindle has the same motion; but, as the whole revolves in one direction, the seven inner circles move slowly in the other, and of these the swiftest is the eighth; next in swiftness are the seventh, sixth, and fifth, which move together; third in swiftness appeared to move according to the law of this reversed motion the fourth; the third appeared fourth and the second fifth. The spindle turns on the knees of Necessity; and on the upper surface of each circle is a siren, who goes round with them, hymning a single tone or note. The eight together form one harmony; and round about, at equal intervals, there is another band, three in number, each sitting upon her throne: these are the Fates, daughters of Necessity, who are clothed in white robes and have chaplets upon their heads, Lachesis and Clotho and Atropos, who accompany with their voices the harmony of the sirens—Lachesis singing of the past, Clotho of the present, Atropos of the future; Clotho from time to time assisting with a touch of her right hand the revolution of the outer circle of the whorl or spindle, and Atropos with her left hand touching and guiding the inner ones, and Lachesis laying hold of either in turn, first with one hand and then with the other.

When Er and the spirits arrived, their duty was to go at once to Lachesis; but first of all there came a prophet who arranged them in order; then he took from the knees of Lachesis lots and samples of lives, and having mounted a high pulpit, spoke as follows: 'Hear the word of Lachesis, the daughter of Necessity. Mortal souls, behold a new cycle of life and mortality. Your genius will not be allotted to you, but you will choose your genius; and let him who draws the first lot have the first choice, and the life which he chooses shall be his destiny. Virtue is free, and as a man honours or dishonours her he will have more or less of her; the responsibility is with the chooser—God is justified.' When the Interpreter had thus spoken he scattered lots indifferently among them all, and each of them took up the lot which fell near him, all but Er himself (he was not allowed), and each as he took his lot perceived the number which he had obtained. Then the Interpreter placed on the ground before them the samples of lives; and there were many more lives than the souls present, and they were of all sorts. There were lives of every animal and of man in every condition. And there were tyrannies among them, some lasting out the tyrant's life, others which broke off in the middle and came to an end in poverty and exile and beggary; and there were lives of famous men, some who were famous for their form

and beauty as well as for their strength and success in games, or, again, for their birth and the
qualities of their ancestors; and some who were
the reverse of famous for the opposite qualities.
And of women likewise; there was not, however,
any definite character in them, because the soul,
when choosing a new life, must of necessity become different. But there was every other quality,
and the all mingled with one another, and also
with elements of wealth and poverty, and disease
and health; and there were mean states also. And
here, my dear Glaucon, is the supreme peril of
our human state; and therefore the utmost care
should be taken. Let each one of us leave every
other kind of knowledge and seek and follow one
thing only, if peradventure he may be able to
learn and may find some one who will make him
able to learn and discern between good and evil,
and so to choose always and everywhere the better life as he has opportunity. He should consider
the bearing of all these things which have been
mentioned severally and collectively upon virtue; he should know what the effect of beauty is
when combined with poverty or wealth in a particular soul, and what are the good and evil consequences of noble and humble birth, of private
and public station, of strength and weakness, of
cleverness and dullness, and of all the natural
and acquired gifts of the soul, and the operation
of them when conjoined; he will then look at the
nature of the soul, and from the consideration
of all these qualities he will be able to determine
which is the better and which is the worse; and
so he will choose, giving the name of evil to the
life which will make his soul more unjust, and
good to the life which will make his soul more
just; all else he will disregard. For we have seen
and know that this is the best choice both in life
and after death. A man must take with him into
the world below an adamantine faith in truth
and right, that there too he may be undazzled by
the desire of wealth or the other allurements of
evil, lest, coming upon tyrannies and similar villainies, he do irremediable wrongs to others and
suffer yet worse himself; but let him know how
to choose the mean and avoid the extremes on
either side, as far as possible, not only in this life

but in all that which is to come. For this is the
way of happiness.

And according to the report of the messenger
from the other world this was what the prophet
said at the time: 'Even for the last comer, if he
chooses wisely and will live diligently, there is appointed a happy and not undesirable existence.
Let not him who chooses first be careless, and let
not the last despair.' And when he had spoken,
he who had the first choice came forward and in
a moment chose the greatest tyranny; his mind
having been darkened by folly and sensuality,
he had not thought out the whole matter before
he chose, and did not at first sight perceive that
he was fated, among other evils, to devour his
own children. But when he had time to reflect,
and saw what was in the lot, he began to beat
his breast and lament over his choice, forgetting
the proclamation of the prophet; for, instead of
throwing the blame of his misfortune on himself, he accused chance and the gods, and everything rather than himself. Now he was one of
those who came from heaven, and in a former
life had dwelt in a well-ordered State, but his virtue was a matter of habit only, and he had no
philosophy. And it was true of others who were
similarly overtaken, that the greater number of
them came from heaven and therefore they had
never been schooled by trial, whereas the pilgrims who came from earth having themselves
suffered and seen others suffer, were not in a
hurry to choose. And owing to this inexperience
of theirs, and also because the lot was a chance,
many of the souls exchanged a good destiny for
an evil or an evil for a good. For if a man had
always on his arrival in this world dedicated
himself from the first to sound philosophy, and
had been moderately fortunate in the number of
the lot, he might, as the messenger reported, be
happy here, and also his journey to another life
and return to this, instead of being rough and
underground, would be smooth and heavenly.
Most curious, he said, was the spectacle—sad and
laughable and strange; for the choice of the souls
was in most cases based on their experience of a
previous life. There he saw the soul which had
once been Orpheus choosing the life of a swan

out of enmity to the race of women, hating to be born of a woman because they had been his murderers; he beheld also the soul of Thamyras choosing the life of a nightingale; birds, on the other hand, like the swan and other musicians, wanting to be men. The soul which obtained the twentieth lot chose the life of a lion, and this was the soul of Ajax the son of Telamon, who would not be a man, remembering the injustice which was done him in the judgment about the arms. The next was Agamemnon, who took the life of an eagle, because, like Ajax, he hated human nature by reason of his sufferings. About the middle came the lot of Atalanta; she, seeing the great fame of an athlete, was unable to resist the temptation: and after her there followed the soul of Epeus the son of Panopeus passing into the nature of a woman cunning in the arts; and far away among the last who chose, the soul of the jester Thersites was putting on the form of a monkey. There came also the soul of Odysseus having yet to make a choice, and his lot happened to be the last of them all. Now the recollection of former toils had disenchanted him of ambition, and he went about for a considerable time in search of the life of a private man who had no cares; he had some difficulty in finding this, which was lying about and had been neglected by everybody else; and when he saw it, he said that he would have done the same had his lot been first instead of last, and that he was delighted to have it. And not only did men pass into animals, but I must also mention that there were animals tame and wild who changed into one another and into corresponding human natures—the good into the gentle and the evil into the savage, in all sorts of combinations.

All the souls had now chosen their lives, and they went in the order of their choice to Lachesis, who sent with them the genius whom they had severally chosen, to be the guardian of their lives and the fulfiller of the choice: this genius led the souls first to Clotho, and drew them within the revolution of the spindle impelled by her hand, thus ratifying the destiny of each; and then, when they were fastened to this, carried them to Atropos, who spun the threads and made them irreversible, whence without turning round they passed beneath the throne of Necessity; and when they had all passed, they marched on in a scorching heat to the plain of Forgetfulness, which was a barren waste destitute of trees and verdure; and then towards evening they encamped by the river of Unmindfulness, whose water no vessel can hold; of this they were all obliged to drink a certain quantity, and those who were not saved by wisdom drank more than was necessary; and each one as he drank forgot all things. Now after they had gone to rest, about the middle of the night there was a thunderstorm and earthquake, and then in an instant they were driven upwards in all manner of ways to their birth, like stars shooting. He himself was hindered from drinking the water. But in what manner or by what means he returned to the body he could not say; only, in the morning, awaking suddenly, he found himself lying on the pyre.

And thus, Glaucon, the tale has been saved and has not perished, and will save us if we are obedient to the word spoken; and we shall pass safely over the river of Forgetfulness and our soul will not be defiled. Wherefore my counsel is, that we hold fast ever to the heavenly way and follow after justice and virtue always, considering that the soul is immortal and able to endure every sort of good and every sort of evil. Thus shall we live dear to one another and to the gods, both while remaining here and when, like conquerors in the games who go round to gather gifts, we receive our reward. And it shall be well with us both in this life and in the pilgrimage of a thousand years which we have been describing.

Symposium (Selections)

The *Symposium* (dated sometime between 385–378 B.C.) recounts a drinking party held at the home of the tragic poet Agathon. The Greek word *symposion* literally means "drinking together." At this particular party, the guests agree that because of their hangovers from the previous evening's festivities, they will go easy on the drinking. Rather than get drunk again they agree to take turns giving speeches in honor of love. The Greek language has several words for "love," but during this symposium the participants will focus on "eros" or desire.

The dialogue is narrated by Apollodorus, a friend of Socrates, who is reporting what he heard about the evening from another friend of Socrates, Aristodemus, who attended the party but did not give a speech. Those who gave speeches during the symposium were: Phaedrus (a friend of Plato); Pausanias (a legal expert); Erixymachus (a physician); Aristophanes (the great comic playwright);

Agathon; Socrates; and Alcibiades (a young, popular, handsome, talented but unscrupulous Athenian politician).

In the excerpts that follow, the theme of the dialogue is introduced, followed by the speeches of Aristophanes and Socrates. As befits the character of a comic playwright, Aristophanes' speech seems to be both poking fun at Greek myths and making a serious point about the nature of love. In the case of Socrates, after questioning Agathon, Socrates recalls how he learned about love from a wise woman seer by the name of Diotima of Mantinea. Whether Diotima was a historical figure or a fictional character created by Plato is a matter of debate. Regardless of the verdict on this question, it is with the teaching of Diotima (as conveyed by Socrates) that the dialogue reaches its greatest degree of complexity and depth in its treatment of love.

This was the style of their conversation as they went along. Socrates dropped behind in a fit of abstraction, and desired Aristodemus, who was waiting, to go on before him. When he reached the house of Agathon he found the doors wide open, and a comical thing happened. A servant coming out met him, and led him at once into the banqueting-hall in which the guests were reclining, for the banquet was about to begin. Welcome, Aristodemus, said Agathon, as soon as he appeared—you are just in time to sup with us; if you come on any other matter put it off, and make one of us, as I was looking for you yesterday and meant to have asked you, if I could have found you. But what have you done with Socrates?

I turned round, but Socrates was nowhere to be seen; and I had to explain that he had been with me a moment before, and that I came by his invitation to the supper.

You were quite right in coming, said Agathon; but where is he himself?

He was behind me just now, as I entered, he said, and I cannot think what has become of him.

Go and look for him, boy, said Agathon, and bring him in; and do you, Aristodemus, meanwhile take the place by Eryximachus.

The servant then assisted him to wash, and he lay down, and presently another servant came in and reported that our friend Socrates had retired into the portico of the neighbouring house. 'There he is fixed,' said he, 'and when I call to him he will not stir.'

How strange, said Agathon; then you must call him again, and keep calling him.

Let him alone, said my informant; he has a way of stopping anywhere and losing himself without any reason. I believe that he will soon appear; do not therefore disturb him.

Well, if you think so, I will leave him, said Agathon. And then, turning to the servants, he added, 'Let us have supper without waiting for him. Serve up whatever you please, for there is no one to give you orders; hitherto I have never left you to yourselves. But on this occasion imagine that you are our hosts, and that I and the company are your guests; treat us well, and then we shall commend you.' After this, supper was served, but still no Socrates; and during the meal Agathon several times expressed a wish to send for him, but Aristodemus objected; and at last when the feast was about half over—for the fit, as usual, was not of long duration—Socrates entered. Agathon, who was reclining alone at the end of the table, begged that he would take the place next to him; that 'I may touch you,' he said, 'and have the benefit of that wise thought which came into your mind in the portico, and is now in your possession; for I am certain that you would not have come away until you had found what you sought.'

How I wish, said Socrates, taking his place as he was desired, that wisdom could be infused by touch, out of the fuller into the emptier man, as water runs through wool out of a fuller cup into an emptier one; if that were so, how greatly should I value the privilege of reclining at your side! For you would have filled me full with a stream of wisdom plenteous and fair; whereas my own is of a very mean and questionable sort, no better than a dream. But yours is bright and full of promise, and was manifested forth in all the splendour of youth the day before yesterday, in the presence of more than thirty thousand Hellenes.

You are mocking, Socrates, said Agathon, and ere long you and I will have to determine who bears off the palm of wisdom—of this Dionysus shall be the judge; but at present you are better occupied with supper.

Socrates took his place on the couch, and supped with the rest; and then libations were offered, and after a hymn had been sung to the god, and there had been the usual ceremonies, they were about to commence drinking, when Pausanias said, And now, my friends, how can we drink with least injury to ourselves? I can assure you that I feel severely the effect of yesterday's potations, and must have time to recover; and I suspect that most of you are in the same predicament, for you were of the party

yesterday. Consider then: How can the drinking be made easiest?

I entirely agree, said Aristophanes, that we should, by all means, avoid hard drinking, for I was myself one of those who were yesterday drowned in drink.

I think that you are right, said Eryximachus, the son of Acumenus; but I should still like to hear one other person speak: Is Agathon able to drink hard?

I am not equal to it, said Agathon.

Then, said Eryximachus, the weak heads like myself, Aristodemus, Phaedrus, and others who never can drink, are fortunate in finding that the stronger ones are not in a drinking mood. (I do not include Socrates, who is able either to drink or to abstain, and will not mind, whichever we do.) Well, as of none of the company seem disposed to drink much, I may be forgiven for saying, as a physician, that drinking deep is a bad practice, which I never follow, if I can help, and certainly do not recommend to another, least of all to any one who still feels the effects of yesterday's carouse.

I always do what you advise, and especially what you prescribe as a physician, rejoined Phaedrus the Myrrhinusian, and the rest of the company, if they are wise, will do the same.

It was agreed that drinking was not to be the order of the day, but that they were all to drink only so much as they pleased.

Then, said Eryximachus, as you are all agreed that drinking is to be voluntary, and that there is to be no compulsion, I move, in the next place, that the flute-girl, who has just made her appearance, be told to go away and play to herself, or, if she likes, to the women who are within (compare Prot.). To-day let us have conversation instead; and, if you will allow me, I will tell you what sort of conversation. This proposal having been accepted, Eryximachus proceeded as follows:—I will begin, he said, after the manner of Melanippe in Euripides, 'Not mine the word' which I am about to speak, but that of Phaedrus. For often he says to me in an indignant tone:— 'What a strange thing it is, Eryximachus, that, whereas other gods have poems and hymns made in their honour, the great and glorious god, Love, has no encomiast among all the poets who are so many. There are the worthy sophists too—the excellent Prodicus for example, who have descanted in prose on the virtues of Heracles and other heroes; and, what is still more extraordinary, I have met with a philosophical work in which the utility of salt has been made the theme of an eloquent discourse; and many other like things have had a like honour bestowed upon them. And only to think that there should have been an eager interest created about them, and yet that to this day no one has ever dared worthily to hymn Love's praises! So entirely has this great deity been neglected.' Now in this Phaedrus seems to me to be quite right, and therefore I want to offer him a contribution; also I think that at the present moment we who are here assembled cannot do better than honour the god Love. If you agree with me, there will be no lack of conversation; for I mean to propose that each of us in turn, going from left to right, shall make a speech in honour of Love. Let him give us the best which he can; and Phaedrus, because he is sitting first on the left hand, and because he is the father of the thought, shall begin.

No one will vote against you, Eryximachus, said Socrates. How can I oppose your motion, who profess to understand nothing but matters of love; nor, I presume, will Agathon and Pausanias; and there can be no doubt of Aristophanes, whose whole concern is with Dionysus and Aphrodite; nor will any one disagree of those whom I see around me. The proposal, as I am aware, may seem rather hard upon us whose place is last; but we shall be contented if we hear some good speeches first. Let Phaedrus begin the praise of Love, and good luck to him. All the company expressed their assent, and desired him to do as Socrates bade him.

Aristodemus did not recollect all that was said, nor do I recollect all that he related to me; but I will tell you what I thought most worthy of remembrance, and what the chief speakers said.

The Speech of Aristophanes

Aristophanes professed to open another vein of discourse; he had a mind to praise Love in another way, unlike that either of Pausanias or Eryximachus. Mankind, he said, judging by their neglect of him, have never, as I think, at all understood the power of Love. For if they had understood him they would surely have built noble temples and altars, and offered solemn sacrifices in his honour; but this is not done, and most certainly ought to be done: since of all the gods he is the best friend of men, the helper and the healer of the ills which are the great impediment to the happiness of the race. I will try to describe his power to you, and you shall teach the rest of the world what I am teaching you. In the first place, let me treat of the nature of man and what has happened to it; for the original human nature was not like the present, but different. The sexes were not two as they are now, but originally three in number; there was man, woman, and the union of the two, having a name corresponding to this double nature, which had once a real existence, but is now lost, and the word 'Androgynous' is only preserved as a term of reproach. In the second place, the primeval man was round, his back and sides forming a circle; and he had four hands and four feet, one head with two faces, looking opposite ways, set on a round neck and precisely alike; also four ears, two privy members, and the remainder to correspond. He could walk upright as men now do, backwards or forwards as he pleased, and he could also roll over and over at a great pace, turning on his four hands and four feet, eight in all, like tumblers going over and over with their legs in the air; this was when he wanted to run fast. Now the sexes were three, and such as I have described them; because the sun, moon, and earth are three; and the man was originally the child of the sun, the woman of the earth, and the man-woman of the moon, which is made up of sun and earth, and they were all round and moved round and round like their parents. Terrible was their might and strength, and the thoughts of their hearts were great, and they made an attack upon the gods; of them is told the tale of Otys and Ephialtes who, as Homer says, dared to scale heaven, and would have laid hands upon the gods. Doubt reigned in the celestial councils. Should they kill them and annihilate the race with thunderbolts, as they had done the giants, then there would be an end of the sacrifices and worship which men offered to them; but, on the other hand, the gods could not suffer their insolence to be unrestrained. At last, after a good deal of reflection, Zeus discovered a way. He said: 'Methinks I have a plan which will humble their pride and improve their manners; men shall continue to exist, but I will cut them in two and then they will be diminished in strength and increased in numbers; this will have the advantage of making them more profitable to us. They shall walk upright on two legs, and if they continue insolent and will not be quiet, I will split them again and they shall hop about on a single leg.' He spoke and cut men in two, like a sorb-apple which is halved for pickling, or as you might divide an egg with a hair; and as he cut them one after another, he bade Apollo give the face and the half of the neck a turn in order that the man might contemplate the section of himself: he would thus learn a lesson of humility. Apollo was also bidden to heal their wounds and compose their forms. So he gave a turn to the face and pulled the skin from the sides all over that which in our language is called the belly, like the purses which draw in, and he made one mouth at the centre, which he fastened in a knot (the same which is called the navel); he also moulded the breast and took out most of the wrinkles, much as a shoemaker might smooth leather upon a last; he left a few, however, in the region of the belly and navel, as a memorial of the primeval state. After the division the two parts of man, each desiring his other half, came together, and throwing their arms about one another, entwined in mutual embraces, longing to grow into one, they were on the point of dying from hunger and self-neglect, because they did not like to do anything apart; and when one of the halves died and the other survived, the survivor sought another mate, man or woman as we call them,—being the sections of entire men or women,—and clung to that. They were being destroyed, when Zeus in pity of them invented a new plan: he turned the parts of generation round to the front, for this had not been always their position,

and they sowed the seed no longer as hitherto like grasshoppers in the ground, but in one another; and after the transposition the male generated in the female in order that by the mutual embraces of man and woman they might breed, and the race might continue; or if man came to man they might be satisfied, and rest, and go their ways to the business of life: so ancient is the desire of one another which is implanted in us, reuniting our original nature, making one of two, and healing the state of man. Each of us when separated, having one side only, like a flat fish, is but the indenture of a man, and he is always looking for his other half. Men who are a section of that double nature which was once called Androgynous are lovers of women; adulterers are generally of this breed, and also adulterous women who lust after men: the women who are a section of the woman do not care for men, but have female attachments; the female companions are of this sort. But they who are a section of the male follow the male, and while they are young, being slices of the original man, they hang about men and embrace them, and they are themselves the best of boys and youths, because they have the most manly nature. Some indeed assert that they are shameless, but this is not true; for they do not act thus from any want of shame, but because they are valiant and manly, and have a manly countenance, and they embrace that which is like them. And these when they grow up become our statesmen, and these only, which is a great proof of the truth of what I am saving. When they reach manhood they are lovers of youth, and are not naturally inclined to marry or beget children,—if at all, they do so only in obedience to the law; but they are satisfied if they may be allowed to live with one another unwedded; and such a nature is prone to love and ready to return love, always embracing that which is akin to him. And when one of them meets with his other half, the actual half of himself, whether he be a lover of youth or a lover of another sort, the pair are lost in an amazement of love and friendship and intimacy, and one will not be out of the other's sight, as I may say, even for a moment: these are the people who pass their whole lives together; yet they could not explain what they desire of one another. For the intense yearning which each of them has towards the other does not appear to be the desire of lover's intercourse, but of something else which the soul of either evidently desires and cannot tell, and of which she has only a dark and doubtful presentiment. Suppose Hephaestus, with his instruments, to come to the pair who are lying side by side and to say to them, 'What do you people want of one another?' they would be unable to explain. And suppose further, that when he saw their perplexity he said: 'Do you desire to be wholly one; always day and night to be in one another's company? for if this is what you desire, I am ready to melt you into one and let you grow together, so that being two you shall become one, and while you live live a common life as if you were a single man, and after your death in the world below still be one departed soul instead of two—I ask whether this is what you lovingly desire, and whether you are satisfied to attain this?'—there is not a man of them who when he heard the proposal would deny or would not acknowledge that this meeting and melting into one another, this becoming one instead of two, was the very expression of his ancient need (compare Arist. Pol.). And the reason is that human nature was originally one and we were a whole, and the desire and pursuit of the whole is called love. There was a time, I say, when we were one, but now because of the wickedness of mankind God has dispersed us, as the Arcadians were dispersed into villages by the Lacedaemonians (compare Arist. Pol.). And if we are not obedient to the gods, there is a danger that we shall be split up again and go about in basso-relievo, like the profile figures having only half a nose which are sculptured on monuments, and that we shall be like tallies. Wherefore let us exhort all men to piety, that we may avoid evil, and obtain the good, of which Love is to us the lord and minister; and let no one oppose him— he is the enemy of the gods who opposes him. For if we are friends of the God and at peace with him we shall find our own true loves, which rarely happens in this world at present. I am serious,

and therefore I must beg Eryximachus not to make fun or to find any allusion in what I am saying to Pausanias and Agathon, who, as I suspect, are both of the manly nature, and belong to the class which I have been describing. But my words have a wider application—they include men and women everywhere; and I believe that if our loves were perfectly accomplished, and each one returning to his primeval nature had his original true love, then our race would be happy. And if this would be best of all, the best in the next degree and under present circumstances must be the nearest approach to such an union; and that will be the attainment of a congenial love. Wherefore, if we would praise him who has given to us the benefit, we must praise the god Love, who is our greatest benefactor, both leading us in this life back to our own nature, and giving us high hopes for the future, for he promises that if we are pious, he will restore us to our original state, and heal us and make us happy and blessed.

The Speech of Socrates/Diotima

Socrates then proceeded as follows:—

In the magnificent oration which you have just uttered, I think that you were right, my dear Agathon, in proposing to speak of the nature of Love first and afterwards of his works—that is a way of beginning which I very much approve. And as you have spoken so eloquently of his nature, may I ask you further, Whether love is the love of something or of nothing? And here I must explain myself: I do not want you to say that love is the love of a father or the love of a mother—that would be ridiculous; but to answer as you would, if I asked is a father a father of something? to which you would find no difficulty in replying, of a son or daughter: and the answer would be right.

Very true, said Agathon.

And you would say the same of a mother?

He assented.

Yet let me ask you one more question in order to illustrate my meaning: Is not a brother to be regarded essentially as a brother of something?

Certainly, he replied.

That is, of a brother or sister?

Yes, he said.

And now, said Socrates, I will ask about Love:—Is Love of something or of nothing?

Of something, surely, he replied.

Keep in mind what this is, and tell me what I want to know—whether Love desires that of which love is.

Yes, surely.

And does he possess, or does he not possess, that which he loves and desires?

Probably not, I should say.

Nay, replied Socrates, I would have you consider whether 'necessarily' is not rather the word. The inference that he who desires something is in want of something, and that he who desires nothing is in want of nothing, is in my judgment, Agathon, absolutely and necessarily true. What do you think?

I agree with you, said Agathon.

Very good. Would he who is great, desire to be great, or he who is strong, desire to be strong?

That would be inconsistent with our previous admissions.

True. For he who is anything cannot want to be that which he is?

Very true.

And yet, added Socrates, if a man being strong desired to be strong, or being swift desired to be swift, or being healthy desired to be healthy, in that case he might be thought to desire something which he already has or is. I give the example in order that we may avoid misconception. For the possessors of these qualities, Agathon, must be supposed to have their respective advantages at the time, whether they choose or not; and who can desire that which he has? Therefore, when a person says, I am well and wish to be well, or I am rich and wish to be rich, and I desire simply to have what I have—to him we shall reply: 'You, my friend, having wealth and health and strength, want to have the continuance of them; for at this moment, whether you choose or no, you have them. And when you say, I desire that which I have and nothing else, is not your meaning that you want to have what you now have in the future?' He must agree with us—must he not?

He must, replied Agathon.

Then, said Socrates, he desires that what he has at present may be preserved to him in the future, which is equivalent to saying that he desires something which is non-existent to him, and which as yet he has not got:

Very true, he said.

Then he and every one who desires, desires that which he has not already, and which is future and not present, and which he has not, and is not, and of which he is in want;—these are the sort of things which love and desire seek?

Very true, he said.

Then now, said Socrates, let us recapitulate the argument. First, is not love of something, and of something too which is wanting to a man?

Yes, he replied.

Remember further what you said in your speech, or if you do not remember I will remind you: you said that the love of the beautiful set in order the empire of the gods, for that of deformed things there is no love—did you not say something of that kind?

Yes, said Agathon.

Yes, my friend, and the remark was a just one. And if this is true, Love is the love of beauty and not of deformity?

He assented.

And the admission has been already made that Love is of something which a man wants and has not?

True, he said.

Then Love wants and has not beauty?

Certainly, he replied.

And would you call that beautiful which wants and does not possess beauty?

Certainly not.

Then would you still say that love is beautiful?

Agathon replied: I fear that I did not understand what I was saying.

You made a very good speech, Agathon, replied Socrates; but there is yet one small question which I would fain ask:—Is not the good also the beautiful?

Yes.

Then in wanting the beautiful, love wants also the good?

I cannot refute you, Socrates, said Agathon:—Let us assume that what you say is true.

Say rather, beloved Agathon, that you cannot refute the truth; for Socrates is easily refuted.

And now, taking my leave of you, I would rehearse a tale of love which I heard from Diotima of Mantineia (compare 1 Alcibiades), a woman wise in this and in many other kinds of knowledge, who in the days of old, when the Athenians offered sacrifice before the coming of the plague, delayed the disease ten years. She was my instructress in the art of love, and I shall repeat to you what she said to me, beginning with the admissions made by Agathon, which are nearly if not quite the same which I made to the wise woman when she questioned me: I think that this will be the easiest way, and I shall take both parts myself as well as I can (compare Gorgias). As you, Agathon, suggested (supra), I must speak first of the being and nature of Love, and then of his works. First I said to her in nearly the same words which he used to me, that Love was a mighty god, and likewise fair; and she proved to me as I proved to him that, by my own showing, Love was neither fair nor good. 'What do you mean, Diotima,' I said, 'is love then evil and foul?' 'Hush,' she cried; 'must that be foul which is not fair?' 'Certainly,' I said. 'And is that which is not wise, ignorant? do you not see that there is a mean between wisdom and ignorance?' 'And what may that be?' I said. 'Right opinion,' she replied; 'which, as you know, being incapable of giving a reason, is not knowledge (for how can knowledge be devoid of reason? nor again, ignorance, for neither can ignorance attain the truth), but is clearly something which is a mean between ignorance and wisdom.' 'Quite true,' I replied. 'Do not then insist,' she said, 'that what is not fair is of necessity foul, or what is not good evil; or infer that because love is not fair and good he is therefore foul and evil; for he is in a mean between them.' 'Well,' I said, 'Love is surely admitted by all to be a great god.' 'By those who know or by those who do not know?' 'By all.' 'And how, Socrates,' she said with a smile, 'can Love be acknowledged to be a great god by those who say that he is not a god at all?' 'And who are they?' I said. 'You and I are two of them,' she replied. 'How can that be?' I said. 'It is quite

intelligible,' she replied; 'for you yourself would acknowledge that the gods are happy and fair—of course you would—would you dare to say that any god was not?' 'Certainly not,' I replied. 'And you mean by the happy, those who are the possessors of things good or fair?' 'Yes.' 'And you admitted that Love, because he was in want, desires those good and fair things of which he is in want?' 'Yes, I did.' 'But how can he be a god who has no portion in what is either good or fair?' 'Impossible.' 'Then you see that you also deny the divinity of Love.'

'What then is Love?' I asked; 'Is he mortal?' 'No.' 'What then?' 'As in the former instance, he is neither mortal nor immortal, but in a mean between the two.' 'What is he, Diotima?' 'He is a great spirit (daimon), and like all spirits he is intermediate between the divine and the mortal.' 'And what,' I said, 'is his power?' 'He interprets,' she replied, 'between gods and men, conveying and taking across to the gods the prayers and sacrifices of men, and to men the commands and replies of the gods; he is the mediator who spans the chasm which divides them, and therefore in him all is bound together, and through him the arts of the prophet and the priest, their sacrifices and mysteries and charms, and all prophecy and incantation, find their way. For God mingles not with man; but through Love all the intercourse and converse of God with man, whether awake or asleep, is carried on. The wisdom which understands this is spiritual; all other wisdom, such as that of arts and handicrafts, is mean and vulgar. Now these spirits or intermediate powers are many and diverse, and one of them is Love.' 'And who,' I said, 'was his father, and who his mother?' 'The tale,' she said, 'will take time; nevertheless I will tell you. On the birthday of Aphrodite there was a feast of the gods, at which the god Poros or Plenty, who is the son of Metis or Discretion, was one of the guests. When the feast was over, Penia or Poverty, as the manner is on such occasions, came about the doors to beg. Now Plenty who was the worse for nectar (there was no wine in those days), went into the garden of Zeus and fell into a heavy sleep, and Poverty considering her own straitened circumstances, plotted to have a child by him, and accordingly she lay down at his side and conceived Love, who partly because he is naturally a lover of the beautiful, and because Aphrodite is herself beautiful, and also because he was born on her birthday, is her follower and attendant. And as his parentage is, so also are his fortunes. In the first place he is always poor, and anything but tender and fair, as the many imagine him; and he is rough and squalid, and has no shoes, nor a house to dwell in; on the bare earth exposed he lies under the open heaven, in the streets, or at the doors of houses, taking his rest; and like his mother he is always in distress. Like his father too, whom he also partly resembles, he is always plotting against the fair and good; he is bold, enterprising, strong, a mighty hunter, always weaving some intrigue or other, keen in the pursuit of wisdom, fertile in resources; a philosopher at all times, terrible as an enchanter, sorcerer, sophist. He is by nature neither mortal nor immortal, but alive and flourishing at one moment when he is in plenty, and dead at another moment, and again alive by reason of his father's nature. But that which is always flowing in is always flowing out, and so he is never in want and never in wealth; and, further, he is in a mean between ignorance and knowledge. The truth of the matter is this: No god is a philosopher or seeker after wisdom, for he is wise already; nor does any man who is wise seek after wisdom. Neither do the ignorant seek after wisdom. For herein is the evil of ignorance, that he who is neither good nor wise is nevertheless satisfied with himself: he has no desire for that of which he feels no want.' 'But who then, Diotima,' I said, 'are the lovers of wisdom, if they are neither the wise nor the foolish?' 'A child may answer that question,' she replied; 'they are those who are in a mean between the two; Love is one of them. For wisdom is a most beautiful thing, and Love is of the beautiful; and therefore Love is also a philosopher or lover of wisdom, and being a lover of wisdom is in a mean between the wise and the ignorant. And of this too his birth is the cause; for his father is wealthy and wise, and his mother poor and foolish. Such, my dear Socrates, is the nature of the

spirit Love. The error in your conception of him was very natural, and as I imagine from what you say, has arisen out of a confusion of love and the beloved, which made you think that love was all beautiful. For the beloved is the truly beautiful, and delicate, and perfect, and blessed; but the principle of love is of another nature, and is such as I have described.'

I said, 'O thou stranger woman, thou sayest well; but, assuming Love to be such as you say, what is the use of him to men?' 'That, Socrates,' she replied, 'I will attempt to unfold: of his nature and birth I have already spoken; and you acknowledge that love is of the beautiful. But some one will say: Of the beautiful in what, Socrates and Diotima?—or rather let me put the question more clearly, and ask: When a man loves the beautiful, what does he desire?' I answered her 'That the beautiful may be his.' 'Still,' she said, 'the answer suggests a further question: What is given by the possession of beauty?' 'To what you have asked,' I replied, 'I have no answer ready.' 'Then,' she said, 'let me put the word "good" in the place of the beautiful, and repeat the question once more: If he who loves loves the good, what is it then that he loves?' 'The possession of the good,' I said. 'And what does he gain who possesses the good?' 'Happiness,' I replied; 'there is less difficulty in answering that question.' 'Yes,' she said, 'the happy are made happy by the acquisition of good things. Nor is there any need to ask why a man desires happiness; the answer is already final.' 'You are right.' I said. 'And is this wish and this desire common to all? and do all men always desire their own good, or only some men?—what say you?' 'All men,' I replied; 'the desire is common to all.' 'Why, then,' she rejoined, 'are not all men, Socrates, said to love, but only some of them? whereas you say that all men are always loving the same things.' 'I myself wonder,' I said, 'why this is.' 'There is nothing to wonder at,' she replied; 'the reason is that one part of love is separated off and receives the name of the whole, but the other parts have other names.' 'Give an illustration,' I said. She answered me as follows: 'There is poetry, which, as you know, is complex and manifold.

All creation or passage of non-being into being is poetry or making, and the processes of all art are creative; and the masters of arts are all poets or makers.' 'Very true.' 'Still,' she said, 'you know that they are not called poets, but have other names; only that portion of the art which is separated off from the rest, and is concerned with music and metre, is termed poetry, and they who possess poetry in this sense of the word are called poets.' 'Very true,' I said. 'And the same holds of love. For you may say generally that all desire of good and happiness is only the great and subtle power of love; but they who are drawn towards him by any other path, whether the path of money-making or gymnastics or philosophy, are not called lovers—the name of the whole is appropriated to those whose affection takes one form only—they alone are said to love, or to be lovers.' 'I dare say,' I replied, 'that you are right.' 'Yes,' she added, 'and you hear people say that lovers are seeking for their other half; but I say that they are seeking neither for the half of themselves, nor for the whole, unless the half or the whole be also a good. And they will cut off their own hands and feet and cast them away, if they are evil; for they love not what is their own, unless perchance there be some one who calls what belongs to him the good, and what belongs to another the evil. For there is nothing which men love but the good. Is there anything?' 'Certainly, I should say, that there is nothing.' 'Then,' she said, 'the simple truth is, that men love the good.' 'Yes,' I said. 'To which must be added that they love the possession of the good?' 'Yes, that must be added.' 'And not only the possession, but the everlasting possession of the good?' 'That must be added too.' 'Then love,' she said, 'may be described generally as the love of the everlasting possession of the good?' 'That is most true.'

'Then if this be the nature of love, can you tell me further,' she said, 'what is the manner of the pursuit? what are they doing who show all this eagerness and heat which is called love? and what is the object which they have in view? Answer me.' 'Nay, Diotima,' I replied, 'if I had known, I should not have wondered at your

wisdom, neither should I have come to learn from you about this very matter.' 'Well,' she said, 'I will teach you:—The object which they have in view is birth in beauty, whether of body or soul.' 'I do not understand you,' I said; 'the oracle requires an explanation.' 'I will make my meaning clearer,' she replied. 'I mean to say, that all men are bringing to the birth in their bodies and in their souls. There is a certain age at which human nature is desirous of procreation—procreation which must be in beauty and not in deformity; and this procreation is the union of man and woman, and is a divine thing; for conception and generation are an immortal principle in the mortal creature, and in the inharmonious they can never be. But the deformed is always inharmonious with the divine, and the beautiful harmonious. Beauty, then, is the destiny or goddess of parturition who presides at birth, and therefore, when approaching beauty, the conceiving power is propitious, and diffusive, and benign, and begets and bears fruit: at the sight of ugliness she frowns and contracts and has a sense of pain, and turns away, and shrivels up, and not without a pang refrains from conception. And this is the reason why, when the hour of conception arrives, and the teeming nature is full, there is such a flutter and ecstasy about beauty whose approach is the alleviation of the pain of travail. For love, Socrates, is not, as you imagine, the love of the beautiful only.' 'What then?' 'The love of generation and of birth in beauty.' 'Yes,' I said. 'Yes, indeed,' she replied. 'But why of generation?' 'Because to the mortal creature, generation is a sort of eternity and immortality,' she replied; 'and if, as has been already admitted, love is of the everlasting possession of the good, all men will necessarily desire immortality together with good: Wherefore love is of immortality.'

All this she taught me at various times when she spoke of love. And I remember her once saying to me, 'What is the cause, Socrates, of love, and the attendant desire? See you not how all animals, birds, as well as beasts, in their desire of procreation, are in agony when they take the infection of love, which begins with the desire of union; whereto is added the care of offspring, on whose behalf the weakest are ready to battle against the strongest even to the uttermost, and to die for them, and will let themselves be tormented with hunger or suffer anything in order to maintain their young. Man may be supposed to act thus from reason; but why should animals have these passionate feelings? Can you tell me why?' Again I replied that I did not know. She said to me: 'And do you expect ever to become a master in the art of love, if you do not know this?' 'But I have told you already, Diotima, that my ignorance is the reason why I come to you; for I am conscious that I want a teacher; tell me then the cause of this and of the other mysteries of love.' 'Marvel not,' she said, 'if you believe that love is of the immortal, as we have several times acknowledged; for here again, and on the same principle too, the mortal nature is seeking as far as is possible to be everlasting and immortal: and this is only to be attained by generation, because generation always leaves behind a new existence in the place of the old. Nay even in the life of the same individual there is succession and not absolute unity: a man is called the same, and yet in the short interval which elapses between youth and age, and in which every animal is said to have life and identity, he is undergoing a perpetual process of loss and reparation—hair, flesh, bones, blood, and the whole body are always changing. Which is true not only of the body, but also of the soul, whose habits, tempers, opinions, desires, pleasures, pains, fears, never remain the same in any one of us, but are always coming and going; and equally true of knowledge, and what is still more surprising to us mortals, not only do the sciences in general spring up and decay, so that in respect of them we are never the same; but each of them individually experiences a like change. For what is implied in the word "recollection," but the departure of knowledge, which is ever being forgotten, and is renewed and preserved by recollection, and appears to be the same although in reality new, according to that law of succession by which all mortal things are preserved, not absolutely the same, but by substitution, the old worn-out mortality leaving another new and similar existence

behind—unlike the divine, which is always the same and not another? And in this way, Socrates, the mortal body, or mortal anything, partakes of immortality; but the immortal in another way. Marvel not then at the love which all men have of their offspring; for that universal love and interest is for the sake of immortality.'

I was astonished at her words, and said: 'Is this really true, O thou wise Diotima?' And she answered with all the authority of an accomplished sophist: 'Of that, Socrates, you may be assured;—think only of the ambition of men, and you will wonder at the senselessness of their ways, unless you consider how they are stirred by the love of an immortality of fame. They are ready to run all risks greater far than they would have run for their children, and to spend money and undergo any sort of toil, and even to die, for the sake of leaving behind them a name which shall be eternal. Do you imagine that Alcestis would have died to save Admetus, or Achilles to avenge Patroclus, or your own Codrus in order to preserve the kingdom for his sons, if they had not imagined that the memory of their virtues, which still survives among us, would be immortal? Nay,' she said, 'I am persuaded that all men do all things, and the better they are the more they do them, in hope of the glorious fame of immortal virtue; for they desire the immortal.

'Those who are pregnant in the body only, betake themselves to women and beget children—this is the character of their love; their offspring, as they hope, will preserve their memory and giving them the blessedness and immortality which they desire in the future. But souls which are pregnant—for there certainly are men who are more creative in their souls than in their bodies—conceive that which is proper for the soul to conceive or contain. And what are these conceptions?—wisdom and virtue in general. And such creators are poets and all artists who are deserving of the name inventor. But the greatest and fairest sort of wisdom by far is that which is concerned with the ordering of states and families, and which is called temperance and justice. And he who in youth has the seed of these implanted in him and is himself inspired, when he comes to maturity desires to beget and generate. He wanders about seeking beauty that he may beget offspring—for in deformity he will beget nothing—and naturally embraces the beautiful rather than the deformed body; above all when he finds a fair and noble and well-nurtured soul, he embraces the two in one person, and to such an one he is full of speech about virtue and the nature and pursuits of a good man; and he tries to educate him; and at the touch of the beautiful which is ever present to his memory, even when absent, he brings forth that which he had conceived long before, and in company with him tends that which he brings forth; and they are married by a far nearer tie and have a closer friendship than those who beget mortal children, for the children who are their common offspring are fairer and more immortal. Who, when he thinks of Homer and Hesiod and other great poets, would not rather have their children than ordinary human ones? Who would not emulate them in the creation of children such as theirs, which have preserved their memory and given them everlasting glory? Or who would not have such children as Lycurgus left behind him to be the saviours, not only of Lacedaemon, but of Hellas, as one may say? There is Solon, too, who is the revered father of Athenian laws; and many others there are in many other places, both among Hellenes and barbarians, who have given to the world many noble works, and have been the parents of virtue of every kind; and many temples have been raised in their honour for the sake of children such as theirs; which were never raised in honour of any one, for the sake of his mortal children.

'These are the lesser mysteries of love, into which even you, Socrates, may enter; to the greater and more hidden ones which are the crown of these, and to which, if you pursue them in a right spirit, they will lead, I know not whether you will be able to attain. But I will do my utmost to inform you, and do you follow if you can. For he who would proceed aright in this matter should begin in youth to visit beautiful forms; and first, if he be guided by his instructor aright, to love one such form only—out of

that he should create fair thoughts; and soon he will of himself perceive that the beauty of one form is akin to the beauty of another; and then if beauty of form in general is his pursuit, how foolish would he be not to recognize that the beauty in every form is one and the same! And when he perceives this he will abate his violent love of the one, which he will despise and deem a small thing, and will become a lover of all beautiful forms; in the next stage he will consider that the beauty of the mind is more honourable than the beauty of the outward form. So that if a virtuous soul have but a little comeliness, he will be content to love and tend him, and will search out and bring to the birth thoughts which may improve the young, until he is compelled to contemplate and see the beauty of institutions and laws, and to understand that the beauty of them all is of one family, and that personal beauty is a trifle; and after laws and institutions he will go on to the sciences, that he may see their beauty, being not like a servant in love with the beauty of one youth or man or institution, himself a slave mean and narrow-minded, but drawing towards and contemplating the vast sea of beauty, he will create many fair and noble thoughts and notions in boundless love of wisdom; until on that shore he grows and waxes strong, and at last the vision is revealed to him of a single science, which is the science of beauty everywhere. To this I will proceed; please to give me your very best attention:

'He who has been instructed thus far in the things of love, and who has learned to see the beautiful in due order and succession, when he comes toward the end will suddenly perceive a nature of wondrous beauty (and this, Socrates, is the final cause of all our former toils)—a nature which in the first place is everlasting, not growing and decaying, or waxing and waning; secondly, not fair in one point of view and foul in another, or at one time or in one relation or at one place fair, at another time or in another relation or at another place foul, as if fair to some and foul to others, or in the likeness of a face or hands or any other part of the bodily frame, or in any form of speech or knowledge, or existing in any other being, as for example, in an animal, or in heaven, or in earth, or in any other place; but beauty absolute, separate, simple, and everlasting, which without diminution and without increase, or any change, is imparted to the ever-growing and perishing beauties of all other things. He who from these ascending under the influence of true love, begins to perceive that beauty, is not far from the end. And the true order of going, or being led by another, to the things of love, is to begin from the beauties of earth and mount upwards for the sake of that other beauty, using these as steps only, and from one going on to two, and from two to all fair forms, and from fair forms to fair practices, and from fair practices to fair notions, until from fair notions he arrives at the notion of absolute beauty, and at last knows what the essence of beauty is. This, my dear Socrates,' said the stranger of Mantineia, 'is that life above all others which man should live, in the contemplation of beauty absolute; a beauty which if you once beheld, you would see not to be after the measure of gold, and garments, and fair boys and youths, whose presence now entrances you; and you and many a one would be content to live seeing them only and conversing with them without meat or drink, if that were possible—you only want to look at them and to be with them. But what if man had eyes to see the true beauty—the divine beauty, I mean, pure and clear and unalloyed, not clogged with the pollutions of mortality and all the colours and vanities of human life—thither looking, and holding converse with the true beauty simple and divine? Remember how in that communion only, beholding beauty with the eye of the mind, he will be enabled to bring forth, not images of beauty, but realities (for he has hold not of an image but of a reality), and bringing forth and nourishing true virtue to become the friend of God and be immortal, if mortal man may. Would that be an ignoble life?'

Such, Phaedrus—and I speak not only to you, but to all of you—were the words of Diotima; and I am persuaded of their truth. And being persuaded of them, I try to persuade others, that in the attainment of this end human nature will not easily find a helper better than love: And therefore, also, I say that every man ought to honour him as I myself honour him, and walk in his ways, and exhort others to do the same, and praise the power and spirit of love according to the measure of my ability now and ever.

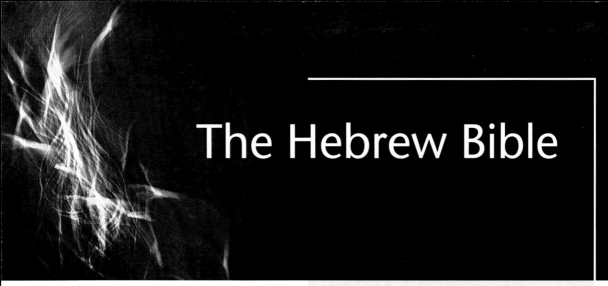

The Hebrew Bible

Editors' Introduction

Although the Bible is normally referred to as if it is a single book, it is well to keep in mind that the text we know as "the Bible" is in fact a collection of writings assembled over an extended period of time by the various religious communities for whom it is the revealed Word of God. Those writings that have been "officially" recognized by the relevant authorities as forming part of scripture are said to be part of the "canon" (from the Latin word for measure or rule) of scripture. The history of the formation of the canon within Judaism and among the various branches of Christianity is complicated and fascinating.

Within the Christian tradition the Bible is understood to consist of two parts, traditionally known as the Old Testament and the New Testament. In recent years (at least in many academic circles) it has become more common to refer to the Old Testament as the Hebrew Bible. One reason for this change has been a concern to avoid any suggestion that the usage "Old" Testament implies that these writings are no longer relevant for Christians or that they are no longer important when seen in light of the New Testament. Another important reason has to do with a heightened sense of interreligious sensitivity. While it is certainly the case that Christianity views the message and events narrated in the New Testament as having brought the story of salvation to its fulfillment, there has also developed a heightened awareness that, however benign the intention behind the usage of Old and New Testaments, such terminology can be offensive to those who understand "Old" in the pejorative sense of passé, superseded, or outdated. To those for whom Judaism is a vibrant, living tradition, and for whom the Hebrew Bible is *the* Bible (and not simply the "Old" part of another tradition's scripture), the description "Old Testament" is not conducive to interreligious dialogue. To speak, then, of the "Hebrew Bible" is also to affirm that this collection of writings has integrity of its own, apart from its incorporation into the Bible used by Christians.

Using the term "Hebrew Bible," however, is not without its problems. Some prefer the term "Jewish Bible," and they point out (rightly) that not all of the books regarded in Judaism as constituting the Bible were actually written in Hebrew (some were written in Aramaic). These are legitimate concerns; but for purposes of this volume we will use "Hebrew Bible" to refer to that collection of texts within Judaism known as the "Tanakh"— those writings recognized as forming the canon of scripture. Within the Hebrew Bible (Tanakh) there are three divisions: the Torah (Teaching), the Neviim (Prophets), and the Ketuvim (Writings). Of these three classes of writings, a primacy is given to the Torah (also referred to as the Pentateuch or the Five Books of Moses). In this reader we have included texts from the Torah (Genesis and Exodus) and from the Ketuvim (Ruth).

The Events, The Personages, The Ideas in The Bible

Formation of the People of God   From 1900 to 1000

PERIODS	MAJOR EVENTS	POLITICS AND SOCIAL LIFE	PERSONAGES	MOVEMENT OF IDEAS
PATRIARCHS 1800–1700	1720 arrival of the HYKSOS in EGYPT	Coming from Mesopotamia, a family of shepherds leads a nomadic life at the edge of the desert and the cultivated lands of Syro-Palestine	**ABRAHAM JACOB**	First ORAL TRADITIONS about the PATRIARCHS (Gn 12—50)—set to writing centuries later, they stress • FIDELITY to vocation • FAITH • PROMISE of a posterity and a land
		The general migration of peoples draws the descendants of Jacob into Egypt	**JOSEPH**	• Successive DETACHMENTS (separation from the clan of Terah, separation from Lot, banishment of Ishmael)
	1560 departure of the HYKSOS	Silence in the Bible about five centuries of history THE HEBREWS IN EGYPT		
EXODUS ABOUT 1250–1225		DELIVERANCE FROM EGYPT. The descendants of Abraham begin to organize themselves into a people • Common adventure in the Sinai desert • Semi-sedentarization near Kadesh	**MOSES**	ORAL TRADITIONS concerning SINAI (Book of Exodus) set to writing a few centuries later Awareness of a SOLIDARITY: • in VOCATION - Conclusion of the Sinai Covenant (Ex 24) • in DAILY LIFE - by the observance of the LAW, core of the most ancient legislative collections (ancient cultual laws: Ex 34: *Code of the Covenant*: Ex 21—23: moral Decalogue: Ex 20 and Dt 5) • in a COMMON HISTORY - regrouping of the most ancient traditions about the origins of the world and the Patriarchs
INSTALLATION IN CANAAN JUDGES 1250–1225		Struggle between the feudal regime in Canaan and the tribes in process of sedentarization The Israelites settle in the mountainous regions (hills of Gilead. mountain of Ephraim, hills of Judah) CONFEDERATION OF THE TWELVE TRIBES, created at the time of the pact of Shechem (Jos 24)	**JOSHUA DEBORAH JEPHTHAH GIDEON SAMSON**	The TRADITIONS are preserved around major sanctuaries • The proud independence of the nomad jealous of his freedom is opposed to the necessary organization required by the sedentary life which is directed toward royalty • Strict Yahwism, the religion of fidelity to a God who guides history confronts the naturalistic religion of the Canaanean Baals, seeking fecundity by means of magical rites • The direct authority of God over his people (Theocracy) and its compatibility with a human royalty These various attitudes are found in the Books of Samuel
		SEMI-NOMADIC ROYALTY: • no capital, administration or professional army • the king, simple military chief intervenes only in case of danger	**SAUL SAMUEL**	

Reprinted by permission of Catholic Book Publishing Corp.

Yahwistic Royalty   1000 to 586

Period	Date	Events	Figures	Literary / Religious development
UNIFIED MONARCHY 1010–931	Around 1060 CAPTURE OF JERUSALEM	MORE CENTRALIZED ROYALTY than that of Saul. The strong personality of DAVID provisionally unites North and South (Israel and Judah) Capital, mercenary army. administration. taxes: the king rules over the entire population in his territory and no longer only over the tribes of Israel	DAVID NATHAN	Administration gives rise to a class of SCRIBES which is at the origin of the first literary period. Parallel development of royalty and classical PROPHETISM ROYAL IDEOLOGY, foundation of MESSIANISM
		Hypertrophy of the royal organization, great splendor at the court: excessive taxes announcing decadence	SOLOMON	Construction of the temple at Jerusalem, religious capital. Apogee of the literary period: • *Royal Psalms* • Collection of the old traditions: (*Yahwist, J*) • Beginning of the wisdom literature: *first Proverbs* • History of succession to throne (2 Sm 9—20 and 1 Kgs 1—2)
THE TWO KINGDOMS	931 SCHISM	SOUTHERN KINGDOM (JUDAH): dynastic stability Sacred character of royalty Struggle with the North over the establishment of their common frontier, then an alliance		
		NORTHERN KINGDOM (ISRAEL): politically more important than Judah. Dynastic instability (19 kings - 9 dynasties) Search for a capital: Shechem. Puma Tirzah (2). Finally Omri founds SAMARIA to foster the opening out to Phoenicia	OMRI ELIJAH ELISHA	Traditions of the North set to writing (*Elohist. E*) *The epic of Elijah and Elisha* (1 Kgs 17—2 Kgs 13)
			AMOS	SOCIAL JUSTICE Announcement of the Day of Yahweh, day of wrath
		Expansion but social inequality: religion controlled by political system, coalitions with neighboring countries against Assyria	HOSEA	LOVE and FIDELITY of Yahweh for his people Struggle against the influence of the religion of the Baals
JUDAH	721 CAPTURE OF SAMARIA by Sargon II		HEZEKIAH ISAIAH	ROYALTY - HOLINESS of Yahweh MESSIANISM: a descendant of David will inaugurate a reign of justice. After the trial, a small "remnant" will return to Yahweh
			MICAH	First core of Deuteronomy (19—27), heritage of the Northern tribes. Uniting of the Yahwist and Elohist tradition - *Proverbs*
		Series of coalitions against ASSYRIA, then against BABYLONIA	JOSIAH JEREMIAH	Interior religion, dialogue with God - suffering Announcement of the NEW COVENANT written on man's heart
	536 CAPTURE OF JERUSALEM			*Deuteronomy* and Deuteronomic reform, first presentation of *Deuteronomic history* (Joshua, Judges, Samuel, Kings) completed during the Exile and at the return the codification of the customs of the Priesthood of Jerusalem, core of Leviticus (*Holiness Code, Lv 17—26*)

JUDAISM FROM 586 TO JESUS CHRIST

Period	Date/Event	Historical situation	Figures	Developments
PREPARATION OF JUDAISM IN EXILE	560 CAPTURE OF JERUSALEM	Babylonia: the ellite of the deported population is gathered into agrecutural colonies	EZEKIEL	Apocalyptic visions and style - the presence of Yahweh is no longer tied to Zion - personal moral responsibility - grandiose per~spectives of restoration after the Exile (demand for purity)
		Palestine: only the inferior classes remain The neighbors (Ammon, Edom) infiltrate into Judah		Meditation on the past - collection of the traditions (J-E-D) Constitution of the *prophetic collections — Priestly History* (P) according to the spirit of Ezekiel and the priests of Jerusalem All this will gradually constitute the "Book of the Word of God" Sacrificial worship is replaced by prayer meetings (beginning of synagogal worship - insistence on the external marks of belonging to the people of God (sabbath, circumcision, fasting)
	538 EDICT OF CYRUS	Babylonia: The exiles gradually settle clown, some enter into administration, others carry on com~merce (archives of a bank)	2nd ISAIAH	Confidence in the almighty Word of Yahweh; Universalist overture Meaning of suffering (songs of the Servant)
ESTABLISH-MENT OF JUDAISM Persian period		RETURN TO PALESTINE Political and economical difficulties Religious com~munity directed by priests	ZERUBBABEL HAGGAI MALACHI	End of prophetism - Predominance of SCRIBES and SAGES End of the work of the Priestly School • Bringing together of the tradition of the *Pentateuch* (J-E-D-P) • Definitive edition of Jos - Jgs - 1 and 2 Sm - 1 and 2 Kgs
		Judah is part of a province of the Persian Empire. but the Judeans have a personal juridic statute: for them the "Law of God" is the "law of the king"	EZRA NEHEMIAH	Severe reform which marks the establishing of JUDAISM, but • Reprise of a UNIVERSALIST overture: *Jonah* • Reprise of the ideas of Dt and return to Messianism: *Chronicles*
	333-323 ALEXANDER THE GREAT			The Sages: • publish their classic teaching: *Proverbs* • pose questions: *Ecclesiastes—Job* • seek to edify: *Ruth-Esther-Tobie* Religious poems: *Song of Songs* - numerous *Psalms*
SPREAD OF JUDAISM Hellenistic period		The central authority imposes Hellenization The Jews resist through fidelity to the law Crisis at the time of the persecution of Anthiochus V The Jewish revolt attains independence Appearance of politico-religious sects: • Sadducees - party of the high priests who admit compromises • Pharisees - strictly faithful to the law • Political extremists (Zealots) and religious extrem-ists (Essenes) separate themselves from them		Importance assumed by the Jewish community of Alexandria: • Translation of the Bible into Greek: the *Septuagint* • God's wisdom in creation and history: *Sirach*
			The MACCABEES John HYRCANUS	Resistance to persecution takes various forms: Armed resistance recounted in *1 Maccabees* • Hope for divine intervention: *2 Maccabees* - *Daniel* - *Judith*
	+63 CAPTURE OF JERUSALEM BY THE ROMANS			In the face of persecution a Sage from Alexandria sings of the Wisdom of God who governs the world and saves his people: *Wisdom*

The New Testament

ROME	DATES	PALESTINE		DATES	SACRED BOOKS
EMPERORS AUGUSTUS	31		HEROD THE GREAT	37	PROBABLE DATES OF REDACTION FOR THE PRINCIPAL BOOKS OF THE NEW TESTAMENT
	6 4	Birth of Jesus Death of Herod the Great	Partition of Palestine	4	
		JUDEA	GALILEE		
		Tetrarchs:			
		HEROD ARCHELAUS	HEROD ANTIPAS	4	
	1			1	
	4	ROMAN PROCURATORS			
TIBERIUS	14				
	26	PONTIUS PILATE			
	30	Crucifixion of Jesus			
	35	Martyrdom of Stephen			
CAIUS CALIGULA	37	Conversion of Saul			
CLAUDIUS	41	1st voyage of Paul	HEROD AGRIPPA 1st King	41	
			Famine (Acts 11:28)	44	
	49	Council of Jerusalem 2nd voyage of Paul			
				50	1 and 2 Thessalonians
		(Gallo proconsul of Achais		52	
				53-54	Galatians
NERO	54	ANTONIUS FELIX			
				56-57	1 Corinthians
				57	2 Corinthians Romans
	58	3rd voyage and arrest of Paul			
		PORCIUS FESTUS		60	Phillipians
				62	Colossians Ephesians Gospels of Mark, Matthew and Luke (between 64 and 80)
Burning of Rome	64				
	64-67	Martyrdom of Peter and Paul			
VESPASIAN	67	Jewish Revolt		65-67	Pastoral Epistles
	70	Destruction of the temple of Jerusalem		70-80	2nd Epistle of Peter Jude
TITUS	79	by the Romans			
DOMITIAN	81				
TRAJAN	98			90-100	Revelation, Letters and Gospel of John

Reprinted by permission of Catholic Book Publishing Corp.

The Pentateuch

The Pentateuch (Greek for "five books") designates the first five books of the Jewish and Christian Bible (Genesis, Exodus, Leviticus, Numbers, and Deuteronomy). Jewish tradition calls the five books Torah (Teaching, Law) because of the centrality of the Sinai covenant and legislation mediated through Moses.

The unity of the Pentateuch comes from the single story it tells. God creates the world and destines human beings for the blessings of progeny and land possession (Gn 1–3). As the human race expands, its evil conduct provokes God to send the flood to wipe out all but righteous Noah's family. After the flood, the world is repopulated from his three sons, Ham, Shem, and Japheth (Gn 4–9). From them are descended the seventy nations of the civilized world whose offense this time (building a city rather than taking their assigned lands, Gn 10–11) provokes God to elect one family from the rest. Abraham and his wife, Sarah, land-less and childless, are promised a child and the land of Canaan. Amid trials and fresh promises, a son (Isaac) is born to them and Abraham takes title to a sliver of Canaanite land, a kind of down payment for later possession (Gn 12–25). Genesis 25–36 tells how their descendant Jacob becomes the father of twelve sons (because of which he is called "Israel"), and Genesis 37–50 tells how the rejected brother Joseph saves the family from famine and brings them to Egypt.

In Egypt, a pharaoh who knew not Joseph subjects "the seventy sons of Jacob" ("the Hebrews") to hard labor, keeping them from their land and destroying their male progeny (Ex 1). Moses is commissioned to lead the people out of Egypt to their own land (Ex 2–6). In ten plagues, the Lord defeats Pharaoh. Free at last, the Hebrews leave Egypt and journey to Mount Sinai (Ex 7–18), where they enter into a covenant to be the people of the Lord and be shaped by the Ten Commandments and other laws (Ex 19–24). Though the people commit apostasy when Moses goes back to the mountain for the plans of the dwelling (tabernacle), Moses' intercession

prevents the abrogation of the covenant by God (Ex 32–34). A principle has been established, however: even the people's apostasy need not end their relationship with God. The book ends with the cloud and the glory taking possession of the tent of meeting (Ex 36:34-38). "The sons of Israel" in Ex 1:1 are the actual sons of Jacob/Israel the patriarch, but at the end of the book they are the nation Israel, for all the elements of nation-hood in antiquity have been granted: a god (and temple), a leader, a land, and an authoritative tradition.

Israel remains at the holy mountain for almost a year. The entire block of material from Ex 19:1 to Nm 10:11 is situated at Sinai. The rituals of Leviticus and Numbers are delivered to Moses at the holy mountain, showing that Israel's worship was instituted by God and part of the very fabric of the people's life. Priestly material in the Book of Exodus (Ex 25–31, 35–40) describes the basic institutions of Israelite worship (the tabernacle, its furniture, and priestly vestments). Leviticus, aptly called in rabbinic tradition the Priests' Manual, lays down the role of priests to teach Israel the distinction between clean and unclean and to see to their holiness. In Nm 10:11–22:1, the journey is resumed, this time from Sinai through the wilderness to Transjordan; Nm 22:2–36:13 tells of events and laws in the plains of Moab.

The final book of the Pentateuch, Deuteronomy, consists of four speeches by Moses to the people who have arrived at the plains of Moab, ready to conquer the land: Dt 1:1 4:43; 4:44–28:68; 29:1–32:52; 33:1–34:12. Each speech is introduced by the formula "This is the law/words/blessing."

The Priestly editor used literary formulas. The formula "These are the generations (the wording can vary) of . . ." occurs five times in the primordial history (Gn 2:4a; 5:1; 6:9; 10:1; 11:10) and five times in the ancestral history (Gn 11:27; 25:12; 25:19; 36:1 [v. 9 is secondary]; 37:2). In Exodus and Numbers the formula (with slight variations) "They departed from (place name) and encamped at (place name)" occurs in two groups of six: A. Ex 12:37a; 13:20; 14:1-2; 15:22a; 16:1; 17:1a; and B. Ex 19:2; Nm 10:12; 20:la; 20:22; 21:10-11; 22:1.

Who wrote the Pentateuch, and when? Up to the seventeenth century, the virtually unanimous answer of Jews and Christians was "Moses" Moses wrote the Pentateuch as David wrote the Psalter and Solomon wrote the wisdom literature. Though scholars had noted inconsistencies (compare Ishmael's age in Gn 16:16 and 21:5, 14) and duplications (Gn 12, 20, and 26), they assumed Mosaic authorship because of the prevalent theory of inspiration: God inspired authors while they wrote. With the rise of historical criticism, scholars began to use the doublets and inconsistencies as clues to different authors and traditions.

By the late nineteenth century, one theory of the sources of the Pentateuch had been worked out that proved acceptable in its main lines to the majority of scholars (apart from Christian and Jewish conservatives) then and now. It can be quickly sketched. In the pre-monarchic period of the Judges (ca. 1220–1020 B.C.), the twelve tribes had an oral form of their story from creation to the taking of the land. With the beginnings of monarchy in the late eleventh and tenth centuries, the oral material was written down, being known as the Yahwist account (from its use of the divine name Yhwh). Its abbreviation, "J," comes from the German spelling of the divine name. In the following century, another account took shape in the Northern Kingdom (called E after its use of Elohim as a divine name); some believe the E source is simply a supplement to J. After the fall of the Northern Kingdom in 722/721 B.C., the E version was taken to Jerusalem where it was combined with the J version to produce J-E. During the exile (conventionally dated 587–539 B.C.) or thereafter, an editor recast J-E to make it relevant for the exiled population. This editor is conventionally known as P (=Priestly) because of the chronological and ritual interests apparent in the work. P can also designate archival material and chronological notices. The audience for the Priestly edition no longer lived in the land and was deeply concerned about its survival and its claim on the land.

Deuteronomy (=D) stands alone in style, genre (preaching rather than narrative), and content. How did it come to be the fifth book of the Pentateuch? The J-E narrative actually ends in Numbers, when Israel arrives at the plains of Moab. Many scholars believe that Deuteronomy was secondarily attached to Numbers by moving the account of Moses' death from its original place in the J-E version in Numbers to the end of Deuteronomy (Dt 34). Deuteronomy was attached to Genesis–Numbers to link it to another great work, the Deuteronomistic History (Joshua to Kings). Deuteronomy is now the fifth book of the Pentateuch and the first book of the Deuteronomistic History.

In the last three decades, the above consensus on the composition of the Pentateuch has come under attack. Some critics are extremely skeptical about the historical value of the so-called early traditions, and a few doubt there ever was a preexilic monarchy of any substance. For such scholars, the Pentateuch is a retrojection from the fourth or third centuries B.C. Other scholars postulate a different sequence of sources, or understand the sources differently.

How should a modern religiously minded person read the Pentateuch? First, readers have before them the most significant thing, the text of the Pentateuch. It is accurately preserved, reasonably well understood, and capable of touching audiences of every age. Take and read! Second, the controversies are about the sources of the Pentateuch, especially their antiquity and character. Many details will never be known, for the evidence is scanty. Indeed, the origin of many great literary works is obscure.

The Pentateuch witnesses to a coherent story that begins with the creation of the world and ends with Israel taking its land. The same story is in the historical Ps 44, 77, 78, 80, 105, 114, and 149, and in the confessions Dt 26:5-9, Jos 24:2-13, and 1 Sm 12:7-13. Though the narrative enthralls and entertains, as all great literature does, it is well to remember that it is a theopolitical charter as well, meant to establish how and why descendants of the patriarchs are a uniquely holy people among the world's nations.

The destruction of the Jerusalem Temple and deportation of Israelites in the sixth century B.C. seemed to invalidate the charter, for Israel no longer possessed its land in any real sense. The last chapter of the ancient narrative—Israel dwelling securely in its land—no longer held true. The story had to be reinterpreted, and the Priestly editor is often credited with doing so. A preface (Gn 1) was added, emphasizing God's intent that human beings continue in existence through their progeny and possess their own land. Good news, surely, to a devastated people wondering whether they would survive and repossess their ancestral land. The ending of the old story was changed to depict Israel at the threshold of the promised land (the plains of Moab) rather than in it. Henceforth, Israel would be a people oriented toward the land rather than possessing it. The revised ending could not be more suitable for Jews and Christians alike. Both peoples can imagine themselves on the threshold of the promised land, listening to the word of God in order to be able to enter it in the future. For Christians particularly, the Pentateuch portrays the pilgrim people waiting for the full realization of the kingdom of God.

The Book of Genesis

Genesis is the first book of the Pentateuch (Genesis, Exodus, Leviticus, Numbers, Deuteronomy), the first section of the Jewish and the Christian Scriptures. Its title in English, "Genesis," comes from the Greek of Gn 2:4, literati.); "the book of the generation (genesis) of the heavens and earth." Its title in the Jewish Scriptures is the opening Hebrew word, *Bereshit,* "in the beginning."

The book has two major sections—the creation and expansion of the human race (2:4—11:9), and the story of Abraham and his descendants (11:10—50:26). The first section deals with God and the nations, and the second deals with God and a particular nation, Israel. The opening creation account (1:1—2:3) lifts up two themes that play major roles in each section—the divine command to the first couple (standing for the whole race) to produce offspring and to possess land (1:28). In the first section, progeny and land appear in the form of births and genealogies (chaps. 2—9) and allotment of land (chaps. 10—11), and in the second, progeny and land appear in the form of promises of descendants and land to the ancestors. Another indication of editing is the formulaic introduction, "this is the story; these are the descendants" (Hebrew *tōledôt*), which occurs five times in Section I (2:4; 5:1; 6:9; 10:1; 10:31) and five times in Section II (11:10; 25:12, 19; 36:1 [v. 9 is an addition]; 37:2).

The Composition of the Book. For the literary sources of Genesis, see "Introduction to the Pentateuch." As far as the sources of Genesis are concerned, contemporay readers can reasonably assume that ancient traditions (J and E) were edited in the sixth or fifth century B.C. for a Jewish audience that had suffered the effects of the exile and was now largely living outside of Palestine. The editor highlighted themes of vital concern to this audience: God intends that every nation have posterity and land; the ancestors of Israel are models for their descendants who also live in hope rather than in full possession of what has been promised; the ancient covenant with God is eternal, remaining valid even when the human party has been unfaithful. By highlighting such concerns, the editor addressed the worries of exiled Israel and indeed of contemporary Jews and Christians.

Genesis I—II. The seven-day creation account in Gn 1:1—2:3 tells of a God whose mere word creates a beautiful universe in which human beings are an integral and important part. Though Gn 2:4—3:24 is often regarded as "the second creation story" the text suggests that the whole of 2:4—11:9 tells one story. The plot of Gn 2—11 (creation, the flood, renewed creation) has been borrowed from creation-flood stories attested in Mesopotamian literature of the second and early first millennia. In the Mesopotamian creation flood stories, the gods created the human race as slaves whose task it was to manage the universe for them—giving them food, clothing, and honor in temple ceremonies. In an unforeseen development, however; the human race grew so numerous and noisy that the gods could not sleep. Deeply angered, the gods decided to destroy the race by a universal flood. One man and his family; however; secretly warned of the flood by his patron god, built a boat and suvived. Soon regretting their impetuous decision, the gods created a revised version of humankind. The new race was created mortal so they would never again grow numerous and bother the gods. The authors of Genesis adapted the creation-flood story in accord with their views of God and humanity. For example, they attributed the fault to human sin rather than to divine miscalculation (6:5–7) and had God reaffirm without change the original creation (9:1–7). In the biblical version God is just, powerful, and not needy.

How should modern readers interpret the creation-flood story in Gn 2—11? The stories are neither history nor myth. "Myth" is an unsuitable term, for it has several different meanings and connotes untruth in popular English. "History" is equally misleading, for it suggests that the events actually took place. The best term is creation-flood story. Ancient Near Eastern thinkers did not have our methods of exploring serious questions. Instead, they used narratives for issues that we would call philosophical and theological. They added and subtracted narrative details and varied the plot as they sought meaning in the ancient stories. Their stories reveal a privileged time, when divine decisions were made that determined the future of the human race. The origin of something was thought to explain its present meaning, e.g., how God acts with justice and generosity; why human beings are rebellious, the nature of sexual attraction and marriage, why there are many peoples and languages. Though the stories may initially strike us as primitive and naive, they are in fact told with skill, compression, and subtlety. They provide profound answers to perennial questions about God and human beings.

Genesis 11—50. One Jewish tradition suggests that God, having been rebuffed in the attempt to forge a relationship with the nations, decided to concentrate on one nation in the hope that it would eventually bring in all the nations. The migration of Abraham's family (11:26–31) is part of the general movement of the human race to take possession of their lands (see 10:32—11:9). Abraham, however; must come into possession of his land in a manner different from the nations, for he will not immediately possess it nor will he have descendants in the manner of the nations, for he is old and his wife is childless (12:1–9). Abraham and Sarah have to live with their God in trust and obedience until at last Isaac is born to them and they manage to buy a sliver of the land (the burial cave at Machpelah, chap. 23). Abraham's humanity and faith offer a wonderful example to the exilic generation.

The historicity of the ancestral stories has been much discussed. Scholars have traditionally dated them sometime in the first half of the second millennium, though a few regard them as late (sixth or fifth century B.C.) and purely fictional. There is unfortunately no direct extra-biblical evidence

confirming (or disproving) the stories. The ancestral stories have affinities, however; to late second-millenium stories of childless ancestors, and their proper names fit linguistic patterns attested in the second millennium. Given the lack of decisive evidence, it is reasonable to accept the Bible's own chronology that the patriarchs were the ancestors of Israel and that they lived well before the exodus that is generally dated in the thirteenth century.

Gn 25:19—35:43 are about Jacob and his twelve sons. The stories are united by a geographical frame: Jacob lives in Canaan until his theft of the right of the firstborn from his brother Esau forces him to flee to Paddan-Aram (alternately Aram-Naharaim). There his uncle Laban tricks him as he earlier tricked his brother: But Jacob is blessed with wealth and sons. He returns to Canaan to receive the final blessing, land, and on the way is reconciled with his brother Esau. As the sons have reached the number of twelve, the patriarch can be given the name Israel (32:28; 35:10). The blessings given to Abraham are reaffirmed to Isaac and to Jacob.

The last cycle of ancestor stories is about Jacob's son Joseph (37:1—50:26, though in chaps. 48—49 the focus swings back to Jacob). The Joseph stories are sophisticated in theme, deftly plotted, and show keen interest in the psychology of the characters. Jacob's favoring of Joseph, the son of his beloved wife Rachel, provokes his brothers to kill him. Joseph escapes death through the intercession of Reuben, the eldest, and of Judah, but is sold into slavery in Egypt. In the immediately following chap. 38, Judah undergoes experiences similar to Joseph's. Joseph, endowed by God with wisdom, becomes second only to Pharaoh in Egypt. From that powerful position, he encounters his unsuspecting brothers who have come to Egypt because of the famine, and tests them to see if they have repented. Joseph learns that they have given up their hatred because of their love for Israel, their father. Judah, who seems to have inherited the mantle of the failed oldest brother Reuben, expresses the brothers' new and profound appreciation of their father and Joseph (chap. 44). At the end of Genesis, the entire family of Jacob/Israel is in Egypt, which prepares for the events in the Book of Exodus.

Genesis in Later Biblical Books. The historical and prophetic books constantly refer to the covenant with the ancestors Abraham, Isaac, and Jacob. Hos 10 sees the traits of Jacob in the behavior of the Israel of his own day. Is 51:2 cites Abraham and Sarah as a model for his dispirited community, for though only a couple, they became a great nation. Jn 1, "In the beginning was the word," alludes to Gn 1:1 (and Pry 8:22) to show that Jesus is creating a new world. St. Paul interprets Jesus as the New Adam in Rom 5:14 and 1 Cor 15:22, 24, whose obedience brings life just as the Old Adam's disobedience brought death. In Rom 4, Paul cites Abraham as someone who was righteous in God's eves centuries before the Law was given at Sinai.

Outline of Genesis:

Preamble. The Creation of the World (1:1—2:3)

I. The Story of the Nations (2:4—11:26)
   A. The Creation of the Man and the Woman, Their Offspring, and the Spread of Civilization (2:4—4:26)
   B. The Pre flood Generations (5:1—6:8)
   C. The Flood and the Renewed Blessing (6:9—9:29)
   D. The Populating of the World and the Prideful City (10:1—11:9)
   E. The Genealogy from Shem to Terah (11:10–26)

II. The Story of the Ancestors of Israel (11:27—50:26)
   A. The Story of Abraham and Sarah (11:27—25:18)
   B. The Story of Isaac and Jacob (25:19—36:43)
   C. The Story of Joseph (37:1—50:26)

The Story of Abraham

CHAPTER 12

Abram's Call and Migration.[1] The Lord said to Abram: Go forth from your land, your relatives, and from your father's house to a land that I will show you. [2] I will make of you a great nation, and I will bless you; I will make your name great, so that you will be a blessing. [3] I will bless those who bless you and curse those who curse you. All the families of the earth will find blessing in you.

[4] Abram went as the Lord directed him, and Lot went with him. Abram was seventy-five years old when he left Haran. [5] Abram took his wife Sarai, his brother's son Lot, all the possessions that they had accumulated, and the persons they had acquired in Haran, and they set out for the land of Canaan. When they came to the land of Canaan, [6] Abram passed through the land as far as the sacred place at Shechem, by the oak of Moreh. The Canaanites were then in the land.

[7] The Lord appeared to Abram and said: To your descendants I will give this land. So Abram built an altar there to the Lord who had appeared to him. [8] From there he moved on to the hill country east of Bethel, pitching his tent with Bethel to the west and Ai to the east. He built an altar there to the Lord and invoked the Lord by name. [9] Then Abram journeyed on by stages to the Negeb.

Abram and Sarai in Egypt. [10] There was famine in the land; so Abram went down to Egypt to sojourn there, since the famine in the land was severe. [11] When he was about to enter Egypt, he said to his wife Sarai: "I know that you are a beautiful woman. [12] When the Egyptians see

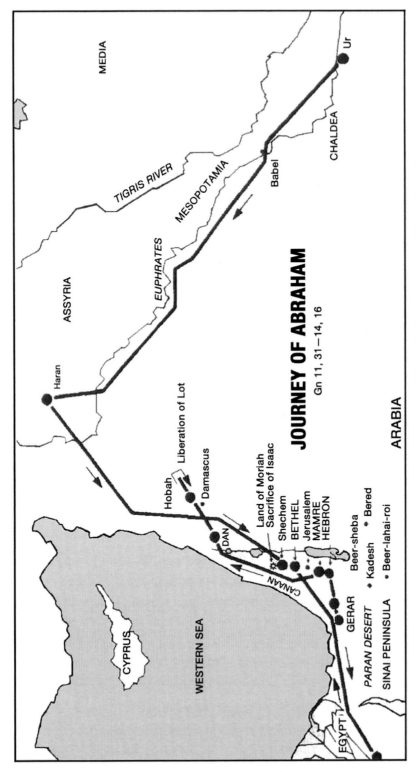

JOURNEY OF ABRAHAM

Gn 11, 31—14, 16

ABRAHAM'S JOURNEY (Gn 11:31—14:16) — **(a)** With his son Abram and his whole family, Terah departs from **Ur** for **Canaan** but settles in **Haran** (11:31). **(b)** Here Abram receives the Lord's call and starts out for **Canaan** (12:1—5). **(c)** At **Shechem** the Lord promises to give this land to Abram's descendants (12:6—7). **(d)** Between **Bethel** and **Ai** Abram builds an altar to the Lord and then journeys to the **Negeb**. A famine drives him into **Egypt** (12:8—20). **(e)** On his return to **Bethel**, he separates from Lot who settles near **Sodom**. Abram settles near the terebinth of Mamre, which is at **Hebron** (13, 1-8). **(f)** When the kings of the Pentapolis capture Lot and his household (see Map opposite p. 19), Abraham overtakes and defeats them at **Dan** and pursues them as far as **Hobah**, north of Damascus (14:12—16).

Reprinted by permission of Catholic Book Publishing Corp

you, they will say, 'She is his wife'; then they will kill me, but let you live. ¹³ Please say, therefore, that you are my sister, so that I may fare well on your account and my life may be spared for your sake." ¹⁴ When Abram arrived in Egypt, the Egyptians saw that the woman was very beautiful. ¹⁵ When Pharaoh's officials saw her they praised her to Pharaoh, and the woman was taken into Pharaoh's house. ¹⁶ Abram fared well on her account, and he acquired sheep, oxen, male and female servants, male and female donkeys, and camels.

¹⁷ But the Lᴏʀᴅ struck Pharaoh and his household with severe plagues because of Sarai, Abram's wife. ¹⁸ Then Pharaoh summoned Abram and said to him: "How could you do this to me! Why did you not tell me she was your wife? ¹⁹ Why did you say, 'She is my sister,' so that I took her for my wife? Now, here is your wife. Take her and leave!"

²⁰ Then Pharaoh gave his men orders concerning Abram, and they sent him away, with his wife and all that belonged to him.

CHAPTER 13

Abram and Lot Part. ¹ From Egypt Abram went up to the Negeb with his wife and all that belonged to him, and Lot went with him. ² Now Abram was very rich in livestock, silver, and gold. ³ From the Negeb he traveled by stages toward Bethel, to the place between Bethel and Ai where his tent had formerly stood, ⁴ the site where he had first built the altar; and there Abram invoked the Lᴏʀᴅ by name. ͨ

⁵ Lot, who went with Abram, also had flocks and herds and tents, ⁶ so that the land could not support them if they stayed together; their possessions were so great that they could not live together. ⁷ There were quarrels between the herders of Abram's livestock and the herders of Lot's livestock. At this time the Canaanites and the Perizzites were living in the land.

⁸ So Abram said to Lot: "Let there be no strife between you and me, or between your herders and my herders, for we are kindred. ⁹ Is not the whole land available? Please separate from me. If you prefer the left, I will go to the right; if you prefer the right, I will go to the left."

¹⁰ Lot looked about and saw how abundantly watered the whole Jordan Plain was as far as Zoar, like the Lᴏʀᴅ's own garden, or like Egypt. This was before the Lᴏʀᴅ had destroyed Sodom and Gomorrah. ¹¹ Lot, therefore, chose for himself the whole Jordan Plain and set out eastward. Thus they separated from each other. ¹² Abram settled in the land of Canaan, while Lot settled among the cities of the Plain, pitching his tents near Sodom. ¹³ Now the inhabitants of Sodom were wicked, great sinners against the Lᴏʀᴅ.

¹⁴ After Lot had parted from him, the Lᴏʀᴅ said to Abram: Look about you, and from where you are, gaze to the north and south, east and west; ¹⁵ all the land that you see I will give to you and your descendants forever. ¹⁶ I will make your descendants like the dust of the earth; if anyone could count the dust of the earth, your descendants too might be counted. ¹⁷ Get up and walk through the land, across its length and breadth, for I give it to you. ¹⁸ Abram moved his tents and went on to settle near the oak of Mamre, which is at Hebron. There he built an altar to the Lᴏʀᴅ.

CHAPTER 15

The Covenant with Abram. ¹ Some time afterward, the word of the Lᴏʀᴅ came to Abram in a vision: Do not fear, Abram! I am your shield; I will make your reward very great.

² But Abram said, "Lᴏʀᴅ Gᴏᴅ, what can you give me, if I die childless and have only a servant of my household, Eliezer of Damascus?" ³ Abram continued, "Look, you have given me no offspring, so a servant of my household will be my heir." ⁴ Then the word of the Lᴏʀᴅ came to him: No, that one will not be your heir; your own offspring will be your heir. ⁵ He took him outside and said: Look up at the sky and count the stars, if you can. Just so, he added, will your descendants

be. ⁶ Abram put his faith in the Lᴏʀᴅ, who attributed it to him as an act of righteousness.

⁷ He then said to him: I am the Lᴏʀᴅ who brought you from Ur of the Chaldeans to give you this land as a possession. ⁸ "Lord Gᴏᴅ," he asked, "how will I know that I will possess it?" ⁹ He answered him: Bring me a three-year-old heifer, a three-year-old female goat, a three-year-old ram, a turtledove, and a young pigeon. ¹⁰ He brought him all these, split them in two, and placed each half opposite the other; but the birds he did not cut up. ¹¹ Birds of prey swooped down on the carcasses, but Abram scared them away. ¹² As the sun was about to set, a deep sleep fell upon Abram, and a great, dark dread descended upon him.

¹³ Then the Lᴏʀᴅ said to Abram: Know for certain that your descendants will reside as aliens in a land not their own, where they shall be enslaved and oppressed for four hundred years. ¹⁴ But I will bring judgment on the nation they must serve, and after this they will go out with great wealth. ¹⁵ You, however, will go to your ancestors in peace; you will be buried at a ripe old age. ¹⁶ In the fourth generation your descendants will return here, for the wickedness of the Amorites is not yet complete.

¹⁷ When the sun had set and it was dark, there appeared a smoking fire pot and a flaming torch, which passed between those pieces. ¹⁸ On that day the Lᴏʀᴅ made a covenant with Abram, saying: To your descendants I give this land, from the Wadi of Egypt to the Great River, the Euphrates, ¹⁹ the land of the Kenites, the Kenizzites, the Kadmonites, ²⁰ the Hittites, the Perizzites, the Rephaim, ²¹ the Amorites, the Canaanites, the Girgashites, and the Jebusites.

CHAPTER 16

Birth of Ishmael. ¹ Abram's wife Sarai had borne him no children. Now she had an Egyptian maidservant named Hagar. ² Sarai said to Abram: "The Lᴏʀᴅ has kept me from bearing children.

Have intercourse with my maid; perhaps I will have sons through her." Abram obeyed Sarai. ³ Thus, after Abram had lived ten years in the land of Canaan, his wife Sarai took her maid, Hagar the Egyptian, and gave her to her husband Abram to be his wife. ⁴ He had intercourse with her, and she became pregnant. As soon as Hagar knew she was pregnant, her mistress lost stature in her eyes. ⁵ So Sarai said to Abram: "This outrage against me is your fault. I myself gave my maid to your embrace; but ever since she knew she was pregnant, I have lost stature in her eyes. May the Lᴏʀᴅ decide between you and me!" ⁶ Abram told Sarai: "Your maid is in your power. Do to her what you regard as right." Sarai then mistreated her so much that Hagar ran away from her.

⁷ The Lᴏʀᴅ's angel found her by a spring in the wilderness, the spring on the road to Shur, ⁸ and he asked, "Hagar, maid of Sarai, where have you come from and where are you going?" She answered, "I am running away from my mistress, Sarai." ⁹ But the Lᴏʀᴅ's angel told her: "Go back to your mistress and submit to her authority. ¹⁰ I will make your descendants so numerous," added the Lᴏʀᴅ's angel, "that they will be too many to count." ¹¹ Then the Lᴏʀᴅ's angel said to her:

"You are now pregnant and shall bear a son;
    you shall name him Ishmael,
For the Lᴏʀᴅ has heeded your affliction.
¹² He shall be a wild ass of a man,
    his hand against everyone,
    and everyone's hand against him;
Alongside all his kindred
    shall he encamp." ᵍ

¹³ To the Lᴏʀᴅ who spoke to her she gave a name, saying, "You are God who sees me"; she meant, "Have I really seen God and remained alive after he saw me?" ¹⁴ That is why the well is called Beer-lahairoi. It is between Kadesh and Bered.

¹⁵ Hagar bore Abram a son, and Abram named the son whom Hagar bore him Ishmael. ¹⁶ Abram was eighty-six years old when Hagar bore him Ishmael.

CHAPTER 17

Covenant of Circumcision. [1] When Abram was ninety-nine years old, the Lord appeared to Abram and said: I am God the Almighty. Walk in my presence and be blameless. [2] Between you and me I will establish my covenant, and I will multiply you exceedingly.

[3] Abram fell face down and God said to him: [4] For my part, here is my covenant with you: you are to become the father of a multitude of nations. [5] No longer will you be called Abram; your name will be Abraham, for I am making you the father of a multitude of nations. [6] I will make you exceedingly fertile; I will make nations of you; kings will stem from you. [7] I will maintain my covenant between me and you and your descendants after you throughout the ages as an everlasting covenant, to be your God and the God of your descendants after you. [8] I will give to you and to your descendants after you the land in which you are now residing as aliens, the whole land of Canaan, as a permanent possession; and I will be their God. [9] God said to Abraham: For your part, you and your descendants after you must keep my covenant throughout the ages. [10] This is the covenant between me and you and your descendants after you that you must keep: every male among you shall be circumcised. [11] Circumcise the flesh of your foreskin. That will be the sign of the covenant between me and you. [12] Throughout the ages, every male among you, when he is eight days old, shall be circumcised, including houseborn slaves and those acquired with money from any foreigner who is not of your descendants. [13] Yes, both the houseborn slaves and those acquired with money must be circumcised. Thus my covenant will be in your flesh as an everlasting covenant. [14] If a male is uncircumcised, that is, if the flesh of his foreskin has not been cut away, such a one will be cut off from his people; he has broken my covenant.

[15] God further said to Abraham: As for Sarai your wife, do not call her Sarai; her name will be Sarah. [16] I will bless her, and I will give you a son by her. Her also will I bless; she will give rise to nations, and rulers of peoples will issue from her. [17] Abraham fell face down and laughed as he said to himself, "Can a child be born to a man who is a hundred years old? Can Sarah give birth at ninety?" [18] So Abraham said to God, "If only Ishmael could live in your favor!" [19] God replied: Even so, your wife Sarah is to bear you a son, and you shall call him Isaac. It is with him that I will maintain my covenant as an everlasting covenant and with his descendants after him. [20] Now as for Ishmael, I will heed you: I hereby bless him. I will make him fertile and will multiply him exceedingly. He will become the father of twelve chieftains, and I will make of him a great nation. [21] But my covenant I will maintain with Isaac, whom Sarah shall bear to you by this time next year. [22] When he had finished speaking with Abraham, God departed from him.

[23] Then Abraham took his son Ishmael and all his slaves, whether born in his house or acquired with his money—every male among the members of Abraham's household—and he circumcised the flesh of their foreskins on that same day, as God had told him to do. [24] Abraham was ninety-nine years old when the flesh of his foreskin was circumcised, [25] and his son Ishmael was thirteen years old when the flesh of his foreskin was circumcised. [26] Thus, on that same day Abraham and his son Ishmael were circumcised; [27] and all the males of his household, including the slaves born in his house or acquired with his money from foreigners, were circumcised with him.

CHAPTER 18

Abraham's Visitors. [1] The Lord appeared to Abraham by the oak of Mamre, as he sat in the entrance of his tent, while the day was growing hot. [2] Looking up, he saw three men standing near him. When he saw them, he ran from the entrance of the tent to greet them; and bowing to the ground, [3] he said: "Sir, if it please you, do not go on past your servant. [4] Let some water be brought, that you may bathe your feet, and then rest under the tree. ⁵ Now that you have come to your servant, let me bring you a little food, that you may refresh yourselves; and afterward you may go on your way." "Very well," they replied, "do as you have said."

⁶ Abraham hurried into the tent to Sarah and said, "Quick, three measures of bran flour! Knead it and make bread." ⁷ He ran to the herd, picked out a tender, choice calf, and gave it to a servant, who quickly prepared it. ⁸ Then he got some curds and milk, as well as the calf that had been prepared, and set these before them, waiting on them under the tree while they ate.

⁹ "Where is your wife Sarah?" they asked him. "There in the tent," he replied. ¹⁰ One of them said, "I will return to you about this time next year, and Sarah will then have a son." Sarah was listening at the entrance of the tent, just behind him. ¹¹ Now Abraham and Sarah were old, advanced in years, and Sarah had stopped having her menstrual periods. ¹² So Sarah laughed to herself and said, "Now that I am worn out and my husband is old, am I still to have sexual pleasure?" ¹³ But the Lord said to Abraham: "Why did Sarah laugh and say, 'Will I really bear a child, old as I am?' ¹⁴ Is anything too marvelous for the Lord to do? At the appointed time, about this time next year, I will return to you, and Sarah will have a son." ¹⁵ Sarah lied, saying, "I did not laugh," because she was afraid. But he said, "Yes, you did."

Abraham Intercedes for Sodom. ¹⁶ With Abraham walking with them to see them on their way, the men set out from there and looked down toward Sodom. ¹⁷ The Lord considered: Shall I hide from Abraham what I am about to do, ¹⁸ now that he is to become a great and mighty nation, and all the nations of the earth are to find blessing in him? ¹⁹ Indeed, I have singled him out that he may direct his children and his household in the future to keep the way of the Lord by doing what is right and just, so that the Lord may put into effect for Abraham the promises he made about him. ²⁰ So the Lord said: The outcry against Sodom and Gomorrah is so great, and their sin so grave, ²¹ that I must go down to see whether or not their actions are as

bad as the cry against them that comes to me. I mean to find out.

²² As the men turned and walked on toward Sodom, Abraham remained standing before the Lord. ²³ Then Abraham drew near and said: "Will you really sweep away the righteous with the wicked? ²⁴ Suppose there were fifty righteous people in the city; would you really sweep away and not spare the place for the sake of the fifty righteous people within it? ²⁵ Far be it from you to do such a thing, to kill the righteous with the wicked, so that the righteous and the wicked are treated alike! Far be it from you! Should not the judge of all the world do what is just?" ²⁶ The Lord replied: If I find fifty righteous people in the city of Sodom, I will spare the whole place for their sake. ²⁷ Abraham spoke up again: "See how I am presuming to speak to my Lord, though I am only dust and ashes! ²⁸ What if there are five less than fifty righteous people? Will you destroy the whole city because of those five?" I will not destroy it, he answered, if I find forty-five there. ²⁹ But Abraham persisted, saying, "What if only forty are found there?" He replied: I will refrain from doing it for the sake of the forty. ³⁰ Then he said, "Do not let my Lord be angry if I go on. What if only thirty are found there?" He replied: I will refrain from doing it if I can find thirty there. ³¹ Abraham went on, "Since I have thus presumed to speak to my Lord, what if there are no more than twenty?" I will not destroy it, he answered, for the sake of the twenty. ³² But he persisted: "Please, do not let my Lord be angry if I speak up this last time. What if ten are found there?" For the sake of the ten, he replied, I will not destroy it.

³³ The Lord departed as soon as he had finished speaking with Abraham, and Abraham returned home.

CHAPTER 19

Destruction of Sodom and Gomorrah. ¹ The two angels reached Sodom in the evening, as Lot was sitting at the gate of Sodom. When

Lot saw them, he got up to greet them; and bowing down with his face to the ground, ² he said, "Please, my lords, come aside into your servant's house for the night, and bathe your feet; you can get up early to continue your journey." But they replied, "No, we will pass the night in the town square." ³ He urged them so strongly, however, that they turned aside to his place and entered his house. He prepared a banquet for them, baking unleavened bread, and they dined.

⁴ Before they went to bed, the townsmen of Sodom, both young and old—all the people to the last man—surrounded the house. ⁵ They called to Lot and said to him, "Where are the men who came to your house tonight? Bring them out to us that we may have sexual relations with them." ⁶ Lot went out to meet them at the entrance. When he had shut the door behind him, ⁷ he said, "I beg you, my brothers, do not do this wicked thing! ⁸ I have two daughters who have never had sexual relations with men. Let me bring them out to you, and you may do to them as you please. But do not do anything to these men, for they have come under the shelter of my roof." ⁹ They replied, "Stand back! This man," they said, "came here as a resident alien, and now he dares to give orders! We will treat you worse than them!" With that, they pressed hard against Lot, moving in closer to break down the door. ¹⁰ But his guests put out their hands, pulled Lot inside with them, and closed the door; ¹¹ they struck the men at the entrance of the house, small and great, with such a blinding light that they were utterly unable to find the doorway.

¹² Then the guests said to Lot: "Who else belongs to you here? Sons-in-law, your sons, your daughters, all who belong to you in the city—take them away from this place! ¹³ We are about to destroy this place, for the outcry reaching the LORD against those here is so great that the LORD has sent us to destroy it." ¹⁴ So Lot went out and spoke to his sons-in-law, who had contracted marriage with his daughters. "Come on, leave this place," he told them; "the LORD is about to destroy the city." But his sons-in-law thought he was joking.

¹⁵ As dawn was breaking, the angels urged Lot on, saying, "Come on! Take your wife with you

and your two daughters who are here, or you will be swept away in the punishment of the city." ¹⁶ When he hesitated, the men, because of the LORD's compassion for him, seized his hand and the hands of his wife and his two daughters and led them to safety outside the city. ¹⁷ As soon as they had brought them outside, they said: "Flee for your life! Do not look back or stop anywhere on the Plain. Flee to the hills at once, or you will be swept away." ¹⁸ "Oh, no, my lords!" Lot replied to them. ¹⁹ "You have already shown favor to your servant, doing me the great kindness of saving my life. But I cannot flee to the hills, or the disaster will overtake and kill me. ²⁰ Look, this town ahead is near enough to escape to. It is only a small place. Let me flee there—is it not a small place?—to save my life." ²¹ "Well, then," he replied, "I grant you this favor too. I will not overthrow the town you have mentioned. ²² Hurry, escape there! I cannot do anything until you arrive there." That is why the town is called Zoar.

²³ The sun had risen over the earth when Lot arrived in Zoar, ²⁴ and the LORD rained down sulfur upon Sodom and Gomorrah, fire from the LORD out of heaven. ²⁵ He overthrew those cities and the whole Plain, together with the inhabitants of the cities and the produce of the soil. ²⁶ But Lot's wife looked back, and she was turned into a pillar of salt.

²⁷ The next morning Abraham hurried to the place where he had stood before the LORD. ²⁸ As he looked down toward Sodom and Gomorrah and the whole region of the Plain, he saw smoke over the land rising like the smoke from a kiln.

²⁹ When God destroyed the cities of the Plain, he remembered Abraham and sent Lot away from the upheaval that occurred when God overthrew the cities where Lot had been living.

Moabites and Ammonites. ³⁰ Since Lot was afraid to stay in Zoar, he and his two daughters went up from Zoar and settled in the hill country, where he lived with his two daughters in a cave. ³¹ The firstborn said to the younger: "Our father is getting old, and there is not a man in the land to have intercourse with us as is the custom everywhere. ³² Come, let us ply our father with wine and then lie with him, that we may ensure posterity by our father." ³³ So that night they plied their father with wine, and the firstborn went in and lay with her father; but he was not aware of her lying down or getting up. ³⁴ The next day the firstborn said to the younger: "Last night I lay with my father. Let us ply him with wine again tonight, and then you go in and lie with him, that we may ensure posterity by our father." ³⁵ So that night, too, they plied their father with wine, and then the younger one went in and lay with him; but he was not aware of her lying down or getting up.

³⁶ Thus the two daughters of Lot became pregnant by their father. ³⁷ The firstborn gave birth to a son whom she named Moab, saying, "From my father." He is the ancestor of the Moabites of today. ³⁸ The younger one, too, gave birth to a son, and she named him Ammon, saying, "The son of my kin." He is the ancestor of the Ammonites of today.

CHAPTER 21

Birth of Isaac. ¹ The LORD took note of Sarah as he had said he would; the LORD did for her as he had promised. ² Sarah became pregnant and bore Abraham a son in his old age, at the set time that God had stated. ³ Abraham gave the name Isaac to this son of his whom Sarah bore him. ⁴ When his son Isaac was eight days old, Abraham circumcised him, as God had commanded. ⁵ Abraham was a hundred years old when his son Isaac was born to him. ⁶ Sarah then said, "God has given me cause to laugh, and all who hear of it will laugh with me. ⁷ Who would ever have told Abraham," she added, "that Sarah would nurse children! Yet I have borne him a son in his old age." ⁸ The child grew and was weaned, and Abraham held a great banquet on the day of the child's weaning.

⁹ Sarah noticed the son whom Hagar the Egyptian had borne to Abraham playing with her son Isaac; ¹⁰ so she demanded of Abraham: "Drive out that slave and her son! No son of that slave is going to share the inheritance with my son Isaac!" ¹¹ Abraham was greatly distressed because it concerned a son of his. ¹² But God said to Abraham: Do not be distressed about the boy or about your slave woman. Obey Sarah, no matter what she asks of you; for it is through Isaac that descendants will bear your name. ¹³ As for the son of the slave woman, I will make a nation of him also, since he too is your offspring.

¹⁴ Early the next morning Abraham got some bread and a skin of water and gave them to Hagar. Then, placing the child on her back, he sent her away. As she roamed aimlessly in the wilderness of Beer-sheba, ¹⁵ the water in the skin was used up. So she put the child down under one of the bushes, ¹⁶ and then went and sat down opposite him, about a bowshot away; for she said to herself, "I cannot watch the child die." As she sat opposite him, she wept aloud. ¹⁷ God heard the boy's voice, and God's angel called to Hagar from heaven: "What is the matter, Hagar? Do not fear; God has heard the boy's voice in this plight of his. ¹⁸ Get up, lift up the boy and hold him by the hand; for I will make of him a great nation." ¹⁹ Then God opened her eyes, and she saw a well of water. She went and filled the skin with water, and then let the boy drink.

²⁰ God was with the boy as he grew up. He lived in the wilderness and became an expert bowman. ²¹ He lived in the wilderness of Paran. His mother got a wife for him from the land of Egypt.

The Covenant at Beer-sheba. ²² At that time Abimelech, accompanied by Phicol, the commander of his army, said to Abraham: "God is with you in everything you do. ²³ So now, swear to me by God at this place that you will not deal falsely with me or with my progeny and posterity, but will act as loyally toward me and the land in which you reside as I have acted toward you." ²⁴ Abraham replied, "I so swear."

²⁵ Abraham, however, reproached Abimelech about a well that Abimelech's servants had seized by force. ²⁶ "I have no idea who did that," Abimelech replied. "In fact, you never told me about it, nor did I ever hear of it until now."

²⁷ Then Abraham took sheep and cattle and gave them to Abimelech and the two made a covenant. ²⁸ Abraham also set apart seven ewe lambs

of the flock, [29] and Abimelech asked him, "What is the purpose of these seven ewe lambs that you have set apart?" [30] Abraham answered, "The seven ewe lambs you shall accept from me that you may be my witness that I dug this well." [31] This is why the place is called Beer-sheba; the two of them took an oath there. [32] When they had thus made the covenant in Beersheba, Abimelech, along with Phicol, the commander of his army, left to return to the land of the Philistines.

[33] Abraham planted a tamarisk at Beersheba, and there he invoked by name the LORD, God the Eternal. [34] Abraham resided in the land of the Philistines for a long time.

CHAPTER 22

The Testing of Abraham. [1] Some time afterward, God put Abraham to the test and said to him: Abraham! "Here I am!" he replied. [2] Then God said: Take your son Isaac, your only one, whom you love, and go to the land of Moriah. There offer him up as a burnt offering on one of the heights that I will point out to you. [3] Early the next morning Abraham saddled his donkey, took with him two of his servants and his son Isaac, and after cutting the wood for the burnt offering, set out for the place of which God had told him.

[4] On the third day Abraham caught sight of the place from a distance. [5] Abraham said to his servants: "Stay here with the donkey, while the boy and I go on over there. We will worship and then come back to you." [6] So Abraham took the wood for the burnt offering and laid it on his son Isaac, while he himself carried the fire and the knife. As the two walked on together, [7] Isaac spoke to his father Abraham. "Father!" he said. "Here I am," he replied. Isaac continued, "Here are the fire and the wood, but where is the sheep for the burnt offering?" [8] "My son," Abraham answered, "God will provide the sheep for the burnt offering." Then the two walked on together.

[9] When they came to the place of which God had told him, Abraham built an altar there and arranged the wood on it. Next he bound his son Isaac, and put him on top of the wood on the altar. [10] Then Abraham reached out and took the knife to slaughter his son. [11] But the angel of the LORD called to him from heaven, "Abraham, Abraham!" "Here I am," he answered. [12] "Do not lay your hand on the boy," said the angel. "Do not do the least thing to him. For now I know that you fear God, since you did not withhold from me your son, your only one." [13] Abraham looked up and saw a single ram caught by its horns in the thicket. So Abraham went and took the ram and offered it up as a burnt offering in place of his son. [14] Abraham named that place Yahwehyireh; hence people today say, "On the mountain the LORD will provide."

[15] A second time the angel of the LORD called to Abraham from heaven [16] and said: "I swear by my very self—oracle of the LORD—that because you acted as you did in not withholding from me your son, your only one, [17] I will bless you and make your descendants as countless as the stars of the sky and the sands of the seashore; your descendants will take possession of the gates of their enemies, [18] and in your descendants all the nations of the earth will find blessing, because you obeyed my command."

[19] Abraham then returned to his servants, and they set out together for Beer-sheba, where Abraham lived.

Nahor's Descendants. [20] Some time afterward, the news came to Abraham: "Milcah too has borne sons to your brother Nahor: [21] Uz, his firstborn, his brother Buz, Kemuel the father of Aram, [22] Chesed, Hazo, Pildash, Jidlaph, and Bethuel." [23] Bethuel became the father of Rebekah. These eight Milcah bore to Nahor, Abraham's brother. [24] His concubine, whose name was Reumah, also bore children: Tebah, Gaham, Tahash, and Maacah.

CHAPTER 25

Death of Abraham. [7] The whole span of Abraham's life was one hundred and seventy-five years. [8] Then he breathed his last, dying at a ripe old age, grown old after a full life; and he was gathered to his people. ⁹ His sons Isaac and Ishmael buried him in the cave of Machpelah, in the field of Ephron, son of Zohar the Hittite, which faces Mamre, ¹⁰ the field that Abraham had bought from the Hittites; there he was buried next to his wife Sarah. ¹¹ After the death of Abraham, God blessed his son Isaac, who lived near Beer-lahai-roi.

Descendants of Ishmael. ¹² These are the descendants of Abraham's son Ishmael, whom Hagar the Egyptian, Sarah's slave, bore to Abraham. ¹³ These are the names of Ishmael's sons, listed in the order of their birth: Ishmael's firstborn Nebaioth, Kedar, Adbeel, Mibsam, ¹⁴ Mishma, Dumah, Massa, ¹⁵ Hadad, Tema, Jetur, Naphish, and Kedemah. ¹⁶ These are the sons of Ishmael, their names by their villages and encampments; twelve chieftains of as many tribal groups.

¹⁷ The span of Ishmael's life was one hundred and thirty-seven years. After he had breathed his last and died, he was gathered to his people. ¹⁸ The Ishmaelites ranged from Havilah, by Shur, which is on the border of Egypt, all the way to Asshur; and they pitched camp alongside their various kindred.

The Story of Joseph

CHAPTER 37

Joseph Sold into Egypt. ¹ Jacob settled in the land where his father had sojourned, the land of Canaan. ² This is the story of the family of Jacob. When Joseph was seventeen years old, he was tending the flocks with his brothers; he was an assistant to the sons of his father's wives Bilhah and Zilpah, and Joseph brought their father bad reports about them ³ Israel loved Joseph best of all his sons, for he was the child of his old age; and he had made him a long ornamented tunic. ⁴ When his brothers saw that their father loved him best of all his brothers, they hated him so much that they could not say a kind word to him.

⁵ Once Joseph had a dream, and when he told his brothers, they hated him even more. ⁶ He said to them, "Listen to this dream I had. ⁷ There we were, binding sheaves in the field, when suddenly my sheaf rose to an upright position, and your sheaves formed a ring around my sheaf and bowed down to it." ⁸ His brothers said to him, "Are you really going to make yourself king over us? Will you rule over us?" So they hated him all the more because of his dreams and his reports.

⁹ Then he had another dream, and told it to his brothers. "Look, I had another dream," he said; "this time, the sun and the moon and eleven stars were bowing down to me." ¹⁰ When he told it to his father and his brothers, his father reproved him and asked, "What is the meaning of this dream of yours? Can it be that I and your mother and your brothers are to come and bow to the ground before you?" ¹¹ So his brothers were furious at him but his father kept the matter in mind.

¹² One day, when his brothers had gone to pasture their father's flocks at Shechem, ¹³ Israel said to Joseph, "Are your brothers not tending our flocks at Shechem? Come and I will send you to them." "I am ready," Joseph answered. ¹⁴ "Go then," he replied; "see if all is well with your brothers and the flocks, and bring back word." So he sent him off from the valley of Hebron. When Joseph reached Shechem, ¹⁵ a man came upon him as he was wandering about in the fields. "What are you looking for?" the man asked him. ¹⁶ "I am looking for my brothers," he answered. "Please tell me where they are tending the flocks." ¹⁷ The man told him, "They have moved on from here; in fact, I heard them say, 'Let us go on to Dothan.'" So Joseph went after his brothers and found them in Dothan. ¹⁸ They saw him from a distance, and before he reached them, they plotted to kill him. ¹⁹ They said to one another: "Here comes that dreamer! ²⁰ Come now, let us kill him and throw him into one of the cisterns here; we

could say that a wild beast devoured him. We will see then what comes of his dreams."

²¹ But when Reuben heard this, he tried to save him from their hands, saying: "We must not take his life." ²² Then Reuben said, "Do not shed blood! Throw him into this cistern in the wilderness; but do not lay a hand on him." His purpose was to save him from their hands and restore him to his father.

²³ So when Joseph came up to his brothers, they stripped him of his tunic, the long ornamented tunic he had on; ²⁴ then they took him and threw him into the cistern. The cistern was empty; there was no water in it.

²⁵ Then they sat down to eat. Looking up, they saw a caravan of Ishmaelites coming from Gilead, their camels laden with gum, balm, and resin to be taken down to Egypt. ²⁶ Judah said to his brothers: "What is to be gained by killing our brother and concealing his blood? ²⁷ Come, let us sell him to these Ishmaelites, instead of doing away with him ourselves. After all, he is our brother, our own flesh." His brothers agreed. ²⁸ Midianite traders passed by, and they pulled Joseph up out of the cistern. They sold Joseph for twenty pieces of silver to the Ishmaelites, who took him to Egypt.

²⁹ When Reuben went back to the cistern and saw that Joseph was not in it, he tore his garments, ³⁰ and returning to his brothers, he exclaimed: "The boy is gone! And I—where can I turn?" ³¹ They took Joseph's tunic, and after slaughtering a goat, dipped the tunic in its blood. ³² Then they sent someone to bring the long ornamented tunic to their father, with the message: "We found this. See whether it is your son's tunic or not." ³³ He recognized it and exclaimed: "My son's tunic! A wild beast has devoured him! Joseph has been torn to pieces!" ³⁴ Then Jacob tore his garments, put sackcloth on his loins, and mourned his son many days. ³⁵ Though his sons and daughters tried to console him, he refused all consolation, saying, "No, I will go down mourning to my son in Sheol." Thus did his father weep for him.

³⁶ The Midianites, meanwhile, sold Joseph in Egypt to Potiphar, an official of Pharaoh and his chief steward.

CHAPTER 39

Joseph's Temptation. ¹ When Joseph was taken down to Egypt, an Egyptian, Potiphar, an official of Pharaoh and his chief steward, bought him from the Ishmaelites who had brought him there. ² The Lᴏʀᴅ was with Joseph and he enjoyed great success and was assigned to the household of his Egyptian master. ³ When his master saw that the Lᴏʀᴅ was with him and brought him success in whatever he did, ⁴ he favored Joseph and made him his personal attendant; he put him in charge of his household and entrusted to him all his possessions. ⁵ From the moment that he put him in charge of his household and all his possessions, the Lᴏʀᴅ blessed the Egyptian's house for Joseph's sake; the Lᴏʀᴅ's blessing was on everything he owned, both inside the house and out. ⁶ Having left everything he owned in Joseph's charge, he gave no thought, with Joseph there, to anything but the food he ate.

Now Joseph was well-built and handsome. ⁷ After a time, his master's wife looked at him with longing and said, "Lie with me." ⁸ But he refused and said to his master's wife, "Look, as long as I am here, my master does not give a thought to anything in the house, but has entrusted to me all he owns. ⁹ He has no more authority in this house than I do. He has withheld from me nothing but you, since you are his wife. How, then, could I do this great wrong and sin against God?" ¹⁰ Although she spoke to him day after day, he would not agree to lie with her, or even be near her.

¹¹ One such day, when Joseph came into the house to do his work, and none of the household servants were then in the house, ¹² she laid hold of him by his cloak, saying, "Lie with me!" But leaving the cloak in her hand, he escaped and ran outside. ¹³ When she saw that he had left his cloak in her hand as he escaped outside, ¹⁴ she cried out to her household servants and told them, "Look! My husband has brought us a Hebrew man to mock us! He came in here to lie with me, but I cried out loudly. ¹⁵ When he heard me scream, he left his cloak beside me and escaped and ran outside."

[16] She kept the cloak with her until his master came home. [17] Then she told him the same story: "The Hebrew slave whom you brought us came to me to amuse himself at my expense. [18] But when I screamed, he left his cloak beside me and escaped outside." [19] When the master heard his wife's story in which she reported, "Thus and so your servant did to me," he became enraged. [20] Joseph's master seized him and put him into the jail where the king's prisoners were confined. And there he sat, in jail.

[21] But the LORD was with Joseph, and showed him kindness by making the chief jailer well-disposed toward him. [22] The chief jailer put Joseph in charge of all the prisoners in the jail. Everything that had to be done there, he was the one to do it. [23] The chief jailer did not have to look after anything that was in Joseph's charge, since the LORD was with him and was bringing success to whatever he was doing.

CHAPTER 40

The Dreams Interpreted. [1] Some time afterward, the royal cupbearer and baker offended their lord, the king of Egypt. [2] Pharaoh was angry with his two officials, the chief cupbearer and the chief baker, [3] and he put them in custody in the house of the chief steward, the same jail where Joseph was confined. [4] The chief steward assigned Joseph to them, and he became their attendant.

After they had been in custody for some time, [5] the cupbearer and the baker of the king of Egypt who were confined in the jail both had dreams on the same night, each his own dream and each dream with its own meaning. [6] When Joseph came to them in the morning, he saw that they looked disturbed. [7] So he asked Pharaoh's officials who were with him in custody in his master's house, "Why do you look so troubled today?" [8] They answered him, "We have had dreams, but there is no one to interpret them." Joseph said to them, "Do interpretations not come from God? Please tell me the dreams."

[9] Then the chief cupbearer told Joseph his dream. "In my dream," he said, "I saw a vine in front of me, [10] and on the vine were three branches. It had barely budded when its blossoms came out, and its clusters ripened into grapes. [11] Pharaoh's cup was in my hand; so I took the grapes, pressed them out into his cup, and put it in Pharaoh's hand." [12] Joseph said to him: "This is its interpretation. The three branches are three days; [13] within three days Pharaoh will single you out and restore you to your post. You will be handing Pharaoh his cup as you formerly did when you were his cupbearer. [14] Only think of me when all is well with you, and please do me the great favor of mentioning me to Pharaoh, to get me out of this place. [15] The truth is that I was kidnapped from the land of the Hebrews, and I have not done anything here that they should have put me into a dungeon."

[16] When the chief baker saw that Joseph had given a favorable interpretation, he said to him: "I too had a dream. In it I had three bread baskets on my head; [17] in the top one were all kinds of bakery products for Pharaoh, but the birds were eating them out of the basket on my head." [18] Joseph said to him in reply: "This is its interpretation. The three baskets are three days; [19] within three days Pharaoh will single you out and will impale you on a stake, and the birds will be eating your flesh."

[20] And so on the third day, which was Pharaoh's birthday, when he gave a banquet to all his servants, he singled out the chief cupbearer and chief baker in the midst of his servants. [21] He restored the chief cupbearer to his office, so that he again handed the cup to Pharaoh; [22] but the chief baker he impaled—just as Joseph had told them in his interpretation. [23] Yet the chief cupbearer did not think of Joseph; he forgot him.

CHAPTER 41

Pharaoh's Dream. [1] After a lapse of two years, Pharaoh had a dream. He was standing by the

Nile, 2 when up out of the Nile came seven cows, fine-looking and fat; they grazed in the reed grass. 3 Behind them seven other cows, poor-looking and gaunt, came up out of the Nile; and standing on the bank of the Nile beside the others, 4 the poor-looking, gaunt cows devoured the seven fine-looking, fat cows. Then Pharaoh woke up.

5 He fell asleep again and had another dream. He saw seven ears of grain, fat and healthy, growing on a single stalk. 6 Behind them sprouted seven ears of grain, thin and scorched by the east wind; 7 and the thin ears swallowed up the seven fat, healthy ears. Then Pharaoh woke up—it was a dream!

8 Next morning his mind was agitated. So Pharaoh had all the magicians and sages of Egypt summoned and recounted his dream to them; but there was no one to interpret it for him. 9 Then the chief cupbearer said to Pharaoh: "Now I remember my negligence! 10 Once, when Pharaoh was angry with his servants, he put me and the chief baker in custody in the house of the chief steward. 11 Later, we both had dreams on the same night, and each of our dreams had its own meaning. 12 There was a Hebrew youth with us, a slave of the chief steward; and when we told him our dreams, he interpreted them for us and explained for each of us the meaning of his dream. 13 Things turned out just as he had told us: I was restored to my post, but the other man was impaled."

14 Pharaoh therefore had Joseph summoned, and they hurriedly brought him from the dungeon. After he shaved and changed his clothes, he came to Pharaoh. 15 Pharaoh then said to Joseph: "I had a dream but there was no one to interpret it. But I hear it said of you, 'If he hears a dream he can interpret it.'" 16 "It is not I," Joseph replied to Pharaoh, "but God who will respond for the well-being of Pharaoh."

17 Then Pharaoh said to Joseph: "In my dream, I was standing on the bank of the Nile, 18 when up from the Nile came seven cows, fat and well-formed; they grazed in the reed grass. 19 Behind them came seven other cows, scrawny, most ill-formed and gaunt. Never have I seen such bad specimens as these in all the land of Egypt! 20 The gaunt, bad cows devoured the first seven fat cows. 21 But when they had consumed them, no one could tell that they had done so, because they looked as bad as before. Then I woke up. 22 In another dream I saw seven ears of grain, full and healthy, growing on a single stalk. 23 Behind them sprouted seven ears of grain, shriveled and thin and scorched by the east wind; 24 and the seven thin ears swallowed up the seven healthy ears. I have spoken to the magicians, but there is no one to explain it to me."

25 Joseph said to Pharaoh: "Pharaoh's dreams have the same meaning. God has made known to Pharaoh what he is about to do. 26 The seven healthy cows are seven years, and the seven healthy ears are seven years—the same in each dream. 27 The seven thin, bad cows that came up after them are seven years, as are the seven thin ears scorched by the east wind; they are seven years of famine. 28 Things are just as I told Pharaoh: God has revealed to Pharaoh what he is about to do. 29 Seven years of great abundance are now coming throughout the land of Egypt; 30 but seven years of famine will rise up after them, when all the abundance will be forgotten in the land of Egypt. When the famine has exhausted the land, 31 no trace of the abundance will be found in the land because of the famine that follows it, for it will be very severe. 32 That Pharaoh had the same dream twice means that the matter has been confirmed by God and that God will soon bring it about.

33 "Therefore, let Pharaoh seek out a discerning and wise man and put him in charge of the land of Egypt. 34 Let Pharaoh act and appoint overseers for the land to organize it during the seven years of abundance. 35 They should collect all the food of these coming good years, gathering the grain under Pharaoh's authority, for food in the cities, and they should guard it. 36 This food will serve as a reserve for the country against the seven years of famine that will occur in the land of Egypt, so that the land may not perish in the famine."

[37] This advice pleased Pharaoh and all his servants. [38] "Could we find another like him," Pharaoh asked his servants, "a man so endowed with the spirit of God?" [39] So Pharaoh said to Joseph: "Since God has made all this known to you, there is no one as discerning and wise as you are. [40] You shall be in charge of my household, and all my people will obey your command. Only in respect to the throne will I outrank you." [41] Then Pharaoh said to Joseph, "Look, I put you in charge of the whole land of Egypt." [42] With that, Pharaoh took off his signet ring and put it on Joseph's finger. He dressed him in robes of fine linen and put a gold chain around his neck. [43] He then had him ride in his second chariot, and they shouted "Abrek!" before him.

Thus was Joseph installed over the whole land of Egypt. [44] "I am Pharaoh," he told Joseph, "but without your approval no one shall lift hand or foot in all the land of Egypt." [45] Pharaoh also bestowed the name of Zaphenath-paneah on Joseph, and he gave him in marriage Asenath, the daughter of Potiphera, priest of Heliopolis. And Joseph went out over the land of Egypt. [46] Joseph was thirty years old when he entered the service of Pharaoh, king of Egypt.

After Joseph left Pharaoh, he went throughout the land of Egypt. [47] During the seven years of plenty, when the land produced abundant crops, [48] he collected all the food of these years of plenty that the land of Egypt was enjoying and stored it in the cities, placing in each city the crops of the fields around it. [49] Joseph collected grain like the sands of the sea, so much that at last he stopped measuring it, for it was beyond measure.

[50] Before the famine years set in, Joseph became the father of two sons, borne to him by Asenath, daughter of Potiphera, priest of Heliopolis. [51] Joseph named his firstborn Manasseh, meaning, "God has made me forget entirely my troubles and my father's house"; [52] and the second he named Ephraim, meaning, "God has made me fruitful in the land of my affliction."

[53] When the seven years of abundance enjoyed by the land of Egypt came to an end, [54] the seven years of famine set in, just as Joseph had said. Although there was famine in all the other countries, food was available throughout the land of Egypt. [55] When all the land of Egypt became hungry and the people cried to Pharaoh for food, Pharaoh said to all the Egyptians: "Go to Joseph and do whatever he tells you." [56] When the famine had spread throughout the land, Joseph opened all the cities that had grain and rationed it to the Egyptians, since the famine had gripped the land of Egypt. [57] Indeed, the whole world came to Egypt to Joseph to buy grain, for famine had gripped the whole world.

CHAPTER 42

The Brothers' First Journey to Egypt.
[1] When Jacob learned that grain rations were for sale in Egypt, he said to his sons: "Why do you keep looking at one another?" [2] He went on, "I hear that grain is for sale in Egypt. Go down there and buy some for us, that we may stay alive and not die." [3] So ten of Joseph's brothers went down to buy grain from Egypt. [4] But Jacob did not send Joseph's brother Benjamin with his brothers, for he thought some disaster might befall him. [5] And so the sons of Israel were among those who came to buy grain, since there was famine in the land of Canaan.

[6] Joseph, as governor of the country, was the one who sold grain to all the people of the land. When Joseph's brothers came, they bowed down to him with their faces to the ground. [7] He recognized them as soon as he saw them. But he concealed his own identity from them and spoke harshly to them. "Where do you come from?" he asked them. They answered, "From the land of Canaan, to buy food."

[8] When Joseph recognized his brothers, although they did not recognize him, [9] he was reminded of the dreams he had about them. He said to them: "You are spies. You have come to see the weak points of the land." [10] "No, my lord," they replied. "On the contrary, your servants have come to buy food. [11] All of us are sons of the same man. We are honest men; your servants have never been spies." [12] But he answered them:

"Not so! It is the weak points of the land that you have come to see." ¹³ "We your servants," they said, "are twelve brothers, sons of a certain man in Canaan; but the youngest one is at present with our father, and the other one is no more." ¹⁴ "It is just as I said," Joseph persisted; "you are spies. ¹⁵ This is how you shall be tested: I swear by the life of Pharaoh that you shall not leave here unless your youngest brother comes here. ¹⁶ So send one of your number to get your brother, while the rest of you stay here under arrest. Thus will your words be tested for their truth; if they are untrue, as Pharaoh lives, you are spies!" ¹⁷ With that, he locked them up in the guardhouse for three days.

¹⁸ On the third day Joseph said to them: "Do this, and you shall live; for I am a God-fearing man. ¹⁹ If you are honest men, let one of your brothers be confined in this prison, while the rest of you go and take home grain for your starving families. ²⁰ But you must bring me your youngest brother. Your words will thus be verified, and you will not die." To this they agreed. ²¹ To one another, however, they said: "Truly we are being punished because of our brother. We saw the anguish of his heart when he pleaded with us, yet we would not listen. That is why this anguish has now come upon us." ²² Then Reuben responded, "Did I not tell you, 'Do no wrong to the boy'? But you would not listen! Now comes the reckoning for his blood." ²² They did not know, of course, that Joseph understood what they said, since he spoke with them through an interpreter. ²⁴ But turning away from them, he wept. When he was able to speak to them again, he took Simeon from among them and bound him before their eyes. ²⁵ Then Joseph gave orders to have their containers filled with grain, their money replaced in each one's sack, and provisions given them for their journey. After this had been done for them, ²⁶ they loaded their donkeys with the grain and departed.

²⁷ At the night encampment, when one of them opened his bag to give his donkey some fodder, he saw his money there in the mouth of his bag. ²⁸ He cried out to his brothers, "My money has been returned! Here it is in my bag!" At

that their hearts sank. Trembling, they asked one another, "What is this that God has done to us?"

²⁹ When they got back to their father Jacob in the land of Canaan, they told him all that had happened to them. ³⁰ "The man who is lord of the land," they said, "spoke to us harshly and put us in custody on the grounds that we were spying on the land. ³¹ But we said to him: 'We are honest men; we have never been spies. ³² We are twelve brothers, sons of the same father; but one is no more, and the youngest one is now with our father in the land of Canaan.' ³³ Then the man who is lord of the land said to us: `This is how I will know if you are honest men: leave one of your brothers with me, then take grain for your starving families and go. ³⁴ When you bring me your youngest brother, and I know that you are not spies but honest men, I will restore your brother to you, and you may move about freely in the land.'"

³⁵ When they were emptying their sacks, there in each one's sack was his moneybag! At the sight of their moneybags, they and their father were afraid. ³⁶ Their father Jacob said to them: "Must you make me childless? Joseph is no more, Simeon is no more, and now you would take Benjamin away! All these things have happened to me!" ³⁷ Then Reuben told his father: "You may kill my own two sons if I do not return him to you! Put him in my care, and I will bring him back to you." ³⁸ But Jacob replied: "My son shall not go down with you. Now that his brother is dead, he is the only one left. If some disaster should befall him on the journey you must make, you would send my white head down to Sheol in grief."

CHAPTER 43

The Second Journey to Egypt. ¹ Now the famine in the land grew severe. ² So when they had used up all the grain they had brought from Egypt, their father said to them, "Go back and buy us a little more food." ³ But Judah replied: "The man strictly warned us, 'You shall not see me unless your brother is with you.' ⁴ If you are willing to let our brother go with us, we will go down to buy food for you. ⁵ But if you are not willing, we will not go down, because the man told us, 'You shall not see me unless your brother is with you.'" ⁶ Israel demanded, "Why did you bring this trouble on me by telling the man that you had another brother?" ⁷ They answered: "The man kept asking about us and our family: 'Is your father still living? Do you have another brother?' We answered him accordingly. How could we know that he would say, `Bring your brother down here'?"

⁸ Then Judah urged his father Israel: "Let the boy go with me, that we may be off and on our way if you and we and our children are to keep from starving to death. ⁹ I myself will serve as a guarantee for him. You can hold me responsible for him. If I fail to bring him back and set him before you, I will bear the blame before you forever. ¹⁰ Had we not delayed, we could have been there and back twice by now!"

¹¹ Israel their father then told them: "If it must be so, then do this: Put some of the land's best products in your baggage and take them down to the man as gifts: some balm and honey, gum and resin, and pistachios and almonds. ¹² Also take double the money along, for you must return the amount that was put back in the mouths of your bags; it may have been a mistake. ¹³ Take your brother, too, and be off on your way back to the man. ¹⁴ May God Almighty grant you mercy in the presence of the man, so that he may let your other brother go, as well as Benjamin. As for me, if I am to suffer bereavement, I shall suffer it."

¹⁵ So the men took those gifts and double the money and Benjamin. They made their way down to Egypt and presented themselves before Joseph. ¹⁶ When Joseph saw them and Benjamin, he told his steward, "Take the men into the house, and have an animal slaughtered and prepared, for they are to dine with me at noon." ¹⁷ Doing as Joseph had ordered, the steward conducted the men to Joseph's house. ¹⁸ But they became apprehensive when they were led to his house. "It must be," they thought, "on account of the money put back in our bags the first time,

that we are taken inside—in order to attack us and take our donkeys and seize us as slaves." ¹⁹ So they went up to Joseph's steward and talked to him at the entrance of the house. ²⁰ "If you please, sir," they said, "we came down here once before to buy food. ²¹ But when we arrived at a night's encampment and opened our bags, there was each man's money in the mouth of his bag— our money in the full amount! We have now brought it back. ²² We have brought other money to buy food. We do not know who put our money in our bags." ²³ He replied, "Calm down! Do not fear! Your God and the God of your father must have put treasure in your bags for you. As for your money, I received it." With that, he led Simeon out to them.

²⁴ The steward then brought the men inside Joseph's house. He gave them water to wash their feet, and gave fodder to their donkeys. ²⁵ Then they set out their gifts to await Joseph's arrival at noon, for they had heard that they were to dine there. ²⁶ When Joseph came home, they presented him with the gifts they had brought inside, while they bowed down before him to the ground. ²⁷ After inquiring how they were, he asked them, "And how is your aged father, of whom you spoke? Is he still alive?" ²⁸ "Your servant our father is still alive and doing well," they said, as they knelt and bowed down. ²⁹ Then Joseph looked up and saw Benjamin, his brother, the son of his mother. He asked, "Is this your youngest brother, of whom you told me?" Then he said to him, "May God be gracious to you, my son!" ³⁰ With that, Joseph hurried out, for he was so overcome with affection for his brother that he was on the verge of tears. So he went into a private room and wept there.

³¹ After washing his face, he reappeared and, now having collected himself, gave the order, "Serve the meal." ³² It was served separately to him, to the brothers, and to the Egyptians who partook of his board. Egyptians may not eat with Hebrews; that is abhorrent to them. ³³ When they were seated before him according to their age, from the oldest to the youngest, they looked at one another in amazement; ³⁴ and

as portions were brought to them from Joseph's table, Benjamin's portion was five times as large as anyone else's. So they drank freely and made merry with him.

CHAPTER 44

Final Test. [1] Then Joseph commanded his steward: "Fill the men's bags with as much food as they can carry, and put each man's money in the mouth of his bag. [2] In the mouth of the youngest one's bag put also my silver goblet, together with the money for his grain." The steward did as Joseph said. [3] At daybreak the men and their donkeys were sent off. [4] They had not gone far out of the city when Joseph said to his steward: "Go at once after the men! When you overtake them, say to them, `Why did you repay good with evil? Why did you steal my silver goblet? [5] Is it not the very one from which my master drinks and which he uses for divination? What you have done is wrong.' "

[6] When the steward overtook them and repeated these words to them, [7] they said to him: "Why does my lord say such things? Far be it from your servants to do such a thing! [8] We even brought back to you from the land of Canaan the money that we found in the mouths of our bags. How could we steal silver or gold from your master's house? [9] If any of your servants is found to have the goblet, he shall die, and as for the rest of us, we shall become my lord's slaves." [10] But he replied, "Now what you propose is fair enough, but only the one who is found to have it shall become my slave, and the rest of you can go free." [11] Then each of them quickly lowered his bag to the ground and opened it; [12] and when a search was made, starting with the oldest and ending with the youngest, the goblet turned up in Benjamin's bag. [13] At this, they tore their garments. Then, when each man had loaded his donkey again, they returned to the city.

[14] When Judah and his brothers entered Joseph's house, he was still there; so they flung themselves on the ground before him. [15] "How could you do such a thing?" Joseph asked them. "Did you not know that such a man as I could discern by divination what happened?" [16] Judah replied: "What can we say to my lord? How can we plead or how try to prove our innocence? God has uncovered your servants' guilt. Here we are, then, the slaves of my lord—the rest of us no less than the one in whose possession the goblet was found." [17] Joseph said, "Far be it from me to act thus! Only the one in whose possession the goblet was found shall become my slave; the rest of you may go back unharmed to your father."

[18] Judah then stepped up to him and said: "I beg you, my lord, let your servant appeal to my lord, and do not become angry with your servant, for you are the equal of Pharaoh. [19] My lord asked his servants, 'Have you a father, or another brother?' [20] So we said to my lord, 'We have an aged father, and a younger brother, the child of his old age. This one's full brother is dead, and since he is the only one by his mother who is left, his father is devoted to him.' [21] Then you told your servants, 'Bring him down to me that I might see him.' [22] We replied to my lord, 'The boy cannot leave his father; his father would die if he left him.' [22] But you told your servants, 'Unless your youngest brother comes down with you, you shall not see me again.' [24] When we returned to your servant my father, we reported to him the words of my lord.

[25] "Later, our father said, 'Go back and buy some food for us.' [26] So we reminded him, `We cannot go down there; only if our youngest brother is with us can we go, for we may not see the man if our youngest brother is not with us.' [27] Then your servant my father said to us, 'As you know, my wife bore me two sons. [28] One of them, however, has gone away from me, and I said, "He must have been torn to pieces by wild beasts!" I have not seen him since. [29] If you take this one away from me too, and a disaster befalls him, you will send my white head down to Sheol in grief.'

[30] "So now, if the boy is not with us when I go back to your servant my father, whose very life is bound up with his, he will die as soon as

he sees that the boy is missing; [31] and your servants will thus send the white head of your servant our father down to Sheol in grief. [32] Besides, I, your servant, have guaranteed the boy's safety for my father by saying, 'If I fail to bring him back to you, father, I will bear the blame before you forever.' [33] So now let me, your servant, remain in place of the boy as the slave of my lord, and let the boy go back with his brothers. [34] How could I go back to my father if the boy were not with me? I could not bear to see the anguish that would overcome my father."

CHAPTER 45

The Truth Revealed. [1] Joseph could no longer restrain himself in the presence of all his attendants, so he cried out, "Have everyone withdraw from me!" So no one attended him when he made himself known to his brothers. [2] But his sobs were so loud that the Egyptians heard him, and so the news reached Pharaoh's house. [3] "I am Joseph," he said to his brothers. "Is my father still alive?" But his brothers could give him no answer, so dumbfounded were they at him.

[4] "Come closer to me," Joseph told his brothers. When they had done so, he said: "I am your brother Joseph, whom you sold into Egypt. [5] But now do not be distressed, and do not be angry with yourselves for having sold me here. It was really for the sake of saving lives that God sent me here ahead of you. [6] The famine has been in the land for two years now, and for five more years cultivation will yield no harvest. [7] God, therefore, sent me on ahead of you to ensure for you a remnant on earth and to save your lives in an extraordinary deliverance. [8] So it was not really you but God who had me come here; and he has made me a father to Pharaoh, lord of all his household, and ruler over the whole land of Egypt.

[9] "Hurry back, then, to my father and tell him: `Thus says your son Joseph: God has made me lord of all Egypt; come down to me without delay. [10] You can settle in the region of Goshen, where you will be near me—you and your

children and children's children, your flocks and herds, and everything that you own. [11] I will provide for you there in the five years of famine that lie ahead, so that you and your household and all that are yours will not suffer want.' [12] Surely, you can see for yourselves, and Benjamin can see for himself, that it is I who am speaking to you. [13] Tell my father all about my high position in Egypt and all that you have seen. But hurry and bring my father down here." [14] Then he threw his arms around his brother Benjamin and wept on his shoulder. [15] Joseph then kissed all his brothers and wept over them; and only then were his brothers able to talk with him.

[16] The news reached Pharaoh's house: "Joseph's brothers have come." Pharaoh and his officials were pleased. [17] So Pharaoh told Joseph: "Say to your brothers: 'This is what you shall do: Load up your animals and go without delay to the land of Canaan. [18] There get your father and your households, and then come to me; I will assign you the best land in Egypt, where you will live off the fat of the land.' [19] Instruct them further: 'Do this. Take wagons from the land of Egypt for your children and your wives and bring your father back here. [20] Do not be concerned about your belongings, for the best in the whole land of Egypt shall be yours.'"

[21] The sons of Israel acted accordingly. Joseph gave them the wagons, as Pharaoh had ordered, and he supplied them with provisions for the journey. [22] He also gave to each of them a set of clothes, but to Benjamin he gave three hundred shekels of silver and five sets of clothes. [23] Moreover, what he sent to his father was ten donkeys loaded with the finest products of Egypt and another ten loaded with grain and bread and provisions for his father's journey. [24] As he sent his brothers on their way, he told them, "Do not quarrel on the way."

[25] So they went up from Egypt and came to the land of Canaan, to their father Jacob. [26] When they told him, "Joseph is still alive—in fact, it is he who is governing all the land of Egypt," he was unmoved, for he did not believe them. [27] But when they recounted to him all that Joseph had told them, and when he saw the wagons that

Joseph had sent to transport him, the spirit of their father Jacob came to life. [28] "Enough," said Israel. "My son Joseph is still alive! I must go and see him before I die."

CHAPTER 46

Migration to Egypt. [1] Israel set out with all that was his. When he arrived at Beer-sheba, he offered sacrifices to the God of his father Isaac. [2] There God, speaking to Israel in a vision by night, called: Jacob! Jacob! He answered, "Here I am." [3] Then he said: I am God, the God of your father. Do not be afraid to go down to Egypt, for there I will make you a great nation. [4] I will go down to Egypt with you and I will also bring you back here, after Joseph has closed your eyes.

[5] So Jacob departed from Beer-sheba, and the sons of Israel put their father and their wives and children on the wagons that Pharaoh had sent to transport him. [6] They took with them their livestock and the possessions they had acquired in the land of Canaan. So Jacob and all his descendants came to Egypt. [7] His sons and his grandsons, his daughters and his granddaughters—all his descendants—he took with him to Egypt.

THE EXODUS FROM EGYPT (c 1320: Ex 12:37—15:21) — **(a)** The Israelites set out from **Rameses** for **Succoth** with their livestock (12:37). **(b)** God does not lead them by way of the Philistines' land, but by the desert near the **Red Sea**. They set out from **Succoth** and encamp at **Etham** on the edge of the desert (13:17-20). **(c)** Following God's command, the people encamp before **Pi-Hahiroth**, between **Migdol** and the sea, in front of **Baal-zephon**. There the Egyptians overtake them (14:1-9). **(d)** The Lord sweeps the seas with a strong east wind throughout the night and turns it into dry land. The Israelites cross over but when the Egyptians try to follow the waters flow back over them (14:21-31).

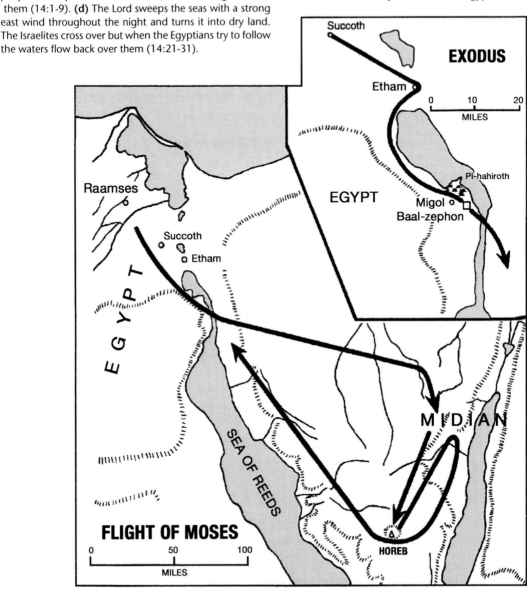

THE FLIGHT OF MOSES (Ex 1:1—12:36) — **(a)** Oppression of Israel in Egypt; the people build the store-cities of **Pithom** and **Rameses**; birth of Moses and his flight into **Midian** (1:1—2:25). **(b)** On the mountain of God, **Horeb**, the Lord appears to Moses, reveals the Divine Name ("I am who am") to him, and gives him the mission of delivering Israel (3:1—4:17). **(c)** Moses returns from **Midian**, and at God's command sets out for **Egypt**; at the **mountain of God**, he meets his brother Aaron and both return to **Egypt** (4:18-31). **(d)** Moses before Pharaoh: the ten plagues; permission to leave Egypt (5:1—12:36).

The Book Of Exodus

The second book of the Pentateuch is called Exodus, from the Greek word for "departure," because its central event was understood by the Septuagint's translators to be the departure of the Israelites from Egypt. Its Hebrew title, Shemoth ("Names"), is from the book's opening phrase, "These are the names. . . ." Continuing the history of Israel from the point where the Book of Genesis leaves off, Exodus recounts the Egyptian oppression of Jacob's ever-increasing descendants and their miraculous deliverance by God through Moses, who led them across the Red Sea to Mount Sinai where they entered into a covenant with the Lord. Covenantal laws and detailed prescriptions for the tabernacle (a portable sanctuary foreshadowing the Jerusalem Temple) and its service are followed by a dramatic episode of rebellion, repentance, and divine mercy. After the broken covenant is renewed, the tabernacle is constructed, and the cloud signifying God's glorious presence descends to cover it.

These events made Israel a nation and confirmed their unique relationship with God. The "law" (Hebrew torah) given by God through Moses to the Israelites at Mount Sinai constitutes the moral, civil, and ritual legislation by which they were to become a holy people. Many elements of it were fundamental to the teaching of Jesus (Mt 5:21–30; 15:4) as well as to New Testament and Christian moral teaching (Rom 13:8–10; 1 Cor 10:1–5; I Pt 2:9).

The principal divisions of Exodus are:

I. Introduction: The Oppression of the Israelites in Egypt (1:1—2:22)
II. The Call and Commission of Moses (2:23—7:7)
III. The Contest with Pharaoh (7:8—13:16)
IV. The Deliverance of the Israelites from Pharaoh and Victory at the Sea (13:17—15:21)
V. The Journey in the Wilderness to Sinai (15:22—18:27)
VI. Covenant and Legislation at Mount Sinai (19:1—31:18)
VII. Israel's Apostasy and God's Renewal of the Covenant (32:1—34:35)
VIII. The Building of the Tabernacle and the Descent of God's Glory upon It (35:1—40:38)

I. INTRODUCTION: THE OPPRESSION OF THE ISRAELITES IN EGYPT

CHAPTER 1

Jacob's Descendants in Egypt. ¹ These are the names of the sons of Israel who, accompanied by their households, entered into Egypt with Jacob: ² Reuben, Simeon, Levi and Judah; ³ Issachar, Zebulun and Benjamin; ⁴ Dan and Naphtali; Gad and Asher. ⁵ The total number of Jacob's direct descendants was seventy." Joseph was already in Egypt.

⁶ Now Joseph and all his brothers and that whole generation died. ⁷ But the Israelites were fruitful and prolific. They multiplied and became so very numerous that the land was filled with them.

The Oppression. ⁸ Then a new king, who knew nothing of Joseph, rose to power in Egypt. ⁹ He said to his people, "See! The Israelite people have multiplied and become more numerous than we are! ¹⁰ Come, let us deal shrewdly with them to stop their increase; otherwise, in time of war they too may join our enemies to fight against us, and so leave the land."

¹¹ Accordingly, they set supervisors over the Israelites to oppress them with forced labor. Thus they had to build for Pharaoh the garrison cities

of Pithom and Raamses. [12] Yet the more they were oppressed, the more they multiplied and spread, so that the Egyptians began to loathe the Israelites. [13] So the Egyptians reduced the Israelites to cruel slavery, [14] making life bitter for them with hard labor, at mortar and brick and all kinds of field work—cruelly oppressed in all their labor.

Command to the Midwives. [15] The king of Egypt told the Hebrew midwives, one of whom was called Shiphrah and the other Puah, [16] "When you act as midwives for the Hebrew women, look on the birthstool: if it is a boy, kill him; but if it is a girl, she may live." [17] The midwives, however, feared God; they did not do as the king of Egypt had ordered them, but let the boys live. [18] So the king of Egypt summoned the midwives and asked them, "Why have you done this, allowing the boys to live?" [19] The midwives answered Pharaoh, "The Hebrew women are not like the Egyptian women. They are robust and give birth before the midwife arrives." [20] Therefore God dealt well with the midwives; and the people multiplied and grew very numerous. [21] And because the midwives feared God, God built up families for them. [22] Pharaoh then commanded all his people, "Throw into the Nile every boy that is born, but you may let all the girls live."

CHAPTER 2

Birth and Adoption of Moses. [1] Now a man of the house of Levi married a Levite woman, [2] and the woman conceived and bore a son. Seeing what a fine child he was, she hid him for three months. [3] But when she could no longer hide him, she took a papyrus basket, daubed it with bitumen and pitch, and putting the child in it, placed it among the reeds on the bank of the Nile. [4] His sister stationed herself at a distance to find out what would happen to him.

[5] Then Pharaoh's daughter came down to bathe at the Nile, while her attendants walked along the bank of the Nile. Noticing the basket among the reeds, she sent her handmaid to fetch it. [6] On opening it, she looked, and there was a baby boy crying! She was moved with pity for him and said, "It is one of the Hebrews' children." [7] Then his sister asked Pharaoh's daughter, "Shall I go and summon a Hebrew woman to nurse the child for you?" [8] Pharaoh's daughter answered her, "Go." So the young woman went and called the child's own mother. [9] Pharaoh's daughter said to her, "Take this child and nurse him for me, and I will pay your wages." So the woman took the child and nursed him. [10] When the child grew, she brought him to Pharaoh's daughter, and he became her son. She named him Moses; for she said, "I drew him out of the water."

Moses' Flight to Midian. [11] On one occasion, after Moses had grown up, when he had gone out to his kinsmen and witnessed their forced labor, he saw an Egyptian striking a Hebrew, one of his own kinsmen. [12] Looking about and seeing no one, he struck down the Egyptian and hid him in the sand. [13] The next day he went out again, and now two Hebrews were fighting! So he asked the culprit, "Why are you striking your companion?" [14] But he replied, "Who has appointed you ruler and judge over us? Are you thinking of killing me as you killed the Egyptian?" Then Moses became afraid and thought, "The affair must certainly be known." [15] When Pharaoh heard of the affair, he sought to kill Moses. But Moses fled from Pharaoh and went to the land of Midian. There he sat down by a well.

[16] Now the priest of Midian had seven daughters, and they came to draw water and fill the troughs to water their father's flock. [17] But shepherds came and drove them away. So Moses rose up in their defense and watered their flock. [18] When they returned to their father Reuel, he said to them, "How is it you have returned so soon today?" [19] They answered, "An Egyptian delivered us from the shepherds. He even drew water for us and watered the flock!" [20] "Where is he?" he asked his daughters. "Why did you leave the man there? Invite him to have something to eat." [21] Moses agreed to stay with him, and the man gave Moses his daughter Zipporah in

marriage. [22] She conceived and bore a son, whom he named Gershom; for he said, "I am a stranger residing in a foreign land."

II. THE CALL AND COMMISSION OF MOSES

The Burning Bush. [23] A long time passed, during which the king of Egypt died. The Israelites groaned under their bondage and cried out, and from their bondage their cry for help went up to God. [24] God heard their moaning and God was mindful of his covenant with Abraham, Isaac and Jacob. [25] God saw the Israelites, and God knew. . . .

CHAPTER 3

[1] Meanwhile Moses was tending the flock of his father-in-law Jethro, the priest of Midian. Leading the flock beyond the wilderness, he came to the mountain of God, Horeb. [2] There the angel of the Lord appeared to him as fire flaming out of a bush. When he looked, although the bush was on fire, it was not being consumed. [3] So Moses decided, "I must turn aside to look at this remarkable sight. Why does the bush not burn up?" [4] When the Lord saw that he had turned aside to look, God called out to him from the bush: Moses! Moses! He answered, "Here I am." [5] God said: Do not come near! Remove your sandals from your feet, for the place where you stand is holy ground. [6] I am the God of your father, he continued, the God of Abraham, the God of Isaac, and the God of Jacob. Moses hid his face, for he was afraid to look at God.

The Call and Commission of Moses. [7] But the Lord said: I have witnessed the affliction of my people in Egypt and have heard their cry against their taskmasters, so I know well what they are suffering. [8] Therefore I have come down to rescue them from the power of the Egyptians and lead them up from that land into a good and spacious land, a land flowing with milk and honey, the country of the Canaanites, the Hittites, the Amorites, the Perizzites, the Girgashites, the Hivites and the Jebusites. [9] Now indeed the outcry of the Israelites has reached me, and I have seen how the Egyptians are oppressing them. [10] Now, go! I am sending you to Pharaoh to bring my people, the Israelites, out of Egypt.

[11] But Moses said to God, "Who am I that I should go to Pharaoh and bring the Israelites out of Egypt?" [12] God answered: I will be with you; and this will be your sign that I have sent you. When you have brought the people out of Egypt, you will serve God at this mountain. [13] "But," said Moses to God, "if I go to the Israelites and say to them, 'The God of your ancestors has sent me to you,' and they ask me, 'What is his name?' what do I tell them?" [14] God replied to Moses: I am who I am. Then he added: This is what you will tell the Israelites: I AM has sent me to you.

[15] God spoke further to Moses: This is what you will say to the Israelites: The Lord, the God of your ancestors, the God of Abraham, the God of Isaac, and the God of Jacob, has sent me to you.

This is my name forever;
  this is my title for all generations.

[16] Go and gather the elders of the Israelites, and tell them, The Lord, the God of your ancestors, the God of Abraham, Isaac, and Jacob, has appeared to me and said: I have observed you and what is being done to you in Egypt; [17] so I have decided to lead you up out of your affliction in Egypt into the land of the Canaanites, the Hittites, the Amorites, the Perizzites, the Girgashites, the Hivites and the Jebusites, a land flowing with milk and honey. [18] They will listen to you. Then you and the elders of Israel will go to the king of Egypt and say to him: The Lord, the God of the Hebrews, has come to meet us. So now, let us go a three days' journey in the wilderness to offer sacrifice to the Lord, our God. [19] Yet I know that the king of Egypt will not allow you to go unless his hand is forced. [20] So I will stretch out my hand and strike Egypt with all the wondrous deeds I will do in its midst. After that he will let you go. [21] I will even make the Egyptians so well-disposed toward this people that, when

you go, you will not go empty-handed. ²² Every woman will ask her neighbor and the resident alien in her house for silver and gold articles and for clothing, and you will put them on your sons and daughters. So you will plunder the Egyptians.

CHAPTER 4

¹ "But," objected Moses, "suppose they do not believe me or listen to me? For they may say, 'The Lord did not appear to you.'" ² The Lord said to him: What is in your hand? "A staff," he answered. ³ God said: Throw it on the ground. So he threw it on the ground and it became a snake, a and Moses backed away from it. ⁴ Then the Lord said to Moses: Now stretch out your hand and take hold of its tail. So he stretched out his hand and took hold of it, and it became a staff in his hand. ⁵ That is so they will believe that the Lord, the God of their ancestors, the God of Abraham, the God of Isaac, and the God of Jacob, did appear to you.

⁶ Again the Lord said to him: Put your hand into the fold of your garment. So he put his hand into the fold of his garment, and when he drew it out, there was his hand covered with scales, like snowflakes. ⁷ Then God said: Put your hand back into the fold of your garment. So he put his hand back into the fold of his garment, and when he drew it out, there it was again like his own flesh. ⁸ If they do not believe you or pay attention to the message of the first sign, they should believe the message of the second sign. ⁹ And if they do not believe even these two signs and do not listen to you, take some water from the Nile and pour it on the dry land. The water you take from the Nile will become blood on the dry land.

Aaron's Office as Assistant. ¹⁰ Moses, however, said to the Lord, "If you please, my Lord, I have never been eloquent, neither in the past nor now that you have spoken to your servant; but I am slow of speech and tongue.'" ¹¹ The Lord said to him: Who gives one person speech? Who makes another mute or deaf, seeing or blind? Is it not I,

the Lord? ¹² Now go, I will assist you in speaking and teach you what you are to say. ¹³ But he said, "If you please, my Lord, send someone else!" ¹⁴ Then the Lord became angry with Moses and said: I know there is your brother, Aaron the Levite, who is a good speaker; even now he is on his way to meet you. When he sees you, he will truly be glad. ¹⁵ You will speak to him and put the words in his mouth. I will assist both you and him in speaking and teach you both what you are to do. ¹⁶ He will speak to the people for you: he will be your spokesman, and you will be as God to him. ¹⁷ Take this staff in your hand; with it you are to perform the signs.

Moses' Return to Egypt. ¹⁸ After this Moses returned to Jethro his father-in-law and said to him, "Let me return to my kindred in Egypt, to see whether they are still living." Jethro replied to Moses, "Go in peace." ¹⁹ Then the Lord said to Moses in Midian: Return to Egypt, for all those who sought your life are dead. ²⁰ So Moses took his wife and his sons, mounted them on the donkey, and started back to the land of Egypt. Moses took the staff of God with him. ²¹ The LORD said to Moses: On your return to Egypt, see that you perform before Pharaoh all the wonders I have put in your power. But I will harden his heart and he will not let the people go. ²² So you will say to Pharaoh, Thus says the Lord: Israel is my son, my firstborn. ²³ I said to you: Let my son go, that he may serve me. Since you refused to let him go, I will kill your son, your firstborn.

²⁴ On the journey, at a place where they spent the night, the Lord came upon Moses and sought to put him to death. ²⁵ But Zipporah took a piece of flint and cut off her son's foreskin and, touching his feet, she said, "Surely you are a spouse of blood to me." ²⁶ So God let Moses alone. At that time she said, "A spouse of blood," in regard to the circumcision.

²⁷ The Lord said to Aaron: Go into the wilderness to meet Moses. So he went; when meeting him at the mountain of God, he kissed him. ²⁸ Moses told Aaron everything the Lord had sent him to say, and all the signs he had commanded him to do. ²⁹ Then Moses and Aaron went and

gathered all the elders of the Israelites. ³⁰ Aaron told them everything the Lᴏʀᴅ had said to Moses, and he performed the signs before the people. ³¹ The people believed, and when they heard that the Lᴏʀᴅ had observed the Israelites and had seen their affliction, they knelt and bowed down.

CHAPTER 5

Pharaoh's Hardness of Heart. ¹ Afterwards, Moses and Aaron went to Pharaoh and said, "Thus says the Lᴏʀᴅ, the God of Israel: Let my people go, that they may hold a feast for me in the wilderness." ² Pharaoh answered, "Who is the Lᴏʀᴅ, that I should obey him and let Israel go? I do not know the Lᴏʀᴅ, and I will not let Israel go." ³ They replied, "The God of the Hebrews has come to meet us. Let us go a three days' journey in the wilderness, that we may offer sacrifice to the Lᴏʀᴅ, our God, so that he does not strike us with the plague or the sword." ⁴ The king of Egypt answered them, "Why, Moses and Aaron, do you make the people neglect their work? Off to your labors!" ⁵ Pharaoh continued, "Look how they are already more numerous than the people of the land, and yet you would give them rest from their labors!"

⁶ That very day Pharaoh gave the taskmasters of the people and their foremen this order: ⁷ "You shall no longer supply the people with straw for their brickmaking as before. Let them go and gather their own straw! ⁸ Yet you shall levy upon them the same quota of bricks as they made previously. Do not reduce it. They are lazy; that is why they are crying, 'Let us go to offer sacrifice to our God.' ⁹ Increase the work for the men, so that they attend to it and not to deceitful words."

¹⁰ So the taskmasters of the people and their foremen went out and told the people, "Thus says Pharaoh, 'I will not provide you with straw. ¹¹ Go and get your own straw from wherever you can find it. But there will not be the slightest reduction in your work.'" ¹² The people, then, scattered throughout the land of Egypt to gather stubble for straw, ¹³ while the taskmasters kept driving them on, saying, "Finish your work, the same daily amount as when the straw was supplied to you." ¹⁴ The Israelite foremen, whom the taskmasters of Pharaoh had placed over them, were beaten, and were asked, "Why have you not completed your prescribed amount of bricks yesterday and today, as before?"

Complaint of the Foremen. ¹⁵ Then the Israelite foremen came and cried out to Pharaoh: "Why do you treat your servants in this manner? ¹⁶ No straw is supplied to your servants, and still we are told, 'Make bricks!' Look how your servants are beaten! It is you who are at fault." ¹⁷ He answered, "Lazy! You are lazy! That is why you keep saying, 'Let us go and offer sacrifice to the Lᴏʀᴅ.' ¹⁸ Now off to work! No straw will be supplied to you, but you must supply your quota of bricks."

¹⁹ The Israelite foremen realized they were in trouble, having been told, "Do not reduce your daily amount of bricks!" ²⁰ So when they left Pharaoh they assailed Moses and Aaron, who were waiting to meet them, ²¹ and said to them, "The Lᴏʀᴅ look upon you and judge! You have made us offensive to Pharaoh and his servants, putting a sword into their hands to kill us."

Renewal of God's Promise. ²² Then Moses again had recourse to the Lᴏʀᴅ and said, "Lᴏʀᴅ, why have you treated this people badly? And why did you send me? ²³ From the time I went to Pharaoh to speak in your name, he has treated this people badly, and you have done nothing to rescue your people."

CHAPTER 6

¹ The Lᴏʀᴅ answered Moses: Now you will see what I will do to Pharaoh. For by a strong hand, he will let them go; by a strong hand, he will drive them from his land.

Confirmation of the Promise to the Ancestors. ² Then God spoke to Moses, and said to him: I am the LORD. ³ As God the Almighty I appeared to Abraham, Isaac, and Jacob, but by my name, LORD, I did not make myself known to them. ⁴ I also established my covenant with them, to give them the land of Canaan, the land in which they were residing as aliens. ⁵ Now that I have heard the groaning of the Israelites, whom the Egyptians have reduced to slavery, I am mindful of my covenant. ⁶ Therefore, say to the Israelites: I am the LORD. I will free you from the burdens of the Egyptians and will deliver you from their slavery. I will redeem you by my outstretched arm and with mighty acts of judgment. ⁷ I will take you as my own people, and I will be your God; and you will know that I, the LORD, am your God who has freed you from the burdens of the Egyptians ⁸ and I will bring you into the land which I swore to give to Abraham, Isaac, and Jacob. I will give it to you as your own possession—I, the LORD! ⁹ But when Moses told this to the Israelites, they would not listen to him because of their dejection and hard slavery.

¹⁰ Then the LORD spoke to Moses: ¹¹ Go, tell Pharaoh, king of Egypt, to let the Israelites leave his land. ¹² However, Moses protested to the LORD, "If the Israelites did not listen to me, how is it possible that Pharaoh will listen to me, poor speaker that I am!" ¹³ But the LORD spoke to Moses and Aaron regarding the Israelites and Pharaoh, king of Egypt, and charged them to bring the Israelites out of the land of Egypt.

Genealogy of Moses and Aaron. ¹⁴ These are the heads of their ancestral houses. The sons of Reuben, the firstborn of Israel: Hanoch, Pallu, Hezron and Carmi; these are the clans of Reuben. ¹⁵ The sons of Simeon: Jemuel, Jamin, Ohad, Jachin, Zohar and Shaul, the son of a Canaanite woman; these are the clans of Simeon. ¹⁶ These are the names of the sons of Levi, in their genealogical order: Gershon, Kohath and Merari. Levi lived one hundred and thirty-seven years.

¹⁷ The sons of Gershon, by their clans: Libni and Shimei. ¹⁸ The sons of Kohath: Amram, Izhar, Hebron and Uzziel. Kohath lived one hundred and thirty-three years. ¹⁹ The sons of Merari: Mahli and Mushi. These are the clans of Levi in their genealogical order.

²⁰ Amram married his aunt Jochebed, who bore him Aaron, Moses, and Miriam. Amram lived one hundred and thirty-seven years. ²¹ The sons of Izhar: Korah, Nepheg and Zichri. ²² The sons of Uzziel: Mishael, Elzaphan and Sithri. ²³ Aaron married Elisheba, Amminadab's daughter, the sister of Nahshon; she bore him Nadab, Abihu, Eleazar and Ithamar. ²⁴ The sons of Korah: Assir, Elkanah and Abiasaph. These are the clans of the Korahites. ²⁵ Eleazar, Aaron's son, married one of Putiel's daughters, who bore him Phinehas. These are the heads of the ancestral houses of the Levites by their clans. ²⁶ These are the Aaron and the Moses to whom the LORD said, "Bring the Israelites out from the land of Egypt, company by company." ²⁷ They are the ones who spoke to Pharaoh, king of Egypt, to bring the Israelites out of Egypt—the same Moses and Aaron.

²⁸ When the LORD spoke to Moses in the land of Egypt ²⁹ the LORD said to Moses: I am the LORD. Say to Pharaoh, king of Egypt, all that I tell you. ³⁰ But Moses protested to the LORD, "Since I am a poor speaker, how is it possible that Pharaoh will listen to me?"

CHAPTER 7

¹ The LORD answered Moses: See! I have made you a god to Pharaoh, and Aaron your brother will be your prophet. ² You will speak all that I command you. In turn, your brother Aaron will tell Pharaoh to let the Israelites go out of his land. ³ Yet I will make Pharaoh so headstrong that, despite the many signs and wonders that I work in the land of Egypt, ⁴ Pharaoh will not listen to you. Therefore I will lay my hand on Egypt and with mighty acts of judgment I will bring my armies, my people the Israelites, out of the land of Egypt. ⁵ All Egyptians will know that I am the LORD, when I stretch out my hand against Egypt and bring the Israelites out of their midst.

⁶ This, then, is what Moses and Aaron did. They did exactly as the LORD had commanded them. ⁷ Moses was eighty years old, and Aaron eighty-three, when they spoke to Pharaoh.

III. THE CONTEST WITH PHARAOH

The Staff Turned Into a Serpent. ⁸ The Lord spoke to Moses and Aaron: ⁹ When Pharaoh demands of you, "Produce a sign or wonder," you will say to Aaron: "Take your staff and throw it down before Pharaoh, and it will turn into a serpent." ¹⁰ Then Moses and Aaron went to Pharaoh and did just as the Lord had commanded. Aaron threw his staff down before Pharaoh and his servants, and it turned into a serpent. ¹¹ Pharaoh, in turn, summoned the wise men and the sorcerers, and they also, the magicians of Egypt, did the same thing by their magic arts. ¹² Each one threw down his staff, and they turned into serpents. But Aaron's staff swallowed their staffs. ¹³ Pharaoh, however, hardened his heart and would not listen to them, just as the Lord had foretold.

First Plague: Water Turned into Blood. ¹⁴ Then the Lord said to Moses: Pharaoh is obstinate in refusing to let the people go. ¹⁵ In the morning, just when he sets out for the water, go to Pharaoh and present yourself by the bank of the Nile, holding in your hand the staff that turned into a snake. ¹⁶ Say to him: The Lord, the God of the Hebrews, sent me to you with the message: Let my people go to serve me in the wilderness. But as yet you have not listened. ¹⁷ Thus says the Lord: This is how you will know that I am the Lord. With the staff here in my hand, I will strike the water in the Nile and it will be changed into blood. ¹⁸ The fish in the Nile will die, and the Nile itself will stink so that the Egyptians will be unable to drink water from the Nile.

¹⁹ The Lord then spoke to Moses: Speak to Aaron: Take your staff and stretch out your hand over the waters of Egypt—its streams, its canals, its ponds, and all its sup-plies of water—that they may become blood. There will be blood throughout the land of Egypt, even in the wooden pails and stone jars.

²⁰ This, then, is what Moses and Aaron did, exactly as the Lord had commanded. Aaron raised his staff and struck the waters in the Nile in full view of Pharaoh and his servants, and all the water in the Nile was changed into blood. ²¹ The fish in the Nile died, and the Nile itself stank so that the Egyptians could not drink water from it. There was blood throughout the land of Egypt. ²² But the Egyptian magicians did the same by their magic arts. So Pharaoh hardened his heart and would not listen to them, just as the Lord had said. ²³ Pharaoh turned away and went into his house, with no concern even for this. ²⁴ All the Egyptians had to dig round about the Nile for drinking water, since they could not drink any water from the Nile.

Second Plague: the Frogs. ²⁵ Seven days passed after the Lord had struck the Nile. ²⁶ Then the Lord said to Moses: Go to Pharaoh and tell him: Thus says the Lord: Let my people go to serve me. ²⁷ If you refuse to let them go, then I will send a plague of frogs over all your territory. ²⁸ The Nile will teem with frogs. They will come up and enter into your palace and into your bedroom and onto your bed, into the houses of your servants, too, and among your people, even into your ovens and your kneading bowls. ²⁹ The frogs will come up over you and your people and all your servants.

CHAPTER 8

¹ The Lord then spoke to Moses: Speak to Aaron: Stretch out your hand with your staff over the streams, the canals, and the ponds, and make frogs overrun the land of Egypt. ² So Aaron stretched out his hand over the waters of Egypt, and the frogs came up and covered the land of Egypt. ³ But the magicians did the same by their magic arts and made frogs overrun the land of Egypt.

⁴ Then Pharaoh summoned Moses and Aaron and said, "Pray to the Lord to remove the frogs from me and my people, and I will let the people go to sacrifice to the Lord." ⁵ Moses answered Pharaoh, "Please designate for me the time when I am to pray for you and your servants and your people, to get rid of the frogs from you and your houses. They will be left only in the Nile."

6 "Tomorrow," he said. Then Moses replied, "It will be as you have said, so that you may know that there is none like the LORD, our God. 7 The frogs will leave you and your houses, your servants and your people; they will be left only in the Nile."

8 After Moses and Aaron left Pharaoh's presence, Moses cried out to the LORD on account of the frogs that he had inflicted on Pharaoh; 9 and the LORD did as Moses had asked. The frogs died off in the houses, the courtyards, and the fields. 10 Heaps of them were piled up, and the land stank. 11 But when Pharaoh saw there was a respite, he became obstinate and would not listen to them, just as the LORD had said.

Third Plague: the Gnats. 12 Thereupon the LORD spoke to Moses: Speak to Aaron: Stretch out your staff and strike the dust of the earth, and it will turn into gnats throughout the land of Egypt. 13 They did so. Aaron stretched out his hand with his staff and struck the dust of the earth, and gnats came upon human being and beast alike. All the dust of the earth turned into gnats throughout the land of Egypt. 14 Though the magicians did the same thing to produce gnats by their magic arts, they could not do so. The gnats were on human being and beast alike, 15 and the magicians said to Pharaoh, "This is the finger of God." Yet Pharaoh hardened his heart and would not listen to them, just as the LORD had said.

Fourth Plague: the Flies. 16 Then the LORD spoke to Moses: Early tomorrow morning present yourself to Pharaoh when he sets out toward the water, and say to him: Thus says the LORD: Let my people go to serve me. 17 For if you do not let my people go, I will send swarms of flies upon you and your servants and your people and your houses. The houses of the Egyptians and the very ground on which they stand will be filled with swarms of flies. 18 But on that day I will make an exception of the land of Goshen, where my people are, and no swarms of flies will be there, so that you may know that I the LORD am in the midst of the land. 19 I will make a distinction between my people and your people. This sign will take place tomorrow.

20 This the LORD did. Thick swarms of flies entered the house of Pharaoh and the houses of his servants; throughout Egypt the land was devastated on account of the swarms of flies.

21 Then Pharaoh summoned Moses and Aaron and said, "Go sacrifice to your God within the land." 22 But Moses replied, "It is not right to do so, for what we sacrifice to the LORD, our God, is abhorrent to the Egyptians. If we sacrifice what is abhorrent to the Egyptians before their very eyes, will they not stone us? 23 We must go a three days' journey in the wilderness and sacrifice to the LORD, our God, as he commands us." 24 Pharaoh said, "I will let you go to sacrifice to the LORD, your God, in the wilderness, provided that you do not go too far away. Pray for me." 25 Moses answered, "As soon as I leave you I will pray to the LORD that the swarms of flies may depart tomorrow from Pharaoh, his servants, and his people. Pharaoh, however, must not act deceitfully again and refuse to let the people go to sacrifice to the LORD." 26 When Moses left Pharaoh, he prayed to the LORD; 27 and the LORD did as Moses had asked, removing the swarms of flies from Pharaoh, his servants, and his people. Not one remained. 28 But once more Pharaoh became obstinate and would not let the people go.

CHAPTER 9

Fifth Plague: the Pestilence. 1 Then the LORD said to Moses: Go to Pharaoh and tell him: Thus says the LORD, the God of the Hebrews: Let my people go to serve me. 2 For if you refuse to let them go and persist in holding them, 3 the hand of the LORD will strike your livestock in the field— your horses, donkeys, camels, herds and flocks— with a very severe pestilence. 4 But the LORD will distinguish between the livestock of Israel and that of Egypt, so that nothing belonging to the Israelites will die. 5 And the LORD set a definite time, saying: Tomorrow the LORD will do this in the land. 6 And on the next day the LORD did it. All the livestock of the Egyptians died, a but not one animal belonging to the Israelites died.

[7] But although Pharaoh found upon inquiry that not even so much as one of the livestock of the Israelites had died, he remained obstinate and would not let the people go.

Sixth Plague: the Boils. [8] So the LORD said to Moses and Aaron: Each of you take handfuls of soot from a kiln, and in the presence of Pharaoh let Moses scatter it toward the sky. [9] It will turn into fine dust over the whole land of Egypt and cause festering boils on human being and beast alike throughout the land of Egypt.

[10] So they took the soot from a kiln and appeared before Pharaoh. When Moses scattered it toward the sky, it caused festering boils on human being and beast alike. [11] Because of the boils the magicians could not stand in Moses' presence, for there were boils on the magicians as well as on the rest of the Egyptians. [12] But the LORD hardened Pharaoh's heart, and he would not listen to them, just as the LORD had said to Moses.

Seventh Plague: the Hail. [13] Then the LORD spoke to Moses: Early tomorrow morning present yourself to Pharaoh and say to him: Thus says the LORD, the God of the Hebrews: Let my people go to serve me, [14] for this time I will unleash all my blows upon you and your servants and your people, so that you may know that there is none like me anywhere on earth. [15] For by now I should have stretched out my hand and struck you and your people with such pestilence that you would have vanished from the earth. [16] But this is why I have let you survive: to show you my power and to make my name resound throughout the earth! [17] Will you continue to exalt yourself over my people and not let them go? [18] At this time tomorrow, therefore, I am going to rain down such fierce hail as there has never been in Egypt from the day it was founded up to the present. [19] Therefore, order your live-stock and whatever else you have in the open fields to be brought to a place of safety. Whatever human being or animal is found in the fields and is not brought to shelter will die when the hail comes down upon them. [20] Those of Pharaoh's servants who feared the word of the LORD hurried their servants and their livestock off to shelter. [21] But those who did not pay attention to the word of the LORD left their servants and their livestock in the fields.

[22] The LORD then said to Moses: Stretch out your hand toward the sky, that hail may fall upon the entire land of Egypt, on human being and beast alike and all the vegetation of the fields in the land of Egypt. [23] So Moses stretched out his staff toward the sky, and the LORD sent forth peals of thunder and hail. Lightning flashed toward the earth, and the LORD rained down hail upon the land of Egypt. [24] There was hail and lightning flashing here and there through the hail, and the hail was so fierce that nothing like it had been seen in Egypt since it became a nation. [25] Throughout the land of Egypt the hail struck down everything in the fields, human being and beast alike; it struck down all the vegetation of the fields and splintered every tree in the fields. [26] Only in the land of Goshen, where the Israelites were, was there no hail.

[27] Then Pharaoh sent for Moses and Aaron and said to them, "I have sinned this time! The LORD is the just one, and I and my people are the ones at fault. [28] Pray to the LORD! Enough of the thunder and hail! I will let you go; you need stay no longer." [29] Moses replied to him, "As soon as I leave the city I will extend my hands to the LORD; the thunder will cease, and there will be no more hail so that you may know that the earth belongs to the LORD. [30] But as for you and your servants, I know that you do not yet fear the LORD God."

[31] Now the flax and the barley were ruined, because the barley was in ear and the flax in bud. [32] But the wheat and the spelt were not ruined, for they grow later.

[33] When Moses had left Pharaoh and gone out of the city, he extended his hands to the LORD. The thunder and the hail ceased, and the rain no longer poured down upon the earth. [34] But Pharaoh, seeing that the rain and the hail and the thunder had ceased, sinned again and became obstinate, both he and his servants. [35] In the hardness of his heart, Pharaoh would not let the Israelites go, just as the LORD had said through Moses.

CHAPTER 10

Eighth Plague: the Locusts. [1] Then the Lord said to Moses: Go to Pharaoh, for I have made him and his servants obstinate in order that I may perform these signs of mine among them [2] and that you may recount to your son and grandson how I made a fool of the Egyptians and what signs I did among them, so that you may know that I am the Lord.

[3] So Moses and Aaron went to Pharaoh and told him, "Thus says the Lord, the God of the Hebrews: How long will you refuse to submit to me? Let my people go to serve me. [4] For if you refuse to let my people go, tomorrow I will bring locusts into your territory. [5] They will cover the surface of the earth, so that the earth itself will not be visible. They will eat up the remnant you saved undamaged from the hail, as well as all the trees that are growing in your fields. [6] They will fill your houses and the houses of your servants and of all the Egyptians—something your parents and your grandparents have not seen from the day they appeared on this soil until today." With that he turned and left Pharaoh.

[7] But Pharaoh's servants said to him, "How long will he be a snare for us? Let the people go to serve the Lord, their God. Do you not yet realize that Egypt is being destroyed?" [8] So Moses and Aaron were brought back to Pharaoh, who said to them, "Go, serve the Lord, your God. But who exactly will go?" [9] Moses answered, "With our young and old we must go; with our sons and daughters, with our flocks and herds we must go. It is a pilgrimage feast of the Lord for us." [10] "The Lord help you," Pharaoh replied, "if I let your little ones go with you! Clearly, you have some evil in mind. [11] By no means! Just you men go and serve the Lord. After all, that is what you have been asking for." With that they were driven from Pharaoh's presence.

[12] The Lord then said to Moses: Stretch out your hand over the land of Egypt for the locusts, that they may come upon it and eat up all the land's vegetation, whatever the hail has left. [13] So Moses stretched out his staff over the land of Egypt, and the Lord drove an east wind over the land all that day and all night. When it was morning, the east wind brought the locusts. [14] The locusts came up over the whole land of Egypt and settled down over all its territory. Never before had there been such a fierce swarm of locusts, nor will there ever be again. [15] They covered the surface of the whole land, so that it became black. They ate up all the vegetation in the land and all the fruit of the trees the hail had spared. Nothing green was left on any tree or plant in the fields throughout the land of Egypt.

[16] Pharaoh hurriedly summoned Moses and Aaron and said, "I have sinned against the Lord, your God, and against you. [17] But now, do forgive me my sin only this once, and pray to the Lord, your God, only to take this death from me." [18] When Moses left Pharaoh, he prayed to the Lord, [19] and the Lord caused the wind to shift to a very strong west wind, which took up the locusts and hurled them into the Red Sea. Not a single locust remained within the whole territory of Egypt. [20] Yet the Lord hardened Pharaoh's heart, and he would not let the Israelites go.

Ninth Plague: the Darkness. [21] Then the Lord said to Moses: Stretch out your hand toward the sky, that over the land of Egypt there may be such darkness that one can feel it. [22] So Moses stretched out his hand toward the sky, and there was dense darkness throughout the land of Egypt for three days. [23] People could not see one another, nor could they get up from where they were, for three days. But all the Israelites had light where they lived.

[24] Pharaoh then summoned Moses and Aaron and said, "Go, serve the Lord. Only your flocks and herds will be detained. Even your little ones may go with you." [25] But Moses replied, "You also must give us sacrifices and burnt offerings to make to the Lord, our God. [26] Our livestock also must go with us. Not an animal must be left behind, for some of them we will select for service to the Lord, our God; but we will not know with which ones we are to serve the Lord until we arrive there." [27] But the Lord hardened

Pharaoh's heart, and he was unwilling to let them go. ²⁸ Pharaoh said to Moses, "Leave me, and see to it that you do not see my face again! For the day you do see my face you will die!" ²⁹ Moses replied, "You are right! I will never see your face again."

CHAPTER 11

Tenth Plague: the Death of the Firstborn. ¹ Then the Lᴏʀᴅ spoke to Moses: One more plague I will bring upon Pharaoh and upon Egypt. After that he will let you depart. In fact, when he finally lets you go, he will drive you away. ² Instruct the people that every man is to ask his neighbor, and every woman her neighbor, for silver and gold articles and for clothing. ³ The Lᴏʀᴅ indeed made the Egyptians well-disposed toward the people; Moses himself was very highly regarded by Pharaoh's servants and the people in the land of Egypt.

⁴ Moses then said, "Thus says the Lᴏʀᴅ: About midnight I will go forth through Egypt. ⁵ Every firstborn in the land of Egypt will die, from the firstborn of Pharaoh who sits on his throne to the firstborn of the slave-girl who is at the handmill, as well as all the firstborn of the animals. ⁶ Then there will be loud wailing throughout the land of Egypt, such as has never been, nor will ever be again. ⁷ But among all the Israelites, among human beings and animals alike, not even a dog will growl, so that you may know that the Lᴏʀᴅ distinguishes between Egypt and Israel. ⁸ All these servants of yours will then come down to me and bow down before me, saying: Leave, you and all your followers! Then I will depart." With that he left Pharaoh's presence in hot anger.

⁹ The Lᴏʀᴅ said to Moses: Pharaoh will not listen to you so that my wonders may be multiplied in the land of Egypt. ¹⁰ Thus, although Moses and Aaron performed all these wonders in Pharaoh's presence, the Lᴏʀᴅ hardened Pharaoh's heart, and he would not let the Israelites go from his land.

CHAPTER 12

The Passover Ritual Prescribed. ¹ The Lᴏʀᴅ said to Moses and Aaron in the land of Egypt: ² This month will stand at the head of your calendar; you will reckon it the first month of the year. ³ Tell the whole community of Israel: On the tenth of this month every family must procure for itself a lamb, one apiece for each household. ⁴ If a household is too small for a lamb, it along with its nearest neighbor will procure one, and apportion the lamb's cost in proportion to the number of persons, according to what each household consumes. ⁵ Your lamb must be a year-old male and without blemish. You may take it from either the sheep or the goats. ⁶ You will keep it until the fourteenth day of this month, and then, with the whole community of Israel assembled, it will be slaughtered during the evening twilight. ⁷ They will take some of its blood and apply it to the two doorposts and the lintel of the houses in which they eat it. ⁸ They will consume its meat that same night, eating it roasted with unleavened bread and bitter herbs. ⁹ Do not eat any of it raw or even boiled in water, but roasted, with its head and shanks and inner organs. ¹⁰ You must not keep any of it beyond the morning; whatever is left over in the morning must be burned up.

¹¹ This is how you are to eat it: with your loins girt, sandals on your feet and your staff in hand, you will eat it in a hurry. It is the Lᴏʀᴅ's Passover. ¹² For on this same night I will go through Egypt, striking down every firstborn in the land, human being and beast alike, and executing judgment on all the gods of Egypt—I, the Lᴏʀᴅ! ¹³ But for you the blood will mark the houses where you are. Seeing the blood, I will pass over you; thereby, when I strike the land of Egypt, no destructive blow will come upon you.

¹⁴ This day will be a day of remembrance for you, which your future generations will celebrate with pilgrimage to the Lᴏʀᴅ; you will celebrate it as a statute forever. ¹⁵ For seven days you must eat unleavened bread. From the very first day

you will have your houses clear of all leaven. For whoever eats leavened bread from the first day to the seventh will be cut off from Israel. [16] On the first day you will hold a sacred assembly, and likewise on the seventh. On these days no sort of work shall be done, except to prepare the food that everyone needs. [17] Keep, then, the custom of the unleavened bread, since it was on this very day that I brought your armies out of the land of Egypt. You must observe this day throughout your generations as a statute forever. [18] From the evening of the fourteenth day of the first month until the evening of the twenty-first day of this month you will eat unleavened bread. [19] For seven days no leaven may be found in your houses; for anyone, a resident alien or a native, who eats leavened food will be cut off from the community of Israel. [20] You shall eat nothing leavened; wherever you dwell you may eat only unleavened bread.

Promulgation of the Passover. [21] Moses summoned all the elders of Israel and said to them, "Go and procure lambs for your families, and slaughter the Passover victims. [22] Then take a bunch of hyssop, and dipping it in the blood that is in the basin, apply some of this blood to the lintel and the two doorposts. And none of you shall go outdoors until morning. [23] For when the LORD goes by to strike down the Egyptians, seeing the blood on the lintel and the two door-posts, the LORD will pass over that door and not let the destroyer come into your houses to strike you down.

[24] "You will keep this practice forever as a statute for yourselves and your descendants. [25] Thus, when you have entered the land which the LORD will give you as he promised, you must observe this rite. [26] When your children ask you, 'What does this rite of yours mean?' [27] you will reply, 'It is the Passover sacrifice for the LORD, who passed over the houses of the Israelites in Egypt; when he struck down the Egyptians, he delivered our houses.'"

Then the people knelt and bowed down, [28] and the Israelites went and did exactly as the LORD had commanded Moses and Aaron.

Death of the Firstborn. [29] And so at midnight the LORD struck down every firstborn in the land of Egypt, from the firstborn of Pharaoh sitting on his throne to the firstborn of the prisoner in the dungeon, as well as all the firstborn of the animals. [30] Pharaoh arose in the night, he and all his servants and all the Egyptians; and there was loud wailing throughout Egypt, for there was not a house without its dead.

Permission to Depart. [31] During the night Pharaoh summoned Moses and Aaron and said, "Leave my people at once, you and the Israelites! Go and serve the LORD as you said. [32] Take your flocks, too, and your herds, as you said, and go; and bless me, too!"

[33] The Egyptians, in a hurry to send them away from the land, urged the people on, for they said, "All of us will die!" [34] The people, therefore, took their dough before it was leavened, in their kneading bowls wrapped in their cloaks on their shoulders. [35] And the Israelites did as Moses had commanded: they asked the Egyptians for articles of silver and gold and for clothing. [36] Indeed the LORD had made the Egyptians so well-disposed toward the people that they let them have whatever they asked for. And so they despoiled the Egyptians.

Departure from Egypt. [37] The Israelites set out from Rameses for Succoth, about six hundred thousand men on foot, not counting the children. [38] A crowd of mixed ancestry also went up with them, with livestock in great abundance, both flocks and herds. [39] The dough they had brought out of Egypt they baked into unleavened loaves. It was not leavened, because they had been driven out of Egypt and could not wait. They did not even prepare food for the journey.

[40] The time the Israelites had stayed in Egypt was four hundred and thirty years. [41] At the end of four hundred and thirty years, on this very date, all the armies of the LORD left the land of Egypt. [42] This was a night of vigil for the LORD, when he brought them out of the land of Egypt; so on this night all Israelites must keep a vigil for the LORD throughout their generations.

Law of the Passover. [43] The LORD said to Moses and Aaron: This is the Passover statute. No foreigner may eat of it. [44] However, every slave bought for money you will circumcise;

then he may eat of it. ⁴⁵ But no tenant or hired worker may eat of it. ⁴⁶ It must be eaten in one house; you may not take any of its meat outside the house. You shall not break any of its bones. ⁴⁷ The whole community of Israel must celebrate this feast. ⁴⁸ If any alien residing among you would celebrate the Passover for the Lord, all his males must be circumcised, and then he may join in its celebration just like the natives. But no one who is uncircumcised may eat of it. ⁴⁹ There will be one law for the native and for the alien residing among you.

⁵⁰ All the Israelites did exactly as the Lord had commanded Moses and Aaron. ⁵¹ On that same day the Lord brought the Israelites out of the land of Egypt company by company.

CHAPTER 13

Consecration of Firstborn. ¹ The Lord spoke to Moses and said: ² Consecrate to me every firstborn; whatever opens the womb among the Israelites, a whether of human being or beast, belongs to me.

³ Moses said to the people, "Remember this day on which you came out of Egypt, out of a house of slavery. For it was with a strong hand that the Lord brought you out from there. Nothing made with leaven may be eaten. ⁴ This day on which you are going out is in the month of Abib. ⁵ Therefore, when the Lord, your God, has brought you into the land of the Canaanites, the Hittites, the Amorites, the Perrizites, the Girgashites, the Hivites, and the Jebusites, which he swore to your ancestors to give you, a land flowing with milk and honey, you will perform the following service in this month. ⁶ For seven days you will eat unleavened bread, and the seventh day will also be a festival to the Lord. ⁷ Unleavened bread may be eaten during the seven days, but nothing leavened and no leaven may be found in your possession in all your territory. ⁸ And on that day you will explain to your son, 'This is because of what the Lord did for me when I came out of Egypt.' ⁹ It will be like a sign on your hand and a

reminder on your forehead, so that the teaching of the Lord will be on your lips: with a strong hand the Lord brought you out of Egypt. ¹⁰ You will keep this statute at its appointed time from year to year.

¹¹ "When the Lord, your God, has brought you into the land of the Canaanites, just as he swore to you and your ancestors, and gives it to you, ¹² you will dedicate to the Lord every newborn that opens the womb; and every firstborn male of your animals will belong to the Lord. ¹³ Every firstborn of a donkey you will ransom with a sheep. If you do not ransom it, you will break its neck. Every human firstborn of your sons you must ransom. ¹⁴ And when your son asks you later on, 'What does this mean?' you will tell him, 'With a strong hand the Lord brought us out of Egypt, out of a house of slavery. ¹⁵ When Pharaoh stubbornly refused to let us go, the Lord killed every firstborn in the land of Egypt, the firstborn of human being and beast alike. That is why I sacrifice to the Lord every male that opens the womb, and why I ransom every firstborn of my sons.' ¹⁶ It will be like a sign on your hand and a band on your forehead that with a strong hand the Lord brought us out of Egypt."

IV. THE DELIVERANCE OF THE ISRAELITES FROM PHARAOH AND VICTORY AT THE SEA

Toward the Red Sea. ¹⁷ Now, when Pharaoh let the people go, God did not lead them by way of the Philistines' land, though this was the nearest; for God said: If the people see that they have to fight, they might change their minds and return to Egypt. ¹⁸ Instead, God rerouted them toward the Red Sea by way of the wilderness road, and the Israelites went up out of the land of Egypt arrayed for battle. ¹⁹ Moses also took Joseph's bones with him, for Joseph had made the Israelites take a solemn oath, saying, "God will surely take care of you, and you must bring my bones up with you from here."

²⁰ Setting out from Succoth, they camped at Etham near the edge of the wilderness.

²¹ The L<small>ORD</small> preceded them, in the daytime by means of a column of cloud to show them the way, and at night by means of a column of fire to give them light. Thus they could travel both day and night. ²² Neither the column of cloud by day nor the column of fire by night ever left its place in front of the people.

CHAPTER 14

¹ Then the L<small>ORD</small> spoke to Moses: ² Speak to the Israelites: Let them turn about and camp before Pi-hahiroth, between Migdol and the sea. Camp in front of Baalzephon, just opposite, by the sea. ³ Pharaoh will then say, "The Israelites are wandering about aimlessly in the land. The wilderness has closed in on them." ⁴ I will so harden Pharaoh's heart that he will pursue them. Thus I will receive glory through Pharaoh and all his army, and the Egyptians will know that I am the L<small>ORD</small>.

This the Israelites did. ⁵ When it was reported to the king of Egypt that the people had fled, Pharaoh and his servants had a change of heart about the people. "What in the world have we done!" they said. "We have released Israel from our service!" ⁶ So Pharaoh harnessed his chariots and took his army with him. ⁷ He took six hundred select chariots and all the chariots of Egypt, with officers on all of them. ⁸ The L<small>ORD</small> hardened the heart of Pharaoh, king of Egypt, so that he pursued the Israelites while they were going out in triumph. ⁹ The Egyptians pursued them—all Pharaoh's horses, his chariots, his horsemen, and his army—and caught up with them as they lay encamped by the sea, at Pi-hahiroth, in front of Baalzephon.

Crossing the Red Sea. ¹⁰ Now Pharaoh was near when the Israelites looked up and saw that the Egyptians had set out after them. Greatly frightened, the Israelites cried out to the L<small>ORD</small>. ¹¹ To Moses they said, "Were there no burial places in Egypt that you brought us to die in the wilderness? What have you done to us, bringing us out of Egypt? ¹² Did we not tell you this in Egypt, when we said, 'Leave us alone that we may serve the Egyptians'? Far better for us to serve the Egyptians than to die in the wilderness." ¹³ But Moses answered the people, "Do not fear! Stand your ground and see the victory the L<small>ORD</small> will win for you today. For these Egyptians whom you see today you will never see again. ¹⁴ The L<small>ORD</small> will fight for you; you have only to keep still."

¹⁵ Then the L<small>ORD</small> said to Moses: Why are you crying out to me? Tell the Israelites to set out. ¹⁶ And you, lift up your staff and stretch out your hand over the sea, and split it in two, that the Israelites may pass through the sea on dry land. ¹⁷ But I will harden the hearts of the Egyptians so that they will go in after them, and I will receive glory through Pharaoh and all his army, his chariots and his horsemen. ¹⁸ The Egyptians will know that I am the L<small>ORD</small>, when I receive glory through Pharaoh, his chariots, and his horsemen.

¹⁹ The angel of God, who had been leading Israel's army, now moved and went around behind them. And the column of cloud, moving from in front of them, took up its place behind them, ²⁰ so that it came between the Egyptian army and that of Israel. And when it became dark, the cloud illumined the night; and so the rival camps did not come any closer together all night long. ²¹ Then Moses stretched out his hand over the sea; and the L<small>ORD</small> drove back the sea with a strong east wind all night long and turned the sea into dry ground. The waters were split, ²² so that the Israelites entered into the midst of the sea on dry land, with the water as a wall to their right and to their left.

Rout of the Egyptians. ²³ The Egyptians followed in pursuit after them—all Pharaoh's horses and chariots and horsemen—into the midst of the sea. ²⁴ But during the watch just before dawn, the L<small>ORD</small> looked down from a column of fiery cloud upon the Egyptian army and threw it into a panic; ²⁵ and he so clogged their chariot wheels that they could drive only with difficulty. With that the Egyptians said, "Let us flee from Israel, because the L<small>ORD</small> is fighting for them against Egypt."

²⁶ Then the L<small>ORD</small> spoke to Moses: Stretch out your hand over the sea, that the water may flow

back upon the Egyptians, upon their chariots and their horsemen. ²⁷ So Moses stretched out his hand over the sea, and at daybreak the sea returned to its normal flow. The Egyptians were fleeing head on toward it when the Lᴏʀᴅ cast the Egyptians into the midst of the sea. ²⁸ As the water flowed back, it covered the chariots and the horsemen. Of all Pharaoh's army which had followed the Israelites into the sea, not even one escaped. ²⁹ But the Israelites had walked on dry land through the midst of the sea, with the water as a wall to their right and to their left. ³⁰ Thus the Lᴏʀᴅ saved Israel on that day from the power of Egypt. When Israel saw the Egyptians lying dead on the seashore ³¹ and saw the great power that the Lᴏʀᴅ had shown against Egypt, the people feared the Lᴏʀᴅ. They believed in the Lᴏʀᴅ and in Moses his servant.

CHAPTER 15

¹ Then Moses and the Israelites sang this song to the Lᴏʀᴅ:

I will sing to the Lᴏʀᴅ, for he is gloriously triumphant;
    horse and chariot he has cast into the sea.
² My strength and my refuge is the Lᴏʀᴅ, and he has become my savior.
    This is my God, I praise him; the God of my father, I extol him.
³ The Lᴏʀᴅ is a warrior,
    Lᴏʀᴅ is his name!
⁴ Pharaoh's chariots and army he hurled into the sea;
    the elite of his officers were drowned in the Red Sea.
⁵ The flood waters covered them,
    they sank into the depths like a stone.
⁶ Your right hand, O Lᴏʀᴅ, magnificent in power,
    your right hand, O Lᴏʀᴅ, shattered the enemy.
⁷ In your great majesty you overthrew your adversaries;

you loosed your wrath to consume them like stubble.
⁸ At the blast of your nostrils the waters piled up,
    the flowing waters stood like a mound,
        the flood waters foamed in the midst of the sea.
⁹ The enemy boasted, "I will pursue and overtake them;
    I will divide the spoils and have my fill of them;
    I will draw my sword; my hand will despoil them!"
¹⁰ When you blew with your breath, the sea covered them;
    like lead they sank in the mighty waters.
¹¹ Who is like you among the gods, O Lᴏʀᴅ?
    Who is like you, magnificent among the holy ones?
    Awe-inspiring in deeds of renown, worker of wonders,
¹²   when you stretched out your right hand, the earth swallowed them!
¹³ In your love you led the people you redeemed;
    in your strength you guided them to your holy dwelling.
¹⁴ The peoples heard and quaked;
    anguish gripped the dwellers in Philistia.
¹⁵ Then were the chieftains of Edom dismayed,
    the nobles of Moab seized by trembling;
    All the inhabitants of Canaan melted away;
¹⁶   terror and dread fell upon them.
    By the might of your arm they became silent like stone,
        while your people, Lᴏʀᴅ, passed over,
        while the people whom you created passed over.
¹⁷ You brought them in, you planted them on the mountain that is your own
    The place you made the base of your throne, Lᴏʀᴅ,
        the sanctuary, Lᴏʀᴅ, your hands established.
¹⁸ May the Lᴏʀᴅ reign forever and ever!

[19] When Pharaoh's horses and chariots and horsemen entered the sea, the LORD made the waters of the sea flow back upon them, though the Israelites walked on dry land through the midst of the sea. [20] Then the prophet Miriam, Aaron's sister, took a tambourine in her hand, while all the women went out after her with tambourines, dancing; [21] and she responded to them:

Sing to the LORD, for he is gloriously
      triumphant;
   horse and chariot he has cast into
      the sea.

V. THE JOURNEY IN THE WILDERNESS TO SINAI

At Marah and Elim. [22] Then Moses led Israel forward from the Red Sea, and they marched out to the wilderness of Shur. After traveling for three days through the wilderness without finding water, [23] they arrived at Marah, where they could not drink its water, because it was too bitter. Hence this place was called Marah. [24] As the people grumbled against Moses, saying, "What are we to drink?" [25] he cried out to the LORD, who pointed out to him a piece of wood. When he threw it into the water, the water became fresh.

It was here that God, in making statutes and ordinances for them, put them to the test. [26] He said: If you listen closely to the voice of the LORD, your God, and do what is right in his eyes: if you heed his commandments and keep all his statutes, I will not afflict you with any of the diseases with which I afflicted the Egyptians; for I, the LORD, am your healer.

[27] Then they came to Elim, where there were twelve springs of water and seventy palm trees, and they camped there near the water.

CHAPTER 16

The Wilderness of Sin. [1] Having set out from Elim, the whole Israelite community came into the wilderness of Sin, which is between Elim and Sinai, on the fifteenth day of the second month after their departure from the land of Egypt. [2] Here in the wilderness the whole Israelite community grumbled against Moses and Aaron. [3] The Israelites said to them, "If only we had died at the LORD's hand in the land of Egypt, as we sat by our kettles of meat and ate our fill of bread! But you have led us into this wilderness to make this whole assembly die of famine!"

The Quail and the Manna. [4] Then the LORD said to Moses: I am going to rain down bread from heaven for you. Each day the people are to go out and gather their daily portion; thus will I test them, to see whether they follow my instructions or not. [5] On the sixth day, however, when they prepare what they bring in, let it be twice as much as they gather on the other days. [6] So Moses and Aaron told all the Israelites, "At evening you will know that it was the LORD who brought you out of the land of Egypt; [7] and in the morning you will see the glory of the LORD, when he hears your grumbling against him. But who are we that you should grumble against us?" [8] And Moses said, "When the LORD gives you meat to eat in the evening and in the morning your fill of bread, and hears the grumbling you utter against him, who then are we? Your grumbling is not against us, but against the LORD."

[9] Then Moses said to Aaron, "Tell the whole Israelite community: Approach the LORD, for he has heard your grumbling." [10] But while Aaron was speaking to the whole Israelite community, they turned in the direction of the wilderness, and there the glory of the LORD appeared in the cloud! [11] The LORD said to Moses: [12] I have heard the grumbling of the Israelites. Tell them: In the evening twilight you will eat meat, and in the morning you will have your fill of bread, and then you will know that I, the LORD, am your God.

[13] In the evening, quail came up and covered the camp. In the morning there was a layer of dew all about the camp, [14] and when the layer of dew evaporated, fine flakes were on the surface of the wilderness, fine flakes like hoarfrost on the ground. [15] On seeing it, the Israelites asked one another, "What is this?" for they did not know

what it was. But Moses told them, "It is the bread which the Lᴏʀᴅ has given you to eat."

Regulations Regarding the Manna.
[16] "Now, this is what the Lᴏʀᴅ has commanded. Gather as much of it as each needs to eat, an omer for each person for as many of you as there are, each of you providing for those in your own tent." [17] The Israelites did so. Some gathered a large and some a small amount. [18] But when they measured it out by the omer, the one who had gathered a large amount did not have too much, and the one who had gathered a small amount did not have too little. They gathered as much as each needed to eat. [19] Moses said to them, "Let no one leave any of it over until morning." [20] But they did not listen to Moses, and some kept a part of it over until morning, and it became wormy and stank. Therefore Moses was angry with them.

[21] Morning after morning they gathered it, as much as each needed to eat; but when the sun grew hot, it melted away. [22] On the sixth day they gathered twice as much food, two omers for each person. When all the leaders of the community came and reported this to Moses, [23] he told them, "That is what the Lᴏʀᴅ has prescribed. Tomorrow is a day of rest, a holy sabbath of the Lᴏʀᴅ. Whatever you want to bake, bake; whatever you want to boil, boil; but whatever is left put away and keep until the morning." [24] When they put it away until the morning, as Moses commanded, it did not stink nor were there worms in it. [25] Moses then said, "Eat it today, for today is the sabbath of the Lᴏʀᴅ. Today you will not find any in the field. [26] Six days you will gather it, but on the seventh day, the sabbath, it will not be there." [27] Still, on the seventh day some of the people went out to gather it, but they did not find any. [28] Then the Lᴏʀᴅ said to Moses: How long will you refuse to keep my commandments and my instructions? [29] Take note! The Lᴏʀᴅ has given you the sabbath. That is why on the sixth day he gives you food for two days. Each of you stay where you are and let no one go out on the seventh day. [30] After that the people rested on the seventh day.

[31] The house of Israel named this food manna. It was like coriander seed, white, and it tasted like wafers made with honey.

[32] Moses said, "This is what the Lᴏʀᴅ has commanded. Keep a full omer of it for your future generations, so that they may see the food I gave you to eat in the wilderness when I brought you out of the land of Egypt." [33] Moses then told Aaron, "Take a jar and put a full omer of manna in it. Then place it before the Lᴏʀᴅ to keep it for your future generations." [34] As the Lᴏʀᴅ had commanded Moses, Aaron placed it in front of the covenant to keep it.

[35] The Israelites ate the manna for forty years, until they came to settled land; they ate the manna until they came to the borders of Canaan. [36] (An omer is one tenth of an ephah.)

CHAPTER 17

Water from the Rock. [1] From the wilderness of Sin the whole Israelite community journeyed by stages, as the Lᴏʀᴅ directed, and encamped at Rephidim.

But there was no water for the people to drink, [2] and so they quarreled with Moses and said, "Give us water to drink." Moses replied to them, "Why do you quarrel with me? Why do you put the Lᴏʀᴅ to a test?" [3] Here, then, in their thirst for water, the people grumbled against Moses, saying, "Why then did you bring us up out of Egypt? To have us die of thirst with our children and our livestock?" [4] So Moses cried out to the Lᴏʀᴅ, "What shall I do with this people? A little more and they will stone me!" [5] The Lᴏʀᴅ answered Moses: Go on ahead of the people, and take along with you some of the elders of Israel, holding in your hand, as you go, the staff with which you struck the Nile. [6] I will be standing there in front of you on the rock in Horeb. Strike the rock, and the water will flow from it for the people to drink. Moses did this, in the sight of the elders of Israel. [7] The place was named Massah and Meribah, because the

Israelites quarreled there and tested the Lord, saying, "Is the Lord in our midst or not?"

Battle with Amalek. [8] Then Amalek came and waged war against Israel in Rephidim. [9] So Moses said to Joshua, "Choose some men for us, and tomorrow go out and engage Amalek in battle. I will be standing on top of the hill with the staff of God in my hand." [10] Joshua did as Moses told him: he engaged Amalek in battle while Moses, Aaron, and Hur climbed to the top of the hill. [11] As long as Moses kept his hands raised up, Israel had the better of the fight, but when he let his hands rest, Amalek had the better of the fight. [12] Moses' hands, however, grew tired; so they took a rock and put it under him and he sat on it. Meanwhile Aaron and Hur supported his hands, one on one side and one on the other, so that his hands remained steady until sunset. [13] And Joshua defeated Amalek and his people with the sword.

[14] Then the Lord said to Moses: Write this down in a book as something to be remembered, and recite it to Joshua: I will completely blot out the memory of Amalek from under the heavens. [15] Moses built an altar there, which he named Yahweh-nissi; [16] for he said, "Take up the banner of the Lord! The Lord has a war against Amalek through the ages."

CHAPTER 18

Meeting with Jethro. [1] Now Moses' father-in-law Jethro, the priest of Midian, heard of all that God had done for Moses and for his people Israel: how the Lord had brought Israel out of Egypt. [2] So his father-in-law Jethro took along Zipporah, Moses' wife—now this was after Moses had sent her back— [3] and her two sons. One of these was named Gershom; for he said, "I am a resident alien in a foreign land." [4] The other was named Eliezer; for he said, "The God of my father is my help; he has rescued me from Pharaoh's sword." [5] Together with Moses' wife and sons, then, his father-in-law Jethro came to him in the wilderness where he was encamped at the mountain of God, [6] and he sent word to Moses, "I, your father-in-law Jethro, am coming to you, along with your wife and her two sons."

[7] Moses went out to meet his father-in-law, bowed down, and then kissed him. Having greeted each other, they went into the tent. [8] Moses then told his father-in-law of all that the Lord had done to Pharaoh and the Egyptians for the sake of Israel, and of all the hardships that had beset them on their journey, and how the Lord had rescued them. [9] Jethro rejoiced over all the goodness that the Lord had shown Israel in rescuing them from the power of the Egyptians. [10] "Blessed be the Lord," he said, "who has rescued you from the power of the Egyptians and of Pharaoh. [11] Now I know that the Lord is greater than all the gods; for he rescued the people from the power of the Egyptians when they treated them arrogantly." [12] Then Jethro, the father-in-law of Moses, brought a burnt offering and sacrifices for God, and Aaron came with all the elders of Israel to share with Moses' father-in-law in the meal before God.

Appointment of Minor Judges. [13] The next day Moses sat in judgment for the people, while they stood around him from morning until evening. [14] When Moses' father-in-law saw all that he was doing for the people, he asked, "What is this business that you are conducting for the people? Why do you sit alone while all the people have to stand about you from morning till evening?" [15] Moses answered his father-in-law, "The people come to me to consult God. [16] Whenever they have a disagreement, they come to me to have me settle the matter between them and make known to them God's statutes and instructions."

[17] "What you are doing is not wise," Moses' father-in-law replied. [18] "You will surely wear yourself out, both you and these people with you. The task is too heavy for you; you cannot do it alone. [19] Now, listen to me, and I will give you some advice, and may God be with you. Act as the people's representative before God, and bring their disputes to God. [20] Enlighten them in

regard to the statutes and instructions, showing them how they are to conduct themselves and what they are to do. ²¹ But you should also look among all the people for able and God-fearing men, trustworthy men who hate dishonest gain, and set them over the people as commanders of thousands, of hundreds, of fifties, and of tens. ²² Let these render decisions for the people in all routine cases. Every important case they should refer to you, but every lesser case they can settle themselves. Lighten your burden by letting them bear it with you! ²³ If you do this, and God so commands you, you will be able to stand the strain, and all these people, too, will go home content."

²⁴ Moses listened to his father-in-law and did all that he had said. ²⁵ He picked out able men from all Israel and put them in charge of the people as commanders of thousands, of hundreds, of fifties, and of tens. ²⁶ They rendered decisions for the people in all routine cases. The more difficult cases they referred to Moses, but all the lesser cases they settled themselves. ²⁷ Then Moses said farewell to his father-in-law, who went off to his own country.

VI. COVENANT AND LEGISLATION AT MOUNT SINAI

CHAPTER 19

Arrival at Sinai. ¹ In the third month after the Israelites' departure from the land of Egypt, on the first day, they came to the wilderness of Sinai. ² After they made the journey from Rephidim and entered the wilderness of Sinai, they then pitched camp in the wilderness.

While Israel was encamped there in front of the mountain, ³ Moses went up to the mountain of God. Then the Lord called to him from the mountain, saying: This is what you will say to the house of Jacob; tell the Israelites: ⁴ You have seen how I treated the Egyptians and how I bore

you up on eagles' wings and brought you to myself. ⁵ Now, if you obey me completely and keep my covenant, you will be my treasured possession among all peoples, though all the earth is mine. ⁶ You will be to me a kingdom of priests, a holy nation. That is what you must tell the Israelites. ⁷ So Moses went and summoned the elders of the people. When he set before them all that the Lord had ordered him to tell them, ⁸ all the people answered together, "Everything the Lord has said, we will do." Then Moses brought back to the Lord the response of the people.

⁹ The Lord said to Moses: I am coming to you now in a dense cloud, so that when the people hear me speaking with you, they will also remain faithful to you.

When Moses, then, had reported the response of the people to the Lord, ¹⁰ the Lord said to Moses: Go to the people and have them sanctify themselves today and tomorrow. Have them wash their garments ¹¹ and be ready for the third day; for on the third day the Lord will come down on Mount Sinai in the sight of all the people. ¹² Set limits for the people all around, saying: Take care not to go up the mountain, or even to touch its edge. All who touch the mountain must be put to death. ¹³ No hand shall touch them, but they must be stoned to death or killed with arrows. Whether human being or beast, they must not be allowed to live. Only when the ram's horn sounds may they go up on the mountain. ¹⁴ Then Moses came down from the mountain to the people and had them sanctify themselves, and they washed their garments. ¹⁵ He said to the people, "Be ready for the third day. Do not approach a woman."

The Great Theophany. ¹⁶ On the morning of the third day there were peals of thunder and lightning, and a heavy cloud over the mountain, and a very loud blast of the shofar, so that all the people in the camp trembled. ¹⁷ But Moses led the people out of the camp to meet God, and they stationed themselves at the foot of the mountain. ¹⁸ Now Mount Sinai was completely enveloped in smoke, because the Lord had come down upon it in fire. The smoke rose from it as though from a kiln, and the whole mountain trembled violently. ¹⁹ The blast of the shofar grew louder and louder, while Moses was speaking and God was answering him with thunder.

²⁰ When the Lord came down upon Mount Sinai, to the top of the mountain, the Lord summoned Moses to the top of the mountain, and Moses went up. ²¹ Then the Lord told Moses: Go down and warn the people not to break through to the Lord in order to see him; otherwise many of them will be struck down. ²² For their part, the priests, who approach the Lord must sanctify themselves; else the Lord will break out in anger against them. ²³ But Moses said to the Lord, "The people cannot go up to Mount Sinai, for you yourself warned us, saying: Set limits around the mountain to make it sacred." ²⁴ So the Lord said to him: Go down and come up along with Aaron. But do not let the priests and the people break through to come up to the Lord; else he will break out against them." ²⁵ So Moses went down to the people and spoke to them.

CHAPTER 20

The Ten Commandments. ¹ Then God spoke all these words:

² I am the Lord your God, who brought you out of the land of Egypt, out of the house of slavery. ³ You shall not have other gods beside me. ⁴ You shall not make for yourself an idol or a likeness of anything in the heavens above or on the earth below or in the waters beneath the earth; ⁵ you shall not bow down before them or serve them. For I, the Lord, your God, am a jealous God, inflicting punishment for their ancestors' wickedness on the children of those who hate me, down to the third and fourth generation; ⁶ but showing love down to the thousandth generation of those who love me and keep my commandments.

⁷ You shall not invoke the name of the Lord, your God, in vain. For the Lord will not leave unpunished anyone who invokes his name in vain.

⁸ Remember the sabbath day—keep it holy. ⁹ Six days you may labor and do all your work,

¹⁰ but the seventh day is a sabbath of the Lord your God. You shall not do any work, either you, your son or your daughter, your male or female slave, your work animal, or the resident alien within your gates. ¹¹ For in six days the Lord made the heavens and the earth, the sea and all that is in them; but on the seventh day he rested. That is why the Lord has blessed the sabbath day and made it holy.

¹² Honor your father and your mother, that you may have a long life in the land the Lord your God is giving you.

¹³ You shall not kill.

¹⁴ You shall not commit adultery.

¹⁵ You shall not steal.

¹⁶ You shall not bear false witness against your neighbor.

¹⁷ You shall not covet your neighbor's house. You shall not covet your neighbor's wife, his male or female slave, his ox or donkey, or anything that belongs to your neighbor.

Moses Accepted as Mediator. ¹⁸ Now as all the people witnessed the thunder and lightning, the blast of the shofar and the mountain smoking, they became afraid and trembled. So they took up a position farther away ¹⁹ and said to Moses, "You speak to us, and we will listen; but do not let God speak to us, or we shall die." ²⁰ Moses answered the people, "Do not be afraid, for God has come only to test you and put the fear of him upon you so you do not sin." ²¹ So the people remained at a distance, while Moses approached the dark cloud where God was.

The Covenant Code. ²² The Lord said to Moses: This is what you will say to the Israelites: You have seen for yourselves that I have spoken to you from heaven. ²³ You shall not make alongside of me gods of silver, nor shall you make for yourselves gods of gold. ²⁴ An altar of earth make for me, and sacrifice upon it your burnt offerings and communion sacrifices, your sheep and your oxen. In every place where I cause my name to be invoked I will come to you and bless you. ²⁵ But if you make an altar of stone for me, do not build it of cut stone, for by putting a chisel to it you profane it. ²⁶ You shall not ascend to my altar by steps, lest your nakedness be exposed.

CHAPTER 21

Laws Regarding Slaves. ¹ These are the ordinances you shall lay before them. ² When you purchase a Hebrew slave, he is to serve you for six years, but in the seventh year he shall leave as a free person without any payment. ³ If he comes into service alone, he shall leave alone; if he comes with a wife, his wife shall leave with him. ⁴ But if his master gives him a wife and she bears him sons or daughters, the woman and her children belong to her master and the man shall leave alone. ⁵ If, however, the slave declares, 'I love my master and my wife and children; I will not leave as a free person,' ⁶ his master shall bring him to God and there, at the door or doorpost, he shall pierce his ear with an awl, thus keeping him as his slave forever.

⁷ When a man sells his daughter as a slave, she shall not go free as male slaves do. ⁸ But if she displeases her master, who had designated her for himself, he shall let her be redeemed. He has no right to sell her to a foreign people, since he has broken faith with her. ⁹ If he designates her for his son, he shall treat her according to the ordinance for daughters. ¹⁰ If he takes another wife, he shall not withhold her food, her clothing, or her conjugal rights. ¹¹ If he does not do these three things for her, she may leave without cost, without any payment.

Personal Injury. ¹² Whoever strikes someone a mortal blow must be put to death. ¹³ However, regarding the one who did not hunt another down, but God caused death to happen by his hand, I will set apart for you a place to which that one may flee. ¹⁴ But when someone kills a neighbor after maliciously scheming to do so, you must take him even from my altar and put him to death. ¹⁵ Whoever strikes father or mother shall be put to death.

¹⁶ A kidnaper, whether he sells the person or the person is found in his possession, shall be put to death.

¹⁷ Whoever curses father or mother shall be put to death.

¹⁸ When men quarrel and one strikes the other with a stone or with his fist, not mortally, but enough to put him in bed, ¹⁹ the one who struck the blow shall be acquitted, provided the other can get up and walk around with the help of his staff. Still, he must compensate him for his recovery time and make provision for his complete healing.

²⁰ When someone strikes his male or female slave with a rod so that the slave dies under his hand, the act shall certainly be avenged. ²¹ If, however, the slave survives for a day or two, he is not to be punished, since the slave is his own property.

²² When men have a fight and hurt a pregnant woman, so that she suffers a miscarriage, but no further injury, the guilty one shall be fined as much as the woman's husband demands of him, and he shall pay in the presence of the judges. ²³ But if injury ensues, you shall give life for life, ²⁴ eye for eye, tooth for tooth, hand for hand, foot for foot, ²⁵ burn for burn, wound for wound, stripe for stripe.

²⁶ When someone strikes his male or female slave in the eye and destroys the use of the eye, he shall let the slave go free in compensation for the eye. ²⁷ If he knocks out a tooth of his male or female slave, he shall let the slave go free in compensation for the tooth.

²⁸ When an ox gores a man or a woman to death, the ox must be stoned; its meat may not be eaten. The owner of the ox, however, shall be free of blame. ²⁹ But if an ox was previously in the habit of goring people and its owner, though warned, would not watch it; should it then kill a man or a woman, not only must the ox be stoned, but its owner also must be put to death. ³⁰ If, however, a fine is imposed on him, he must pay in ransom for his life whatever amount is imposed on him. ³¹ This ordinance applies if it is a boy or a girl that the ox gores. ³² But if it is a male or a female slave that it gores, he must pay the owner of the slave thirty shekels of silver, and the ox must be stoned.

Property Damage. ³³ When someone uncovers or digs a cistern and does not cover it over again, should an ox or a donkey fall into it, 34 the owner of the cistern must make good by restoring the value of the animal to its owner, but the dead animal he may keep.

35 When one man's ox hurts another's ox and it dies, they shall sell the live ox and divide this money as well as the dead animal equally between them. 36 But if it was known that the ox was previously in the habit of goring and its owner would not watch it, he must make full restitution, an ox for an ox; but the dead animal he may keep.

37 When someone steals an ox or a sheep and slaughters or sells it, he shall restore five oxen for the one ox, and four sheep for the one sheep.

CHAPTER 22

1 [If a thief is caught in the act of house-breaking and beaten to death, there is no bloodguilt involved. 2 But if after sunrise he is thus beaten, there is bloodguilt.] He must make full restitution. If he has nothing, he shall be sold to pay for his theft. 3 If what he stole is found alive in his possession, be it an ox, a donkey or a sheep, he shall make twofold restitution.

4 When someone causes a field or a vineyard to be grazed over, by sending his cattle to graze in another's field, he must make restitution with the best produce of his own field or vineyard. 5 If a fire breaks out, catches on to thorn bushes, and consumes shocked grain, standing grain, or the field itself, the one who started the fire must make full restitution.

Trusts and Loans. 6 When someone gives money or articles to another for safekeeping and they are stolen from the latter's house, the thief, if caught, must make twofold restitution. 7 If the thief is not caught, the owner of the house shall be brought to God, to swear that he himself did not lay hands on his neighbor's property. 8 In every case of dishonest appropriation, whether it be about an ox, or a donkey, or a sheep, or a garment, or anything else that has disappeared, where another claims that the thing is his, the claim of both parties shall be brought before God; the one whom God convicts must make twofold restitution to the other.

9 When someone gives an ass, or an ox, or a sheep, or any other animal to another for safekeeping, if it dies, or is maimed or snatched away, without anyone witnessing the fact, 10 there shall be an oath before the LORD between the two of them that the guardian did not lay hands on his neighbor's property; the owner must accept the oath, and no restitution is to be made. 11 But if the guardian has actually stolen from it, then he must make restitution to the owner. 12 If it has been killed by a wild beast, let him bring it as evidence; he need not make restitution for the mangled animal.

13 When someone borrows an animal from a neighbor, if it is maimed or dies while the owner is not present, that one must make restitution. 14 But if the owner is present, that one need not make restitution. If it was hired, this was covered by the price of its hire.

Social Laws. 15 When a man seduces a virgin who is not betrothed, and lies with her, he shall make her his wife by paying the bride price. 16 If her father refuses to give her to him, he must still pay him the bride price for virgins.

17 You shall not let a woman who practices sorcery live.

18 Anyone who lies with an animal shall be put to death.

19 Whoever sacrifices to any god, except to the LORD alone, shall be put under the ban.

20 You shall not oppress or afflict a resident alien, for you were once aliens residing in the land of Egypt. 22 You shall not wrong any widow or orphan. 22 If ever you wrong them and they cry out to me, I will surely listen to their cry. 23 My wrath will flare up, and I will kill you with the sword; then your own wives will be widows, and your children orphans.

24 If you lend money to my people, the poor among you, you must not be like a money lender; you must not demand interest from them. 25 If you take your neighbor's cloak as a pledge, you shall return it to him before sunset; 26 for this is his only covering; it is the cloak for his body.

What will he sleep in? If he cries out to me, I will listen; for I am compassionate.

²⁷ You shall not despise God, nor curse a leader of your people.

²⁸ You shall not delay the offering of your harvest and your press. You shall give me the firstborn of your sons. ²⁹ You must do the same with your oxen and your sheep; for seven days the firstling may stay with its mother, but on the eighth day you must give it to me.

³⁰ You shall be a people sacred to me. Flesh torn to pieces in the field you shall not eat; you must throw it to the dogs.

CHAPTER 23

¹ You shall not repeat a false report. Do not join your hand with the wicked to be a witness supporting violence. ² You shall not follow the crowd in doing wrong. When testifying in a lawsuit, you shall not follow the crowd in perverting justice. ³ You shall not favor the poor in a lawsuit.

⁴ When you come upon your enemy's ox or donkey going astray, you must see to it that it is returned. ⁵ When you notice the donkey of one who hates you lying down under its burden, you should not desert him; you must help him with it.

⁶ You shall not pervert justice for the needy among you in a lawsuit. ⁷ You shall keep away from anything dishonest. The innocent and the just you shall not put to death, for I will not acquit the guilty. ⁸ Never take a bribe, for a bribe blinds the clear-sighted and distorts the words of the just. ⁹ You shall not oppress a resident alien; you well know how it feels to be an alien, since you were once aliens yourselves in the land of Egypt.

Religious Laws. ¹⁰ For six years you may sow your land and gather in its produce. ¹¹ But the seventh year you shall let the land lie untitled and fallow, that the poor of your people may eat of it and their leftovers the wild animals may eat. So also shall you do in regard to your vineyard and your olive grove.

¹² For six days you may do your work, but on the seventh day you must rest, that your ox and your donkey may have rest, and that the son of your maidservant and the resident alien may be refreshed. ¹³ Give heed to all that I have told you.

You shall not mention the name of any other god; it shall not be heard from your lips. ¹⁴ Three times a year you shall celebrate a pilgrim feast to me. ¹⁵ You shall keep the feast of Unleavened Bread. As I have commanded you, you must eat unleavened bread for seven days at the appointed time in the month of Abib, for it was then that you came out of Egypt. No one shall appear before me empty-handed. ¹⁶ You shall also keep the feast of the grain harvest with the first fruits of the crop that you sow in the field; and finally, the feast of Ingathering at the end of the year, when you collect your produce from the fields. ¹⁷ Three times a year shall all your men appear before the Lord God.

¹⁸ You shall not offer the blood of my sacrifice with anything leavened; nor shall the fat of my feast be kept overnight till the next day. ¹⁹ The choicest first fruits of your soil you shall bring to the house of the Lord, your God.

You shall not boil a young goat in its mother's milk.

Reward of Fidelity. ²⁰ See, I am sending an angel before you, to guard you on the way and bring you to the place I have prepared. ²¹ Be attentive to him and obey him. Do not rebel against him, for he will not forgive your sin. My authority is within him. ²² If you obey him and carry out all I tell you, I will be an enemy to your enemies and a foe to your foes.

²³ My angel will go before you and bring you to the Amorites, Hittites, Perizzites, Canaanites, Hivites and Jebusites; and I will wipe them out. ²⁴ Therefore, you shall not bow down to their gods and serve them, nor shall you act as they do; rather, you must demolish them and smash their sacred stones. ²⁵ You shall serve the Lord, your God; then he will bless your food and drink, and I will remove sickness from your midst; ²⁶ no woman in your land will be barren or miscarry; and I will give you a full span of life.

²⁷ I will have the terror of me precede you, so that I will throw into panic every nation you reach. I will make all your enemies turn from you in flight, ²⁸ and ahead of you I will send hornets to drive the Hivites, Canaanites and Hittites out of your way. ²⁹ But I will not drive them all out before you in one year, lest the land become desolate and the wild animals multiply against you. ³⁰ Little by little I will drive them out before you, until you have grown numerous enough to take possession of the land. ³¹ I will set your boundaries from the Red Sea to the sea of the Philistines, and from the wilderness to the Euphrates; all who dwell in this land I will hand over to you and you shall drive them out before you. ³² You shall not make a covenant with them or their gods. ³³ They must not live in your land. For if you serve their gods, this will become a snare to you.

CHAPTER 24

Ratification of the Covenant. ¹ Moses himself was told: Come up to the LORD, you and Aaron, with Nadab, Abihu, and seventy of the elders of Israel. You shall bow down at a distance. ² Moses alone is to come close to the LORD; the others shall not come close, and the people shall not come up with them.

³ When Moses came to the people and related all the words and ordinances of the LORD, they all answered with one voice, "We will do everything that the LORD has told us." ⁴ Moses then wrote down all the words of the LORD and, rising early in the morning, he built at the foot of the mountain an altar and twelve sacred stones for the twelve tribes of Israel. ⁵ Then, having sent young men of the Israelites to offer burnt offerings and sacrifice young bulls as communion offerings to the LORD, ⁶ Moses took half of the blood and put it in large bowls; the other half he splashed on the altar. ⁷ Taking the book of the covenant, he read it aloud to the people, who answered, "All that the LORD has said, we will hear and do." ⁸ Then he took the blood and splashed it on the people, saying, "This is the blood of the covenant which the LORD has made with you according to all these words."

⁹ Moses then went up with Aaron, Nadab, Abihu, and seventy elders of Israel, ¹⁰ and they beheld the God of Israel. Under his feet there appeared to be sapphire tilework, as clear as the sky itself. ¹¹ Yet he did not lay a hand on these chosen Israelites. They saw God, and they ate and drank.

Moses on the Mountain. ¹² The LORD said to Moses: Come up to me on the mountain and, while you are there, I will give you the stone tablets on which I have written the commandments intended for their instruction. ¹³ So Moses set out with Joshua, his assistant, and went up to the mountain of God. ¹⁴ He told the elders, "Wait here for us until we return to you. Aaron and Hur are with you. Anyone with a complaint should approach them." ¹⁵ Moses went up the mountain. Then the cloud covered the mountain. ¹⁶ The glory of the LORD settled upon Mount Sinai. The cloud covered it for six days, and on the seventh day he called to Moses from the midst of the cloud. ¹⁷ To the Israelites the glory of the LORD was seen as a consuming fire on the top of the mountain. ¹⁸ But Moses entered into the midst of the cloud and went up on the mountain. He was on the mountain for forty days and forty nights.

The Book of Ruth

The Book of Ruth is named for the Moabite woman who commits herself to the Israelite people by an oath to her mother-in-law Naomi and becomes the great-grandmother of David by marriage to Boaz of Bethlehem. Thus she is an ancestor in the messianic line that leads to Jesus (Mt 1:5).

The book portrays the love and loyalty of human beings in working their way through tragic circumstances to participation in the community of the faithful people of God. The key is responsible and loving decision-making: Ruth's loyalty (2:11), her generosity (1:15–17; 2:2, 7) and her willingness to take risks for the sake of righteousness set in motion a chain of beneficial events, while behind the scenes God blesses each step in the developing drama. Ruth is so frequently designated "the Moabite" in the book that the audience of the story is constantly reminded of the universality of the embrace of salvation.

In the Greek and Latin canons, Ruth follows Judges, to which it is related by its opening time reference ("Once back in the time of the judges . . ."), and precedes Samuel, serving as transition from Israel as tribal union to monarchy. In the present sequence of the Hebrew canon it is placed among the "Writings" immediately after the Book of Proverbs, which ends with a powerful portrayal of "the woman of worth" (Pry 31:10–31; cf. Ru 3:11). Ruth is the primary liturgical text in Judaism for the celebration of the feast of Weeks (Shabuot).

The beauty of the story's construction, its use of dialogue (nearly two-thirds of the text), and the sheer drama of its content mark it as one of the classic short stories of world literature. Based on the recollection of an historical figure, a story is developed which grips its audience with profound insight into divine and human relationships. The story is presented from a point some time after the course of events, as is indicated by the explanation of an obscure custom in 4:7. Wherever and whenever it was told, its claim of God's universal concern for humankind and the attractiveness of caring human responsibility shines forth.

The date of composition is disputed. Many authors date it early in the monarchy, and valid arguments can be presented for that position. Others argue for a postexilic date; they see the favorable presentation of a Moabite woman who became David's grandmother as a counter to the stringent measures of Ezra and Nehemiah against marriage with Moabites and other non-Jews (Ezr 9—10; Neh 13:23–29).

CHAPTER 1

Naomi in Moab. [1] Once back in the time of the judges there was a famine in the land; so a man from Bethlehem of Judah left home with his wife and two sons to reside on the plateau of Moab. [2] The man was named Elimelech, his wife Naomi, and his sons Mahlon and Chilion; they were Ephrathites from Bethlehem of Judah. Some time after their arrival on the plateau of Moab, [3] Elimelech, the husband of Naomi, died, and she was left with her two sons. [4] They married Moabite women, one named Orpah, the other Ruth. When they had lived there about ten years, [5] both Mahlon and Chilion died also, and the woman was left with neither her two boys nor her husband.

[6] She and her daughters-in-law then prepared to go back from the plateau of Moab because word had reached her there that the LORD had seen to his people's needs and given them food. [7] She and her two daughters-in-law left the place where they had been living. On the road back to the land of Judah, [8] Naomi said to her daughters-in-law, "Go back, each of you to your mother's house. May the LORD show you the same kindness as you have shown to the deceased and to

me. [9] May the LORD guide each of you to find a husband and a home in which you will be at rest." She kissed them good-bye, but they wept aloud, [10] crying, "No! We will go back with you, to your people." [11] Naomi replied, "Go back, my daughters. Why come with me? Have I other sons in my womb who could become your husbands? [12] Go, my daughters, for I am too old to marry again. Even if I had any such hope, or if tonight I had a husband and were to bear sons, [13] would you wait for them and deprive yourselves of husbands until those sons grew up? No, my daughters, my lot is too bitter for you, because the LORD has extended his hand against me." [14] Again they wept aloud; then Orpah kissed her mother-in-law good-bye, but Ruth clung to her.

[15] "See now," she said, "your sister-in-law has gone back to her people and her god. Go back after your sister-in-law!" [16] But Ruth said, "Do not press me to go back and abandon you!

> Wherever you go I will go, wherever you lodge
>   I will lodge.
> Your people shall be my people and your God,
>   my God.

[17] Where you die I will die, and there be buried.

May the LORD do thus to me, and more, if even death separates me from you!" [18] Naomi then ceased to urge her, for she saw she was determined to go with her.

The Return to Bethlehem. [19] So they went on together until they reached Bethlehem. On their arrival there, the whole town was excited about them, and the women asked: "Can this be Naomi?" [20] But she said to them, "Do not call me Naomi ['Sweet']. Call me Mara ['Bitter'], for the Almighty has made my life very bitter. [21] I went away full, but the LORD has brought me back empty. Why should you call me 'Sweet,' since the LORD has brought me to trial, and the Almighty has pronounced evil sentence on me." [22] Thus it was that Naomi came back with her Moabite daughter-in-law Ruth, who accompanied her back from the plateau of Moab. They arrived in Bethlehem at the beginning of the barley harvest.

CHAPTER 2

The Meeting. [1] Naomi had a powerful relative named Boaz," through the clan of her husband Elimelech. [2] Ruth the Moabite said to Naomi, "I would like to go and glean grain in the field of anyone who will allow me." Naomi said to her, "Go ahead, my daughter." [3] So she went. The field she entered to glean after the harvesters happened to be the section belonging to Boaz, of the clan of Elimelech. [4] Soon, along came Boaz from Bethlehem and said to the harvesters, "The LORD be with you," and they replied, "The LORD bless you." [5] Boaz asked the young man overseeing his harvesters, "Whose young woman is this?" [6] The young man overseeing the harvesters answered, "She is the young Moabite who came back with Naomi from the plateau of Moab. [7] She said, 'I would like to gather the gleanings into sheaves after the harvesters.' Ever since she came this morning she has remained here until now, with scarcely a moment's rest."

[8] Boaz then spoke to Ruth, "Listen, my daughter. Do not go to glean in anyone else's field; you are not to leave here. Stay here with my young women. [9] Watch to see which field is to be harvested, and follow them. Have I not commanded the young men to do you no harm? When you are thirsty, go and drink from the vessels the young people have filled." [10] Casting herself prostrate upon the ground, she said to him, "Why should I, a foreigner, be favored with your attention?" [11] Boaz answered her: "I have had a complete account of what you have done for your mother-in-law after your husband's death; you have left your father and your mother and the land of your birth, and have come to a people whom previously you did not know. [12] May the LORD reward what you have done! May you receive a full reward from the LORD, the God of Israel, under whose wings you have come for refuge." [13] She said, "May I prove worthy of your favor, my lord. You have comforted me. You have spoken to the heart of your servant—and I am not even one of your servants!" [14] At mealtime Boaz said to her,

"Come here and have something to eat; dip your bread in the sauce." Then as she sat near the harvesters, he handed her some roasted grain and she ate her fill and had some left over. [15] As she rose to glean, Boaz instructed his young people: "Let her glean among the sheaves themselves without scolding her, [16] and even drop some handfuls and leave them for her to glean; do not rebuke her."

[17] She gleaned in the field until evening, and when she beat out what she had gleaned it came to about an ephah of barley, [18] which she took into the town and showed to her mother-in-law. Next she brought out what she had left over from the meal and gave it to her. [19] So her mother-in-law said to her, "Where did you glean today? Where did you go to work? May the one who took notice of you be blessed!" Then she told her mother-in-law with whom she had worked. "The man at whose place I worked today is named Boaz," she said. [20] "May he be blessed by the Lord, who never fails to show kindness to the living and to the dead," Naomi exclaimed to her daughter-in-law. She continued, "This man is a near relative of ours, one of our redeemers." [21] "He even told me," added Ruth the Moabite, "Stay with my young people until they complete my entire harvest." [22] "You would do well, my daughter," Naomi rejoined, "to work with his young women; in someone else's field you might be insulted." [23] So she stayed gleaning with Boaz's young women until the end of the barley and wheat harvests.

CHAPTER 3

Ruth Again Presents Herself. When Ruth was back with her mother-in-law, [1] Naomi said to her, "My daughter, should I not be seeking a pleasing home for you? [2] Now! Is not Boaz, whose young women you were working with, a relative of ours? This very night he will be winnowing barley at the threshing floor. [3] Now, go bathe and anoint yourself; then put on your best attire and go down to the threshing floor. Do not make yourself known to the man before he has finished eating and drinking. [4] But when he lies down, take note of the place where he lies; then go uncover a place at his feet and you lie down. He will then tell you what to do." [5] "I will do whatever you say," Ruth replied. [6] She went down to the threshing floor and did just as her mother-in-law had instructed her.

[7] Boaz ate and drank to his heart's content, and went to lie down at the edge of the pile of grain. She crept up, uncovered a place at his feet, and lay down. [8] Midway through the night, the man gave a start and groped about, only to find a woman lying at his feet. [9] "Who are you?" he asked. She replied, "I am your servant Ruth. Spread the wing of your cloak over your servant, for you are a redeemer." [10] He said, "May the Lord bless you, my daughter! You have been even more loyal now than before in not going after the young men, whether poor or rich. [11] Now rest assured, my daughter, I will do for you whatever you say; all my townspeople know you to be a worthy woman. [12] Now, I am in fact a redeemer, but there is another redeemer closer than I. [13] Stay where you are for tonight, and tomorrow, if he will act as redeemer for you, good. But if he will not, as the Lord lives, I will do it myself. Lie there until morning." [14] So she lay at his feet until morning, but rose before anyone could recognize another, for Boaz had said, "Let it not be known that this woman came to the threshing floor." [15] Then he said to her, "Take off the shawl you are wearing; hold it firmly." When she did so, he poured out six measures of barley and helped her lift the bundle; then he himself left for the town.

[16] She, meanwhile, went home to her mother-in-law, who asked, "How did things go, my daughter?" So she told her all the man had done for her, [17] and concluded, "He gave me these six measures of barley and said, 'Do not go back to your mother-in-law empty.'" [18] Naomi then said, "Wait here, my daughter, until you learn what happens, for the man will not rest, but will settle the matter today."

CHAPTER 4

Boaz Marries Ruth. ¹ Boaz went to the gate and took a seat there. Along came the other redeemer of whom he had spoken. Boaz called to him by name, "Come, sit here." And he did so. ² Then Boaz picked out ten of the elders of the town and asked them to sit nearby. When they had done this, ³ he said to the other redeemer: "Naomi, who has come back from the plateau of Moab, is putting up for sale the piece of land that belonged to our kinsman Elimelech. ⁴ So I thought I would inform you. Before those here present, including the elders of my people, purchase the field; act as redeemer. But if you do not want to do it, tell me so, that I may know, for no one has a right of redemption prior to yours, and mine is next." He answered, "I will act as redeemer."

⁵ Boaz continued, "When you acquire the field from Naomi, you also acquire responsibility for Ruth the Moabite, the widow of the late heir, to raise up a family for the deceased on his estate." ⁶ The redeemer replied, "I cannot exercise my right of redemption for that would endanger my own estate. You do it in my place, for I cannot." ⁷ Now it used to be the custom in Israel that, to make binding a contract of redemption or exchange, one party would take off a sandal and give it to the other. This was the form of attestation in Israel. ⁸ So the other redeemer, in saying to Boaz, "Acquire it for yourself," drew off his sandal. ⁹ Boaz then said to the elders and to all the people, "You are witnesses today that I have acquired from Naomi all the holdings of Elimelech, Chilion and Mahlon. ¹⁰ I also acquire Ruth the Moabite, the widow of Mahlon, as my wife, in order to raise up a family for her late husband on his estate, so that the name of the deceased may not perish from his people and his place. Do you witness this today?" ¹¹ All those at the gate, including the elders, said, "We do. May the LORD make this woman come into your house like Rachel and Leah, who between them built up the house of Israel. Prosper in Ephrathah! Bestow a name in Bethlehem! ¹² With the offspring the LORD will give you from this young woman, may your house become like the house of Perez, whom Tamar bore to Judah."

¹³ Boaz took Ruth. When they came together as husband and wife, the LORD enabled her to conceive and she bore a son. ¹⁴ Then the women said to Naomi, "Blessed is the LORD who has not failed to provide you today with a redeemer. May he become famous in Israel! ¹⁵ He will restore your life and be the support of your old age, for his mother is the daughter-in-law who loves you. She is worth more to you than seven sons!" ¹⁶ Naomi took the boy, cradled him against her breast, and cared for him. ¹⁷ The neighbor women joined the celebration: "A son has been born to Naomi!" They named him Obed. He was the father of Jesse, the father of David.

¹⁸ These are the descendants of Perez: Perez was the father of Hezron, ¹⁹ Hezron was the father of Ram, Ram was the father of Amminadab, ²⁰ Amminadab was the father of Nahshon, Nahshon was the father of Salma, ²¹ Salma was the father of Boaz, Boaz was the father of Obed, ²² Obed was the father of Jesse, and Jesse became the father of David.

ENDNOTES

The Story of Abraham

12:1—3 *Go forth . . . find blessing in you:* the syntax of the Hebrew suggests that the blessings promised to Abraham are contingent on his going to Canaan.

12:2 The call of Abraham begins a new history of blessing (18:18; 22:15–18), which is passed on in each instance to the chosen successor (26:2–4; 28:14). This call evokes the last story in the primeval history (11:1–9) by reversing its themes: Abraham goes forth rather than settle down; it is God rather than Abraham who will make a name for him; the families of the earth will find blessing in him.

12:3 *Will find blessing in you:* the Hebrew conjugation of the verb here and in 18:18 and 28:14 can be either reflexive ("shall bless themselves by you" = people will invoke Abraham as an example of someone blessed by God) or passive ("by you all the families of earth will be blessed" = the religious privileges of Abraham and his descendants ultimately will be extended to the nations). In 22:18 and 26:4, another conjugation of the same verb is used in a similar context that is undoubtedly reflexive ("bless themselves"). Many scholars suggest that the two passages in which the sense is clear should determine the interpretation of the three ambiguous passages: the privileged blessing enjoyed by Abraham and his descendants will awaken in all peoples the desire to enjoy those same blessings. Since the term is understood in a passive sense in the New Testament (Acts 3:25; Gal 3:8), it is rendered here by a neutral expression that admits of both meanings.

12:5 The ancestors appear in Genesis as pastoral nomads living at the edge of settled society, and having occasional dealings with the inhabitants, sometimes even moving into towns for brief periods. Unlike modern nomads such as the Bedouin, however, ancient pastoralists fluctuated between following the herds and sedentary life, depending on circumstances. Pastoralists could settle down and farm and later resume a pastoral way of life. Indeed, there was a symbiotic relationship between pastoralists and villagers, each providing goods to the other. *Persons:* servants and others who formed the larger household under the leadership of Abraham; cf. 14:14.

12:6 Abraham's journey to the center of the land, Shechem, then to Bethel, and then to the Negeb, is duplicated in Jacob's journeys (33:18; 35:1, 6, 27; 46:1) and in the general route of the conquest under Joshua (Jos 7:2; 8:9, 30). Abraham's journey is a symbolic "conquest" of the land he has been promised. In building altars here (vv. 7, 8) and elsewhere, Abraham acknowledges his God as Lord of the land.

12:9 *The Negeb:* the semidesert land south of Judah.

12:10—13:1 Abraham and Sarah's sojourn in Egypt and encounter with Pharaoh foreshadow their descendants' experience, suggesting a divine design in which they must learn to trust. The story of Sarah, the ancestor in danger, is told again in chap. 20, and also in 26:1–11 with Rebekah instead of Sarah. Repetition of similar events is not unusual in literature that has been orally shaped.

12:13 *You are my sister:* the text does not try to excuse Abraham's deception, though in 20:12 a similar deception is somewhat excused.

12:16 *Camels:* domesticated camels did not come into common use in the ancient Near East until the end of the second millennium B.C. Thus the mention of camels here (24:11–64; 30:43; 31:17, 34; 32:8, 16; 37:25) is seemingly an anachronism.

15:1—21 In the first section (vv. 1—6), Abraham is promised a son and heir, and in the second (vv. 7—21), he is promised a land. The structure is similar in both: each of the two promises is not immediately accepted; the first is met with a complaint (vv. 2—3) and the second with a request for a sign (v.8). God's answer differs in each section—a sign in v.5 and an oath in vv. 9—21. Some scholars believe that the Genesis promises of progeny and land were originally separate and only later combined, but progeny and land are persistent concerns especially of ancient peoples and it is hard to imagine one without the other.

15:6 Abraham's act of faith in God's promises was regarded as an act of righteousness, i.e., as fully expressive of his relationship with God. St. Paul (Rom 4:1—25; Gal 3:6—9) makes Abraham's faith a model for Christians.

15:9—17 Cutting up animals was a well-attested way of making a treaty in antiquity. Jer 34:17–20 shows the rite is a form of self-imprecation in which violators invoke the fate of the animals upon themselves. The eighth-century B.C. Sefire treaty from Syria reads, "As this calf is cut up, thus Matti'el shall be cut up." The smoking fire pot and the flaming torch (v. 17), which represent God, pass between the pieces, making God a signatory to the covenant.

15:13—16 The verses clarify the promise of the land by providing a timetable of its possession: after four hundred years of servitude, your descendants will actually possess the land in the fourth generation (a patriarchal generation seems to be one hundred years). The iniquity of the current inhabitants (called here the Amorites) has not yet reached the point where God must intervene in punishment. Another table is given in Ex 12:40, which is not compatible with this one.

15:16 *Generation:* the Hebrew term *dor* is commonly rendered as "generation," but it may signify a period of varying length. A "generation" is the period between the birth of children and the birth of their parents, normally about twenty to twenty-five years. The actual length of a generation can vary, however; in Jb 42:16 it is thirty-five and in Nm 32:13 it is forty. The meaning may be life spans, which in Gn 6:3 is one hundred twenty years and in Is 65:20 is one hundred years.

15:18—21 The *Wadi,* i.e., a gully or ravine, of *Egypt* is the Wadi-el-`Arish, which is the boundary between the settled land and the Sinai desert. Some scholars suggest that the boundaries are those of a Davidic empire at its greatest extent; others that they are idealized boundaries. Most lists of the ancient inhabitants of the promised land give three, six, or seven peoples, but vv. 19—21 give a grand total of ten.

16:1—16 In the previous chapter Abraham was given a timetable of possession of the land, but nothing was said about when the child was to be born. In this chapter, Sarah takes matters into her own hands, for she has been childless ten years since the promise (cf. 12:4 with 16:16). The story is about the two women, Sarah the infertile mistress and Hagar the fertile slave; Abraham has only a single sentence. In the course of the story, God intervenes directly on the side of Hagar, for she is otherwise without resources.

16:2 The custom of an infertile wife providing her husband with a concubine to produce children is widely attested in ancient Near Eastern law; e.g., an Old Assyrian marriage contract states that the wife must provide her husband with a concubine if she does not bear children within two years.

16:4 Because barrenness was at that time normally blamed on the woman and regarded as a disgrace, it is not surprising that Hagar looks down on Sarah. Ancient Near Eastern legal practice addresses such cases of insolent slaves and allows disciplining of them. Prv 30:23 uses as an example of intolerable behavior "a maidservant when she ousts her mistress."

16:7 *The Lord's angel:* a manifestation of God in human form; in v. 13 the messenger is identified with God. See note on Ex 3:2.

16:11 *Ishmael:* in Hebrew the name means "God has heard." It is the same Hebrew verb that is translated "heeded" in the next clause. In other ancient Near Eastern texts, the name commemorated the divine answer to the parents' prayer to have a child, but here it is broadened to mean that God has "heard" Hagar's plight. In vv. 13–14, the verb "to see" is similarly broadened to describe God's special care for those in need.

16:12 *Alongside:* lit., "against the face of"; the same phrase is used of the lands of Ishmael's descendants in 25:18. It can be translated "in opposition to" (Dt 21:16; Jb 1:11; 6:28; 21:31), but here more likely means that Ishmael's settlement was near but not in the promised land.

16:13 *God who sees me:* Hebrew *el-ro'i* is multivalent, meaning either "God of seeing," i.e., extends his protection to me, or "God sees," which can imply seeing human suffering (29:32; Ex 2:25; Is 57:18; 58:3). It is probable that Hagar means to express both of these aspects. *Remained alive:* for the ancient notion that a person died on seeing God, see Gn 32:31; Ex 20:19; Dt 4:33; Jgs 13:22.

16:14 *Beer-lahai-roi:* possible translations of the name of the well include: "spring of the living one who sees me"; "the well of the living sight"; or "the one who sees me lives." See note on v. 13.

17:1–27 The Priestly source gathers the major motifs of the story so far and sets them firmly within a covenant context; the word "covenant" occurs thirteen times. There are links to the covenant with Noah (v. 1 = 6:9; v. 7 = 9:9; v. 11 = 9:12–17). In this chapter, vv. 1–8 promise progeny and land; vv. 9–14 are instructions about circumcision; vv. 15–21 repeat the promise of a son to Sarah and distinguish this promise from that to Hagar; vv. 22–27 describe Abraham's carrying out the commands. *The Almighty:* traditional rendering of Hebrew *El Shaddai,* which is P's favorite designation of God in the period of the ancestors. Its etymology is uncertain, but its root meaning is probably "God, the One of the Mountains."

17:5 Abram and Abraham are merely two forms of the same name, both meaning, "the father is exalted"; another variant

form is Abiram (Nm 16:1; 1 Kgs 16:34). The additional *-ha-* in the form Abraham is explained by popular etymology as coming from *ab-hamon goyim,* "father of a multitude of nations."

17:10 *Circumcised:* circumcision was widely practiced in the ancient world, usually as an initiation rite for males at puberty. By shifting the time of circumcision to the eighth day after birth, biblical religion made it no longer a "rite of passage" but the sign of the eternal covenant between God and the community descending from Abraham.

17:15 Sarai and Sarah are variant forms of the same name, both meaning "princess."

17:17 *Laughed: yishaq,* which is also the Hebrew form of the name "Isaac"; similar explanations of the name are given in Gn 18:12 and 21:6.

18:1 Chapters 18 and 19 combined form a continuous narrative, concluding the story of Abraham and his nephew Lot that began in 13:2-18. The mysterious men visit Abraham in Mamre to promise him and Sarah a child the following year (18:1–15) and then visit Lot in Sodom to investigate and then to punish the corrupt city (19:1–29). Between the two visits, Abraham questions God about the justice of punishing Sodom (18:16–33). At the end of the destruction of Sodom, there is a short narrative about Lot as the ancestor of Moab and the Ammonites (19:30–38).

18:3 Abraham addresses the leader of the group, whom he does not yet recognize as the Lord; in the next two verses he speaks to all three men. The other two are later (Gn 19:1) identified as angels. The shifting numbers and identification of the visitors are a narrative way of expressing the mysterious presence of God.

18:6 *Three measures:* Hebrew *seah;* three seahs equal one ephah, about half a bushel.

18:8 *Curds:* a type of soft cheese or yogurt.

18:10 *One of them:* i.e., the Lord.

18:12 *Sarah laughed:* a play on the verb "laugh," which prefigures the name of Isaac; see note on 17:17.

18:20 The immorality of the cities was already hinted at in 13:13, when Lot made his choice to live there. The "outcry" comes from the victims of the injustice and violence rampant in the city, which will shortly be illustrated in the treatment of the visitors. The outcry of the Hebrews under the harsh treatment of Pharaoh (Ex 3:7) came up to God who reacts in anger at mistreatment of the poor (cf. Ex 22:21–23; Is 5:7). Sodom and Gomorrah became types of sinful cities in biblical literature. Is 1:9–10; 3:9 sees their sin as lack of social justice, Ez 16:46–51, as disregard for the poor, and Jer 23:14, as general immorality. In the Genesis story, the sin is violation of the sacred duty of hospitality by the threatened rape of Lot's guests.

19:1–29 The story takes place in one day (counting a day from the previous evening): evening (v. 1), dawn (v. 15), and sunrise (v. 23). The passage resembles Jgs 19:15–25, which suggests dependence of one story on the other.

19:2 *My lords:* Lot does not yet know that the men are God's messengers; cf. 18:3.

19:8 *Let me bring them out to you:* the authority of a patriarch within his house was virtually absolute. Lot's extreme response of offering his daughters to a violent mob seems to be motivated by the obligation of hospitality.

19:11 *Blinding light:* an extraordinary flash that temporarily dazed the wicked men and revealed to Lot the true nature of his guests.

19:14 It is uncertain whether Lot's sons-in-law were fully married to his daughters or only "engaged" to them (Israelite "engagement" was the first part of the marriage ceremony), or even whether the daughters involved were the same as, or different from, the two daughters who were still in their father's house.

19:20 *A small place:* the Hebrew word *misar,* lit., "a little thing," has the same root consonants as the name of the town Zoar in v. 22.

19:25 *Overthrew:* this term, lit., "turned upside down," is used consistently to describe the destruction of the cities of the Plain. The imagery of earthquake and subsequent fire fits the geology of this region.

19:28–29 In a deft narrative detail, Abraham looks down from the height east of Hebron, from which he could easily see the region at the southern end of the Dead Sea, where the cities of the Plain were probably located.

19:30–38 This Israelite tale about the origin of Israel's neighbors east of the Jordan and the Dead Sea was told partly to ridicule these ethnically related but rival nations and partly to give popular etymologies for their names. The stylized nature of the story is seen in the names of the daughters ("the first-born" and "the younger"), the ease with which they fool their father, and the identical descriptions of the encounters.

19:37 *From my father:* in Hebrew, me'abi, similar in sound to the name "Moab."

19:38 *The son of my kin:* in Hebrew, *ben-ammi,* similar in sound to the name "Ammonites."

21:1–21 The long-awaited birth of Isaac parallels the birth of Ishmael in chap. 16, precipitating a rivalry and expulsion as in that chapter. Though this chapter is unified, the focus of vv. 1–7 is exclusively on Sarah and Isaac, and the focus of vv. 8–21 is exclusively on Hagar and Ishmael. The promise of a son to the barren Sarah and elderly Abraham has been central to the previous chapters and now that promise comes true with the birth of Isaac. The other great promise, that of land, will be resolved, at least in an anticipatory way, in Abraham's purchase of the cave at Machpelah in chap. 23. The parallel births of the two boys has influenced the Lucan birth narratives of John the Baptist and Jesus (Lk 1–2).

21:6 *Laugh:* for the third time (cf. 17:17 and 18:12) there is laughter, playing on the similarity in Hebrew between the pronunciation of the name Isaac and words associated with laughter.

21:11 *A son of his:* Abraham is the father of both boys, but Sarah is the mother only of Isaac. Abraham is very concerned that Ishmael have a sufficient inheritance.

21:13 *I will make a nation of him also:* Ishmael's descendants are named in 25:12–18.

21:14 *Placing the child on her back:* a reading based on an emendation of the traditional Hebrew text. In the traditional Hebrew text, Abraham put the bread and the waterskin on Hagar's back, while her son apparently walked beside her. In this way the traditional Hebrew text harmonizes the data of the Priestly source, in which Ishmael would have been at least four-teen years old when Isaac was born; compare 16:16 with 21:5; cf. 17:25. But in the present Elohist (?) story, Ishmael is obviously a little boy, not much older than Isaac; cf. vv. 15, 18.

21:22 Of the two related promises of progeny and land, that of progeny has been fulfilled in the previous chapter. Now the claim on the land begins to be solidified by Abimelech's recognition of Abraham's claim on the well at Beer-sheba; it will be furthered by Abraham's purchase of the cave at Machpelah in chap. 23. Two levels of editing are visible in the story: (1) no. 22–24, 27, 32, the general covenant with Abimelech; (2) vv. 25–26, 28–30, 31, Abraham's claim on the well. Both versions play on the root of the Hebrew word *Sheba',* which means "seven" and "swear," and the place name Beer-sheba.

21:23 *This place:* Beer-sheba (v. 31). Abimelech had come from Gerar (20:2), about thirty miles west of Beer-Sheba.

21:32 *Philistines:* one of the Sea Peoples, who migrated from Mycenaean Greece around 1200 B.C. and settled on the coastland of Canaan, becoming a principal rival of Israel. Non-biblical texts do not use the term "Philistine" before ca. 1200 B.C.; it is probable that this usage and those in chap. 26 are anachronistic, perhaps applying a later ethnic term for an earlier, less-known one.

21:33 *God the Eternal:* in Hebrew, *'el 'olam,* perhaps the name of the deity of the pre-Israelite sanctuary at Beer-sheba, but used by Abraham as a title of God; cf. Is 40:28.

22:1–19 The divine demand that Abraham sacrifice to God the son of promise is the greatest of his trials; after the successful completion of the test, he has only to buy a burial site for Sarah and find a wife for Isaac. The story is widely recognized as a literary masterpiece, depicting in a few lines God as the absolute Lord, inscrutable yet ultimately gracious, and Abraham, acting in moral grandeur as the great ancestor of Israel. Abraham speaks simply, with none of the wordy evasions of chaps. 13 and 21. The style is laconic; motivations and thoughts are not explained, and the reader cannot but wonder at the scene. In vv. 15–18, the angel repeats the seventh and climactic promise. *Moriah:* the mountain is not given a precise geographical location here, though 2 Chr 3:1 identifies Moriah as the mountain of Jerusalem where Solomon built the Temple; Abraham is thus the first to worship there. The word "Moriah" is a play on the verb "to see" (Heb. *ra'ah*); the wordplay is continued in v. 8, "God will provide (lit., "see")" and in v. 14, Yahweh-yireh, meaning "the LORD will see/provide."

22:9 *Bound:* the Hebrew verb is *'agad,* from which is derived the noun Akedah, "the binding (of Isaac)," the traditional Jewish name for this incident.

22:13 While the Bible recognizes that firstborn males belong to God (Ex 13:11–16; 34:19–20), and provides an alternate sacrifice to redeem firstborn sons, the focus here is on Abraham's being tested by God (v. 1). But the widely attested practice of child sacrifice underscores, for all its horror today, the realism of the test.

22:14 *Yahweh-yireh:* a Hebrew expression meaning "the LORD will see/provide." See note on vv. 1–19.

22:15–19 The seventh and climactic statement of the blessings to Abraham. Unlike the other statements, which were purely promissory, this one is presented as a reward for Abraham's extraordinary trust.

22:20–24 The descendants to the second generation of Nahor, Abraham's brother, who married Milcah. Of Terah's three sons (11:27), the oldest, Abraham, fathered Isaac (21:1–7), and the youngest, Haran (who died in Ur), fathered Lot. Abraham is now told that Nahor had eight children by Milcah and four by his concubine Reumah. Apart from the notice about the children born to Abraham by his second wife, Keturah (25:1–6), all the information about Terah's family to the second generation is now complete. It is noteworthy that Jacob will, like Nahor, have eight children by his wives and four by his concubines.

25:12 Like the conclusion of the Jacob story (chap. 36), where the numerous descendants of the rejected Esau are listed, the descendants of the rejected Ishmael conclude the story.

25:18 *Pitched camp:* lit., "fell"; the same Hebrew verb is used in Jgs 7:12 in regard to the hostile encampment of desert tribes. The present passage shows the fulfillment of the prediction contained in Gn 16:12.

The Story of Joseph

37:1 The statement points ahead to 47:27, "Thus Israel settled in the land of Egypt, in the region of Goshen" These two statements frame the Joseph narrative; the later material (47:28—49:33) is about Jacob; chap. 50 brings to a conclusion themes remaining from the earlier story. One aim of the Joseph story is to explain how Israel came to Egypt after sojourning so long in Canaan.

37:2 The Joseph story is great literature not only in its themes but in its art. The stories show an interest in the psychology of the characters; everyone acts "in character" yet there is never a doubt that a divine purpose is bringing events to their conclusion. According to a literary analysis, vv. 1–4 set the scene; vv. 5–36 introduce the dramatic tension in the form of a conflict within the family; chaps. 38—41 describe the journeys away from their family of the eponymous ancestors of the two great tribes of later times, Judah (chap. 38) and Joseph (chaps. 39—41) and their preliminary conclusions; chaps. 42—44 detail the famine and journeys for food (chaps. 42, 43) that bring the brothers and (indirectly) the father into fresh contact with a mature Joseph who now has the power of life and death over them; 45:1—47:27 is the resolution (reconciliation of Joseph to his brothers) and the salvation of the family.

37:3 Jacob's favoring Joseph over his other sons is a cause of the brothers' attempt on his life. Throughout the story, Jacob is unaware of the impact of his favoritism on his other sons (cf. vv. 33–35; 42:36). *Long ornamented tunic:* the meaning of the Hebrew phrase is unclear. In 2 Sm 13:18–19, it is the distinctive dress of unmarried royal daughters. The "coat of many colors" in the Septuagint became the traditional translation. Ancient depictions of Semites in formal dress show them with long, ornamented robes and that is the most likely meaning here. Possibly, the young Joseph is given a coat that symbolizes honor beyond his years. Later, Pharaoh will clothe Joseph in a robe that symbolizes honor (41:42).

37:5–10 Joseph's dreams of ruling his brothers appear at first glance to be merely adolescent grandiosity, and they bring him only trouble. His later successes make it clear, however, that they were from God. Another confirmation of their divine source is the doubling of dreams (cf. 41:32).

37:21–36 The chapter thus far is from the Yahwist source, as are also vv. 25–28a. But vv. 21–24 and 28b–36 are from another source (sometimes designated the Elohist source). In the latter, Reuben tries to rescue Joseph, who is taken in Reuben's absence by certain Midianites; in the Yahwist source, it is Judah who saves Joseph's life by having him sold to certain Ishmaelites. Although the two variant forms in which the story was handed down in early oral tradition differ in these minor points, they agree on the essential fact that Joseph was brought as a slave into Egypt because of the jealousy of his brothers.

37:28 *They sold Joseph . . . silver:* editors tried to solve the confusion, created by different sources, by supposing that it was the Midianite traders who pulled Joseph out of the pit and sold him to Ishmaelites. In all probability, one source had the brothers selling Joseph to Ishmaelites, whereas the other had them cast him into the pit whence he was taken by Midianite traders.

37:29 *Tore his garments:* the traditional sign of mourning in the ancient Near East.

37:35 *Sheol:* see note on Ps 6:6.

40:1 Joseph interprets the dreams of the Pharaoh's two officials. His ability to interpret the dreams shows that God is still with him and points forward to his role of dream interpreter for Pharaoh in chap. 41.

40:13 *Single you out:* lit., "lift up your head" (see also vv. 19, 20).

41:1–57 Joseph correctly interprets Pharaoh's dream and becomes second in command over all Egypt.

41:8 *Magicians:* one of the tasks of the "magicians" was interpreting dreams. The interpretation of dreams was a long-standing practice in Egypt. A manual of dream interpretation has been found, written in the early second millennium and re-published later in which typical dreams are given ("If a man sees himself in a dream . . .") followed by a judgment of "good" or "bad." Interpreters were still needed for dreams, however, and Pharaoh complains that none of his dream interpreters can interpret his unprecedented dream. The same term will be used of Pharaoh's magicians in Exodus.

41:42 *Signet ring:* a finger ring in which was set a stamp seal, different from the cylinder seal such as Judah wore; see note on 38:18. By receiving Pharaoh's signet ring, Joseph was made vizier of Egypt (v. 43); the vizier was known as "seal-bearer of the king of Lower Egypt." The gold chain was a symbol of high office in ancient Egypt.

41:43 *Abrek:* apparently a cry of homage, though the word's derivation and actual meaning are uncertain.

41:45 *Zaphenath-paneah:* a Hebrew transcription of an Egyptian name meaning "the god speaks and he (the newborn child) lives" Asenath: means "belonging to (the Egyptian goddess) Neith." *Potiphera:* means "he whom Ra (the Egyptian god) gave"; a shorter form of the same name was borne by Joseph's master (37:36). *Heliopolis:* in Hebrew, *On,* a city seven miles northeast of modern Cairo, site of the chief temple of the sun god; it is mentioned also in v. 50; 46:20; Ez 30:17.

41:51 *Manasseh:* an allusion to this name is in the Hebrew expression, *nishshani,* "he made me forget."

41:52 *Ephraim:* related to the Hebrew expression *hiphrani,* "(God) has made me fruitful." The name originally meant something like "fertile land."

42:1–38 The first journey of the brothers to Egypt. Its cause is famine, which was also the reason Abraham and Sarah undertook their dangerous journey to Egypt. The brothers bow to Joseph in v. 6, which fulfills Joseph's dream in 37:5–11. Endowed with wisdom, Joseph begins a process of instruction or "discipline" for his brothers that eventually forces them to recognize the enormity of their sin against him and the family. He controls their experience of the first journey with the result that the second journey in chaps. 43—44 leads to full acknowledgment and reconciliation.

42:9, 12 *Weak points:* lit., "the nakedness of the land"; the military weakness of the land, like human nakedness, should not be seen by strangers.

43:1–34 The second journey to Egypt. Joseph the sage has carefully prepared the brothers for a possible reconciliation. In this chapter and the following one Judah steps forward as the hero, in contrast to chaps. 37 and 42 where Reuben was the hero. Here Judah serves as guarantee for Benjamin.

43:32 *Separately to him:* that Joseph did not eat with the other Egyptians was apparently a matter of rank.

43:34 *Five times as large as:* probably an idiomatic expression for "much larger than." Cf. 45:22.

44:1–34 Joseph's pressure on his brothers and Judah's great speech. Judah has the longest speech in the Book of Genesis; it summarizes the recent past (vv. 18–29), shows the pain Joseph's actions have imposed on their aged father (vv. 30–32), and ends with the offer to take the place of Benjamin as servant of Joseph (vv. 33–34). The role of Judah in the entire story is exceedingly important and is easily underrated: he tries to rescue Joseph (37:26–27), his "going down away from the brothers" is parallel to Joseph's (chap. 38) and prepares him (as it prepares Joseph) for the reconciliation, his speech in chap. 44 persuades Joseph to reveal himself and be reconciled to his brothers. Here, Judah effectively replaces Reuben as a spokesman for the brothers. Jacob in his testament (chap. 49) devotes the most attention to Judah and Joseph. In one sense, the story can be called the story of Joseph and Judah.

44:5 *Divination:* seeking omens through liquids poured into a cup or bowl was a common practice in the ancient Near East; cf. v. 15. Even though divination was frowned on in later Israel (Lv 19:31), it is in this place an authentic touch which is ascribed to Joseph, the wisest man in Egypt.

44:16 *Guilt:* in trying to do away with Joseph when he was young.

44:19 *My lord asked his servants:* such frequently repeated expressions in Judah's speech show the formal court style used by a subject in speaking to a high official.

45:1–28 Joseph reveals his identity and the family is reconciled.

45:8 Father to Pharaoh: a term applied to a vizier in ancient Egypt.

45:9–15 In these verses, as in 46:31—47:5a, all from the Yahwist source, Joseph in his own name invites his father and brothers to come to Egypt. Only after their arrival is Pharaoh informed of the fact. On the other hand, in 45:16–20, which scholars have traditionally attributed to the Elohist source, it is Pharaoh himself who invites Joseph's family to migrate to his domain.

45:10 *The region of Goshen:* the meaning of the term is unknown. It is found in no Egyptian source. It is generally thought to be in the modern Wadi Tumilat in the eastern part of the Nile Delta.

46:1—47:26 Jacob and his family settle in Egypt. Joseph's economic policies.

46:37 *I am God:* more precisely according to the Hebrew text, "I am El." "El" is here a divine name, not the common noun "god."

The Book of Exodus

1:1 *Sons of Israel:* here literally the first-generation sons of Jacob/Israel. Cf. v. 5. However, beginning with v. 7 the same Hebrew phrase refers to Jacob's more remote descendants; hence, from there on, it is ordinarily rendered "the Israelites." *Households:* the family in its fullest sense, including wives, children and servants.

1:2 Jacob's sons are listed here according to their respective mothers. Cf. Gn 29:31; 30:20; 35:16–26.

1:5 *Direct descendants:* lit., "persons coming from Jacob's loins"; hence, wives of Jacob's sons and servants are not included. Cf. Gn 46:26. Seventy: Gn 46:26, along with the Septuagint for the verse, agrees on a total of sixty-six coming down to Egypt with Jacob, but in v. 27 the Hebrew text adds the two sons born to Joseph in Egypt and presupposes Jacob himself and Joseph for a total of seventy; the Septuagint adds "nine sons" born to Joseph to get a total of seventy-five. This is the figure the Septuagint and 4QEx[a] have here in v.5.

1:7 *Fruitful . . . multiplied . . . the land was filled with them:* the language used here to indicate the fecundity of the Israelite population echoes the divine blessing bestowed upon humanity at creation (Gn 1:28) and after the flood (Gn 9:1) as well as suggesting fulfillment of the promises to the ancestors Abraham, Isaac, and Jacob (Gn 12:2; 13:16; 15:5; 28:14; passim).

1:8 *Who knew nothing of Joseph:* the nuance intended by the Hebrew verb "know" here goes beyond precise determination. The idea may be not simply that a new king came to power who had not heard of Joseph but that this king ignored the services that Joseph had rendered to Egypt, repudiating the special relationship that existed between Joseph and his predecessor on the throne.

1:10 *Increase:* Pharaoh's actions thereby immediately pit him against God's will for the Israelites to multiply; see note on v. 7 above.

1:11 *Pharaoh:* not a personal name, but a title common to all the kings of Egypt.

1:14 *Mortar:* either the wet clay with which the bricks were made, as in Na 3:14, or the cement used between the bricks in building, as in Gn 11:3.

1:16 *Birthstool:* apparently a pair of stones on which the mother is seated for childbirth opposite the midwife. The Hebrew word elsewhere is used to refer to the stones of a potter's wheel.

2:1 *Now a man:* the chapter begins abruptly, without names for the man or woman (in contrast to the midwives of 1:15), who in 6:20 are identified as Amram and Jochebed.

2:3 *Basket:* the same Hebrew word is used in Gn 6:14 and throughout the flood narrative for Noah's ark, but nowhere else in the Bible. Here, however, the "ark" or "chest" was made of papyrus stalks. Presumably the allusion to Genesis is intentional. Just as Noah and his family were preserved safe from the threatening waters of the flood in the ark he built, so now Moses is preserved from the threatening waters of the Nile in the ark prepared by his mother. Among the reeds: the Hebrew noun for "reed" is overwhelmingly used in the phrase "Reed Sea," traditionally translated "Red Sea."

2:9 *And I will pay your wages:* the idea that the child's mother will be paid for nursing her child—and by Pharaoh's own daughter—heightens the narrative's irony.

2:10 *When the child grew:* while v. 9 implies that the boy's mother cared for him as long as he needed to be nursed (presumably, between two and four years), the same verb appears in v. 11 to describe the attainment of adulthood. And he became her son: Pharaoh's daughter adopts Moses, thus adding to the irony of the account. The king of Egypt had ordered the killing of all the sons of the Hebrews, and one now becomes the son of his own daughter! *Moses:* in Hebrew, *mosheh.* There is a play on words here: Hebrew *mosheh* echoes *meshithihu* ("I drew him out"). However, the name Moses actually has nothing to do with that Hebrew verb, but is probably derived from Egyptian "beloved" or "has been born," preserved in such Pharaonic names as Thutmoses (meaning approximately "Beloved of the god Thoth" or "The god Thoth is born, has given birth to [the child]").The original meaning of Moses' name was no longer remembered (if it was Egyptian, it may have contained an Egyptian divine element as well, perhaps the name of the Nile god Hapi), and a secondary explanation was derived from this story (or gave rise to it, if the drawing from the water of the Nile was intended to foreshadow the Israelites' escape from Egypt through the Red Sea).

2:11 *After Moses had grown up:* cf. 7:7, where Moses is said to be eighty years old at the time of his mission to Pharaoh. *Striking:* probably in the sense of "flogging"; in v. 12, however, the some verb is used in the sense of "killing."

2:15 *Land of Midian:* the territory under the control of a confederation made up, according to Nm 31:8, of five Midianite tribes. According to Gn 25:1–2, Midian was a son of Abraham by Keturah. In view of the extreme hostility in later periods between Israel and Midian (cf. Nm 31; Jgs 6—8), the relationship is striking, as is the account here in Exodus of good relations between Moses and no less than a Midianite priest.

2:18 *Reuel:* also called Jethro. Cf. 3:1; 4:18; 18:1.

2:19 *An Egyptian:* Moses was probably wearing Egyptian dress, or spoke Egyptian to Reuel's daughters.

2:22 *Gershom:* the name is explained unscientifically as if it came from the Hebrew word *ger,* "sojourner, resident alien," and the Hebrew word *sham,* "there." *Stranger residing:* Hebrew *ger,* one who seeks and finds shelter and a home away from his or her own people or land.

2:25 *God knew:* in response to the people's cry, God, mindful of the covenant, looks on their plight and acknowledges firsthand the depth of their suffering (see 3:7). In vv. 23–25, traditionally attributed to the Priestly writer, God is mentioned five times, in contrast to the rest of chaps. 1—2, where God is rarely mentioned. These verses serve as a fitting transition to Moses' call in chap. 3.

3:1—4:17 After the introduction to the narrative in 2:23–25, the commissioning itself falls into three sections: God's appearance under the aspect of a burning bush (3:1–6); the explicit commission (3:7–10); and an extended dialogue between Moses and God, in the course of which Moses receives the revelation of God's personal name. Although in the J source of the Pentateuch people have known and invoked God's personal name in worship since the time of Seth (Gn 4:26), for the E and P sources (see 6:2–4), God first makes this name publicly available here through Moses.

3:1 *The mountain of God, Horeb:* traditionally, "Horeb" is taken to be an alternate name in E source material and Deuteronomy (e.g., Dt 1:2) for what in J and P is known as Mount Sinai, the goal of the Israelites' journey after leaving Egypt and the site of the covenant God makes with Israel. However, it is not clear that originally the two names reflect the same mountain, nor even that "Horeb" refers originally to a mountain and not simply the dry, ruined region (from Hebrew horeb, "dryness, devastation") around the mountain. Additionally, the position of "Horeb" at the end of the verse may indicate that the identification of the "mountain of God" with Horeb (= Sinai?) represents a later stage in the evolution of the tradition about God's meeting with Moses. The phrase "mountain of God" simply anticipates the divine apparitions which would take place there, both on this occasion and after the Israelites' departure from Egypt; alternatively, it means that the place was already sacred or a place of pilgrimage in pre-Israelite times. In any case, the narrative offers no indications of its exact location.

3:2 *The angel of the LORD:* Hebrew *mal'ak* or "messenger" is regularly translated *angelus* by the Septuagint, from which the English word "angel" is derived, but the Hebrew term lacks connotations now popularly associated with "angel" (such as wings). Although angels frequently assume human form (cf. Gn 18–19), the term is also used to indicate the visual form under which God occasionally appeared and spoke to people, referred to indifferently in some Old Testament texts either as

God's "angel," *mal'ak,* or as God. Cf. Gn 16:7, 13; Ex 14:19, 24–25; Nm 22:22–35; Jgs 6:11–18. *The bush:* Hebrew *seneh,* perhaps "thorny bush," occurring only here in as. 2–4 and in Dt 33:16. Its use here is most likely a wordplay on Sinai (Hebrew *sinay*), implying a popular etymology for the name of the sacred mountain.

3:6 *God of your father:* a frequently used epithet in Genesis (along with the variants "my father" and "your father") for God as worshiped by the ancestors. As is known from its usage outside of the Bible in the ancient Near East, it suggests a close, personal relationship between the individual and the particular god in question, who is both a patron and a protector, a god traditionally revered by the individual's family and whose worship is passed down from father to son. *The God of Abraham . . . Jacob:* this precise phrase (only here and in v. 15; 4:5) stresses the continuity between the new rev-elation to Moses and the earlier religious experience of Israel's ancestors, identifying the God who is now addressing Moses with the God who promised land and numerous posterity to the ancestors. Cf. Mt 22:32; Mk 12:26; Lk 20:37. *Afraid to look at God:* the traditions about Moses are not uniform in regard to his beholding or not being able to look at God (cf. 24:11; 33:11, 18–23; 34:29–35). Here Moses' reaction is the natural and spontaneous gesture of a person suddenly confronted with a direct experience of God. Aware of his human frailty and the gulf that separates him from the God who is holy, he hides his face. To encounter the divine was to come before an awesome and mysterious power unlike any other a human being might experience and, as such, potentially threatening to one's very identity or existence (see Gn 32:30).

3:8 *I have come down:* cf. Gn 11:5, 7; 18:21. *Flowing with milk and honey:* an expression denoting agricultural prosperity, which seems to have been proverbial in its application to the land of Canaan. Cf. Ex 13:5; Nm 13:27; Jos 5:6; Jer 11:5; 32:22; Ez 20:6, 15.

3:11 *Who am I:* this question is always addressed by an inferior to a superior (to the ruler in 1 Sm 18:18; to God in 2 Sm 7:18 and its parallel, 1 Chr 17:16; 1 Chr 29:14; 2 Chr 2:5). In response to some special opportunity or invitation, the question expresses in a style typical of the ancient Near East the speaker's humility or gratitude or need of further assistance, but never unwillingness or an outright refusal to respond. Instead the question sets the stage for further support from the superior should that be needed (as here).

3:12 *Sign:* a visible display of the power of God. The ancient notion of a sign from God does not coincide with the modern understanding of "miracle," which suggests some disruption in the laws governing nature. While most any phenomenon can become a vehicle for displaying the purposes and providence of God, here the sign intended to confirm Moses' commission by God seems to be the burning bush itself. Since normally the giving of such a sign would follow the commission rather than precede it (see Jgs 6:11–24), some see Israel's service of God at Sinai after the exodus from Egypt as the confirmatory sign, albeit retroactively. It is more likely, however, that its mention here is intended to establish the present episode with Moses

alone as a prefiguration of God's fiery theophany to all Israel on Mount Sinai. *Serve God:* Hebrew *'-b-d,* "serve," includes among its meanings both the notion of "serving or working for another" and the notion of "worship."The implication here is that the Israelites' service/worship of God is incompatible with their service to Pharaoh.

3:14 *I am who I am:* Moses asks in v. 13 for the name of the One speaking to him, but God responds with a wordplay which preserves the utterly mysterious character of the divine being even as it appears to suggest something of the inner meaning of God's name: *'ehyeh* "I am" or "I will be(come)" for "*Yhwh,*" the personal name of the God of Israel. While the phrase "I am who I am" resists unraveling, it nevertheless suggests an etymological linking between the name "Yhwh" and an earlier form of the Hebrew verbal root *h-y-h* "to be." On that basis many have interpreted the name "Yhwh" as a third-person form of the verb meaning "He causes to be, creates," itself perhaps a shortened form of a longer liturgical name such as "(God who) creates (the heavenly armies)." Note in this connection the invocation of Israel's God as "Lord (*Yhwh*) of Hosts" (e.g.,1 Sm 17:45). In any case, out of reverence for God's proper name, the term *Adonai,* "my Lord," was later used as a substitute. The word Lord (in small capital letters) indicates that the Hebrew text has the sacred name (*Yhwh*), the tetragrammaton. The word "Jehovah" arose from a false reading of this name as it is written in the current Hebrew text. The Septuagint has *egō eimi ho ōn,* "I am the One who is" (*ōn* being the participle of the verb "to be"). This can be taken as an assertion of God's aseity or self-existence, and has been understood as such by the Church, since the time of the Fathers, as a true expression of God's being, even though it is not precisely the meaning of the Hebrew.

3:22 *Articles:* probably jewelry.

4:12 *Assist you in speaking:* lit., "be with your mouth"; cf. v.15, lit., "be with your mouth and with his mouth."

4:13 *Send someone else:* lit., "send by means of him whom you will send," that is, "send whom you will."

4:16 *Spokesman:* lit., "mouth"; Aaron was to serve as a mouthpiece for Moses, as a prophet does for God; hence the relation between Moses and Aaron is compared to that between God and his prophet: Moses "will be as God to," i.e., lit.,"will become God for him." Cf. 7:1.

4:17 *This staff:* probably the same as that of vv. 2–4; but some understand that a new staff is now given by God to Moses.

4:18 *Jethro:* the Hebrew text has "Jether," apparently a variant form of "Jethro" found in the same verse. *To see whether they are still living:* Moses did not tell his father-in-law his main reason for returning to Egypt.

4:21 *Harden his heart:* in the biblical view, the heart, whose actual function in the circulation of blood was unknown, typically performs functions associated today more with the brain than with the emotions. Therefore, while it may be used in connection with various emotional states ranging from joy to sadness, it very commonly designates the seat of intellectual and volitional activities. For God to harden Pharaoh's heart is to harden his resolve against the Israelites' desire to leave. In the ancient world, actions which are out of character are routinely attributed not to the person but to some "outside" superhuman power acting upon the person (Jgs 14:16;1 Sm 16:10). Uncharacteristically negative actions or states are explained in the same way (1 Sm 16:14). In this instance, the opposition of Pharaoh, in the face of God's displays of power, would be unintelligible to the ancient Israelites unless he is seen as under some divine constraint. But this does not diminish Pharaoh's own responsibility. In the anthropology of the ancient Israelites there is no opposition between individual responsibility and God's sovereignty over all of creation. Cf. Rom 9:17–18.

4:24–26 This story continues to perplex commentators and may have circulated in various forms before finding its place here in Exodus. Particularly troublesome is the unique phrase "spouse of blood." Nevertheless, v. 26, which apparently comes from the hand of a later commentator on the original story, is intended to offer some clarification. It asserts that when Zipporah used the problematic expression (addressing it either to Moses or her son), she did so with reference to the circumcision performed on her son—the only place in the Bible where this rite is performed by a woman. Whatever the precise meaning of the phrase "spouse of blood," circumcision is the key to understanding it as well as the entire incident. One may conclude, therefore, that God was angry with Moses for having failed to keep the divine command given to Abraham in Gn 17:10–12 and circumcise his son. Moses' life is spared when his wife circumcises their son.

4:25 *Touching his feet:* a euphemism most probably for the male sexual organ (see 2 Kgs 18:27; Is 7:20); whether the genitals of the child (after Zipporah circumcised him) or of Moses (after the circumcision of his son) is not clear.

4:31 *Observed . . . their affliction:* the same phrases used in God's dialogue with Moses in 3:16—17.

5:1 *Hold a feast:* the Hebrew verb used here, hagag ("to celebrate a feast or a festival"; see 12:14; 23:14), refers to a community celebration marked above all by a procession to the sanctuary. It is used especially of three major feasts: Unleavened Bread, Pentecost (in 23:16, "the Feast of Harvest," but customarily "the Feast of Weeks" [*Shavuot*]), and Succoth/Sukkoth (in 34:16, "the Feast of Ingathering," but more frequently "of Booths, or Tabernacles," as in Dt 16:13, 16; 31:10; Lv 23:34; Zec 14:16; passim) and—along with the related noun *hag*—the Passover in 12:14. See 23:14—18; 34:18—25.

5:2 *I do not know the Lord:* whether or not he had heard of the Lord, the God of Israel, Pharaoh here refuses to acknowledge the Lord's authority. See note on 1:8.

5:5 *They are already more numerous:* a recollection of Pharaoh's earlier words to his subjects in 1:9.

5:6 *The taskmasters of the people and their foremen:* the former were higher officials and probably Egyptians; the latter were lower officials (perhaps recordkeepers or clerks), chosen from the Israelites themselves. Cf. v. 14.

5:7 Straw was mixed with clay to give sun-dried bricks greater cohesion and durability.

5:10 *Thus says Pharaoh:* the standard formula for prophetic oracles, but with Pharaoh rather than the Lord as the subject.

This heightens the sense of personal conflict between Pharaoh, who acts as if he were God, and the Lord, whose claims are spurned by Pharaoh.

5:15 *Cried out to Pharaoh:* the Hebrew verb translated "cry out" and its related noun are normally used of appeals to God by Moses (8:8; 14:15; 15:25; 17:4), the people (3:7, 9; 14:10), or an oppressed individual (22:22, 26). Here, by implication, these minor Israelite officials appeal to Pharaoh as if he were their God. See v. 10.

6:1 *By a strong hand:* by God's hand or Pharaoh's hand? The Hebrew is ambiguous; although it may be an allusion to God's hand of 3:19-20, both interpretations are possible.

6:2—7:7 According to the standard source criticism of the Pentateuch, 6:2—7:7 represents a Priestly version of the JE call narrative in 3:1—4:17. But in context the present account does more than simply repeat the earlier passage. See note below.

6:3 *God the Almighty:* in Hebrew, El Shaddai. This traditional translation does not have a firm philological basis. *But by my name . . . I did not make myself known to them:* although the text implies that the name Lord was unknown previously, in context the emphasis in the passage falls on the understanding of God that comes with knowledge of the name. In this way God responds to the worsening plight of the Israelites and Moses' complaint in 5:23 that God has done nothing at all to rescue them.

6:12 *Poor speaker:* lit., "uncircumcised of lips": a metaphor expressing the hindrance of good communication expressed as "slow of speech and tongue" (4:10). Also used as a metaphor for impeded "heart" (Lv 26:41; Dt 10:16).

6:14 The purpose of the genealogy here is to give the line from which Moses and Aaron sprang, with special emphasis placed on the line of Aaron. Reuben and Simeon are mentioned first because, as older brothers of Levi, their names occur before his in the genealogy.

6:20 *His aunt:* more exactly, "his father's sister." Later on such a marriage was forbidden. Cf. Lv 18:12. Hence, the Greek and Latin versions render here, "his cousin."

6:25 *Phinehas:* according to Nm 25:13, Phinehas was given by God "the covenant of an everlasting priesthood" because of his zeal for God when the Israelites committed apostasy by worshiping the Baal of Pear in the plains of Moab (see Nm 25:1–18).

7:1 *Prophet:* Hebrew *nabi*, one who can legitimately speak for God and in God's name to another or others. Just as God spoke to Moses, so Moses will speak to Aaron, who will be a "prophet" to Pharaoh. Cf. 4:16.

7:14—12:30 After a brief preface (vv. 8–13) drawn from the Priestly source, a narrative depicting the series of ten disasters that God brings upon Pharaoh because of his stubbornness ensues. Although most of these disasters, known traditionally as the "ten plagues of Egypt," could be interpreted as naturally occurring phenomena, they are clearly represented by the biblical authors as extraordinary events indicative of God's intervention on behalf of Israel and as occurring exactly according to Moses' commands. See Ps 78:43–51 and 105:27–36 for poetic versions of these plagues, which also differ significantly from the account here.

7:14 *Pharaoh is obstinate:* lit., "Pharaoh's heart is heavy" (*kabed*); thus not precisely the same Hebrew idiom as found in vv.13 and 22, "stubborn," lit.,"Pharaoh's heart was hard(ened)" (hazaq) (cf. the related idiom with Pharaoh as the object, e.g., 4:21).

7:15 *The staff that turned into a snake:* the allusion is to 4:2–4 rather than 7:9–12. The latter comes from the hand of the Priestly writer and features Aaron—with his staff—as the principal actor.

7:22 *The Egyptian magicians did the same:* this is an exaggeration, presumably influenced by the similar statement in v. 11; whereas the magicians could turn their staffs into snakes after Aaron had done so, after Aaron's sign there should not have been any water in Egypt still unchanged to blood for the magicians "to do the same" with it (cf. v. 24).

8:12, 17 *Gnats, flies:* it is uncertain what species of troublesome insects are meant here in vv. 12–14 and then in vv. 17–27, the identification as "gnat" (vv. 12–14) and as "fly" (vv. 17–27) being based on the rendering of the Septuagint. Others suggest "lice" in vv. 12–14, while rabbinic literature renders Hebrew *'arob* in vv. 17–27 as a "mixture of wild animals." In the Hebrew of the Old Testament, the word occurs only in the context of the plagues (see also Ps 78:45 and 105:31).

8:15 *The finger of God:* previously the magicians had, for the most part, been able to replicate the signs and wonders Moses performed to manifest God's power—turning their staffs into snakes (7:11–12), turning water into blood (7:22), and producing frogs to overrun the land of Egypt (8:3). But now for the first time they are unable to compete, and confess a power greater than their own is at work. Cf. Lk 11:20.

8:19 *A distinction:* while some uncertainty surrounds the Hebrew here rendered as "distinction," it is clear that now the Israelites begin to be set apart from the Egyptians, a separation that reaches a climax in the death of the Egyptian firstborn (11:7).

8:22 Perhaps Moses is deceiving the Pharaoh much like the "God-fearing" midwives (1:16—20), although ancient historians writing about Egypt some time after the period in which the exodus is set do note Egyptian prohibitions on sacrificing cattle or slaughtering sacred animals. As such, the Egyptians might well have fiercely resented certain sacrificial practices of the Israelites. Certain animals were held sacred in Egypt, as the representations of various deities.

9:9 *Boils:* the exact nature of the disease is not clear. Semitic cognates, for example, suggest the Hebrew root means "to be hot" and thus point to some sort of inflammation. The fact that soot taken from the kiln is the agent of the disease would point in the same direction. See further Lv 13:18–23; Dt 28:35; 2 Kgs 20:7.

9:16 *To show you:* some ancient versions such as the Septuagint read, "to show through you." Cf. Rom 9:17.

9:28 *Thunder:* lit., "divine voices," "voices of God," or the like.

10:10 *The Lord help you . . . :* lit., "May the Lord be with you in the same way as I let you . . ."; a sarcastic blessing intended as a curse.

10:11 Pharaoh realized that if the men alone went they would have to return to their families. He suspected that the Hebrews had no intention of returning.

10:13 *East wind:* coming across the desert from Arabia, the strong east wind brings Egypt the burning sirocco and, at times, locusts. Cf. 14:21.

10:19 *The Red Sea:* the traditional translation, cf. Septuagint and other Versions; but the Hebrew literally means "sea of reeds" or "reedy sea," which could probably be applied to a number of bodies of shallow water, most likely somewhat to the north of the present deep Red Sea.

10:21 Darkness: commentators note that at times a storm from the south, called the khamsin, blackens the sky of Egypt with sand from the Sahara; the dust in the air is then so thick that the darkness can, in a sense, "be felt." But such observations should not obscure the fact that for the biblical author what transpires in each of the plagues is clearly something extraordinary, an event which witnesses to the unrivaled power of Israel's God.

10:26 *Service:* as is obvious from v. 25, the service in question here is the offering of sacrifice. The continued use of the verb *'bd* "to serve" and related nouns for both the people's bondage in Egypt and their subsequent service to the Lord dramatizes the point of the conflict between Pharaoh and the God of Israel, who demands from the Israelites an attachment which is exclusive. See Lv 25:55.

11:5 *Handmill:* two pieces of stone were used to grind grain. A smaller upper stone was moved back and forth over a larger stationary stone.This menial work was done by slaves and captives.

12:1–20 This section, which interrupts the narrative of the exodus, contains later legislation concerning the celebration of Passover.

12:2 As if to affirm victory over Pharaoh and sovereignty over the Israelites, the Lord proclaims a new calendar for Israel. This month: Abib, the month of "ripe grain" Cf. 13:4; 23:15; 34:18; Dt 16:1. It occurred near the vernal equinox, March–April. Later it was known by the Babylonian name of Nisan. Cf. Neh 2:1; Est 3:7.

12:4 *The lamb's cost:* some render the Hebrew, "reckon for the lamb the number of persons required to eat it." Cf. v. 10.

12:15 *Cut off:* a common Priestly term, not easily reduced to a simple English equivalent, since its usage appears to involve a number of associated punishments, some or all of which may come into play in any instance of the term's use. These included the excommunication of the offender from the Israelite community, the premature death of the offender, the eventual eradication of the offender's posterity, and finally the loss by the offender of all ancestral holdings.

12:22 *Hyssop:* a plant with many small woody branches that was convenient for a sprinkling rite.

12:32 *Bless me, too:* in a final and humiliating admission of defeat, once again Pharaoh asks Moses to intercede for him (cf. 8:24). However, Pharaoh may be speaking sarcastically.

12:38 *Mixed ancestry:* not simply descendants of Jacob; cf. Nm 11:4; Lv 24:10–11.

12:40 *In Egypt:* according to the Septuagint and the Samaritan Pentateuch "in Canaan and Egypt," thus reckoning from the time of Abraham. Cf. Gal 3:17.

12:46 *You shall not break any of its bones:* the application of these words to Jesus on the cross (Jn 19:36) sees the Paschal lamb as a prophetic type of Christ, sacrificed to free men and women from the bondage of sin. Cf. also 1 Cor 5:7; 1 Pt 1:19.

12:49 *One law:* the first appearance of the word *torah*, traditionally translated as "law," though it can have the broader meaning of "teaching" or "instruction" Elsewhere, too, it is said that the "alien" is to be accorded the same treatment as the Israelite (e.g., Lv 19:34).

13:4 *Abib:* "ear (of grain)," the old Canaanite name for this month; Israel later called it "Nisan." It was the first month in their liturgical calendar (cf. 12:2).

13:5 *The following service:* the celebration of the feast of Unleavened Bread now constitutes the Israelites' service, in contrast to the "service" they performed for Pharaoh as his slaves.

13:9 *Sign:* while here observance of the feast of Unleavened Bread is likened only metaphorically to a physical sign of one's piety that can be worn as a kind of badge in commemoration of the exodus, from ancient times Jews have seen in this verse also the basis for the wearing of phylacteries. These are small receptacles for copies of biblical verses which Jewish men bind to the arms and forehead as a kind of mnemonic device for the observance of the Law.

13:17 *By way of the Philistines' land:* the most direct route from Egypt to Palestine, along the shore of the Mediterranean.

13:21 *A column of cloud . . . a column of fire:* probably one and the same extraordinary phenomenon, a central nucleus of fire surrounded by smoke; only at night was its luminous nature visible; cf. 40:38.

14:2 *Pi-hahiroth . . . Migdol . . . Baal-zephon:* these places have not been definitively identified. Even the relative position of Pi-hahiroth and Baal-zephon is not clear; perhaps the former was on the west shore of the sea, where the Israelites were, and the latter on the opposite shore.

14:7 *Officers:* cf. 1 Kgs 9:22; Ez 23:15. The Hebrew word *shalish*, rendered in 1 Kgs 9:22 as "adjutant," has yet to have its meaning convincingly established. Given the very possible etymological connection with the number "three," others suggest the translation "three-man crew" or, less likely, the "third man in the chariot" although Egyptian chariots carried two-man crews. The author of the text may have been describing the chariots of his experience without direct historical knowledge of Egyptian ways.

14:9 *Horsemen:* the usage here may be anachronistic, since horsemen, or cavalry, play a part in warfare only at the end of the second millennium B.C.

14:19 *Angel of God:* Hebrew *mal'ak ha'elohim* (Septuagint *ho angelos tou theou*) here refers not to an independent spiritual being but to God's power at work in the world; corresponding to the column of cloud/fire, the expression more clearly preserves a sense of distance between God and God's creatures. The two halves of the verse are parallel and may come from different narrative sources.

14:20 The reading of the Hebrew text here is uncertain. The image is of a darkly glowing storm cloud, ominously bright, keeping the two camps apart.

15:1–21 This poem, regarded by many scholars as one of the oldest compositions in the Bible, was once an independent work. It has been inserted at this important juncture in the large narrative of Exodus to celebrate God's saving power, having miraculously delivered the people from their enemies, and ultimately leading them to the promised land.

Although the victory it describes over the Egyptians at the sea bears a superficial resemblance in v. 8 to the preceding depiction of the water standing like a wall (14:22), the poem (as opposed to the following prose verse, v. 19) suggests a different version of the victory at sea than that found in chap. 14. There is no splitting of the sea in an act reminiscent of the Lord's combat at creation with the sea monsters Rahab and Leviathan (Jb 9:13; 26:12; Ps 74:13–14; 89:11; Is 51:9–10); nor is there mention of an east wind driving the waters back so that the Israelites can cross. In this version it is by means of a storm at sea, caused by a ferocious blast from his nostrils, that the Lord achieves a decisive victory against Pharaoh and his army (vv. 1–12). The second half of the poem (vv. 13–18) describes God's guidance into the promised land.

15:4 *Red Sea:* the traditional translation of the Hebrew *yam suph*, which actually means "Sea of Reeds" or "reedy sea." The location is uncertain, though in view of the route taken by the Israelites from Egypt to Sinai, it could not have been the Red Sea, which is too far south. It was probably a smaller body of water south of the Gulf of Suez. The term occurs also in Exodus at 10:19; 13:18; and 23:31.

15:13 *Love:* the very important Hebrew term *hesed* carries a variety of nuances depending on context: love, kindness, faithfulness. It is often rendered "steadfast love." It implies a relationship that generates an obligation and therefore is at home in a covenant context. Cf. 20:6.

15:16 *Passed over:* an allusion to the crossing of the Jordan River (cf. Jos 3—5), written as if the entry into the promised land had already occurred. This verse suggests that at one time there was a ritual enactment of the conquest at a shrine near the Jordan River which included also a celebration of the victory at the sea.

15:21 *She responded:* Miriam's refrain echoes the first verse of this song and was probably sung as an antiphon after each verse.

15:22 *Red Sea:* see note on v. 4.

16:1 *On the fifteenth day of the second month:* just one full month after their departure from Egypt. Cf. 12:2, 51; Nm 33:3–4. The Septuagint takes the date to be the beginning of the Israelites' grumbling.

16:4 *Bread from heaven:* as a gift from God, the manna is said to come down from the sky. Cf. Ps 78:24–25; Wis 16:20. Perhaps it was similar to a natural substance that is still found in small quantities on the Sinai peninsula—probably the honey-like resin from the tamarisk tree—but here it is, at least in part, clearly an extraordinary sign of God's providence. With reference to Jn 6:32, 49–52, the Christian tradition has regarded the manna as a type of the Eucharist. Test: as the text stands, it seems to leave open the question whether the test concerns trusting in God to provide them with the daily gift of food or observing the sabbath instructions.

16:15 *What is this:* the Hebrew *man hu* is thus rendered by the ancient versions, which understood the phrase as a popular etymology of the Hebrew word *man,* "manna"; but some render *man hu,* "This is manna."

16:16 *Omer:* a dry measure of approximately two quarts.

16:18 Paul cites this passage as an example of equitable sharing (2 Cor 8:15).

16:31 *Coriander seed:* small, round, aromatic seeds of bright brown color; the comparison, therefore, refers merely to the size and shape, not to the taste or color of the manna.

16:33 *Jar:* according to the Greek translation, which is followed in Heb 9:4, this was a golden vessel.

16:34 *The covenant:* i.e., the ark of the covenant, in which were placed the two tablets of the Ten Commandments. Cf. 25:16, 21–22.

16:36 *Omer . . . ephah:* see note on Is 5:10.

17:7 *Massah . . . Meribah:* Hebrew words meaning, respectively, "the place of the test" and "the place of strife, of quarreling"

17:8 *Amalek:* the Amalekites appear in the Bible as early inhabitants of southern Palestine and the Sinai peninsula prior to the appearance of the Israelites in the region. Cf. Nm 24:20.

17:15 *Yahweh-nissi:* meaning, "the Lord is my banner."

17:16 *Take up the banner of the LORD:* lit., "a hand on the LORD's banner," apparently a war cry for the Israelite troops in the conduct of Holy War; however, the Hebrew text is difficult to interpret.

18:2 *Moses had sent her back:* a later gloss which attempts to harmonize Zipporah's presence with Jethro here in this story and the account of Moses' return to Egypt with Zipporah in 4:20.

18:5 The allusion to meeting Moses encamped at the mountain of God, prior to the arrival of the Israelites at Sinai in chap. 19, might well suggest a different narrative context for this story from an earlier stage of the biblical tradition's development. It is noteworthy that immediately after the Sinai pericope (Ex 19:1—Nm 10:28), recounting the theophany at Sinai and the giving of the law, the narrative of Israel's march through the wilderness resumes with an apparent doublet of the visit by Moses' father-in-law (Nm 10:29–32).

18:12 That a non-Israelite, such as Jethro, should bless Israel's God by way of acknowledging what God had done for Israel (v. 10) is not entirely surprising; but the Midianite priest's sacrifice to the God of Israel, including his presiding over a sacrificial meal with Aaron and the elders of Israel, is unusual, suggesting that he was himself already a worshiper of Yhwh, Israel's God. Note further in this connection the role Jethro takes in the following narrative (vv. 13–27) in instituting a permanent judiciary for the Israelites. *Burnt offering:* a sacrifice wholly burnt up as an offering to God.

18:19–20 By emphasizing Moses' mediatorial role for the people before God in regard to God's statutes and instructions,

this story about the institution of Israel's judiciary prepares for Moses' role in the upcoming revelation of the law at Sinai.

18:23 *And God so commands you:* i.e., and God approves.

19:2 Apparently from a different source (P) than v. 1, which notes the date, v. 2 from the J source includes a second notice of the arrival in the wilderness of Sinai. The Israelites now will be camped at Sinai from this point on all the way to Nm 10:10. This is a striking indication of the centrality and importance of the Sinai narrative in the overall composition of the Pentateuch.

19:5 *Covenant:* while covenants between individuals and between nations are ubiquitous in the ancient Near East, the adaptation of this concept to express the relationship that will henceforth characterize God's relationship to Israel represents an important innovation of biblical faith. Other gods might "choose" nations to fulfill a special destiny or role in the world; but only Israel's God is bound to a people by covenant. Thereby Israel's identity as a people is put upon a foundation that does not depend upon the vicissitudes of Israelite statehood or the normal trappings of national existence. Israel will be a covenant people.

19:6 *Kingdom of priests:* inasmuch as this phrase is parallel to "holy nation," it most likely means that the whole Israelite nation is set apart from other nations and so consecrated to God, or holy, in the way priests are among the people (cf. Is 61:6; 1 Pt 2:5, 9).

19:13 *May they go up on the mountain:* in vv. 12–13a, a later Priestly reshaping of an earlier version of the instructions governing how the people are to prepare for the encounter with God (vv. 10–11, 13b), the people are to be restrained from ascending the mountain, which is suffused with the holiness of God and too dangerous for their approach. In the earlier version, as v. 13b suggests, the sanctified people must come near, in order to hear God speaking with Moses (v. 9) and in this way receive confirmation of his special relationship with God.

19:16 *Shofar:* a ram's horn used like a trumpet for signaling both for liturgical and military purposes.

19:20–25 At this point the Priestly additions of vv. 12–13a are elaborated with further Priestly instructions, which include the priests' sanctifying themselves apart from the people (v. 22) and Aaron accompanying Moses to the top of the mountain (v. 24).

20:1–17 The precise numbering and division of these precepts into "ten commandments" is somewhat uncertain. Traditionally among Catholics and Lutherans vv. 1–6 are considered as only one commandment, and v. 17 as two. The Anglican, Greek Orthodox, and Reformed churches count vv. 1–6 as two, and v. 17 as one. Cf. Dt 5:6–21. The traditional designation as "ten" is not found here but in 34:28 (and also Dt 4:13 and 10:4), where these precepts are alluded to literally as "the ten words." That they were originally written on two tablets appears in Ex 32:15–16; 34:28–29; Dt 4:13; 10:2–4.

The present form of the commands is a product of a long development, as is clear from the fact that the individual precepts vary considerably in length and from the slightly different formulation of Dt 5:6–21 (see especially vv. 12–15 and 21).

Indeed they represent a mature formulation of a traditional morality. Why this specific selection of commands should be set apart is not entirely clear. None of them is unique in the Old Testament and all of the laws which follow are also from God and equally binding on the Israelites. Even so, this collection represents a privileged expression of God's moral demands on Israel and is here set apart from the others as a direct, unmediated communication of God to the Israelites and the basis of the covenant being concluded on Sinai.

20:3 *Beside me:* this commandment is traditionally understood as an outright denial of the existence of other gods except the God of Israel; however, in the context of the more general prohibitions in vv. 4–5, v. 3 is, more precisely, God's demand for Israel's exclusive worship and allegiance.

The Hebrew phrase underlying the translation "beside me" is, nonetheless, problematic and has been variously translated, e.g., "except me," "in addition to me," "in preference to me," "in defiance of me," and "in front of me" or "before my face." The latter translation, with its concrete, spatial nuances, has suggested to some that the prohibition once sought to exclude from the Lord's sanctuary the cult images or idols of other gods, such as the asherah, or stylized sacred tree of life, associated with the Canaanite goddess Asherah (34:13). Over the course of time, as an. 4–5 suggest, the original scope of v. 3 was expanded.

20:4 *Or a likeness of anything:* compare this formulation to that found in Dt 5:8, which understands this phrase and the following phrases as specifications of the prohibited idol (Hebrew pesel), which usually refers to an image that is carved or hewn rather than cast.

20:5 *Jealous:* demanding exclusive allegiance. *Inflicting punishment . . . the third and fourth generation:* the intended emphasis is on God's mercy by the contrast between punishment and mercy ("to the thousandth generation"—v. 6). Other Old Testament texts repudiate the idea of punishment devolving on later generations (cf. Dt 24:16; Jer 31:29–30; Ez 18:2–4). Yet it is known that later generations may suffer the punishing effects of sins of earlier generations, but not the guilt.

20:7 *In vain:* i.e., to no good purpose, a general framing of the prohibition which includes swearing falsely, especially in the context of a legal proceeding, but also goes beyond it (cf. Lv 24:16; Prv 30:8–9).

20:8 *Keep it holy:* i.e., to set it apart from the other days of the week, in part, as the following verse explains, by not doing work that is ordinarily done in the course of a week. The special importance of this command can be seen in the fact that, together with vv. 9–11, it represents the longest of the Decalogue's precepts.

20:11 Here, in a formulation which reflects Priestly theology, the veneration of the sabbath is grounded in God's own hallowing of the sabbath in creation. Compare 31:13; Dt 5:15.

20:12–17 The Decalogue falls into two parts: the preceding precepts refer to God, the following refer primarily to one's fellow Israelites.

20:13 *Kill:* as frequent instances of killing in the context of war or certain crimes (see vv. 12–18) demonstrate in the Old Testament, not all killing comes within the scope of the commandment. For this reason, the Hebrew verb translated here as "kill" is often understood as "murder," although it is in fact used in the Old Testament at times for unintentional acts of killing (e.g., Dt 4:41; Jos 20:3) and for legally sanctioned killing (Nm 35:30). The term may originally have designated any killing of another Israelite, including acts of manslaughter, for which the victim's kin could exact vengeance. In the present context, it denotes the killing of one Israelite by another, motivated by hatred or the like (Nm 35:20; cf. Hos 6:9).

20:22—23:33 This collection consists of the civil and religious laws, both apodictic (absolute) and casuistic (conditional), which were given to the people through the mediation of Moses. They will be written down by Moses in 24:4.

20:24 *Where I cause my name to be invoked:* i.e., at the sacred site where God wishes to be worshiped. Dt 12 will demand the centralization of all sacrificial worship in one place chosen by God.

21:1 *Ordinances:* judicial precedents to be used in settling questions of law and custom. More than half of the civil and religious laws in this collection (20:22—23:33), designated in 24:7 as "the book of the covenant," have parallels in the cuneiform laws of the ancient Near East. It is clear that Israel participated in a common legal culture with its neighbors.

21:2 *Slave:* an Israelite could become a slave of another Israelite as a means of paying a debt, or an Israelite could be born into slavery due to a parent's status as a slave. Here a time limit is prescribed for such slavery; other stipulations (vv. 20–21, 26–27) tried to reduce the evils of slavery, but slavery itself is not condemned in the Old Testament.

21:6 *To God:* the ritual of the piercing of the slave's ear, which signified a lifetime commitment to the master, probably took place at the door of the household, where God as protector of the household was called upon as a witness. Another possible location for the ritual would have been the door of the sanctuary, where God or judges would have witnessed the slave's promise of lifetime obedience to his master.

21:8 *Designated her:* intended her as a wife of second rank.

21:12–14 Unintentional homicide is to be punished differently from premeditated, deliberate murder. One who kills unintentionally can seek asylum by grasping the horns of the altar at the local sanctuary. In later Israelite history, when worship was centralized in Jerusalem, cities throughout the realm were designated as places of refuge. Apparently the leaders of the local community were to determine whether or not the homicide was intentional.

21:15 The verb used most often signifies a violent, sometimes deadly, attack. The severe penalty assigned is intended to safeguard the integrity of the family.

21:17 *Curses:* not merely an angrily uttered expletive at one's parents, but a solemn juridical formula of justifiable retribution which was considered to be legally binding and guaranteed by God.

21:22–25 This law of talion is applied here in the specific case of a pregnant woman who, as an innocent bystander, is injured by two fighting men. The law of talion is not held up as a general principle to be applied throughout the book of the covenant. (But see note on Lv 24:19–20.) Here this principle of rigorous accountability aimed to prevent injury to a woman about to give birth by apparently requiring the assailant to have his own wife injured as she was about to bring new life into his family. However, it is debatable whether talion was ever understood or applied literally in Israel. In his Sermon on the Mount, Jesus challenges his audience to find a deeper form of justice than the supposed equilibrium offered by talion (Mt 5:38–40).

21:30 *Ransom:* the amount of money or material goods required to restore the relationship between the relatives of the victim and the negligent owner of the goring ox.

22:1–2 *If a thief is caught:* this seems to be a fragment of what was once a longer law on housebreaking, which has been inserted here into the middle of a law on stealing animals. At night the house-holder would be justified in killing a burglar outright, but not so in the daytime, when the burglar could more easily be caught alive. *He must make full restitution:* this stood originally immediately after 21:37.

22:7 *Brought to God:* either within the household or at the sanctuary, the owner of the house is required to take an oath before God. 22:16 The bride price for virgins: fifty shekels according to Dt 22:29.

22:27 *Despise God:* a turning away from God's authority and so failing to honor God (cf.1 Sm 2:30).

23:14 These three feasts—Passover/Unleavened Bread, Weeks (Pentecost), and Booths (Tabernacles or Succoth/ Sukkoth)—are also listed in 34:18–26; Lv 23; Dt 16.

23:15 *Appear before me:* the original expression was "see my face"; so also in several other places, as 23:17; 34:23–24; Dt 16:16; 31:11.

23:19 *Boil a young goat in its mother's milk:* this command, repeated in 34:26 and Dt 14:21, is difficult to understand. It may originate from a taboo that forbade killing the young that were still nursing from the mother, or that forbade the mixing of life and death: the slaughtered young goat with the milk that previously had nourished its life. The Jewish dietary custom of keeping meat and dairy products separate is based on this command.

23:21 *My authority is within him:* lit., "My name is within him."

23:24 *Sacred stones:* objects that symbolized the presence of Canaanite deities. In general, standing stones served as memorials for deities, persons, or significant events such as military victories or covenant-making. See 24:4.

23:28 *Hornets:* the Hebrew *sir'ah* is a disputed term, but according to ancient interpreters it refers to hornets that were unleashed against the enemy to sting them and cause panic (cf. Dt 7:20; Jos 24:12; Wis 12:8). Others associate the word with plagues or troublesome afflictions.

23:31 *The sea of the Philistines:* the Mediterranean. Only in the time of David and Solomon did the territory of Israel come near to reaching such distant borders.

24:4 *Sacred stones:* stone shafts or slabs, erected as symbols of the fact that each of the twelve tribes had entered into this covenant with God; see 23:24; Gn 28:18.

24:11 *They saw God:* the ancients thought that the sight of God would bring instantaneous death. Cf. 33:20; Gn 16:13; 32:31; Jgs 6:22–23;13:22. *Ate and drank:* partook of the sacrificial meal.

The Book of Ruth

1:1–2 *Back in the time of the judges:* the story looks back three generations before King David (4:17) into the time of the tribal confederation described in the Book of Judges. David's Moabite connections are implied in 1 Sm 22:3–4. *Bethlehem of Judah:* Bethlehem, a town in which part of the Judean clan-division called Ephrathah lived; cf. 1 Chr 2:50–51; 4:4; Mi 5:1. Jos 19:15 mentions a different Bethlehem in the north. *The plateau of Moab:* on the east side of the Jordan valley rift, where the hills facing west get more rain, and where agricultural conditions differ from those in Judah. *Ephrathites:* a reminder of David's origins; cf. Mi 5:1.

1:5 *Boys:* the way the storyteller chooses certain words as guides is shown here; "boy" will not appear again until 4:16.

1:6 *Had seen to his people's needs:* lit., "had visited his people."

1:8 *Mother's house:* the women's part of the home, but also perhaps the proper location for arranging marriage; Sg 3:4; 8:2; Gn 24:28. *Kindness:* Hebrew *hesed.* The powerful relationship term used here will recur in 2:20 and 3:10; kindness operates on both the divine-human and human-human level in Ruth.

1:11 *Other sons . . . husbands:* a reference to a customary practice known from Dt 25:5–10, levirate marriage, which assigns responsibility to the brother-in-law to produce heirs in order to perpetuate the name and hold the patrimonial land of a man who died childless. How far the responsibility extended beyond blood brothers is unclear; cf. Gn 38:8 and the upcoming scene in Ru 4:5-6. Naomi imagines the impossible: were she to have more sons they could take Ruth and Orpah as their wives.

1:16–17 Ruth's adherence to her mother-in-law in 1:14 is now expressed in a profound oath of loyalty, culminating in a formulary found frequently in Samuel and Kings; cf. especially 1 Sm 20:13. *Even death:* burial in Naomi's family tomb means that not even death will separate them.

1:21 Naomi's despair is made clear by her play on the meaning of her name in v. 20 and now by her accusation, like that in many psalms and in Job, that God has acted harshly toward her. The language belongs to the realm of judicial proceedings. By crying out in this way, the faithful Israelite opens the door to change, since the cry assumes that God hears and will do something about such seemingly unjust circumstances.

1:22 Barley and wheat harvests come in succession, from as early as April–May into June–July; Dt 16:9–12 suggests that the grain harvest lasts about seven weeks. The time reference leads effectively to the next episode.

2:1 Kinship ties and responsibilities now become very important. Boaz is introduced as one of a group surrounding Naomi through her husband's kin who are expected to extend care. The particular term used here (*moda'*, "relative") is picked up in 3:2; otherwise, most of the terminology about this responsibility to care will use the vocabulary of redeeming (*go'el*, "redeemer").

2:2 Israelite custom made provision for the poor, the widow, the stranger and the orphan to gather what was left behind by the harvesters, and instructed farmers not to cut to the edges of their fields, for the sake of these marginalized; Lv 19:9–10; 23:22; Dt 24:19-22.

2:4 The story brings Boaz upon the scene quickly, but he moves among his workers with the grace of a man of prominence, greeting them and being received with courtesy. The Hebrew blessing formulas used are frequent in Jewish and Christian liturgies.

2:7 The verse is somewhat garbled, but the points are clear that Ruth has been appropriately deferential in seeking permission to glean, and has worked steadily since arriving. Or perhaps she has waited patiently until Boaz arrives to gain permission.

2:13 *Servant:* only here is the language of servanthood used. Ruth has spoken with very deferential words to Boaz, but then seems to think that she has assumed too much.

2:17 *Ephah:* see note on Is 5:10.

2:20 For the first time, the story uses the Hebrew word *go'el,* "redeemer," for the responsibilities of the circle of kinship surrounding Naomi and Ruth and their deceased relatives. Involved are the recovery or retention of family land (Lv 25:25; 27:9–33; Jer 32:6–25), release of a relative from voluntary servitude to pay debts (Lv 25:47–55), and "redeeming blood" or vengeance, attested in passages which regulate such vengeance. No explicit connection is made elsewhere in the Bible between marriage responsibilities and redeeming.

3:2 Ruth's determined action to bring relief to Naomi's and her own circumstances now impels Naomi to move, using means available in Israelite custom which no one in the story has up to this point brought into play.

3:4 *Uncover a place at his feet:* Naomi advocates a course of action that will lead Boaz to act. Israelite custom and moral expectations strongly suggest that there is no loss of virtue involved in the scene.

3:9 *Spread the wing of your cloak:* Ez 16:8 makes it clear that this is a request for marriage. Ruth connects it to "redeemer" responsibility. A wordplay on "wing" links what Boaz is asked to do to what he has asked God to do for Ruth in 2:12.

3:11 *Worthy woman:* the language corresponds to the description of Boaz in 2:1 (lit., "strong and worthy"); the two worthy people are linked in character to one another, as they have already proven to be in their generous behavior toward the ones in need of their care. The townspeople, lit., "all the gate of my people," will ratify this at the gate in the sequel.

3:12 *Another redeemer closer than I:* Boaz knows of a closer relative who would have a prior right to buy the field and marry Ruth.

4:1 The gate of an Israelite town was the place where commercial and other legal matters were dealt with in publicly witnessed fashion.

4:2 *Ten of the elders:* to serve as judges in legal matters as well as witnesses of the settlement of business affairs; cf. Dt 25:7–9.

4:4 Although the laws governing inheritance by Israelite widows are not specified in the Bible, Naomi seems to have the right of disposal of a piece of Elimelech's land. The redemption custom in Lv 25:25 would then guide the procedure.

4:5–6 Although redemption and levirate practices are not otherwise linked in the Bible, they belong in the same area of need. Boaz claims that buying Elimelech's field obligates the other redeemer to produce an heir for Mahlon, who would then inherit the land. That would jeopardize this redeemer's overall holdings, since he would lose the land he had paid for. He can afford the first step but not the second, and cedes his responsibility to Boaz, who is willing to do both.

4:7 *Take off a sandal:* the legislation in Dt 25:8–10 provides that if a "redeemer" refuses to carry out the obligation of marrying his brother's wife, the woman shall strip off his sandal as a gesture of insult. In later years, when the obligation of carrying out this function of the "redeemer" was no longer keenly felt, the removal of the sandal may have become a formalized way of renouncing the rights/obligations of the "redeemer," as in this text.

4:12 Gn 38 contains a story about Tamar similar to Ruth's in levirate marriage. Judah, under less laudable circumstances, fulfills the same role as Boaz will, and Perez, son of Judah and Tamar, perpetuates the line. Thus two non-Israelite women, Tamar and Ruth, are important links in David's genealogy.

4:16 *Cradled him:* the child belongs to Naomi in the sense that he now becomes the redeemer in the family, as stated in 4:14. This tender act by Naomi is not necessarily adoptive and differs from the relationship in Gn 30:3; cf. Nm 11:12. Naomi now has a "boy" to replace her two lost "boys" in 1:5.

The New Testament

Editors' Introduction

The New Testament forms the second part of the Christian Bible. It consists of twenty-seven books, written in the first and second centuries within the various Christian communities scattered throughout the Roman Empire. Central to the New Testament writings are the gospels of Mark, Matthew, Luke, and John. These gospels are not so much biographies of Jesus as they are narratives that offer a theological presentation of the significance of his message and life. While the four gospels agree on the central meaning of the "Jesus event," they offer four different theological interpretations of that event. Although there is ongoing scholarly debate concerning the precise dating of the gospels, there is a fairly widespread consensus that the *Gospel According to Mark* is the earliest (around 70 AD), followed by Luke (80–90), Matthew (80–90), and John (90–100 AD). In the case of the *Gospel According to Luke,* the author wrote an additional narrative, the *Acts of the Apostles,* chronicling the spread of the Jesus movement after his death, resurrection, and ascension.

The New Testament canon also includes twenty-one letters. These letters are, for the most part, written in the name of one of the important leaders of the early Christian movement and addressed to a particular local community of Christians. The letters frequently offer advice, instruction, clarification, admonition, and encouragement to the members of the various communities with regard to living a Christian life. Of these letters, fourteen have been attributed to St. Paul. However, among these, only seven are considered by biblical scholars to be of undisputed Pauline authorship.

The last book of the New Testament (and of the entire Christian Bible) is the *Book of Revelation,* also referred to as the *Apocalypse of John.* Written during a time of intense persecution of Christians by Roman authorities, it is a visionary, highly symbolic work that has puzzled interpreters and provided inspiration and hope for persecuted Christians throughout the centuries. It has also been a favorite book among sectarian, fringe movements within Christianity, who readily apply its dramatic portrayal of God's final overthrowing of evil to their own victory over their enemies.

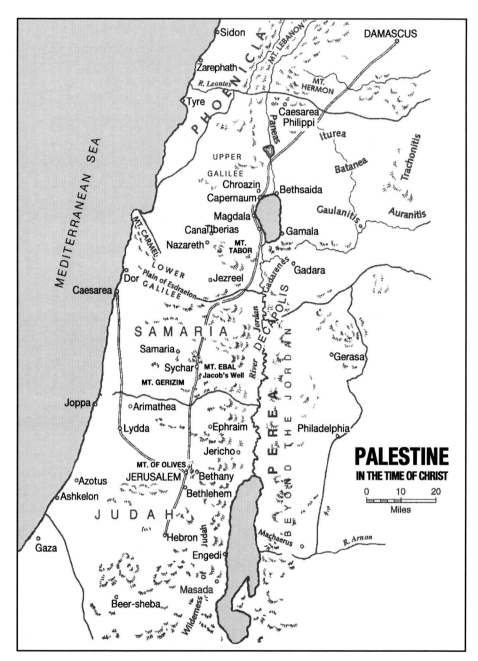

PALESTINE IN THE TIME OF CHRIST
IN THE TIME OF CHRIST

0   10   20
Miles

PALESTINE IN THE TIME OF CHRIST (37 B.C.—36 A.D.) —**(a)** Herod the Great becomes king under the Romans in 37 (and is kept by Caesar Augustus in 29). Herod's reign is one of continual fear of plots and he does not hesitate to execute his own relatives and children, while erecting magnificent edifices. **(b)** Jesus is born sometime before Herod's death (7–6 B.C.?). **(c)** In 4 B.C. Herod's kingdom is divided among his sons. Archelaus becomes ethnarch of Judea but is deposed in 6 A.D. and **Judea** and **Samaria** become part of the Roman province of Syria. Antipas becomes tetrarch of **Galilee** and **Perea** until 39 A.D. Philip becomes tetrarch of **Trachonitis** until his death in 34 A.D. **(d)** In 7 A.D. Annas is made high priest. **(e)** In 15 A.D. Tiberius Caesar becomes Roman Emperor. **(f)** In 26 A.D. Joseph Caiaphas is made high priest. **(g)** In 26 A.D. Pontius Pilate is sent as governor of Judea and outrages the Jews by letting the Romans bring ensigns into the temple.

The Gospel According to Luke

The Gospel according to Luke is the first part of a two-volume work that continues the biblical history of God's dealings with humanity found in the Old Testament, showing how God's promises to Israel have been fulfilled in Jesus and how the salvation promised to Israel and accomplished by Jesus has been extended to the Gentiles. The stated purpose of the two volumes is to provide Theophilus and others like him with certainty—assurance—about earlier instruction they have received (1:4). To accomplish his purpose, Luke shows that the preaching and teaching of the representatives of the early church are grounded in the preaching and teaching of Jesus, who during his historical ministry (Acts 1:21–22) prepared his specially chosen followers and commissioned them to be witnesses to his resurrection and to all else that he did (Acts 10:37–42). This continuity between the historical ministry of Jesus and the ministry of the apostles is Luke's way of guaranteeing the fidelity of the Church's teaching to the teaching of Jesus.

Luke's story of Jesus and the church is dominated by a historical perspective. This history is first of all salvation history. God's divine plan for human salvation was accomplished during the period of Jesus, who through the events of his life (22:22) fulfilled the Old Testament prophecies (4:21; 18:31; 22:37; 24:26–27, 44), and this salvation is now extended to all humanity in the period of the church (Acts 4:12). This salvation history, moreover, is a part of human history. Luke relates the story of Jesus and the church to events in contemporary Palestinian (Lk 1:5; 3:1–2; Acts 4:6) and Roman (Lk 2:1–2; 3:1; Acts 11:28; 18:2, 12) history for, as Paul says in Acts 26:26, "this was not done in a corner" Finally, Luke relates the story of Jesus and the church to contemporaneous church history. Luke is concerned with presenting Christianity as a legitimate form of worship in the Roman world, a religion that is capable of meeting the spiritual needs of a world empire like that of Rome. To this end, Luke depicts the Roman governor Pilate declaring Jesus innocent of any wrongdoing three times (Acts 23:29; 25:25; 26:31–32). At the same time Luke argues in Acts that Christianity is the logical development and proper fulfillment of Judaism and is therefore deserving of the same toleration and freedom traditionally accorded Judaism by Rome (Acts 13:16–41; 23:6–9 24:10–21; 26:2–23).

The prominence given to the period of the church in the story has important consequences for Luke's interpretation of the teachings of Jesus. By presenting the time of the church as a distinct phase of salvation history, Luke accordingly shifts the early Christian emphasis away from the expectation of an imminent parousia to the day-to-day concerns of the Christian community in the world. He does this in the gospel by regularly emphasizing the words "each day" (Lk 9:23; cf. Mk 8:34; Lk 11:3; 16:19; 19:47) in the sayings of Jesus. Although Luke still believes the parousia to be a reality that will come unexpectedly (12:38, 45–46), he is more concerned with presenting the words and deeds of Jesus as guides for the conduct of Christian disciples in the interim period between the ascension and the parousia and with presenting Jesus himself as the model of Christian life and piety.

Throughout the gospel, Luke calls upon the Christian disciple to identify with the master Jesus, who is caring and tender toward the poor and lowly, the outcast, the sinner; and the afflicted, toward all those who recognize their dependence on God (4:18; 6:20–23; 7:36–50; 14:12–14; 15:1–32; 16:19–31; 18:9–14; 19:1–10; 21:1–4), but who is severe toward the proud and self-righteous, and particularly toward those who place their material wealth before the service of God and his people (6:24–26; 12:13–21; 16:13–15, 19–31; 18:9–14, 15–25; cf. 1:50–53). No gospel writer is more concerned than Luke with the mercy and compassion of Jesus (7:41–43; 10:29–37; 13.6–9; 15:11–32). No gospel writer is more concerned with the role of the Spirit in the life of Jesus and the Christian disciple (1:35, 41; 2:25–27; 4:1, 14, 18; 10:21; 11:13; 24:49), with the importance of prayer (3:21; 5:16; 6.12; 9:28; 11:1–13; 18:1–8), or with Jesus' concern for women (7:11–17, 36–50; 8:2–3; 10:38–42). While Jesus calls all humanity to repent (5:32; 10:13; 11:32; 13:1–5; 15:7–10; 16:30; 17:3–4; 24:47), he is particularly demanding of those who would be his disciples. Of them he demands absolute and total detachment from family and material possessions (9:57–62; 12:32–34; 14:25–35). To all who respond in faith and repentance to the word Jesus preaches, he brings salvation (2:30–32; 3:6; 7:50; 8:48, 50; 17:19; 19:9) and peace (2:14; 7:50; 8:48; 19:38, 42) and life (10:25–28; 18:26–30).

Early Christian tradition, from the late second century on, identifies the author of this gospel and of the Acts of the Apostles as Luke, a Syrian from Antioch, who is mentioned in the New Testament in Col 4:14, Phlm 24 and 2 Tm 4:11. The prologue of the gospel makes it clear that Luke is not part of the first generation of Christian disciples but is himself dependent upon the traditions he received from those who were eyewitnesses and ministers of the word (1:2). His two-volume work marks him as someone who was highly literate both in the Old Testament traditions according to the Greek versions and in Hellenistic Greek writings.

Among the likely sources for the composition of this gospel (1:3) were the Gospel of Mark, a written collection of sayings of Jesus known also to the author of the Gospel of Matthew, and other special traditions that were used by Luke alone among the gospel writers. Some hold that Luke used Mark only as a complementary source for rounding out the material he took from other traditions. Because of its dependence on the Gospel of Mark and because details in Luke's Gospel (13:35a; 19:43–44; 21:20; 23:28–31) imply that the author was acquainted with the destruction of the city of Jerusalem by the Romans in A.D. 70, the Gospel of Luke is dated by most scholars after that date; many propose A.D. 80–90 as the time of composition.

Luke's consistent substitution of Greek names for the Aramaic or Hebrew names occurring in his sources (e.g., Lk 23:33; Mk 15:22; Lk 18:41; Mk 10:51), his omission from the gospel of specifically Jewish Christian concerns found in his sources (e.g., Mk 7:1–23), his interest in Gentile Christians (2:30–32; 3:6, 38; 4:16–30; 13:28–30; 14:15–24; 17:11–19 24:47–48), and his incomplete knowledge of Palestinian geography, customs, and practices are among the characteristics of this gospel that suggest that Luke was a non-Palestinian writing to a non-Palestinian audience that was largely made up of Gentile Christians.

The principal divisions of the Gospel according to Luke are the following:

   I. The Prologue (1:1–4)

   II. The Infancy Narrative (1:5—2:52)

   III. The Preparation for the Public Ministry (3:1—4:13)

   IV. The Ministry in Galilee (4:14—9:50)

   V. The Journey to Jerusalem: Luke's Travel Narrative (9:51—19:27)

   VI. The Teaching Ministry in Jerusalem (19:28—21:38)

   VII. The Passion Narrative (22:1—23:56)

   VIII. The Resurrection Narrative (24:1–53)

I: THE PROLOGUE

CHAPTER 1

[1] Since many have undertaken to compile a narrative of the events that have been fulfilled among us, [2] just as those who were eyewitnesses from the beginning and ministers of the word have handed them down to us, [3] I too have decided, after investigating everything accurately anew, to write it down in an orderly sequence for you, most excellent Theophilus, [4] so that you may realize the certainty of the teachings you have received.

II: THE INFANCY NARRATIVE

Announcement of the Birth of John.
[5] In the days of Herod, King of Judea, there was a priest named Zechariah of the priestly division of Abijah; his wife was from the daughters of Aaron, and her name was Elizabeth. [6] Both were righteous in the eyes of God, observing all the commandments and ordinances of the Lord blamelessly. [7] But they had no child, because Elizabeth was barren and both were advanced in years. [8] Once when he was serving as priest in his division's turn before God, [9] according to the practice of the priestly service, he was chosen by lot to enter the sanctuary of the Lord to burn incense. [10] Then, when the whole assembly of the people was praying outside at the hour of the incense offering, [11] the angel of the Lord appeared to him, standing at the right of the altar of incense. [12] Zechariah was troubled by what he saw, and fear came upon him. [13] But the angel said to him, "Do not be afraid, Zechariah, because your prayer has been heard. Your wife Elizabeth will bear you a son, and you shall name him John. [14] And you will have joy and gladness, and many will rejoice at his birth, [15] for he will be great in the sight of [the] Lord. He will drink neither wine nor strong drink. He will be filled with the holy Spirit even from his mother's womb, [16] and he will turn many of the children of Israel to the Lord their God. [17] He will go before him in the spirit and power of Elijah to turn the hearts of fathers toward children and the disobedient to the understanding of the righteous, to prepare a people fit for the Lord." [18] Then Zechariah said to the angel, "How shall I know this? For I am an old man, and my wife is advanced in years." [19] And the angel said to him in reply, "I am Gabriel, who stand before God. I was sent to speak to you and to announce to you this good news. [20] But now you will be speechless and unable to talk until the day these things take place, because you did not believe my words, which will be fulfilled at their proper time."

[21] Meanwhile the people were waiting for Zechariah and were amazed that he stayed so long in the sanctuary. [22] But when he came out, he was unable to speak to them, and they realized that he had seen a vision in the sanctuary. He was gesturing to them but remained mute. [23] Then, when his days of ministry were completed, he went home. [24] After this time his wife Elizabeth conceived, and she went into seclusion for five months, saying, [25] "So has the Lord done for me at a time when he has seen fit to take away my disgrace before others."

Announcement of the Birth of Jesus.
[26] In the sixth month, the angel Gabriel was sent from God to a town of Galilee called Nazareth, [27] to a virgin betrothed to a man named Joseph, of the house of David, and the virgin's name was Mary. [28] And coming to her, he said, "Hail, favored one! The Lord is with you." [29] But she was greatly troubled at what was said and pondered what sort of greeting this might be. [30] Then the angel said to her, "Do not be afraid, Mary, for you have found favor with God. [31] Behold, you will conceive in your womb and bear a son, and you shall name him Jesus. [32] He will be great and will be called Son of the Most High, and the Lord God will give him the throne of David his father, [33] and he will rule over the house of Jacob forever, and of his kingdom there will be no end." [34] But Mary said to the angel, "How can this be, since I

have no relations with a man?" [35] And the angel said to her in reply, "The holy Spirit will come upon you, and the power of the Most High will overshadow you. Therefore the child to be born will be called holy, the Son of God. [36] And behold, Elizabeth, your relative, has also conceived a son in her old age, and this is the sixth month for her who was called barren; [37] for nothing will be impossible for God." [38] Mary said, "Behold, I am the handmaid of the Lord. May it be done to me according to your word." Then the angel departed from her.

Mary Visits Elizabeth. [39] During those days Mary set out and traveled to the hill country in haste to a town of Judah, [40] where she entered the house of Zechariah and greeted Elizabeth. [41] When Elizabeth heard Mary's greeting, the infant leaped in her womb, and Elizabeth, filled with the holy Spirit, [42] cried out in a loud voice and said, "Most blessed are you among women, and blessed is the fruit of your womb. [43] And how does this happen to me, that the mother of my Lord should come to me? [44] For at the moment the sound of your greeting reached my ears, the infant in my womb leaped for joy. [45] Blessed are you who believed that what was spoken to you by the Lord would be fulfilled."

The Canticle of Mary. [46] And Mary said:

"My soul proclaims the greatness of the Lord;
[47]   my spirit rejoices in God my savior.
[48] For he has looked upon his handmaid's
        lowliness;
    behold, from now on will all ages call me
        blessed.
[49] The Mighty One has done great things for me,
    and holy is his name.
[50] His mercy is from age to age
    to those who fear him.
[51] He has shown might with his arm, dispersed
        the arrogant of mind and heart.
[52] He has thrown down the rulers from their
        thrones
    but lifted up the lowly.
[53] The hungry he has filled with good things;
    the rich he has sent away empty.
[54] He has helped Israel his servant,

remembering his mercy,
[55] according to his promise to our fathers,
    to Abraham and to his descendants
        forever."

[56] Mary remained with her about three months and then returned to her home.

The Birth of John. [57] When the time arrived for Elizabeth to have her child she gave birth to a son. [58] Her neighbors and relatives heard that the Lord had shown his great mercy toward her, and they rejoiced with her. [59] When they came on the eighth day to circumcise h the child, they were going to call him Zechariah after his father, [60] but his mother said in reply, "No. He will be called John." [61] But they answered her, "There is no one among your relatives who has this name." [62] So they made signs, asking his father what he wished him to be called. [63] He asked for a tablet and wrote, "John is his name," and all were amazed. [64] Immediately his mouth was opened, his tongue freed, and he spoke blessing God. [65] Then fear came upon all their neighbors, and all these matters were discussed throughout the hill country of Judea. [66] All who heard these things took them to heart, saying, "What, then, will this child be?" For surely the hand of the Lord was with him.

The Canticle of Zechariah. [67] Then Zechariah his father, filled with the holy Spirit, prophesied, saying:

[68] "Blessed be the Lord, the God of Israel, for he
        has visited and brought redemption to his
        people.
[69] He has raised up a horn for our salvation
    within the house of David his servant,
[70] even as he promised through the mouth
        of his holy prophets from of old:
[71]   salvation from our enemies and from
        the hand of all who hate us,
[72] to show mercy to our fathers
    and to be mindful of his holy covenant
[73] and of the oath he swore to Abraham our
        father,
    and to grant us that,
[74] rescued from the hand of enemies,
    without fear we might worship him

75 in holiness and righteousness
    before him all our days.
76 And you, child, will be called prophet of the
    Most High,
      for you will go before the Lord to prepare
      his ways,
77 to give his people knowledge of salvation
    through the forgiveness of their sins,
78 because of the tender mercy of our God
    by which the daybreak from on high
      will visit us
79 to shine on those who sit in darkness and
    death's shadow,
    to guide our feet into the path of peace."

80 The child grew and became strong in spirit, and he was in the desert until the day of his manifestation to Israel.

CHAPTER 2

The Birth of Jesus. 1 In those days a decree went out from Caesar Augustus that the whole world should be enrolled. 2 This was the first enrollment, when Quirinius was governor of Syria. 3 So all went to be enrolled, each to his own town. 4 And Joseph too went up from Galilee from the town of Nazareth to Judea, to the city of David that is called Bethlehem, because he was of the house and family of David, 5 to be enrolled with Mary, his betrothed, who was with child. 6 While they were there, the time came for her to have her child, 7 and she gave birth to her firstborn son. She wrapped him in swaddling clothes and laid him in a manger, because there was no room for them in the inn.

8 Now there were shepherds in that region living in the fields and keeping the night watch over their flock. 9 The angel of the Lord appeared to them and the glory of the Lord shone around them, and they were struck with great fear. 10 The angel said to them, "Do not be afraid; for behold, I proclaim to you good news of great joy that will be for all the people. 11 For today in the city of David a savior has been born for you who is Messiah and Lord. 12 And this will be a sign for you: you will find an infant wrapped in swaddling clothes and lying in a manger." 13 And suddenly there was a multitude of the heavenly host with the angel, praising God and saying:

14 "Glory to God in the highest
    and on earth peace to those on whom
      his favor rests."

The Visit of the Shepherds. 15 When the angels went away from them to heaven, the shepherds said to one another, "Let us go, then, to Bethlehem to see this thing that has taken place, which the Lord has made known to us." 16 So they went in haste and found Mary and Joseph, and the infant lying in the manger. 17 When they saw this, they made known the message that had been told them about this child. 18 All who heard it were amazed by what had been told them by the shepherds. 19 And Mary kept all these things, reflecting on them in her heart. 20 Then the shepherds returned, glorifying and praising God for all they had heard and seen, just as it had been told to them.

The Circumcision and Naming of Jesus. 21 When eight days were completed for his circumcision, he was named Jesus, the name given him by the angel before he was conceived in the womb.

The Presentation in the Temple. 22 When the days were completed for their purification according to the law of Moses, they took him up to Jerusalem to present him to the Lord, 23 just as it is written in the law of the Lord, "Every male that opens the womb shall be consecrated to the Lord," 24 and to offer the sacrifice of "a pair of turtledoves or two young pigeons," in accordance with the dictate in the law of the Lord.

25 Now there was a man in Jerusalem whose name was Simeon. This man was righteous and devout, awaiting the consolation of Israel, and the holy Spirit was upon him. 26 It had been revealed to him by the holy Spirit that he should not see death before he had seen the Messiah of the Lord. 27 He came in the Spirit into the temple; and when the parents brought in the child Jesus to perform the custom of the law in regard to

him, [28] he took him into his arms and blessed God, saying:

[29] "Now, Master, you may let your servant go
        in peace, according to your word,
[30] for my eyes have seen your salvation,
[31]   which you prepared in sight of all the
            peoples,
[32] a light for revelation to the Gentiles,
            and glory for your people Israel."

[33] The child's father and mother were amazed at what was said about him; [34] and Simeon blessed them and said to Mary his mother, "Behold, this child is destined for the fall and rise of many in Israel, and to be a sign that will be contradicted [35] (and you yourself a sword will pierce) so that the thoughts of many hearts may be revealed." [36] There was also a prophetess, Anna, the daughter of Phanuel, of the tribe of Asher. She was advanced in years, having lived seven years with her husband after her marriage, [37] and then as a widow until she was eighty-four. She never left the temple, but worshiped night and day with fasting and prayer. [38] And coming forward at that very time, she gave thanks to God and spoke about the child to all who were awaiting the redemption of Jerusalem.

The Return to Nazareth. [39] When they had fulfilled all the prescriptions of the law of the Lord, they returned to Galilee, to their own town of Nazareth.' [40] The child grew and became strong, filled with wisdom; and the favor of God was upon him.

The Boy Jesus in the Temple. [41] Each year his parents went to Jerusalem for the feast of Passover, [42] and when he was twelve years old, they went up according to festival custom. [43] After they had completed its days, as they were returning, the boy Jesus remained behind in Jerusalem, but his parents did not know it. [44] Thinking that he was in the caravan, they journeyed for a day and looked for him among their relatives and acquaintances, [45] but not finding him, they returned to Jerusalem to look for him. [46] After three days they found him in the temple, sitting in the midst of the teachers, listening to them and asking them questions, [47] and all who

heard him were astounded at his understanding and his answers. [48] When his parents saw him, they were astonished, and his mother said to him, "Son, why have you done this to us? Your father and I have been looking for you with great anxiety." [49] And he said to them, "Why were you looking for me? Did you not know that I must be in my Father's house?" [50] But they did not understand what he said to them. [51] He went down with them and came to Nazareth, and was obedient to them; and his mother kept all these things in her heart. [52] And Jesus advanced [in] wisdom and age and favor before God and man.

III: THE PREPARATION FOR THE PUBLIC MINISTRY

CHAPTER 3

The Preaching of John the Baptist. [1] In the fifteenth year of the reign of Tiberius Caesar, when Pontius Pilate was governor of Judea, and Herod was tetrarch of Galilee, and his brother Philip tetrarch of the region of Ituraea and Trachonitis, and Lysanias was tetrarch of Abilene, [2] during the high priesthood of Annas and Caiaphas, the word of God came to John the son of Zechariah in the desert. [3] He went throughout [the] whole region of the Jordan, proclaiming a baptism of repentance for the forgiveness of sins, [4] as it is written in the book of the words of the prophet Isaiah:

"A voice of one crying out in the desert:
'Prepare the way of the Lord,
    make straight his paths.
[5] Every valley shall be filled
        and every mountain and hill shall be
            made low.
    The winding roads shall be made straight,
        and the rough ways made smooth,
[6] and all flesh shall see the salvation of God.'"

[7] He said to the crowds who came out to be baptized by him, "You brood of vipers! Who warned you to flee from the coming wrath? [8] Produce

good fruits as evidence of your repentance; and do not begin to say to yourselves, `We have Abraham as our father,' for I tell you, God can raise up children to Abraham from these stones. [9] Even now the ax lies at the root of the trees. Therefore every tree that does not produce good fruit will be cut down and thrown into the fire."

[10] And the crowds asked him, "What then should we do?" [11] He said to them in reply, "Whoever has two tunics should share with the person who has none. And whoever has food should do likewise." [12] Even tax collectors came to be baptized and they said to him, "Teacher, what should we do?" [13] He answered them, "Stop collecting more than what is prescribed." [14] Soldiers also asked him, "And what is it that we should do?" He told them, "Do not practice extortion, do not falsely accuse anyone, and be satisfied with your wages."

[15] Now the people were filled with expectation, and all were asking in their hearts whether John might be the Messiah. [16] John answered them all, saying, "I am baptizing you with water, but one mightier than I is coming. I am not worthy to loosen the thongs of his sandals. He will baptize you with the holy Spirit and fire. [17] His winnowing fan is in his hand to clear his threshing floor and to gather the wheat into his barn, but the chaff he will burn with unquenchable fire." [18] Exhorting them in many other ways, he preached good news to the people. [19] Now Herod the tetrarch, who had been censured by him because of Herodias, his brother's wife, and because of all the evil deeds Herod had committed, [20] added still another to these by [also] putting John in prison.

The Baptism of Jesus. [21] After all the people had been baptized and Jesus also had been baptized and was praying, heaven was opened [22] and the holy Spirit descended upon him in bodily form like a dove. And a voice came from heaven, "You are my beloved Son; with you I am well pleased."

The Genealogy of Jesus. [23] When Jesus began his ministry he was about thirty years of age. He was the son, as was thought, of Joseph, the son of Heli, [24] the son of Matthat, the son of Levi, the son of Melchi, the son of Jannai, the son of Joseph, [25] the son of Mattathias, the son of Amos, the son of Nahum, the son of Esli, the son of Naggai, [26] the son of Maath, the son of Mattathias, the son of Semein, the son of Josech, the son of Joda, [27] the son of Joanan, the son of Rhesa, the son of Zerubbabel, the son of Shealtiel, the son of Neri, [28] the son of Melchi, the son of Addi, the son of Cosam, the son of Elmadam, the son of Er, [29] the son of Joshua, the son of Eliezer, the son of Jorim, the son of Matthat, the son of Levi, [30] the son of Simeon, the son of Judah, the son of Joseph, the son of Jonam, the son of Eliakim, [31] the son of Melea, the son of Menna, the son of Mattatha, the son of Nathan, the son of David, [32] the son of Jesse," the son of Obed, the son of Boaz, the son of Sala, the son of Nahshon, [33] the son of Amminadab, the son of Admin, the son of Arni, the son of Hezron, the son of Perez, the son of Judah, [34] the son of Jacob, the son of Isaac, the son of Abraham, the son of Terah, the son of Nahor, [35] the son of Serug, the son of Reu, the son of Peleg, the son of Eber, the son of Shelah, [36] the son of Cainan, the son of Arphaxad, the son of Shem, the son of Noah, the son of Lamech, [37] the son of Methuselah, the son of Enoch, the son of Jared, the son of Mahalaleel, the son of Cainan, [38] the son of Enos, the son of Seth, the son of Adam, the son of God.

CHAPTER 4

The Temptation of Jesus. [1] Filled with the holy Spirit, Jesus returned from the Jordan and was led by the Spirit into the desert [2] for forty days, to be tempted by the devil. He ate nothing during those days, and when they were over he was hungry. [3] The devil said to him, "If you are the Son of God, command this stone to become bread." [4] Jesus answered him, "It is written, 'One does not live by bread alone.'" [5] Then he took him up and showed him all the kingdoms of the world in a single instant. [6] The devil said to him, "I shall give to you all this power and their glory; for it has been handed over to me, and I may give it to whomever I wish. [7] All this will be yours, if you worship me." [8] Jesus said to him in reply, "It is written:

'You shall worship the Lord, your God,
and him alone shall you serve.'"

[9] Then he led him to Jerusalem, made him stand on the parapet of the temple, and said to him, "If you are the Son of God, throw yourself down from here, [10] for it is written:

'He will command his angels concerning
you,
to guard you,'

[11] and:
'With their hands they will support you,
lest you dash your foot against a stone.'"

[12] Jesus said to him in reply, "It also says, 'You shall not put the Lord, your God, to the test.'" [13] When the devil had finished every temptation, he departed from him for a time.

IV: THE MINISTRY
IN GALILEE

The Beginning of the Galilean Ministry.
[14] Jesus returned to Galilee in the power of the Spirit, and news of him spread throughout the whole region. [15] He taught in their synagogues and was praised by all.

The Rejection at Nazareth. [16] He came to Nazareth, where he had grown up, and went according to his custom into the synagogue on the sabbath day. He stood up to read [17] and was handed a scroll of the prophet Isaiah. He unrolled the scroll and found the passage where it was written:

[18] "The Spirit of the Lord is upon me, because
he has anointed me to bring glad tidings
to the poor.
He has sent me to proclaim liberty to captives
and recovery of sight to the blind, to let
the oppressed go free,
[19] and to proclaim a year acceptable to the Lord."

[20] Rolling up the scroll, he handed it back to the attendant and sat down, and the eyes of all in the synagogue looked intently at him. [21] He said to them, "Today this scripture passage is fulfilled in your hearing." [22] And all spoke highly of him and were amazed at the gracious words that came from his mouth. They also asked, "Isn't this the son of Joseph?" [23] He said to them, "Surely you will quote me this proverb, 'Physician, cure yourself,' and say, 'Do here in your native place the things that we heard were done in Capernaum.'" [24] And he said, "Amen, I say to you, no prophet is accepted in his own native place. [25] Indeed, I tell you, there were many widows in Israel in the days of Elijah when the sky was closed for three and a half years and a severe famine spread over the entire land. [26] It was to none of these that Elijah was sent, but only to a widow in Zarephath in the land of Sidon. [27] Again, there were many lepers in Israel during the time of Elisha the prophet; yet not one of them was cleansed, but only Naaman the Syrian." [28] When the people in the synagogue heard this, they were all filled with fury. [29] They rose up, drove him out of the town, and led him to the brow of the hill on which their town had been built, to hurl him down headlong. [30] But he passed through the midst of them and went away.

The Cure of a Demoniac. [31] Jesus then went down to Capernaum, a town of Galilee. He taught them on the Sabbath, [32] and they were astonished at his teaching because he spoke with authority. [33] In the synagogue there was a man with the spirit of an unclean demon, " and he cried out in a loud voice, [34] "Ha! What have you to do with us, Jesus of Nazareth? Have you come to destroy us? I know who you are—the Holy One of God!" [35] Jesus rebuked him and said, "Be quiet! Come out of him!" Then the demon threw the man down in front of them and came out of him without doing him any harm. [36] They were all amazed and said to one another, "What is there about his word? For with authority and power he commands the unclean spirits, and they come out." [37] And news of him spread everywhere in the surrounding region.

The Cure of Simon's Mother-in-Law.
[38] After After he left the synagogue, he entered

the house of Simon. Simon's mother-in-law was afflicted with a severe fever, and they interceded with him about her. [39] He stood over her, rebuked the fever, and it left her. She got up immediately and waited on them.

Other Healings. [40] At sunset, all who had people sick with various diseases brought them to him. He laid his hands on each of them and cured them. [41] And demons also came out from many, shouting, "You are the Son of God." But he rebuked them and did not allow them to speak because they knew that he was the Messiah.

Jesus Leaves Capernaum. [42] At day-break, Jesus left and went to a deserted place. The crowds went looking for him, and when they came to him, they tried to prevent him from leaving them. [43] But he said to them, "To the other towns also I must proclaim the good news of the kingdom of God, because for this purpose I have been sent." [44] And he was preaching in the synagogues of Judea.

CHAPTER 5

The Call of Simon the Fisherman. [1] While the crowd was pressing in on Jesus and listening to the word of God, he was standing by the Lake of Gennesaret. [2] He saw two boats there alongside the lake; the fishermen had disembarked and were washing their nets. [3] Getting into one of the boats, the one belonging to Simon, he asked him to put out a short distance from the shore. Then he sat down and taught the crowds from the boat. [4] After he had finished speaking, he said to Simon, "Put out into deep water and lower your nets for a catch." [5] Simon said in reply, "Master, we have worked hard all night and have caught nothing, but at your command I will lower the nets." [6] When they had done this, they caught a great number of fish and their nets were tearing. [7] They signaled to their partners in the other boat to come to help them. They came and filled both boats so that they were in danger of sinking. [8] When Simon Peter saw this, he fell at the knees of Jesus and said, "Depart from me,

Lord, for I am a sinful man." [9] For astonishment at the catch of fish they had made seized him and all those with him, [10] and likewise James and John, the sons of Zebedee, who were partners of Simon. Jesus said to Simon, "Do not be afraid; from now on you will be catching men." [11] When they brought their boats to the shore, they left everything and followed him.

The Cleansing of a Leper. [12] Now there was a man full of leprosy in one of the towns where he was; and when he saw Jesus, he fell prostrate, pleaded with him, and said, "Lord, if you wish, you can make me clean." [13] Jesus stretched out his hand, touched him, and said, "I do will it. Be made clean." And the leprosy left him immediately. [14] Then he ordered him not to tell anyone, but "Go, show yourself to the priest and offer for your cleansing what Moses prescribed; that will be proof for them." [15] The report about him spread all the more, and great crowds assembled to listen to him and to be cured of their ailments, [16] but he would withdraw to deserted places to pray.

The Healing of a Paralytic. [17] One day as Jesus was teaching, Pharisees and teachers of the law were sitting there who had come from every village of Galilee and Judea and Jerusalem, and the power of the Lord was with him for healing. [18] And some men brought on a stretcher a man who was paralyzed; they were trying to bring him in and set [him] in his presence. [19] But not finding a way to bring him in because of the crowd, they went up on the roof and lowered him on the stretcher through the tiles into the middle in front of Jesus. [20] When he saw their faith, he said, "As for you, your sins are forgiven." [21] Then the scribes and Pharisees began to ask themselves, "Who is this who speaks blasphemies? Who but God alone can forgive sins?" [22] Jesus knew their thoughts and said to them in reply, "What are you thinking in your hearts? [23] Which is easier, to say, 'Your sins are forgiven,' or to say, 'Rise and walk'? [24] But that you may know that the Son of Man has authority on earth to forgive sins"—he said to the man who was paralyzed, "I say to you, rise, pick up your stretcher, and go home." [25] He stood up immediately before them, picked up what he had been lying on, and went home, glorifying God. ²⁶ Then astonishment seized them all and they glorified God, and, struck with awe, they said, "We have seen incredible things today."

The Call of Levi. ²⁷ After this he went out and saw a tax collector named Levi sitting at the customs post. He said to him, "Follow me." ²⁸ And leaving everything behind, he got up and followed him. ²⁹ Then Levi gave a great banquet for him in his house, and a large crowd of tax collectors and others were at table with them. ³⁰ The Pharisees and their scribes complained to his disciples, saying, "Why do you eat and drink with tax collectors and sinners?" ³¹ Jesus said to them in reply, "Those who are healthy do not need a physician, but the sick do. ³² I have not come to call the righteous to repentance but sinners."

The Question about Fasting. ³³ And they said to him, "The disciples of John fast often and offer prayers, and the disciples of the Pharisees do the same; but yours eat and drink." ³⁴ Jesus answered them, "Can you make the wedding guests fast while the bridegroom is with them? ³⁵ But the days will come, and when the bridegroom is taken away from them, then they will fast in those days." ³⁶ And he also told them a parable. "No one tears a piece from a new cloak to patch an old one. Otherwise, he will tear the new and the piece from it will not match the old cloak. ³⁷ Likewise, no one pours new wine into old wineskins. Otherwise, the new wine will burst the skins, and it will be spilled, and the skins will be ruined. ³⁸ Rather, new wine must be poured into fresh wineskins. ³⁹ [And] no one who has been drinking old wine desires new, for he says, 'The old is good.'"

CHAPTER 6

Debates about the Sabbath. ¹ While he was going through a field of grain on a sabbath, his disciples were picking the heads of grain, rubbing them in their hands, and eating them. ² Some Pharisees said, "Why are you doing what is unlawful on the sabbath?" ³ Jesus said to them in reply, "Have you not read what David did when he and those [who were] with him were hungry? ⁴ [How] he went into the house of God, took the bread of offering, which only the priests could lawfully eat, ate of it, and shared it with his companions." ⁵ Then he said to them, "The Son of Man is lord of the sabbath."

⁶ On another sabbath he went into the synagogue and taught, and there was a man there whose right hand was withered. ⁷ The scribes and the Pharisees watched him closely to see if he would cure on the sabbath so that they might discover a reason to accuse him. ⁸ But he realized their intentions and said to the man with the withered hand, "Come up and stand before us." And he rose and stood there. ⁹ Then Jesus said to them, "I ask you, is it lawful to do good on the sabbath rather than to do evil, to save life rather than to destroy it?" ¹⁰ Looking around at them all, he then said to him, "Stretch out your hand." He did so and his hand was restored. ¹¹ But they became enraged and discussed together what they might do to Jesus.

The Mission of the Twelve. ¹² In those days he departed to the mountain to pray, and he spent the night in prayer to God. ¹³ When day came, he called his disciples to himself, and from them he chose Twelve, whom he also named apostles: ¹⁴ Simon, whom he named Peter, and his brother Andrew, James, John, Philip, Bartholomew, ¹⁵ Matthew, Thomas, James the son of Alphaeus, Simon who was called a Zealot, ¹⁶ and Judas the son of James, and Judas Iscariot, who became a traitor.

Ministering to a Great Multitude. ¹⁷ And he came down with them and stood on a stretch of level ground. A great crowd of his disciples and a large number of the people from all Judea and Jerusalem and the coastal region of Tyre and Sidon ¹⁸ came to hear him and to be healed of their diseases; and even those who were tormented by unclean spirits were cured. ¹⁹ Everyone in the crowd sought to touch him because power came forth from him and healed them all.

Sermon on the Plain. ²⁰ And raising his eyes toward his disciples he said:

"Blessed are you who are poor,
> for the kingdom of God is yours.

²¹ Blessed are you who are now hungry, for you
> will be satisfied.

Blessed are you who are now weeping, for
> you will laugh.

²² Blessed are you when people hate you,
> and when they exclude and insult you,
> and denounce your name as evil
> on account of the Son of Man.

²³ Rejoice and leap for joy on that day! Behold, your reward will be great in heaven. For their ancestors treated the prophets in the same way.

²⁴ But woe to you who are rich,
> for you have received your consolation.

²⁵ But woe to you who are filled now,
> for you will be hungry.

Woe to you who laugh now,
> for you will grieve and weep.

²⁶ Woe to you when all speak well of you,
> for their ancestors treated the false
> > prophets in this way.

Love of Enemies. ²⁷ "But to you who hear I say, love your enemies, do good to those who hate you, ²⁸ bless those who curse you, pray for those who mistreat you. ²⁹ To the person who strikes you on one cheek, offer the other one as well, and from the person who takes your cloak, do not withhold even your tunic. ³⁰ Give to everyone who asks of you, and from the one who takes what is yours do not demand it back. ³¹ Do to others as you would have them do to you." ³² For if you love those who love you, what credit is that to you? Even sinners love those who love them. ³³ And if you do good to those who do good to you, what credit is that to you? Even sinners do the same. ³⁴ If you lend money to those from whom you expect repayment, what credit [is] that to you? Even sinners lend to sinners, and get back the same amount. ³⁵ But rather, love your enemies and do good to them, and lend expecting nothing back; then your reward will be great and you will be children of the Most High, for he himself is kind to the ungrateful and the wicked. ³⁶ Be merciful, just as [also] your Father is merciful.

Judging Others. ³⁷ "Stop judging and you will not be judged. Stop condemning and you will not be condemned. Forgive and you will be forgiven. ³⁸ Give and gifts will be given to you; a good measure, packed together, shaken down, and overflowing, will be poured into your lap. For the measure with which you measure will in return be measured out to you." ³⁹ And he told them a parable, "Can a blind person guide a blind person? Will not both fall into a pit?" ⁴⁰ No disciple is superior to the teacher; but when fully trained, every disciple will be like his teacher. ⁴¹ Why do you notice the splinter in your brother's eye, but do not perceive the wooden beam in your own? ⁴² How can you say to your brother, 'Brother, let me remove that splinter in your eye,' when you do not even notice the wooden beam in your own eye? You hypocrite! Remove the wooden beam from your eye first; then you will see clearly to remove the splinter in your brother's eye.

A Tree Known by Its Fruit. ⁴³ "A good tree does not bear rotten fruit, nor does a rotten tree bear good fruit. ⁴⁴ For every tree is known by its own fruit. For people do not pick figs from thornbushes, nor do they gather grapes from brambles. ⁴⁵ A good person out of the store of goodness in his heart produces good, but an evil person out of a store of evil produces evil; for from the fullness of the heart the mouth speaks.

The Two Foundations. ⁴⁶ "Why do you call me, 'Lord, Lord,' but not do what I command? ⁴⁷ I will show you what someone is like who comes to me, listens to my words, and acts on them. ⁴⁸ That one is like a person building a house, who dug deeply and laid the foundation on rock; when the flood came, the river burst against that house but could not shake it because it had been well built. ⁴⁹ But the one who listens and does not act is like a person who built a house on the ground without a foundation. When the river burst against it, it collapsed at once and was completely destroyed."

CHAPTER 7

The Healing of a Centurion's Slave. [1] When he had finished all his words to the people, he entered Capernaum. [2] A centurion there had a slave who was ill and about to die, and he was valuable to him. [3] When he heard about Jesus, he sent elders of the Jews to him, asking him to come and save the life of his slave. [4] They approached Jesus and strongly urged him to come, saying, "He deserves to have you do this for him, [5] for he loves our nation and he built the synagogue for us." [6] And Jesus went with them, but when he was only a short distance from the house, the centurion sent friends to tell him, "Lord, do not trouble yourself, for I am not worthy to have you enter under my roof. [7] Therefore, I did not consider myself worthy to come to you; but say the word and let my servant be healed. [8] For I too am a person subject to authority, with soldiers subject to me. And I say to one, 'Go,' and he goes; and to another, 'Come here,' and he comes; and to my slave, 'Do this,' and he does it." [9] When Jesus heard this he was amazed at him and, turning, said to the crowd following him, "I tell you, not even in Israel have I found such faith." [10] When the messengers returned to the house, they found the slave in good health.

Raising of the Widow's Son. [11] Soon afterward he journeyed to a city called Nain, and his disciples and a large crowd accompanied him. [12] As he drew near to the gate of the city, a man who had died was being carried out, the only son of his mother, and she was a widow. A large crowd from the city was with her. [13] When the Lord saw her, he was moved with pity for her and said to her, "Do not weep." [14] He stepped forward and touched the coffin; at this the bearers halted, and he said, "Young man, I tell you, arise!" [15] The dead man sat up and began to speak, and Jesus gave him to his mother. [16] Fear seized them all, and they glorified God, exclaiming, "A great prophet has arisen in our midst," and "God has visited his people." [17] This report about him spread through the whole of Judea and in all the surrounding region.

The Messengers from John the Baptist. [18] The disciples of John told him about all these things. John summoned two of his disciples [19] and sent them to the Lord to ask, "Are you the one who is to come, or should we look for another?" [20] When the men came to him, they said, "John the Baptist has sent us to you to ask, `Are you the one who is to come, or should we look for another?'" [21] At that time he cured many of their diseases, sufferings, and evil spirits; he also granted sight to many who were blind. [22] And he said to them in reply, "Go and tell John what you have seen and heard: the blind regain their sight, the lame walk, lepers are cleansed, the deaf hear, the dead are raised, the poor have the good news pro-claimed to them. [23] And blessed is the one who takes no offense at me."

Jesus' Testimony to John. [24] When the messengers of John had left, Jesus began to speak to the crowds about John. "What did you go out to the desert to see—a reed swayed by the wind? [25] Then what did you go out to see? Someone dressed in fine garments? Those who dress luxuriously and live sumptuously are found in royal palaces. [26] Then what did you go out to see? A prophet? Yes, I tell you, and more than a prophet. [27] This is the one about whom scripture says:

'Behold, I am sending my messenger
  ahead of you,
  he will prepare your way before you.'

[28] I tell you, among those born of women, no one is greater than John; yet the least in the kingdom of God is greater than he." [29] (All the people who listened, including the tax collectors, and who were baptized with the baptism of John, acknowledged the righteousness of God; [30] but the Pharisees and scholars of the law, who were not baptized by him, rejected the plan of God for themselves.)

[31] "Then to what shall I compare the people of this generation? What are they like? [32] They are

like children who sit in the marketplace and call to one another,

> 'We played the flute for you, but you did not dance.
> We sang a dirge, but you did not weep.'

[33] For John the Baptist came neither eating food nor drinking wine, and you said, 'He is possessed by a demon.' [34] The Son of Man came eating and drinking and you said, `Look, he is a glutton and a drunkard, a friend of tax collectors and sinners.' [35] But wisdom is vindicated by all her children."

The Pardon of the Sinful Woman. [36] A Pharisee invited him to dine with him, and he entered the Pharisee's house and reclined at table. [37] Now there was a sinful woman in the city who learned that he was at table in the house of the Pharisee. Bringing an alabaster flask of ointment, [38] she stood behind him at his feet weeping and began to bathe his feet with her tears. Then she wiped them with her hair, kissed them, and anointed them with the ointment. [39] When the Pharisee who had invited him saw this he said to himself, "If this man were a prophet, he would know who and what sort of woman this is who is touching him, that she is a sinner." [40] Jesus said to him in reply, "Simon, I have something to say to you." "Tell me, teacher," he said. [41] "Two people were in debt to a certain creditor; one owed five hundred days' wages and the other owed fifty. [42] Since they were unable to repay the debt, he forgave it for both. Which of them will love him more?" [43] Simon said in reply, "The one, I suppose, whose larger debt was forgiven." He said to him, "You have judged rightly." [44] Then he turned to the woman and said to Simon, "Do you see this woman? When I entered your house, you did not give me water for my feet, but she has bathed them with her tears and wiped them with her hair. [45] You did not give me a kiss, but she has not ceased kissing my feet since the time I entered. [46] You did not anoint my head with oil, but she anointed my feet with ointment. [47] So I tell you, her many sins have been forgiven; hence, she has shown great love. But the one to

whom little is forgiven, loves little." [48] He said to her, "Your sins are forgiven." [49] The others at table said to themselves, "Who is this who even forgives sins?" [50] But he said to the woman, "Your faith has saved you; go in peace."

CHAPTER 8

Galilean Women Follow Jesus. [1] Afterward he journeyed from one town and village to another, preaching and proclaiming the good news of the kingdom of God. Accompanying him were the Twelve [2] and some women who had been cured of evil spirits and infirmities, Mary, called Magdalene, from whom seven demons had gone out, [3] Joanna, the wife of Herod's steward Chuza, Susanna, and many others who provided for them out of their resources.

The Parable of the Sower. [4] When a large crowd gathered, with people from one town after another journeying to him, he spoke in a parable. [5] "A sower went out to sow his seed. And as he sowed, some seed fell on the path and was trampled, and the birds of the sky ate it up. [6] Some seed fell on rocky ground, and when it grew, it withered for lack of moisture. [7] Some seed fell among thorns, and the thorns grew with it and choked it. [8] And some seed fell on good soil, and when it grew, it produced fruit a hundredfold." After saying this, he called out, "Whoever has ears to hear ought to hear."

The Purpose of the Parables. [9] Then his disciples asked him what the meaning of this parable might be. [10] He answered, "Knowledge of the mysteries of the kingdom of God has been granted to you; but to the rest, they are made known through parables so that 'they may look but not see, and hear but not understand.'

The Parable of the Sower Explained. [11] "This is the meaning of the parable. The seed is the word of God. [12] Those on the path are the ones who have heard, but the devil comes and takes away the word from their hearts that they may not believe and be saved. ¹³ Those on rocky ground are the ones who, when they hear, receive the word with joy, but they have no root; they believe only for a time and fall away in time of trial. ¹⁴ As for the seed that fell among thorns, they are the ones who have heard, but as they go along, they are choked by the anxieties and riches and pleasures of life, and they fail to produce mature fruit. ¹⁵ But as for the seed that fell on rich soil, they are the ones who, when they have heard the word, embrace it with a generous and good heart, and bear fruit through perseverance.

The Parable of the Lamp. ¹⁶ "No one who lights a lamp conceals it with a vessel or sets it under a bed; rather, he places it on a lampstand so that those who enter may see the light. ¹⁷ For there is nothing hidden that will not become visible, and nothing secret that will not be known and come to light. ¹⁸ Take care, then, how you hear. To anyone who has, more will be given, and from the one who has not, even what he seems to have will be taken away."

Jesus and His Family. ¹⁹ Then his mother and his brothers came to him but were unable to join him because of the crowd. ²⁰ He was told, "Your mother and your brothers are standing outside and they wish to see you." ²¹ He said to them in reply, "My mother and my brothers are those who hear the word of God and act on it."

The Calming of a Storm at Sea. ²² One day he got into a boat with his disciples and said to them, "Let us cross to the other side of the lake." So they set sail, ²³ and while they were sailing he fell asleep. A squall blew over the lake, and they were taking in water and were in danger. ²⁴ They came and woke him saying, "Master, master, we are perishing!" He awakened, rebuked the wind and the waves, and they subsided and there was a calm. ²⁵ Then he asked them, "Where is your faith?" But they were filled with awe and amazed and said to one another, "Who then is this, who commands even the winds and the sea, and they obey him?"

The Healing of the Gerasene Demoniac. ²⁶ Then they sailed to the territory of the Gerasenes, which is opposite Galilee. ²⁷ When he came ashore a man from the town who was possessed by demons met him. For a long time he had not worn clothes; he did not live in a house, but lived among the tombs. ²⁸ When he saw Jesus, he cried out and fell down before him; in a loud voice he shouted, "What have you to do with me, Jesus, son of the Most High God? I beg you, do not torment me!" ²⁹ For he had ordered the unclean spirit to come out of the man. (It had taken hold of him many times, and he used to be bound with chains and shackles as a restraint, but he would break his bonds and be driven by the demon into deserted places.) ³⁰ Then Jesus asked him, "What is your name?" He replied, "Legion," because many demons had entered him. ³¹ And they pleaded with him not to order them to depart to the abyss.

³² A herd of many swine was feeding there on the hillside, and they pleaded with him to allow them to enter those swine; and he let them. ³³ The demons came out of the man and entered the swine, and the herd rushed down the steep bank into the lake and was drowned. ³⁴ When the swineherds saw what had happened, they ran away and reported the incident in the town and throughout the countryside. ³⁵ People came out to see what had happened and, when they approached Jesus, they discovered the man from whom the demons had come out sitting at his feet. He was clothed and in his right mind, and they were seized with fear. ³⁶ Those who witnessed it told them how the possessed man had been saved. ³⁷ The entire population of the region of the Gerasenes asked Jesus to leave them because they were seized with great fear. So he got into a boat and returned. ³⁸ The man from whom the demons had come out begged to remain with him, but he sent him away, saying, ³⁹ "Return home and recount what God has done for you." The man went off and proclaimed throughout the whole town what Jesus had done for him.

Jairus's Daughter and the Woman with a Hemorrhage. ⁴⁰ When Jesus returned, the crowd welcomed him, for they were all waiting for him. ⁴¹ And a man named Jairus, an official of the synagogue, came forward. He fell at the feet of Jesus and begged him to come to his house,

⁴² because he had an only daughter, about twelve years old, and she was dying. As he went, the crowds almost crushed him. ⁴³ And a woman afflicted with hemorrhages for twelve years, who [had spent her whole livelihood on doctors and] was unable to be cured by anyone, ⁴⁴ came up behind him and touched the tassel on his cloak. Immediately her bleeding stopped. ⁴⁵ Jesus then asked, "Who touched me?" While all were denying it, Peter said, "Master, the crowds are pushing and pressing in upon you." ⁴⁶ But Jesus said, "Someone has touched me; for I know that power has gone out from me." ⁴⁷ When the woman realized that she had not escaped notice, she came forward trembling. Falling down before him, she explained in the presence of all the people why she had touched him and how she had been healed immediately. ⁴⁸ He said to her, "Daughter, your faith has saved you; go in peace."

⁴⁹ While he was still speaking, someone from the synagogue official's house arrived and said, "Your daughter is dead; do not trouble the teacher any longer." ⁵⁰ On hearing this, Jesus answered him, "Do not be afraid; just have faith and she will be saved." ⁵¹ When he arrived at the house he allowed no one to enter with him except Peter and John and James, and the child's father and mother. ⁵² All were weeping and mourning for her, when he said, "Do not weep any longer, for she is not dead, but sleeping." ⁵³ And they ridiculed him, because they knew that she was dead. ⁵⁴ But he took her by the hand and called to her, "Child, arise!" ⁵⁵ Her breath returned and she immediately arose. He then directed that she should be given something to eat. ⁵⁶ Her parents were astounded, and he instructed them to tell no one what had happened.

CHAPTER 9

The Mission of the Twelve. ¹ He summoned the Twelve and gave them power and authority over all demons and to cure diseases, ² and he sent them to proclaim the kingdom of God and to heal [the sick]. ³ He said to them, "Take nothing for the journey, neither walking stick, nor sack, nor food, nor money, and let no one take a second tunic. ⁴ Whatever house you enter, stay there and leave from there. ⁵ And as for those who do not welcome you, when you leave that town, shake the dust from your feet in testimony against them." ⁶ Then they set out and went from village to village proclaiming the good news and curing diseases everywhere.

Herod's Opinion of Jesus. ⁷ Herod the tetrarch heard about all that was happening, and he was greatly perplexed because some were saying, "John has been raised from the dead"; ⁸ others were saying, "Elijah has appeared"; still others, "One of the ancient prophets has arisen." ⁹ But Herod said, "John I beheaded. Who then is this about whom I hear such things?" And he kept trying to see him.

The Return of the Twelve and the Feeding of the Five Thousand. ¹⁰ When the apostles returned, they explained to him what they had done. He took them and withdrew in private to a town called Bethsaida. ¹¹ The crowds, meanwhile, learned of this and followed him. He received them and spoke to them about the kingdom of God, and he healed those who needed to be cured. ¹² As the day was drawing to a close, the Twelve approached him and said, "Dismiss the crowd so that they can go to the surrounding villages and farms and find lodging and provisions; for we are in a deserted place here." ¹³ He said to them, "Give them some food yourselves." They replied, "Five loaves and two fish are all we have, unless we ourselves go and buy food for all these people." ¹⁴ Now the men there numbered about five thousand. Then he said to his disciples, "Have them sit down in groups of [about] fifty." ¹⁵ They did so and made them all sit down. ¹⁶ Then taking the five loaves and the two fish, and looking up to heaven, he said the blessing over them, broke them, and gave them to the disciples to set before the crowd. ¹⁷ They all ate and were satisfied. And when the leftover fragments were picked up, they filled twelve wicker baskets.

Peter's Confession about Jesus. ¹⁸ Once when Jesus was praying in solitude, and the disciples were with him, he asked them, "Who do the crowds say that I am?" ¹⁹ They said in reply, "John the Baptist; others, Elijah; still others, 'One of the ancient prophets has arisen.' ²⁰ Then he said to them, "But who do you say that I am?" Peter said in reply, "The Messiah of God." ²¹ He rebuked them and directed them not to tell this to anyone.

The First Prediction of the Passion. ²² He said, "The Son of Man must suffer greatly and be rejected by the elders, the chief priests, and the scribes, and be killed and on the third day be raised."

The Conditions of Discipleship. ²² Then he said to all, "If anyone wishes to come after me, he must deny himself and take up his cross daily and follow me. ²⁴ For whoever wishes to save his life will lose it, but whoever loses his life for my sake will save it. ²⁵ What profit is there for one to gain the whole world yet lose or forfeit himself? ²⁶ Whoever is ashamed of me and of my words, the Son of Man will be ashamed of when he comes in his glory and in the glory of the Father and of the holy angels. ²⁷ Truly I say to you, there are some standing here who will not taste death until they see the kingdom of God."

The Transfiguration of Jesus. ²⁸ About eight days after he said this, he took Peter, John, and James and went up the mountain to pray. ²⁹ While he was praying his face changed in appearance and his clothing became dazzling white. ³⁰ And behold, two men were conversing with him, Moses and Elijah, ³¹ who appeared in glory and spoke of his exodus that he was going to accomplish in Jerusalem. ³² Peter and his companions had been overcome by sleep, but becoming fully awake, they saw his glory and the two men standing with him. ³³ As they were about to part from him, Peter said to Jesus, "Master, it is good that we are here; let us make three tents, one for you, one for Moses, and one for Elijah." But he did not know what he was saying. ³⁴ While he was still speaking, a cloud came and cast a shadow over them, and they became frightened when they entered the cloud. ³⁵ Then from the cloud came a voice that said, "This is my chosen Son; listen to him." ³⁶ After the voice had spoken, Jesus was found alone. They fell silent and did not at that time tell anyone what they had seen.

The Healing of a Boy with a Demon. ³⁷ On the next day, when they came down from the mountain, a large crowd met him. ³⁸ There was a man in the crowd who cried out, "Teacher, I beg you, look at my son; he is my only child. ³⁹ For a spirit seizes him and he suddenly screams and it convulses him until he foams at the mouth; it releases him only with difficulty, wearing him out. ⁴⁰ I begged your disciples to cast it out but they could not." ⁴¹ Jesus said in reply, "O faithless and perverse generation, how long will I be with you and endure you? Bring your son here." ⁴² As he was coming forward, the demon threw him to the ground in a convulsion; but Jesus rebuked the unclean spirit, healed the boy, and returned him to his father. ⁴³ And all were astonished by the majesty of God.

The Second Prediction of the Passion. While they were all amazed at his every deed, he said to his disciples, ⁴⁴ "Pay attention to what I am telling you. The Son of Man is to be handed over to men." ⁴⁵ But they did not understand this saying; its meaning was hidden from them so that they should not understand it, and they were afraid to ask him about this saying.

The Greatest in the Kingdom. ⁴⁶ An argument arose among the disciples about which of them was the greatest. ⁴⁷ Jesus realized the intention of their hearts and took a child and placed it by his side ⁴⁸ and said to them, "Whoever receives this child in my name receives me, and whoever receives me receives the one who sent me. For the one who is least among all of you is the one who is the greatest."

Another Exorcist. ⁴⁹ Then John said in reply, "Master, we saw someone casting out demons in your name and we tried to prevent him because he does not follow in our company." ⁵⁰ Jesus said to him, "Do not prevent him, for whoever is not against you is for you."

V: THE JOURNEY TO JERUSALEM: LUKE'S TRAVEL NARRATIVE

Departure for Jerusalem; Samaritan Inhospitality. [51] When the days for his being taken up were fulfilled, he resolutely determined to journey to Jerusalem, [52] and he sent messengers ahead of him. On the way they entered a Samaritan village to prepare for his reception there, [53] but they would not welcome him because the destination of his journey was Jerusalem. [54] When the disciples James and John saw this they asked, "Lord, do you want us to call down fire from heaven to consume them?" [55] Jesus turned and rebuked them, [56] and they journeyed to another village.

The Would-be Followers of Jesus. [57] As they were proceeding on their journey someone said to him, "I will follow you wherever you go." [58] Jesus answered him, "Foxes have dens and birds of the sky have nests, but the Son of Man has nowhere to rest his head." [59] And to another he said, "Follow me." But he replied, "[Lord,] let me go first and bury my father." [60] But he answered him, "Let the dead bury their dead. But you, go and proclaim the kingdom of God." [61] And another said, "I will follow you, Lord, but first let me say farewell to my family at home." [62] [To him] Jesus said, "No one who sets a hand to the plow and looks to what was left behind is fit for the kingdom of God."

CHAPTER 10

The Mission of the Seventy-two. [1] After this the Lord appointed seventy[-two] others whom he sent ahead of him in pairs to every town and place he intended to visit. [2] He said to them, "The harvest is abundant but the laborers are few; so ask the master of the harvest to send out laborers for his harvest. [3] Go on your way; behold, I am sending you like lambs among wolves. [4] Carry no money bag, no sack, no sandals; and greet no one along the way. [5] Into whatever house you enter, first say, 'Peace to this household.' [6] If a peaceful person lives there, your peace will rest on him; but if not, it will return to you. [7] Stay in the same house and eat and drink what is offered to you, for the laborer deserves his payment. Do not move about from one house to another. [8] Whatever town you enter and they welcome you, eat what is set before you, [9] cure the sick in it and say to them, 'The kingdom of God is at hand for you.' [10] Whatever town you enter and they do not receive you, go out into the streets and say, [11] 'The dust of your town that clings to our feet, even that we shake off against you.' Yet know this: the kingdom of God is at hand. [12] I tell you, it will be more tolerable for Sodom on that day than for that town.

Reproaches to Unrepentant Towns. [13] "Woe to you, Chorazin! Woe to you, Bethsaida! For if the mighty deeds done in your midst had been done in Tyre and Sidon, they would long ago have repented, sitting in sackcloth and ashes. [14] But it will be more tolerable for Tyre and Sidon at the judgment than for you. [15] And as for you, Capernaum, 'Will you be exalted to heaven? You will go down to the netherworld.'" [16] Whoever listens to you listens to me. Whoever rejects you rejects me. And whoever rejects me rejects the one who sent me."

Return of the Seventy-two. [17] The seventy [-two] returned rejoicing, and said, "Lord, even the demons are subject to us because of your name." [18] Jesus said, "I have observed Satan fall like lightning from the sky. [19] Behold, I have given you the power 'to tread upon serpents' and scorpions and upon the full force of the enemy and nothing will harm you. [20] Nevertheless, do not rejoice because the spirits are subject to you, but rejoice because your names are written in heaven."

Praise of the Father. [21] At that very moment he rejoiced [in] the holy Spirit and said, "I give you praise, Father, Lord of heaven and earth, for although you have hidden these things from the wise and the learned you have revealed them to the childlike. Yes, Father, such has been your gracious will. [22] All things have been handed over to me by my Father. No one knows who the Son is except the Father, and who the Father is except the Son and anyone to whom the Son wishes to reveal him."

The Privileges of Discipleship. [23] Turning to the disciples in private he said, "Blessed are the eyes that see what you see. [24] For I say to you, many prophets and kings desired to see what you see, but did not see it, and to hear what you hear, but did not hear it."

The Greatest Commandment. [25] There was a scholar of the law who stood up to test him and said, "Teacher, what must I do to inherit eternal life?" [26] Jesus said to him, "What is written in the law? How do you read it?" [27] He said in reply, "You shall love the Lord, your God, with all your heart, with all your being, with all your strength, and with all your mind, and your neighbor as yourself." [28] He replied to him, "You have answered correctly; do this and you will live."

The Parable of the Good Samaritan. [29] But because he wished to justify himself, he said to Jesus, "And who is my neighbor?" [30] Jesus replied, "A man fell victim to robbers as he went down from Jerusalem to Jericho. They stripped and beat him and went off leaving him half-dead. [31] A priest happened to be going down that road, but when he saw him, he passed by on the opposite side. [32] Likewise a Levite came to the place, and when he saw him, he passed by on the opposite side. [33] But a Samaritan traveler who came upon him was moved with compassion at the sight. [34] He approached the victim, poured oil and wine over his wounds and bandaged them. Then he lifted him up on his own animal, took him to an inn and cared for him. [35] The next day he took out two silver coins and gave them to the innkeeper with the instruction, 'Take care of him. If you spend more than what I have given you, I shall repay you on my way back.' [36] Which of these three, in your opinion, was neighbor to the robbers' victim?" [37] He answered, "The one who treated him with mercy." Jesus said to him, "Go and do likewise."

Martha and Mary. [38] As they continued their journey he entered a village where a woman whose name was Martha welcomed him. [39] She had a sister named Mary [who] sat beside the Lord at his feet listening to him speak. [40] Martha, burdened with much serving, came to him and said, "Lord, do you not care that my sister has left me by myself to do the serving? Tell her to help me." [41] The Lord said to her in reply, "Martha, Martha, you are anxious and worried about many things. [42] There is need of only one thing. Mary has chosen the better part and it will not be taken from her."

CHAPTER 11

The Lord's Prayer. [1] He was praying in a certain place, and when he had finished, one of his disciples said to him, "Lord, teach us to pray just as John taught his disciples." [2] He said to them, "When you pray, say:

> Father, hallowed be your name,
>   your kingdom come.
> [3]   Give us each day our daily bread
> [4]   and forgive us our sins
>   for we ourselves forgive everyone in
>   debt to us,
>   and do not subject us to the final test."

Further Teachings on Prayer. [5] And he said to them, "Suppose one of you has a friend to whom he goes at midnight and says, 'Friend, lend me three loaves of bread, [6] for a friend of mine has arrived at my house from a journey and I have nothing to offer him,' [7] and he says in reply from within, 'Do not bother me; the door has already been locked and my children and I are already in bed. I cannot get up to give you anything.' [8] I tell you, if he does not get up to give him the loaves because of their friendship, he will get up to give him whatever he needs because of his persistence.

The Answer to Prayer. [9] "And I tell you, ask and you will receive; seek and you will find;

knock and the door will be opened to you. ¹⁰ For everyone who asks, receives; and the one who seeks, finds; and to the one who knocks, the door will be opened. ¹¹ What father among you would hand his son a snake when he asks for a fish? ¹² Or hand him a scorpion when he asks for an egg? ¹³ If you then, who are wicked, know how to give good gifts to your children, how much more will the Father in heaven give the holy Spirit to those who ask him?"

Jesus and Beelzebul. ¹⁴ He was driving out a demon [that was] mute, and when the demon had gone out, the mute person spoke and the crowds were amazed. ¹⁵ Some of them said, "By the power of Beelzebul, the prince of demons, he drives out demons." ¹⁶ Others, to test him, asked him for a sign from heaven. ¹⁷ But he knew their thoughts and said to them, 'Every kingdom divided against itself will be laid waste and house will fall against house. ¹⁸ And if Satan is divided against himself, how will his kingdom stand? For you say that it is by Beelzebul that I drive out demons. ¹⁹ If I, then, drive out demons by Beelzebul, by whom do your own people drive them out? Therefore they will be your judges. ²⁰ But if it is by the finger of God that [I] drive out demons, then the kingdom of God has come upon you. ²¹ When a strong man fully armed guards his palace, his possessions are safe. ²² But when one stronger than he attacks and overcomes him, he takes away the armor on which he relied and distributes the spoils. ²³ Whoever is not with me is against me, and whoever does not gather with me scatters.

The Return of the Unclean Spirit. ²⁴ "When an unclean spirit goes out of someone, it roams through arid regions searching for rest but, finding none, it says, 'I shall return to my home from which I came.' ²⁵ But upon returning, it finds it swept clean and put in order. ²⁶ Then it goes and brings back seven other spirits more wicked than itself who move in and dwell there, and the last condition of that person is worse than the first."

True Blessedness. ²⁷ While he was speaking, a woman from the crowd called out and said to him, "Blessed is the womb that carried you and the breasts at which you nursed." ²⁸ He replied, "Rather, blessed are those who hear the word of God and observe it."

The Demand for a Sign. ²⁹ While still more people gathered in the crowd, he said to them, "This generation is an evil generation; it seeks a sign, but no sign will be given it, except the sign of Jonah. ³⁰ Just as Jonah became a sign to the Ninevites, so will the Son of Man be to this generation. ³¹ At the judgment the queen of the south will rise with the men of this generation and she will condemn them, because she came from the ends of the earth to hear the wisdom of Solomon, and there is something greater than Solomon here. ³² At the judgment the men of Nineveh will arise with this generation and condemn it, because at the preaching of Jonah they repented, and there is something greater than Jonah here.

The Simile of Light. ³³ "No one who lights a lamp hides it away or places it [under a bushel basket], but on a lampstand so that those who enter might see the light. ³⁴ The lamp of the body is your eye. When your eye is sound, then your whole body is filled with light, but when it is bad, then your body is in darkness. ³⁵ Take care, then, that the light in you not become darkness. ³⁶ If your whole body is full of light, and no part of it is in darkness, then it will be as full of light as a lamp illuminating you with its brightness."

Denunciation of the Pharisees and Scholars of the Law. ³⁷ After he had spoken, a Pharisee invited him to dine at his home. He entered and reclined at table to eat. ³⁸ The Pharisee was amazed to see that he did not observe the prescribed washing before the meal. ³⁹ The Lord said to him, "Oh you Pharisees! Although you cleanse the outside of the cup and the dish, inside you are filled with plunder and evil. ⁴⁰ You fools! Did not the maker of the outside also make the inside? ⁴¹ But as to what is within, give alms, and behold, everything will be clean for you. ⁴² Woe to you Pharisees! You pay tithes of mint and of rue and of every garden herb, but you pay no attention to judgment and to love for God.

These you should have done, without overlooking the others. [44] Woe to you Pharisees! You love the seat of honor in synagogues and greetings in marketplaces. [44] Woe to you! You are like unseen graves over which people unknowingly walk."

[45] Then one of the scholars of the law said to him in reply, "Teacher, by saying this you are insulting us too." [46] And he said, "Woe also to you scholars of the law! You impose on people burdens hard to carry, but you yourselves do not lift one finger to touch them. [47] Woe to you! You build the memorials of the prophets whom your ancestors killed. [48] Consequently, you bear witness and give consent to the deeds of your ancestors, for they killed them and you do the building. [49] Therefore, the wisdom of God said, `I will send to them prophets and apostles; some of them they will kill and persecute' [50] in order that this generation might be charged with the blood of all the prophets shed since the foundation of the world, [51] from the blood of Abel to the blood of Zechariah who died between the altar and the temple building. Yes, I tell you, this generation will be charged with their blood! [52] Woe to you, scholars of the law! You have taken away the key of knowledge. You yourselves did not enter and you stopped those trying to enter." [53] When he left, the scribes and Pharisees began to act with hostility toward him and to interrogate him about many things, [54] for they were plotting to catch him at something he might say.

CHAPTER 12

The Leaven of the Pharisees. [1] Meanwhile, so many people were crowding together that they were trampling one another underfoot. He began to speak, first to his disciples, "Beware of the leaven—that is, the hypocrisy—of the Pharisees.

Courage under Persecution. [2] "There is nothing concealed that will not be revealed, nor secret that will not be known. [3] Therefore whatever you have said in the darkness will be heard in the light, and what you have whispered behind closed doors will be proclaimed on the housetops. [4] I tell you, my friends, do not be afraid of those who kill the body but after that can do no more. [5] I shall show you whom to fear. Be afraid of the one who after killing has the power to cast into Gehenna; yes, I tell you, be afraid of that one. [6] Are not five sparrows sold for two small coins? Yet not one of them has escaped the notice of God. [7] Even the hairs of your head have all been counted. Do not be afraid. You are worth more than many sparrows. [8] I tell you, everyone who acknowledges me before others the Son of Man will acknowledge before the angels of God. [9] But whoever denies me before others will be denied I before the angels of God.

Sayings about the Holy Spirit. [10] "Everyone who speaks a word against the Son of Man will be forgiven, but the one who blasphemes against the holy Spirit will not be forgiven. [11] When they take you before synagogues and before rulers and authorities, do not worry about how or what your defense will be or about what you are to say. [12] For the holy Spirit will teach you at that moment what you should say."

Saying against Greed. [13] Someone in the crowd said to him, "Teacher, tell my brother to share the inheritance with me." [14] He replied to him, "Friend, who appointed me as your judge and arbitrator?" [15] Then he said to the crowd, "Take care to guard against all greed, for though one may be rich, one's life does not consist of possessions."

Parable of the Rich Fool. [16] Then he told them a parable. "There was a rich man whose land produced a bountiful harvest. [17] He asked himself, 'What shall I do, for I do not have space to store my harvest?' [18] And he said, 'This is what I shall do: I shall tear down my barns and build larger ones. There I shall store all my grain and other goods [19] and I shall say to myself, "Now as for you, you have so many good things stored up for many years, rest, eat, drink, be merry!" [20] But God said to him, 'You fool, this night your life will be demanded of you; and the things you have prepared, to whom will they belong?' [21] Thus will it be for the one who stores up treasure for himself but is not rich in what matters to God."

Dependence on God. [22] He said to [his] disciples, "Therefore I tell you, do not worry about your life and what you will eat, or about your body and what you will wear. [23] For life is more than food and the body more than clothing. [24] Notice the ravens: they do not sow or reap; they have neither storehouse nor barn, yet God feeds them. How much more important are you than birds! [25] Can any of you by worrying add a moment to your lifespan? [26] If even the smallest things are beyond your control, why are you anxious about the rest? [27] Notice how the flowers grow. They do not toil or spin. But I tell you, not even Solomon in all his splendor was dressed like one of them." [28] If God so clothes the grass in the field that grows today and is thrown into the oven tomorrow, will he not much more provide for you, O you of little faith? [29] As for you, do not seek what you are to eat and what you are to drink, and do not worry anymore. [30] All the nations of the world seek for these things, and your Father knows that you need them. [31] Instead, seek his kingdom, and these other things will be given you besides. [32] Do not be afraid any longer, little flock, for your Father is pleased to give you the kingdom. [33] Sell your belongings and give alms. Provide money bags for yourselves that do not wear out, an inexhaustible treasure in heaven that no thief can reach nor moth destroy. [34] For where your treasure is, there also will your heart be.

Vigilant and Faithful Servants. [35] "Gird your loins and light your lamps [36] and be like servants who await their master's return from a wedding, ready to open immediately when he comes and knocks. [37] Blessed are those servants whom the master finds vigilant on his arrival. Amen, I say to you, he will gird himself, have them recline at table, and proceed to wait on them. [38] And should he come in the second or third watch and find them prepared in this way, blessed are those servants. [39] Be sure of this: if the master of the house had known the hour when the thief was coming, he would not have let his house be broken into. [40] You also must be prepared, for at an hour you do not expect, the Son of Man will come."

[41] Then Peter said, "Lord, is this parable meant for us or for everyone?" [42] And the Lord replied, "Who, then, is the faithful and prudent steward whom the master will put in charge of his servants to distribute [the] food allowance at the proper time? [43] Blessed is that servant whom his master on arrival finds doing so. [44] Truly, I say to you, he will put him in charge of all his property. [45] But if that servant says to himself, 'My master is delayed in coming,' and begins to beat the menservants and the maidservants, to eat and drink and get drunk, [46] then that servant's master will come on an unexpected day and at an unknown hour and will punish him severely and assign him a place with the unfaithful. [47] That servant who knew his master's will but did not make preparations nor act in accord with his will shall be beaten severely; [48] and the servant who was ignorant of his master's will but acted in a way deserving of a severe beating shall be beaten only lightly. Much will be required of the person entrusted with much, and still more will be demanded of the person entrusted with more.

Jesus: A Cause of Division. [49] "I have come to set the earth on fire, and how I wish it were already blazing! [50] There is a baptism with which I must be baptized, and how great is my anguish until it is accomplished! [51] Do you think that I have come to establish peace on the earth? No, I tell you, but rather division. [52] From now on a household of five will be divided, three against two and two against three; [53] a father will be divided against his son and a son against his father, a mother against her daughter and a daughter against her mother, a mother-in-law against her daughter-in-law and a daughter-in-law against her mother-in-law"

Signs of the Times. [54] He also said to the crowds, "When you see [a] cloud rising in the west you say immediately that it is going to rain—and so it does; [55] and when you notice that the wind is blowing from the south you say that it is going to be hot—and so it is. [56] You hypocrites! You know how to interpret the appearance of the earth and the sky; why do you not know how to interpret the present time?

Settlement with an Opponent. [57] "Why do you not judge for yourselves what is right? [58] If you are to go with your opponent before a magistrate, make an effort to settle the matter on the way; otherwise your opponent will turn you over to the judge, and the judge hand you over to the constable, and the constable throw you into prison. [59] I say to you, you will not be released until you have paid the last penny."

CHAPTER 13

A Call to Repentance. [1] At that time some people who were present there told him about the Galileans whose blood Pilate had mingled with the blood of their sacrifices. [2] He said to them in reply, "Do you think that because these Galileans suffered in this way they were greater sinners than all other Galileans? [3] By no means! But I tell you, if you do not repent, you will all perish as they did! [4] Or those eighteen people who were killed when the tower at Siloam fell on them—do you think they were more guilty than everyone else who lived in Jerusalem? [5] By no means! But I tell you, if you do not repent, you will all perish as they did!"

The Parable of the Barren Fig Tree. [6] And he told them this parable: "There once was a person who had a fig tree planted in his orchard, and when he came in search of fruit on it but found none, [7] he said to the gardener, 'For three years now I have come in search of fruit on this fig tree but have found none. [So] cut it down. Why should it exhaust the soil?' [8] He said to him in reply, 'Sir, leave it for this year also, and I shall cultivate the ground around it and fertilize it; [9] it may bear fruit in the future. If not you can cut it down..'"

Cure of a Crippled Woman on the Sabbath. [10] He was teaching in a synagogue on the sabbath. [11] And a woman was there who for eighteen years had been crippled by a spirit; she was bent over, completely incapable of standing erect. [12] When Jesus saw her, he called to her and said, "Woman, you are set free of your infirmity." [13] He laid his hands on her, and she at once stood up straight and glorified God. [14] But the leader of the synagogue, indignant that Jesus had cured on the sabbath, said to the crowd in reply, "There are six days when work should be done. Come on those days to be cured, not on the sabbath day." [15] The Lord said to him in reply, "Hypocrites! Does not each one of you on the sabbath untie his ox or his ass from the manger and lead it out for watering? [16] This daughter of Abraham, whom Satan has bound for eighteen years now, ought she not to have been set free on the sabbath day from this bondage?" [17] When he said this, all his adversaries were humiliated; and the whole crowd rejoiced at all the splendid deeds done by him.

The Parable of the Mustard Seed. [18] Then he said, "What is the kingdom of God like? To what can I compare it? [19] It is like a mustard seed that a person took and planted in the garden. When it was fully grown, it became a large bush and 'the birds of the sky dwelt in its branches.' "

The Parable of the Yeast. [20] Again he said, "To what shall I compare the kingdom of God? [21] It is like yeast that a woman took and mixed [in] with three measures of wheat flour until the whole batch of dough was leavened."

The Narrow Door; Salvation and Rejection. [22] He passed through towns and villages, teaching as he went and making his way to Jerusalem. [23] Someone asked him, "Lord, will only a few people be saved?" He answered them, [24] "Strive to enter through the narrow door, for many, I tell you, will attempt to enter but will not be strong enough. [25] After the master of the house has arisen and locked the door, then will you stand outside knocking and saying, 'Lord, open the door for us.' He will say to you in reply, 'I do not know where you are from.' [26] And you will say, 'We ate and drank in your company and you taught in our streets.' [27] Then he will say to you, 'I do not know where [you] are from. Depart from me, all you evildoers!' [28] And there will be wailing and grinding of teeth when you see Abraham, Isaac, and Jacob and all the prophets in the kingdom of God and you yourselves cast out. [29] And people will come from the east and the west and from the north and the south and will recline at table in the kingdom of God. [30] For behold, some are last who will be first, and some are first who will be last."

Herod's Desire to Kill Jesus. [31] At that time some Pharisees came to him and said, "Go away, leave this area because Herod wants to kill you." [32] He replied, "Go and tell that fox, 'Behold, I cast out demons and I perform healings today and tomorrow, and on the third day I accomplish my purpose. [33] Yet I must continue on my way today, tomorrow, and the following day, for it is impossible that a prophet should die outside of Jerusalem.'

The Lament over Jerusalem. [34] "Jerusalem, Jerusalem, you who kill the prophets and stone those sent to you, how many times I yearned to gather your children together as a hen gathers her brood under her wings, but you were unwilling! [35] Behold, your house will be abandoned. [But] I tell you, you will not see me until [the time comes when] you say, 'Blessed is he who comes in the name of the Lord.'

CHAPTER 14

Healing of the Man with Dropsy on the Sabbath. [1] On a sabbath he went to dine at the home of one of the leading Pharisees, and the people there were observing him carefully. [2] In front of him there was a man suffering from dropsy. [3] Jesus spoke to the scholars of the law and Pharisees in reply, asking, "Is it lawful to cure on the sabbath or not?" [4] But they kept silent; so he took the man and, after he had healed him, dismissed him. [5] Then he said to them, "Who among you, if your son or ox falls into a cistern, would not immediately pull him out on the sabbath day?" [6] But they were unable to answer his question.'

Conduct of Invited Guests and Hosts. [7] He told a parable to those who had been invited, noticing how they were choosing the places of honor at the table. [8] "When you are invited by someone to a wedding banquet, do not recline at

table in the place of honor. A more distinguished guest than you may have been invited by him, [9] and the host who invited both of you may approach you and say, 'Give your place to this man,' and then you would proceed with embarrassment to take the lowest place. [10] Rather, when you are invited, go and take the lowest place so that when the host comes to you he may say, 'My friend, move up to a higher position.' Then you will enjoy the esteem of your companions at the table. [11] For everyone who exalts himself will be humbled, but the one who humbles himself will be exalted." [12] Then he said to the host who invited him, "When you hold a lunch or a dinner, do not invite your friends or your brothers or your relatives or your wealthy neighbors, in case they may invite you back and you have repayment. [13] Rather, when you hold a banquet, invite the poor, the crippled, the lame, the blind; [14] blessed indeed will you be because of their inability to repay you. For you will be repaid at the resurrection of the righteous."

The Parable of the Great Feast. [15] One of his fellow guests on hearing this said to him, "Blessed is the one who will dine in the kingdom of God." [16] He replied to him, "A man gave a great dinner to which he invited many. [17] When the time for the dinner came, he dispatched his servant to say to those invited, `Come, everything is now ready.' [18] But one by one, they all began to excuse themselves. The first said to him, 'I have purchased a field and must go to examine it; I ask you, consider me excused.' [19] And another said, 'I have purchased five yoke of oxen and am on my way to evaluate them; I ask you, consider me excused.' [20] And another said, 'I have just married a woman, and therefore I cannot come.' [21] The servant went and reported this to his master. Then the master of the house in a rage commanded his servant, 'Go out quickly into the streets and alleys of the town and bring in here the poor and the crippled, the blind and the lame.' [22] The servant reported, 'Sir, your orders have been carried out and still there is room.' [23] The master then ordered the servant, 'Go out to the highways and hedgerows and make people come in that my home may be filled. [24] For, I tell you, none of those men who were invited will taste my dinner.'"

Sayings on Discipleship. 25 Great crowds were traveling with him, and he turned and addressed them, 26 "If any one comes to me without hating his father and mother, wife and children, brothers and sisters, and even his own life, he cannot be my disciple.'" 27 Whoever does not carry his own cross and come after me cannot be my disciple." 28 Which of you wishing to construct a tower does not first sit down and calculate the cost to see if there is enough for its completion? 29 Otherwise, after laying the foundation and finding himself unable to finish the work the onlookers should laugh at him 30 and say, 'This one began to build but did not have the resources to finish.' 31 Or what king marching into battle would not first sit down and decide whether with ten thousand troops he can successfully oppose another king advancing upon him with twenty thousand troops? 32 But if not, while he is still far away, he will send a delegation to ask for peace terms. 33 In the same way, everyone of you who does not renounce all his possessions cannot be my disciple.

The Simile of Salt. 34 "Salt is good, but if salt itself loses its taste, with what can its flavor be restored? 35 It is fit neither for the soil nor for the manure pile; it is thrown out. Whoever has ears to hear ought to hear."

CHAPTER 15

The Parable of the Lost Sheep. 1 The tax collectors and sinners were all drawing near to listen to him, 2 but the Pharisees and scribes began to complain, saying, "This man welcomes sinners and eats with them." 3 So to them he addressed this parable. 4 "What man among you having a hundred sheep and losing one of them would not leave the ninety-nine in the desert and go after the lost one until he finds it? 5 And when he does find it, he sets it on his shoulders with great joy 6 and, upon his arrival home, he calls together his friends and neighbors and says to

them, 'Rejoice with me because I have found my lost sheep.' 7 I tell you, in just the same way there will be more joy in heaven over one sinner who repents than over ninety-nine righteous people who have no need of repentance.

The Parable of the Lost Coin. 8 "Or what woman having ten coins and losing one would not light a lamp and sweep the house, searching carefully until she finds it? 9 And when she does find it, she calls together her friends and neighbors and says to them, 'Rejoice with me because I have found the coin that I lost.' 10 In just the same way, I tell you, there will be rejoicing among the angels of God over one sinner who repents."

The Parable of the Lost Son. 11 Then he said, "A man had two sons, 12 and the younger son said to his father, 'Father, give me the share of your estate that should come to me.' So the father divided the property between them. 13 After a few days, the younger son collected all his belongings and set off to a distant country where he squandered his inheritance on a life of dissipation. 14 When he had freely spent everything, a severe famine struck that country, and he found himself in dire need. 15 So he hired himself out to one of the local citizens who sent him to his farm to tend the swine. 16 And he longed to eat his fill of the pods on which the swine fed, but nobody gave him any. 17 Coming to his senses he thought, 'How many of my father's hired workers have more than enough food to eat, but here am I, dying from hunger. 18 I shall get up and go to my father and I shall say to him, "Father, I have sinned against heaven and against you. 19 I no longer deserve to be called your son; treat me as you would treat one of your hired workers." 20 So he got up and went back to his father. While he was still a long way off, his father caught sight of him, and was filled with compassion. He ran to his son, embraced him and kissed him. 21 His son said to him, 'Father, I have sinned against heaven and against you; I no longer deserve to be called your son.' 22 But his father ordered his servants, 'Quickly bring the finest robe and put it on him; put a ring on his finger and sandals on his feet. 23 Take the fattened calf and slaughter it. Then let us celebrate with a feast, 24 because this son of mine was dead, and has come to life again; he was lost, and has been found.' Then the celebration began. ²⁵ Now the older son had been out in the field and, on his way back, as he neared the house, he heard the sound of music and dancing. ²⁶ He called one of the servants and asked what this might mean. ²⁷ The servant said to him, `Your brother has returned and your father has slaughtered the fattened calf because he has him back safe and sound.' ²⁸ He became angry, and when he refused to enter the house, his father came out and pleaded with him. ²⁹ He said to his father in reply, `Look, all these years I served you and not once did I disobey your orders; yet you never gave me even a young goat to feast on with my friends. ³⁰ But when your son returns who swallowed up your property with prostitutes, for him you slaughter the fattened calf.' ³¹ He said to him, 'My son, you are here with me always; everything I have is yours. ³² But now we must celebrate and rejoice, because your brother was dead and has come to life again; he was lost and has been found.'"

CHAPTER 16

The Parable of the Dishonest Steward. ¹ Then he also said to his disciples, "A rich man had a steward who was reported to him for squandering his property. ² He summoned him and said, 'What is this I hear about you? Prepare a full account of your stewardship, because you can no longer be my steward.' ³ The steward said to himself, 'What shall I do, now that my master is taking the position of steward away from me? I am not strong enough to dig and I am ashamed to beg. ⁴ I know what I shall do so that, when I am removed from the stewardship, they may welcome me into their homes.' ⁵ He called in his master's debtors one by one. To the first he said, 'How much do you owe my master?' ⁶ He replied, 'One hundred measures of olive oil.' He said to him, 'Here is your promissory note. Sit down and quickly write one for fifty.' ⁷ Then to another he said, 'And you, how much do you owe?' He

replied, 'One hundred kors of wheat.' He said to him, 'Here is your promissory note; write one for eighty.' ⁸ And the master commended that dishonest steward for acting prudently.

Application of the Parable. "For the children of this world are more prudent in dealing with their own generation than are the children of light. ⁹ I tell you, make friends for yourselves with dishonest wealth, so that when it fails, you will be welcomed into eternal dwellings. ¹⁰ The person who is trustworthy in very small matters is also trustworthy in great ones; and the person who is dishonest in very small matters is also dishonest in great ones. ¹¹ If, therefore, you are not trustworthy with dishonest wealth, who will trust you with true wealth? ¹² If you are not trustworthy with what belongs to another, who will give you what is yours? ¹³ No servant can serve two masters. He will either hate one and love the other, or be devoted to one and despise the other. You cannot serve God and mammon."

A Saying Against the Pharisees. ¹⁴ The Pharisees, who loved money, heard all these things and sneered at him. ¹⁵ And he said to them, "You justify yourselves in the sight of others, but God knows your hearts; for what is of human esteem is an abomination in the sight of God.

Sayings about the Law. ¹⁶ "The law and the prophets lasted until John; but from then on the kingdom of God is proclaimed, and everyone who enters does so with violence. ¹⁷ It is easier for heaven and earth to pass away than for the smallest part of a letter of the law to become invalid.

Sayings about Divorce. ¹⁸ "Everyone who divorces his wife and marries another commits adultery, and the one who marries a woman divorced from her husband commits adultery.

The Parable of the Rich Man and Lazarus. ¹⁹ "There was a rich man who dressed in purple garments and fine linen and dined sumptuously each day. ²⁰ And lying at his door was a poor man named Lazarus, covered with sores, ²¹ who would gladly have eaten his fill of the scraps that fell from the rich man's table. Dogs even used to come and lick his sores. ²² When the poor man died, he was carried away by angels to the bosom of Abraham. The rich man also died and was buried, ²³ and from the netherworld, where he was in torment, he raised his eyes and saw Abraham far off and Lazarus at his side. ²⁴ And he cried out, 'Father Abraham, have pity on me. Send Lazarus to dip the tip of his finger in water and cool my tongue, for I am suffering torment in these flames.' ²⁵ Abraham replied, 'My child, remember that you received what was good during your lifetime while Lazarus likewise received what was bad; but now he is comforted here, whereas you are tormented. ²⁶ Moreover, between us and you a great chasm is established to prevent anyone from crossing who might wish to go from our side to yours or from your side to ours.' ²⁷ He said, 'Then I beg you, father, send him to my father's house, ²⁸ for I have five brothers, so that he may warn them, lest they too come to this place of torment.' ²⁹ But Abraham replied, 'They have Moses and the prophets. Let them listen to them.' ³⁰ He said, 'Oh no, father Abraham, but if someone from the dead goes to them, they will repent.' ³¹ Then Abraham said, 'If they will not listen to Moses and the prophets, neither will they be persuaded if someone should rise from the dead.'"

CHAPTER 17

Temptations to Sin. ¹ He said to his disciples, "Things that cause sin will inevitably occur, but woe to the person through whom they occur. ² It would be better for him if a millstone were put around his neck and he be thrown into the sea than for him to cause one of these little ones to sin. ³ Be on your guard! If your brother sins, rebuke him; and if he repents, forgive him. ⁴ And if he wrongs you seven times in one day and returns to you seven times saying, 'I am sorry,' you should forgive him."

Saying of Faith. ⁵ And the apostles said to the Lord, "Increase our faith." ⁶ The Lord replied, "If you have faith the size of a mustard seed, you would say to [this] mulberry tree, 'Be uprooted and planted in the sea,' and it would obey you.

Attitude of a Servant. ⁷ "Who among you would say to your servant who has just come in from plowing or tending sheep in the field, 'Come here immediately and take your place at table'? ⁸ Would he not rather say to him, 'Prepare something for me to eat. Put on your apron and wait on me while I eat and drink. You may eat and drink when I am finished'? ⁹ Is he grateful to that servant because he did what was commanded? ¹⁰ So should it be with you. When you have done all you have been commanded, say, 'We are unprofitable servants; we have done what we were obliged to do.'"

The Cleansing of Ten Lepers. ¹¹ As he continued his journey to Jerusalem, he traveled through Samaria and Galilee. ¹² As he was entering a village, ten lepers met [him]. They stood at a distance from him ¹³ and raised their voice, saying, "Jesus, Master! Have pity on us!" ¹⁴ And when he saw them, he said, "Go show yourselves to the priests." As they were going they were cleansed. ¹⁵ And one of them, realizing he had been healed, returned, glorifying God in a loud voice; ¹⁶ and he fell at the feet of Jesus and thanked him. He was a Samaritan. ¹⁷ Jesus said in reply, "Ten were cleansed, were they not? Where are the other nine? ¹⁸ Has none but this foreigner returned to give thanks to God?" ¹⁹ Then he said to him, "Stand up and go; your faith has saved you."

The Coming of the Kingdom of God. ²⁰ Asked by the Pharisees when the kingdom of God would come, he said in reply, "The coming of the kingdom of God cannot be observed, ²¹ and no one will announce, 'Look, here it is,' or, 'There it is: For behold, the kingdom of God is among you."

The Day of the Son of Man. ²² Then he said to his disciples, "The days will come when you will long to see one of the days of the Son of Man, but you will not see it. ²³ There will be those who will say to you, 'Look, there he is,' [or] 'Look, here he is.' Do not go off, do not run in pursuit. ²⁴ For just as lightning flashes and lights up the sky from one side to the other, so will the Son of Man be [in his day]. ²⁵ But first he must suffer greatly and be rejected by this generation.'" [26] As it was in the days of Noah, so it will be in the days of the Son of Man; [27] they were eating and drinking, marrying and giving in marriage up to the day that Noah entered the ark, and the flood came and destroyed them all. [28] Similarly, as it was in the days of Lot: they were eating, drinking, buying, selling, planting, building; [29] on the day when Lot left Sodom, fire and brimstone rained from the sky to destroy them all. [30] So it will be on the day the Son of Man is revealed. [31] On that day, a person who is on the housetop and whose belongings are in the house must not go down to get them, and likewise a person in the field must not return to what was left behind. [32] Remember the wife of Lot. [33] Whoever seeks to preserve his life will lose it, but whoever loses it will save it. [34] I tell you, on that night there will be two people in one bed; one will be taken, the other left. [35] And there will be two women grinding meal together; one will be taken, the other left." [36] [37] They said to him in reply, "Where, Lord?" He said to them, "Where the body is, there also the vultures will gather."

CHAPTER 18

The Parable of the Persistent Widow.
[1] Then he told them a parable about the necessity for them to pray always without becoming weary. He said, [2] "There was a judge in a certain town who neither feared God nor respected any human being. [3] And a widow in that town used to come to him and say, 'Render a just decision for me against my adversary.' [4] For a long time the judge was unwilling, but eventually he thought, 'While it is true that I neither fear God nor respect any human being, [5] because this widow keeps bothering me I shall deliver a just decision for her lest she finally come and strike me.'" [6] The Lord said, "Pay attention to what the dishonest judge says. [7] Will not God then secure the rights of his chosen ones who call out to him day and night? Will he be slow to answer them?

[8] I tell you, he will see to it that justice is done for them speedily. But when the Son of Man comes, will he find faith on earth?"

The Parable of the Pharisee and the Tax Collector. [9] He then addressed this parable to those who were convinced of their own righteousness and despised everyone else. [10] "Two people went up to the temple area to pray; one was a Pharisee and the other was a tax collector. [11] The Pharisee took up his position and spoke this prayer to himself, 'O God, I thank you that I am not like the rest of humanity—greedy, dishonest, adulterous—or even like this tax collector. [12] I fast twice a week, and I pay tithes on my whole income.' [13] But the tax collector stood off at a distance and would not even raise his eyes to heaven but beat his breast and prayed, 'O God, be merciful to me a sinner.' [14] I tell you, the latter went home justified, not the former; for everyone who exalts himself will be humbled, and the one who humbles himself will be exalted."

Saying on Children and the Kingdom.
[15] People were bringing even infants to him that he might touch them, and when the disciples saw this, they rebuked them. [16] Jesus, however, called the children to himself and said, "Let the children come to me and do not prevent them; for the kingdom of God belongs to such as these. [17] Amen, I say to you, whoever does not accept the kingdom of God like a child will not enter it."

The Rich Official. [18] An official asked him this question, "Good teacher, what must I do to inherit eternal life?" [19] Jesus answered him, "Why do you call me good? No one is good but God alone. [20] You know the commandments, 'You shall not commit adultery; you shall not kill; you shall not steal; you shall not bear false witness; honor your father and your mother.'" [21] And he replied, "All of these I have observed from my youth." [22] When Jesus heard this he said to him, "There is still one thing left for you: sell all that you have and distribute it to the poor, and you will have a treasure in heaven. Then come, follow me." [23] But when he heard this he became quite sad, for he was very rich.

On Riches and Renunciation. [24] Jesus looked at him [now sad] and said, "How hard it is for those who have wealth to enter the kingdom of God! [25] For it is easier for a camel to pass through the eye of a needle than for a rich person to enter the kingdom of God." [26] Those who heard this said, "Then who can be saved?" [27] And he said, "What is impossible for human beings is possible for God." [28] Then Peter said, "We have given up our possessions and followed you." [29] He said to them, "Amen, I say to you, there is no one who has given up house or wife or brothers or parents or children for the sake of the kingdom of God [30] who will not receive [back] an overabundant return in this present age and eternal life in the age to come."

The Third Prediction of the Passion. [31] Then he took the Twelve aside and said to them, "Behold, we are going up to Jerusalem and everything written by the prophets about the Son of Man will be fulfilled. [32] He will be handed over to the Gentiles and he will be mocked and insulted and spat upon; [33] and after they have scourged him they will kill him, but on the third day he will rise." [34] But they understood nothing of this; the word remained hidden from them and they failed to comprehend what he said.

The Healing of the Blind Beggar. [35] Now as he approached Jericho a blind man was sitting by the roadside begging, [36] and hearing a crowd going by, he inquired what was happening. [37] They told him, "Jesus of Nazareth is passing by." [38] He shouted, "Jesus, Son of David, have pity on me!" [39] The people walking in front rebuked him, telling him to be silent, but he kept calling out all the more, "Son of David, have pity on me!" [40] Then Jesus stopped and ordered that he be brought to him; and when he came near, Jesus asked him, [41] "What do you want me to do for you?" He replied, "Lord, please let me see." [42] Jesus told him, "Have sight; your faith has saved you." [43] He immediately received his sight and followed him, giving glory to God. When they saw this, all the people gave praise to God.

CHAPTER 19

Zacchaeus the Tax Collector. [1] He came to Jericho and intended to pass through the town. [2] Now a man there named Zacchaeus, who was a chief tax collector and also a wealthy man, [3] was seeking to see who Jesus was; but he could not see him because of the crowd, for he was short in stature. [4] So he ran ahead and climbed a sycamore tree in order to see Jesus, who was about to pass that way. [5] When he reached the place, Jesus looked up and said to him, "Zacchaeus, come down quickly, for today I must stay at your house." [6] And he came down quickly and received him with joy. [7] When they all saw this, they began to grumble, saying, "He has gone to stay at the house of a sinner." [8] But Zacchaeus stood there and said to the Lord, "Behold, half of my possessions, Lord, I shall give to the poor, and if I have extorted anything from anyone I shall repay it four times over." [9] And Jesus said to him, "Today salvation has come to this house because this man too is a descendant of Abraham. [10] For the Son of Man has come to seek and to save what was lost."

The Parable of the Ten Gold Coins. [11] While they were listening to him speak, he proceeded to tell a parable because he was near Jerusalem and they thought that the kingdom of God would appear there immediately. [12] So he said, "A nobleman went off to a distant country to obtain the kingship for himself and then to return. [13] He called ten of his servants and gave them ten gold coins and told them, 'Engage in trade with these until I return.' [14] His fellow citizens, however, despised him and sent a delegation after him to announce, 'We do not want this man to be our king.' [15] But when he returned after obtaining the kingship, he had the servants called, to whom he had given the money, to learn what they had gained by trading. [16] The first came forward and said, 'Sir, your gold coin has earned ten additional ones.' [17] He replied, 'Well done, good servant! You have been faithful in this very small matter; take charge of ten cities.' [18] Then the second came and reported, 'Your gold coin, sir, has earned five more.' [19] And to this servant too he said, 'You, take charge of five cities.' [20] Then the other servant came and said, 'Sir, here is your gold coin; I kept it stored away in a handkerchief, [21] for I was afraid of you, because you are a demanding person; you take up what you did not lay down and you harvest what you did not plant.' [22] He said to him, 'With your own words I shall condemn you, you wicked servant. You knew I was a demanding person, taking up what I did not lay down and harvesting what I did not plant; [23] why did you not put my money in a bank? Then on my return I would have collected it with interest.' [24] And to those standing by he said, 'Take the gold coin from him and give it to the servant who has ten.' [25] But they said to him, 'Sir, he has ten gold coins.' [26] 'I tell you, to everyone who has, more will be given, but from the one who has not, even what he has will be taken away. [27] Now as for those enemies of mine who did not want me as their king, bring them here and slay them before me.'"

VI: THE TEACHING MINISTRY IN JERUSALEM

The Entry into Jerusalem. [28] After he had said this, he proceeded on his journey up to Jerusalem. [29] As he drew near to Bethphage and Bethany at the place called the Mount of Olives, he sent two of his disciples. [30] He said, "Go into the village opposite you, and as you enter it you will find a colt tethered on which no one has ever sat. Untie it and bring it here. [31] And if anyone should ask you, 'Why are you untying it?' you will answer, 'The Master has need of it.'" [32] So those who had been sent went off and found everything just as he had told them. [33] And as they were untying the colt, its owners said to them, "Why are you untying this colt?" [34] They answered, "The Master has need of it." [35] So they brought it to Jesus, threw their cloaks over the colt, and helped Jesus to mount. [36] As he rode along, the people were spreading their cloaks on the road; [37] and now as he was approaching the slope of the Mount of Olives, the whole multitude of his disciples began to praise God aloud with joy for all the mighty deeds they had seen. [38] They proclaimed:

> "Blessed is the king who comes in the name
>   of the Lord.
> Peace in heaven and glory in the highest."

[39] Some of the Pharisees in the crowd said to him, "Teacher, rebuke your disciples." [40] He said in reply, "I tell you, if they keep silent, the stones will cry out!"

The Lament for Jerusalem. [41] As he drew near, he saw the city and wept over it, [42] saying, "If this day you only knew what makes for peace—but now it is hidden from your eyes. [43] For the days are coming upon you when your enemies will raise a palisade against you; they will encircle you and hem you in on all sides. [44] They will smash you to the ground and your children within you, and they will not leave one stone upon another within you because you did not recognize the time of your visitation."

The Cleansing of the Temple. [45] Then Jesus entered the temple area and proceeded to drive out those who were selling things, [46] saying to them, "It is written, 'My house shall be a house of prayer, but you have made it a den of thieves.'" [47] And every day he was teaching in the temple area. The chief priests, the scribes, and the leaders of the people, meanwhile, were seeking to put him to death, [48] but they could find no way to accomplish their purpose because all the people were hanging on his words.

CHAPTER 20

The Authority of Jesus Questioned. [1] One day as he was teaching the people in the temple area and proclaiming the good news, the chief priests and scribes, together with the elders, approached him [2] and said to him, "Tell us, by what authority are you doing these things? Or who is the one who gave you this authority?" [3] He said to them in reply, "I shall ask you a question. Tell me, [4] was John's baptism of heavenly or of human origin?" [5] They discussed this among themselves, and said, "If we say, 'Of heavenly origin,' he will say, 'Why did you not believe him?' [6] But if we say, 'Of human origin,' then all the people will stone us, for they are convinced that John was a prophet." [7] So they answered that they did not know from where it came. [8] Then Jesus said to them, "Neither shall I tell you by what authority I do these things."

The Parable of the Tenant Farmers.
[9] Then he proceeded to tell the people this parable. "[A] man planted a vineyard, leased it to tenant farmers, and then went on a journey for a long time. [10] At harvest time he sent a servant to the tenant farmers to receive some of the produce of the vineyard. But they beat the servant and sent him away empty-handed. [11] So he proceeded to send another servant, but him also they beat and insulted and sent away empty-handed. [12] Then he proceeded to send a third, but this one too they wounded and threw out. [13] The owner of the vineyard said, 'What shall I do? I shall send my beloved son; maybe they will respect him.' [14] But when the tenant farmers saw him they said to one another, 'This is the heir. Let us kill him that the inheritance may become ours.' [15] So they threw him out of the vineyard and killed him. What will the owner of the vineyard do to them? [16] He will come and put those tenant farmers to death and turn over the vineyard to others." When the people heard this, they exclaimed, "Let it not be so!" [17] But he looked at them and asked, "What then does this scripture passage mean:

'The stone which the builders rejected
    has become the cornerstone'?

[18] Everyone who falls on that stone will be dashed to pieces; and it will crush anyone on whom it falls." [19] The scribes and chief priests sought to lay their hands on him at that very hour, but they feared the people, for they knew that he had addressed this parable to them.

Paying Taxes to the Emperor. [20] They watched him closely and sent agents pretending to be righteous who were to trap him in speech, in order to hand him over to the authority and power of the governor. [21] They posed this question to him, "Teacher, we know that what you say and teach is correct, and you show no partiality, but teach the way of God in accordance with the truth. [22] Is it lawful for us to pay tribute to Caesar or not?" [23] Recognizing their craftiness he said to them, [24] "Show me a denarius; whose image and name does it bear?" They replied, "Caesar's." [25] So he said to them, "Then repay to Caesar what belongs to Caesar and to God what belongs to God." [26] They were unable to trap him by something he might say before the people, and so amazed were they at his reply that they fell silent.

The Question about the Resurrection.
[27] Some Sadducees, those who deny that there is a resurrection, came forward and put this question to him, [28] saying, "Teacher, Moses wrote for us, 'If someone's brother dies leaving a wife but no child, his brother must take the wife and raise up descendants for his brother.' [29] Now there were seven brothers; the first married a woman but died childless. [30] Then the second [31] and the third married her, and likewise all the seven died childless. [32] Finally the woman also died. [33] Now at the resurrection whose wife will that woman be? For all seven had been married to her." [34] Jesus said to them, "The children of this age marry and are given in marriage; [35] but those who are deemed worthy to attain to the coming age and to the resurrection of the dead neither marry nor are given in marriage. [36] They can no longer die, for they are like angels; and they are the children of God because they are the ones who will rise. [37] That the dead will rise even Moses made known in the passage about the bush, when he called 'Lord' the God of Abraham, the God of Isaac, and the God of Jacob; [38] and he is not God of the dead, but of the living, for to him all are alive." [39] Some of the scribes said in reply, "Teacher, you have answered well." [40] And they no longer dared to ask him anything.

The Question about David's Son. [41] "Then he said to them, "How do they claim that the Messiah is the Son of David? [42] For David himself in the Book of Psalms says:

'The Lord said to my lord,
"Sit at my right hand
[43]   till I make your enemies your footstool."'

[44] Now if David calls him 'lord,' how can he be his son?"

Denunciation of the Scribes. [45] Then, within the hearing of all the people, he said to [his] disciples, [46] "Be on guard against the scribes, who like to go around in long robes and love greetings in marketplaces, seats of honor in synagogues, and places of honor at banquets. [47] They devour the houses of widows and, as a pretext, recite lengthy prayers. They will receive a very severe condemnation."

CHAPTER 21

The Poor Widow's Contribution. [1] When he looked up he saw some wealthy people putting their offerings into the treasury [2] and he noticed a poor widow putting in two small coins. [3] He said, "I tell you truly, this poor widow put in more than all the rest; [4] for those others have all made offerings from their surplus wealth, but she, from her poverty, has offered her whole livelihood."

The Destruction of the Temple Foretold. [5] While some people were speaking about how the temple was adorned with costly stones and votive offerings, he said, [6] "All that you see here—the days will come when there will not be left a stone upon another stone that will not be thrown down."

The Sign of the End. [7] Then they asked him, "Teacher, when will this happen? And what sign will there be when all these things are about to happen?" [8] He answered, "See that you not be deceived, for many will come in my name, saying, 'I am he,' and 'The time has come.' Do not follow them! [9] "When you hear of wars and insurrections, do not be terrified; for such things must happen first, but it will not immediately be the end." [10] Then he said to them, "Nation will rise against nation, and kingdom against kingdom. [11] There will be powerful earthquakes, famines, and plagues from place to place; and awesome sights and mighty signs will come from the sky.

The Coming Persecution. [12] "Before all this happens, however, they will seize and persecute you, they will hand you over to the synagogues and to prisons, and they will have you led before kings and governors because of my name. [13] It will lead to your giving testimony. [14] Remember, you are not to prepare your defense beforehand, [15] for I myself shall give you a wisdom in speaking that all your adversaries will be powerless to resist or refute. [16] You will even be handed over by parents, brothers, relatives, and friends, and they will put some of you to death. [17] You will be hated by all because of my name, [18] but not a hair on your head will be destroyed. [19] By your perseverance you will secure your lives.

The Great Tribulation. [20] "When you see Jerusalem surrounded by armies, know that its desolation is at hand. [21] Then those in Judea must flee to the mountains. Let those within the city escape from it, and let those in the countryside not enter the city, [22] for these days are the time of punishment when all the scriptures are fulfilled. [23] Woe to pregnant women and nursing mothers in those days, for a terrible calamity will come upon the earth and a wrathful judgment upon this people. [24] They will fall by the edge of the sword and be taken as captives to all the Gentiles; and Jerusalem will be trampled underfoot by the Gentiles until the times of the Gentiles are fulfilled.

The Coming of the Son of Man. [25] "There will be signs in the sun, the moon, and the stars, and on earth nations will be in dismay, perplexed by the roaring of the sea and the waves. [26] People will die of fright in anticipation of what is coming upon the world, for the powers of the heavens will be shaken." [27] And then they will see the Son of Man coming in a cloud with power and great glory. [28] But when these signs begin to happen, stand erect and raise your heads because your redemption is at hand."

The Lesson of the Fig Tree. [29] He taught them a lesson. "Consider the fig tree and all the other trees. [30] When their buds burst open, you see for yourselves and know that summer is now near; [31] in the same way, when you see these things happening, know that the kingdom of God is near. [32] Amen, I say to you, this generation will not pass away until all these things have taken place. [33] Heaven and earth will pass away, but my words will not pass away.

Exhortation to be Vigilant. [34] "Beware that your hearts do not become drowsy from carousing and drunkenness and the anxieties of daily life, and that day catch you by surprise [35] like a trap. For that day will assault everyone who lives on the face of the earth. [36] Be vigilant at all times and pray that you have the strength to escape the tribulations that are imminent and to stand before the Son of Man."

Ministry in Jerusalem. [37] During the day, Jesus was teaching in the temple area, but at night he would leave and stay at the place called the Mount of Olives. [38] And all the people would get up early each morning to listen to him in the temple area.

VII: THE PASSION NARRATIVE

CHAPTER 22

The Conspiracy Against Jesus. [1] Now the feast of Unleavened Bread, called the Passover, was drawing near, [2] and the chief priests and the scribes were seeking a way to put him to death, for they were afraid of the people. [3] Then Satan entered into Judas, the one surnamed Iscariot, who was counted among the Twelve, [4] and he went to the chief priests and temple guards to discuss a plan for handing him over to them. [5] They were pleased and agreed to pay him money. [6] He accepted their offer and sought a

favorable opportunity to hand him over to them in the absence of a crowd.

Preparations for the Passover. [7] When the day of the Feast of Unleavened Bread arrived, the day for sacrificing the Passover lamb, [8] he sent out Peter and John, instructing them, "Go and make preparations for us to eat the Passover." [9] They asked him, "Where do you want us to make the preparations?" [10] And he answered them, "When you go into the city, a man will meet you carrying a jar of water. Follow him into the house that he enters [11] and say to the master of the house, 'The teacher says to you, "Where is the guest room where I may eat the Passover with my disciples?"' [12] He will show you a large upper room that is furnished. Make the preparations there." [13] Then they went off and found everything exactly as he had told them, and there they prepared the Passover.

The Last Supper. [14] When the hour came, he took his place at table with the apostles. [15] He said to them, "I have eagerly desired to eat this Passover with you before I suffer, [16] for, I tell you, I shall not eat it [again] until there is fulfillment in the kingdom of God." [17] Then he took a cup, gave thanks, and said, "Take this and share it among yourselves; [18] for I tell you [that] from this time on I shall not drink of the fruit of the vine until the kingdom of God comes." [19] Then he took the bread, said the blessing, broke it, and gave it to them, saying, "This is my body, which will be given for you; do this in memory of me." [20] And likewise the cup after they had eaten, saying, "This cup is the new covenant in my blood, which will be shed for you.

The Betrayal Foretold. [21] "And yet behold, the hand of the one who is to betray me is with me on the table; [22] for the Son of Man indeed goes as it has been determined; but woe to that man by whom he is betrayed." [22] And they began to debate among themselves who among them would do such a deed.

The Role of the Disciples. [24] Then an argument broke out among them about which of them should be regarded as the greatest. [25] He said to them, "The kings of the Gentiles lord it over them and those in authority over them are addressed as 'Benefactors'; ²⁶ but among you it shall not be so. Rather, let the greatest among you be as the youngest, and the leader as the servant. ²⁷ For who is greater: the one seated at table or the one who serves? Is it not the one seated at table? I am among you as the one who serves. ²⁸ It is you who have stood by me in my trials; ²⁹ and I confer a kingdom on you, just as my Father has conferred one on me, ³⁰ that you may eat and drink at my table in my kingdom; and you will sit on thrones judging the twelve tribes of Israel.

Peter's Denial Foretold. ³¹ "Simon, Simon, behold Satan has demanded to sift all of you like wheat, ³² but I have prayed that your own faith may not fail; and once you have turned back, you must strengthen your brothers." ³³ He said to him, "Lord, I am prepared to go to prison and to die with you." ³⁴ But he replied, "I tell you, Peter, before the cock crows this day, you will deny three times that you know me."

Instructions for the Time of Crisis. ³⁵ He said to them, "When I sent you forth without a money bag or a sack or sandals, were you in need of anything?" "No, nothing," they replied. ³⁶ He said to them, "But now one who has a money bag should take it, and likewise a sack, and one who does not have a sword should sell his cloak and buy one. ³⁷ For I tell you that this scripture must be fulfilled in me, namely, `He was counted among the wicked'; and indeed what is written about me is coming to fulfillment." ³⁸ Then they said, "Lord, look, there are two swords here." But he replied, "It is enough!"

The Agony in the Garden. ³⁹ Then going out he went, as was his custom, to the Mount of Olives, and the disciples followed him ⁴⁰ When he arrived at the place he said to them, "Pray that you may not undergo the test." ⁴¹ After withdrawing about a stone's throw from them and kneeling, he prayed, ⁴² saying, "Father, if you are willing, take this cup away from me; still, not my will but yours be done." [⁴³ And to strengthen him an angel from heaven appeared to him. ⁴⁴ He was in such agony and he prayed so fervently that his sweat became like drops of blood falling on the ground.] ⁴⁵ When he rose from prayer and returned to his disciples, he found them sleeping from grief. ⁴⁶ He said to them, "Why are you sleeping? Get up and pray that you may not undergo the test."

The Betrayal and Arrest of Jesus. ⁴⁷ While he was still speaking, a crowd approached and in front was one of the Twelve, a man named Judas. He went up to Jesus to kiss him. ⁴⁸ Jesus said to him, "Judas, are you betraying the Son of Man with a kiss?" ⁴⁹ His disciples realized what was about to happen, and they asked, "Lord, shall we strike with a sword?" ⁵⁰ And one of them struck the high priest's servant and cut off his right ear. ⁵¹ But Jesus said in reply, "Stop, no more of this!" Then he touched the servant's ear and healed him. ⁵² And Jesus said to the chief priests and temple guards and elders who had come for him, "Have you come out as against a robber, with swords and clubs? ⁵³ Day after day I was with you in the temple area, and you did not seize me; but this is your hour, the time for the power of darkness."

Peter's Denial of Jesus. ⁵⁴ After arresting him they led him away and took him into the house of the high priest; Peter was following at a distance. ⁵⁵ They lit a fire in the middle of the courtyard and sat around it, and Peter sat down with them. ⁵⁶ When a maid saw him seated in the light, she looked intently at him and said, "This man too was with him." ⁵⁷ But he denied it saying, "Woman, I do not know him." ⁵⁸ A short while later someone else saw him and said, "You too are one of them"; but Peter answered, "My friend, I am not." ⁵⁹ About an hour later, still another insisted, "Assuredly, this man too was with him, for he also is a Galilean." ⁶⁰ But Peter said, "My friend, I do not know what you are talking about." Just as he was saying this, the cock crowed, ⁶¹ and the Lord turned and looked at Peter; and Peter remembered the word of the Lord, how he had said to him, "Before the cock crows today, you will deny me three times." ⁶² He went out and began to weep bitterly. ⁶³ The men who held Jesus in custody were ridiculing and beating him. ⁶⁴ They blindfolded him and questioned him, saying, "Prophesy! Who is it that struck you?" ⁶⁵ And they reviled him in saying many other things against him.

Jesus before the Sanhedrin. ⁶⁶ When day came the council of elders of the people met, both chief priests and scribes, and they brought him before their Sanhedrin. ⁶⁷ They said, "If you are the Messiah, tell us," but he replied to them, "If I tell you, you will not believe, ⁶⁸ and if I question, you will not respond. ⁶⁹ But from this time on the Son of Man will be seated at the right hand of the power of God." ⁷⁰ They all asked, "Are you then the Son of God?" He replied to them, "You say that I am." ⁷¹ Then they said, "What further need have we for testimony? We have heard it from his own mouth."

CHAPTER 23

Jesus before Pilate. ¹ Then the whole assembly of them arose and brought him before Pilate. ² They brought charges against him, saying, "We found this man misleading our people; he opposes the payment of taxes to Caesar and maintains that he is the Messiah, a king." ³ Pilate asked him, "Are you the king of the Jews?" He said to him in reply, "You say so." ⁴ Pilate Pilate then addressed the chief priests and the crowds, "I find this man not guilty." ⁵ But they were adamant and said, "He is inciting the people with his teaching throughout all Judea, from Galilee where he began even to here."

Jesus before Herod. ⁶ On hearing this Pilate asked if the man was a Galilean; ⁷ and upon learning that he was under Herod's jurisdiction, he sent him to Herod who was in Jerusalem at that time. ⁸ Herod was very glad to see Jesus; he had been wanting to see him for a long time, for he had heard about him and had been hoping to see him perform some sign. ⁹ He questioned him at length, but he gave him no answer. ¹⁰ The chief priests and scribes, meanwhile, stood by accusing him harshly. ¹¹ [Even] Herod and his soldiers treated him contemptuously and mocked him, and after clothing him in resplendent garb, he sent him back to Pilate. ¹² Herod and Pilate became friends that very day, even though they had been enemies formerly. ¹³ Pilate then summoned the chief priests, the rulers, and the people ¹⁴ and said to them, "You brought this man to me and accused him of inciting the people to revolt. I have conducted my investigation in your presence and have not found this man guilty of the charges you have brought against him, ¹⁵ nor did Herod, for he sent him back to us. So no capital crime has been committed by him. ¹⁶ Therefore I shall have him flogged and then release him." [¹⁷]

The Sentence of Death. ¹⁸ But all together they shouted out, "Away with this man! Release Barabbas to us." ¹⁹ (Now Barabbas had been imprisoned for a rebellion that had taken place in the city and for murder.) ²⁰ Again Pilate addressed them, still wishing to release Jesus, ²¹ but they continued their shouting, "Crucify him! Crucify him!" ²² Pilate addressed them a third time, "What evil has this man done? I found him guilty of no capital crime. Therefore I shall have him flogged and then release him." ²³ With loud shouts, however, they persisted in calling for his crucifixion, and their voices prevailed. ²⁴ The verdict of Pilate was that their demand should be granted. ²⁵ So he released the man who had been imprisoned for rebellion and murder, for whom they asked, and he handed Jesus over to them to deal with as they wished.

The Way of the Cross. ²⁶ As they led him away they took hold of a certain Simon, a Cyrenian, who was coming in from the country; and after laying the cross on him, they made him carry it behind Jesus. ²⁷ A large crowd of people followed Jesus, including many women who mourned and lamented him. ²⁸ "Jesus turned to them and said, "Daughters of Jerusalem, do not weep for me; weep instead for yourselves and for your children, ²⁹ for indeed, the days are coming when people will say, 'Blessed are the barren, the wombs that never bore and the breasts that never nursed.' ³⁰ At that time people will say to the mountains, 'Fall upon us!' and to the hills, 'Cover us!' ³¹ for if these things are done when the wood is green what will happen when it is dry?" ³² Now two others, both criminals, were led away with him to be executed.

The Crucifixion. ³³ When they came to the place called the Skull, they crucified him and the criminals there, one on his right, the other on his left. [34] [Then Jesus said, "Father, forgive them, they know not what they do."] They divided his garments by casting lots. [35] The people stood by and watched; the rulers, meanwhile, sneered at him and said, "He saved others, let him save himself if he is the chosen one, the Messiah of God." [36] Even the soldiers jeered at him. As they approached to offer him wine [37] they called out, "If you are King of the Jews, save yourself." [38] Above him there was an inscription that read, "This is the King of the Jews." [39] Now one of the criminals hanging there reviled Jesus, saying, "Are you not the Messiah? Save yourself and us." [40] The other, however, rebuking him, said in reply, "Have you no fear of God, for you are subject to the same condemnation? [41] And indeed, we have been condemned justly, for the sentence we received corresponds to our crimes, but this man has done nothing criminal." [42] Then he said, "Jesus, remember me when you come into your kingdom." [43] He replied to him, "Amen, I say to you, today you will be with me in Paradise."

The Death of Jesus. [44] It was now about noon and darkness came over the whole land until three in the afternoon [45] because of an eclipse of the sun. Then the veil of the temple was torn down the middle. [46] Jesus cried out in a loud voice, "Father, into your hands I commend my spirit"; and when he had said this he breathed his last. [47] The centurion who witnessed what had happened glorified God and said, "This man was innocent beyond doubt." [48] When all the people who had gathered for this spectacle saw what had happened, they returned home beating their breasts; [49] but all his acquaintances stood at a distance, including the women who had followed him from Galilee and saw these events.

The Burial of Jesus. [50] Now there was a virtuous and righteous man named Joseph who, though he was a member of the council, [51] had not consented to their plan of action. He came from the Jewish town of Arimathea and was awaiting the kingdom of God. [52] He went to Pilate and asked for the body of Jesus. [53] After he had taken the body down, he wrapped it in a linen cloth and laid him in a rock-hewn tomb in which no one had yet been buried. [54] It was the day of preparation, and the sabbath was about to begin. [55] The women who had come from Galilee with him followed behind, and when they had seen the tomb and the way in which his body was laid in it, [56] they returned and prepared spices and perfumed oils. Then they rested on the sabbath according to the commandment.

VIII: THE RESURRECTION NARRATIVE

CHAPTER 24

The Resurrection of Jesus. [1] But at day-break on the first day of the week they took the spices they had prepared and went to the tomb. [2] They found the stone rolled away from the tomb; [3] but when they entered, they did not find the body of the Lord Jesus. [4] While they were puzzling over this, behold, two men in dazzling garments appeared to them. [5] They were terrified and bowed their faces to the ground. They said to them, "Why do you seek the living one among the dead? [6] He is not here, but he has been raised. Remember what he said to you while he was still in Galilee, [7] that the Son of Man must be handed over to sinners and be crucified, and rise on the third day." [8] And they remembered his words. [9] Then they returned from the tomb and announced all these things to the eleven and to all the others. [10] The women were Mary Magdalene, Joanna, and Mary the mother of James; the others who accompanied them also told this to the apostles, [11] but their story seemed like nonsense and they did not believe them. [12] But Peter got up and ran to the tomb, bent down, and saw the burial cloths alone; then he went home amazed at what had happened.

The Appearance on the Road to Emmaus. [13] Now that very day two of them were going to a village seven miles from Jerusalem called Emmaus, [14] and they were conversing about all the things that had occurred. [15] And it happened that while they were conversing and debating, Jesus himself drew near and walked with them, [16] but their eyes were prevented from recognizing him. [17] He asked them, "What are you discussing as you walk along?" They stopped, looking downcast. [18] One of them, named Cleopas, said to him in reply, "Are you the only visitor to Jerusalem who does not know of the things that have taken place there in these days?" [19] And he replied to them, "What sort of things?" They said to him, "The things that happened to Jesus the Nazarene, who was a prophet mighty in deed and word before God and all the people, [20] how our chief priests and rulers both handed him over to a sentence of death and crucified him. [21] But we were hoping that he would be the one to redeem Israel; and besides all this, it is now the third day since this took place. [22] Some women from our group, however, have astounded us: they were at the tomb early in the morning [23] and did not find his body; they came back and reported that they had indeed seen a vision of angels who announced that he was alive. [24] Then some of those with us went to the tomb and found things just as the women had described, but him they did not see." [25] And he said to them, "Oh, how foolish you are! How slow of heart to believe all that the prophets spoke! [26] Was it not necessary that the Messiah should suffer these things and enter into his glory?" [27] Then beginning with Moses and all the prophets, he interpreted to them what referred to him in all the scriptures. [28] As they approached the village to which they were going, he gave the impression that he was going on farther. [29] But they urged him, "Stay with us, for it is nearly evening and the day is almost over." So he went in to stay with them. [30] And it happened that, while he was with them at table, he took bread, said the blessing, broke it, and gave it to them. [31] With that their eyes were opened and they recognized him, but he vanished from their sight. [32] Then they said to each other, "Were not our hearts burning [within us] while he spoke to us on the way and opened the scriptures to us?" [33] So they set out at once and returned to Jerusalem where they found gathered together the eleven and those with them [34] who were saying, "The Lord has truly been raised and has appeared to Simon!" [35] Then the two recounted what had taken place on the way and how he was made known to them in the breaking of the bread.

The Appearance to the Disciples in Jerusalem. [36] While they were still speaking about this, he stood in their midst and said to them, "Peace be with you." [37] But they were startled and terrified and thought that they were seeing a ghost. [38] Then he said to them, "Why are you troubled? And why do questions arise in your hearts? [39] Look at my hands and my feet, that it is I myself. Touch me and see, because a ghost does not have flesh and bones as you can see I have." [40] And as he said this, he showed them his hands and his feet. [41] While they were still incredulous for joy and were amazed, he asked them, "Have you anything here to eat?" [42] They gave him a piece of baked fish; [43] he took it and ate it in front of them. [44] He said to them, "These are my words that I spoke to you while I was still with you, that everything written about me in the law of Moses and in the prophets and psalms must be fulfilled." [45] Then he opened their minds to understand the scriptures. [46] And he said to them, "Thus it is written that the Messiah would suffer and rise from the dead on the third day [47] and that repentance, for the forgiveness of sins, would be preached in his name to all the nations, beginning from Jerusalem. [48] You are witnesses of these things. [49] And [behold] I am sending the promise of my Father upon you; but stay in the city until you are clothed with power from on high."

The Ascension. [50] Then he led them [out] as far as Bethany, raised his hands, and blessed them. [51] As he blessed them he parted from them and was taken up to heaven. [52] They did him homage and then returned to Jerusalem with great joy, [53] and they were continually in the temple praising God.

The Acts of the Apostles (Selections)

I: THE PREPARATION FOR THE CHRISTIAN MISSION

CHAPTER 1

The Promise of the Spirit. [1] In the first book, Theophilus, I dealt with all that Jesus did and taught [2] until the day he was taken up, after giving instructions through the holy Spirit to the apostles whom he had chosen. [3] He presented himself alive to them by many proofs after he had suffered, appearing to them during forty days and speaking about the kingdom of God. [4] While meeting with them, he enjoined them not to depart from Jerusalem, but to wait for "the promise of the Father about which you have heard me speak; [5] for John baptized with water, but in a few days you will be baptized with the holy Spirit."

The Ascension of Jesus. [6] When they had gathered together they asked him, "Lord, are you at this time going to restore the kingdom to Israel?" [7] He answered them, "It is not for you to know the times or seasons that the Father has established by his own authority. [8] But you will receive power when the holy Spirit comes upon you, and you will be my witnesses in Jerusalem, throughout Judea and Samaria, and to the ends of the earth." [9] When he had said this, as they were looking on, he was lifted up, and a cloud took him from their sight. [10] While they were looking intently at the sky as he was going, suddenly two men dressed in white garments stood beside them. [11] They said, "Men of Galilee, why are you standing there looking at the sky? This Jesus who has been taken up from you into heaven will return in the same way as you have seen him going into heaven." [12] Then they returned to Jerusalem from the mount called Olivet, which is near Jerusalem, a sabbath day's journey away.

The First Community in Jerusalem. [13] When they entered the city they went to the upper room where they were staying, Peter and John and James and Andrew, Philip and Thomas, Bartholomew and Matthew, James son of Alphaeus, Simon the Zealot, and Judas son of James. [14] All these devoted themselves with one accord to prayer, together with some women, and Mary the mother of Jesus, and his brothers.

The Choice of Judas's Successor. [15] During those days Peter stood up in the midst of the brothers (there was a group of about one hundred and twenty persons in the one place). He said, [16] "My brothers, the scripture had to be fulfilled which the holy Spirit spoke beforehand through the mouth of David, concerning Judas, who was the guide for those who arrested Jesus. [17] He was numbered among us and was allotted a share in this ministry. [18] He bought a parcel of land with the wages of his iniquity, and falling headlong, he burst open in the middle, and all his insides spilled out. [19] This became known to everyone who lived in Jerusalem, so that the parcel of land was called in their language 'Akeldama,' that is, Field of Blood. [20] For it is written in the Book of Psalms:

'Let his encampment become desolate,
    and may no one dwell in it.'

And:

'May another take his office.'

[21] Therefore, it is necessary that one of the men who accompanied us the whole time the Lord Jesus came and went among us, [22] beginning from the baptism of John until the day on which he was taken up from us, become with us a witness to his resurrection." [23] So they proposed two, Joseph called Barsabbas, who was also known as Justus, and Matthias. [24] Then they prayed, "You, Lord, who know the hearts of all, show which one of these two you have chosen [25] to take the place in this apostolic ministry from which Judas turned away to go to his own place." [26] Then they gave lots to them, and the lot fell upon Matthias, and he was counted with the eleven apostles.

CHAPTER 2

The Coming of the Spirit. ¹ When the time for Pentecost was fulfilled, they were all in one place together. ² And suddenly there came from the sky a noise like a strong driving wind, and it filled the entire house in which they were. ³ Then there appeared to them tongues as of fire, which parted and came to rest on each one of them. ⁴ And they were all filled with the holy Spirit and began to speak in different tongues, as the Spirit enabled them to proclaim.

⁵ Now there were devout Jews from every nation under heaven staying in Jerusalem. ⁶ At this sound, they gathered in a large crowd, but they were confused because each one heard them speaking in his own language. ⁷ They were astounded, and in amazement they asked, "Are not all these people who are speaking Galileans? ⁸ Then how does each of us hear them in his own native language? ⁹ We are Parthians, Medes, and Elamites, inhabitants of Mesopotamia, Judea and Cappadocia, Pontus and Asia, ¹⁰ Phrygia and Pamphylia, Egypt and the districts of Libya near Cyrene, as well as travelers from Rome, ¹¹ both Jews and converts to Judaism, Cretans and Arabs, yet we hear them speaking in our own tongues of the mighty acts of God." ¹² They were all astounded and bewildered, and said to one another, "What does this mean?" ¹³ But others said, scoffing, "They have had too much new wine."

II: THE MISSION IN JERUSALEM

Peter's Speech at Pentecost. ¹⁴ Then Peter stood up with the Eleven, raised his voice, and proclaimed to them, "You who are Jews, indeed all of you staying in Jerusalem. Let this be known to you, and listen to my words. ¹⁵ These people are not drunk, as you suppose, for it is only nine o'clock in the morning. ¹⁶ No, this is what was spoken through the prophet Joel:

¹⁷ 'It will come to pass in the last days,' God says,
    'that I will pour out a portion of my spirit upon all flesh.
Your sons and your daughters shall prophesy,
    your young men shall see visions,
    your old men shall dream dreams.
¹⁸ Indeed, upon my servants and my handmaids
    I will pour out a portion of my spirit in those days,
    and they shall prophesy.
¹⁹ And I will work wonders in the heavens above
    and signs on the earth below:
    blood, fire, and a cloud of smoke.
²⁰ The sun shall be turned to darkness,
    and the moon to blood,
    before the coming of the great and splendid day of the Lord,
²¹ and it shall be that everyone shall be saved who calls on
    the name of the Lord.'

²² You who are Israelites, hear these words. Jesus the Nazorean was a man commended to you by God with mighty deeds, wonders, and signs, which God worked through him in your midst, as you yourselves know. ²³ This man, delivered up by the set plan and foreknowledge of God, you killed, using lawless men to crucify him. ²⁴ But God raised him up, releasing him from the throes of death, because it was impossible for him to be held by it. ²⁵ For David says of him:

'I saw the Lord ever before me, "'
    with him at my right hand I shall not be disturbed.
²⁶ Therefore my heart has been glad and my tongue has exulted;
    my flesh, too, will dwell in hope,
²⁷ because you will not abandon my soul to the netherworld,
    nor will you suffer your holy one to see corruption.
²⁸ You have made known to me the paths of life;
    you will fill me with joy in your presence.'

²⁹ My brothers, one can confidently say to you about the patriarch David that he died and was buried, and his tomb is in our midst to this day. ³⁰ But since he was a prophet and knew that God had sworn an oath to him that he would set one of his descendants upon his throne, ³¹ he foresaw and spoke of the resurrection of the Messiah, that neither was he abandoned to the netherworld nor did his flesh see corruption. ³² God raised this Jesus; of this we are all witnesses. ³³ Exalted at the right hand of God, he received the promise of the holy Spirit from the Father and poured it forth, as you [both] see and hear. ³⁴ For David did not go up into heaven, but he himself said:

'The Lord said to my Lord, "Sit at my right hand

³⁵ until I make your enemies your foot-stool."'

³⁶ Therefore let the whole house of Israel know for certain that God has made him both Lord and Messiah, this Jesus whom you crucified."

³⁷ Now when they heard this, they were cut to the heart, and they asked Peter and the other apostles, "What are we to do, my brothers?" ³⁸ Peter [said] to them, "Repent and be baptized, every one of you, in the name of Jesus Christ for the forgiveness of your sins; and you will receive the gift of the holy Spirit. ³⁹ For the promise is made to you and to your children and to all those far off, whomever the Lord our God will call." ⁴⁰ He testified with many other arguments, and was exhorting them, "Save yourselves from this corrupt generation." ⁴¹ Those who accepted his message were baptized, and about three thousand persons were added that day.

Communal Life. ⁴² They devoted themselves to the teaching of the apostles and to the communal life, to the breaking of the bread and to the prayers. ⁴³ Awe came upon everyone, and many wonders and signs were done through the apostles. ⁴⁴ All who believed were together and had all things in common; ⁴⁵ they would sell their property and possessions and divide them among all according to each one's need. ⁴⁶ Every day they devoted themselves to meeting together in the temple area and to breaking bread in their homes. They ate their meals with exultation and sincerity of heart, ⁴⁷ praising God and enjoying favor with all the people. And every day the Lord added to their number those who were being saved.

CHAPTER 3

Cure of a Crippled Beggar. ¹ Now Peter and John were going up to the temple area for the three o'clock hour of prayer. ² And a man crippled from birth was carried and placed at the gate of the temple called "the Beautiful Gate" every day to beg for alms from the people who entered the temple. ³ When he saw Peter and John about to go into the temple, he asked for alms. ⁴ But Peter looked intently at him, as did John, and said, "Look at us." ⁵ He paid attention to them, expecting to receive something from them. ⁶ Peter said, "I have neither silver nor gold, but what I do have I give you: in the name of Jesus Christ the Nazorean, [rise and] walk." ⁷ Then Peter took him by the right hand and raised him up, and immediately his feet and ankles grew strong. ⁸ He leaped up, stood, and walked around, and went into the temple with them, walking and jumping and praising God. ⁹ When all the people saw him walking and praising God, ¹⁰ they recognized him as the one who used to sit begging at the Beautiful Gate of the temple, and they were filled with amazement and astonishment at what had happened to him.

Peter's Speech. ¹¹ As he clung to Peter and John, all the people hurried in amazement toward them in the portico called "Solomon's Portico." ¹² When Peter saw this, he addressed the people, "You Israelites, why are you amazed at this, and why do you look so intently at us as if we had made him walk by our own power or piety? ¹³ The God of Abraham, [the God] of Isaac, and [the God] of Jacob, the God of our ancestors, has glorified his servant Jesus whom you handed over and denied in Pilate's presence, when he had decided to release him. ¹⁴ You denied the Holy and Righteous One and asked that a murderer be released to you. ¹⁵ The author of life you put to death, but God raised him from the dead; of this we are witnesses. ¹⁶ And by faith in his name, this man, whom you see and know, his name has made strong, and the faith that comes through it has given him this perfect health, in the presence of all of you. ¹⁷ Now I know, brothers, that you acted out of ignorance, just as your leaders did; ¹⁸ but God has thus brought to fulfillment what he had announced beforehand through the mouth of all the prophets, that his Messiah would suffer. ¹⁹ Repent, therefore, and be converted, that your sins may be wiped away, ²⁰ and that the Lord may grant you times of refreshment and send you the Messiah already appointed for you, Jesus, ²¹ whom heaven must receive until the times of universal restoration of which God spoke through the mouth of his holy prophets from of old. ²² For Moses said:

'A prophet like me will the Lord, your God,
   raise up for you
      from among your own kinsmen;
to him you shall listen in all that he may
      say to you.
²³ Everyone who does not listen to that prophet
      will be cut off from the people.'

²⁴ Moreover, all the prophets who spoke, from Samuel and those afterwards, also announced these days. ²⁵ You are the children of the prophets and of the covenant that God made with your ancestors when he said to Abraham, 'In your offspring all the families of the earth shall be blessed.' ²⁶ For you first, God raised up his servant and sent him to bless you by turning each of you from your evil ways."

CHAPTER 4

¹ While they were still speaking to the people, the priests, the captain of the temple guard, and the Sadducees confronted them, ² disturbed that they were teaching the people and proclaiming in Jesus the resurrection of the dead. ³ They laid hands on them and put them in custody until

the next day, since it was already evening. ⁴ But many of those who heard the word came to believe and [the] number of men grew to [about] five thousand.

Before the Sanhedrin. ⁵ On the next day, their leaders, elders, and scribes were assembled in Jerusalem, ⁶ with Annas the high priest, Caiaphas, John, Alexander, and all who were of the high-priestly class. ⁷ They brought them into their presence and questioned them, "By what power or by what name have you done this?" ⁸ Then Peter, filled with the holy Spirit, answered them, "Leaders of the people and elders: ⁹ If we are being examined today about a good deed done to a cripple, namely, by what means he was saved, ¹⁰ then all of you and all the people of Israel should know that it was in the name of Jesus Christ the Nazorean whom you crucified, whom God raised from the dead; in his name this man stands before you healed. ¹¹ He is 'the stone rejected by you, the builders, which has become the cornerstone.' ¹² There is no salvation through anyone else, nor is there any other name under heaven given to the human race by which we are to be saved."

¹³ Observing the boldness of Peter and John and perceiving them to be uneducated, ordinary men, they were amazed, and they recognized them as the companions of Jesus. ¹⁴ Then when they saw the man who had been cured standing there with them, they could say nothing in reply. ¹⁵ So they ordered them to leave the Sanhedrin, and conferred with one another, saying, ¹⁶ "What are we to do with these men? Everyone living in Jerusalem knows that a remarkable sign was done through them, and we cannot deny it. ¹⁷ But so that it may not be spread any further among the people, let us give them a stern warning never again to speak to anyone in this name."

¹⁸ So they called them back and ordered them not to speak or teach at all in the name of Jesus. ¹⁹ Peter and John, however, said to them in reply, "Whether it is right in the sight of God for us to obey you rather than God, you be the judges. ²⁰ It is impossible for us not to speak about what we have seen and heard." ²¹ After threatening them further, they released them, finding no way

to punish them, on account of the people who were all praising God for what had happened. [22] For the man on whom this sign of healing had been done was over forty years old.

Prayer of the Community. [23] After their release they went back to their own people and reported what the chief priests and elders had told them. [24] And when they heard it, they raised their voices to God with one accord and said, "Sovereign Lord, maker of heaven and earth and the sea and all that is in them, [25] you said by the holy Spirit through the mouth of our father David, your servant:

'Why did the Gentiles rage
and the peoples entertain folly?
[26] The kings of the earth took their stand
and the princes gathered together
against the Lord and against his
anointed.'

[27] Indeed they gathered in this city against your holy servant Jesus whom you anointed, Herod and Pontius Pilate, together with the Gentiles and the peoples of Israel, [28] to do what your hand and [your] will had long ago planned to take place. [29] And now, Lord, take note of their threats, and enable your servants to speak your word with all boldness, [30] as you stretch forth [your] hand to heal, and signs and wonders are done through the name of your holy servant Jesus." [31] As they prayed, the place where they were gathered shook, and they were all filled with the holy Spirit and continued to speak the word of God with boldness.

Life in the Christian Community. [32] The community of believers was of one heart and mind, and no one claimed that any of his possessions was his own, but they had everything in common. [33] With great power the apostles bore witness to the resurrection of the Lord Jesus, and great favor was accorded them all. [34] There was no needy person among them, for those who owned property or houses would sell them, bring the proceeds of the sale, [35] and put them at the feet of the apostles, and they were distributed to each according to need.

[36] Thus Joseph, also named by the apostles Barnabas (which is translated "son of encouragement"), a Levite, a Cypriot by birth, [37] sold a piece of property that he owned, then brought the money and put it at the feet of the apostles.

ENDNOTES

The Gospel According to Luke

1:1–4 The Gospel according to Luke is the only one of the synoptic gospels to begin with a literary prologue. Making use of a formal, literary construction and vocabulary, the author writes the prologue in imitation of Hellenistic Greek writers and, in so doing, relates his story about Jesus to contemporaneous Greek and Roman literature. Luke is not only interested in the words and deeds of Jesus, but also in the larger context of the birth, ministry, death, and resurrection of Jesus as the fulfillment of the promises of God in the Old Testament. As a second- or third-generation Christian, Luke acknowledges his debt to earlier *eyewitnesses and ministers of the word,* but claims that his contribution to this developing tradition is a complete and accurate account, told in an orderly manner, and intended to provide Theophilus ("friend of God," literally) and other readers with certainty about earlier teachings they have received.

1:5–2:52 Like the Gospel according to Matthew, this gospel opens with an infancy narrative, a collection of stories about the birth and childhood of Jesus. The narrative uses early Christian traditions about the birth of Jesus, traditions about the birth and circumcision of John the Baptist, and canticles such as the Magnificat (1:46–55) and Benedictus (1:67–79), composed of phrases drawn from the Greek Old Testament. It is largely, however, the composition of Luke who writes in imitation of Old Testament birth stories, combining historical and legendary details, literary ornamentation and interpretation of scripture, to answer in advance the question, "Who is Jesus Christ?" The focus of the narrative, therefore, is primarily christological. In this section Luke announces many of the themes that will become prominent in the rest of the gospel: the centrality of Jerusalem and the temple, the journey motif, the universality of salvation, joy and peace, concern for the lowly, the importance of women, the presentation of Jesus as savior, Spirit-guided revelation and prophecy, and the fulfillment of Old Testament promises. The account presents parallel scenes (diptychs) of angelic announcements of the birth of John the Baptist and of Jesus, and of the birth, circumcision, and presentation of John and Jesus. In this parallelism, the ascendency of Jesus over John is stressed: John is prophet of the Most High (1:76); Jesus Is Son of the Most High (1:32). John is great in the sight of the Lord (1:15); Jesus will be Great (a LXX attribute, used absolutely, of God) (1:32). John will go before the Lord (1:16–17); Jesus will be Lord (1:43; 2:11).

1:5 *In the days of Herod, King of Judea:* Luke relates the story of salvation history to events in contemporary world history. Here and in 3:1–2 he connects his narrative with events in Palestinian history; in 2:1–2 and 3:1 he casts the Jesus story in the light of events of Roman history. Herod the Great, the son of the Idumean Antipater, was declared "King of Judea" by the Roman Senate in 40 B.C., but became the undisputed ruler of Palestine only in 37 B.C. He continued as king until his death in 4 B.C. Priestly division of Abijah: a reference to the eighth of the twenty-four divisions of priests who, for a week at a time, twice a year, served in the Jerusalem temple.

1:7 *They had no child:* though childlessness was looked upon in contemporaneous Judaism as a curse or punishment for sin, it is intended here to present Elizabeth in a situation similar to that of some of the great mothers of important Old Testament figures: Sarah (Gn 15:3;16:1); Rebekah (Gn 25:21); Rachel (Gn 29:31; 30:1); the mother of Samson and wife of Manoah (Jgs 13:2–3); Hannah (1 Sm 1:2).

1:13 *Do not be afraid:* a stereotyped Old Testament phrase spoken to reassure the recipient of a heavenly vision (Gn 15:1; Jos 1:9; Dn 10:12, 19 and elsewhere in v. 30; 2:10). *You shall name him John:* the name means "Yahweh has shown favor," an indication of John's role in salvation history.

1:15 *He will drink neither wine nor strong drink:* like Samson (Jgs 13:4–5) and Samuel (1 Sm 1:11 LXX and 4QSama), John is to be consecrated by Nazirite vow and set apart for the Lord's service.

1:17 *He will go before him in the spirit and power of Elijah:* John is to be the messenger sent before Yahweh, as described in Mal 3:1–2. He is cast, moreover, in the role of the Old Testament fiery reformer, the prophet Elijah, who according to Mal 3:23 is sent before "the great and terrible day of the Lord comes."

1:19 *I am Gabriel:* "the angel of the Lord" is identified as Gabriel, the angel who in Dn 9:20–25 announces the seventy weeks of years and the coming of an anointed one, a prince. By alluding to Old Testament themes in vv. 17, 19 such as the coming of the day of the Lord and the dawning of the messianic era, Luke is presenting his interpretation of the significance of the births of John and Jesus.

1:20 *You will be speechless and unable to talk:* Zechariah's becoming mute is the sign given in response to his question in v. 18. When Mary asks a similar question in v. 34, unlike Zechariah who was punished for his doubt, she, in spite of her doubt, is praised and reassured (vv. 35–37).

1:26–38 The announcement to Mary of the birth of Jesus is parallel to the announcement to Zechariah of the birth of John. In both the angel Gabriel appears to the parent who is troubled by the vision (vv. 11–12, 26–29) and then told by the angel not to fear (vv. 13, 30). After the announcement is made (vv. 14–17, 31–33) the parent objects (vv. 18, 34) and a sign is given to confirm the announcement (vv. 20, 36). The particular focus of the announcement of the birth of Jesus is on his identity as Son of David (vv. 32–33) and Son of God (vv. 32, 35).

1:32 *Son of the Most High:* cf. v. 76 where John is described as "prophet of the Most High." "Most High" is a title for God commonly used by Luke (Lk 1:35, 76; 6:35; 8:28; Acts 7:48; 16:17).

1:34 Mary's questioning response is a denial of sexual relations and is used by Luke to lead to the angel's declaration about the Spirit's role in the conception of this child (v. 35). According to Luke, the virginal conception of Jesus takes place through the holy Spirit, the power of God, and therefore Jesus has a unique relationship to Yahweh: he is Son of God.

1:36–37 The sign given to Mary in confirmation of the angel's announcement to her is the pregnancy of her aged relative Elizabeth. If a woman past the childbearing age could become pregnant, why, the angel implies, should there be doubt about Mary's pregnancy, for nothing will be impossible for God.

1:43 Even before his birth, Jesus is identified in Luke as the Lord.

1:45 *Blessed are you who believed:* Luke portrays Mary as a believer whose faith stands in contrast to the disbelief of Zechariah (v. 20). Mary's role as believer in the infancy narrative should be seen in connection with the explicit mention of her presence among "those who believed" after the resurrection at the beginning of the Acts of the Apostles (Acts 1:14).

1:46–55 Although Mary is praised for being the mother of the Lord and because of her belief, she reacts as the servant in a psalm of praise, the Magnificat. Because there is no specific connection of the canticle to the context of Mary's pregnancy and her visit to Elizabeth, the Magnificat (with the possible exception of v. 48) may have been a Jewish Christian hymn that Luke found appropriate at this point in his story. Even if not composed by Luke, it fits in well with themes found elsewhere in Luke: joy and exultation in the Lord; the lowly being singled out for God's favor; the reversal of human fortunes; the fulfillment of Old Testament promises. The loose connection between the hymn and the context is further seen in the fact that a few Old Latin manuscripts identify the speaker of the hymn as Elizabeth, even though the overwhelming textual evidence makes Mary the speaker.

1:57–66 The birth and circumcision of John above all emphasize John's incorporation into the people of Israel by the sign of the covenant (Gn 17:1–12). The narrative of John's circumcision also prepares the way for the subsequent description of the circumcision of Jesus in 2:21. At the beginning of his two-volume work Luke shows those who play crucial roles in the inauguration of Christianity to be wholly a part of the people of Israel. At the end of the Acts of the Apostles (Acts 21:20; 22:3; 23:6–9; 24:14–16; 26:2–8, 22–23) he will argue that Christianity is the direct descendant of Pharisaic Judaism.

1:59 The practice of Palestinian Judaism at this time was to name the child at birth; moreover, though naming a male child after the father is not completely unknown, the usual practice was to name the child after the grandfather (see v. 61). The naming of the child John and Zechariah's recovery from his loss of speech should be understood as fulfilling the angel's announcement to Zechariah in vv. 13, 20.

1:68–79 Like the canticle of Mary (vv. 46; 55) the canticle of Zechariah is only loosely connected with its context. Apart from vv. 76–77, the hymn in speaking of a horn for our salvation (v. 69) and the daybreak from on high (v. 78) applies more closely to Jesus and his work than to John. Again like Mary's canticle, it is largely composed of phrases taken from the Greek Old Testament and may have been a Jewish Christian hymn of praise that Luke adapted to fit the present context by inserting vv. 76–77 to give Zechariah's reply to the question asked in v. 66. 1:69 A horn for our salvation: the horn is a common Old Testament figure for strength (Ps 18:3; 75:5–6; 89:18; 112:9; 148:14). This description is applied to God in Ps 18:2 and is here transferred to Jesus. The connection of the phrase with

the house of David gives the title messianic overtones and may indicate an allusion to a phrase in Hannah's song of praise (1 Sm 2:10), "the horn of his anointed."

1:76 *You will go before the Lord:* here the Lord is most likely a reference to Jesus (contrast vv. 15–17 where Yahweh is meant) and John is presented as the precursor of Jesus.

1:78 *The daybreak from on high:* three times in the LXX (Jer 23:5; Zec 3:8; 6:12), the Greek word used here for *daybreak* translates the Hebrew word for "scion, branch," an Old Testament messianic title.

2:1–2 Although universal registrations of Roman citizens are attested in 28 B.C., 8 B.C., and A.D. 14 and enrollments in individual provinces of those who are not Roman citizens are also attested, such a universal census of the Roman world under Caesar Augustus is unknown outside the New Testament. Moreover, there are notorious historical problems connected with Luke's dating the census when *Quirinius was governor of Syria,* and the various attempts to resolve the difficulties have proved unsuccessful. P. Sulpicius Quirinius became legate of the province of Syria in A.D. 6–7 when Judea was annexed to the province of Syria. At that time, a provincial census of Judea was taken up. If Quirinius had been legate of Syria previously, it would have to have been before 10 B.C. because the various legates of Syria from 10 B.C. to 4 B.C. (the death of Herod) are known, and such a dating for an earlier census under Quirinius would create additional problems for dating the beginning of Jesus' ministry (3:1, 23). A previous legateship after 4 B.C. (and before A.D. 6) would not fit with the dating of Jesus' birth in the days of Herod (Lk 1:5; Mt 2:1). Luke may simply be combining Jesus' birth in Bethlehem with his vague recollection of a census under Quirinius (see also Acts 5:37) to underline the significance of this birth for the whole Roman world: through this child born in Bethlehem peace and salvation come to the empire.

2:1 *Caesar Augustus:* the reign of the Roman emperor Caesar Augustus is usually dated from 27 B.C. to his death in A.D. 14. According to Greek inscriptions, Augustus was regarded in the Roman Empire as "savior" and "god," and he was credited with establishing a time of peace, the *pax Augusta,* throughout the Roman world during his long reign. It is not by chance that Luke relates the birth of Jesus to the time of Caesar Augustus: the real savior (v. 11) and peace-bearer (v. 14; see also 19:38) is the child born in Bethlehem. The great emperor is simply God's agent (like the Persian king Cyrus in Is 44:28–45:1) who provides the occasion for God's purposes to be accomplished. *The whole world:* that is, the whole Roman world: Rome, Italy, and the Roman provinces.

2:7 *Firstborn son:* the description of Jesus as firstborn son does not necessarily mean that Mary had other sons. It is a legal description indicating that Jesus possessed the rights and privileges of the firstborn son (Gn 27; Ex 13:2; Nm 3:12–13; 18:15–16; Dt 21:15–17). See notes on Mt 1:25; Mk 6:3. *Wrapped him in swaddling clothes:* there may be an allusion here to the birth of another descendant of David, his son Solomon, who though a great king was wrapped in swaddling clothes like any other infant (Wis 7:4–6). *Laid him in a manger:* a feeding trough for animals. A possible allusion to Is 1:3 LXX.

2:8–20 The announcement of Jesus' birth to the shepherds is in keeping with Luke's theme that the lowly are singled out as the recipients of God's favors and blessings (see also 1:48, 52).

2:11 *The basic message of the infancy narrative is contained in the angel's announcement:* this child is savior, Messiah, and Lord. Luke is the only synoptic gospel writer to use the title savior for Jesus (Lk 2:11; Acts 5:31; 13:23; see also Lk 1:69; 19:9; Acts 4:12). As savior, Jesus is looked upon by Luke as the one who rescues humanity from sin and delivers humanity from the condition of alienation from God. The title *christos,* "Christ" is the Greek equivalent of the Hebrew *masiah,* "Messiah," "anointed one." Among certain groups in first-century Palestinian Judaism, the title was applied to an expected royal leader from the line of David who would restore the kingdom to Israel (see Acts 1:6). The political overtones of the title are played down in Luke and instead the Messiah of the Lord (v. 26) or the Lord's anointed is the one who now brings salvation to all humanity, Jew and Gentile (vv. 29–32). Lord is the most frequently used title for Jesus in Luke and Acts. In the New Testament it is also applied to Yahweh, as it is in the Old Testament. When used of Jesus it points to his transcendence and dominion over humanity.

2:14 *On earth peace to those on whom his favor rests:* the peace that results from the Christ event is for those whom God has favored with his grace. This reading is found in the oldest representatives of the Western and Alexandrian text traditions and is the preferred one; the Byzantine text tradition, on the other hand, reads: "on earth peace, good will toward men." The peace of which Luke's gospel speaks (v. 14; 7:50; 8:48; 10:5–6; 19:38, 42; 24:36) is more than the absence of war of the *pax Augusta;* it also includes the security and well-being characteristic of peace in the Old Testament.

2:21 Just as John before him had been incorporated into the people of Israel through his circumcision, so too this child (see note on 1:57–66).

2:22–40 The presentation of Jesus in the temple depicts the parents of Jesus as devout Jews, faithful observers of the law of the Lord (vv. 23–24, 39), i.e., the law of Moses. In this respect, they are described in a fashion similar to the parents of John (1:6) and Simeon (v. 25) and Anna (vv. 36–37).

2:22 *Their purification:* syntactically, *their* must refer to Mary and Joseph, even though the Mosaic law never mentions the purification of the husband. Recognizing the problem, some Western scribes have altered the text to read "his purification," understanding the presentation of Jesus in the temple as a form of purification; the Vulgate version has a Latin form that could be either "his" or "her." According to the Mosaic law (Lv 12:2–8), the woman who gives birth to a boy is unable for forty days to touch anything sacred or to enter the temple area by reason of her legal impurity. At the end of this period she is required to offer a year-old lamb as a burnt offering and a turtledove or young pigeon as an expiation of sin. The woman who could not afford a lamb offered instead two turtledoves or two young pigeons, as Mary does here. *They took him up to Jerusalem to present him to the Lord:* as the firstborn son (v. 7) Jesus was consecrated to the Lord as the law required (Ex 13:2, 12), but there was no requirement that this be done

at the temple. The concept of a presentation at the temple is probably derived from 1 Sm 1:24–28, where Hannah offers the child Samuel for sanctuary services. The law further stipulated (Nm 3:47–48) that the firstborn son should be redeemed by the parents through their payment of five shekels to a member of a priestly family. About this legal requirement Luke is silent.

2:25 *Awaiting the consolation of Israel:* Simeon here and later Anna who speak about the child to all who were awaiting the redemption of Jerusalem represent the hopes and expectations of faithful and devout Jews who at this time were looking forward to the restoration of God's rule in Israel. The birth of Jesus brings these hopes to fulfillment.

2:35 *(And you yourself a sword will pierce):* Mary herself will not be untouched by the various reactions to the role of Jesus (v. 34). Her blessedness as mother of the Lord will be challenged by her son who describes true blessedness as "hearing the word of God and observing it" (11:27–28 and 8:20–21).

2:41–52 This story's concern with an incident from Jesus' youth is unique in the canonical gospel tradition. It presents Jesus in the role of the faithful Jewish boy, raised in the traditions of Israel, and fulfilling all that the law requires. With this episode, the infancy narrative ends just as it began, in the setting of the Jerusalem temple.

2:49 I must be in my Father's house: this phrase can also be translated, "I must be about my Father's work." In either translation, Jesus refers to God as his Father. His divine sonship, and his obedience to his heavenly Father's will, take precedence over his ties to his family.

3:1–20 Although Luke is indebted in this section to his sources, the Gospel of Mark and a collection of sayings of John the Baptist, he has clearly marked this introduction to the ministry of Jesus with his own individual style. Just as the gospel began with a long periodic sentence (1:1–4), so too this section (vv. 1–2). He casts the call of John the Baptist in the form of an Old Testament prophetic call (v. 2) and extends the quotation from Isaiah found in Mk 1:3 (Is 40:3) by the addition of Is 40:4–5 in vv. 5–6. In doing so, he presents his theme of the universality of salvation, which he has announced earlier in the words of Simeon (2:30–32). Moreover, in describing the expectation of the people (v. 15), Luke is characterizing the time of John's preaching in the same way as he had earlier described the situation of other devout Israelites in the infancy narrative (2:25–26, 37–38). In vv. 7–18 Luke presents the preaching of John the Baptist who urges the crowds to reform in view of the coming wrath (vv. 7, 9: eschatological preaching), and who offers the crowds certain standards for reforming social conduct (vv. 10–14: ethical preaching), and who announces to the crowds the coming of *one mightier than* he (vv. 15–18: messianic preaching).

3:1 *Tiberius Caesar:* Tiberius succeeded Augustus as emperor in A.D. 14 and reigned until A.D. 37. The fifteenth year of his reign, depending on the method of calculating his first regnal year, would have fallen between A.D. 27 and 29. *Pontius Pilate:* prefect of Judea from A.D. 26 to 36. The Jewish historian Josephus describes him as a greedy and ruthless prefect who had little regard for the local Jewish population and their religious practices (see 13:1). *Herod:* i.e., Herod Antipas, the son of Herod the Great. He ruled over Galilee and Perea from 4 B.C. to A.D. 39. His official title tetrarch means lit., "ruler of a quarter," but came to designate any subordinate prince. Philip: also a son of Herod the Great, tetrarch of the territory to the north and east of the Sea of Galilee from 4 B.C. to A.D. 34. Only two small areas of this territory are mentioned by Luke. Lysanias: nothing is known about this Lysanias who is said here to have been tetrarch of Abilene, a territory northwest of Damascus.

3:2 *During the high priesthood of Annas and Caiaphas:* after situating the call of John the Baptist in terms of the civil rulers of the period, Luke now mentions the religious leadership of Palestine (see note on 1:5). Annas had been high priest A.D. 6–15. After being deposed by the Romans in A.D. 15 he was succeeded by various members of his family and eventually by his son-in-law, Caiaphas, who was high priest A.D. 18–36. Luke refers to Annas as high priest at this time (but see Jn 18:13, 19), possibly because of the continuing influence of Annas or because the title continued to be used for the ex-high priest. *The word of God came to John:* Luke is alone among the New Testament writers in associating the preaching of John with a call from God. Luke is thereby identifying John with the prophets whose ministries began with similar calls. In 7:26 John will be described as "more than a prophet"; he is also the precursor of Jesus (7:27), a transitional figure inaugurating the period of the fulfillment of prophecy and promise.

3:4 The Essenes from Qumran used the same passage to explain why their community was in the desert studying and observing the law and the prophets (1QS 8:12–15).

3:16 *He will baptize you with the holy Spirit and fire:* in contrast to John's baptism with water, Jesus is said to baptize with the holy Spirit and with fire. From the point of view of the early Christian community, the Spirit and fire must have been understood in the light of the fire symbolism of the pouring out of the Spirit at Pentecost (Acts 2:1–4); but as part of John's preaching, the Spirit and fire should be related to their purifying and refining characteristics (Ez 36:25–27; Mal 3:2–3).

3:19–20 Luke separates the ministry of John the Baptist from that of Jesus by reporting the imprisonment of John before the baptism of Jesus (vv. 21–22). Luke uses this literary device to serve his understanding of the periods of salvation history. With John the Baptist, the time of promise, the period of Israel, comes to an end; with the baptism of Jesus and the descent of the Spirit upon him, the time of fulfillment, the period of Jesus, begins. In his second volume, the Acts of the Apostles, Luke will introduce the third epoch in salvation history, the period of the church.

3:21–22 This episode in Luke focuses on the heavenly message identifying Jesus as Son and, through the allusion to Is 42:1, as Servant of Yahweh. The relationship of Jesus to the Father has already been announced in the infancy narrative (1:32, 35; 2:49); it occurs here at the beginning of Jesus' Galilean ministry and will reappear in 9:35 before another major section of Luke's gospel, the travel narrative (9:51–19:27). Elsewhere in Luke's writings (Lk 4:18; Acts 10:38), this incident will be interpreted as a type of anointing of Jesus.

3:21 *Was praying:* Luke regularly presents Jesus at prayer at important points in his ministry: here at his baptism; at the choice of the Twelve (6:12); before Peter's confession (9:18); at the transfiguration (9:28); when he teaches his disciples to pray (11:1); at the Last Supper (22:32); on the Mount of Olives (22:41); on the cross (23:46).

3:22 *You are my beloved Son; with you I am well pleased:* this is the best attested reading in the Greek manuscripts. The Western reading, "You are my Son, this day I have begotten you," is derived from Ps 2:7.

3:23–38 Whereas Mt 1:2 begins the genealogy of Jesus with Abraham to emphasize Jesus' bonds with the people of Israel, Luke's universalism leads him to trace the descent of Jesus beyond Israel to Adam and beyond that to God (v. 38) to stress again Jesus' divine sonship.

3:31 *The son of Nathan, the son of David:* in keeping with Jesus' prophetic role in Luke and Acts (e.g., Lk 7:16, 39; 9:8; 13:33; 24:19; Acts 3:22–23; 7:37) Luke traces Jesus' Davidic ancestry through the prophet Nathan (see 2 Sm 7:2) rather than through King Solomon, as Mt 1:6-7.

4:1 *Filled with the holy Spirit:* as a result of the descent of the Spirit upon him at his baptism (3:21–22), Jesus is now equipped to overcome the devil. Just as the Spirit is prominent at this early stage of Jesus' ministry (vv. 1, 14, 18), so too it will be at the beginning of the period of the church in Acts (Acts 1:4; 2:4, 17).

4:2 *For forty days:* the mention of forty days recalls the forty years of the wilderness wanderings of the Israelites during the Exodus (Dt 8:2).

4:9 *To Jerusalem:* the Lucan order of the temptations concludes on the parapet of the temple in Jerusalem, the city of destiny in Luke–Acts. It is in Jerusalem that Jesus will ultimately face his destiny (9:51; 13:33).

4:13 For a time, the devil's opportune time will occur before the passion and death of Jesus (22:3, 31–32, 53).

4:14 *News of him spread:* a Lucan theme; see 4:37; 5:15; 7:17.

4:16–30 Luke has transposed to the beginning of Jesus' ministry an incident from his Marcan source, which situated it near the end of the Galilean ministry (Mk 6:1–6a). In doing so, Luke turns the initial admiration (v. 22) and subsequent rejection of Jesus (vv. 28–29) into a foreshadowing of the whole future ministry of Jesus. Moreover, the rejection of Jesus in his own home-town hints at the greater rejection of him by Israel (Acts 13:46).

4:16 *According to his custom:* Jesus' practice of regularly attending synagogue is carried on by the early Christians' practice of meeting in the temple (Acts 2:46; 3:1; 5:12).

4:18 *The Spirit of the Lord is upon me, because he has anointed me:* see note on 3:21–22. As this incident develops, Jesus is portrayed as a prophet whose ministry is compared to that of the prophets Elijah and Elisha. Prophetic anointings are known in first-century Palestinian Judaism from the Qumran literature that speaks of prophets as God's anointed ones. *To bring glad tidings to the poor:* more than any other gospel writer Luke is concerned with Jesus' attitude toward the economically and socially poor (see 6:20, 24; 12:16–21; 14:12–14; 16:19–26;

19:8). At times, the poor in Luke's gospel are associated with the downtrodden, the oppressed and afflicted, the forgotten and the neglected (4:18; 6:20–22; 7:22; 14:12–14), and it is they who accept Jesus' message of salvation.

4:21 *Today this scripture passage is fulfilled in your hearing:* this sermon inaugurates the time of fulfillment of Old Testament prophecy. Luke presents the ministry of Jesus as fulfilling Old Testament hopes and expectations (7:22); for Luke, even Jesus' suffering, death, and resurrection are done in fulfillment of the scriptures (Lk 24:25–27, 44–46; Acts 3:18).

4:23 *The things that we heard were done in Capernaum:* Luke's source for this incident reveals an awareness of an earlier ministry of Jesus in Capernaum that Luke has not yet made use of because of his transposition of this Nazareth episode to the beginning of Jesus' Galilean ministry. It is possible that by use of the future tense *you will quote me . . . ,* Jesus is being portrayed as a prophet.

4:25–26 *The references to Elijah and Elisha serve several purposes in this episode:* they emphasize Luke's portrait of Jesus as a prophet like Elijah and Elisha; they help to explain why the initial admiration of the people turns to rejection; and they provide the scriptural justification for the future Christian mission to the Gentiles.

4:26 *A widow in Zarephath in the land of Sidon:* like Naaman the Syrian in v. 27, a non-Israelite becomes the object of the prophet's ministry.

4:31–44 The next several incidents in Jesus' ministry take place in Capernaum and are based on Luke's source, Mk 1:21–39. To the previous portrait of Jesus as prophet (vv. 16–30) they now add a presentation of him as teacher (vv. 31–32), exorcist (vv. 32–37, 41), healer (vv. 38–40), and proclaimer of God's kingdom (v. 43).

4:34 *What have you to do with us? Have you come to destroy us?:* the question reflects the current belief that before the day of the Lord control over humanity would be wrested from the evil spirits, evil destroyed, and God's authority over humanity reestablished. The synoptic gospel tradition presents Jesus carrying out this task.

4:38 *The house of Simon:* because of Luke's arrangement of material, the reader has not yet been introduced to Simon (cf. Mk 1:16–18, 29–31). Situated as it is before the call of Simon (5:1–11), it helps the reader to understand Simon's eagerness to do what Jesus says (5:5) and to follow him (5:11).

4:41 *They knew that he was the Messiah:* that is, the Christ (see note on 2:11).

4:42 *They tried to prevent him from leaving them:* the reaction of these strangers in Capernaum is presented in contrast to the reactions of those in his hometown who rejected him (vv. 28–30).

4:44 *In the synagogues of Judea:* instead of *Judea,* which is the best reading of the manuscript tradition, the Byzantine text tradition and other manuscripts read "Galilee," a reading that harmonizes Luke with Mt 4:23 and Mk 1:39. Up to this point Luke has spoken only of a ministry of Jesus in Galilee. Luke may be using *Judea* to refer to the land of Israel, the territory of the Jews, and not to a specific portion of it.

5:1–11 This incident has been transposed from his source, Mk 1:16–20, which places it immediately after Jesus makes his appearance in Galilee. By this transposition Luke uses this example of Simon's acceptance of Jesus to counter the earlier rejection of him by his hometown people, and since several incidents dealing with Jesus' power and authority have already been narrated, Luke creates a plausible context for the acceptance of Jesus by Simon and his partners. Many commentators have noted the similarity between the wondrous catch of fish reported here (4:4–9) and the post-resurrectional appearance of Jesus in Jn 21:1–11. There are traces in Luke's story that the post-resurrectional context is the original one: in 4:8 Simon addresses Jesus as *Lord* (a post-resurrectional title for Jesus–see Lk 24:34; Acts 2:36–that has been read back into the historical ministry of Jesus) and recognizes himself as a sinner (an appropriate recognition for one who has denied knowing Jesus–22:54–62). As used by Luke, the incident looks forward to Peter's leadership in Luke–Acts (Lk 6:14; 9:20; 22:31–32; 24:34; Acts 1:15; 2:14–40; 10:11–18; 15:7–12) and symbolizes the future success of Peter as fisherman (Acts 2:41).

5:11 *They left everything:* in Mk 1:16–20 and Mt 4:18–22 the fishermen who follow Jesus leave their nets and their father; in Luke, they leave everything (see also 5:28; 12:33; 14:33; 18:22), an indication of Luke's theme of complete detachment from material possessions.

5:14 *Show yourself to the priest . . . what Moses pre-scribed:* this is a reference to Lv 14:2–9 that gives detailed instructions for the purification of one who had been a victim of leprosy and thereby excluded from contact with others (see Lv 13:45–46, 49; Nm 5:2–3).

5:17–6:11 From his Marcan source, Luke now introduces a series of controversies with Pharisees: controversy over Jesus' power to forgive sins (5:17–26); controversy over his eating and drinking with tax collectors and sinners (5:27–32); controversy over not fasting (5:33–36); and finally two episodes narrating controversies over observance of the sabbath (6:1–11).

5:19 *Through the tiles:* Luke has adapted the story found in Mark to his non-Palestinian audience by changing "opened up the roof" (Mk 2:4 a reference to Palestinian straw and clay roofs) to *through the tiles,* a detail that reflects the Hellenistic Greco-Roman house with tiled roof.

5:20 *As for you, your sins are forgiven:* life., "O man, your sins are forgiven you." The connection between the forgiveness of sins and the cure of the paralytic reflects the belief of first-century Palestine (based on the Old Testament: Ex 20:5; Dt 5:9) that sickness and infirmity are the result of sin, one's own or that of one's ancestors (see also Lk 13:2; Jn 5:14; 9:2).

5:28 *Leaving everything behind:* see note on v. 11. 5:34–35

5:34 *Wedding guests:* lit., "sons of the bridal chamber."

5:39 *The old is good:* this saying is meant to be ironic and offers an explanation for the rejection by some of the new wine that Jesus offers: satisfaction with old forms will prevent one from sampling the new.

6:1–11 The two episodes recounted here deal with gathering grain and healing, both of which were forbidden on the sabbath. In his defense of his disciples' conduct and his own charitable deed, Jesus argues that satisfying human needs such as hunger and performing works of mercy take precedence even over the sacred sabbath rest.

6:12 *Spent the night in prayer:* see note on Lk 3:21.

6:13 *He chose Twelve:* the identification of this group as the Twelve is a part of early Christian tradition (see 1 Cor 15:5), and in Matthew and Luke, the Twelve are associated with the twelve tribes of Israel (Lk 22:29–30; Mt 19:28). After the fall of Judas from his position among the Twelve, the need is felt on the part of the early community to reconstitute this group before the Christian mission begins at Pentecost (Acts 1:15–26). From Luke's perspective, they are an important group who because of their association with Jesus from the time of his baptism to his ascension (Acts 1:21–22) provide the continuity between the historical Jesus and the church of Luke's day and who as the original eyewitnesses guarantee the fidelity of the church's beliefs and practices to the teachings of Jesus (1:1–4). *Whom he also named apostles:* only Luke among the gospel writers attributes to Jesus the bestowal of the name *apostles* upon the Twelve. See note on Mt 10:2–4. "Apostle" becomes a technical term in early Christianity for a missionary sent out to preach the word of God. Although Luke seems to want to restrict the title to the Twelve (only in Acts 4:4, 14 are Paul and Barnabas termed apostles), other places in the New Testament show an awareness that the term was more widely applied (1 Cor 15:5–7; Gal 1:19; 1 Cor 1:1; 9:1; Rom 16:7).

6:15 *Simon who was called a Zealot:* the Zealots were the instigators of the First Revolt of Palestinian Jews against Rome in A.D. 66–70. Because the existence of the Zealots as a distinct group during the lifetime of Jesus is the subject of debate, the meaning of the identification of Simon as a Zealot is unclear.

6:16 *Judas Iscariot:* the name Iscariot may mean "man from Kerioth."

6:17 *The coastal region of Tyre and Sidon:* not only Jews from Judea and Jerusalem, but even Gentiles from outside Palestine come to hear Jesus (see 2:31–32; 3:6; 4:24–27).

6:20–49 Luke's "Sermon on the Plain" is the counterpart to Matthew's "Sermon on the Mount" (Mt 5:1–7:27). It is addressed to the disciples of Jesus, and, like the sermon in Matthew, it begins with beatitudes (vv. 20–22) and ends with the parable of the two houses (vv. 46–49). Almost all the words of Jesus reported by Luke are found in Matthew's version, but because Matthew includes sayings that were related to specifically Jewish Christian problems (e.g., Mt 5:17–20; 6:1–8, 16–18) that Luke did not find appropriate for his predominantly Gentile Christian audience, the "Sermon on the Mount" is considerably longer. Luke's sermon may be outlined as follows: an introduction consisting of blessings and woes (vv. 20–26); the love of one's enemies (vv. 27–36); the demands of loving one's neighbor (vv. 37–42); good deeds as proof of one's goodness (vv. 43–45); a parable illustrating the result of listening to and acting on the words of Jesus (vv. 46–49). At the core of the sermon is Jesus' teaching on the love of one's enemies (vv. 27–36) that has as its source of motivation God's graciousness and compassion for all humanity (vv. 35–36) and Jesus' teaching on the love of one's neighbor (vv. 37–42) that is characterized by forgiveness and generosity.

6:20–26 The introductory portion of the sermon consists of blessings and woes that address the real economic and social conditions of humanity (the poor–the rich; the hungry–the satisfied; those grieving–those laughing; the outcast–the socially acceptable). By contrast, Matthew emphasizes the religious and spiritual values of disciples in the kingdom inaugurated by Jesus ("poor in spirit," Mt 5:5; "hunger and thirst for righteousness," Mt 5:6). In the sermon, blessed extols the fortunate condition of persons who are favored with the blessings of God; the woes, addressed as they are to the disciples of Jesus, threaten God's profound displeasure on those so blinded by their present fortunate situation that they do not recognize and appreciate the real values of God's kingdom. In all the blessings and woes, the present condition of the persons addressed will be reversed in the future.

7:1–8:3 The episodes in this section present a series of reactions to the Galilean ministry of Jesus and reflect some of Luke's particular interests: the faith of a Gentile (7: 1–10); the prophet Jesus' concern for a widowed mother (7:11–17); the ministry of Jesus directed to the afflicted and unfortunate of Is 61:1 (7:18–23); the relation between John and Jesus and their role in God's plan for salvation (7:24–35); a forgiven sinner's manifestation of love (7:36–50); the association of women with the ministry of Jesus (8:1–3).

7:1–10 This story about the faith of the centurion, a Gentile who cherishes the Jewish nation (v. 5), prepares for the story in Acts of the conversion by Peter of the Roman centurion Cornelius who is similarly described as one who is generous to the Jewish nation (Acts 10:2). See also Acts 10:34–35 in the speech of Peter: "God shows no partiality . . . the person who fears him and acts righteously is acceptable to him."

7:6 *I am not worthy to have you enter under my roof:* to enter the house of a Gentile was considered unclean for a Jew; cf. Acts 10:28.

7:11–17 In the previous incident Jesus' power was displayed for a Gentile whose servant was dying; in this episode it is displayed toward a widowed mother whose only son has already died. Jesus' power over death prepares for his reply to John's disciples in v. 22: "the dead are raised." This resuscitation in alluding to the prophet Elijah's resurrection of the only son of a widow of Zarephath (1 Kgs 17:8–24) leads to the reaction of the crowd: "A great prophet has arisen in our midst" (v. 16).

7:18–23 In answer to John's question, *Are you the one who, is to come?*–a probable reference to the return of the fiery prophet of reform, Elijah, "before the day of the Lord comes, the great and terrible day" (Mal 3:19)–Jesus responds that his role is rather to bring the blessings spoken of in Is 61:1 to the oppressed and neglected of society (v. 22; cf. 4:18).

7:23 *Blessed is the one who takes no offense at me:* this beatitude is pronounced on the person who recognizes Jesus' true identity in spite of previous expectations of what "the one who is to come" would be like.

7:24–30 In his testimony to John, Jesus reveals his understanding of the relationship between them: John is the precursor of Jesus (v. 27); John is the messenger spoken of in Mal 3:1 who in Mal 3:19 is identified as Elijah. Taken with the previous episode, it can be seen that Jesus identifies John as precisely the person John envisioned Jesus to be: the Elijah who prepares the way for the coming of the day of the Lord.

7:36–50 In this story of the pardoning of the sinful woman Luke presents two different reactions to the ministry of Jesus. A Pharisee, suspecting Jesus to be a prophet, invites Jesus to a festive banquet in his house, but the Pharisee's self-righteousness leads to little forgiveness by God and consequently little love shown toward Jesus. The sinful woman, on the other hand, manifests a faith in God (v. 50) that has led her to seek forgiveness for her sins, and because so much was forgiven, she now overwhelms Jesus with her display of love; cf. the similar contrast in attitudes in 18:9–14. The whole episode is a powerful lesson on the relation between forgiveness and love.

7:36 *Reclined at table:* the normal posture of guests at a banquet. Other oriental banquet customs alluded to in this story include the reception by the host with a kiss (v. 45), washing the feet of the guests (v. 44), and the anointing of the guests' heads (v. 46).

7:41 *Days' wages:* one denarius is the normal daily wage of a laborer.

7:47 *Her many sins have been forgiven; hence, she has shown great love:* lit., "her many sins have been forgiven, seeing that she has loved much." That the woman's sins have been forgiven is attested by the great love she shows toward Jesus. Her love is the consequence of her forgiveness. This is also the meaning demanded by the parable in vv. 41–43.

8:1–3 Luke presents Jesus as an itinerant preacher traveling in the company of the Twelve and of the Galilean women who are sustaining them out of their means. These Galilean women will later accompany Jesus on his journey to Jerusalem and become witnesses to his death (23:49) and resurrection (24:9–11, where Mary Magdalene and Joanna are specifically mentioned; cf. also Acts 1:14). The association of women with the ministry of Jesus is most unusual in the light of the attitude of first-century Palestinian Judaism toward women. The more common attitude is expressed in Jn 4:27, and early rabbinic documents caution against speaking with women in public.

8:4–21 The focus in this section is on how one should hear the word of God and act on it. It includes the parable of the sower and its explanation (vv. 4–15), a collection of sayings on how one should act on the word that is heard (vv. 16–18), and the identification of the mother and brothers of Jesus as the ones who hear the word and act on it (vv. 19–21).

8:16–18 These sayings continue the theme of responding to the word of God. Those who hear the word must become a light to others (v. 16); even the mysteries of the kingdom that have been made known to the disciples (vv. 9–10) must come to light (v. 17); a generous and persevering response to the word of God leads to a still more perfect response to the word.

8:21 The family of Jesus is not constituted by physical relationship with him but by obedience to the word of God. In this, Luke agrees with the Marcan parallel (Mk 3:31–35), although by omitting Mk 3:33 and especially Mk 3:20–21 Luke has softened the Marcan picture of Jesus' natural family.

Probably he did this because Mary has already been presented in 1:38 as the obedient handmaid of the Lord who fulfills the requirement for belonging to the eschatological family of Jesus; cf. also 11:27–28.

8:22–56 This section records four miracles of Jesus that manifest his power and authority: (1) the calming of a storm on the lake (vv. 22–25); (2) the exorcism of a demoniac (vv. 26–39); (3) the cure of a hemorrhaging woman (vv. 40–48); (4) the raising of Jairus's daughter to life (vv. 49–56). They parallel the same sequence of stories at Mk 4:35–5:43.

8:26 *Gerasenes:* other manuscripts read Gadarenes or Gergesenes. *Opposite Galilee:* probably Gentile territory (note the presence in the area of pigs–unclean animals to Jews) and an indication that the person who receives salvation (v. 36) is a Gentile.

8:30 *What is your name?:* the question reflects the popular belief that knowledge of the spirit's name brought control over the spirit. *Legion:* to Jesus' question the demon replies with a Latin word transliterated into Greek. The Roman legion at this period consisted of 5,000 to 6,000 foot soldiers; hence the name implies a very large number of demons.

8:31 *Abyss:* the place of the dead (Rom 10:7) or the prison of Satan (Rev 20:3) or the subterranean "watery deep" that symbolizes the chaos before the order imposed by creation (Gn 1:2).

8:35 *Sitting at his feet:* the former demoniac takes the position of a disciple before the master (Lk 10:39; Acts 22:3).

8:40–56 Two interwoven miracle stories, one a healing and the other a resuscitation, present Jesus as master over sickness and death. In the Lucan account, faith in Jesus is responsible for the cure (v. 48) and for the raising to life (v. 50).

8:42 *An only daughter:* cf. the son of the widow of Nain whom Luke describes as an "only" son (7:12; see also 9:38).

8:43 Afflicted with hemorrhages for twelve years: according to the Mosaic law (Lv 15:25–30) this condition would render the woman unclean and unfit for contact with other people.

8:52 *Sleeping:* her death is a temporary condition; cf. Jn 11:11–14.

9:1–6 Armed with the power and authority that Jesus himself has been displaying in the previous episodes, the Twelve are now sent out to continue the work that Jesus has been performing throughout his Galilean ministry: (1) proclaiming the kingdom (4:43; 8:1); (2) exorcising demons (4:33–37, 41; 8:26–39) and (3) healing the sick (4:38–40; 5:12–16, 17–26; 6:6–10; 7:1–10, 17, 22; 8:40–56).

9:3 *Take nothing for the journey:* the absolute detachment required of the disciple (14:33) leads to complete reliance on God (12:22–31).

9:7–56 This section in which Luke gathers together incidents that focus on the identity of Jesus is introduced by a question that Herod is made to ask in this gospel: "Who then is this about whom I hear such things?" (v. 9) In subsequent episodes, Luke reveals to the reader various answers to Herod's question: Jesus is one in whom God's power is present and who provides for the needs of God's people (vv. 10–17); Peter declares Jesus to be "the Messiah of God" (vv. 18–21); Jesus says he is the suffering Son of Man (vv. 22, 43–45); Jesus is the Master to be followed, even to death (vv. 23–27); Jesus is God's son, his Chosen One (vv. 28–36).

9:7 *Herod the tetrarch:* see note on 3:1.

9:9 *And he kept trying to see him:* this indication of Herod's interest in Jesus prepares for 13:31–33 and for 23:8–12 where Herod's curiosity about Jesus' power to perform miracles remains unsatisfied.

9:16 *Then taking . . . :* the actions of Jesus recall the institution of the Eucharist in 22:19; 9:18–22 This incident is based on Mk 8:27–33, but Luke has eliminated Peter's refusal to accept Jesus as suffering Son of Man (Mk 8:32) and the rebuke of Peter by Jesus (Mk 8:33). Elsewhere in the gospel, Luke softens the harsh portrait of Peter and the other apostles found in his Marcan source (cf. 22:39–46, which similarly lacks a rebuke of Peter that occurs in the source, Mk 14:37–38).

9:18 *When Jesus was praying in solitude:* see note on 3:21.

9:23 *Daily:* this is a Lucan addition to a saying of Jesus, removing the saying from a context that envisioned the imminent suffering and death of the disciple of Jesus (as does the saying in Mk 8:34–35) to one that focuses on the demands of daily Christian existence.

9:28–36 Situated shortly after the first announcement of the passion, death, and resurrection, this scene of Jesus' transfiguration provides the heavenly confirmation to Jesus' declaration that his suffering will end in glory (v. 32).

9:28 *Up the mountain to pray:* the "mountain" is the regular place of prayer in Luke (see 6:12; 22:39–41).

9:30 *Moses and Elijah:* the two figures represent the Old Testament law and the prophets. At the end of this episode, the heavenly voice will identify Jesus as the one to be listened to now (v. 35).

9:31 *His exodus that he was going to accomplish in Jerusalem:* Luke identifies the subject of the conversation as the *exodus* of Jesus, a reference to the death, resurrection, and ascension of Jesus that will take place in Jerusalem, the city of destiny (see v. 51). The mention of exodus, however, also calls to mind the Israelite Exodus from Egypt to the promised land.

9:32 *They saw his glory:* the glory that is proper to God is here attributed to Jesus (see 24:26).

9:33 *Let us make three tents:* in a possible allusion to the feast of Tabernacles, Peter may be likening his joy on the occasion of the transfiguration to the joyful celebration of this harvest festival.

9:34 Over them: it is not clear whether them refers to Jesus, Moses, and Elijah, or to the disciples.

9:35 Like the heavenly voice that identified Jesus at his baptism prior to his undertaking the Galilean ministry (3:22), so too here before the journey to the city of destiny is begun (v. 51) the heavenly voice again identifies Jesus as Son. *Listen to him:* the two representatives of Israel of old depart (v. 33) and Jesus is left alone (v. 36) as the teacher whose words must be heeded (see also Acts 3:22).

9:36 *At that time:* i.e., before the resurrection.

9:46–50 These two incidents focus on attitudes that are opposed to Christian discipleship: rivalry and intolerance of outsiders.

9:51–18:14 The Galilean ministry of Jesus finishes with the previous episode and a new section of Luke's gospel begins, the journey to Jerusalem. This journey is based on Mk 10:1–52 but Luke uses his Marcan source only in 18:15–19:27. Before that point he has inserted into his gospel a distinctive collection of sayings of Jesus and stories about him that he has drawn from Q, a collection of sayings of Jesus used also by Matthew, and from his own special traditions. All of the material collected in this section is loosely organized within the framework of a journey of Jesus to Jerusalem, the city of destiny, where his exodus (suffering, death, resurrection, ascension) is to take place (9:31), where salvation is accomplished, and from where the proclamation of God's saving word is to go forth (Lk 24:47; Acts 1:8). Much of the material in the Lucan travel narrative is teaching for the disciples. During the course of this journey Jesus is preparing his chosen Galilean witnesses for the role they will play after his exodus (9:31): they are to be his witnesses to the people (Acts 10:39; 13:31) and thereby provide certainty to the readers of Luke's gospel that the teachings they have received are rooted in the teachings of Jesus (1:1–4).

9:51–55 Just as the Galilean ministry began with a rejection of Jesus in his hometown, so too the travel narrative begins with the rejection of him by Samaritans. In this episode Jesus disassociates himself from the attitude expressed by his disciples that those who reject him are to be punished severely. The story alludes to 2 Kgs 1:10, 12 where the prophet Elijah takes the course of action Jesus rejects, and Jesus thereby rejects the identification of himself with Elijah.

9:51 *Days for his being taken up:* like the reference to his exodus in v. 31 this is probably a reference to all the events (suffering, death, resurrection, ascension) of his last days in Jerusalem. *He resolutely determined:* lit., "he set his face."

9:52 *Samaritan:* Samaria was the territory between Judea and Galilee west of the Jordan river. For ethnic and religious reasons, the Samaritans and the Jews were bitterly opposed to one another (see Jn 4:9).

9:57–62 In these sayings Jesus speaks of the severity and the unconditional nature of Christian discipleship. Even family ties and filial obligations, such as burying one's parents, cannot distract one no matter how briefly from proclaiming the kingdom of God. The first two sayings are paralleled in Mt 8:19–22.

9:60 *Let the dead bury their dead:* i.e., let the spiritually dead (those who do not follow) bury their physically dead.

10:1–12 Only the Gospel of Luke contains two episodes in which Jesus sends out his followers on a mission: the first (9:1–6) is based on the mission in Mk 6:66–13 and recounts the sending out of the Twelve; here in vv. 1–12 a similar report based on Q becomes the sending out of seventy-two in this gospel. The episode continues the theme of Jesus preparing witnesses to himself and his ministry. These witnesses include not only the Twelve but also the seventy-two who may represent the Christian mission in Luke's own day. Note that the instructions given to the Twelve and to the seventy-two are similar and that what is said to the seventy-two in v. 4 is directed to the Twelve in 22:35.

10:1 *Seventy[-two]:* important representatives of the Alexandrian and Caesarean text types read "seventy," while other important Alexandrian texts and Western readings have "seventy-two."

10:4 *Carry no money bag . . . greet no one along the way:* because of the urgency of the mission and the singlemindedness required of missionaries, attachment to material possessions should be avoided and even customary greetings should not distract from the fulfillment of the task.

10:5 *First say, 'Peace to this household':* see notes on Lk 2:14.

10:6 *A peaceful person:* lit., "a son of peace."

10:13–16 The call to repentance that is a part of the proclamation of the kingdom brings with it a severe judgment for those who hear it and reject it.

10:15 *The netherworld:* the underworld, the place of the dead (Acts 2:27, 31) here contrasted with heaven.

10:18 *I have observed Satan fall like lightning:* the effect of the mission of the seventy-two is characterized by the Lucan Jesus as a symbolic fall of Satan. As the kingdom of God is gradually being established, evil in all its forms is being defeated; the dominion of Satan over humanity is at an end.

10:21 *Revealed them to the childlike:* a restatement of the theme announced in 8:10: the mysteries of the kingdom are revealed to the disciples.

10:25–37 In response to a question from a Jewish legal expert about inheriting eternal life, Jesus illustrates the superiority of love over legalism through the story of the good Samaritan. The law of love proclaimed in the "Sermon on the Plain" (6:27–36) is exemplified by one whom the legal expert would have considered ritually impure (see Jn 4:9). Moreover, the identity of the "neighbor" requested by the legal expert (v. 29) turns out to be a Samaritan, the enemy of the Jew (see note on 9:52).

10:25 *Scholar of the law:* an expert in the Mosaic law, and probably a member of the group elsewhere identified as the scribes (5:21).

10:31–32 *Priest . . . Levite:* those religious representatives of Judaism who would have been expected to be models of "neighbor" to the victim pass him by.

10:38–42 The story of Martha and Mary further illustrates the importance of hearing the words of the teacher and the concern with women in Luke.

10:39 *Sat beside the Lord at his feet:* it is remarkable for first-century Palestinian Judaism that a woman would assume the posture of a disciple at the master's feet (see also Lk 8:35; Acts 22:3), and it reveals a characteristic attitude of Jesus toward women in this gospel (see 8:2–3).

10:42 *There is need of only one thing:* some ancient versions read, "there is need of few things"; another important, although probably inferior, reading found in some manuscripts is, "there is need of few things, or of one"

11:1–13 Luke presents three episodes concerned with prayer. The first (vv. 1–4) recounts Jesus teaching his disciples the Christian communal prayer, the "Our Father"; the second (vv. 5–8), the importance of persistence in prayer; the third (vv. 9–13), the effectiveness of prayer.

11:1–4 The Matthean form of the "Our Father" occurs in the "Sermon on the Mount" (Mt 6:9–15); the shorter Lucan version is presented while Jesus is at prayer (see note on 3:21) and his disciples ask him to teach them to pray just as John taught his disciples to pray. In answer to their question, Jesus presents them with an example of a Christian communal prayer that stresses the fatherhood of God and acknowledges him as the one to whom the Christian disciple owes daily sustenance (v.3), forgiveness (v. 4), and deliverance from the final trial (v. 4).

11:2 *Your kingdom come:* in place of this petition, some early church Fathers record: "May your holy Spirit come upon us and cleanse us," a petition that may reflect the use of the "Our Father" in a baptismal liturgy.

11:13 *The holy Spirit:* this is a Lucan editorial alteration of a traditional saying of Jesus (see Mt 7:11). Luke presents the gift of the holy Spirit as the response of the Father to the prayer of the Christian disciple.

11:19 *Your own people:* the Greek reads "your sons" Other Jewish exorcists (see Acts 19:13–20), who recognize that the power of God is active in the exorcism, would themselves convict the accusers of Jesus.

11:22 *One stronger:* i.e., Jesus. Cf. 3:16 where John the Baptist identifies Jesus as "more powerful than I."

11:27–28 The beatitude in v. 28 should not be interpreted as a rebuke of the mother of Jesus; see note on 8:21. Rather, it emphasizes (like 2:35) that attentiveness to God's word is more important than biological relationship to Jesus.

11:29–32 The "sign of Jonah" in Luke is the preaching of the need for repentance by a prophet who comes from afar. Cf. Mt 12:38–42 (and see notes there) where the "sign of Jonah" is interpreted by Jesus as his death and resurrection.

11:37–54 This denunciation of the Pharisees (vv. 39–44) and the scholars of the law (vv. 45–52) is set by Luke in the context of Jesus' dining at the home of a Pharisee. Controversies with or reprimands of Pharisees are regularly set by Luke within the context of Jesus' eating with Pharisees (see 5:29–39; 7:36–50; 14:1–24).

11:44 *Unseen graves:* contact with the dead or with human bones or graves (see Nm 19:16) brought ritual impurity. Jesus presents the Pharisees as those who insidiously lead others astray through their seeming attention to the law.

11:45 *Scholars of the law:* see note on 10:25.

11:49 *I will send to them prophets and apostles:* Jesus connects the mission of the church (apostles) with the mission of the Old Testament prophets who often suffered the rebuke of their contemporaries.

11:51 *From the blood of Abel to the blood of Zechariah:* the murder of Abel is the first murder recounted in the Old Testament (Gn 4:8). The Zechariah mentioned here may be the Zechariah whose murder is recounted in 2 Chr 24:20–22, the last murder presented in the Hebrew canon of the Old Testament.

12:2–9 Luke presents a collection of sayings of Jesus exhorting his followers to acknowledge him and his mission fearlessly and assuring them of God's protection even in times of persecution. They are paralleled in Mt 10:26–33.

12:6 *Two small coins:* the Roman copper coin, the assarion (Latin *as*), was worth about one-sixteenth of a denarius (see note on 7:41).

12:10–12 The sayings about the holy Spirit are set in the context of fearlessness in the face of persecution (vv. 2–9; cf. Mt 12:31–32). The holy Spirit will be presented in Luke's second volume, the Acts of the Apostles, as the power responsible for the guidance of the Christian mission and the source of courage in the face of persecution.

12:13–34 Luke has joined together sayings contrasting those whose focus and trust in life is on material possessions, symbolized here by the rich fool of the parable (vv. 16–21), with those who recognize their complete dependence on God Is. 21), those whose radical detachment from material possessions symbolizes their heavenly treasure (vv. 33–34).

12:21 *Rich in what matters to God:* lit., "rich for God."

12:35–48 This collection of sayings relates to Luke's understanding of the end time and the return of Jesus. Luke emphasizes for his readers the importance of being faithful to the instructions of Jesus in the period before the parousia.

12:45 *My master is delayed in coming:* this statement indicates that early Christian expectations for the imminent return of Jesus had undergone some modification. Luke cautions his readers against counting on such a delay and acting irresponsibly. Cf. the similar warning in Mt 24:48.

12:49–53 Jesus' proclamation of the kingdom is a refining and purifying fire. His message that meets with acceptance or rejection will be a source of conflict and dissension even within families.

12:50 *Baptism:* i.e., his death.

12:59 *The last penny:* Greek, *lepton,* a very small amount. Mt 5:26 has for "the last penny" the Greek word *kodrantēs* (Latin *quadrans,* "farthing").

13:1–5 The death of the Galileans at the hands of Pilate (v. 1) and the accidental death of those on whom the tower fell (v. 4) are presented by the Lucan Jesus as timely reminders of the need for all to repent, for the victims of these tragedies should not be considered outstanding sinners who were singled out for punishment.

13:1 The slaughter of the Galileans by Pilate is unknown outside Luke; but from what is known about Pilate from the Jewish historian Josephus, such a slaughter would be in keeping with the character of Pilate. Josephus reports that Pilate had disrupted a religious gathering of the Samaritans on Mount Gerizim with a slaughter of the participants (*Antiquities* 18, 4,1 #86–87), and that on another occasion Pilate had killed many Jews who had opposed him when he appropriated money from the temple treasury to build an aqueduct in Jerusalem (*Jewish War* 2, 9, 4 #175–77; *Antiquities* 18, 3, 2 #60–62).

13:4 Like the incident mentioned in v. 1 nothing of this accident in Jerusalem is known outside Luke and the New Testament.

13:6–9 Following on the call to repentance in vv. 1–5, the parable of the barren fig tree presents a story about the continuing patience of God with those who have not yet given evidence of their repentance (see 3:8). The parable may also be alluding to the delay of the end time, when punishment will be meted out, and the importance of preparing for the end of the age because the delay will not be permanent (vv. 8–9).

13:10–17 The cure of the crippled woman on the sabbath and the controversy that results furnishes a parallel to an incident that will be reported by Luke in 14:1–6, the cure of the man with dropsy on the sabbath. A characteristic of Luke's style is the juxtaposition of an incident that reveals Jesus' concern for a man with an incident that reveals his concern for a woman; cf., e.g., 7:11–17 and 8:49–56.

13:15–16 If the law as interpreted by Jewish tradition allowed for the untying of bound animals on the sabbath, how much more should this woman who has been bound by Satan's power be freed on the sabbath from her affliction.

13:16 *Whom Satan has bound:* affliction and infirmity are taken as evidence of Satan's hold on humanity. The healing ministry of Jesus reveals the gradual wresting from Satan of control over humanity and the establishment of God's kingdom.

13:18–21 Two parables are used to illustrate the future proportions of the kingdom of God that will result from its deceptively small beginning in the preaching and healing ministry of Jesus. They are paralleled in Mt 13:31–33 and Mk 4:30–32.

13:22–30 These sayings of Jesus follow in Luke upon the parables of the kingdom (vv. 18–21) and stress that great effort is required for entrance into the kingdom (v. 24) and that there is an urgency to accept the present opportunity to enter because the narrow door will not remain open indefinitely (v. 25). Lying behind the sayings is the rejection of Jesus and his message by his Jewish contemporaries (v. 26) whose places at table in the kingdom will be taken by Gentiles from the four corners of the world (v. 29). Those called last (the Gentiles) will precede those to whom the invitation to enter was first extended (the Jews). See also 14:15–24.

13:32 Nothing, not even Herod's desire to kill Jesus, stands in the way of Jesus' role in fulfilling God's will and in establishing the kingdom through his exorcisms and healings.

13:33 *It is impossible that a prophet should die outside of Jerusalem:* Jerusalem is the city of destiny and the goal of the journey of the prophet Jesus. Only when he reaches the holy city will his work be accomplished.

14:1–6 See note on 13:10–17.

14:2 *Dropsy:* an abnormal swelling of the body because of the retention and accumulation of fluid.

14:5 *Your son or ox:* this is the reading of many of the oldest and most important New Testament manuscripts. Because of the strange collocation of *son* and *ox,* some copyists have altered it to "your ass or ox," on the model of the saying in 13:15.

14:7–14 The banquet scene found only in Luke provides the opportunity for these teachings of Jesus on humility and presents a setting to display Luke's interest in Jesus' attitude toward the rich and the poor (see notes on 4:18; 6:20–26; 12:13–34).

14:15–24 The parable of the great dinner is a further illustration of the rejection by Israel, God's chosen people, of Jesus' invitation to share in the banquet in the kingdom and the extension of the invitation to other Jews whose identification as the poor, crippled, blind, and lame (v. 21) classifies them among those who recognize their need for salvation, and to Gentiles (v. 23). A similar parable is found in Mt 22:1–10.

14:25–33 This collection of sayings, most of which are peculiar to Luke, focuses on the total dedication necessary for the disciple of Jesus. No attachment to family (v. 26) or possessions (v. 33) can stand in the way of the total commitment demanded of the disciple. Also, acceptance of the call to be a disciple demands readiness to accept persecution and suffering (v. 27) and a realistic assessment of the hardships and costs (vv. 28–32).

14:26 *Hating his father . . . :* cf. the similar saying in Mt 10:37. The disciple's family must take second place to the absolute dedication involved in following Jesus (see also 9:59–62).

14:34–35 The simile of salt follows the sayings of Jesus that demanded of the disciple total dedication and detachment from family and possessions and illustrates the condition of one who does not display this total commitment. The halfhearted disciple is like salt that cannot serve its intended purpose.

15:1–32 To the parable of the lost sheep (vv. 1–7) that Luke shares with Matthew (Mt 18:12–14), Luke adds two parables (the lost coin, vv. 8–10; the prodigal son, vv. 11–32) from his own special tradition to illustrate Jesus' particular concern for the lost and God's love for the repentant sinner.

15:8 *Ten coins:* lit., "ten drachmas." A drachma was a Greek silver coin.

16:1–8a The parable of the dishonest steward has to be understood in the light of the Palestinian custom of agents acting on behalf of their masters and the usurious practices common to such agents. The dishonesty of the steward consisted in the squandering of his master's property (v. 1) and not in any subsequent graft. The master commends the dishonest steward who has forgone his own usurious commission on the business transaction by having the debtors write new notes that reflected only the real amount owed the master (i.e., minus the steward's profit). The dishonest steward acts in this way in order to ingratiate himself with the debtors because he knows he is being dismissed from his position In. 3). The parable, then, teaches the prudent use of one's material goods in light of an imminent crisis.

16:6 *One hundred measures:* lit., "one hundred baths." A bath is a Hebrew unit of liquid measurement equivalent to eight or nine gallons.

16:7 *One hundred kors:* a *kor* is a Hebrew unit of dry measure for grain or wheat equivalent to ten or twelve bushels.

16:8b–13 Several originally independent sayings of Jesus are gathered here by Luke to form the concluding application of the parable of the dishonest steward.

16:8b–9 The first conclusion recommends the prudent use of one's wealth (in the light of the coming of the end of the age) after the manner of the children of this world, represented in the parable by the dishonest steward.

16:9 *Dishonest wealth:* lit., "mammon of iniquity." Mammon is the Greek transliteration of a Hebrew or Aramaic word that is usually explained as meaning "that in which one trusts." The characterization of this wealth as dishonest expresses a tendency of wealth to lead one to dishonesty. *Eternal dwellings:* or, "eternal tents," i.e., heaven.

16:10–12 The second conclusion recommends constant fidelity to those in positions of responsibility.

16:13 The third conclusion is a general statement about the incompatibility of serving God and being a slave to riches. To be dependent upon wealth is opposed to the teachings of Jesus who counseled complete dependence on the Father as one of the characteristics of the Christian disciple (12:22–39). God and mammon: see note on v. 9. Mammon is used here as if it were itself a god.

16:14–18 The two parables about the use of riches in chap. 16 are separated by several isolated sayings of Jesus on the hypocrisy of the Pharisees (vv. 14–15), on the law (vv. 16–17), and on divorce (v. 18).

16:14–15 The Pharisees are here presented as examples of those who are slaves to wealth (see v.13) and, consequently, they are unable to serve God.

16:16 John the Baptist is presented in Luke's gospel as a transitional figure between the period of Israel, the time of promise, and the period of Jesus, the time of fulfillment. With John, the fulfillment of the old Testament promises has begun.

16:19–31 The parable of the rich man and Lazarus again illustrates Luke's concern with Jesus' attitude toward the rich and the poor. The reversal of the fates of the rich man and Lazarus (vv. 22–23) illustrates the teachings of Jesus in Luke's "Sermon on the Plain" (6:20–21, 24–25).

16:19 The oldest Greek manuscript of Luke dating from ca. A.D. 175–225 records the name of the rich man as an abbreviated form of "Nineveh," but there is very little textual support in other manuscripts for this reading. "Dives" of popular tradition is the Latin Vulgate's translation for "rich man" (vv. 19–31).

16:23 *The netherworld:* see note on 10:15.

16:30–31 A foreshadowing in Luke's gospel of the rejection of the call to repentance even after Jesus' resurrection.

17:3 *Be on your guard:* the translation takes v. 3a as the conclusion to the saying on scandal in vv. 1–2. It is not impossible that it should be taken as the beginning of the saying on forgiveness in vv. 3b–4.

17:7–10 These sayings of Jesus, peculiar to Luke, which continue his response to the apostles' request to increase their faith (vv. 5–6), remind them that Christian disciples can make no claim on God's graciousness; in fulfilling the exacting demands of discipleship, they are only doing their duty.

17:11–19 This incident recounting the thankfulness of the cleansed Samaritan leper is narrated only in Luke's gospel and provides an instance of Jesus holding up a non-Jew (v. 18) as an example to his Jewish contemporaries (cf. 10:33 where a similar purpose is achieved in the story of the good Samaritan). Moreover, it is the faith in Jesus manifested by the foreigner that has brought him salvation (v. 19; cf. the similar relationship between faith and salvation in 7:50; 8:48, 50).

17:11 *Through Samaria and Galilee:* or, "between Samaria and Galilee."

17:14 See note on 5:14.

17:20–37 To the question of the Pharisees about the time of the coming of God's kingdom, Jesus replies that the kingdom is *among you* (vv. 20–21). The emphasis has thus been shifted from an imminent observable coming of the kingdom to something that is already present in Jesus' preaching and healing ministry. Luke has also appended further traditional sayings of Jesus about the unpredictable suddenness of the day of the Son of Man, and assures his readers that in spite of the delay of that day (12:45), it will bring judgment unexpectedly on those who do not continue to be vigilant.

17:21 *Among you:* the Greek preposition translated as among can also be translated as "within." In the light of other statements in Luke's gospel about the presence of the kingdom (see 10:9, 11; 11:20) "among" is to be preferred.

17:36 The inclusion of v. 36, "There will be two men in the field; one will be taken, the other left behind," in some Western manuscripts appears to be a scribal assimilation to Mt 24:40.

18:1–14 The particularly Lucan material in the travel narrative concludes with two parables on prayer. The first (vv. 1–8) teaches the disciples the need of persistent prayer so that they not fall victims to apostasy (v. 8). The second (vv. 9–14) condemns the self-righteous, critical attitude of the Pharisee and teaches that the fundamental attitude of the Christian disciple must be the recognition of sinfulness and complete dependence on God's graciousness. The second parable recalls the story of the pardoning of the sinful woman (7:36–50) where a similar contrast is presented between the critical attitude of the Pharisee Simon and the love shown by the pardoned sinner.

18:5 *Strike me:* the Greek verb translated as strike means "to strike under the eye" and suggests the extreme situation to which the persistence of the widow might lead. It may, however, be used here in the much weaker sense of "to wear one out."

18:15–19:27 Luke here includes much of the material about the journey to Jerusalem found in his Marcan source (Mk 10:1–52) and adds to it the story of Zacchaeus (19:1–10) from his own particular tradition and the parable of the gold coins (minas) (19:11–27) from Q, the source common to Luke and Matthew.

18:15–17 The sayings on children furnish a contrast to the attitude of the Pharisee in the preceding episode (vv. 9–14) and that of the wealthy official in the following one (vv. 18–23) who think that they can lay claim to God's favor by their own merit. The attitude of the disciple should be marked by the receptivity and trustful dependence characteristic of the child.

18:22 Detachment from material possessions results in the total dependence on God demanded of one who would inherit eternal life. *Sell all that you have:* the original saying (cf. Mk 10:21) has characteristically been made more demanding by Luke's addition of "all."

18:31–33 The details included in this third announcement of Jesus' suffering and death suggest that the literary formulation of the announcement has been directed by the knowledge of the historical passion and death of Jesus.

18:31 *Everything written by the prophets . . . will be fulfilled:* this is a Lucan addition to the words of Jesus found in the Marcan source (Mk 10:32–34). Luke understands the events of Jesus' last days in Jerusalem to be the fulfillment of Old Testament prophecy, but, as is usually the case in Luke–Acts, the author does not specify which Old Testament prophets he has in mind; cf. Lk 24:25, 27, 44; Acts 3:8; 13:27; 26:22–23.

18:38 *Son of David:* the blind beggar identifies Jesus with a title that is related to Jesus' role as Messiah (see note on 2:11). Through this Son of David, salvation comes to the blind man. Note the connection between salvation and house of David mentioned earlier in Zechariah's canticle (1:69).

19:1–10 The story of the tax collector Zacchaeus is unique to this gospel. While a rich man (v. 2), Zacchaeus provides a contrast to the rich man of 18:18–23 who cannot detach himself from his material possessions to become a follower of Jesus. Zacchaeus, according to Luke, exemplifies the proper attitude toward wealth: he promises to give half of his possessions to the poor (8) and consequently is the recipient of salvation (vv. 9–10).

19:9 *A descendant of Abraham:* lit., "a son of Abraham." The tax collector Zacchaeus, whose repentance is attested by his determination to amend his former ways, shows himself to be a true descendant of Abraham, the true heir to the promises of God in the Old Testament. Underlying Luke's depiction of Zacchaeus as a descendant of Abraham, the father of the Jews (1:73; 16:22–31), is his recognition of the central place occupied by Israel in the plan of salvation.

19:10 This verse sums up for Luke his depiction of the role of Jesus as savior in this gospel.

19:11–27 In this parable Luke has combined two originally distinct parables: (1) a parable about the conduct of faithful and productive servants (vv. 13,15b–26) and (2) a parable about a rejected king (vv. 12, 14–15a, 27). The story about the conduct of servants occurs in another form in Mt 25:14–20. The story about the rejected king may have originated with a contemporary historical event. After the death of Herod the Great, his son Archelaus traveled to Rome to receive the title of king. A delegation of Jews appeared in Rome before Caesar Augustus to oppose the request of Archelaus. Although not given the title of king, Archelaus was made ruler over Judea and Samaria. As the story is used by Luke, however, it furnishes a correction to the expectation of the imminent end of the age and of the establishment of the kingdom in Jerusalem (v. 11). Jesus is not on his way to Jerusalem to receive the kingly power; for that, he most go away and only after returning from the distant country (a reference to the parousia) will reward and judgment take place.

19:13 *Ten gold coins:* lit., "ten minas." A mina was a monetary unit that in ancient Greece was the equivalent of one hundred drachmas.

19:28–21:38 With the royal entry of Jesus into Jerusalem, a new section of Luke's gospel begins, the ministry of Jesus in Jerusalem before his death and resurrection. Luke suggests that this was a lengthy ministry in Jerusalem (19:47; 20:1; 21:37–38; 22:53) and it is characterized by Jesus' daily teaching in the temple (21:37–38). For the story of the entry of Jesus into Jerusalem, see also Mt 21:1–11; Mk 11:1–10; Jn 12:12–19.

19:38 *Blessed is the king who comes in the name of the Lord:* only in Luke is Jesus explicitly given the title king when he enters Jerusalem in triumph. Luke has inserted this title into the words of Ps 118:26 that heralded the arrival of the pilgrims coming to the holy city and to the temple. Jesus is thereby acclaimed as king (see 1:32) and as the one who comes (see Mal 3:1; Lk 7:19). *Peace in heaven . . . :* the acclamation of the disciples of Jesus in Luke echoes the announcement of the angels at the birth of Jesus (2:14). The peace Jesus brings is associated with the salvation to be accomplished here in Jerusalem.

19:39 Rebuke your disciples: this command, found only in Luke, was given so that the Roman authorities would not interpret the acclamation of Jesus as king as an uprising against them; cf. 23:2–3.

19:41–44 The lament for Jerusalem is found only in Luke. By not accepting Jesus (the one who mediates peace), Jerusalem will not find peace but will become the victim of devastation.

19:43–44 Luke may be describing the actual disaster that befell Jerusalem in A.D. 70 when it was destroyed by the Romans during the First Revolt.

19:45–46 Immediately upon entering the holy city, Jesus in a display of his authority enters the temple (see Mal 3:1–3) and lays claim to it after cleansing it that it might become a proper place for his teaching ministry in Jerusalem (19:47; 20:1; 21:37; 22:53). See Mt 21:12–17; Mk 11:15–19; Jn 2:13–17.

20:1–47 The Jerusalem religious leaders or their representatives, in an attempt to incriminate Jesus with the Romans and to discredit him with the people, pose a number of questions to him (about his authority, v. 2; about payment of taxes, v. 22; about the resurrection, vv. 28–33).

20:9–19 This parable about an absentee landlord and a tenant farmers' revolt reflects the social and economic conditions of rural Palestine in the first century. The synoptic gospel writers use the parable to describe how the rejection of the landlord's son becomes the occasion for the vineyard to be taken away from those to whom it was entrusted (the religious leadership of Judaism that rejects the teaching and preaching of Jesus; v. 19).

20:15 *They threw him out of the vineyard and killed him:* cf. Mk 12:8. Luke has altered his Marcan source and reports that the murder of the son takes place outside the vineyard to reflect the tradition of Jesus' death outside the walls of the city of Jerusalem (see Heb 13:12).

20:20 *The governor:* i.e., Pontius Pilate, the Roman administrator responsible for the collection of taxes and maintenance of order in Palestine.

20:22 Through their question the agents of the Jerusalem religious leadership hope to force Jesus to take sides on one of the sensitive political issues of first-century Palestine. The issue of nonpayment of taxes to Rome becomes one of the focal points of the First Jewish Revolt (A.D. 66–70) that resulted in the Roman destruction of Jerusalem and the temple.

20:24 *Denarius:* a Roman silver coin (see note on 7:41).

20:28–33 The Sadducees' question, based on the law of levirate marriage recorded in Dt 25:5–10, ridicules the idea of the resurrection. Jesus rejects their naive understanding of the resurrection (vv. 35–36) and then argues on behalf of the resurrection of the dead on the basis of the written law (vv. 37–38) that the Sadducees accept.

20:36 *Because they are the ones who will rise:* lit., "being sons of the resurrection."

20:41–44 After successfully answering the three questions of his opponents, Jesus now asks them a question. Their inability to respond implies that they have forfeited their position and authority as the religious leaders of the people because they do not understand the scriptures. This series of controversies between the religious leadership of Jerusalem and Jesus reveals Jesus as the authoritative teacher whose words are to be listened to (see 9:35).

21:1–4 The widow is another example of the poor ones in this gospel whose detachment from material possessions and dependence on God leads to their blessedness (6:20). Her simple offering provides a striking contrast to the pride and pretentiousness of the scribes denounced in the preceding section (20:45–47). The story is taken from Mk 12:41–44.

21:5–36 Jesus' eschatological discourse in Luke is inspired by Mk 13 but Luke has made some significant alterations to the words of Jesus found there. Luke maintains, though in a modified form, the belief in the early expectation of the end of the age (see vv. 27, 28, 31, 32, 36), but, by focusing attention throughout the gospel on the importance of the day-to-day following of Jesus and by reinterpreting the meaning of some of the signs of the end from Mk 13 he has come to terms with what seemed to the early Christian community to be a delay of the parousia. Mark, for example, described the desecration of the Jerusalem temple by the Romans (Mk 13:14) as the apocalyptic symbol (see Dn 9:27; 12:11) accompanying the end of the age and the coming of the Son of Man. Luke (vv. 20–24), however, removes the apocalyptic setting and separates the historical destruction of Jerusalem from the signs of the coming of the Son of Man by a period that he refers to as "the times of the Gentiles" (v. 24).

21:8 *The time has come:* in Luke, the proclamation of the imminent end of the age has itself become a false teaching.

21:12 *Before all this happens . . . :* to Luke and his community, some of the signs of the end just described (vv. 10–11) still lie in the future. Now in dealing with the persecution of the disciples (vv. 12–19) and the destruction of Jerusalem (vv. 20–24) Luke is pointing to eschatological signs that have already been fulfilled.

21:15 *A wisdom in speaking:* lit., "a mouth and wisdom." 21:20–24 The actual destruction of Jerusalem by Rome in A.D. 70 upon which Luke and his community look back provides the assurance that, just as Jesus' prediction of Jerusalem's destruction was fulfilled, so too will be his announcement of their final redemption (vv. 27–28).

21:24 *The times of the Gentiles:* a period of indeterminate length separating the destruction of Jerusalem from the cosmic signs accompanying the coming of the Son of Man.

21:26 *The powers of the heavens:* the heavenly bodies mentioned in v. 25 and thought of as cosmic armies.

22:1–23:56a The passion narrative. Luke is still dependent upon Mark for the composition of the passion narrative but has incorporated much of his own special tradition into the narrative. Among the distinctive sections in Luke are: (1) the tradition of the institution of the Eucharist (22:15–20); (2) Jesus' farewell discourse (22:21–38); (3) the mistreatment and interrogation of Jesus (22:63–71); (4) Jesus before Herod and his second appearance before Pilate (23:6–16); (5) words addressed to the women followers on the way to the crucifixion (23:27–32); (6) words to the penitent thief (23:39–41); (7) the death of Jesus (23:46, 47b–49). Luke stresses the innocence of Jesus (23:4, 14–15, 22) who is the victim of the powers of evil (22:3,31, 53) and who goes to his death in fulfillment of his Father's will (22:42, 46). Throughout the narrative Luke emphasizes the mercy, compassion, and healing power of Jesus (22:51; 23:43) who does not go to death lonely and deserted, but is accompanied by others who follow him on the way of the cross (23:26–31, 49).

22:3 *Satan entered into Judas:* see note on 4:13.

22:15 *This Passover:* Luke clearly identifies this last supper of Jesus with the apostles as a Passover meal that commemorated the deliverance of the Israelites from slavery in Egypt. Jesus reinterprets the significance of the Passover by setting it in the context of the kingdom of God (v. 16). The "deliverance" associated with the Passover finds its new meaning in the blood that will be shed (v. 20).

22:17 Because of a textual problem in no. 19–20 some commentators interpret this cup as the eucharistic cup.

22:19c–20 *Which will be given . . . do this in memory of me:* these words are omitted in some important Western text manuscripts and a few Syriac manuscripts. Other ancient text types, including the oldest papyrus manuscript of Luke dating from the late second or early third century, contain the longer reading presented here. The Lucan account of the words of institution of the Eucharist bears a close resemblance to the words of institution in the Pauline tradition (see 1 Cor 11:23–26).

22:24–38 The Gospel of Luke presents a brief farewell discourse of Jesus; compare the lengthy farewell discourses and prayer in Jn 13–17.

22:25 *Benefactors':* this word occurs as a title of rulers in the Hellenistic world.

22:31–32 Jesus' prayer for Simon's faith and the commission to strengthen his brothers anticipates the post-resurrectional prominence of Peter in the first half of Acts, where he appears as the spokesman for the Christian community and the one who begins the mission to the Gentiles (Acts 10–11).

22:31 *All of you:* lit., "you." The translation reflects the meaning of the Greek text that uses a second person plural pronoun here.

22:36 In contrast to the ministry of the Twelve and of the seventy-two during the period of Jesus (9:3; 10:4), in the future period of the church the missionaries must be prepared for the opposition they will face in a world hostile to their preaching.

22:38 *It is enough!:* the farewell discourse ends abruptly with these words of Jesus spoken to the disciples when they take literally what was intended as figurative language about being prepared to face the world's hostility.

22:43–44 These verses, though very ancient, were probably not part of the original text of Luke. They are absent from the oldest papyrus manuscripts of Luke and from manuscripts of wide geographical distribution.

22:51 *And healed him:* only Luke recounts this healing of the injured servant.

22:61 Only Luke recounts that *the Lord turned and looked at Peter.* This look of Jesus leads to Peter's weeping bitterly over his denial (v. 62).

22:66–71 Luke recounts one daytime trial of Jesus (vv. 66–71) and hints at some type of preliminary nighttime investigation (vv. 54–65). Mark (and Matthew who follows Mark) has transferred incidents of this day into the nighttime interrogation with the result that there appear to be two Sanhedrin trials of Jesus in Mark (and Matthew).

22:66 *Sanhedrin:* the word is a Hebraized form of a Greek word meaning a "council," and refers to the elders, chief priests, and scribes who met under the high priest's leadership to decide religious and legal questions that did not pertain to Rome's interests. Jewish sources are not clear on the competence of the Sanhedrin to sentence and to execute during this period.

23:1–5, 13–25 Twice Jesus is brought before Pilate in Luke's account, and each time Pilate explicitly declares Jesus innocent of any wrongdoing (vv. 4,14, 22). This stress on the innocence of Jesus before the Roman authorities is also characteristic of John's gospel (Jn 18:38; 19:4, 6). Luke presents the Jerusalem Jewish leaders as the ones who force the hand of the Roman authorities by. 1–2, 5, 10, 13, 18, 21, 23–25).

23:6–12 The appearance of Jesus before Herod is found only in this gospel. Herod has been an important figure in Luke (9:7–9; 13:31–33) and has been presented as someone who has been curious about Jesus for a long time. His curiosity goes unrewarded. It is faith in Jesus, not curiosity, that is rewarded (7:50; 8:48, 50; 17:19).

23:17 This verse, "He was obliged to release one prisoner for them at the festival," is not part of the original text of Luke. It is an explanatory gloss from Mk 15:6 (also Mt 27:15) and is not found in many early and important Greek manuscripts.

23:26–32 An important Lucan theme throughout the gospel has been the need for the Christian disciple to follow in the foot-steps of Jesus. Here this theme comes to the fore with the story of Simon of Cyrene who takes up the cross and follows Jesus (see 9:23; 14:27) and with the large crowd who likewise follow Jesus on the way of the cross.

23:34 *[Then Jesus said, "Father, forgive them, they know not what they do."]:* this portion of v. 34 does not occur in the oldest papyrus manuscript of Luke and in other early Greek manuscripts and ancient versions of wide geographical distribution.

23:39–43 This episode is recounted only in this gospel. The penitent sinner receives salvation through the crucified Jesus.

Jesus' words to the penitent thief reveal Luke's understanding that the destiny of the Christian is "to be with Jesus."

23:44 *Noon . . . three in the afternoon:* lit., the sixth and ninth hours.

23:47 *This man was innocent:* or, "This man was righteous."

24:1–53 *The resurrection narrative in Luke consists of five sections:* (1) the women at the empty tomb (23:56b–24:12); (2) the appearance to the two disciples on the way to Emmaus (vv. 13–35); (3) the appearance to the disciples in Jerusalem (vv. 36–43); (4) Jesus' final instructions (vv. 44–49); (5) the ascension (vv. 50–53). In Luke, all the resurrection appearances take place in and around Jerusalem; moreover, they are all recounted as having taken place on Easter Sunday. A consistent theme throughout the narrative is that the suffering, death, and resurrection of Jesus were accomplished in fulfillment of Old Testament promises and of Jewish hopes (vv. 19a, 21,26–27, 44, 46). In his second volume, Acts, Luke will argue that Christianity is the fulfillment of the hopes of Pharisaic Judaism and its logical development (see Acts 24:10–21).

24:6 *He is not here, but he has been raised:* this part of the verse is omitted in important representatives of the Western text tradition, but its presence in other text types and the slight difference in wording from Mt 28:6 and Mk 16:6 argue for its retention.

24:9 The women in this gospel do not flee from the tomb and tell no one, as in Mk 16:8 but return and tell the disciples about their experience. The initial reaction to the testimony of the women is disbelief (v. 11).

24:12 This verse is missing from the Western textual tradition but is found in the best and oldest manuscripts of other text types.

24:13–35 This episode focuses on the interpretation of scripture by the risen Jesus and the recognition of him in the breaking of the bread. The references to the quotations of scripture and explanation of it (vv. 25–27), the kerygmatic proclamation (v. 34), and the liturgical gesture (v. 30) suggest that the episode is primarily catechetical and liturgical rather than apologetic.

24:13 *Seven miles:* lit., "sixty stades." A stade was 607 feet. Some manuscripts read "160 stades" or more than eighteen miles. The exact location of Emmaus is disputed.

24:16 A consistent feature of the resurrection stories is that the risen Jesus was different and initially unrecognizable (Lk 24:37; Mk 16:12; Jn 20:14; 21:4).

24:26 *That the Messiah should suffer . . . :* Luke is the only New Testament writer to speak explicitly of a suffering Messiah (Lk 24:26, 46; Acts 3:18; 17:3; 26:23). The idea of a suffering Messiah is not found in the Old Testament or in other Jewish literature prior to the New Testament period, although the idea is hinted at in Mk 8:31–33.

24:36–43, 44–49 The Gospel of Luke, like each of the other gospels (Mt 28:16–20; Mk 16:14–15; Jn 20:19–23), focuses on an important appearance of Jesus to the Twelve in which they are commissioned for their future ministry. As in vv. 6, 12, so in vv. 36, 40 there are omissions in the Western text.

24:39–42 The apologetic purpose of this story is evident in the concern with the physical details and the report that Jesus ate food.

24:46 See note on v. 26.

24:49 *The promise of my Father:* i.e., the gift of the holy Spirit.

24:50–53 Luke brings his story about the time of Jesus to a close with the report of the ascension. He will also begin the story of the time of the church with a recounting of the ascension. In the gospel, Luke recounts the ascension of Jesus on Easter Sunday night, thereby closely associating it with the resurrection. In Acts 1:3, 9–11; 13:31 he historicizes the ascension by speaking of a forty-day period between the resurrection and the ascension. The Western text omits some phrases in vv. 51, 52 perhaps to avoid any chronological conflict with Acts 1 about the time of the ascension.

24:53 The Gospel of Luke ends as it began (1:9), in the Jerusalem temple.

The Acts of the Apostles

1:1–26 This introductory material (vv. 1–2) connects Acts with the Gospel of Luke, shows that the apostles were instructed by the risen Jesus (vv. 3–5), points out that the parousia or second coming in glory of Jesus will occur as certainly as his ascension occurred (vv. 6–11), and lists the members of the Twelve, stressing their role as a body of divinely mandated witnesses to his life, teaching, and resurrection (vv. 12–26).

1:3 *Appearing to them during forty days:* Luke considered especially sacred the interval in which the appearances and instructions of the risen Jesus occurred and expressed it therefore in terms of the sacred number forty (cf. Dt 8:2). In his gospel, however, Luke connects the ascension of Jesus with the resurrection by describing the ascension on Easter Sunday evening (Lk 24:50–53). What should probably be understood as one event (resurrection, glorification, ascension, sending of the Spirit—the paschal mystery) has been historicized by Luke when he writes of a visible ascension of Jesus after forty days and the descent of the Spirit at Pentecost. For Luke, the ascension marks the end of the appearances of Jesus except for the extraordinary appearance to Paul. With regard to Luke's understanding of salvation history, the ascension also marks the end of the time of Jesus (Lk 24:50–53) and signals the beginning of the time of the church.

1:4 *The promise of the Father:* the holy Spirit, as is clear from the next verse. This gift of the Spirit was first promised in Jesus' final instructions to his chosen witnesses in Luke's gospel (Lk 24:49) and formed part of the continuing instructions of the risen Jesus on the kingdom of God, of which Luke speaks in v. 3.

1:6 The question of the disciples implies that in believing Jesus to be the Christ (see note on Lk 2:11) they had expected him to be a political leader who would restore self-rule to Israel during his historical ministry. When this had not taken place, they ask if it is to take place at this time, the period of the church.

1:7 This verse echoes the tradition that the precise time of the parousia is not revealed to human beings; cf. Mk 13:32; 1 Thes 5:1–3.

1:8 Just as Jerusalem was the city of destiny in the Gospel of Luke (the place where salvation was accomplished), so here at the beginning of Acts, Jerusalem occupies a central position.

It is the starting point for the mission of the Christian disciples to "the ends of the earth," the place where the apostles were situated and the doctrinal focal point in the early days of the community (15:2, 6). The ends of the earth: for Luke, this means Rome.

1:18 Luke records a popular tradition about the death of Judas that differs from the one in Mt 27:5, according to which Judas hanged himself. Here, although the text is not certain, Judas is depicted as purchasing a piece of property with the betrayal money and being killed on it in a fall.

1:26 The need to replace Judas was probably dictated by the symbolism of the number twelve, recalling the twelve tribes of Israel. This symbolism also indicates that for Luke (see Lk 22:30) the Christian church is a reconstituted Israel.

2:1–41 Luke's pentecostal narrative consists of an introduction (vv. 1–13), a speech ascribed to Peter declaring the resurrection of Jesus and its messianic significance (vv. 14–36), and a favorable response from the audience (vv. 37–41). It is likely that the narrative telescopes events that took place over a period of time and on a less dramatic scale. The Twelve were not originally in a position to proclaim publicly the messianic office of Jesus without incurring immediate reprisal from those religious authorities in Jerusalem who had brought about Jesus' death precisely to stem the rising tide in his favor.

2:2 *There came from the sky a noise like a strong driving wind:* wind and spirit are associated in Jn 3:8. The sound of a great rush of wind would herald a new action of God in the history of salvation.

2:3 *Tongues as of fire:* see Ex 19:18 where fire symbolizes the presence of God to initiate the covenant on Sinai. Here the holy Spirit acts upon the apostles, preparing them to proclaim the new covenant with its unique gift of the Spirit (v. 38).

2:4 *To speak in different tongues:* ecstatic prayer in praise of God, interpreted in no. 6, 11 as speaking in foreign languages, symbolizing the worldwide mission of the church.

2:14–36 The first of six discourses in Acts (along with 3:12–26; 4:8–12; 5:29–32; 10:34–43; 13:16–41) dealing with the resurrection of Jesus and its messianic import. Five of these are attributed to Peter, the final one to Paul. Modern scholars term these discourses in Acts the "kerygma," the Greek word for proclamation (cf. 1 Cor 15:11).

2:33 *At the right hand of God:* or "by the right hand of God."

2:38 Repent and be baptized: repentance is a positive concept, a change of mind and heart toward God reflected in the actual goodness of one's life. It is in accord with the apostolic teaching derived from Jesus (v. 42) and ultimately recorded in the four gospels. Luke presents baptism in Acts as the expected response to the apostolic preaching about Jesus and associates it with the conferring of the Spirit (1:5; 10:448; 11:16).

2:42–47 The first of three summary passages (along with 4:32–37; 5:12–16) that outline, somewhat idyllically, the chief characteristics of the Jerusalem community: adherence to the teachings of the Twelve and the centering of its religious life in the eucharistic liturgy (v. 42); a system of distribution of goods that led wealthier Christians to sell their possessions when the needs of the community's poor required it (v. 44 and the note

on 4:32–37); and continued attendance at the temple, since in this initial stage there was little or no thought of any dividing line between Christianity and Judaism (v. 46).

3:1–4:31 This section presents a series of related events: the dramatic cure of a lame beggar (3:1–10) produces a large audience for the kerygmatic discourse of Peter (3:11–26). The Sadducees, taking exception to the doctrine of resurrection, have Peter, John, and apparently the beggar as well, arrested (4:1–4) and brought to trial before the Sanhedrin. The issue concerns the authority by which Peter and John publicly teach religious doctrine in the temple (4:5–7). Peter replies with a brief summary of the kerygma, implying that his authority is prophetic (4:8–12). The court warns the apostles to abandon their practice of invoking prophetic authority in the name of Jesus (4:13-18). When Peter and John reply that the prophetic role cannot be abandoned to satisfy human objections, the court nevertheless releases them, afraid to do otherwise since the beggar, lame from birth and over forty years old, is a well-known figure in Jerusalem and the facts of his cure are common property (4:19–22). The narrative concludes with a prayer of the Christian community imploring divine aid against threats of persecution (4:23–31).

3:1 *For the three o'clock hour of prayer:* lit., "at the ninth hour of prayer." With the day beginning at 6 A.M., the ninth hour would be 3 P.M.

3:8–10 The miracle has a dramatic cast; it symbolizes the saving power of Christ and leads the beggar to enter the temple, where he hears Peter's proclamation of salvation through Jesus.

3:13 Has glorified: through the resurrection and ascension of Jesus, God reversed the judgment against him on the occasion of his trial. **Servant:** the Greek word can also be rendered as "son" or even "child" here and also in v. 26; 4:25 (applied to David); 4:27; and 4:30. Scholars are of the opinion, however, that the original concept reflected in the words identified Jesus with the suffering Servant of the Lord of Is 52:13–53:12.

3:14 *The Holy and Righteous One:* so designating Jesus emphasizes his special relationship to the Father (see Lk 1:35; 4:34) and emphasizes his sinlessness and religious dignity that are placed in sharp contrast with the guilt of those who rejected him in favor of Barabbas.

3:15 *The author of life:* other possible translations of the Greek title are "leader of life" or "pioneer of life." The title clearly points to Jesus as the source and originator of salvation.

3:17 *Ignorance:* a Lucan motif, explaining away the actions not only of the people but also of their leaders in crucifying Jesus. On this basis the presbyters in Acts could continue to appeal to the Jews in Jerusalem to believe in Jesus, even while affirming their involvement in his death because they were unaware of his messianic dignity. See also 13:27 and Lk 23:34.

3:18 *Through the mouth of all the prophets:* Christian prophetic insight into the Old Testament saw the crucifixion and death of Jesus as the main import of messianic prophecy. The Jews themselves did not anticipate a suffering Messiah; they usually understood the Servant Song in Is 52:13–53:12 to signify their own suffering as a people. In his typical fashion (cf.

Lk 18:31; 24:25, 27, 44), Luke does not specify the particular Old Testament prophecies that were fulfilled by Jesus. See also note on Lk 24:26.

3:20 *The Lord . . . and send you the Messiah already appointed for you, Jesus:* an allusion to the parousia or second coming of Christ, judged to be imminent in the apostolic age.This reference to its nearness is the only explicit one in Acts. Some scholars believe that this verse preserves a very early christology, in which the title "Messiah" (Greek "Christ") is applied to him as of his parousia, his second coming (contrast 2:36). This view of a future messiahship of Jesus is not found elsewhere in the New Testament.

3:21 *The times of universal restoration:* like "the times of refreshment" (v. 20), an apocalyptic designation of the messianic age, fitting in with the christology of v. 20 that associates the messiahship of Jesus with his future coming.

3:22 A loose citation of Dt 18:15, which teaches that the Israelites are to learn the will of Yahweh from no one but their prophets. At the time of Jesus, some Jews expected a unique prophet to come in fulfillment of this text. Early Christianity applied this tradition and text to Jesus and used them especially in defense of the divergence of Christian teaching from traditional Judaism.

4:1 *The priests, the captain of the temple guard, and the Sadducees:* the priests performed the temple liturgy; the temple guard was composed of Levites, whose captain ranked next after the high priest. The Sadducees, a party within Judaism at this time, rejected those doctrines, including bodily resurrection, which they believed alien to the ancient Mosaic religion. The Sadducees were drawn from priestly families and from the lay aristocracy.

4:11 Early Christianity applied this citation from Ps 118:22 to Jesus; cf. Mk 12:10; 1 Pt 2:7.

4:12 In the Roman world of Luke's day, salvation was often attributed to the emperor who was hailed as "savior" and "god." Luke, in the words of Peter, denies that deliverance comes through anyone other than Jesus.

4:27 *Herod:* Herod Antipas, ruler of Galilee and Perea from 4 B.C. to A.D. 39, who executed John the Baptist and before whom Jesus was arraigned; cf. Lk 23:6–12.

4:31 *The place . . . shook:* the earthquake is used as a sign of the divine presence in Ex 19:18; Is 6:4. Here the shaking of the building symbolizes God's favorable response to the prayer. Luke may have had as an additional reason for using the symbol in this sense the fact that it was familiar in the Hellenistic world. Ovid and Virgil also employ it.

4:32–37 This is the second summary characterizing the Jerusalem community (see note on 2:42–47). It emphasizes the system of the distribution of goods and introduces Barnabas, who appears later in Acts as the friend and companion of Paul, and who, as noted here (v. 37), endeared himself to the community by a donation of money through the sale of property. This sharing of material possessions continues a practice that Luke describes during the historical ministry of Jesus (Lk 8:3) and is in accord with the sayings of Jesus in Luke's gospel (Lk 12:33; 16:9, 11, 13).

The *Bhagavad Gita*

Editors' Introduction

The selected chapters from the *Bhagavad Gita* that you are about to read are drawn from one of the most popular spiritual classics of the Hindu tradition. Often translated as "The Song of God" or "The Song Celestial," the *Gita*, an abbreviated title for the more formal *Bhagavad Gita,* is part of one of the most popular epics of Indian culture, the *Mahabharata* (the *Ramayana* being the other). Mistakenly, most Westerners think that both the *Gita* and the *Mahabharata* are sacred scriptures of the Hindu tradition, but this is in fact not the case. Rather, the *Mahabharata* is one of India's great epics, not unlike the *Iliad* or the *Odyssey* are for ancient Greece and subsequently for Western culture in general, in which are embodied in mythological and symbolic form the history, culture and spiritual values that are the foundation of India's rich and diverse religious heritage. While not a scripture per se, the Gita is more properly classified as *bhaktic* or "devotional" literature. Along with teaching religious moral values, the *Gita* is designed to inspire the reader to strive for moksha or "spiritual liberation" from the world of *maya* or illusion. As part of its classification as bhaktic literature, Hindus all over the world chant from the *Gita* during religious ceremonies often called *puja*, which means "worship" in Sanskrit, the sacred language of many Hindu doctrinal and liturgical texts.

Even though the *Gita* is not a scripture, its eighteen chapters are replete with the theology and worldview of Hinduism as most specifically embodied in the *Vedas,* the oldest of the Hindu scriptures, and the *Upanishads,* a corpus of metaphysical and theological writings of later development that are also classified as "scripture" in the Hindu tradition. In terms of the *Bhagavad Gita,* while the ideas and values drawn from the *Vedas* are included in its chapters, it is really the *Upanishads* that are its main source of theological and cosmological inspiration. Also included are some metaphysical ideas mutually shared with Buddhism, which developed out of its mother tradition Hinduism in the same way that Christianity developed out of Judaism, its mother tradition.

Though the *Gita* contains much theology, its essence is ethical and the truths it seeks to impart are presented in the form of an ethical dilemma set within the context of war fought on a vast battlefield, all of which can be taken as metaphors or symbols for the spiritual journey and the perils that come along with the quest for Ultimate Reality or *Brahman,* a word which comes close to the concept of "God" in the Abrahamic traditions of Judaism, Christianity, or Islam. However, unlike the one God of the Abrahamic faiths, *Brahman* is not conceived of in Hinduism as a personal God but more as the impersonal ground or source of all existence and life or as unconditioned Absolute Truth with a capital "T" that is ultimately beyond all human conception. Yet, this does not mean that in Hinduism there is no concept of a personal God who enters into relationship with human beings and who communicates with them intimately through visions, dreams, ritual and devotional practices, and in response to prayer. Rather, *Brahman,* the impersonal absolute, does in fact relate to human beings in very personal ways through the *avatars* or divine incarnations that appear on Earth as needed in the form of various male, female, and androgynous deities, and sometimes even as half-human, half-animal incarnations. The half-human, half-elephant god *Ganesha* is a perfect example of the latter. It is as Lord Krishna, an avatar of *Vishnu,* a hypostasis of *Brahman* that God relates personally with Arjuna, the chief protagonist of the *Bhagavad Gita.*

If asked to sum up the teachings of the *Gita* in one simple maxim, it is "your business is with the deed not with the result." This is the primary lesson about the spiritual quest and about life in general that is taught through the chapters of the *Gita.* It is this maxim that Lord Krishna teaches to Arjuna, the third son of King Pandu, of the Pandavas dynasty when he is about to begin a war that was precipitated when Arjuna's one hundred cousins, who belonged to the Kaurava dynasty, refused to return even a few villages to the five Pandava brothers after their return from enforced exile. Standing on his side of the battlefield with Lord Krishna beside him as his chief advisor, Arjuna looks at his uncles, cousins, and friends standing on the other side of the battlefield. At that crucial moment, Arjuna wonders whether or not he is "morally prepared or justified in killing his blood relations" despite the fact that it was Arjuna and his brother Bhima who had courageously prepared for this war. One way or the other, Arjuna was certain that he would be victorious in this war since he had Lord Krishna, one of the incarnations of Vishnu, on his side. Yet, just as the battle is about to begin, Arjuna puts it on hold to have a conversation with Krishna about the battle he is about to begin and whether or not it is the right thing to do. The conversation ends with Krishna convincing Arjuna that in the grand scheme of things, he is nothing but a pawn and the best that Arjuna can do is his duty and not to question God's will. In so doing, Lord Krishna provides a philosophy of

life that gives Arjuna the courage to begin the battle that had become temporarily stalled because he (Arjuna) had lost his nerve.

The spiritual and moral teachings that undergird this story of war are what you are about to read in the eleven chapters that follow and as you enter into the drama of the *Gita.*

By way of cultural background, the *Bhagavad Gita* was first translated into English and published by Charles Wilkins in November of 1784. An improvement of the original translation from the Sanskrit was subsequently done by Frederich Max Mueller (1823–1900), the German Sanskrit scholar, who included the updated translation in his *Sacred Books of the East* series published by Oxford University Press. The *Bhagavad Gita* is one of the most widely read texts of the world. It has inspired many prominent Americans, among them, Henry David Thoreau, Ralph Waldo Emerson, Walt Whitman, and, in the twentieth century, Martin Luther King, Jr.

Along with the *Bible,* specifically the Beatitudes attributed to Jesus in the Synoptic Gospels of Matthew and Luke, the *Bhagavad Gita* was the other main spiritual source that inspired Mohandas K. Gandhi's Satyagraha (soul force) movement of non-violent resistance that played a major role in India's struggle for independence from the British Empire. The *Gita* was also a main source of inspiration for the twentieth century Indian poet, philosopher, and Nobel Peace Prize laureate Rabindranath Tagore. In the second half of the twentieth century, the *Gita* exerted an immense influence, especially in the 1950s, on such Beat poets and writers as Allen Ginsberg, Jack Kerouac, and Gary Snyder. In the 1960s, the *Bhagavad Gita* played a major role among the American counterculture, mostly through the *Hare Krishna* movement. Chiefly through the writings of Christopher Isherwood and Alan Watts, the *Bhagavad Gita* introduced Indian religious values and Vedanta philosophy to generations of artists, poets, political activists and religious seekers of all stripes.

The Bhagavad Gita (Selections)

CHAPTER I.

Dhritarâshtra said

What did my people and the Pândavas do, O Sañgaya! when they assembled together on the holy field of Kurukshetra, desirous to do battle?

Sañgaya said:

Seeing the army of the Pândavas drawn up in battle-array, the prince Duryodhana approached the preceptor, and spoke these words: 'O preceptor! observe this grand army of the sons of Pându, drawn up in battle-array by your talented pupil, the son of Drupada. In it are heroes bearing large bows, the equals of Bhîma and Arguna in battle—namely, Yuyudhâna, Virâta, and Drupada, the master of a great chariot, and Dhrishtaketu, Kekitâna, and the valiant king of Kâsî, Purugit and Kuntibhoga, and that eminent man Saibya; the heroic Yudhâmanyu, the valiant Uttamaugas, the son of Subhadrâ, and the sons of Draupadî—all masters of great chariots. And now, O best of Brâhmanas! learn who are most distinguished among us, and are leaders of my army. I will name them to you, in order that you may know them well. Yourself, and Bhîshma, and Karna, and Kripa the victor of many battles; Asvatthâman, and Vikarna, and also the son of Somadatta, and many other brave men, who have given up their lives for me, who fight with various weapons, and are all dexterous in battle. Thus our army which is protected by Bhîshma is unlimited; while this army of theirs which is protected by Bhîma is very limited. And therefore do ye all, occupying respectively the positions assigned to you, protect Bhîshma only.'

Then his powerful grandsire, Bhîshma, the oldest of the Kauravas, roaring aloud like a lion, blew his conch, thereby affording delight to Duryodhana. And then all at once, conchs, and kettledrums, and tabors, and trumpets were played upon; and there was a tumultuous din. Then, too, Mâdhava and the son of Pându (Arguna), seated in a grand chariot to which white steeds were yoked, blew their heavenly conchs. Hrishîkesa blew the Pâñkaganya, and Dhanañgaya the Devadatta, and Bhîma, (the doer) of fearful deeds, blew the great conch Paundra. King Yudhishthira, the son of Kuntî, blew the Anantavigaya, and Nakula and Sahadeva respectively the Sughosha and Manipushpaka. And the king of Kâsî, too, who has an excellent bow, and Sikhandin, the master of a great car, and Dhrishtadyumna, Virâta, and the unconquered Sâtyaki, and Drupada, and the sons of Draupadî, and the son of Subhadrâ, of mighty arms, blew conchs severally from all sides, O king of the earth! That tumultuous din rent the hearts of all the people of Dhritarâshtra's party, causing reverberations throughout heaven and earth. Then seeing the people of Dhritarâshtra's party regularly marshalled, the son of Pându, whose standard is the ape, raised his bow, after the discharge of missiles had commenced, and O king of the earth! spake these words to Hrishîkesa: 'O undegraded one! station my chariot between the two armies, while I observe those, who stand here desirous to engage in battle, and with whom, in the labours of this struggle, I must do battle. I will observe those who are assembled here and who are about to engage in battle, wishing to do service in battle to the evil-minded son of Dhritarâshtra.'

Sañgaya said:

Thus addressed by Gudâkesa, O descendant of Bharata! Hrishîkesa stationed that excellent chariot between the two armies, in front of Bhîshma and Drona and of all the kings of the earth, and said O son of Prithâ! look at these assembled Kauravas.' There the son of Prithâ saw in both armies, fathers and grandfathers, preceptors, maternal uncles, brothers, sons, grandsons, companions, fathers-in-law, as well as friends.

And seeing all those kinsmen standing there, the son of Kuntî was overcome by excessive pity, and spake thus despondingly.

Arguna said:

Seeing these kinsmen, O Krishna! standing here desirous to engage in battle, my limbs droop down; my mouth is quite dried up; a tremor comes on my body; and my hairs stand on end; the Gândîva bow slips from my hand; my skin burns intensely. I am unable, too, to stand up; my mind whirls round, as it were; O Kesava! I see adverse omens; and I do not perceive any good to accrue after killing my kinsmen in the battle. I do not wish for victory, O Krishna! nor sovereignty, nor pleasures: what is sovereignty to us, O Govinda! what enjoyments, and even life? Even those, for whose sake we desire sovereignty, enjoyments, and pleasures, are standing here for battle, abandoning life and wealth-preceptors, fathers, sons as well as grandfathers, maternal uncles, fathers-in-law, grandsons, brothers-in-law, as also other relatives. These I do not wish to kill, though they kill me, O destroyer of Madhu! even for the sake of sovereignty over the three worlds, how much less then for this earth alone? What joy shall be ours, O Ganârdana! after killing Dhritarâshtra's sons? Killing these felons we shall only incur sin. Therefore it is not proper for us to kill our own kinsmen, the sons of Dhritarâshtra. For how, O Mâdhava! shall we be happy after killing our own relatives? Although having their consciences corrupted by avarice, they do not see the evils flowing from the extinction of a family, and the sin in treachery to friends, still, O Ganârdana! should not we, who do see the evils flowing from the extinction of a family, learn to refrain from that sin? On the extinction of a family, the eternal rites of families are destroyed. Those rites being destroyed, impiety predominates over the whole family. In consequence of the predominance of impiety, O Krishna! the women of the family become corrupt; and the women becoming corrupt, O descendant of Vrishni! intermingling of castes results; that intermingling necessarily leads the family and the

destroyers of the family to hell; for when the ceremonies of offering the bowls of food and water to them fail, their ancestors fall down to hell. By these transgressions of the destroyers of families, which occasion interminglings of castes, the eternal rites of castes and rites, of families are subverted. And O Ganârdana! we have heard that men whose family-rites are subverted, must necessarily live in hell. Alas! we are engaged in committing a heinous sin, seeing that we are making efforts for killing our own kinsmen out of greed of the pleasures of sovereignty. If the sons of Dhritarâshtra, weapon in hand, should kill me in battle, me weaponless and not defending myself, that would be better for me.

Sañgaya said:

Having spoken thus, Arguna cast aside his bow together with the arrows, on the battlefield, and sat down in his chariot, with a mind agitated by grief.

CHAPTER II.

Sañgaya said:

To him, who was thus overcome with pity, and dejected, and whose eyes were full of tears and turbid, the destroyer of Madhu spoke these words.

The Deity said:

How comes it that this delusion, O Arguna! which is discarded by the good, which excludes from heaven, and occasions infamy, has overtaken you in this place of peril? Be not effeminate, O son of Prithâ! it is not worthy of you. Cast off this base weakness of heart, and arise, O terror of your foes!

Arguna said:

How, O destroyer of Madhu! shall I encounter with arrows in the battle Bhîshma and Drona—both, O destroyer of enemies! entitled to reverence? Not killing my preceptors—men of great glory—it is better to live even on alms in this world. But killing them, though they are avaricious of worldly goods, I should only enjoy blood-tainted enjoyments. Nor do we know which of the two is better for us—whether that we should vanquish them, or that they should vanquish us. Even those, whom having killed, we do not wish to live—even those sons of Dhritarâshtra stand arrayed against us. With a heart contaminated by the taint of helplessness, with a mind confounded about my duty, I ask you. Tell me what is assuredly good for me. I am your disciple; instruct me, who have thrown myself on your indulgence. For I do not perceive what is to dispel that grief which will dry up my organs after I shall have obtained a prosperous kingdom on earth without a foe, or even the sovereignty of the gods.

Sañgaya said:

Having spoken thus to Hrishîkesa, O terror of your foes! Gudâkesa said to Govinda, 'I shall not engage in battle;' and verily remained silent. To him thus desponding between the two armies, O descendant of Bharata! Hrishîkesa spoke these words with a slight smile.

The Deity said:

You have grieved for those who deserve no grief, and you talk words of wisdom. Learned men grieve not for the living nor the dead. Never did I not exist, nor you, nor these rulers of men; nor will any one of us ever hereafter cease to be. As, in this body, infancy and youth and old age come to the embodied self, so does the acquisition of another body; a sensible man is not deceived about that the contacts of the senses, O son of Kuntî! which produce cold and heat, pleasure and pain, are not permanent, they are ever coming and going. Bear them, O descendant of Bharata! For, O chief of men! that sensible man whom they pain and pleasure being alike to him afflict not, he merits immortality. There is no existence for that which is unreal; there is no non-existence for that which is real. And the correct conclusion about both is perceived by those who perceive the truth. Know that to be indestructible which pervades all this; the destruction of that inexhaustible principle none can bring about. These bodies appertaining to the embodied self which is eternal, indestructible, and indefinable, are said to be perishable; therefore do engage in battle, O descendant of Bharata! He who thinks it to be the killer and he who thinks it to be killed, both know nothing. It kills not, is not killed. It is not born, nor does it ever die, nor, having existed, does it exist no more. Unborn, everlasting, unchangeable, and primeval, it is not killed when the body is killed. O son of Prithâ! how can that man who knows it thus to be indestructible, everlasting, unborn, and inexhaustible, how and whom can he kill, whom can he cause to be killed? As a man, casting off old clothes, puts on others and new ones, so the embodied self casting off old bodies, goes to others and new ones. Weapons do not divide it into pieces; fire does not burn it, waters do not moisten it; the wind does not dry it up. It is not divisible; it is not combustible; it is not to be moistened; it is not to be dried up. It is everlasting, all-pervading, stable, firm, and eternal. It is said to be unperceived, to be unthinkable, to be unchangeable. Therefore knowing it to be such, you ought not to grieve, But even if you think that it is constantly born, and constantly dies, still, O you of mighty arms! you ought not to grieve thus. For to one that is born, death is certain; and to one that dies, birth is certain. Therefore about this unavoidable thing, you ought not to grieve. The source of things, O descendant of Bharata! is unperceived; their middle state is perceived; and their end again is unperceived. What occasion is there for any lamentation regarding them? One looks upon it as a wonder; another similarly speaks of it as a wonder; another too hears of it as a wonder; and even after having heard of it, no one does really know it. This embodied self, O descendant of Bharata! within every one's body is ever indestructible. Therefore you ought not to grieve for any being. Having regard to your own duty also, you ought not to falter, for there is nothing better for a Kshatriya than a righteous battle. Happy those Kshatriyas, O son of Prithâ! who can find such a battle to fight—come of itself—an open door to heaven! But if you will not fight this righteous battle, then you will have abandoned your own duty and your fame, and you will incur sin. All beings, too, will tell of your everlasting infamy; and to one who has been honoured, infamy is a greater evil than death. Warriors who are masters of great chariots will think that you abstained from the battle through fear, and having been highly thought of by them, you will fall down to littleness. Your enemies, too, decrying your power, will speak much about you that should not be spoken. And what, indeed, more lamentable than that? Killed, you will obtain heaven; victorious, you will enjoy the earth. Therefore arise, O son of Kuntî! resolved to engage in battle. Looking alike on pleasure and pain, on gain and loss, on victory and defeat, then prepare for battle, and thus you will not incur sin. The knowledge here declared to you is that relating to the Sânkhya. Now hear that relating to the Yoga. Possessed of this knowledge, O son of Prithâ! you will cast off the bonds of action. In this path to final emancipation nothing that is commenced becomes abortive; no obstacles exist; and even a little of this form of piety protects one from great danger. There is here, O descendant of Kuru! but one state of mind consisting in firm understanding. But the states of mind of those who have no firm understanding are many-branched and endless. The state of mind consisting in firm understanding regarding steady contemplation does not belong to those, O son of Prithâ! who are strongly attached to worldly pleasures and power, and whose minds are drawn away by that flowery talk which is full of ordinances of specific acts for the attainment of those pleasures and that power, and which promises birth as the fruit of acts—that flowery talk which those unwise ones utter, who are enamoured of Vedic words, who say there is nothing else, who are full of desires, and whose goal is heaven. The Vedas merely relate to the effects of the three qualities; do you, O Arguna! rise above those effects of the three qualities, and be free from the pairs of opposites, always preserve

courage, be free from anxiety for new acquisitions or protection of old acquisitions, and be self-controlled. To the instructed Brâhmana, there is in all the Vedas as much utility as in a reservoir of water into which waters flow from all sides. Your business is with action alone; not by any means with fruit. Let not the fruit of action be your motive to action. Let not your attachment be fixed on inaction. Having recourse to devotion, O Dhanañgaya! perform actions, casting off all attachment, and being equable in success or ill-success; such equability is called devotion. Action, O Dhanañgaya! is far inferior to the devotion of the mind. In that devotion seek shelter. Wretched are those whose motive to action is the fruit of action. He who has obtained devotion in this world casts off both merit and sin. Therefore apply yourself to devotion; devotion in all actions is wisdom. The wise who have obtained devotion cast off the fruit of action; and released from the shackles of repeated births, repair to that seat where there is no unhappiness. When your mind shall have crossed beyond the taint of delusion, then will you become indifferent to all that you have heard or will hear. When your mind, confounded by what you have heard, will stand firm and steady in contemplation, then will you acquire devotion.

Arguna said:

What are the characteristics, O Kesava! of one whose mind is steady, and who is intent on contemplation? How should one of steady mind speak, how sit, how move?

The Deity said:

When a man, O son of Prithâ! abandons all the desires of his heart, and is pleased in his self only and by his self, he is then called one of steady mind. He whose heart is not agitated in the midst of calamities, who has no longing for pleasures, and from whom the feelings of affection, fear, and wrath have departed, is called a sage of steady mind. His mind is steady, who, being without attachments anywhere, feels no exultation and no aversion on encountering the various agreeable and disagreeable things of this world). A man's mind is steady, when he withdraws his senses from all objects of sense, as the tortoise withdraws its limbs from all sides. Objects of sense draw back from a person who is abstinent; not so the taste for those objects. But even the taste departs from him, when he has seen the Supreme. The boisterous senses, O son of Kuntî! carry away by force the mind even of a wise man, who exerts himself for final emancipation. Restraining them all, a man should remain engaged in devotion, making me his only resort. For his mind is steady whose senses are under his control. The man who ponders over objects of sense forms an attachment to them; from that attachment is produced desire; and from desire anger is produced; from anger results want of discrimination; from want of discrimination, confusion of the memory; from confusion of the memory, loss of reason; and in consequence of loss of reason. he is utterly ruined. But the self-restrained man who moves among objects with senses under the control of his own self, and free from affection and aversion, obtains tranquillity. When there is tranquillity, all his miseries are destroyed, for the mind of him whose heart is tranquil soon becomes steady. He who is not self-restrained has no steadiness of mind; nor has he who is not self-restrained perseverance in the pursuit of self-knowledge; there is no tranquillity for him who does not persevere in the pursuit of self-knowledge; and whence can there be happiness for one who is not tranquil? For the heart which follows the rambling senses leads away his judgment, as the wind leads a boat astray upon the waters. Therefore, O you of mighty arms! his mind is steady whose senses are restrained on all sides from objects of sense. The self-restrained man is awake, when it is night for all beings; and when all beings are awake, that is the night of the right-seeing sage. He into whom all objects of desire enter, as waters enter the ocean, which, though replenished, still keeps its position unmoved, he only obtains tranquillity; not he who desires those objects of desire. The man who, casting off all desires, lives free from attachments, who is free from egoism, and from the feeling that this or that is mine, obtains

tranquillity. This, O son of Prithâ! is the Brahmic state; attaining to this, one is never deluded; and remaining in it in one's last moments, one attains brahma-nirvâna the Brahmic bliss.

CHAPTER III.

Arguna said:

If, O Ganârdana! devotion is deemed by you to be superior to action, then why, O Kesava! do you prompt me to this fearful action? You seem, indeed, to confuse my mind by equivocal words. Therefore, declare one thing determinately, by which I may attain the highest good.

The Deity said:

O sinless one! I have already declared, that in this world there is a twofold path—that of the Sânkhyas by devotion in the shape of true knowledge; and that of the Yogins by devotion in the shape of action. A man does not attain freedom from action merely by not engaging in action; nor does he attain perfection by mere renunciation. For nobody ever remains even for an instant without performing some action; since the qualities of nature constrain everybody, not having free-will in the matter, to some action. The deluded man who, restraining the organs of action, continues to think in his mind about objects of sense, is called a hypocrite. But he, O Arguna! who restraining his senses by his mind and being free from attachments, engages in devotion in the shape of action, with the organs of action, is far superior. Do you perform prescribed action, for action is better than inaction, and the support of your body, too, cannot be accomplished with inaction. This world is fettered by all action other than action for the purpose of the sacrifice. Therefore, O son of Kuntî! do you, casting off attachment, perform action for that purpose. The Creator, having in olden times created men together with the sacrifice, said: 'Propagate with this. May it be the giver to you of the things you desire. Please the gods with this, and may those gods please you. Pleasing each other, you will attain the highest good. For pleased with the sacrifices, the gods will give you the enjoyments you desire. And he who enjoys himself without giving them what they have given, is, indeed, a thief.' The good, who eat the leavings of a sacrifice, are released from all sins. But the unrighteous ones, who prepare food for themselves only, incur sin. From food are born all creatures; from rain is the production of food; rain is produced by sacrifices; sacrifices are the result of action; know that action has its source in the Vedas; the Vedas come from the Indestructible. Therefore the all-comprehending Vedas are always concerned with sacrifices. He who in this world does not turn round the wheel revolving thus, is of sinful life, indulging his senses, and, O son of Prithâ! he lives in vain. But the man who is attached to his self only, who is contented in his self, and is pleased with his self, has nothing to do. He has no interest at all in what is done, and none whatever in what is not done, in this world; nor is any interest of his dependent on any being. Therefore always perform action, which must be performed, without attachment. For a man, performing action without attachment, attains the Supreme. By action alone, did Ganaka and the rest work for perfection. And having regard also to the keeping of people to their duties you should perform action. Whatever a great man does, that other men also do. And people follow whatever he receives as authority. There is nothing, O son of Prithâ! for me to do in all the three worlds, nothing to acquire which has not been acquired. Still I do engage in action. For should I at any time not engage without sloth in action, men would follow in my path from all sides, O son of Prithâ! If I did not perform actions, these worlds would be destroyed, I should be the cause of caste interminglings; and I should be ruining these people. As the ignorant act, O descendant of Bharata! with attachment to action, so should a wise man act without attachment, wishing to keep the people to their duties. A wise man should not shake the convictions of the ignorant who are attached to action, but acting with devotion himself should

make them apply themselves to all action. He whose mind is deluded by egoism thinks himself the doer of the actions, which, in every way, are done by the qualities of nature. But he, O you of mighty arms! who knows the truth about the difference from qualities and the difference from actions, forms no attachments, believing that qualities deal with qualities. But those who are deluded by the qualities of nature form attachments to the actions of the qualities. A man of perfect knowledge should not shake these men of imperfect knowledge in their convictions. Dedicating all actions to me with a mind knowing the relation of the supreme and individual self, engage in battle without desire, without any feeling that this or that is mine, and without any mental trouble. Even those men who always act on this opinion of mine, full of faith, and without carping, are released from all actions. But those who carp at my opinion and do not act upon it, know them to be devoid of discrimination, deluded as regards all knowledge, and ruined. Even a man of knowledge acts consonantly to his own nature. All beings follow nature. What will restraint effect? Every sense has its affections and aversions towards its objects fixed. One should not become subject to them, for they are one's opponents. One's own duty, though defective, is better than another's duty well performed. Death in performing one's own duty is preferable; the performance of the duty of others is dangerous.

Arguna said:

But by whom, O descendant of Vrishni! is man impelled, even though unwilling, and, as it were, constrained by force, to commit sin?

The Deity said:

It is desire, it is wrath, born from the quality of passion; it is very ravenous, very sinful. Know that that is the foe in this world. As fire is enveloped by smoke, a mirror by dust, the fœtus by the womb, so is this enveloped by desire. Knowledge, O son of Kuntî! is enveloped by this constant foe of the man of knowledge, in the shape of desire, which is like a fire and insatiable. The senses, the mind, and the understanding are said to be its seat; with these it deludes the embodied self after enveloping knowledge. Therefore, O chief of the descendants of Bharata! first restrain your senses, then cast off this sinful thing which destroys knowledge and experience. It has been said, Great are the senses, greater than the senses is the mind, greater than the mind is the understanding. What is greater than the understanding is that. Thus knowing that which is higher than the understanding, and restraining yourself by yourself, O you of mighty arms! destroy this unmanageable enemy in the shape of desire.

CHAPTER IV.

The Deity said:

This everlasting system of devotion I declared to the sun, the sun declared it to Manu, and Manu communicated it to Ikshvâku. Coming thus by steps, it became known to royal sages. But, O terror of your foes! that devotion was lost to the world by long lapse of time. That same primeval devotion I have declared to you to-day, seeing. that you are my devotee and friend, for it is the highest mystery.

Arguna said:

Later is your birth the birth of the sun is prior. How then shall I understand that you declared this first?

The Deity said:

I have passed through many births, O Arguna I and you also. I know them all, but you, O terror of your foes! do not know them. Even though I am unborn and inexhaustible in my essence, even though I am lord of all beings, still I take up the control of my own nature, and am born by means of my delusive power. Whensoever, O descendant of Bharata! piety languishes, and impiety is in the ascendant, I create myself. I am born age after age, for the protection of the good, for the destruction of evil-doers, and the establishment of piety. Whoever truly knows thus my divine

birth and work, casts off this body and is not born again. He comes to me, O Arguna! Many from whom affection, fear, and wrath have departed, who are full of me, who depend on me, and who are purified by the penance of knowledge, have come into my essence. I serve men in the way in which they approach me. In every way, O son of Prithâ! men follow in my path. Desiring the success of actions, men in this world worship the divinities, for in this world of mortals, the success produced by action is soon obtained. The fourfold division of castes was created by me according to the apportionment of qualities and duties. But though I am its author, know me to be inexhaustible, and not the author. Actions defile me not. I have no attachment to the fruit of actions. He who knows me thus is not tied down by actions. Knowing this, the men of old who wished for final emancipation, performed action. Therefore do you, too, perform action as was done by men of old in olden times. Even sages are confused as to what is action, what inaction. Therefore I will speak to you about action, and learning that, you will be freed from this world of evil. One must possess knowledge about action; one must also possess knowledge about prohibited action; and again one must possess knowledge about inaction. The truth regarding action is abstruse. He is wise among men, he is possessed of devotion, and performs all actions, who sees inaction in action, and action in inaction. The wise call him learned, whose acts are all free from desires and fancies, and whose actions are burnt down by the fire of knowledge. Forsaking all attachment to the fruit of action, always contented, dependent on none, he does nothing at all, though he engages in action. Devoid of expectations, restraining the mind and the self, and casting off all belongings, he incurs no sin, performing actions merely for the sake of the body. Satisfied with earnings coming spontaneously, rising above the pairs of opposites, free from all animosity, and equable on success or ill-success, he is not fettered down, even though he performs actions. The acts of one who is devoid of attachment, who is free, whose mind is fixed on knowledge, and who performs action for the purpose of the sacrifice are all destroyed. Brahman is the oblation; with Brahman as a sacrificial instrument it is offered up; Brahman is in the fire; and by Brahman it is thrown; and Brahman, too, is the goal to which he proceeds who meditates on Brahman in the action. Some devotees perform the sacrifice to the gods, some offer up the sacrifice by the sacrifice itself in the fire of Brahman. Others offer up the senses, such as the sense of hearing and others, in the fires of restraint; others offer up the objects of sense, such as sound and so forth, into the fires of the senses. Some again offer up all the operations of the senses and the operations of the life-breaths into the fire of devotion by self-restraint, kindled by knowledge. Others perform the sacrifice of wealth, the sacrifice of penance, the sacrifice of concentration of mind, the sacrifice of Vedic study, and of knowledge, and others are ascetics of rigid vows. Some offer up the upward life-breath into the downward life-breath, and the downward life-breath into the upper life-breath, and stopping up the motions of the upward and downward life-breaths, devote themselves to the restraint of the life-breaths. Others, who take limited food, offer up the life-breaths into the life-breaths. All of these, conversant with the sacrifice, have their sins destroyed by the sacrifice. Those who eat the nectar-like leavings of the sacrifice repair to the eternal Brahman. This world is not for those who perform no sacrifice, whence then the other, O best of the Kauravas! Thus sacrifices of various sorts are laid down in the Vedas. Know them all to be produced from action, and knowing this you will be released from the fetters of this world. The sacrifice of knowledge, O terror of your foes! is superior to the sacrifice of wealth, for action, O son of Prithâ! is wholly and entirely comprehended in knowledge. That you should learn by salutation, question, and service. The men of knowledge who perceive the truth will teach knowledge to you. Having learnt that, O son of Pându! you will not again fall thus into delusion; and by means of it, you will see all beings, without exception, first in yourself, and then in me. Even if you are the most sinful of all sinful men, you will cross over all trespasses by means of the boat of knowledge alone. As a fire well kindled, O Arguna! reduces fuel to ashes, so the fire of knowledge reduces all actions to ashes. For there is in this world no means of sanctification like knowledge, and that one perfected by devotion finds within one's self in time. He who has faith, whose senses are restrained, and who is assiduous, obtains knowledge. Obtaining knowledge, he acquires, without delay, the highest tranquillity. He who is ignorant and devoid of faith, and whose self is full of misgivings, is ruined. Not this world, not the next, nor happiness, is for him whose self is full of misgivings. Actions, O Dhanañgaya! do not fetter one who is self-possessed, who has renounced action by devotion, and who has destroyed misgivings by knowledge. Therefore, O descendant of Bharata! destroy, with the sword of knowledge, these misgivings of yours which fill your mind, and which are produced from ignorance. Engage in devotion. Arise!

CHAPTER V.

Arguna said:

O Krishna! you praise renunciation of actions and also the pursuit of them. Tell me determinately which one of these two is superior.

The Deity said:

Renunciation and pursuit of action are both instruments of happiness. But of the two, pursuit of action is superior to renunciation of action. He should be understood to be always an ascetic, who has no aversion and no desire. For, O you of mighty arms! he who is free from the pairs of opposites is easily released from all bonds. Children—not wise men—talk of sankhya and yoga as distinct. One who pursues either well obtains the fruit of both. The seat which the sânkhyas obtain is reached by the yogas also. He sees truly, who sees the sânkhya and yoga as one. Renunciation, O you of mighty arms! is difficult to reach without devotion; the sage possessed of devotion attains Brahman without delay. He who is possessed of devotion, whose self is pure, who has restrained his self, and who has controlled his senses, and who identifies his self with every being, is not tainted though he performs actions. The man of devotion, who knows the truth, thinks he does nothing at all, when he sees, hears, touches, smells, eats, moves, sleeps, breathes, talks, throws out, takes, opens or closes the eyelids; he holds that the senses deal with the objects of the senses. He who, casting off all attachment, performs actions dedicating them to Brahman, is not tainted by sin, as the lotus-leaf is not tainted by water. Devotees, casting off attachment, perform actions for attaining purity of self, with the body, the mind, the understanding, or even the senses—all free from egoistic notions. He who is possessed of devotion, abandoning the fruit of actions, attains the highest tranquillity. He who is without devotion, and attached to the fruit of action, is tied down by reason of his acting in consequence of some desire. The self-restrained, embodied self lies at ease within the city of nine portals, renouncing all actions by the mind, not doing nor causing any thing to be done. The Lord is not the cause of actions, or of the capacity of performing actions amongst men, or of the connexion of action and fruit. But nature only works. The Lord receives no one's sin, nor merit either. Knowledge is enveloped by ignorance, hence all creatures are deluded. But to those who have destroyed that ignorance by knowledge of the self, such knowledge, like the sun, shows forth that supreme principle. And those whose mind is centred on it, whose very self it is, who are thoroughly devoted to it, and whose final goal it is, go never to return, having their sins destroyed by knowledge. The wise look upon a Brâhmana possessed of learning and humility, on a cow, an elephant, a dog, and a Svapâka, as alike. Even here, those have conquered the material world, whose mind rests in equability; since Brahman is free from defects and equable, therefore they rest in Brahman. He who knows Brahman, whose mind is steady, who is not deluded, and who rests in Brahman, does not exult on finding anything agreeable, nor

does he grieve on finding anything disagreeable. One whose self is not attached to external objects, obtains the happiness that is in one's self; and by means of concentration of mind, joining one's self with the Brahman, one obtains indestructible happiness. For the enjoyments born of contact between senses and their objects are, indeed, sources of misery; they have a beginning as well as an end. O son of Kuntî! a wise man feels no pleasure in them. He who even in this world, before his release from the body, is able to bear the agitations produced from desire and wrath, is a devoted man, he is a happy man. The devotee whose happiness is within himself, whose recreation is within himself, and whose light of knowledge also is within himself, becoming one with the Brahman, obtain the Brahmic bliss. The sages whose sins have perished, whose misgivings are destroyed, who are self-restrained, and who are intent on the welfare of all beings, obtain the Brahmic bliss. To the ascetics, who are free from desire and wrath, and whose minds are restrained, and who have knowledge of the self, the Brahmic bliss is on both sides of death. The sage who excludes from his mind external objects, concentrates the visual power between the brows, and making the upward and downward life-breaths even, confines their movements within the nose, who restrains senses, mind, and understanding, whose highest goal is final emancipation, from whom desire, fear, and wrath have departed, is, indeed, forever released from birth and death. He knowing me to be the enjoyer of all sacrifices and penances, the great Lord of all worlds, and the friend of all beings, attains tranquility.

CHAPTER VI.

The Deity said:

He who, regardless of the fruit of actions, performs the actions which ought to be performed, is the devotee and renouncer; not he who discards the sacred fires, nor he who performs no acts. Know, O son of Pându! that what is called renunciation is devotion; for nobody becomes a devotee who has not renounced all fancies. To the sage who wishes to rise to devotion, action is said to be a means, and to him, when he has risen to devotion, tranquillity is said to be a means. When one does not attach oneself to objects of sense, nor to action, renouncing all fancies, then is one said to have risen to devotion. A man should elevate his self by his self; he should not debase his self, for even a man's own self is his friend, a man's own self is also his enemy. To him who has subjugated his self by his self, his self is a friend; but to him who has not restrained his self, his own self behaves inimically, like an enemy. The self of one who has subjugated his self and is tranquil, is absolutely concentrated on itself, in the midst of cold and heat, pleasure and pain, as well as honour and dishonour. The devotee whose self is contented with knowledge and experience, who is unmoved, who has restrained his senses, and to whom a sod, a stone, and gold are alike, is said to be devoted. And he is esteemed highest, who thinks alike about well-wishers, friends, and enemies, and those who are indifferent, and those who take part with both sides, and those who are objects of hatred, and relatives, as well as about the good and the sinful. A devotee should constantly devote his self to abstraction, remaining in a secret place, alone, with his mind and self restrained, without expectations, and without belongings. Fixing his seat firmly in a clean place, not too high nor too low, and covered over with a sheet of cloth, a deerskin, and blades of Kusa grass,—and there seated on that seat, fixing his mind exclusively on one point, with the workings of the mind and senses restrained, he should practice devotion for purity of self. Holding his body, head, and neck even and unmoved, remaining steady, looking at the tip of his own nose, and not looking about in all directions, with a tranquil self, devoid of fear, and adhering to the rules of Brahmakârins, he should restrain his mind, and concentrate it on me, and sit down engaged in devotion, regarding me as his final goal. Thus constantly devoting his self to abstraction, a devotee whose mind is restrained, attains that tranquillity which culminates in

final emancipation, and assimilation with me. Devotion is not his, O Arguna! who eats too much, nor his who eats not at all; not his who is addicted to too much sleep, nor his who is ever awake. That devotion which destroys all misery is his, who takes due food and exercise, who toils duly in all works, and who sleeps and awakes in due time. When a man's mind well restrained becomes steady upon the self alone, then he being indifferent to all objects of desire, is said to be devoted. As a light standing in a windless place flickers not, that is declared to be the parallel for a devotee, whose mind is restrained, and who devotes his self to abstraction. That mental condition, in which the mind restrained by practice of abstraction, ceases to work; in which too, one seeing the self by the self, is pleased in the self; in which one experiences that infinite happiness which transcends the senses, and which can be grasped by the understanding only; and adhering to which, one never swerves from the truth; acquiring which, one thinks no other acquisition higher than it; and adhering to which, one is not shaken off even by great misery; that should be understood to be called devotion in which there is a severance of all connexion with pain. That devotion should be practised with steadiness and with an undesponding heart. Abandoning, without exception, all desires, which are produced from fancies, and restraining the whole group of the senses on all sides by the mind only, one should by slow steps become quiescent, with a firm resolve coupled with courage; and fixing his mind upon the self, should think of nothing. Wherever the active and unsteady mind breaks forth, there one should ever restrain it, and fix it steadily on the self alone. The highest happiness comes to such a devotee, whose mind is fully tranquil, in whom the quality of passion has been suppressed, who is free from sin, and who is become one with the Brahman. Thus constantly devoting his self to abstraction, a devotee, freed from sin, easily obtains that supreme happiness—contact with the Brahman. He who has devoted his self to abstraction, by devotion, looking alike on everything, sees the self abiding in all beings, and all beings in the self. To him who sees me in everything, and everything in me, I am never lost, and he is not lost to me. The devotee who worships me abiding in all beings, holding that all is one, lives in me, however he may be living. That devotee, O Arguna! is deemed to be the best, who looks alike on pleasure or pain, whatever it may be, in all creatures, comparing all with his own pleasure or pain.

Arguna said:

I cannot see, O destroyer of Madhu! how the sustained existence is to be secured of this devotion by means of equanimity which you have declared-in consequence of fickleness. For, O Krishna! the mind is fickle, boisterous strong, and obstinate; and I think that to restrain it is as difficult as to restrain the wind.

The Deity said:

Doubtless, O you of mighty arms! the mind is difficult to restrain, and fickle. Still, O son of Kuntî! it may be restrained by constant practice and by indifference to worldly objects. It is my belief, that devotion is hard to obtain for one who does not restrain his self. But by one who is self-restrained and assiduous, it can be obtained through proper expedients.

Arguna said:

What is the end of him, O Krishna! who does not attain the consummation of his devotion, being not assiduous, and having a mind shaken off from devotion, though full of faith? Does he, fallen from both paths, go to ruin like a broken cloud, being, O you of mighty arms! without support, and deluded on the path leading to the Brahman? Be pleased, O Krishna! to entirely destroy this doubt of mine, for none else than you can destroy this doubt.

The Deity said:

O son of Prithâ! neither in this world nor the next, is ruin for him; for, O dear friend! none who performs good deeds comes to an evil end. He who is fallen from devotion attains the worlds of those who perform meritorious acts, dwells there for many a year, and is afterwards born into a family of holy and illustrious men. Or he is even born into a family of talented devotees; for such a birth as that in this world is more difficult to obtain. There he comes into contact with the knowledge which belonged to him in his former body, and then again, O descendant of Kuru! he works for perfection. For even though reluctant, he is led away by the self-same former practice, and although he only wishes to learn devotion, he rises above the fruits of action laid down in the divine word. But the devotee working with great efforts, and cleared of his sins, attains perfection after many births, and then reaches the supreme goal. The devotee is esteemed higher than the performers of penances, higher even than the men of knowledge, and the devotee is higher than the men of action; therefore, O Arguna! become a devotee. And even among all devotees, he who, being full of faith, worships me, with his inmost self intent on me, is esteemed by me to be the most devoted.

CHAPTER VII.

The Deity said:

O son of Prithâ! now hear how you can without doubt know me fully, fixing your mind on me, and resting in me, and practising devotion. I will now tell you exhaustively about knowledge together with experience; that being known, there is nothing further left in this world to know. Among thousands of men, only some work for perfection; and even of those who have reached perfection, and who are assiduous, only some know me truly. Earth, water, fire, air, space, mind, understanding, and egoism, thus is my nature divided eightfold. But this is a lower form of my nature. Know that there is another form of my nature, and higher than this, which is animate, O you of mighty arms! and by which this universe is upheld. Know that all things have these for their source. I am the producer and the destroyer of the whole universe. There is nothing else, O Dhanañgaya! higher than myself; all this is woven upon me, like numbers of pearls upon a thread. I am the taste in water, O son of Kuntî! I am the light of the sun and moon. I am 'Om' in all the Vedas, sound in space, and manliness in human beings; I am the fragrant smell in the earth, refulgence in the fire; I am life in all beings, and penance in those who perform penance. Know me, O son of Prithâ! to be the eternal seed of all beings; I am the discernment of the discerning ones, and I the glory of the glorious. I am also the strength, unaccompanied by fondness or desire, of the strong. And, O chief of the descendants of Bharata! I am love unopposed to piety among all beings. And all entities which are of the quality of goodness, and those which are of the quality of passion and of darkness, know that they are, indeed, all from me; I am not in them, but they are in me. The whole universe deluded by these three states of mind, developed from the qualities, does not know me, who am beyond them and inexhaustible; for this delusion of mine, developed from the qualities, is divine and difficult to transcend. Those cross beyond this delusion who resort to me alone. Wicked men, doers of evil acts, who are deluded, who are deprived of their knowledge by this delusion, and who incline to the demoniac state of mind, do not resort to me. But, O Arguna! doers of good acts of four classes worship me: one who is distressed, one who is seeking after knowledge, one who wants wealth, and one, O chief of the descendants of Bharata! who is possessed of knowledge. Of these, he who is possessed of knowledge, who is always devoted, and whose worship is addressed to one Being only, is esteemed highest. For to the man of knowledge I am dear above all things, and he is dear to me. All these are noble! But the man possessed of knowledge is deemed by me to be my own self. For he with his self devoted to abstraction, has taken to me as the goal than which there is nothing higher. At the end of many lives, the man possessed of knowledge approaches me, believing that Vâsudeva is everything. Such a high-souled man is very hard to find. Those who are deprived of knowledge by various desires approach other

divinities, observing various regulations, and controlled by their own natures. Whichever form of deity any worshipper wishes to worship with faith, to that form I render his faith steady. Possessed of that faith, he seeks to propitiate the deity in that form, and obtains from it those beneficial things which he desires, though they are really given by me. But the fruit thus obtained by them, who have little judgment, is perishable. Those who worship the divinities go to the divinities, and my worshippers, too, go to me. The undiscerning ones, not knowing my transcendent and inexhaustible essence, than which there is nothing higher, think me, who am unperceived, to have become perceptible. Surrounded by the delusion of my mystic power, I am not manifest to all. This deluded world knows not me unborn and inexhaustible. I know, O Arguna! the things which have been, those which are, and those which are to be. But me nobody knows. All beings, O terror of your foes! are deluded at the time of birth by the delusion, O descendant of Bharata! caused by the pairs of opposites arising from desire and aversion. But the men of meritorious actions, whose sins have terminated, worship me, being released from the delusion caused by the pairs of opposites, and being firm in their beliefs. Those who, resting on me, work for release from old age and death, know the Brahman, the whole Adhyâtma, and all action. And those who know me with the Adhibhûta, the Adhidaiva, and the Adhiyagña, having minds devoted to abstraction, know me at the time of departure from this world.

CHAPTER VIII.

Arguna said:

What is that Brahman, what the Adhyâtma, and what, O best of beings! is action? And what is called the Adhibhûta? And who is the Adhiyagña, and how in this body, O destroyer of Madhu? And how, too, are you to be known at the time of departure from this world by those who restrain their selfs?

The Deity said:

The Brahman is the supreme, the indestructible. Its manifestation as an individual self is called the Adhyâtma. The offering of an oblation to any divinity, which is the cause of the production and development of all things, is named action. The Adhibhûta is all perishable things. The Adhidaivata is the primal being. And the Adhiyagña, O best of embodied beings! is I myself in this body. And he who leaves this body and departs from this world remembering me in his last moments, comes into my essence. There is no doubt of that. Also whichever form of deity he remembers when he finally leaves this body, to that he goes, O son of Kuntî! having been used to ponder on it. Therefore, at all times remember me, and engage in battle. Fixing your mind and understanding on me, you will come to me, there is no doubt. He who thinks of the supreme divine Being, O son of Prithâ! with a mind not running to other objects, and possessed of abstraction in the shape of continuous meditation about the supreme, goes to him. He who, possessed of reverence for the supreme Being with a steady mind, and with the power of devotion, properly concentrates the life-breath between the brows, and meditates on the ancient Seer, the ruler, more minute than the minutest atom, the supporter of all, who is of an unthinkable form, whose brilliance is like that of the sun, and who is beyond all darkness, he attains to that transcendent and divine Being. I will tell you briefly about the seat, which those who know the Vedas declare to be indestructible; which entered by ascetics from whom all desires have departed; and wishing for which, people pursue the mode of life of Brahmakârins. He who leaves the body and departs from this world, stopping up all passages, and confining the mind within the heart, placing the life-breath in the head, and adhering to uninterrupted meditation, repeating the single syllable 'Om,' signifying the eternal Brahman, and meditating on me, he reaches the highest goal. To the devotee who

constantly practises abstraction, O son of Prithâ! and who with a mind not turned to anything else, is ever and constantly meditating on me, I am easy of access. The high-souled ones, who achieve the highest perfection, attaining to me, do not again come to life, which is transient, a home of woes. All worlds, O Arguna! up to the world of Brahman, are destined to return. But, O son of Kuntî! after attaining to me, there is no birth again. Those who know a day of Brahman to end after one thousand ages, and the night to terminate after one thousand ages, are the persons who know day and night. On the advent of day, all perceptible things are produced from the unperceived; and on the advent of night they dissolve in that same principle called the unperceived. This same assemblage of entities, being produced again and again, dissolves on the advent of night, and, O son of Prithâ! issues forth on the advent of day, without a will of its own. But there is another entity, unperceived and eternal, and distinct from this unperceived principle, which is not destroyed when all entities are destroyed. It is called the unperceived, the indestructible; they call it the highest goal. Attaining to it, none returns. That is my supreme abode. That supreme Being, O son of Prithâ! he in whom all these entities dwell, and by whom all this is permeated, is to be attained to by reverence not directed to another. I will state the times, O descendant of Bharata! at which devotees departing from this world go, never to return, or to return. The fire, the flame, the day, the bright fortnight, the six months of the northern solstice, departing from the world in these, those who know the Brahman go to the Brahman. Smoke, night, the dark fortnight, the six months of the southern solstice, dying in these, the devotee goes to the lunar light and returns. These two paths, bright and dark, are deemed to be eternal in this world. By the one, a man goes never to return, by the other he comes back. Knowing these two paths, O son of Prithâ! no devotee is deluded. Therefore at all times be possessed of devotion, O Arguna! A devotee knowing all this, obtains all the holy fruit which is prescribed for study of the Vedas, for sacrifices, and also for penances and gifts, and he attains to the highest and primeval seat.

CHAPTER IX.

Now I will speak to you, who are not given to carping, of that most mysterious knowledge, accompanied by experience, by knowing which you will be released from evil. It is the chief among the sciences, the chief among the mysteries. It is the best means of sanctification. It is imperishable, not opposed to the sacred law. It is to be apprehended directly, and is easy to practise. O terror of your foes! those men who have no faith in this holy doctrine, return to the path of this mortal world, without attaining to me. This whole universe is pervaded by me in an unperceived form. All entities live in me, but I do not live in them. Nor yet do all entities live in me. See my divine power. Supporting all entities and producing all entities, my self lives not in those entities. As the great and ubiquitous atmosphere always remains in space, know that similarly all entities live in me. At the expiration of a Kalpa, O son of Kuntî! all entities enter my nature; and at the beginning of a Kalpa, I again bring them forth. Taking the control of my own nature, I bring forth again and again this whole collection of entities, without a will of its own, by the power of nature. But, O Arguna! these actions do not fetter me, who remain like one unconcerned, and who am unattached to those actions. Nature gives birth to movables and immovables through me, the supervisor, and by reason of that, O son of Kuntî! the universe revolves. Deluded people of vain hopes, vain acts, vain knowledge, whose minds are disordered, and who are inclined to the delusive nature of Asuras and Râkshasas, not knowing my highest nature as great lord of all entities, disregard me as I have assumed a human body. But the high-souled ones, O son of Prithâ! who are inclined to the godlike nature, knowing me as the inexhaustible source of all entities, worship me with minds not turned elsewhere. Constantly glorifying me, and exerting themselves, firm in their vows, and saluting me with reverence, they worship me, being always devoted. And others again, offering up the sacrifice of knowledge, worship me as one, as distinct, and as all-pervading in numerous forms. I am the Kratu, I am the Yagña, I am the Svadhâ, I the product of the herbs. I am the sacred verse. I too am the sacrificial butter, and I the fire, I the offering. I am the father of this universe, the mother, the creator, the grandsire, the thing to be known, the means of sanctification, the syllable Om, the Rik, Sâman, and Yagus also; the goal, the sustainer, the lord, the supervisor, the residence, the asylum, the friend, the source, and that in which it merges, the support, the receptacle, and the inexhaustible seed. I cause heat and I send forth and stop showers. I am immortality and also death; and I, O Arguna! am that which is and that which is not. Those who know the three branches of knowledge, who drink the Soma juice, whose sins are washed away, offer sacrifices and pray to me for a passage into heaven; and reaching the holy world of the lord of gods, they enjoy in the celestial regions the celestial pleasures of the gods. And having enjoyed that great heavenly world, they enter the mortal world when their merit is exhausted. Thus those who wish for objects of desire, and resort to the ordinances of the three Vedas, obtain as the fruit going and coming. To those men who worship me, meditating on me and on no one else, and who are constantly devoted, I give new gifts and preserve what is acquired by them. Even those, O son of Kuntî! who being devotees of other divinities worship with faith, worship me only, but irregularly. For I am the enjoyer as well as the lord of all sacrifices. But they know me not truly, therefore do they fall. Those who make vows to the gods go to the gods; those who make vows to the manes go to the manes, those who worship the Bhûtas go to the Bhûtas; and those likewise who worship me go to me. Whoever with devotion offers me leaf, flower, fruit, water, that, presented with devotion, I accept from him whose self is pure. Whatever you do, O son of Kuntî!

whatever you eat, whatever sacrifice you make, whatever you give, whatever penance you perform, do that as offered to me. Thus will you be released from the bonds of action, the fruits of which are agreeable or disagreeable. And with your self possessed of this devotion, this renunciation, you will be released from the bonds of action and will come to me. I am alike to all beings; to me none is hateful, none dear. But those who worship me with devotion dwell in me, and I too in them. Even if a very ill-conducted man worships me, not worshipping any one else, he must certainly be deemed to be good, for he has well resolved. He soon becomes devout of heart, and obtains lasting tranquillity. You may affirm, O son of Kuntî! that my devotee is never ruined. For, O son of Prithâ! even those who are of sinful birth, women, Vaisyas; and Sûdras likewise, resorting to me, attain the supreme goal. What then need be said of holy Brâhmanas and royal saints who are my devotees? Coming to this transient unhappy world, worship me. Place your mind on me, become my devotee, my worshipper; reverence me, and thus making me your highest goal, and devoting your self to abstraction, you will certainly come to me.

CHAPTER X.

Yet again, O you of mighty arms! listen to my excellent words, which, out of a wish for your welfare, I speak to you who are delighted with them. Not the multitudes of gods, nor the great sages know my source; for I am in every way the origin of the gods and great sages. Of all mortals, he who knows me to be unborn, without beginning, the great lord of the world, being free from delusion, is released from all sins. Intelligence, knowledge, freedom from delusion, forgiveness, truth, restraint of the senses, tranquillity, pleasure, pain, birth, death, fear, and also security, harmlessness, equability, contentment, penance, making gifts, glory, disgrace, all these different tempers of living beings are from me alone. The seven great sages, and likewise the four ancient Manus, whose descendants are all these people in the world, were all born from my mind, partaking of my powers. Whoever correctly knows these powers and emanations of mine, becomes possessed of devotion free from indecision; of this there is no doubt. The wise, full of love, worship me, believing that I am the origin of all, and that all moves on through me. Placing their minds on me, offering their lives to me, instructing each other, and speaking about me, they are always contented and happy. To these, who are constantly devoted, and who worship with love, I give that knowledge by which they attain to me. And remaining in their hearts, I destroy, with the brilliant lamp of knowledge, the darkness born of ignorance in such men only, out of compassion for them.

Arguna said:

You are the supreme Brahman, the supreme goal, the holiest of the holy. All sages, as well as the divine sage Nârada, Asita, Devala, and Vyâsa, call you the eternal being, divine, the first god, the unborn, the all-pervading. And so, too, you tell me yourself, O Kesava! I believe all this that you tell me to be true; for, O lord! neither the gods nor demons understand your manifestation. You only know your self by your self. O best of beings! creator of all things! lord of all things! god of gods! lord of the universe! be pleased to declare without, exception your divine emanations, by which emanations you stand pervading all these worlds. How shall I know you, O you of mystic power! always meditating on you? And in what various entities, O lord! should I meditate on you? Again, O Ganârdana! do you yourself declare your powers and emanations; because hearing this nectar, I still feel no satiety.

The Deity said:

Well then, O best of Kauravas! I will state to you my own divine emanations; but only the chief ones, for there is no end to the extent of my emanations. I am the self, O Gudâkesa! seated in the hearts of all beings. I am the beginning and the middle and the end also of all beings. I am Vishnu among the Âdityas, the beaming sun among the shining bodies; I am Marîki among the Maruts, and the moon among the lunar mansions. Among the Vedas, I am the Sâma-veda. I am Indra among the gods. And I am mind among the senses. I am consciousness in living beings. And I am Sankara among the Rudras, the lord of wealth among Yakshas and Rakshases. And I am fire among the Vasus, and Meru among the high-topped mountains. And know me, O Arguna! to be Brihaspati, the chief among domestic priests. I am Skanda among generals. I am the ocean among reservoirs of water. I am Bhrigu among the great sages. I am the single syllable (Om) among words. Among sacrifices I am the Gapa sacrifice; the Himâlaya among the firmly-fixed mountains; the Asvattha among all trees, and Nârada among divine sages; Kitraratha among the heavenly choristers, the sage Kapila among the Siddhas. Among horses know me to be Ukkaissravas, brought forth by the labours for the nectar; and Airâvata among the great elephants, and the ruler. of men among men. I am the thunderbolt among weapons, the wish-giving cow among cows. And I am love which generates. Among serpents I am Vâsuki. Among Nâga snakes I am Ananta; I am Varuna among aquatic beings. And I am Aryaman among the manes, and Yama among rulers. Among demons, too, I am Pralhâda. I am the king of death Kâla, time among those that count. Among beasts I am the lord of beasts, and the son of Vinatâ among birds. I am the wind among those that blow. I am Râma among those that wield weapons. Among fishes I am Makara, and among streams the Gâhnavî. Of created things I am the beginning and the end and the middle also, O Arguna! Among sciences, I am the science of the Adhyâtma, and I am the argument of controversialists. Among letters I am the letter A, and among the group of compounds the copulative compound. I myself am time inexhaustible, and I the creator whose faces are in all directions. I am death who seizes all, and the source of what is to be. And among females, fame, fortune, speech, memory, intellect, courage. forgiveness. Likewise among Sâman hymns, I am the Brihat-sâman, and I the Gâyatrî among metres. I am Mârgasîrsha among the months, the spring among the seasons; of cheats, I am the game of dice; I am the glory of the glorious, I am victory, I am industry, I am the goodness of the good. I am Vâsudeva among the descendants of Vrishni, and Arguna among the Pândavas. Among sages also, I am Vyâsa; and among the discerning ones, I am the discerning Usanas. I am the rod of those that restrain, and the policy of those that desire victory. I am silence respecting secrets. I am the knowledge of those that have knowledge And, O Arguna! I am also that which is the seed of all things. There is nothing movable or immovable which can exist without me. O terror of your foes! there is no end to my divine emanations. Here I have declared the extent of those emanations only in part. Whatever thing there is of power, or glorious, or splendid, know all that to be produced from portions of my energy. Or rather, O Arguna! what have you to do, knowing all this at large? I stand supporting all this by but a single portion of myself.

CHAPTER XI.

Arguna said:

In consequence of the excellent and mysterious words concerning the relation of the supreme and individual soul, which you have spoken for my welfare, this delusion of mine is gone away. O you whose eyes are like lotus leaves! I have heard from you at large about the production and dissolution of things, and also about your inexhaustible greatness. O highest lord! what you have said about yourself is so. I wish, O best of beings! to see your divine form. If, O lord! you think that it is possible for me to look upon it, then, O lord of the possessors of mystic power! show your inexhaustible form to me.

The Deity said:

In hundreds and in thousands see my forms, O son of Prithâ! various, divine, and of various colours and shapes. See the Âdityas, Vasus, Rudras, the two Asvins, and Maruts likewise. And O descendant of Bharata! see wonders, in numbers, unseen before. Within my body, O Gudâkesa! see to-day the whole universe, including everything movable and immovable, all in one, and whatever else you wish to see. But you will not be able to see me with merely, this eye of yours. I give you an eye divine. Now see my divine power.

Sañgaya said

Having spoken thus, O king! Hari, the great lord of the possessors of mystic power, then showed to the son of Prithâ his supreme divine form, having many mouths and eyes, having within it many wonderful sights, having many celestial ornaments, having many celestial weapons held erect, wearing celestial flowers and vestments, having an anointment of celestial perfumes, full of every wonder, the infinite deity with faces in all directions. If in the heavens, the lustre of a thousand suns burst forth all at once, that would be like the lustre of that mighty one. There the son of Pându then observed in the body of the god of gods the whole universe all in one, and divided into numerous divisions. Then Dhanañgaya filled with amazement, and with hair standing on end, bowed his head before the god, and spoke with joined hands.

Arguna said:

O god! I see within your body the gods, as also all the groups of various beings; and the lord Brahman seated on his lotus seat, and all the sages and celestial snakes. I see you, who are of countless forms, possessed of many arms, stomachs, mouths, and eyes on all sides. And, O lord of the universe! O you of all forms! I do not see your end or middle or beginning. I see you bearing a coronet and a mace and a discus—a mass of glory, brilliant on all sides, difficult to look at, having on all sides the effulgence of a blazing fire or sun, and indefinable. You are indestructible, the supreme one to be known. You are the highest support of this universe. You are the inexhaustible protector of everlasting piety. I believe you to be the eternal being. I see you void of beginning, middle, end—of infinite power, of unnumbered arms, having the sun and moon for eyes, having a mouth like a blazing fire, and heating the universe with your radiance. For this space between heaven and earth and all the quarters are pervaded by you alone. Looking at this wonderful and terrible form of yours, O high-souled one! the three worlds are affrighted. For here these groups of gods are entering into you. Some being afraid are praying with joined hands, and the groups of great sages and Siddhas are saying 'Welfare!' and praising you with abundant hymns of praise. The Rudras, and Âdityas, the Vasus, the Sâdhyas, the Visvas, the two Asvins, the Maruts, and the Ushmapas, and the groups of Gandharvas, Yakshas, demons, and Siddhas are all looking at you amazed. Seeing your mighty form, with many mouths and eyes, with many arms, thighs, and feet, with many stomachs, and fearful with many jaws, all people, and I likewise, are much alarmed, O you of mighty arms! Seeing you, O Vishnu! touching the skies, radiant, possessed of many hues, with a gaping mouth, and with large blazing eyes, I am much alarmed in my inmost self, and feel no courage, no tranquillity. And seeing your mouths terrible by the jaws, and resembling the fire of destruction, I cannot recognise the various directions, I feel no comfort. Be gracious, O lord of gods! who pervadest the universe. And all these sons of Dhritarâshtra, together with all the bands of kings, and Bhîshma and Drona, and this charioteer's son likewise, together with our principal warriors also, are rapidly entering your mouths, fearful and horrific by reason of your jaws. And some with their heads smashed are seen to be stuck in the spaces between the teeth. As the many rapid currents of a river's waters run towards the sea alone, so do these heroes of the human world enter your mouths blazing all round. As butterflies, with increased velocity, enter a blazing fire to their destruction, so too do these people enter your mouths with increased velocity only to their destruction. Swallowing all these people, you are licking them over and over again from all sides, with your blazing mouths. Your fierce splendours, O Vishnu! filling the whole universe with their effulgence, are heating it. Tell me who you are in this fierce form. Salutations be to thee, O chief of the gods! Be gracious. I wish to know you, the primeval, one, for I do not understand your actions.

The Deity said:

I am death, the destroyer of the worlds, fully developed, and I am now active about the overthrow of the worlds. Even without you, the warriors standing in the adverse hosts, shall all cease to be. Therefore, be up, obtain glory, and vanquishing your foes, enjoy a prosperous kingdom. All these have been already killed by me. Be only the instrument, O Savyasâkin! Drona, and Bhîshma, and Gayadratha, and Karna, and likewise other valiant warriors also, whom I have killed, do you kill. Be not alarmed. Do fight. And in the battle you will conquer your foes.

Sañgaya said:

Hearing these words of Kesava, the wearer of the coronet, trembling, and with joined hands, bowed down; and sorely afraid, and with throat choked up, he again spoke to Krishna after saluting him.

Arguna said:

It is quite proper, O Hrishîkesa! that the universe is delighted and charmed by your renown, that the demons run away affrighted in all directions, and that all the assemblages of Siddhas bow down to you. And why, O high-souled one! should they not bow down to you who are greater than Brahman, and first cause? O infinite lord of gods! O you pervading the universe! you are the indestructible, that which is, that which is not, and what is beyond them. You are the primal god, the ancient being, you are the highest support of this universe. You are that which has knowledge, that which is the object of knowledge, you are the highest goal. By you is this universe pervaded., O you of infinite forms! You are the wind, Yama, fire, Varuna, the moon, you Pragâpati, and the great

grandsire. Obeisance be to thee a thousand times, and again and again obeisance to thee! In front and from behind obeisance to thee! Obeisance be to thee from all sides, O you who are all! You are of infinite power, of unmeasured glory; you pervade all, and therefore you are all! Whatever I have said contemptuously,—for instance, 'O Krishna!' 'O Yâdava!' 'O friend!'—thinking you to be my friend, and not knowing your greatness as shown in this universal form, or through friendliness, or incautiously; and whatever disrespect I have shown you for purposes of merriment, on occasions of play, sleep, dinner, or sitting together, whether alone or in the presence of friends,—for all that, O undegraded one! I ask pardon of you who are indefinable. You are the father of the world-movable and immovable,—you its great and venerable master; there is none equal to you, whence can there be one greater, O you whose power is unparalleled in all the three worlds? Therefore I bow and prostrate myself, and would propitiate you, the praiseworthy lord. Be pleased, O god! to pardon my guilt as a father that of his son, a friend that of his friend, or a husband that of his beloved. I am delighted at seeing what I had never seen before, and my heart is also alarmed by fear. Show me that same form, O god! Be gracious, O lord of gods! O you pervading the universe! I wish to see you bearing the coronet and the mace, with the discus in hand, just the same as before. O you of thousand arms! O you of all forms! assume that same four-handed form.

The Deity said:

O Arguna! being pleased with you, I have by my own mystic power shown you this supreme form, full of glory, universal, infinite, primeval, and which has not been seen before by any one else but you, O you hero among the Kauravas! I cannot be seen in this form by any one but you, even by the help of the study of the Vedas, or of sacrifices, nor by gifts, nor by actions, nor by fierce penances. Be not alarmed, be not perplexed, at seeing this form of mine, fearful like this. Free from fear and with delighted heart, see now again that same form of mine.

Sañgaya said:

Having thus spoken to Arguna, Vâsudeva again showed his own form, and the high-souled one becoming again of a mild form, comforted him who had been affrighted.

Arguna said:

O Ganardana! seeing this mild, human form of yours, I am now in my right mind, and have come to my normal state.

The Deity said:

Even the gods are always desiring to see this form of mine, which it is difficult to get a sight of, and which you have seen. I cannot be seen, as you have seen me, by means of the Vedas, not by penance, not by gift, nor yet by sacrifice. But, O Arguna! by devotion to me exclusively, I can in this form be truly known, seen, and assimilated with, O terror of your foes! He who performs acts for propitiating me, to whom I am the highest object, who is my devotee, who is free from attachment, and who has no enmity towards any being, he, O son of Pându! comes to me.

St. Augustine: *The Confessions*

Editors' Introduction

While recognized as an extraordinary autobiographical account of conversion, *The Confessions* of St. Augustine can also be understood as an extended prayer to and before God. We tend to think of personal prayer as a private matter, but here Augustine invites us to reflect along with him as he reviews his life in the presence of the God to whom he is praying.

If we understand the book in this way, we can better grasp the meaning of its title. On one level, *The Confessions* embodies the common usage of the term "confession" as a statement of repentance for one's sins. There is certainly plenty of this in the text. In fact, some readers are mystified by the seemingly inordinate length with which the author decries the sins of his past—sins that do not strike at least some readers as being particularly egregious or harmful. (Here's a hint—pay attention to Augustine's story of the pears.) But this confession of sin is only one aspect of what Augustine wishes to convey to his readers through these reflections. "Confession" can also be understood as a form of praise, and this is perhaps the most important meaning it has for Augustine here. His confession of the bad deeds from his past is meant to illuminate the tremendous goodness and mercy of God—a God who he experiences as having freed him from his earlier, inauthentic ways of life. Augustine's prayer is a prayer of praise and thanksgiving to God for helping him to be free to become his true self. For Augustine, that true self

cannot be understood apart from his relationship to the One who has freed and enlightened him.

Augustine was born in 354 A.D. in the northern African city of Thagaste (modern day Souk Ahras in Algeria). His mother, Monica, was a Christian, and his father, Patricius, was a pagan. At this time, northern Africa was part of the Roman Empire. Around the age of seventeen he was sent to Carthage (in what is now Tunisia) for higher studies in classical literature and rhetoric. While in Carthage he began to live with a woman (whose name we do not know) with whom he had a son, Adeodatus ("Godsend"). It appears that he and his companion loved one another deeply, and that they remained mutually faithful during the course of their fourteen year relationship.

Although his mother was a Christian, Augustine was not baptized, and he seems to have been little affected by the Christian message during his youth and teenage years. While there is sometimes a tendency to focus on the misadventures and sins of his early years (an image he did much to perpetuate himself, in order to highlight the significance of his conversion), it is important to keep in mind that Augustine was someone who was always searching and who always thought seriously about philosophical, moral, and religious questions. When he was nineteen he came across a treatise called the *Hortensius* written by the Roman philosopher Cicero. This book inspired him with a desire to seek wisdom, and it can be truly said of Augustine that while this desire would sometimes be submerged by other concerns, it never left him. His was a probing intellect, and his life unfolded as a search for answers to the most serious questions. One episode in his ongoing intellectual journey occurred during his years in Carthage when he was attracted to a group called the Manichees. Manicheanism was a religious/philosophical system that originated in Persia. Manichean teaching was dualistic, believing that the world was the scene of a struggle between an evil power and a power of good. According to this view, God was good but incapable of conquering evil. Another dualistic feature of Manicheanism was a sharp contrast between matter and spirit. For seriously committed Manichees, this entailed a very negative view of the material world, and it was their belief that salvation involved freeing oneself as much as possible from the concerns of the flesh.

Having completed his education, Augustine found employment teaching rhetoric in Carthage. Dissatisfied with the behavior of his students, he made his way to Rome in 383, in the hope that education might be viewed more seriously there. Once again disappointed, he applied for and won a professorship in the northern Italian city of Milan. There he encountered two influences that would prove to be crucial in his process of conversion: Neo-Platonic philosophy and the preaching of St. Ambrose, bishop of Milan. Neo-Platonism is a complex philosophical teaching; some of what attracted Augustine to it was the idea of life as a journey of ascent toward union with divine reality and the idea of God as an entirely spiritual substance. With regard to this latter idea, the notion that "real" was not the same thing as "body" came as a tremendous intellectual breakthrough for him. Through Ambrose, Augustine came to appreciate the importance of the Bible, a book he had previously viewed as unsophisticated in comparison with philosophy.

Despite these movements of intellectual conversion, Augustine remained at this time an ambitious young man eager to make a name for himself in Milan. Whether at his mother's urging, by his own decision, or through a mutually agreed upon arrangement, it was decided that his long-time companion (the mother of his son) would

return to Africa. If Augustine was going to move up in society he needed to contract a "proper" marriage, and he needed to marry someone with a substantial dowry. While Augustine's behavior toward his partner is hardly defensible, it should be kept in mind that in fourth century Roman society it was relatively common for a young man to live with a female companion for an extended period of time and then to leave her when he contracted a legal marriage. Marriage at this time was often entered into for financial reasons and as a way of joining two families together. Be careful not to read contemporary ideas about romantic love or Christian commitment into the practices of late Roman society. Augustine's mother Monica arranged a marriage, but since the promised bride was still too young to marry, Augustine would have to wait two years between the time of sending away his partner and his arranged marriage. This he found difficult to do, and he soon began to live with another woman.

Despite these circumstances, Augustine remained unsettled and searching morally, spiritually, and intellectually. His friend Alypius helped to convince him that he (Augustine) was not made for marriage, so he broke off the plan for the arranged marriage and ended the relationship with the woman with whom he was living. Through friends he also became acquainted with various accounts of personal conversion, including the story of St. Anthony of the Desert (an Egyptian saint/monk who lived from 251 to 356). Augustine found himself deeply moved by these conversion narratives. He was now on the verge of a decisive breakthrough. The moment came in the summer of 386. Highly agitated and suffering from a good deal of personal confusion and anguish, Augustine (along with Alypius) went out into the garden adjoining the place where he was living. There, coming from a nearby house, he heard the voice of a young child singing over and over again the words "Pick it up and read." Augustine picked up a volume containing the letters of St. Paul, opened it randomly to a page, and found there words that he took to be addressed to him by God. Augustine, his son Adeodatus,

Alypius, and several other friends were baptized by St. Ambrose on Easter 387.

Within a year Augustine decided to return to Africa. On the way there, in the Italian city of Ostia, his mother died. Shortly after he returned to Africa, his son died at age seventeen. In 391, he was ordained a priest in Hippo Regius (present day Annaba in Algeria), and in 395 he was named bishop of the city. He served as bishop until his death in 430. Intense and energetic as always, he immersed himself in the pastoral care of his people, wrote voluminously, and preached with great effectiveness. He died as the Vandals (a Germanic tribe) were laying siege to his city. The Roman world that had shaped him in so many ways was, if not disappearing, about to be deeply transformed. Through *The Confessions* and his other writings he would exert a profound influence on the new world that would emerge from the ruins of Rome.

The Confessions (Selections)

BOOK ONE

In God's searching presence, Augustine undertakes to plumb the depths of his memory to trace the mysterious pilgrimage of grace which his life has been—and to praise God for his constant and omnipotent grace. In a mood of sustained prayer, he recalls what he can of his infancy, his learning to speak, and his childhood experiences in school. He concludes with a paean of grateful praise to God.

CHAPTER I

1. "Great art thou, O Lord, and greatly to be praised; great is thy power, and infinite is thy wisdom." And man desires to praise thee, for he is a part of thy creation; he bears his mortality about with him and carries the evidence of his sin and the proof that thou dost resist the proud. Still he desires to praise thee, this man who is only a small part of thy creation. Thou hast prompted him, that he should delight to praise thee, for thou hast made us for thyself and restless is our heart until it comes to rest in thee. Grant me, O Lord, to know and understand whether first to invoke thee or to praise thee; whether first to know thee or call upon thee. But who can invoke thee, knowing thee not? For he who knows thee not may invoke thee as another than thou art. It may be that we should invoke thee in order that we may come to know thee. But "how shall they call on him in whom they have not believed? Or how shall they believe without a preacher?" Now, "they shall praise the Lord who seek him," for "those who seek shall find him," and, finding him, shall praise him. I will seek thee, O Lord, and call upon thee. I call upon thee, O Lord, in my faith which thou hast given me, which thou hast inspired in me through the humanity of thy Son, and through the ministry of thy preacher.

CHAPTER II

2. And how shall I call upon my God—my God and my Lord? For when I call on him I ask him to come into me. And what place is there in me into which my God can come? How could God, the God who made both heaven and earth, come into me? Is there anything in me, O Lord my God, that can contain thee? Do even the heaven and the earth, which thou hast made, and in which thou didst make me, contain thee? Is it possible that, since without thee nothing would be which does exist, thou didst make it so that whatever exists has some capacity to receive thee? Why, then, do I ask thee to come into me, since I also am and could not be if thou wert not in me? For I am not, after all, in hell—and yet thou art there too, for "if I go down into hell, thou art there." Therefore I would not exist—I would simply not be at all—unless I exist in thee, from whom and by whom and in whom all things are. Even so, Lord; even so. Where do I call thee to, when I am already in thee? Or from whence wouldst thou come into me? Where, beyond heaven and earth, could I go that there my God might come to me—he who hath said, "I fill heaven and earth"?

BOOK TWO

He concentrates here on his sixteenth year, a year of idleness, lust, and adolescent mischief. The memory of stealing some pears prompts a deep probing of the motives and aims of sinful acts. "I became to myself a wasteland."

CHAPTER I

1. I wish now to review in memory my past wickedness and the carnal corruptions of my soul—not because I still love them, but that I may love thee, O my God. For love of thy love I do this, recalling in the bitterness of self-examination my wicked ways, that thou mayest grow sweet to me, thou sweetness without deception! Thou sweetness happy and assured! Thus thou mayest gather me up out of those fragments in which I was torn to pieces, while I turned away from thee, O Unity, and lost myself among "the many." For as I became a youth, I longed to be satisfied with worldly things, and I dared to grow wild in a succession of various and shadowy loves. My form wasted away, and I became corrupt in thy eyes, yet I was still pleasing to my own eyes—and eager to please the eyes of men.

CHAPTER II

2. But what was it that delighted me save to love and to be loved? Still I did not keep the moderate way of the love of mind to mind—the bright path of friendship. Instead, the mists of passion steamed up out of the puddly concupiscence of the flesh, and the hot imagination of puberty, and they so obscured and overcast my heart that I was unable to distinguish pure affection from unholy desire. Both boiled confusedly within me, and dragged my unstable youth down over the cliffs of unchaste desires and plunged me into a gulf of infamy. Thy anger had come upon me, and I knew it not. I had been deafened by the clanking of the chains of my mortality, the punishment for my soul's pride, and I wandered farther from thee, and thou didst permit me to do so. I was tossed to and fro, and wasted, and poured out, and I boiled over in my fornications—and yet thou didst hold thy peace, O my tardy Joy! Thou didst still hold thy peace, and I wandered still farther from thee into more and yet more barren fields of sorrow, in proud dejection and restless lassitude.

3. If only there had been someone to regulate my disorder and turn to my profit the fleeting beauties of the things around me, and to fix a bound to their sweetness, so that the tides of my youth might have spent themselves upon the shore of marriage! Then they might have been tranquilized and satisfied with having children, as thy law prescribes, O Lord—O thou who dost

form the offspring of our death and art able also with a tender hand to blunt the thorns which were excluded from thy paradise! For thy omnipotence is not far from us even when we are far from thee. Now, on the other hand, I might have given more vigilant heed to the voice from the clouds: "Nevertheless, such shall have trouble in the flesh, but I spare you," and, "It is good for a man not to touch a woman," and, "He that is unmarried cares for the things that belong to the Lord, how he may please the Lord; but he that is married cares for the things that are of the world, how he may please his wife." I should have listened more attentively to these words, and, thus having been "made a eunuch for the Kingdom of Heaven's sake," I would have with greater happiness expected thy embraces.

4. But, fool that I was, I foamed in my wickedness as the sea and, forsaking thee, followed the rushing of my own tide, and burst out of all thy bounds. But I did not escape thy scourges. For what mortal can do so? Thou wast always by me, mercifully angry and flavoring all my unlawful pleasures with bitter discontent, in order that I might seek pleasures free from discontent. But where could I find such pleasure save in thee, O Lord—save in thee, who dost teach us by sorrow, who woundest us to heal us, and dost kill us that we may not die apart from thee. Where was I, and how far was I exiled from the delights of thy house, in that sixteenth year of the age of my flesh, when the madness of lust held full sway in me—that madness which grants indulgence to human shamelessness, even though it is forbidden by thy laws—and I gave myself entirely to it? Meanwhile, my family took no care to save me from ruin by marriage, for their sole care was that I should learn how to make a powerful speech and become a persuasive orator.

CHAPTER III

5. Now, in that year my studies were interrupted. I had come back from Madaura, a neighboring city where I had gone to study grammar and rhetoric; and the money for a further term at Carthage was being got together for me. This project was more a matter of my father's ambition than of his means, for he was only a poor citizen of Tagaste.

To whom am I narrating all this? Not to thee, O my God, but to my own kind in thy presence—to that small part of the human race who may chance to come upon these writings. And to what end? That I and all who read them may understand what depths there are from which we are to cry unto thee. For what is more surely heard in thy ear than a confessing heart and a faithful life?

Who did not extol and praise my father, because he went quite beyond his means to supply his son with the necessary expenses for a far journey in the interest of his education? For many far richer citizens did not do so much for their children. Still, this same father troubled himself not at all as to how I was progressing toward thee nor how chaste I was, just so long as I was skillful in speaking—no matter how barren I was to thy tillage, O God, who art the one true and good Lord of my heart, which is thy field.

6.   During that sixteenth year of my age, I lived with my parents, having a holiday from school for a time—this idleness imposed upon me by my parents' straitened finances. The thornbushes of lust grew rank about my head, and there was no hand to root them out. Indeed, when my father saw me one day at the baths and perceived that I was becoming a man, and was showing the signs of adolescence, he joyfully told my mother about it as if already looking forward to grandchildren, rejoicing in that sort of inebriation in which the world so often forgets thee, its Creator, and falls in love with thy creature instead of thee—the inebriation of that invisible wine of a perverted will which turns and bows down to infamy. But in my mother's breast thou hadst already begun to build thy temple and the foundation of thy holy habitation—whereas my father was only a catechumen, and that but recently. She was, therefore, startled with a holy fear and trembling: for though I had not yet been baptized, she feared those crooked ways in which they walk who turn their backs to thee and not their faces.

7.   Woe is me! Do I dare affirm that thou didst hold thy peace, O my God, while I wandered farther away from thee? Didst thou really then hold thy peace? Then whose words were they but thine which by my mother, thy faithful handmaid, thou didst pour into my ears? None of them, however, sank into my heart to make me do anything. She deplored and, as I remember, warned me privately with great solicitude, "not to commit fornication; but above all things never to defile another man's wife." These appeared to me but womanish counsels, which I would have blushed to obey. Yet they were from thee, and I knew it not. I thought that thou wast silent and that it was only she who spoke. Yet it was through her that thou didst not keep silence toward me; and in rejecting her counsel I was rejecting thee—I, her son, "the son of thy handmaid, thy servant." But I did not realize this, and rushed on headlong with such blindness that, among my friends, I was ashamed to be less shameless than they, when I heard them boasting of their disgraceful exploits—yes, and glorying all the more the worse their baseness was. What is worse, I took pleasure in such exploits, not for the pleasure's sake only but mostly for praise. What is worthy of vituperation except vice itself? Yet I made myself out worse than I was, in order that I might not go lacking for praise. And when in anything I had not sinned as the worst ones in the group, I would still say that I had done what I had not done, in order not to appear contemptible because I was more innocent than they; and not to drop in their esteem because I was more chaste.

8.   Behold with what companions I walked the streets of Babylon! I rolled in its mire and lolled about on it, as if on a bed of spices and precious ointments. And, drawing me more closely to the very center of that city, my invisible enemy trod me down and seduced me, for I was easy to seduce. My mother had already fled out of the midst of Babylon and was progressing, albeit slowly, toward its outskirts. For in counseling me to chastity, she did not bear in mind what her husband had told her about me. And although she knew that my passions were destructive even then and dangerous for the future, she did not think they should be restrained by the bonds of conjugal affection—if, indeed, they could not be cut away to the quick. She took no heed of this, for she was afraid lest a wife should prove a hindrance and a burden to my hopes. These were not her hopes of the world to come, which my mother had in thee, but the hope of learning, which both my parents were too anxious that I should acquire—my father, because he had little or no thought of thee, and only vain thoughts for me; my mother, because she thought that the usual course of study would not only be no hindrance but actually a furtherance toward my eventual return to thee. This much I conjecture, recalling as well as I can the temperaments of my parents. Meantime, the reins of discipline were slackened on me, so that without the restraint of due severity, I might play at whatsoever I fancied, even to the point of dissoluteness. And in all this there was that mist which shut out from my sight the brightness of thy truth, O my God; and my iniquity bulged out, as it were, with fatness!

CHAPTER IV

9. Theft is punished by thy law, O Lord, and by the law written in men's hearts, which not even ingrained wickedness can erase. For what thief will tolerate another thief stealing from him? Even a rich thief will not tolerate a poor thief who is driven to theft by want. Yet I had a desire to commit robbery, and did so, compelled to it by neither hunger nor poverty, but through a contempt for well-doing and a strong impulse to iniquity. For I pilfered something which I already had in sufficient measure, and of much better quality. I did not desire to enjoy what I stole, but only the theft and the sin itself.

There was a pear tree close to our own vineyard, heavily laden with fruit, which was not tempting either for its color or for its flavor. Late one night—having prolonged our games in the streets until then, as our bad habit was—a group of young scoundrels, and I among them, went to shake and rob this tree. We carried off a huge load of pears, not to eat ourselves, but to dump out to the hogs, after barely tasting some of them ourselves. Doing this pleased us all the more because it was forbidden. Such was my heart, O God, such was my heart—which thou didst pity even in that bottomless pit. Behold, now let my heart confess to thee what it was seeking there, when I was being gratuitously wanton, having no inducement to evil but the evil itself. It was foul, and I loved it. I loved my own undoing. I loved my error—not that for which I erred but the error itself. A depraved soul, falling away from security in thee to destruction in itself, seeking nothing from the shameful deed but shame itself.

CHAPTER V

10. Now there is a comeliness in all beautiful bodies, and in gold and silver and all things. The sense of touch has its own power to please and the other senses find their proper objects in physical sensation. Worldly honor also has its own glory, and so do the powers to command and to overcome: and from these there springs up the desire for revenge. Yet, in seeking these pleasures, we must not depart from thee, O Lord, nor deviate from thy law. The life which we live here has its own peculiar attractiveness because it has a certain measure of comeliness of its own and a harmony with all these inferior values. The bond of human friendship has a sweetness of its own, binding many souls together as one. Yet because of these values, sin is committed, because we have an inordinate preference for these goods of a lower order and neglect the better and the higher good—neglecting thee, O our Lord God, and thy truth and thy law. For these inferior values have their delights, but not at all equal to my God, who hath made them all. For in him do the righteous delight and he is the sweetness of the upright in heart.

11. When, therefore, we inquire why a crime was committed, we do not accept the explanation unless it appears that there was the desire to obtain some of those values which we designate inferior, or else a fear of losing them. For truly they are beautiful and comely, though in comparison with the superior and celestial goods they are abject and contemptible. A man has murdered another man—what was his motive? Either he desired his wife or his property or else he would steal to support himself; or else he was afraid of losing something to him; or else, having been injured, he was burning to be revenged. Would a man commit murder without a motive, taking delight simply in the act of murder? Who would believe such a thing? Even for that savage and brutal man [Catiline], of whom it was said that he was gratuitously wicked and cruel, there is still a motive assigned to his deeds. "Lest through idleness," he says, "hand or heart should grow inactive." And to what purpose? Why, even this: that, having once got possession of the city through his practice of his wicked ways, he might gain honors, empire, and wealth, and thus be exempt from the fear of the laws and from financial difficulties in supplying the needs of his family—and from the consciousness of his own wickedness. So it seems that even Catiline himself loved not his own villainies, but something else, and it was this that gave him the motive for his crimes.

CHAPTER VI

12.   What was it in you, O theft of mine, that I, poor wretch, doted on—you deed of darkness—in that sixteenth year of my age? Beautiful you were not, for you were a theft. But are you anything at all, so that I could analyze the case with you? Those pears that we stole were fair to the sight because they were thy creation, O Beauty beyond compare, O Creator of all, O thou good God—God the highest good and my true good. Those pears were truly pleasant to the sight, but it was not for them that my miserable soul lusted, for I had an abundance of better pears. I stole those simply that I might steal, for, having stolen them, I threw them away. My sole gratification in them was my own sin, which I was pleased to enjoy; for, if any one of these pears entered my mouth, the only good flavor it had was my sin in eating it. And now, O Lord my God, I ask what it was in that theft of mine that caused me such delight; for behold it had no beauty of its own—certainly not the sort of beauty that exists in justice and wisdom, nor such as is in the mind, memory senses, and the animal life of man; nor yet the kind that is the glory and beauty of the stars in their courses; nor the beauty of the earth, or the sea—teeming with spawning life, replacing in birth that which dies and decays. Indeed, it did not have that false and shadowy beauty which attends the deceptions of vice.

13.   For thus we see pride wearing the mask of high-spiritedness, although only thou, O God, art high above all. Ambition seeks honor and glory, whereas only thou shouldst be honored above all, and glorified forever. The powerful man seeks to be feared, because of his cruelty; but who ought really to be feared but God only? What can be forced away or withdrawn out of his power—when or where or whither or by whom? The enticements of the wanton claim the name of love; and yet nothing is more enticing than thy love, nor is anything loved more healthfully than thy truth, bright and beautiful above all. Curiosity prompts a desire for knowledge, whereas it is only thou who knowest all things supremely. Indeed, ignorance and foolishness themselves go masked under the names of simplicity and innocence; yet there is no being that has true simplicity like thine, and none is innocent as thou art. Thus it is that by a sinner's own deeds he is himself harmed. Human sloth pretends to long for rest, but what sure rest is there save in the Lord? Luxury would fain be called plenty and abundance; but thou art the fullness and unfailing abundance of unfading joy. Prodigality presents a show of liberality; but thou art the most lavish giver of all good things. Covetousness desires to possess much; but thou art already the possessor of all things. Envy contends that its aim is for excellence; but what is so excellent as thou? Anger seeks revenge; but who avenges more justly than thou? Fear recoils at the unfamiliar and the sudden changes which threaten things beloved, and is wary for its own security; but what can happen that is unfamiliar or sudden to thee? Or who can deprive thee of what thou lovest? Where, really, is there unshaken security save with thee? Grief languishes for things lost in which desire had taken delight, because it wills to have nothing taken from it, just as nothing can be taken from thee.

14. Thus the soul commits fornication when she is turned from thee, and seeks apart from thee what she cannot find pure and untainted until she returns to thee. All things thus imitate thee—but pervertedly—when they separate themselves far from thee and raise themselves up against thee. But, even in this act of perverse imitation, they acknowledge thee to be the Creator of all nature, and recognize that there is no place whither they can altogether separate themselves from thee. What was it, then, that I loved in that theft? And wherein was I imitating my Lord, even in a corrupted and perverted way? Did I wish, if only by gesture, to rebel against thy law, even though I had no power to do so actually—so that, even as a captive, I might produce a sort of counterfeit liberty, by doing with impunity deeds that were forbidden, in a deluded sense of omnipotence? Behold this servant of thine, fleeing from his Lord and following a shadow! O rottenness! O monstrousness of life and abyss of death! Could I find pleasure only in what was unlawful, and only because it was unlawful?

CHAPTER VII

15. "What shall I render unto the Lord" for the fact that while my memory recalls these things my soul no longer fears them? I will love thee, O Lord, and thank thee, and confess to thy name, because thou hast put away from me such wicked and evil deeds. To thy grace I attribute it and to thy mercy, that thou hast melted away my sin as if it were ice. To thy grace also I attribute whatsoever of evil I did not commit—for what might I not have done, loving sin as I did, just for the sake of sinning? Yea, all the sins that I confess now to have been forgiven me, both those which I committed willfully and those which, by thy

providence, I did not commit. What man is there who, when reflecting upon his own infirmity, dares to ascribe his chastity and innocence to his own powers, so that he should love thee less—as if he were in less need of thy mercy in which thou forgivest the transgressions of those that return to thee? As for that man who, when called by thee, obeyed thy voice and shunned those things which he here reads of me as I recall and confess them of myself, let him not despise me—for I, who was sick, have been healed by the same Physician by whose aid it was that he did not fall sick, or rather was less sick than I. And for this let him love thee just as much—indeed, all the more—since he sees me restored from such a great weakness of sin by the selfsame Saviour by whom he sees himself preserved from such a weakness.

CHAPTER VIII

16. What profit did I, a wretched one, receive from those things which, when I remember them now, cause me shame—above all, from that theft, which I loved only for the theft's sake? And, as the theft itself was nothing, I was all the more wretched in that I loved it so. Yet by myself alone I would not have done it—I still recall how I felt about this then—I could not have done it alone. I loved it then because of the companionship of my accomplices with whom I did it. I did not, therefore, love the theft alone—yet, indeed, it was only the theft that I loved, for the companionship was nothing. What is this paradox? Who is it that can explain it to me but God, who illumines my heart and searches out the dark corners thereof? What is it that has prompted my mind to inquire about it, to discuss and to reflect upon all this? For had I at that time loved the pears that I stole and wished to enjoy them, I might have done so alone, if I could have been satisfied with the mere act of theft by which my pleasure was served. Nor did I need to have that itching of my own passions inflamed by the encouragement of my accomplices. But since the pleasure I got was not from the pears, it was in the crime itself, enhanced by the companionship of my fellow sinners.

CHAPTER IX

17.   By what passion, then, was I animated? It was undoubtedly depraved and a great misfortune for me to feel it. But still, what was it? "Who can understand his errors?"

We laughed because our hearts were tickled at the thought of deceiving the owners, who had no idea of what we were doing and would have strenuously objected. Yet, again, why did I find such delight in doing this which I would not have done alone? Is it that no one readily laughs alone? No one does so readily; but still sometimes, when men are by themselves and no one else is about, a fit of laughter will overcome them when something very droll presents itself to their sense or mind. Yet alone I would not have done it—alone I could not have done it at all.

Behold, my God, the lively review of my soul's career is laid bare before thee. I would not have committed that theft alone. My pleasure in it was not what I stole but, rather, the act of stealing. Nor would I have enjoyed doing it alone—indeed I would not have done it! O friendship all unfriendly! You strange seducer of the soul, who hungers for mischief from impulses of mirth and wantonness, who craves another's loss without any desire for one's own profit or revenge—so that, when they say, "Let's go, let's do it," we are ashamed not to be shameless.

CHAPTER X

18.   Who can unravel such a twisted and tangled knottiness? It is unclean. I hate to reflect upon it. I hate to look on it. But I do long for thee, O Righteousness and Innocence, so beautiful and comely to all virtuous eyes—I long for thee with an insatiable satiety. With thee is perfect rest, and life unchanging. He who enters into thee enters into the joy of his Lord, and shall have no fear and shall achieve excellence in the Excellent. I fell away from thee, O my God, and in my youth I wandered too far from thee, my true support. And I became to myself a wasteland.

BOOK THREE

The story of his student days in Carthage, his discovery of Cicero's Hortensius, the enkindling of his philosophical interest, his infatuation with the Manichean heresy, and his mother's dream which foretold his eventual return to the true faith and to God.

CHAPTER I

1.   I came to Carthage, where a caldron of unholy loves was seething and bubbling all around me. I was not in love as yet, but I was in love with love; and, from a hidden hunger, I hated myself for not feeling more intensely a sense of hunger. I was looking for something to love, for I was in love with loving, and I hated security and a smooth way, free from snares. Within me I had a dearth of that inner food which is thyself, my God—although that dearth caused me no hunger. And I remained without any appetite for incorruptible food—not because I was already filled with it, but because the emptier I became the more I loathed it. Because of this my soul was unhealthy; and, full of sores, it exuded itself forth, itching to be scratched by scraping on the things of the senses. Yet, had these things no soul, they would certainly not inspire our love.

To love and to be loved was sweet to me, and all the more when I gained the enjoyment of the body of the person I loved. Thus I polluted the spring of friendship with the filth of concupiscence and I dimmed its luster with the slime of lust. Yet, foul and unclean as I was, I still craved, in excessive vanity, to be thought elegant and urbane. And I did fall precipitately into the love I was longing for. My God, my mercy, with how much bitterness didst thou, out of thy infinite goodness, flavor that sweetness for me! For I was not only beloved but also I secretly reached the climax of enjoyment; and yet I was joyfully bound with troublesome tics, so that I could be scourged with the burning iron rods of jealousy, suspicion, fear, anger, and strife.

CHAPTER II

2.   Stage plays also captivated me, with their sights full of the images of my own miseries: fuel for my own fire. Now, why does a man like to be made sad by viewing doleful and tragic scenes, which he himself could not by any means endure? Yet, as a spectator, he wishes to experience from them a sense of grief, and in this very sense of grief his pleasure consists. What is this but wretched madness? For a man is more affected by these actions the more he is spuriously involved in these affections. Now, if he should suffer them in his own person, it is the custom to call this "misery." But when he suffers with another, then it is called "compassion." But what kind of compassion is it that arises from viewing fictitious and unreal sufferings? The spectator is not expected to aid the sufferer but merely to grieve for him. And the more he grieves the more he applauds the actor of these fictions. If the misfortunes of the characters—whether historical or entirely imaginary—are represented so as not to touch the feelings of the spectator, he goes away disgusted and complaining. But if his feelings are deeply touched, he sits it out attentively, and sheds tears of joy.

3.   Tears and sorrow, then, are loved. Surely every man desires to be joyful. And, though no one is willingly miserable, one may, nevertheless, be pleased to be merciful so that we love their sorrows because without them we should have nothing to pity. This also springs from that same vein of friendship. But whither does it go? Whither does it flow? Why does it run into that torrent of pitch which seethes forth those huge tides of loathsome lusts in which it is changed and altered past recognition, being diverted and corrupted from its celestial purity by its own will? Shall, then, compassion be repudiated? By no means! Let us, however, love the sorrows of others. But let us beware of uncleanness, O my soul, under the protection of my God, the God of our fathers, who is to be praised and exalted—let us beware of uncleanness. I have not yet ceased to have compassion. But in those days in the theaters I sympathized with lovers when they sinfully enjoyed one another, although this was done fictitiously in the play. And when they lost one another, I grieved with them, as if pitying them, and yet had delight in both grief and pity. Nowadays I feel much more pity for one who delights in his wickedness than for one who counts himself unfortunate because he fails to obtain some harmful pleasure or suffers the loss of some miserable felicity. This, surely, is the truer compassion, but the sorrow I feel in it has no delight for me. For although he that grieves with the unhappy should be commended for his work of love, yet he who has the power of real compassion would still prefer that there be nothing for him to grieve about. For if good will were to be ill will—which it cannot be—only then could he who is truly and sincerely compassionate wish that there were some unhappy people so that he might commiserate them. Some grief may then be justified, but none of it loved. Thus it is that thou dost act, O Lord God, for thou lovest souls far more purely than we do and art more incorruptibly compassionate, although thou art never wounded by any sorrow. Now "who is sufficient for these things?"

4.   But at that time, in my wretchedness, I loved to grieve; and I sought for things to grieve about. In another man's misery, even though it was feigned and impersonated on the stage, that performance of the actor pleased me best and attracted me most powerfully which moved me to tears. What marvel then was it that an unhappy sheep, straying from thy flock and impatient of thy care, I became infected with a foul disease? This is the reason for my love of griefs: that they would not probe into me too deeply (for I did not love to suffer in myself such things as I loved to look at), and they were the sort of grief which came from hearing those fictions, which affected only the surface of my emotion. Still, just as if they had been poisoned fingernails, their scratching was followed by inflammation, swelling, putrefaction, and corruption. Such was my life! But was it life, O my God?

CHAPTER III

5.   And still thy faithful mercy hovered over me from afar. In what unseemly iniquities did I wear myself out, following a sacrilegious curiosity, which, having deserted thee, then began to drag me down into the treacherous abyss, into the beguiling obedience of devils, to whom I made offerings of my wicked deeds. And still in all this thou didst not fail to scourge me. I dared, even while thy solemn rites were being celebrated inside the walls of thy church, to desire and to plan a project which merited death as its fruit. For this thou didst chastise me with grievous punishments, but nothing in comparison with my fault, O thou my greatest mercy, my God, my refuge from those terrible dangers in which I wandered with stiff neck, receding farther from thee, loving my own ways and not thine—loving a vagrant liberty!

6.   Those studies I was then pursuing, generally accounted as respectable, were aimed at distinction in the courts of law—to excel in which, the more crafty I was, the more I should be praised. Such is the blindness of men that they even glory in their blindness. And by this time I had become a master in the School of Rhetoric, and I rejoiced proudly in this honor and became inflated with arrogance. Still I was relatively sedate, O Lord, as thou knowest, and had no share in the wreckings of "The Wreckers" (for this stupid and diabolical name was regarded as the very badge of gallantry) among whom I lived with a sort of ashamed embarrassment that I was not even as they were. But I lived with them, and at times I was delighted with their friendship, even when I abhorred their acts (that is, their "wrecking") in which they insolently attacked the modesty of strangers, tormenting them by uncalled-for jeers, gratifying their mischievous mirth. Nothing could more nearly resemble the actions of devils than these fellows. By what name, therefore, could they be more aptly called

than "wreckers"?—being themselves wrecked first, and altogether turned upside down. They were secretly mocked at and seduced by the deceiving spirits, in the very acts by which they amused themselves in jeering and horseplay at the expense of others.

CHAPTER IV

7.   Among such as these, in that unstable period of my life, I studied the books of eloquence, for it was in eloquence that I was eager to be eminent, though from a reprehensible and vainglorious motive, and a delight in human vanity. In the ordinary course of study I came upon a certain book of Cicero's, whose language almost all admire, though not his heart. This particular book of his contains an exhortation to philosophy and was called *Hortensius*. Now it was this book which quite definitely changed my whole attitude and turned my prayers toward thee, O Lord, and gave me new hope and new desires. Suddenly every vain hope became worthless to me, and with an incredible warmth of heart I yearned for an immortality of wisdom and began now to arise that I might return to thee. It was not to sharpen my tongue further that I made use of that book. I was now nineteen; my father had been dead two years, and my mother was providing the money for my study of rhetoric. What won me in it [i.e., the *Hortensius*] was not its style but its substance.

8.   How ardent was I then, my God, how ardent to fly from earthly things to thee! Nor did I know how thou wast even then dealing with me. For with thee is wisdom. In Greek the love of wisdom is called "philosophy," and it was with this love that that book inflamed me. There are some who seduce through philosophy, under a great, alluring, and honorable name, using it to color and adorn their own errors. And almost all who did this, in Cicero's own time and earlier, are censored and pointed out in his book. In it there is also manifest that most salutary admonition of thy Spirit, spoken by thy good and pious servant: "Beware lest any man spoil you through philosophy and vain deceit, after the tradition of men, after the rudiments of the world, and not after Christ: for in him all the fullness of the Godhead dwells bodily." Since at that time, as thou knowest, O Light of my heart, the words of the apostle were unknown to me, I was delighted with Cicero's exhortation, at least enough so that I was stimulated by it, and enkindled and inflamed to love, to seek, to obtain, to hold, and to embrace, not this or that sect, but wisdom itself, wherever it might be. Only this checked my ardor: that the name of Christ was not in it. For this name, by thy mercy, O Lord, this name of my Saviour thy Son, my tender heart had piously drunk in, deeply treasured even with my mother's milk. And whatsoever was lacking that name, no matter how erudite, polished, and truthful, did not quite take complete hold of me.

CHAPTER V

9.   I resolved, therefore, to direct my mind to the Holy Scriptures, that I might see what they were. And behold, I saw something not comprehended by the proud, not disclosed to children, something lowly in the hearing, but sublime in the doing, and veiled in mysteries. Yet I was not of the number of those who could enter into it or bend my neck to follow its steps. For then it was quite different from what I now feel. When I then turned toward the Scriptures, they appeared to me to be quite unworthy to be compared with the dignity of Tully. For my inflated pride was repelled by their style, nor could the sharpness of my wit penetrate their inner meaning. Truly they were of a sort to aid the growth of little ones, but I scorned to be a little one and, swollen with pride, I looked upon myself as fully grown.

CHAPTER VI

10.   Thus I fell among men, delirious in their pride, carnal and voluble, whose mouths were the snares of the devil—a trap made out of a mixture of the syllables of thy name and the names of our Lord Jesus Christ and of the Paraclete. These names were never out of their mouths, but only as sound and the clatter of tongues, for their

heart was empty of truth. Still they cried, "Truth, Truth," and were forever speaking the word to me. But the thing itself was not in them. Indeed, they spoke falsely not only of thee—who truly art the Truth—but also about the basic elements of this world, thy creation. And, indeed, I should have passed by the philosophers themselves even when they were speaking truth concerning thy creatures, for the sake of thy love, O Highest Good, and my Father, O Beauty of all things beautiful.

O Truth, Truth, how inwardly even then did the marrow of my soul sigh for thee when, frequently and in manifold ways, in numerous and vast books, [the Manicheans] sounded out thy name though it was only a sound! And in these dishes—while I starved for thee—they served up to me, in thy stead, the sun and moon thy beauteous works—but still only thy works and not thyself; indeed, not even thy first work. For thy spiritual works came before these material creations, celestial and shining though they are. But I was hungering and thirsting, not even after those first works of thine, but after thyself the Truth, "with whom is no variableness, neither shadow of turning." Yet they still served me glowing fantasies in those dishes. And, truly, it would have been better to have loved this very sun—which at least is true to our sight—than those illusions of theirs which deceive the mind through the eye. And yet because I supposed the illusions to be from thee I fed on them—not with avidity, for thou didst not taste in my mouth as thou art, and thou wast not these empty fictions. Neither was I nourished by them, but was instead exhausted. Food in dreams appears like our food awake; yet the sleepers are not nourished by it, for they are asleep. But the fantasies of the Manicheans were not in any way like thee as thou hast spoken to me now. They were simply fantastic and false. In comparison to them the actual bodies which we see with our fleshly sight, both celestial and terrestrial, are far more certain. These true bodies even the beasts and birds perceive as well as we do and they are more certain than the images we form about them. And again, we do with more certainty form our conceptions about them than, from them, we go on by means of them to imagine of other greater and infinite bodies which have no existence. With such empty husks was I then fed, and yet was not fed.

But thou, my Love, for whom I longed in order that I might be strong, neither art those bodies that we see in heaven nor art thou those which we do not see there, for thou hast created them all and yet thou reckonest them not among thy greatest works. How far, then, art thou from those fantasies of mine, fantasies of bodies which have no real being at all! The images of those bodies which actually exist are far more certain than these fantasies. The bodies themselves are more certain than the images, yet even these thou art not. Thou art not even the soul, which is the life of bodies; and, clearly, the life of the body is better than the body itself. But thou art the life of souls, life of lives, having life in thyself, and never changing, O Life of my soul.

11.   Where, then, wast thou and how far from me? Far, indeed, was I wandering away from thee, being barred even from the husks of those swine whom I fed with husks. For how much better were the fables of the grammarians and poets than these snares [of the Manicheans]! For verses and poems and "the flying Medea" are still more profitable truly than these men's "five elements," with their various colors, answering to "the five caves of darkness" (none of which exist and yet in which they slay the one who believes in them). For verses and poems I can turn into food for the mind, for though I sang about "the flying Medea" I never believed it, but those other things [the fantasies of the Manicheans] I did believe. Woe, woe, by what steps I was dragged down to "the depths of hell"—toiling and fuming because of my lack of the truth, even when I was seeking after thee, my God! To thee I now confess it, for thou didst have mercy on me when I had not yet confessed it. I sought after thee, but not according to the understanding of the mind, by means of which thou hast willed that I should excel the beasts, but only after the guidance of my physical senses. Thou wast more inward to me than the most inward part of me; and higher than my highest reach. I came upon that brazen woman, devoid of prudence, who, in Solomon's obscure parable, sits at the door of the house on a seat and says, "Stolen waters are sweet, and bread eaten in secret is pleasant." This woman seduced me, because she found my soul outside its own door, dwelling on the sensations of my flesh and ruminating on such food as I had swallowed through these physical senses.

CHAPTER VII

12.   For I was ignorant of that other reality, true Being. And so it was that I was subtly persuaded to agree with these foolish deceivers when they put their questions to me: "Whence comes evil?" and, "Is God limited by a bodily shape, and has he hairs and nails?" and, "Are those patriarchs to be esteemed righteous who had many wives at one time, and who killed men and who sacrificed living creatures?" In my ignorance I was much disturbed over these things and, though I was retreating from the truth, I appeared to myself to be going toward it, because I did not yet know that evil was nothing but a privation of good (that, indeed, it has no being); and how should I have seen this when the sight of my eyes went no farther than physical objects, and the sight of my mind reached no farther than to phantasms? And I did not know that God is a spirit who has no parts extended in length and breadth, whose being has no mass—for every mass is less in a part than in a whole—and if it be an infinite mass it must be less in such parts as are limited by a certain space than in its infinity. It cannot therefore be wholly everywhere as Spirit is, as God is. And I was entirely ignorant as to what is that principle within us by which we are like God, and which is rightly said in Scripture to be made "after God's image."

13.   Nor did I know that true inner righteousness—which does not judge according to custom but by the measure of the most perfect law of God Almighty—by which the mores of various places and times were adapted to those places and times (though the law itself is the same always and everywhere, not one thing in one place and another in another). By this inner righteousness Abraham and Isaac, and Jacob and Moses and David, and all those commended by the mouth of God were righteous and were judged unrighteous only by foolish men who were judging by human judgment and gauging their judgment of the mores of the whole human race by the narrow norms of their own mores. It is as if a man in an armory, not knowing what piece goes on what part of the body, should put a greave on his head and a helmet on his shin and then complain because they did not fit. Or as if, on some holiday when afternoon business was forbidden, one were to grumble at not being allowed to go on selling as it had been lawful for him to do in the forenoon. Or, again, as if, in a house, he sees a servant handle something that the butler is not permitted to touch, or when something is done behind a stable that would be prohibited in a dining room, and then a person should be indignant that in one house and one family the same things are not allowed to every member of the household. Such is the case with those who cannot endure to hear that something was lawful for righteous men in former times that is not so now; or that God, for certain temporal reasons, commanded then one thing to them and another now to these: yet both would be serving the same righteous will. These people should see that in one man, one day, and one house, different things are fit for different members; and a thing that was formerly lawful may become, after a time, unlawful—and something allowed or commanded in one place that is justly prohibited and punished in another. Is justice, then, variable and changeable? No, but the times over which she presides are not all alike because they are different times. But men, whose days upon the earth are few, cannot by their own perception harmonize the causes of former ages and other nations, of which they had no experience, and compare them with these of which they do have experience; although in one and the same body, or day, or family, they can readily see that what is suitable for each member, season, part, and person may differ. To the one they take exception; to the other they submit.

14.   These things I did not know then, nor had I observed their import. They met my eyes on every side, and I did not see. I composed poems, in which I was not free to place each foot just anywhere, but in one meter one way, and in another meter another way, nor even in any one verse was the same foot allowed in all places. Yet the art by which I composed did not have different principles for each of these different cases, but the same law throughout. Still I did not see how, by that righteousness to which good and holy men submitted, all those things that God had commanded were gathered, in a far more excellent and sublime way, into one moral order; and it did not vary in any essential respect, though it did not in varying times prescribe all things at once but, rather, distributed and prescribed what was proper for each. And, being blind, I blamed those pious fathers, not only for making use of present things as God had commanded and inspired them to do, but also for foreshadowing things to come, as God revealed it to them.

BOOK FOUR

This is the story of his years among the Manicheans. It includes the account of his teaching at Tagaste, his taking a mistress, the attractions of astrology, the poignant loss of a friend which leads to a searching analysis of grief and transience. He reports on his first book, *De pulchro et apto,* and his introduction to Aristotle's *Categories* and other books of philosophy and theology, which he mastered with great ease and little profit.

CHAPTER I

1.   During this period of nine years, from my nineteenth year to my twenty-eighth, I went astray and led others astray. I was deceived and deceived others, in varied lustful projects—sometimes publicly, by the teaching of what men style "the liberal arts"; sometimes secretly, under the false guise of religion. In the one, I was proud of myself; in the other, superstitious; in all, vain! In my public life I was striving after the emptiness of popular fame, going so far as to seek theatrical applause, entering poetic contests, striving for the straw garlands and the vanity of theatricals and intemperate desires. In my private life I was seeking to be purged from these corruptions of ours by carrying food to those who were called "elect" and "holy," which, in the laboratory of their stomachs, they should make into angels and gods for us, and by them we might be set free. These projects I followed out and practiced with my friends, who were both deceived with me and by me. Let the proud laugh at me, and those who have not yet been savingly cast down and stricken by thee, O my God. Nevertheless, I would confess to thee my shame to thy glory. Bear with me, I beseech thee, and give me the grace to retrace in my present memory the devious ways of my past errors and thus be able to "offer to thee the sacrifice of thanksgiving." For what am I to myself without thee but a guide to my own downfall? Or what am I, even at the best, but one suckled on thy milk and feeding on thee, O Food that never perishes? What indeed is any man, seeing that he is but a man? Therefore, let the strong and the mighty laugh at us, but let us who are "poor and needy" confess to thee.

CHAPTER II

2. During those years I taught the art of rhetoric. Conquered by the desire for gain, I offered for sale speaking skills with which to conquer others. And yet, O Lord, thou knowest that I really preferred to have honest scholars (or what were esteemed as such) and, without tricks of speech, I taught these scholars the tricks of speech—not to be used against the life of the innocent, but sometimes to save the life of a guilty man. And thou, O God, didst see me from afar, stumbling on that slippery path and sending out some flashes of fidelity amid much smoke—guiding those who loved vanity and sought after lying, being myself their companion.

In those years I had a mistress, to whom I was not joined in lawful marriage. She was a woman I had discovered in my wayward passion, void as it was of understanding, yet she was the only one; and I remained faithful to her and with her I discovered, by my own experience, what a great difference there is between the restraint of the marriage bond contracted with a view to having children and the compact of a lustful love, where children are born against the parents' will—although once they are born they compel our love.

3. I remember too that, when I decided to compete for a theatrical prize, some magician—I do not remember him now—asked me what I would give him to be certain to win. But I detested and abominated such filthy mysteries, and answered "that, even if the garland was of imperishable gold, I would still not permit a fly to be killed to win it for me." For he would have slain certain living creatures in his sacrifices, and by those honors would have invited the devils to help me. This evil thing I refused, but not out of a pure love of thee, O God of my heart, for I knew not how to love thee because I knew not how to conceive of anything beyond corporeal splendors. And does not a soul, sighing after such idle fictions, commit fornication against thee, trust in false things, and "feed on the winds"? But still I would not have sacrifices offered to devils on my behalf, though I was myself still offering them sacrifices of a sort by my own [Manichean] superstition. For what else is it "to feed on the winds" but to feed on the devils, that is, in our wanderings to become their sport and mockery?

CHAPTER IV

7. In those years, when I first began to teach rhetoric in my native town, I had gained a very dear friend, about my own age, who was associated with me in the same studies. Like myself, he was just rising up into the flower of youth. He had grown up with me from childhood and we had been both school fellows and playmates. But he was not then my friend, nor indeed ever became my friend, in the true sense of the term;

for there is no true friendship save between those thou dost bind together and who cleave to thee by that love which is "shed abroad in our hearts through the Holy Spirit who is given to us." Still, it was a sweet friendship, being ripened by the zeal of common studies. Moreover, I had turned him away from the true faith—which he had not soundly and thoroughly mastered as a youth—and turned him toward those superstitious and harmful fables which my mother mourned in me. With me this man went wandering off in error and my soul could not exist without him. But behold thou wast close behind thy fugitives—at once a God of vengeance and a Fountain of mercies, who dost turn us to thyself by ways that make us marvel. Thus, thou didst take that man out of this life when he had scarcely completed one whole year of friendship with me, sweeter to me than all the sweetness of my life thus far.

8.   Who can show forth all thy praise for that which he has experienced in himself alone? What was it that thou didst do at that time, O my God; how unsearchable are the depths of thy judgments! For when, sore sick of a fever, he long lay unconscious in a death sweat and everyone despaired of his recovery, he was baptized without his knowledge. And I myself cared little, at the time, presuming that his soul would retain what it had taken from me rather than what was done to his unconscious body. It turned out, however, far differently, for he was revived and restored. Immediately, as soon as I could talk to him—and I did this as soon as he was able, for I never left him and we hung on each other overmuch—I tried to jest with him, supposing that he also would jest in return about that baptism which he had received when his mind and senses were inactive, but which he had since learned that he had received. But he recoiled from me, as if I were his enemy, and, with a remarkable and unexpected freedom, he admonished me that, if I desired to continue as his friend, I must cease to say such things. Confounded and confused, I concealed my feelings till he should get well and his health recover enough to allow me to deal with him as I wished. But he was snatched away

from my madness, that with thee he might be preserved for my consolation. A few days after, during my absence, the fever returned and he died.

9.   My heart was utterly darkened by this sorrow and everywhere I looked I saw death. My native place was a torture room to me and my father's house a strange unhappiness. And all the things I had done with him—now that he was gone—became a frightful torment. My eyes sought him everywhere, but they did not see him; and I hated all places because he was not in them, because they could not say to me, "Look, he is coming," as they did when he was alive and absent. I became a hard riddle to myself, and I asked my soul why she was so downcast and why this disquieted me so sorely. But she did not know how to answer me. And if I said, "Hope thou in God," she very properly disobeyed me, because that dearest friend she had lost was as an actual man, both truer and better than the imagined deity she was ordered to put her hope in. Nothing but tears were sweet to me and they took my friend's place in my heart's desire.

CHAPTER V

10.   But now, O Lord, these things are past and time has healed my wound. Let me learn from thee, who art Truth, and put the ear of my heart to thy mouth, that thou mayest tell me why weeping should be so sweet to the unhappy. Hast thou—though omnipresent—dismissed our miseries from thy concern? Thou abidest in thyself while we are disquieted with trial after trial. Yet unless we wept in thy ears, there would be no hope for us remaining. How does it happen that such sweet fruit is plucked from the bitterness of life, from groans, tears, sighs, and lamentations? Is it the hope that thou wilt hear us that sweetens it? This is true in the case of prayer, for in a prayer there is a desire to approach thee. But is it also the case in grief for a lost love, and in the kind of sorrow that had then overwhelmed me? For I had neither a hope of his coming back to life, nor in all my tears did I seek this. I simply grieved and wept, for I was miserable and had lost my joy. Or is weeping a bitter thing that gives us pleasure because of our aversion to the things we once enjoyed and this only as long as we loathe them?

BOOK FIVE

A year of decision. Faustus comes to Carthage and Augustine is disenchanted in his hope for solid demonstration of the truth of Manichean doctrine. He decides to flee from his known troubles at Carthage to troubles yet unknown at Rome. His experiences at Rome prove disappointing and he applies for a teaching post at Milan. Here he meets Ambrose, who confronts him as an impressive witness for Catholic Christianity and opens out the possibilities of the allegorical interpretation of Scripture. Augustine decides to become a Christian catechumen.

CHAPTER VIII

14.   Thou didst so deal with me, therefore, that I was persuaded to go to Rome and teach there what I had been teaching at Carthage. And how I was persuaded to do this I will not omit to confess to thee, for in this also the profoundest workings of thy wisdom and thy constant mercy toward us must be pondered and acknowledged. I did not wish to go to Rome because of the richer fees and the higher dignity which my friends promised me there—though these considerations did affect my decision. My principal and almost sole motive was that I had been informed that the students there studied more quietly and were better kept under the control of stern discipline, so that they did not capriciously and impudently rush into the classroom of a teacher not their own—indeed, they were not admitted at all without the permission of the teacher. At Carthage, on the contrary, there was a shameful and intemperate license among the students. They burst in rudely and, with furious gestures, would disrupt the discipline which the teacher had established for the good of his pupils. Many outrages they

perpetrated with astounding effrontery, things that would be punishable by law if they were not sustained by custom. Thus custom makes plain that such behavior is all the more worthless because it allows men to do what thy eternal law never will allow. They think that they act thus with impunity, though the very blindness with which they act is their punishment, and they suffer far greater harm than they inflict.

The manners that I would not adopt as a student I was compelled as a teacher to endure in others. And so I was glad to go where all who knew the situation assured me that such conduct was not allowed. But thou, "O my refuge and my portion in the land of the living," didst goad me thus at Carthage so that I might thereby be pulled away from it and change my worldly habitation for the preservation of my soul. At the same time, thou didst offer me at Rome an enticement, through the agency of men enchanted with this death-in-life—by their insane conduct in the one place and their empty promises in the other. To correct my wandering footsteps, thou didst secretly employ their perversity and my own. For those who disturbed my tranquillity were blinded by shameful madness and also those who allured me elsewhere had nothing better than the earth's cunning. And I who hated actual misery in the one place sought fictitious happiness in the other.

15.   Thou knewest the cause of my going from one country to the other, O God, but thou didst not disclose it either to me or to my mother, who grieved deeply over my departure and followed me down to the sea. She clasped me tight in her embrace, willing either to keep me back or to go with me, but I deceived her, pretending that I had a friend whom I could not leave until he had a favorable wind to set sail. Thus I lied to my mother—and such a mother!—and escaped. For this too thou didst mercifully pardon me—fool that I was—and didst preserve me from the waters of the sea for the water of thy grace; so that, when I was purified by that, the fountain of my mother's eyes, from which she had daily watered the ground for me as she prayed to thee, should be dried. And, since she refused to return without me, I persuaded her, with some difficulty, to remain that night in a place quite close to our ship, where there was a shrine in memory of the blessed Cyprian. That night I slipped away secretly, and she remained to pray and weep. And what was it, O Lord, that she was asking of thee in such a flood of tears but that thou wouldst not allow me to sail? But thou, taking thy own secret counsel and noting the real point to her desire, didst not grant what she was then asking in order to grant to her the thing that she had always been asking.

The wind blew and filled our sails, and the shore dropped out of sight. Wild with grief, she was there the next morning and filled thy ears with complaints and groans which thou didst disregard, although, at the very same time, thou wast using my longings as a means and wast hastening me on to the fulfillment of all longing. Thus the earthly part of her love to me was justly purged by the scourge of sorrow. Still, like all mothers—though even more than others—she loved to have me with her, and did not know what joy thou wast preparing for her through my going away. Not knowing this secret end, she wept and mourned and saw in her agony the inheritance of Eve—seeking in sorrow what she had brought forth in sorrow. And yet, after accusing me of perfidy and cruelty, she still continued her intercessions for me to thee. She returned to her own home, and I went on to Rome.

CHAPTER IX

16.   And lo, I was received in Rome by the scourge of bodily sickness; and I was very near to falling into hell, burdened with all the many and grievous sins I had committed against thee, myself, and others—all over and above that fetter of original sin whereby we all die in Adam. For thou hadst forgiven me none of these things in Christ, neither had he abolished by his cross the enmity that I had incurred from thee through my sins. For how could he do so by the crucifixion of a phantom, which was all I supposed him to be? The death of my soul was as real then as

the death of his flesh appeared to me unreal. And the life of my soul was as false, because it was as unreal as the death of his flesh was real, though I believed it not.

My fever increased, and I was on the verge of passing away and perishing; for, if I had passed away then, where should I have gone but into the fiery torment which my misdeeds deserved, measured by the truth of thy rule? My mother knew nothing of this; yet, far away, she went on praying for me. And thou, present everywhere, didst hear her where she was and had pity on me where I was, so that I regained my bodily health, although I was still disordered in my sacrilegious heart. For that peril of death did not make me wish to be baptized. I was even better when, as a lad, I entreated baptism of my mother's devotion, as I have already related and confessed. But now I had since increased in dishonor, and I madly scoffed at all the purposes of thy medicine which would not have allowed me, though a sinner such as I was, to die a double death. Had my mother's heart been pierced with this wound, it never could have been cured, for I cannot adequately tell of the love she had for me, or how she still travailed for me in the spirit with a far keener anguish than when she bore me in the flesh.

17.   I cannot conceive, therefore, how she could have been healed if my death (still in my sins) had pierced her inmost love. Where, then, would have been all her earnest, frequent, and ceaseless prayers to thee? Nowhere but with thee. But couldst thou, O most merciful God, despise the "contrite and humble heart" of that pure and prudent widow, who was so constant in her alms, so gracious and attentive to thy saints, never missing a visit to church twice a day, morning and evening—and this not for vain gossiping, nor old wives' fables, but in order that she might listen to thee in thy sermons, and thou to her in her prayers? Couldst thou, by whose gifts she was so inspired, despise and disregard the tears of such a one without coming to her aid—those tears by which she entreated thee, not for gold or silver, and not for any changing or fleeting good, but for the salvation of the soul of her son? By no means, O Lord. It is certain that thou wast near and wast hearing and wast carrying out the plan by which thou hadst predetermined it should be done. Far be it from thee that thou shouldst have deluded her in those visions and the answers she had received from thee—some of which I have mentioned, and others not—which she kept in her faithful heart, and, forever beseeching, urged them on thee as if they had thy own signature. For thou, "because thy mercy endureth forever," hast so condescended to those whose debts thou hast pardoned that thou likewise dost become a debtor by thy promises.

CHAPTER X

18.   Thou didst restore me then from that illness, and didst heal the son of thy handmaid in his body, that he might live for thee and that thou mightest endow him with a better and more certain health. After this, at Rome, I again joined those deluding and deluded "saints"; and not their "hearers" only, such as the man was in whose house I had fallen sick, but also with those whom they called "the elect." For it still seemed to me "that it is not we who sin, but some other nature sinned in us." And it gratified my pride to be beyond blame, and when I did anything wrong not to have to confess that I had done wrong—"that thou mightest heal my soul because it had sinned against thee"—and I loved to excuse my soul and to accuse something else inside me (I knew not what) but which was not I. But, assuredly, it was I, and it was my impiety that had divided me against myself. That sin then was all the more incurable because I did not deem myself a sinner. It was an execrable iniquity, O God Omnipotent, that I would have preferred to have thee defeated in me, to my destruction, than to be defeated by thee to my salvation. Not yet, therefore, hadst thou set a watch upon my mouth and a door around my lips that my heart might not incline to evil speech, to make excuse for sin with men that work iniquity. And, therefore, I continued still in the company of their "elect."

19.   But now, hopeless of gaining any profit from that false doctrine, I began to hold more loosely and negligently even to those points which I had decided to rest content with, if I could find nothing better. I was now half inclined to believe that those philosophers whom they call "The Academics" were wiser than the rest in holding that we ought to doubt everything, and in maintaining that man does not have the power of comprehending any certain truth, for, although I had not yet understood their meaning, I was fully persuaded that they thought just as they are commonly reputed to do. And I did not fail openly to dissuade my host from his confidence which I observed that he had in those fictions of which the works of Mani are full. For all this, I was still on terms of more intimate friendship with these people than with others who were not of their heresy. I did not indeed defend it with my former ardor; but my familiarity with that group—and there were many of them concealed in Rome at that time—made me slower to seek any other way. This was particularly easy since I had no hope of finding in thy Church the truth from which they had turned me aside, O Lord of heaven and earth, Creator of all things visible and invisible. And it still seemed to me most unseemly to believe that thou couldst have the form of human flesh and be bounded by the bodily shape of our limbs. And when I desired to meditate on my God, I did not know what to think of but a huge extended body—for what did not have bodily extension did not seem to me to exist—and this was the greatest and almost the sole cause of my unavoidable errors.

20.   And thus I also believed that evil was a similar kind of substance, and that it had its own hideous and deformed extended body—either in a dense form which they called the earth or in a thin and subtle form as, for example, the substance of the air, which they imagined as some malignant spirit penetrating that earth. And because my piety—such as it was—still compelled me to believe that the good God never created any evil substance, I formed the idea of two masses, one opposed to the other, both infinite but with the evil more contracted and the good more expansive. And from this diseased beginning, the other sacrileges followed after.

For when my mind tried to turn back to the Catholic faith, I was cast down, since the Catholic faith was not what I judged it to be. And it seemed to me a greater piety to regard thee, my God—to whom I make confession of thy mercies—as infinite in all respects save that one: where the extended mass of evil stood opposed to thee, where I was compelled to confess that thou art finite—than if I should think that thou couldst be confined by the form of a human body on every side. And it seemed better to me to believe that no evil had been created by thee—for in my ignorance evil appeared not only to be some kind of substance but a corporeal one at that. This was because I had, thus far, no conception of mind, except as a subtle body diffused throughout local spaces. This seemed better than to believe that anything could emanate from thee which had the character that I considered evil to be in its nature. And I believed that our Saviour himself also—thy Only Begotten—had been brought forth, as it were, for our salvation out of the mass of thy bright shining substance. So that I could believe nothing about him except what I was able to harmonize with these vain imaginations. I thought, therefore, that such a nature could not be born of the Virgin Mary without being mingled with the flesh, and I could not see how the divine substance, as I had conceived it, could be mingled thus without being contaminated. I was afraid, therefore, to believe that he had been born in the flesh, lest I should also be compelled to believe that he had been contaminated by the flesh. Now will thy spiritual ones smile blandly and lovingly at me if they read these confessions. Yet such was I.

CHAPTER XI

21. Furthermore, the things they censured in thy Scriptures I thought impossible to be defended. And yet, occasionally, I desired to confer on various matters with someone well learned in those books, to test what he thought of them. For already the words of one Elpidius, who spoke and disputed face to face against these same Manicheans, had begun to impress me, even when I was at Carthage; because he brought forth things out of the Scriptures that were not easily withstood, to which their answers appeared to me feeble. One of their answers they did not give forth publicly, but only to us in private—when they said that the writings of the New Testament had been tampered with by unknown persons who desired to ingraft the Jewish law into the Christian faith. But they themselves never brought forward any uncorrupted copies. Still thinking in corporeal categories and very much ensnared and to some extent stifled, I was borne down by those conceptions of bodily substance. I panted under this load for the air of thy truth, but I was not able to breathe it pure and undefiled.

CHAPTER XII

22. I set about diligently to practice what I came to Rome to do—the teaching of rhetoric. The first task was to bring together in my home a few people to whom and through whom I had begun to be known. And lo, I then began to learn that other offenses were committed in Rome which I had not had to bear in Africa. Just as I had been told, those riotous disruptions by young blackguards were not practiced here. Yet, now, my friends told me, many of the Roman students—breakers of faith, who, for the love of money, set a small value on justice—would conspire together and suddenly transfer to another teacher, to evade paying their master's fees. My heart hated such people, though not with a "perfect hatred"; for doubtless I hated them more because I was to suffer from them than on account of their own illicit acts. Still, such people are base indeed; they fornicate against thee, for they love the transitory mockeries of temporal things and the filthy gain which begrimes the hand that grabs it; they embrace the fleeting world and scorn thee, who abidest and invitest us to return to thee and who pardonest the prostituted human soul when it does return to thee. Now I hate such crooked and perverse men, although I love them if they will be corrected and come to prefer the learning they obtain to money and, above all, to prefer thee to such learning, O God, the truth and fullness of our positive good, and our most pure peace. But then the wish was stronger in me for my own sake not to suffer evil from them than was my desire that they should become good for thy sake.

CHAPTER XIII

23.   When, therefore, the officials of Milan sent to Rome, to the prefect of the city, to ask that he provide them with a teacher of rhetoric for their city and to send him at the public expense, I applied for the job through those same persons, drunk with the Manichean vanities, to be freed from whom I was going away—though neither they nor I were aware of it at the time. They recommended that Symmachus, who was then prefect, after he had proved me by audition, should appoint me.

And to Milan I came, to Ambrose the bishop, famed through the whole world as one of the best of men, thy devoted servant. His eloquent discourse in those times abundantly provided thy people with the flour of thy wheat, the gladness of thy oil, and the sober intoxication of thy wine. To him I was led by thee without my knowledge, that by him I might be led to thee in full knowledge. That man of God received me as a father would, and welcomed my coming as a good bishop should. And I began to love him, of course, not at the first as a teacher of the truth, for I had entirely despaired of finding that in thy Church—but as a friendly man. And I studiously listened to him—though not with the right motive—as he preached to the people. I was trying to discover whether his eloquence came up to his reputation, and whether it flowed fuller or thinner than others said it did. And thus I hung on his words intently, but, as to his subject matter, I was only a careless and contemptuous listener. I was delighted with the charm of his speech, which was more erudite,

though less cheerful and soothing, than Faustus' style. As for subject matter, however, there could be no comparison, for the latter was wandering around in Manichean deceptions, while the former was teaching salvation most soundly. But "salvation is far from the wicked," such as I was then when I stood before him. Yet I was drawing nearer, gradually and unconsciously.

CHAPTER XIV

24.   For, although I took no trouble to learn what he said, but only to hear how he said it—for this empty concern remained foremost with me as long as I despaired of finding a clear path from man to thee—yet, along with the eloquence I prized, there also came into my mind the ideas which I ignored; for I could not separate them. And, while I opened my heart to acknowledge how skillfully he spoke, there also came an awareness of how truly he spoke—but only gradually. First of all, his ideas had already begun to appear to me defensible; and the Catholic faith, for which I supposed that nothing could be said against the onslaught of the Manicheans, I now realized could be maintained without presumption. This was especially clear after I had heard one or two parts of the Old Testament explained allegorically—whereas before this, when I had interpreted them literally, they had "killed" me spiritually. However, when many of these passages in those books were expounded to me thus, I came to blame my own despair for having believed that no reply could be given to those who hated and scoffed at the Law and the Prophets. Yet I did not see that this was reason enough to follow the Catholic way, just because it had learned advocates who could answer objections adequately and without absurdity. Nor could I see that what I had held to heretofore should now be condemned, because both sides were equally defensible. For that way did not appear to me yet vanquished; but neither did it seem yet victorious.

25.   But now I earnestly bent my mind to require if there was possible any way to prove the Manicheans guilty of falsehood. If I could have conceived of a spiritual substance, all their strongholds would have collapsed and been cast out of my mind. But I could not. Still, concerning the body of this world, nature as a whole—now that I was able to consider and compare such things more and more—I now decided that the majority of the philosophers held the more probable views. So, in what I thought was the method of the Academics—doubting everything and fluctuating between all the options—I came to the conclusion that the Manicheans were to be abandoned. For I judged, even in that period of doubt, that I could not remain in a sect to which I preferred some of the philosophers. But I refused to commit the cure of my fainting soul to the philosophers, because they were without the saving name of Christ. I resolved, therefore, to become a catechumen in the Catholic Church—which my parents had so much urged upon me—until something certain shone forth by which I might guide my course.

BOOK SEVEN

The conversion to Neoplatonism. Augustine traces his growing disenchantment with the Manichean conceptions of God and evil and the dawning understanding of God's incorruptibility. But his thought is still bound by his materialistic notions of reality. He rejects astrology and turns to the study of Neoplatonism. There follows an analysis of the differences between Platonism and Christianity and a remarkable account of his appropriation of Plotinian wisdom and his experience of a Plotinian ecstasy. From this, he comes finally to the diligent study of the Bible, especially the writings of the apostle Paul. His pilgrimage is drawing toward its goal, as he begins to know Jesus Christ and to be drawn to him in hesitant faith.

CHAPTER I

1. Dead now was that evil and shameful youth of mine, and I was passing into full manhood. As I increased in years, the worse was my vanity. For I could not conceive of any substance but the sort I could see with my own eyes. I no longer thought of thee, O God, by the analogy of a human body. Ever since I inclined my ear to philosophy I had avoided this error—and the truth on this point I rejoiced to find in the faith of our spiritual mother, thy Catholic Church. Yet I could not see how else to conceive thee. And I, a man—and such a man!-sought to conceive thee, the sovereign and only true God. In my inmost heart, I believed that thou art incorruptible and inviolable and unchangeable, because—though I knew not how or why—I could still see plainly and without doubt that the corruptible is inferior to the incorruptible, the inviolable obviously superior to its opposite, and the unchangeable better than the changeable.

My heart cried out violently against all fantasms, and with this one clear certainty I endeavored to brush away the swarm of unclean flies that swarmed around the eyes of my mind. But behold they were scarcely scattered before they gathered again, buzzed against my face, and beclouded my vision. I no longer thought of God in the analogy of a human body, yet I was constrained to conceive thee to be some kind of body in space, either infused into the world, or infinitely diffused beyond the world—and this was the incorruptible, inviolable, unchangeable substance, which I thought was better than the corruptible, the violable, and the changeable. For whatever I conceived to be deprived of the dimensions of space appeared to me to be nothing, absolutely nothing; not even a void, for if a body is taken out of space, or if space is emptied of all its contents (of earth, water, air, or heaven), yet it remains an empty space—a spacious nothing, as it were.

2. Being thus gross-hearted and not clear even to myself, I then held that whatever had neither length nor breadth nor density nor solidity, and did not or could not receive such dimensions, was absolutely nothing. For at that time my mind dwelt only with ideas, which resembled the forms with which my eyes are still familiar, nor could I see that the act of thought, by which I formed those ideas, was itself immaterial, and yet it could not have formed them if it were not itself a measurable entity.

So also I thought about thee, O Life of my life, as stretched out through infinite space, interpenetrating the whole mass of the world, reaching out beyond in all directions, to immensity without end; so that the earth should have thee, the heaven have thee, all things have thee, and all of them be limited in thee, while thou art placed nowhere at all. As the body of the air above the earth does not bar the passage of the light of the sun, so that the light penetrates it, not by bursting nor dividing, but filling it entirely, so I imagined that the body of heaven and air and sea, and even of the earth, was all open to thee and, in all its greatest parts as well as the smallest, was ready to receive thy presence by a secret inspiration which, from within or without all, orders all things thou hast created. This was my conjecture, because I was unable to think of anything else; yet it was untrue. For in this way a greater part of the earth would contain a greater part of thee; a smaller part, a smaller fraction of thee. All things would be full of thee in such a sense that there would be more of thee in an elephant than in a sparrow, because one is larger than the other and fills a larger space. And this would make the portions of thyself present in the several portions of the world in fragments, great to the great, small to the small. But thou art not such a one. But as yet thou hadst not enlightened my darkness.

BOOK EIGHT

Conversion to Christ. Augustine is deeply impressed by Simplicianus' story of the conversion to Christ of the famous orator and philosopher, Marius Victorinus. He is stirred to emulate him, but finds himself still enchained by his incontinence and preoccupation with worldly affairs. He is then visited by a court official, Ponticianus, who tells him and Alypius the stories of the conversion of Anthony and also of two imperial "secret service agents." These stories throw him into a violent turmoil, in which his divided will struggles against himself. He almost succeeds in making the decision for continence, but is still held back. Finally, a child's song, overheard by chance, sends him to the Bible; a text from Paul resolves the crisis; the conversion is a fact. Alypius also makes his decision, and the two inform the rejoicing Monica.

CHAPTER I

1.   O my God, let me remember with gratitude and confess to thee thy mercies toward me. Let my bones be bathed in thy love, and let them say: "Lord, who is like unto thee? Thou hast broken my bonds in sunder, I will offer unto thee the sacrifice of thanksgiving." And how thou didst break them I will declare, and all who worship thee shall say, when they hear these things: "Blessed be the Lord in heaven and earth, great and wonderful is his name."

Thy words had stuck fast in my breast, and I was hedged round about by thee on every side. Of thy eternal life I was now certain, although I had seen it "through a glass darkly." And I had been relieved of all doubt that there is an incorruptible substance and that it is the source of every other substance. Nor did I any longer crave greater certainty about thee, but rather greater steadfastness in thee.

But as for my temporal life, everything was uncertain, and my heart had to be purged of the old leaven. "The Way"—the Saviour himself—pleased me well, but as yet I was reluctant to pass through the strait gate.

And thou didst put it into my mind, and it seemed good in my own sight, to go to Simplicianus, who appeared to me a faithful servant of thine, and thy grace shone forth in him. I had also been told that from his youth up he had lived in entire devotion to thee. He was already an old man, and because of his great age, which he had passed in such a zealous discipleship in thy way, he appeared to me likely to have gained much wisdom—and, indeed, he had. From all his experience, I desired him to tell me—setting before him all my agitations—which would be the most fitting way for one who felt as I did to walk in thy way.

2. For I saw the Church full; and one man was going this way and another that. Still, I could not be satisfied with the life I was living in the world. Now, indeed, my passions had ceased to excite me as of old with hopes of honor and wealth, and it was a grievous burden to go on in such servitude. For, compared with thy sweetness and the beauty of thy house—which I loved—those things delighted me no longer. But I was still tightly bound by the love of women; nor did the apostle forbid me to marry, although he exhorted me to something better, wishing earnestly that all men were as he himself was.

But I was weak and chose the easier way, and for this single reason my whole life was one of inner turbulence and listless indecision, because from so many influences I was compelled—even though unwilling—to agree to a married life which bound me hand and foot. I had heard from the mouth of Truth that "there are eunuchs who have made themselves eunuchs for the Kingdom of Heaven's sake" but, said he, "He that is able to receive it, let him receive it." Of a certainty, all men are vain who do not have the knowledge of God, or have not been able, from the good things that are seen, to find him who is good. But I was no longer fettered in that vanity. I had surmounted it, and from the united testimony of thy whole creation had found thee, our Creator, and thy Word—God with thee, and together with thee and the Holy Spirit, one God—by whom thou hast created all things. There is still another sort of wicked men, who "when they knew God, they glorified him not as God, neither were thankful." Into this also I had fallen, but thy right hand held me up and bore me away, and thou didst place me where I might recover. For thou hast said to men, "Behold the fear of the Lord, this is wisdom," and, "Be not wise in your own eyes," because "they that profess themselves to be wise become fools." But I had now found the goodly pearl; and I ought to have sold all that I had and bought it—yet I hesitated.

CHAPTER II

3. I went, therefore, to Simplicianus, the spiritual father of Ambrose (then a bishop), whom Ambrose truly loved as a father. I recounted to him all the mazes of my wanderings, but when I mentioned to him that I had read certain books of the Platonists which Victorinus—formerly professor of rhetoric at Rome, who died a Christian, as I had been told—had translated into Latin, Simplicianus congratulated me that I had not fallen upon the writings of other philosophers, which were full of fallacies and deceit, "after the beggarly elements of this world," whereas in the Platonists, at every turn, the pathway led to belief in God and his Word.

Then, to encourage me to copy the humility of Christ, which is hidden from the wise and revealed to babes, he told me about Victorinus himself, whom he had known intimately at Rome. And I cannot refrain from repeating what he told me about him. For it contains a glorious proof of thy grace, which ought to be confessed to thee: how that old man, most learned, most skilled in all the liberal arts; who had read, criticized, and explained so many of the writings of the philosophers; the teacher of so many noble senators; one who, as a mark of his distinguished service in office had both merited and obtained a statue in the Roman Forum—which men of this world esteem a great honor—this man who, up to an advanced age, had been a worshiper of idols, a communicant in the sacrilegious rites to which almost all the nobility of Rome were wedded; and who had inspired the people with the love of Osiris and

"The dog Anubis, and a medley crew

Of monster gods who 'gainst Neptune stand in arms

'Gainst Venus and Minerva, steel-clad Mars,"

whom Rome once conquered, and now worshiped; all of which old Victorinus had with thundering eloquence defended for so many years—despite all this, he did not blush to become a child of thy Christ, a babe at thy font, bowing his neck to the yoke of humility and submitting his forehead to the ignominy of the cross.

4.   O Lord, Lord, "who didst bow the heavens and didst descend, who didst touch the mountains and they smoked," by what means didst thou find thy way into that breast? He used to read the Holy Scriptures, as Simplicianus said, and thought out and studied all the Christian writings most studiously. He said to Simplicianus—not openly but secretly as a friend—"You must know that I am a Christian." To which Simplicianus replied, "I shall not believe it, nor shall I count you among the Christians, until I see you in the Church of Christ." Victorinus then asked, with mild mockery, "Is it then the walls that make Christians?" Thus he often would affirm that he was already a Christian, and as often Simplicianus made the same answer; and just as often his jest about the walls was repeated. He was fearful of offending his friends, proud demon worshipers, from the height of whose Babylonian dignity, as from the tops of the cedars of Lebanon which the Lord had not yet broken down, he feared that a storm of enmity would descend upon him.

But he steadily gained strength from reading and inquiry, and came to fear lest he should be denied by Christ before the holy angels if he now was afraid to confess him before men. Thus he came to appear to himself guilty of a great fault, in being ashamed of the sacraments of the humility of thy Word, when he was not ashamed of the sacrilegious rites of those proud demons, whose pride he had imitated and whose rites he had shared. From this he became bold-faced against vanity and shamefaced toward the truth. Thus, suddenly and unexpectedly, he said to Simplicianus—as he himself told me—"Let us go to the church; I wish to become a Christian." Simplicianus went with him, scarcely able to contain himself for joy. He was admitted to the first sacraments of instruction, and not long afterward gave in his name that he might receive the baptism of regeneration. At this Rome marveled and the Church rejoiced. The proud saw and were enraged; they gnashed their teeth and melted away! But the Lord God was thy servant's

hope and he paid no attention to their vanity and lying madness.

5.   Finally, when the hour arrived for him to make a public profession of his faith—which at Rome those who are about to enter into thy grace make from a platform in the full sight of the faithful people, in a set form of words learned by heart—the presbyters offered Victorinus the chance to make his profession more privately, for this was the custom for some who were likely to be afraid through bashfulness. But Victorinus chose rather to profess his salvation in the presence of the holy congregation. For there was no salvation in the rhetoric which he taught: yet he had professed that openly. Why, then, should he shrink from naming thy Word before the sheep of thy flock, when he had not shrunk from uttering his own words before the mad multitude?

So, then, when he ascended the platform to make his profession, everyone, as they recognized him, whispered his name one to the other, in tones of jubilation. Who was there among them that did not know him? And a low murmur ran through the mouths of all the rejoicing multitude: "Victorinus! Victorinus!" There was a sudden burst of exaltation at the sight of him, and suddenly they were hushed that they might hear him. He pronounced the true faith with an excellent boldness, and all desired to take him to their very heart—indeed, by their love and joy they did take him to their heart. And they received him with loving and joyful hands.

CHAPTER III

6.   O good God, what happens in a man to make him rejoice more at the salvation of a soul that has been despaired of and then delivered from greater danger than over one who has never lost hope, or never been in such imminent danger? For thou also, O most merciful Father, "dost rejoice more over one that repents than over ninety and nine just persons that need no repentance." And we listen with much delight whenever we hear how the lost sheep is brought home again on the shepherd's shoulders while the angels rejoice; or when the piece of money is restored to its place in the treasury and the neighbors rejoice with the woman who found it. And the joy of the solemn festival of thy house constrains us to tears when it is read in thy house: about the younger son who "was dead and is alive again, was lost and is found." For it is thou who rejoicest both in us and in thy angels, who are holy through holy love. For thou art ever the same because thou knowest unchangeably all things which remain neither the same nor forever.

7. What, then, happens in the soul when it takes more delight at finding or having restored to it the things it loves than if it had always possessed them? Indeed, many other things bear witness that this is so—all things are full of witnesses, crying out, "So it is." The commander triumphs in victory; yet he could not have conquered if he had not fought; and the greater the peril of the battle, the more the joy of the triumph. The storm tosses the voyagers, threatens shipwreck, and everyone turns pale in the presence of death. Then the sky and sea grow calm, and they rejoice as much as they had feared. A loved one is sick and his pulse indicates danger; all who desire his safety are themselves sick at heart; he recovers, though not able as yet to walk with his former strength; and there is more joy now than there was before when he walked sound and strong. Indeed, the very pleasures of human life—not only those which rush upon us unexpectedly and involuntarily, but also those which are voluntary and planned—men obtain by difficulties. There is no pleasure in caring and drinking unless the pains of hunger and thirst have preceded. Drunkards even eat certain salt meats in order to create a painful thirst—and when the drink allays this, it causes pleasure. It is also the custom that the affianced bride should not be immediately given in marriage so that the husband may not esteem her any less, whom as his betrothed he longed for.

8. This can be seen in the case of base and dishonorable pleasure. But it is also apparent in pleasures that are permitted and lawful: in the sincerity of honest friendship; and in him who was dead and lived again, who had been lost and was found. The greater joy is everywhere preceded by the greater pain. What does this mean, O Lord my God, when thou art an everlasting joy to thyself, and some creatures about thee are ever rejoicing in thee? What does it mean that this portion of creation thus ebbs and flows, alternately in want and satiety? Is this their mode of being and is this all thou hast allotted to them: that, from the highest heaven to the lowest earth, from the beginning of the world to the end, from the angels to the worm, from the first movement to the last, thou wast assigning to all their proper places and their proper seasons—to all the kinds of good things and to all thy just works? Alas, how high thou art in the highest and how deep in the deepest! Thou never departest from us, and yet only with difficulty do we return to thee.

CHAPTER IV

9. Go on, O Lord, and act: stir us up and call us back; inflame us and draw us to thee; stir us up and grow sweet to us; let us now love thee, let us run to thee. Are there not many men who, out of a deeper pit of darkness than that of Victorinus, return to thee—who draw near to thee and are illuminated by that light which gives those who receive it power from thee to become thy sons? But if they are less well-known, even those who know them rejoice less for them. For when many rejoice together the joy of each one is fuller, in that they warm one another, catch fire from each other; moreover, those who are well-known influence many toward salvation and take the lead with many to follow them. Therefore, even those who took the way before them rejoice over them greatly, because they do not rejoice over them alone. But it ought never to be that in thy tabernacle the persons of the rich should be welcome before the poor, or the nobly born before the rest—since "thou hast rather chosen the weak things of the world to confound the strong; and hast chosen the base things of the world and things that are despised, and the things that are not, in order to bring to nought the things that are." It was even "the least of the apostles" by whose tongue thou didst sound forth these words. And when Paulus the proconsul had his pride overcome by the on-slaught of the apostle and he was made to pass under the easy yoke of thy Christ and became an officer of the great King, he also desired to be called Paul instead of Saul, his former name, in testimony to such a great victory. For the en-emy is more overcome in one on whom he has a greater hold, and whom he has hold of more completely. But the proud he controls more read-ily through their concern about their rank and, through them, he controls more by means of their influence. The more, therefore, the world prized the heart of Victorinus (which the devil had held in an impregnable stronghold) and the tongue of Victorinus (that sharp, strong weapon with which the devil had slain so many), all the more exultingly should thy sons rejoice because our King hath bound the strong man, and they saw his vessels taken from him and cleansed, and made fit for thy honor and "profitable to the Lord for every good work."

CHAPTER V

10.   Now when this man of thine, Simplicianus, told me the story of Victorinus, I was eager to imi-tate him. Indeed, this was Simplicianus' purpose in telling it to me. But when he went on to tell how, in the reign of the Emperor Julian, there was a law passed by which Christians were for-bidden to teach literature and rhetoric; and how Victorinus, in ready obedience to the law, chose to abandon his "school of words" rather than thy Word, by which thou makest eloquent the tongues of the dumb—he appeared to me not so much brave as happy, because he had found a rea-son for giving his time wholly to thee. For this was what I was longing to do; but as yet I was bound by the iron chain of my own will. The enemy held fast my will, and had made of it a chain, and had bound me tight with it. For out of the perverse will came lust, and the service of lust ended in habit, and habit, not resisted, became necessity.

By these links, as it were, forged together—which is why I called it "a chain"—a hard bondage held me in slavery. But that new will which had begun to spring up in me freely to worship thee and to enjoy thee, O my God, the only certain Joy, was not able as yet to overcome my former willful-ness, made strong by long indulgence. Thus my two wills—the old and the new, the carnal and the spiritual—were in conflict within me; and by their discord they tore my soul apart.

11.   Thus I came to understand from my own experience what I had read, how "the flesh lusts against the Spirit, and the Spirit against the flesh." I truly lusted both ways, yet more in that which I approved in myself than in that which I disapproved in myself. For in the latter it was not now really I that was involved, because here I was rather an unwilling sufferer than a willing actor. And yet it was through me that habit had become an armed enemy against me, because I had willingly come to be what I unwillingly found myself to be.

Who, then, can with any justice speak against it, when just punishment follows the sinner? I had now no longer my accustomed excuse that, as yet, I hesitated to forsake the world and serve thee because my perception of the truth was un-certain. For now it was certain. But, still bound to the earth, I refused to be thy soldier; and was as much afraid of being freed from all entangle-ments as we ought to fear to be entangled.

12.   Thus with the baggage of the world I was sweetly burdened, as one in slumber, and my musings on thee were like the efforts of those who desire to awake, but who are still overpowered with drowsiness and fall back into deep slumber. And as no one wishes to sleep forever (for all men rightly count waking better)—yet a man will usu-ally defer shaking off his drowsiness when there is a heavy lethargy in his limbs; and he is glad to sleep on even when his reason disapproves, and the hour for rising has struck—so was I assured that it was much better for me to give myself up to thy love than to go on yielding myself to my own lust. Thy love satisfied and vanquished me;

my lust pleased and fettered me. I had no answer to thy calling to me, "Awake, you who sleep, and arise from the dead, and Christ shall give you light." On all sides, thou didst show me that thy words are true, and I, convicted by the truth, had nothing at all to reply but the drawling and drowsy words: "Presently; see, presently. Leave me alone a little while." But "presently, presently," had no present; and my "leave me alone a little while" went on for a long while. In vain did I "delight in thy law in the inner man" while "another law in my members warred against the law of my mind and brought me into captivity to the law of sin which is in my members." For the law of sin is the tyranny of habit, by which the mind is drawn and held, even against its will. Yet it deserves to be so held because it so willingly falls into the habit. "O wretched man that I am! Who shall deliver me from the body of this death" but thy grace alone, through Jesus Christ our Lord?

CHAPTER VI

13. And now I will tell and confess unto thy name, O Lord, my helper and my redeemer, how thou didst deliver me from the chain of sexual desire by which I was so tightly held, and from the slavery of worldly business. With increasing anxiety I was going about my usual affairs, and daily sighing to thee. I attended thy church as frequently as my business, under the burden of which I groaned, left me free to do so. Alypius was with me, disengaged at last from his legal post, after a third term as assessor, and now waiting for private clients to whom he might sell his legal advice as I sold the power of speaking (as if it could be supplied by teaching). But Nebridius had consented, for the sake of our friendship, to teach under Verecundus—a citizen of Milan and professor of grammar, and a very intimate friend of us all—who ardently desired, and by right of friendship demanded from us, the faithful aid he greatly needed. Nebridius was not drawn to this by any desire of gain—for he could have made much more out of his learning had he been so inclined—but as he was a most sweet and kindly friend, he was unwilling, out of respect for the

duties of friendship, to slight our request. But in this he acted very discreetly, taking care not to become known to those persons who had great reputations in the world. Thus he avoided all distractions of mind, and reserved as many hours as possible to pursue or read or listen to discussions about wisdom.

14. On a certain day, then, when Nebridius was away—for some reason I cannot remember—there came to visit Alypius and me at our house one Ponticianus, a fellow countryman of ours from Africa, who held high office in the emperor's court. What he wanted with us I do not know; but we sat down to talk together, and it chanced that he noticed a book on a game table before us. He took it up, opened it, and, contrary to his expectation, found it to be the apostle Paul, for he imagined that it was one of my wearisome rhetoric textbooks. At this, he looked up at me with a smile and expressed his delight and wonder that he had so unexpectedly found this book and only this one, lying before my eyes; for he was indeed a Christian and a faithful one at that, and often he prostrated himself before thee, our God, in the church in constant daily prayer. When I had told him that I had given much attention to these writings, a conversation followed in which he spoke of Anthony, the Egyptian monk, whose name was in high repute among thy servants, although up to that time not familiar to me. When he learned this, he lingered on the topic, giving us an account of this eminent man, and marveling at our ignorance. We in turn were amazed to hear of thy wonderful works so fully manifested in recent times—almost in our own—occurring in the true faith and the Catholic Church. We all wondered—we, that these things were so great, and he, that we had never heard of them.

15. From this, his conversation turned to the multitudes in the monasteries and their manners so fragrant to thee, and to the teeming solitudes of the wilderness, of which we knew nothing at all. There was even a monastery at Milan, outside the city's walls, full of good brothers under the fostering care of Ambrose—and we were ignorant of it. He went on with his story, and we listened intently and in silence. He then told us how, on a certain afternoon, at Trier, when the emperor was occupied watching the gladiatorial games, he and three comrades went out for a walk in the gardens close to the city walls. There, as they chanced to walk two by two, one strolled away with him, while the other two went on by themselves. As they rambled, these first two came upon a certain cottage where lived some of thy servants, some of the "poor in spirit" ("of such is the Kingdom of Heaven"), where they found the book in which was written the life of Anthony! One of them began to read it, to marvel and to be inflamed by it. While reading, he meditated on embracing just such a life, giving up his worldly employment to seek thee alone. These two belonged to the group of officials called "secret service agents." Then, suddenly being overwhelmed with a holy love and a sober shame and as if in anger with himself, he fixed his eyes on his friend, exclaiming: "Tell me, I beg you, what goal are we seeking in all these toils of ours? What is it that we desire? What is our motive in public service? Can our hopes in the court rise higher than to be `friends of the emperor'? But how frail, how beset with peril, is that pride! Through what dangers must we climb to a greater danger? And when shall we succeed? But if I chose to become a friend of God, see, I can become one now." Thus he spoke, and in the pangs of the travail of the new life he turned his eyes again onto the page and continued reading; he was inwardly changed, as thou didst see, and the world dropped away from his mind, as soon became plain to others. For as he read with a heart like a stormy sea, more than once he groaned. Finally he saw the better course, and resolved on it. Then, having become thy servant, he said to his friend: "Now I have broken loose from those hopes we had, and I am determined to serve God; and I enter into that service from this hour in this place. If you are reluctant to imitate me, do not oppose me." The other replied that he would continue bound in his friendship, to share in so great a service for so great a prize. So both became thine, and began to "build a tower", counting the cost—namely,

of forsaking all that they had and following thee. Shortly after, Ponticianus and his companion, who had walked with him in the other part of the garden, came in search of them to the same place, and having found them reminded them to return, as the day was declining. But the first two, making known to Ponticianus their resolution and purpose, and how a resolve had sprung up and become confirmed in them, entreated them not to take it ill if they refused to join themselves with them. But Ponticianus and his friend, although not changed from their former course, did nevertheless (as he told us) bewail themselves and congratulated their friends on their godliness, recommending themselves to their prayers. And with hearts inclining again toward earthly things, they returned to the palace. But the other two, setting their affections on heavenly things, remained in the cottage. Both of them had affianced brides who, when they heard of this, likewise dedicated their virginity to thee.

CHAPTER VII

16.   Such was the story Ponticianus told. But while he was speaking, thou, O Lord, turned me toward myself, taking me from behind my back, where I had put myself while unwilling to exercise self-scrutiny. And now thou didst set me face to face with myself, that I might see how ugly I was, and how crooked and sordid, bespotted and ulcerous. And I looked and I loathed myself; but whither to fly from myself I could not discover. And if I sought to turn my gaze away from myself, he would continue his narrative, and thou wouldst oppose me to myself and thrust me before my own eyes that I might discover my iniquity and hate it. I had known it, but acted as though I knew it not—I winked at it and forgot it.

17.   But now, the more ardently I loved those whose wholesome affections I heard reported— that they had given themselves up wholly to thee to be cured—the more did I abhor myself when compared with them. For many of my years—perhaps twelve—had passed away since my nineteenth, when, upon the reading of Cicero's *Hortensius*, I was roused to a desire for wisdom. And here I was, still postponing the abandonment of this world's happiness to devote myself to the search. For not just the finding alone, but also the bare search for it, ought to have been preferred above the treasures and kingdoms of this world; better than all bodily pleasures, though they were to be had for the taking. But, wretched youth that I was—supremely wretched even in the very outset of my youth—I had entreated chastity of thee and had prayed, "Grant me chastity and continence, but not yet." For I was afraid lest thou shouldst hear me too soon, and too soon cure me of my disease of lust which I desired to have satisfied rather than extinguished. And I had wandered through perverse ways of godless superstition—not really sure of it, either, but preferring it to the other, which I did not seek in piety, but opposed in malice.

18. And I had thought that I delayed from day to day in rejecting those worldly hopes and following thee alone because there did not appear anything certain by which I could direct my course. And now the day had arrived in which I was laid bare to myself and my conscience was to chide me: "Where are you, O my tongue? You said indeed that you were not willing to cast off the baggage of vanity for uncertain truth. But behold now it is certain, and still that burden oppresses you. At the same time those who have not worn themselves out with searching for it as you have, nor spent ten years and more in thinking about it, have had their shoulders unburdened and have received wings to fly away." Thus was I inwardly confused, and mightily confounded with a horrible shame, while Ponticianus went ahead speaking such things. And when he had finished his story and the business he came for, he went his way. And then what did I not say to myself, within myself? With what scourges of rebuke did I not lash my soul to make it follow me, as I was struggling to go after thee? Yet it drew back. It refused. It would not make an effort. All its arguments were exhausted and confuted. Yet it resisted in sullen disquiet, fearing the cutting off of that habit by which it was being wasted to death, as if that were death itself.

CHAPTER VIII

19. Then, as this vehement quarrel, which I waged with my soul in the chamber of my heart, was raging inside my inner dwelling, agitated both in mind and countenance, I seized upon Alypius and exclaimed: "What is the matter with us? What is this? What did you hear? The uninstructed start up and take heaven, and we—with all our learning but so little heart—see where we wallow in flesh and blood! Because others have gone before us, are we ashamed to follow, and not rather ashamed at our not following?" I scarcely knew what I said, and in my excitement I flung away from him, while he gazed at me in silent astonishment. For I did not sound like myself: my face, eyes, color, tone expressed my meaning more clearly than my words.

There was a little garden belonging to our lodging, of which we had the use—as of the whole house—for the master, our landlord, did not live there. The tempest in my breast hurried me out into this garden, where no one might interrupt the fiery struggle in which I was engaged with myself, until it came to the outcome that thou knewest though I did not. But I was mad for health, and dying for life; knowing what evil thing I was, but not knowing what good thing I was so shortly to become.

I fled into the garden, with Alypius following step by step; for I had no secret in which he did not share, and how could he leave me in such distress? We sat down, as far from the house as possible. I was greatly disturbed in spirit, angry at myself with a turbulent indignation because I had not entered thy will and covenant, O my God, while all my bones cried out to me to enter, extolling it to the skies. The way therein is not by ships or chariots or feet—indeed it was not as far as I had come from the house to the place where we were seated. For to go along that road and indeed to reach the goal is nothing else but the will to go. But it must be a strong and single will, not staggering and swaying about this way and that—a changeable, twisting, fluctuating will, wrestling with itself while one part falls as another rises.

20.   Finally, in the very fever of my indecision, I made many motions with my body; like men do when they will to act but cannot, either because they do not have the limbs or because their limbs are bound or weakened by disease, or incapacitated in some other way. Thus if I tore my hair, struck my forehead, or, entwining my fingers, clasped my knee, these I did because I willed it. But I might have willed it and still not have done it, if the nerves had not obeyed my will. Many things then I did, in which the will and power to do were not the same. Yet I did not do that one thing which seemed to me infinitely more desirable, which before long I should have power to will because shortly when I willed, I would will with a single will. For in this, the power of willing is the power of doing; and as yet I could not do it. Thus my body more readily obeyed the slightest wish of the soul in moving its limbs at the order of my mind than my soul obeyed itself to accomplish in the will alone its great resolve.

CHAPTER IX

21.   How can there be such a strange anomaly? And why is it? Let thy mercy shine on me, that I may inquire and find an answer, amid the dark labyrinth of human punishment and in the darkest contritions of the sons of Adam. Whence such an anomaly? And why should it be? The mind commands the body, and the body obeys. The mind commands itself and is resisted. The mind commands the hand to be moved and there is such readiness that the command is scarcely distinguished from the obedience in act. Yet the mind is mind, and the hand is body. The mind commands the mind to will, and yet though it be itself it does not obey itself. Whence this strange anomaly and why should it be? I repeat: The will commands itself to will, and could not give the command unless it wills; yet what is commanded is not done. But actually the will does not will entirely; therefore it does not command entirely. For as far as it wills, it commands. And as far as it does not will, the thing commanded is not done. For the will commands that there be an act of will—not another, but itself. But it does not

command entirely. Therefore, what is commanded does not happen; for if the will were whole and entire, it would not even command it to be, because it would already be. It is, therefore, no strange anomaly partly to will and partly to be unwilling. This is actually an infirmity of mind, which cannot wholly rise, while pressed down by habit, even though it is supported by the truth. And so there are two wills, because one of them is not whole, and what is present in this one is lacking in the other.

CHAPTER X

22.   Let them perish from thy presence, O God, as vain talkers, and deceivers of the soul perish, who, when they observe that there are two wills in the act of deliberation, go on to affirm that there are two kinds of minds in us: one good, the other evil. They are indeed themselves evil when they hold these evil opinions—and they shall become good only when they come to hold the truth and consent to the truth that thy apostle may say to them: "You were formerly in darkness, but now are you in the light in the Lord." But they desired to be light, not "in the Lord," but in themselves. They conceived the nature of the soul to be the same as what God is, and thus have become a thicker darkness than they were; for in their dread arrogance they have gone farther away from thee, from thee "the true Light, that lights every man that comes into the world." Mark what you say and blush for shame; draw near to him and be enlightened, and your faces shall not be ashamed.

While I was deliberating whether I would serve the Lord my God now, as I had long purposed to do, it was I who willed and it was also I who was unwilling. In either case, it was I. I neither willed with my whole will nor was I wholly unwilling. And so I was at war with myself and torn apart by myself. And this strife was against my will; yet it did not show the presence of another mind, but the punishment of my own. Thus it was no more I who did it, but the sin that dwelt in me—the punishment of a sin freely committed by Adam, and I was a son of Adam.

23. For if there are as many opposing natures as there are opposing wills, there will not be two but many more. If any man is trying to decide whether he should go to their conventicle or to the theater, the Manicheans at once cry out, "See, here are two natures—one good, drawing this way, another bad, drawing back that way; for how else can you explain this indecision between conflicting wills?" But I reply that both impulses are bad—that which draws to them and that which draws back to the theater. But they do not believe that the will which draws to them can be anything but good. Suppose, then, that one of us should try to decide, and through the conflict of his two wills should waver whether he should go to the theater or to our Church. Would not those also waver about the answer here? For either they must confess, which they are unwilling to do, that the will that leads to our church is as good as that which carries their own adherents and those captivated by their mysteries; or else they must imagine that there are two evil natures and two evil minds in one man, both at war with each other, and then it will not be true what they say, that there is one good and another bad. Else they must be converted to the truth, and no longer deny that when anyone deliberates there is one soul fluctuating between conflicting wills.

24. Let them no longer maintain that when they perceive two wills to be contending with each other in the same man the contest is between two opposing minds, of two opposing substances, from two opposing principles, the one good and the other bad. Thus, O true God, thou dost reprove and confute and convict them. For both wills may be bad: as when a man tries to decide whether he should kill a man by poison or by the sword; whether he should take possession of this field or that one belonging to someone else, when he cannot get both; whether he should squander his money to buy pleasure or hold onto his money through the motive of covetousness; whether he should go to the circus or to the theater, if both are open on the same day; or, whether he should take a third course, open at the same time, and rob another man's house; or, a fourth option, whether he should commit adultery, if he has the opportunity—all these things concurring in the same space of time and all being equally longed for, although impossible to do at one time. For the mind is pulled four ways by four antagonistic wills—or even more, in view of the vast range of human desires—but even the Manicheans do not affirm that there are these many different substances. The same principle applies as in the action of good wills. For I ask them, "Is it a good thing to have delight in reading the apostle, or is it a good thing to delight in a sober psalm, or is it a good thing to discourse on the gospel?" To each of these, they will answer, "It is good." But what, then, if all delight us equally and all at the same time? Do not different wills distract the mind when a man is trying to decide what he should choose? Yet they are all good, and are at variance with each other until one is chosen. When this is done the whole united will may go forward on a single track instead of remaining as it was before, divided in many ways. So also, when eternity attracts us from above, and the pleasure of earthly delight pulls us down from below, the soul does not will either the one or the other with all its force, but still it is the same soul that does not will this or that with a united will, and is therefore pulled apart with grievous perplexities, because for truth's sake it prefers this, but for custom's sake it does not lay that aside.

CHAPTER XI

25. Thus I was sick and tormented, reproaching myself more bitterly than ever, rolling and writhing in my chain till it should be utterly broken. By now I was held but slightly, but still was held. And thou, O Lord, didst press upon me in my inmost heart with a severe mercy, redoubling the lashes of fear and shame; lest I should again give way and that same slender remaining tie not be broken off, but recover strength and enchain me yet more securely.

I kept saying to myself, "See, let it be done now; let it be done now." And as I said this I all but came to a firm decision. I all but did it—yet

I did not quite. Still I did not fall back to my old condition, but stood aside for a moment and drew breath. And I tried again, and lacked only a very little of reaching the resolve—and then somewhat less, and then all but touched and grasped it. Yet I still did not quite reach or touch or grasp the goal, because I hesitated to die to death and to live to life. And the worse way, to which I was habituated, was stronger in me than the better, which I had not tried. And up to the very moment in which I was to become another man, the nearer the moment approached, the greater horror did it strike in me. But it did not strike me back, nor turn me aside, but held me in suspense.

26.   It was, in fact, my old mistresses, trifles of trifles and vanities of vanities, who still enthralled me. They tugged at my fleshly garments and softly whispered: "Are you going to part with us? And from that moment will we never be with you any more? And from that moment will not this and that be forbidden you forever?" What were they suggesting to me in those words "this or that"? What is it they suggested, O my God? Let thy mercy guard the soul of thy servant from the vileness and the shame they did suggest! And now I scarcely heard them, for they were not openly showing themselves and opposing me face to face; but muttering, as it were, behind my back; and furtively plucking at me as I was leaving, trying to make me look back at them. Still they delayed me, so that I hesitated to break loose and shake myself free of them and leap over to the place to which I was being called—for unruly habit kept saying to me, "Do you think you can live without them?"

27.   But now it said this very faintly; for in the direction I had set my face, and yet toward which I still trembled to go, the chaste dignity of continence appeared to me—cheerful but not wanton, modestly alluring me to come and doubt nothing, extending her holy hands, full of a multitude of good examples—to receive and embrace me. There were there so many young men and maidens, a multitude of youth and every age, grave widows and ancient virgins; and continence herself in their midst: not barren, but a fruitful mother of children—her joys—by thee, O Lord, her husband. And she smiled on me with a challenging smile as if to say: "Can you not do what these young men and maidens can? Or can any of them do it of themselves, and not rather in the Lord their God? The Lord their God gave me to them. Why do you stand in your own strength, and so stand not? Cast yourself on him; fear not. He will not flinch and you will not fall. Cast yourself on him without fear, for he will receive and heal you." And I blushed violently, for I still heard the muttering of those "trifles" and hung suspended. Again she seemed to speak: "Stop your ears against those unclean members of yours, that they may be mortified. They tell you of delights, but not according to the law of the Lord thy God." This struggle raging in my heart was nothing but the contest of self against self. And Alypius kept close beside me, and awaited in silence the outcome of my extraordinary agitation.

CHAPTER XII

28.   Now when deep reflection had drawn up out of the secret depths of my soul all my misery and had heaped it up before the sight of my heart, there arose a mighty storm, accompanied by a mighty rain of tears. That I might give way fully to my tears and lamentations, I stole away from Alypius, for it seemed to me that solitude was more appropriate for the business of weeping. I went far enough away that I could feel that even his presence was no restraint upon me. This was the way I felt at the time, and he realized it. I suppose I had said something before I started up and he noticed that the sound of my voice was choked with weeping. And so he stayed alone, where we had been sitting together, greatly astonished. I flung myself down under a fig tree—how I know not—and gave free course to my tears. The streams of my eyes gushed out an acceptable sacrifice to thee. And, not indeed in these words, but to this effect, I cried to thee: "And thou, O Lord, how long? How long, O Lord? Wilt thou be angry forever? Oh, remember not against us our former iniquities." For I felt that I was still enthralled by them. I sent up these sorrowful cries: "How long, how long? Tomorrow and tomorrow? Why not now? Why not this very hour make an end to my uncleanness?"

29 I was saying these things and weeping in the most bitter contrition of my heart, when suddenly I heard the voice of a boy or a girl I know not which—coming from the neighboring house, chanting over and over again, "Pick it up, read it; pick it up, read it." Immediately I ceased weeping and began most earnestly to think whether it was usual for children in some kind of game to sing such a song, but I could not remember ever having heard the like. So, damming the torrent of my tears, I got to my feet, for I could not but think that this was a divine command to open the Bible and read the first passage I should light upon. For I had heard how Anthony, accidentally coming into church while the gospel was being read, received the admonition as if what was read had been addressed to him: "Go and sell what you have and give it to the poor, and you shall have treasure in heaven; and come and follow me." By such an oracle he was forthwith converted to thee.

So I quickly returned to the bench where Alypius was sitting, for there I had put down the apostle's book when I had left there. I snatched it up, opened it, and in silence read the paragraph on which my eyes first fell: "Not in rioting and drunkenness, not in chambering and wantonness, not in strife and envying, but put on the Lord Jesus Christ, and make no provision for the flesh to fulfill the lusts thereof." I wanted to read no further, nor did I need to. For instantly, as the sentence ended, there was infused in my heart something like the light of full certainty and all the gloom of doubt vanished away.

30. Closing the book, then, and putting my finger or something else for a mark I began—now with a tranquil countenance—to tell it all to Alypius. And he in turn disclosed to me what had been going on in himself, of which I knew nothing. He asked to see what I had read. I showed him, and he looked on even further than I had read. I had not known what followed. But indeed it was this, "Him that is weak in the faith, receive." This he applied to himself, and told me so. By these words of warning he was strengthened, and by exercising his good resolution and purpose—all very much in keeping with his character, in which, in these respects, he was always far different from and better than I—he joined me in full commitment without any restless hesitation.

Then we went in to my mother, and told her what happened, to her great joy. We explained to her how it had occurred—and she leaped for joy triumphant; and she blessed thee, who art "able to do exceedingly abundantly above all that we ask or think." For she saw that thou hadst granted her far more than she had ever asked for in all her pitiful and doleful lamentations. For thou didst so convert me to thee that I sought neither a wife nor any other of this world's hopes, but set my feet on that rule of faith which so many years before thou hadst showed her in her dream about me. And so thou didst turn her grief into gladness more plentiful than she had ventured to desire, and dearer and purer than the desire she used to cherish of having grandchildren of my flesh.

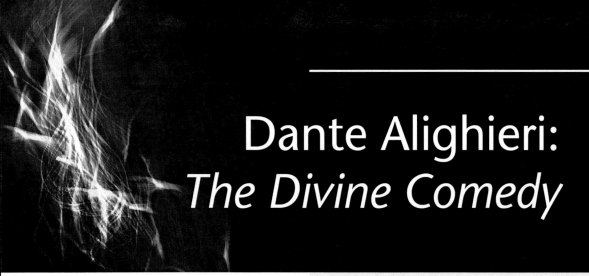

Dante Alighieri: *The Divine Comedy*

Editors' Introduction

From the tortures of hell, through the painful process of purification in purgatory, to a vision of paradise that tests the limits of what can be expressed in language, Dante's poem has left a lasting imprint on the imagination of western culture.

It is likely that Dante would have found this to be entirely appropriate. He was not a man given to modesty with regard to his talent. He believed that he had something important to say about the human condition, something that transcended the circumstances of his particular time and place. Even though many of the characters we encounter in *Inferno, Purgatory,* and *Paradise* may be unfamiliar to us due to the fact that they are figures from the ancient and medieval worlds, or because they are associated with events taking place on the Italian peninsula during Dante's lifetime, he believed that his readers could draw important lessons from the situations he described, lessons applicable to people at all times. While there is no doubt that he was addressing the circumstances of his time, he also understood himself as having a prophetic role, offering wisdom to the world on matters of religion, politics, culture, philosophy, and society. To understand how he came to take this role upon himself, we need to know something about his earlier life.

At the time Dante was born (1265) in Florence, there was no single nation known as Italy. The Italian peninsula consisted of various territories and city-states, many of which were frequently being fought over by kings, popes, and the townspeople themselves. Dante would have considered himself primarily a citizen of Florence; this city-state was his "homeland." As a child he followed a normal course of education for the time, studying grammar, rhetoric, and classical and medieval literature. The most influential event of his childhood was his encounter with Beatrice Portinari. He first met her when they were both eight years old, and he became smitten by her. When he saw her nine years later, she became even more firmly ensconced in his imagination as the epitome of grace and beauty. Beatrice's death in 1290 grieved Dante deeply, and as a distraction from grief he busied himself with the study of philosophy and theology. In *The Divine Comedy* Beatrice will appear as one of the primary agents of Dante's salvation, a virtual female Christ figure.

As a young man Dante had already begun to study and write poetry. He married Gemma Donati when he was twenty, and together they had four children. With the death of his father in 1285, Dante became responsible for his entire family, leading him to take a more public and political role in the life of his city. This involvement was to have significant and ultimately, unfortunate consequences for him. The two predominant political factions in Florence were the Guelfs and the Ghibellines; the Guelfs were further divided into the Black and the White factions ("Black" and "White" having nothing to do with race or color here). Dante became a prominent White Guelf, reaching the height of his influence in 1300, when he was elected one of the seven priors (basically a councilman/leader) of Florence. It was a time of tremendous violence and strife. In 1302, while on a diplomatic mission to Rome to dissuade the pope from inviting French troops to enter Tuscany (the region in which Florence is located), the Black Guelf party came to power in Florence, and Dante was condemned to exile on the basis of trumped up charges of political corruption. If he had ever returned to Florence, he would have been executed.

Dante never again returned to the city he loved, remaining in exile until his death in 1321. At first he found it difficult to adjust to life away from Florence. He moved from place to place, eventually settling in the Italian city of Ravenna, where he died and was buried. Exile forced Dante to think more deeply about his life and to reflect upon the disorders of his time. Out of these reflections came the work we know as *The Divine Comedy*. He began the work around 1308 and completed it shortly before his death. Dante called his work *Commedia;* the adjective "Divine" was suggested later by the Italian Renaissance writer Boccaccio. The title "Commedia" does not mean that the poem is funny ("funny" is not a word that normally comes to mind when thinking about the *Commedia*); rather it indicates that the poem ends happily, as Dante the pilgrim is caught up in his vision of God.

For those with just a passing familiarity with Dante, there is sometimes a tendency to reduce his understanding of life to that which is presented in *Inferno*. That would be a serious mistake. Always bear in mind that two thirds of the work is about conversion and salvation. Dante was well acquainted with human sin and evil, but he was able to look beyond these realities and to offer hope for the redemption of the world. Nor is there anything escapist about Dante's message. When, in *Paradise,* he ascends to his final vision of God, it is not with the intention of fleeing from the world; rather, the vision will become the guiding principle for the transformed perspective that he will now bring to his life. He very much believed in God's victory over sin and death, and he insisted that with divine help the world could become a place of order and harmony, far removed from the petty and destructive internecine conflicts that so marred the society in which he lived. For those accustomed to thinking of poetry as an art form with only peripheral relevance to what we consider the "real world," Dante's conception of his mission may seem odd. Yet it was precisely as a poet that he took upon himself the mantle of a prophet. He used his unsurpassed imaginative powers to create a work in which he recounted his own painful process of conversion and challenged his readers both then and now to change their lives—not out of fear of divine punishment (in Dante, people are punished *by* their sins rather than *for* their sins), but out of the conviction that the final word about human affairs is a word of grace.

Inferno

Inferno is the first and most widely read of the three works that comprise *The Divine Comedy.* Its geography can be imagined as a funnel lined with various concentric circles in which sins of ever increasing severity are punished. There are three major divisions within *Inferno,* based upon the three different types of sins. After Limbo, Circles Two through Five are reserved for those who have sinned due to some form of incontinence or lack of self-restraint with regard to something that in itself is a good. For example, food is something natural and healthy for people, but indulged in to excess it becomes the sin of gluttony. Canto V (included below) describes the fate of those who suffer from the sin of lust, which, in Dante's view, is an excess of a desire natural to human beings.

Circle Six is a place of transition in which heretics dwell. The Seventh Circle is inhabited by those who have committed sins of violence. In Circles Eight and Nine Dante writes of those who are guilty of various forms of fraud, including flatterers, grafters, hypocrites, thieves, and traitors. Always bear in mind that for Dante sin is understood to be not only damaging to the person it infects, but also (and in some ways more importantly) to the community to which the sinner belongs. This is one of the reasons why Dante views sins of fraud to be so serious—the dishonesty of the fraudulent makes genuine community impossible, since once the bond of trust is broken, society deteriorates.

Canto I

Halfway through his life, Dante the Pilgrim wakes to find himself lost in a dark wood. Terrified at being alone in so dismal a valley, he wanders until he comes to a hill bathed in sunlight, and his fear begins to leave him. But when he starts to climb the hill his path is blocked by three fierce beasts: first a Leopard, then a Lion, and finally a She-Wolf. They fill him with fear and drive him back down to the sunless wood. At that moment the figure of a man appears before him; it is the shade of Virgil, and the Pilgrim begs for help. Virgil tells him that he cannot overcome the beasts which obstruct his path; they must remain until a "Greyhound" comes who will drive them back to Hell. Rather by another path will the Pilgrim reach the sunlight, and Virgil promises to guide him on that path through Hell and Purgatory, after which another spirit, more fit than Virgil, will lead him to Paradise. The Pilgrim begs Virgil to lead on, and the Guide starts ahead. The Pilgrim follows.

Midway along the journey of our life
   I woke to find myself in a dark wood,
   for I had wandered off from the straight path.   3

How hard it is to tell what it was like,
   this wood of wilderness, savage and stubborn
   (the thought of it brings back all my old fears),   6

1. The imaginary date of the poem's beginning is the night before Good Friday in 1300, the year of the papal jubilee proclaimed by Boniface VIII. Born in 1265, Dante would be thirty-five years old, which is half the seventy years allotted to man in the Bible.

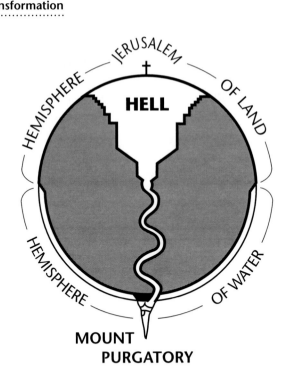

a bitter place! Death could scarce be bitterer. But
   if I would show the good that came of it
   I must talk about things other than the good.   9

How I entered there I cannot truly say,
   I had become so sleepy at the moment
   when I first strayed, leaving the path of truth;   12

but when I found myself at the foot of a hill,
   at the edge of the wood's beginning, down in the valley,
   where I first felt my heart plunged deep in fear,   15

I raised my head and saw the hilltop shawled in
   morning rays of light sent from the planet
   that leads men straight ahead on every road.   18

And then only did terror start subsiding
   in my heart's lake, which rose to heights of fear
   that night I spent in deepest desperation.   21

31–51. The three beasts that block the Pilgrim's path could symbolize the three major divisions of Hell. The spotted Leopard (32) represents Fraud (cf. Canto XVI, 106–108) and reigns over the Eighth and Ninth Circles where the Fraudulent are punished (Cantos XVIII–XXXIV). The Lion (45) symbolizes all forms of Violence that are punished in the Seventh Circle (XII–XVII). The She-Wolf (49) represents the different types of Concupisence or Incontinence that are punished in Circles Two to Five (V–VIII).

Just as a swimmer, still with panting breath, now
    safe upon the shore, out of the deep,
      might turn for one last look at the dangerous waters,   24

so I, although my mind was turned to flee,
    turned round to gaze once more upon the pass
      that never let a living soul escape.   27

I rested my tired body there awhile
    and then began to climb the barren slope
      (I dragged my stronger foot and limped along).   30

Beyond the point the slope begins to rise
    sprang up a leopard, trim and very swift!
      It was covered by a pelt of many spots.   33

And, everywhere I looked, the beast was there
    blocking my way, so time and time again
      I was about to turn and go back down.   36

The hour was early in the morning then,
    the sun was climbing up with those same stars
      that had accompanied it on the world's first day,   39

the day Divine Love set their beauty turning;
    so the hour and sweet season of creation
      encouraged me to think I could get past   42

that gaudy beast, wild in its spotted pelt,
    but then good hope gave way and fear returned
      when the figure of a lion loomed up before me,   45

and he was coming straight toward me, it seemed,
    with head raised high, and furious with hunger
      the air around him seemed to fear his presence.   48

And now a she-wolf came, that in her leanness
    seemed racked with every kind of greediness
      (how many people she has brought to grief!).   51

This last beast brought my spirit down so low
    with fear that seized me at the sight of her,
      I lost all hope of going up the hill.   54

As a man who, rejoicing in his gains,
    suddenly seeing his gain turn into loss,
      will grieve as he compares his then and now,   57

so she made me do, that relentless beast;
    coming toward me, slowly, step by step,
    she forced me back to where the sun is mute.   60

While I was rushing down to that low place,
    my eyes made out a figure coming toward me
    of one grown faint, perhaps from too much silence.   63

And when I saw him standing in this wasteland,
    "Have pity on my soul," I cried to him,
    "whichever you are, shade or living man!"   66

"No longer living man, though once I was,"
    he said, "and my parents were from Lombardy,
    both of them were Mantuans by birth.   69

I was born, though somewhat late, *sub Julio,*
    and lived in Rome when good Augustus reigned,
    when still the false and lying gods were worshipped.   72

I was a poet and sang of that just man,
    son of Anchises, who sailed off from Troy
    after the burning of proud Ilium.   75

But why retreat to so much misery?
    Why not climb up this blissful mountain here,
    the beginning and the source of all man's joy?"   78

"Are you then Virgil, are you then that fount
    from which pours forth so rich a stream of words?"
    I said to him, bowing my head modestly.   81

"O light and honor of the other poets,
    may my long years of study, and that deep love
    that made me search your verses, help me now!   84

You are my teacher, the first of all my authors,
    and you alone the one from whom I took
    the noble style that was to bring me honor.   87

You see the beast that forced me to retreat;
    save me from her, I beg you, famous sage,
    she makes me tremble, the blood throbs in my veins."   90

---

62. The approaching figure represents (though not exclusively, for he has other meanings) Reason or Natural Philosophy. The Pilgrim cannot proceed to the light of Divine Love (the mountaintop) until he has overcome the three beasts of his sin; and because it is impossible for man to cope with the beasts unaided, Virgil has been summoned to guide the Pilgrim.

63. The voice of Reason has been silent in the Pilgrim's ear for a long time.

"But you must journey down another road,"
    he answered, when he saw me lost in tears,
    "if ever you hope to leave this wilderness;   93

this beast, the one you cry about in fear,
    allows no soul to succeed along her path,
    she blocks his way and puts an end to him.   96

She is by nature so perverse and vicious,
    her craving belly is never satisfied,
    still hungering for food the more she eats.   99

She mates with many creatures, and will go on
    mating with more until the greyhound comes
    and tracks her down to make her die in anguish.   102

He will not feed on either land or money:
    his wisdom, love, and virtue shall sustain him;
    he will be born between Feltro and Feltro.   105

He comes to save that fallen Italy
    for which the maid Camilla gave her life
    and Turnus, Nisus, Euryalus died of wounds.   108

And he will hunt for her through every city
    until he drives her back to Hell once more,
    whence Envy first unleashed her on mankind.   111

And so, I think it best you follow me
    for your own good, and I shall be your guide
    and lead you out through an eternal place   114

where you will hear desperate cries, and see
    tormented shades, some old as Hell itself,
    and know what second death is, from their screams.   117

---

91. Dante must choose another road because, in order to arrive at the Divine Light, it is necessary first to recognize the true nature of sin, renounce it, and pay penance for it.

101–111. The Greyhound has been identified with Henry VII, Charles Martel, and even Dante himself. It seems more plausible that the Greyhound represents Can Grande della Scala, the ruler of Verona from 1308 to 1329, whose "wisdom, love, and virtue" (104) were certainly well-known to Dante. Whoever the Greyhound may be, the prophecy would seem to indicate in a larger sense the establishment of a spiritual kingdom on earth in which "wisdom, love, and virtue" will replace the bestial sins of the world. Perhaps Dante had no specific person in mind.

107. Camilla was the valiant daughter of King Metabus, who was slain while fighting against the Trojans (*Aeneid* XI).

108. Turnus was the king of the Rutulians. Nisus and Euryalus were young Trojan warriors slain during a nocturnal raid on the camp of the Rutulians.

117. The "second" death is that of the soul, which occurs when the soul is damned.

And later you will see those who rejoice
    while they are burning, for they have hope of coming,
    whenever it may be, to join the blessèd—   120

to whom, if you too wish to make the climb,
    a spirit, worthier than I, must take you;
    I shall go back, leaving you in her care,   123

because that Emperor dwelling on high
    will not let me lead any to His city,
    since I in life rebelled against His law.   126

Everywhere He reigns, and there He rules;
    there is His city, there is His high throne.
    Oh, happy the one He makes His citizen!"   129

And I to him: "Poet, I beg of you,
    in the name of God, that God you never knew,
    save me from this evil place and worse,   132

lead me there to the place you spoke about
    that I may see the gate Saint Peter guards
    and those whose anguish you have told me of."   135

Then he moved on, and I moved close behind him.

Canto II

But the pilgrim begins to waver; he expresses to Virgil his misgivings about his ability to undertake the journey proposed by Virgil. His predecessors have been Aeneas and Saint Paul, and he feels unworthy to take his place in their company. But Virgil rebukes his cowardice, and relates the chain of events that led him to come to Dante. The Virgin Mary took pity on the Pilgrim in his despair and instructed Saint Lucia to aid him. The Saint turned to Beatrice because of Dante's great love for her, and Beatrice in turn went down to Hell, into Limbo, and asked Virgil to guide her friend until that time when she herself would become his guide. The Pilgrim takes heart at Virgil's explanation and agrees to follow him.

The day was fading and the darkening air
    was releasing all the creatures on our earth
    from their daily tasks, and I, one man alone,   3

---

122. Just as Virgil, the pagan Roman poet, cannot enter the Christian Paradise because he lived before the birth of Christ and lacks knowledge of Christian salvation, so Reason can only guide the Pilgrim to a certain point: In order to enter Paradise, the Pilgrim's guide must be Christian Grace or Revelation (Theology) in the figure of Beatrice.

124. Note the pagan terminology of Virgil's reference to God: It expresses, as best it can, his unenlightened conception of the Supreme Authority.

was making ready to endure the battle
  of the journey, and of the pity it involved,
  which my memory, unerring, shall now retrace.   6

O Muses! O high genius! Help me now!
  O memory that wrote down what I saw,
  here your true excellence shall be revealed!   9

Then I began: "O poet come to guide me,
  tell me if you think my worth sufficient
  before you trust me to this arduous road.   12

You wrote about young Sylvius's father,
  who went beyond, with flesh corruptible,
  with all his senses, to the immortal realm;   15

but if the Adversary of all evil
  was kind to him, considering who he was,
  and the consequence that was to come from him,   18

this cannot seem, to thoughtful men, unfitting,
  for in the highest heaven he was chosen
  father of glorious Rome and of her empire,   21

and both the city and her lands, in truth,
  were established as the place of holiness
  where the successors of great Peter sit.   24

And from this journey you celebrate in verse,
  Aeneas learned those things that were to bring
  victory for him, and for Rome, the Papal seat;   27

then later the Chosen Vessel, Paul, ascended
  to ring back confirmation of that faith
  which is the first step on salvation's road.   30

But why am I to go? Who allows me to?
  I am not Aeneas, I am not Paul,
  neither I nor any man would think me worthy;   33

and so, if I should undertake the journey,
  I fear it might turn out an act of folly
  you are wise, you see more than my words express."   36

28–30. In his Second Epistle to the Corinthians (12:2–4), the apostle Paul alludes to his mystical elevation to the third heaven and to the arcane messages pronounced there.

As one who unwills what he willed, will change
    his purpose with some new second thought,
    completely quitting what he first had started,   39

so I did, standing there on that dark slope,
    thinking, ending the beginning of that venture
    I was so quick to take up at the start.   42

"If I have truly understood your words,"
    that shade of magnanimity replied,
    "your soul is burdened with that cowardice   45

which often weighs so heavily on man,
    it turns him from a noble enterprise
    like a frightened beast that shies at its own shadow,   48

To free you from this fear, let me explain
    the reason I came here, the words I heard
    that first time I felt pity for your soul: 51

I was among those dead who are suspended,
    when a lady summoned me. She was so blessed
    and beautiful, I implored her to command me.   54

With eyes of light more bright than any star,
    in low, soft tones she started to address me
    in her own language, with an angel's voice: 57

'O noble soul, courteous Mantuan,
    whose fame the world continues to preserve
    and will preserve as long as world there is,   60

my friend, who is no friend of Fortune's, strays
    on a desert slope; so many obstacles
    have crossed his path, his fright has turned him back   63

I fear he may have gone so far astray,
    from what report has come to me in Heaven,
    that I may have started to his aid too late.   66

Now go, and with your elegance of speech,
    with whatever may be needed for his freedom,
    give him your help, and thereby bring me solace.   69

I am Beatrice, who urges you to go;
    I come from the place I am longing to return to;
    love moved me, as it moves me now to speak.   72

When I return to stand before my Lord,
  often I shall sing your praises to Him.'
  And then she spoke no more. And I began, 75

'O Lady of Grace, through whom alone mankind
  may go beyond all worldly things contained
  within the sphere that makes the smallest round, 78

your plea fills me with happy eagerness
  to have obeyed already would still seem late!
  You needed only to express your wish. 81

But tell me how you dared to make this journey
  all the way down to this point of spacelessness,
  away from your spacious home that calls you back.' 84

'Because your question searches for deep meaning,
  I shall explain in simple words,' she said,
  'just why I have no fear of coming here. 87

A man must stand in fear of just those things
  that truly have the power to do us harm,
  of nothing else, for nothing else is fearsome. 90

God gave me such a nature through His Grace,
  the torments you must bear cannot affect me,
  nor are the fires of Hell a threat to me. 93

A gracious lady sits in Heaven grieving
  for what happened to the one I send you to,
  and her compassion breaks Heaven's stern decree. 96

She called Lucia and making her request,
  she said, "Your faithful one is now in need
  of you, and to you I now commend his soul." 99

Lucia, the enemy of cruelty,
  hastened to make her way to where I was,
  sitting by the side of ancient Rachel, 102

and said to me: "Beatrice, God's true praise,
  will you not help the one whose love was such
  it made him leave the vulgar crowd for you? 105

94. The lady is the Virgin Mary.

102. In the Dantean Paradise Rachel is seated by Beatrice.

Do you not hear the pity of his weeping,
    do you not see what death it is that threatens him
    along that river the sea shall never conquer?"   108

There never was a wordly person living
    more anxious to promote his selfish gains
    than I was at the sound of words like these—   111

to leave my holy seat and come down here
    and place my trust in you, in your noble speech
    that honors you and all those who have heard it!'   114

When she had finished reasoning, she turned
    her shining eyes away, and there were tears.
    How eager then I was to come to you!   117

And I have come to you just as she wished,
    and I have freed you from the beast that stood
    blocking the quick way up the mount of bliss.   120

So what is wrong? Why, why do you delay?
    Why are you such a coward in your heart,
    why aren't you bold and free of all your fear,   123

when three such gracious ladies, who are blessed,
    watch out for you up there in Heaven's court,
    and my words, too, bring promise of such good?"   126

As little flowers from the frosty night
    are closed and limp, and when the sun shines down
    on them, they rise to open on their stem,   129

my wilted strength began to bloom within me,
    and such warm courage flowed into my heart
    that I spoke like a man set free of fear.   132

"O she, compassionate, who moved to help me!
    And you, all kindness, in obeying quick
    those words of truth she brought with her for you—   135

you and the words you spoke have moved my heart
    with such desire to continue onward
    that now I have returned to my first purpose.   138

Let us start, for both our wills, joined now, are one.
    You are my guide, you are my lord and teacher."
    These were my words to him and, when he moved,   141

I entered on that deep and rugged road.

Canto III

As the two poets enter the vestibule that leads to Hell itself, Dante sees the inscription above the gate, and he hears the screams of anguish from the damned souls. Rejected by God and not accepted by the powers of Hell, the first group of souls are "nowhere," because of their cowardly refusal to make a choice in life. Their punishment is to follow a banner at a furious pace forever, and to be tormented by flies and hornets. The Pilgrim recognizes several of these shades but mentions none by name. Next they come to the River Acheron, where they are greeted by the infernal boatman, Charon. Among those doomed souls who are to be ferried across the river, Charon sees the living man and challenges him, but Virgil lets it be known that his companion must pass. Then across the landscape rushes a howling wind, which blasts the Pilgrim out of his senses, and he falls to the ground.

I AM THE WAY INTO THE DOLEFUL CITY,
   I AM THE WAY INTO ETERNAL GRIEF,
   I AM THE WAY TO A FORSAKEN RACE.   3

JUSTICE IT WAS THAT MOVED MY GREAT CREATOR;
   DIVINE OMNIPOTENCE CREATED ME,
   AND HIGHEST WISDOM JOINED WITH PRIMAL LOVE.   6

BEFORE ME NOTHING BUT ETERNAL THINGS
   WERE MADE, AND I SHALL LAST ETERNALLY.
   ABANDON EVERY HOPE, ALL YOU WHO ENTER.   9

I saw these words spelled out in somber colors
   inscribed along the ledge above a gate;
   "Master," I said, "these words I see are cruel."   12

He answered me, speaking with experience:
   "Now here you must leave all distrust behind;
   let all your cowardice die on this spot.   15

We are at the place where earlier I said
   you could expect to see the suffering race
   of souls who lost the good of intellect."   18

Placing his hand on mine, smiling at me
   in such a way that I was reassured,
   he led me in, into those mysteries.   21

Here sighs and cries and shrieks of lamentation
   echoed throughout the starless air of Hell;
   at first these sounds resounding made me weep: 24

5–6. Divine Omnipotence, Highest Wisdom, and Primal Love are, respectively, the Father, the Son, and the Holy Ghost. Thus, the gate of Hell was created by the Trinity moved by Justice.

18. Souls who have lost sight of God.

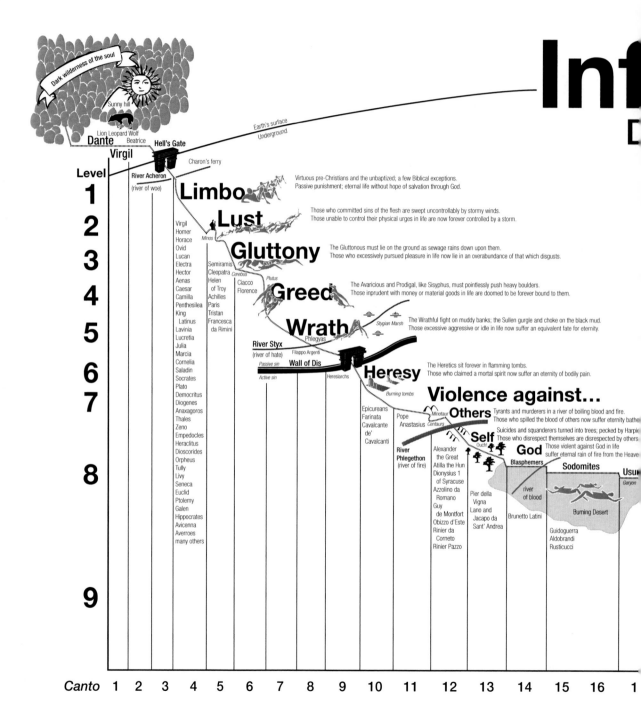

Inf

D

Copyright © 2011 by Ryan Flynn. Reprinted by permission of Ryan Flynn.

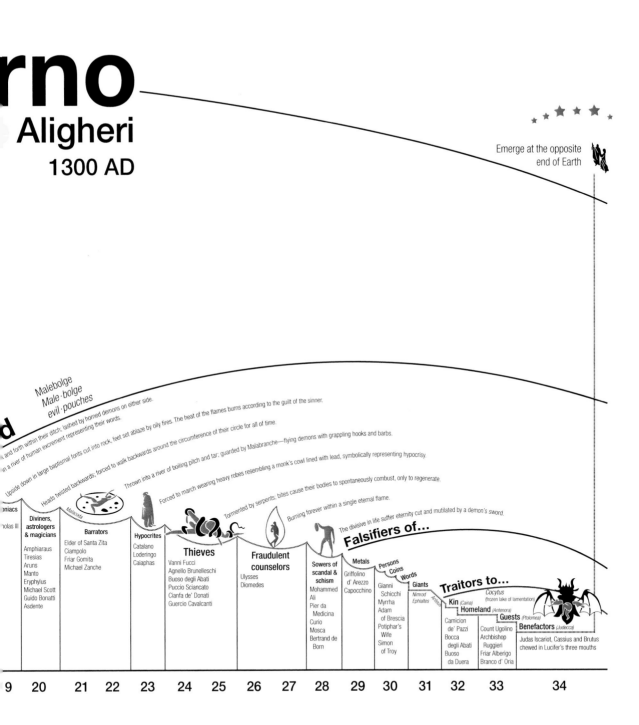

rno
Aligheri
1300 AD

Emerge at the opposite
end of Earth

Malebolge
Male·bolge
evil·pouches

...k and forth within their ditch, lashed by horned demons on either side.

...in a river of human excrement, representing their words.

...Upside down in large baptismal fonts cut into rock, feet set ablaze by oily fires. The heat of the flames burns according to the guilt of the sinner.

Heads twisted backwards, forced to walk backwards around the circumference of their circle for all of time.

Thrown into a river of boiling pitch and tar; guarded by Malabranche—flying demons with grappling hooks and barbs.

Forced to march wearing heavy robes resembling a monk's cowl lined with lead, symbolically representing hypocrisy.

Tormented by serpents; bites cause their bodies to spontaneously combust, only to regenerate.

Burning forever within a single eternal flame.

The divisive in life suffer eternity cut and mutilated by a demon's sword.

Falsifiers of...

Traitors to...

...oniacs

...holas III

**Diviners,
astrologers
& magicians**

Amphiaraus
Tiresias
Aruns
Manto
Eryphylus
Michael Scott
Guido Bonatti
Asdente

Malacoda

Barrators

Elder of Santa Zita
Ciampolo
Friar Gomita
Michael Zanche

Hypocrites

Catalano
Loderingo
Caiaphas

Thieves

Vanni Fucci
Agnello Brunelleschi
Buoso degli Abati
Puccio Sciancato
Cianfa de' Donati
Guercio Cavalcanti

Ulysses
Diomedes

**Fraudulent
counselors**

**Sowers of
scandal &
schism**

Mohammed
Ali
Pier da
Medicina
Curio
Mosca
Bertrand de
Born

Metals
Griffolino
d' Arezzo
Capocchino

Persons
Coins
Gianni
Schicchi
Myrrha
Adam
of Brescia
Potiphar's
Wife
Simon
of Troy

Words

Giants
Nimrod
Ephialtes

Antaeus

Kin *(Caina)*

Homeland *(Antenora)*

Camicion
de' Pazzi
Bocca
degli Abati
Buoso
da Duera

Cocytus
(frozen lake of lamentation)

Guests *(Ptolomea)*

Count Ugolino
Archbishop
Ruggieri
Friar Alberigo
Branco d' Oria

Benefactors *(Judecca)*

Judas Iscariot, Cassius and Brutus
chewed in Lucifer's three mouths

| 9 | 20 | 21 | 22 | 23 | 24 | 25 | 26 | 27 | 28 | 29 | 30 | 31 | 32 | 33 | 34 |

tongues confused, a language strained in anguish
   with cadences of anger, shrill outcries
   and raucous groans that joined with sounds of hands,   27

raising a whirling storm that turns itself
   forever through that air of endless black,
   like grains of sand swirling when a whirlwind blows.   30

And I, in the midst of all this circling horror,
   began, "Teacher, what are these sounds I hear?
   What souls are these so overwhelmed by grief?"   33

And he to me: "This wretched state of being
   is the fate of those sad souls who lived a life
   but lived it with no blame and with no praise.   36

They are mixed with that repulsive choir of angels
   neither faithful nor unfaithful to their God,
   who undecided stood but for themselves.   39

Heaven, to keep its beauty, cast them out,
   but even Hell itself would not receive them,
   for fear the damned might glory over them."   42

And I. "Master, what torments do they suffer
   that force them to lament so bitterly?"
   He answered: "I will tell you in few words: 45

these wretches have no hope of truly dying,
   and this blind life they lead is so abject
   it makes them envy every other fate.   48

The world will not record their having been there;
   Heaven's mercy and its justice turn from them.
   Let's not discuss them; look and pass them by."   51

And so I looked and saw a kind of banner
   rushing ahead, whirling with aimless speed
   as though it would not ever take a stand;   54

behind it an interminable train
   of souls pressed on, so many that I wondered
   how death could have undone so great a number.   57

52–69. In the *Inferno* divine retribution assumes the form of the *contrapasso,* i.e., the just punishment of sin, effected by a process either resembling or contrasting to the sin itself. In this canto the *contrapasso* opposes the sin of neutrality, or inactivity: The souls who in their early lives had no banner, no leader to follow, now run forever after one.

When I had recognized a few of them,
    I saw the shade of the one who must have been
    the coward who had made the great refusal.   60

At once I understood, and I was sure
    this was that sect of evil souls who were
    hateful to God and to His enemies.   63

These wretches, who had never truly lived,
    went naked, and were stung and stung again
    by the hornets and the wasps that circled them   66

and made their faces run with blood in streaks;
    their blood, mixed with their tears, dripped to their feet,
    and disgusting maggots collected in the pus.   69

And when I looked beyond this crowd I saw
    a throng upon the shore of a wide river,
    which made me ask, "Master, I would like to know: 72

who are these people, and what law is this
    that makes those souls so eager for the crossing
    as I can see, even in this dim light?"   75

And he: "All this will be made plain to you
    as soon as we shall come to stop awhile
    upon the sorrowful shore of Acheron."   78

And I, with eyes cast down in shame, for fear
    that I perhaps had spoken out of turn,
    said nothing more until we reached the river.   81

And suddenly, coming toward us in a boat,
    a man of years whose ancient hair was white
    shouted at us, "Woe to you, perverted souls!   84

Give up all hope of ever seeing Heaven:
    I come to lead you to the other shore,
    into eternal darkness, ice, and fire.   87

And you, the living soul, you over there,
    get away from all these people who are dead."
    But when he saw I did not move aside,   90

---

60. The coward could be Pontius Pilate, who refused to pass sentence on Christ.

he said, "Another way, by other ports,
    not here, shall you pass to reach the other shore;
    a lighter skiff than this must carry you."   93

And my guide, "Charon, this is no time for anger!
    It is so willed, there where the power is
    for what is willed; that's all you need to know."   96

These words brought silence to the woolly cheeks
    of the ancient steersman of the livid marsh,
    whose eyes were set in glowing wheels of fire.   99

But all those souls there, naked, in despair,
    changed color and their teeth began to chatter
    at the sound of his announcement of their doom.   102

They were cursing God, cursing their own parents,
    the human race, the time, the place, the seed
    of their beginning, and their day of birth.   105

Then all together, weeping bitterly,
    they packed themselves along the wicked shore
    that waits for every man who fears not God.   108

The devil, Charon, with eyes of glowing coals,
    summons them all together with a signal,
    and with an oar he strikes the laggard sinner.   111

As in autumn when the leaves begin to fall,
    one after the other (until the branch
    is witness to the spoils spread on the ground),   114

so did the evil seed of Adam's Fall
    drop from that shore to the boat, one at a time,
    at the signal, like the falcon to its lure.   117

Away they go across the darkened waters,
    and before they reach the other side to land,
    a new throng starts collecting on this side.   120

"My son," the gentle master said to me,
    "all those who perish in the wrath of God
    assemble here from all parts of the earth;   123

124–126. It is perhaps a part of the punishment that the souls of all the damned are eager for their punishment to begin; those who were so willing to sin on earth, are in hell damned with a willingness to receive their just retribution.

they want to cross the river, they are eager;
    it is Divine Justice that spurs them on,
    turning the fear they have into desire.   126

A good soul never comes to make this crossing,
    so, if Charon grumbles at the sight of you,
    you see now what his words are really saying."   129

He finished speaking, and the grim terrain
    shook violently; and the fright it gave me
    even now in recollection makes me sweat.   132

Out of the tear-drenched land a wind arose
    which blasted forth into a reddish light,
    knocking my senses out of me completely,   135

and I fell as one falls tired into sleep.

Canto IV

Waking from his swoon, the Pilgrim is led by Virgil to the First Circle of Hell, known as Limbo, where the sad shades of the virtuous non-Christians dwell. The souls here, including Virgil, suffer no physical torment, but they must live, in desire, without hope of seeing God. Virgil tells about Christ's descent into Hell and His salvation of several Old Testament figures.

A heavy clap of thunder! I awoke
    from the deep sleep that drugged my mind—startled,
    the way one is when shaken out of sleep.   3

I turned my rested eyes from side to side,
    already on my feet and, staring hard,
    I tried my best to find out where I was,   6

and this is what I saw: I found myself
    upon the brink of grief's abysmal valley
    that collects the thunderings of endless cries.   9

So dark and deep and nebulous it was,
    try as I might to force my sight below,
    I could not see the shape of anything.   12

"Let us descend into the sightless world,"
    began the poet (his face was deathly pale):
    "I will go first, and you will follow me."   15

And I, aware of his changed color, said:
   "But how can I go on if you are frightened?
   You are my constant strength when I lose heart."   18

And he to me: "The anguish of the souls
   that are down here paints my face with pity
   which you have wrongly taken to be fear.   21

Let us go, the long road urges us."
   He entered then, leading the way for me
   down to the first circle of the abyss.   24

Down there, to judge only by what I heard,
   there were no wails but just the sounds of sighs
   rising and trembling through the timeless air,   27

the sounds of sighs of untormented grief
   burdening these groups, diverse and teeming,
   made up of men and women and of infants.   30

Then the good master said, "You do not ask
   what sort of souls are these you see around you.
   Now you should know before we go on farther,   33

they have not sinned. But their great worth alone
   was not enough, for they did not know Baptism,
   which is the gateway to the faith you follow,   36

and if they came before the birth of Christ,
   they did not worship God the way one should;
   I myself am a member of this group.   39

For this defect, and for no other guilt,
   we here are lost. In this alone we suffer:
   cut off from hope, we live on in desire."   42

The words I heard weighed heavy on my heart;
   to think that souls as virtuous as these
   were suspended in that limbo, and forever!   45

"Tell me, my teacher, tell me, O my master,"
   I began (wishing to have confirmed by him
   the teachings of unerring Christian doctrine),   48

"did any ever leave here, through his merit
   or with another's help, and go to bliss?"
   And he, who understood my hidden question,   51

answered: "I was a novice in this place
    when I saw a mighty lord descend to us
    who wore the sign of victory as his crown.   54

He took from us the shade of our first parent,
    of Abel, his good son, of Noah, too,
    and of obedient Moses, who made the laws;   57

Abram, the Patriarch, David the King,
    Israel with his father and his children,
    with Rachel, whom he worked so hard to win;   60

and many more he chose for blessedness;
    and you should know, before these souls were taken,
    no human soul had ever reached salvation."   63

Canto V

From limbo Virgil leads his ward down to the threshold of the Second Circle of Hell, where for the first time he will see the damned in Hell being punished for their sins. There, barring their way, is the hideous figure of Minòs, the bestial judge of Dante's underworld; but after strong words from Virgil, the poets are allowed to pass into the dark space of this circle, where can be heard the wailing voices of the Lustful, whose punishment consists in being forever whirled about in a dark, stormy wind. After seeing a thousand or more famous lovers—including Semiramis, Dido, Helen, Achilles, and Paris—the Pilgrim asks to speak to two figures he sees together. They are Francesca da Rimini and her lover, Paolo, and the scene in which they appear is probably the most famous episode of the *Inferno*. At the end of the scene, the Pilgrim, who has been overcome by pity for the lovers, faints to the ground.

This way I went, descending from the first
    into the second round, that holds less space
    but much more pain—stinging the soul to wailing.   3

There stands Minòs grotesquely, and he snarls,
    examining the guilty at the entrance;
    he judges and dispatches, tail in coils.   6

By this I mean that when the evil soul
    appears before him, it confesses all,
    and he, who is the expert judge of sins,   9

---

4. Minòs was the son of Zeus and Europa. As king of Crete he was revered for his wisdom and judicial gifts. For these qualities he became chief magistrate of the underworld in classical literature. (See Virgil, *Aeneid* VI, 432–433.) Although Dante did not alter Minòs' official function, he transformed him into a demonic figure, both in his physical characteristics and in his bestial activity.

knows to what place in Hell the soul belongs;
    the times he wraps his tail around himself
    tell just how far the sinner must go down.   12

The damned keep crowding up in front of him:
    they pass along to judgment one by one;
    they speak, they hear, and then are hurled below.   15

"O you who come to the place where pain is host,"
    Minòs spoke out when he caught sight of me,
    putting aside the duties of his office,   18

"be careful how you enter and whom you trust
    it's easy to get in, but don't be fooled!"
    And my guide said to him: "Why keep on shouting?   21

Do not attempt to stop his fated journey; it
    is so willed there where the power is
    for what is willed; that's all you need to know."   24

And now the notes of anguish start to play
    upon my ears; and now I find myself
    where sounds on sounds of weeping pound at me.   27

I came to a place where no light shone at all,
    bellowing like the sea racked by a tempest,
    when warring winds attack it from both sides.   30

The infernal storm, eternal in its rage,
    sweeps and drives the spirits with its blast:
    it whirls them, lashing them with punishment.   33

When they are swept back past their place of judgment,
    then come the shrieks, laments, and anguished cries;
    there they blaspheme God's almighty power.   36

I learned that to this place of punishment
    all those who sin in lust have been condemned,
    those who make reason slave to appetite;   39

and as the wings of starlings in the winter
    bear them along in wide-spread, crowded flocks,
    so does that wind propel the evil spirits: 42

31–32. The *contrapasso* or punishment suggests that lust (the "infernal storm") is pursued without the light of reason (in the darkness).

now here, then there, and up and down, it drives them
    with never any hope to comfort them
    hope not of rest but even of suffering less.   45

And just like cranes in flight, chanting their lays,
    stretching an endless line in their formation,
    I saw approaching, crying their laments,   48

spirits carried along by the battling winds.
    And so I asked, "Teacher, tell me, what souls
    are these punished in the sweep of the black wind?"   51

"The first of those whose story you should know,"
    my master wasted no time answering,
    "was empress over lands of many tongues;   54

her vicious tastes had so corrupted her
    she licensed every form of lust with laws
    to cleanse the stain of scandal she had spread;   57

she is Semiramis, who, legend says,
    was Ninus' wife as well as his successor;
    she governed all the land the Sultan rules.   60

The next is she who killed herself for love
    and broke faith with the ashes of Sichaeus;
    and there is Cleopatra, who loved men's lusting.   63

See Helen there, the root of evil woe
    lasting long years, and see the great Achilles,
    who lost his life to love, in final combat;   66

see Paris, Tristan"—then, more than a thousand
    he pointed out to me, and named them all,
    those shades whom love cut off from life on earth.   69

---

64. Helen of Troy.

65–66. Enticed by the beauty of Polyxena, a daughter of the Trojan king, Achilles desired her to be his wife, but Hecuba, Polyxena's mother, arranged a counterplot with Paris so that when Achilles entered the temple for his presumed marriage, he was treacherously slain by Paris.

67. Paris was the son of Priam, king of Troy, whose abduction of Helen ignited the Trojan War. Tristan was the central figure of numerous medieval French, German, and Italian romances. Sent as a messenger by his uncle, King Mark of Cornwall, to obtain Isolt for him in marriage, Tristan became enamored of her, and she of him. After Isolt's marriage to Mark, the lovers continued their love affair, and in order to maintain its secrecy they necessarily employed many deceits and ruses. According to one version, Mark, increasingly suspicious of their attachment, finally discovered them together and ended the incestuous relationship by mortally wounding Tristan with a lance.

After I heard my teacher call the names
    of all these knights and ladies of ancient times,
    pity confused my senses, and I was dazed.   72

I began: "Poet, I would like, with all my heart,
    to speak to those two there who move together
    and seem to be so light upon the winds."   75

And he: "You'll see when they are closer to us;
    if you entreat them by that love of theirs
    that carries them along, they'll come to you."   78

When the winds bent their course in our direction
    I raised my voice to them, "O wearied souls,
    come speak with us if it be not forbidden."   81

As doves, called by desire to return
    to their sweet nest, with wings raised high and poised,
    float downward through the air, guided by will,   84

so these two left the flock where Dido is
    and came toward us through the malignant air,
    such was the tender power of my call.   87

"O living creature, gracious and so kind,
    who makes your way here through this dingy air
    to visit us who stained the world with blood,   90

if we could claim as friend the King of Kings,
    we would beseech him that he grant you peace,
    you who show pity for our atrocious plight.   93

Whatever pleases you to hear or speak
    we will hear and we will speak about with you
    as long as the wind, here where we are, is silent.   96

The place where I was born lies on the shore
    where the river Po with its attendant streams
    descends to seek its final resting place.   99

Love, quick to kindle in the gentle heart,
    seized this one for the beauty of my body,
    torn from me. (How it happened still offends me!)   102

---

74. The two are Francesca, daughter of Guido Vecchio da Polenta, lord of Ravenna; and Paolo Malatesta, third son of Malatesta da Verrucchio, lord of Rimini. Around 1275 the aristocratic Francesca was married for political reasons to Gianciotto, the physically deformed second son of Malatesta da Verrucchio. In time a love affair developed between Francesca and Gianciotto's younger brother, Paolo. One day the betrayed husband discovered them in an amorous embrace and slew them both.

Love, that excuses no one loved from loving,
   seized me so strongly with delight in him
   that, as you see, he never leaves my side. 105

Love led us straight to sudden death together.
   Caïna awaits the one who quenched our lives."
   These were the words that came from them to us. 108

When those offended souls had told their story,
   I bowed my head and kept it bowed until
   the poet said, "What are you thinking of?" 111

When finally I spoke, I sighed, "Alas,
   all those sweet thoughts, and oh, how much desiring
   brought these two down into this agony." 114

And then I turned to them and tried to speak;
   I said, "Francesca, the torment that you suffer
   brings painful tears of pity to my eyes. 117

But tell me, in that time of your sweet sighing
   how, and by what signs, did love allow you
   to recognize your dubious desires?" 120

And she to me: "There is no greater pain
   than to remember, in our present grief,
   past happiness (as well your teacher knows)! 123

But if your great desire is to learn
   the very root of such a love as ours,
   I shall tell you, but in words of flowing tears. 126

One day we read, to pass the time away,
   of Lancelot, of how he fell in love;
   we were alone, innocent of suspicion. 129

Time and again our eyes were brought together
   by the book we read; our faces flushed and paled.
   To the moment of one line alone we yielded: 132

it was when we read about those longed-for lips
   now being kissed by such a famous lover,
   that this one (who shall never leave my side) 135

---

107. Caïna was one of the four divisions of Cocytus, the lower part of Hell, wherein those souls who treacherously betrayed their kin are tormented.

then kissed my mouth, and trembled as he did.
　　Our Galehot was that book and he who wrote it.
　　That day we read no further." And all the while   138

the one of the two spirits spoke these words,
　　the other wept, in such a way that pity
　　blurred my senses; I swooned as though to die,   141

and fell to Hell's floor as a body, dead, falls.

Canto XIX deals with a form of fraud known as simony. Simony is a sin in which an individual tries to make money by selling or profiting from the exercise of church offices. Consequently, we find reference in this canto to several popes Dante considered guilty of this crime. His attitude toward them is quite harsh, since he believed that the corruption of the church had terrible consequences for the good of society. You will notice that the sinners we encounter in Cantos XIX and XXI are found in concentric ditches called bolgia (from the Italian word for pouch). In various places there are stone bridges over the bolgia over which Dante and Virgil can cross as they descend deeper into hell.

Canto XIX

From the bridge above the Third *Bolgia* can be seen a rocky landscape below filled with holes, from each of which protrude a sinner's legs and feet; flames dance across their soles. When the Pilgrim expresses curiosity about a particular pair of twitching legs, Virgil carries him down into the *bolgia* so that the Pilgrim himself may question the sinner. The legs belong to Pope Nicholas III, who astounds the Pilgrim by mistaking him for Boniface VIII, the next pope, who, as soon as he dies, will fall to the same hole, thereby pushing Nicholas farther down. He predicts that soon after Boniface, Pope Clement V will come, stuffing both himself and Boniface still deeper. To Nicholas's rather rhetoric-filled speech the Pilgrim responds with equally high language, inveighing against the Simonists, the evil churchmen who are punished here. Virgil is much pleased with his pupil and, lifting him in an affectionate embrace, he carries him to the top of the arch above the next *bolgia*.

O Simon Magus! O scum that followed him!
　　Those things of God that rightly should be wed
　　to holiness, you, rapacious creatures,   3

for the price of gold and silver, prostitute.
　　Now, in your honor, I must sound my trumpet
　　for here in the third pouch is where you dwell.   6

1–6. As related in Acts (8:9–24), Simon the magician, having observed the descent of the Holy Spirit upon the apostles John and Peter, desired to purchase this power for himself, whereupon Peter harshly admonished him for even thinking that the gift of God might be bought. Derived from this sorcerer's name, the word "simony" (74) refers to those offenses involving the sale or fraudulent possession of ecclesiastical offices.

We had already climbed to see this tomb,
  and were standing high above it on the bridge,
  exactly at the mid-point of the ditch.   9

O Highest Wisdom, how you demonstrate
  your art in Heaven, on earth, and here in Hell!
  How justly does your power make awards!   12

I saw along the sides and on the bottom
  the livid-colored rock all full of holes;
  all were the same in size, and each was round.   15

To me they seemed no wider and no deeper
  than those inside my lovely San Giovanni,
  in which the priest would stand or baptize from;   18

and one of these, not many years ago,
  I smashed for someone who was drowning in it:
  let this be mankind's picture of the truth!   21

From the mouth of every hole were sticking out
  a single sinner's feet, and then the legs
  up to the calf—the rest was stuffed inside.   24

The soles of every sinner's feet were flaming; their
  naked legs were twitching frenziedly
  they would have broken any chain or rope.   27

Just as a flame will only move along
  an object's oily outer peel, so here
  the fire slid from heel to toe and back.   30

"Who is that one, Master, that angry wretch,
  who is writhing more than any of his comrades,"
  I asked, "the one licked by a redder flame?"   33

And he to me, "If you want to be carried down
  along that lower bank to where he is,
  you can ask him who he is and why he's here."   36

And I, "My pleasure is what pleases you:
  you are my lord, you know that from your will
  I would not swerve. You even know my thoughts."   39

---

25. Just as the Simonists' perversion of the Church is symbolized by their "perverted" immersion in holes resembling baptismal fonts, so their "baptism" is perverted: instead of the head being moistened with water, the feet are "baptized" with oil and fire.

When we reached the fourth bank, we began to turn
   and, keeping to the left, made our way down
   to the bottom of the holed and narrow ditch.   42

The good guide did not drop me from his side
   until he brought me to the broken rock
   of that one who was fretting with his shanks.   45

"Whatever you are, holding your upside down,
   O wretched soul, stuck like a stake in ground,
   make a sound or something," I said, "if you can."   48

I stood there like a priest who is confessing
   some vile assassin who, fixed in his ditch,
   has called him back again to put off dying.   51

He cried: "Is that you, here, already, upright?
   Is that you here already upright, Boniface?
   By many years the book has lied to me!   54

Are you fed up so soon with all that wealth
   for which you did not fear to take by guile
   the Lovely Lady, then tear her asunder?"   57

I stood there like a person just made fun of,
   dumbfounded by a question for an answer,
   not knowing how to answer the reply.   60

Then Virgil said: "Quick, hurry up and tell him:
   'I'm not the one, I'm not the one you think!'"
   And I answered just the way he told me to.   63

The spirit heard, and twisted both his feet,
   then, sighing with a grieving, tearful voice,
   he said: "Well then, what do you want of me?   66

---

53. From the foreknowledge granted to the infernal shades, the speaker shows that Pope Boniface VIII, upon his death in 1303, will take his place in that very receptacle wherein he himself is now being tormented. The Pilgrim's voice, so close at hand, has caused the sinner to believe that his successor has arrived unexpectedly before his time (three years, in fact) and, consequently, that the Divine Plan of Events, the Book of Fate (54), has lied to him.

    Having obtained the abdication of Pope Celestine V, Boniface gained the support of Charles II of Nantes and thus was assured of his election to the papacy (1294). In addition to misusing the Church's influence in his dealings with Charles, Boniface VIII freely distributed ecclesiastical offices among his family and confidants. As early as 1300 he was plotting the destruction of the Whites, the Florentine political faction to which Dante belonged.

57. The "Lovely Lady" is the Church.

If it concerns you so to learn my name
    that for this reason you came down the bank,
    know that I once was dressed in the great mantle.   69

But actually I was the she-bear's son,
    so greedy to advance my cubs, that wealth
    I pocketed in life, and here, myself.   72

Beneath my head are pushed down all the others
    who came, sinning in simony, before me,
    squeezed tightly in the fissures of the rock.   75

I, in my turn, shall join the rest below
    as soon as he comes, the one I thought you were
    when, all too quick, I put my question to you.   78

But already my feet have baked a longer time
    (and I have been stuck upside-down like this)
    than he will stay here planted with feet aflame: 81

soon after him shall come one from the West,
    a lawless shepherd, one whose fouler deeds
    make him a fitting cover for us both.   84

He shall be another Jason, like the one
    in Maccabees: just as his king was pliant,
    so France's king shall soften to this priest."   87

I do not know, perhaps I was too bold here,
    but I answered him in tune with his own words:
    "Well, tell me now: what was the sum of money   90

that holy Peter had to pay our Lord
    before He gave the keys into his keeping?
    Certainly He asked no more than 'Follow me.'   93

67–72. Gian Gaetano degli Orsini (lit. "of the little bears," hence the designation "she-bear's son" and the reference to "my cubs") became Pope Nicholas III in 1277. As a cardinal he won renown for his integrity; however, in the short three years between ascent to the papal throne and his death he became notorious for his simoniacal practices.

77. The man still to come is Boniface VIII. (See above, note on line 53.)

82–84. The "lawless shepherd" is Pope Clement V of Gascony, who, upon his death in 1314, will join Nicholas and Boniface in eternal torment.

85–87. Having obtained the high priesthood of the Jews by bribing King Antiochus of Syria, Jason neglected the sacrifices and sanctuary of the temple and introduced Greek modes of life into his community. As Jason had fraudulently acquired his position, so had Menelaus, who offered more money to the king, supplanted Jason (2 Maccabees 47:7–27). As Jason obtained office from King Antiochus fraudulently, so shall Clement acquire his from Philp.

Nor did Peter or the rest extort gold coins
    or silver from Matthias when he was picked
    to fill the place the evil one had lost.   96

So stay stuck there, for you are rightly punished,
    and guard with care the money wrongly gained
    that made you stand courageous against Charles.   99

And were it not for the reverence I have
    for those highest of all keys that you once held
    in the happy life—if this did not restrain me,   102

I would use even harsher words than these,
    for your avarice brings grief upon the world,
    crushing the good, exalting the depraved.   105

You shepherds it was the Evangelist had in mind
    when the vision came to him of her who sits
    upon the waters playing whore with kings: 108

that one who with the seven heads was born
    and from her ten horns managed to draw strength
    so long as virtue was her bridegroom's joy.   111

You have built yourselves a God of gold and silver!
    How do you differ from the idolator,
    except he worships one, you worship hundreds?   114

O Constantine, what evil did you sire,
    not by your conversion, but by the dower
    that the first wealthy Father got from you!"   117

94–96. After the treachery and subsequent expulsion of Judas, the apostles cast lots in order to replenish their number. Thus, by the will of God, not through monetary payment, was Matthias elected to the vacated post (Acts 1:15–26).

106–111. St. John the Evangelist relates his vision of the dissolute Imperial City of Rome. To Dante, she "who sits / upon the waters" represents the Church, which has been corrupted by the simoniacal activities of many popes (the "shepherds" of the Church). The seven heads symbolize the seven Holy Sacraments; the ten horns represent the Ten Commandments.

115–117. Constantine the Great, emperor of Rome (306–387), was converted to Christianity in the year 312. Having conquered the eastern Mediterranean lands, he transferred the capital of the Roman Empire to Constantinople (360). This move, according to tradition, stemmed from Constantine's decision to place the western part of the empire under the jurisdiction of the Church in order to repay Pope Sylvester ("the first wealthy Father") for healing him of leprosy. The so-called "Donation of Constantine," though it was proved in the fifteenth century to be a complete fabrication on the part of the clergy, was universally accepted as the truth in the Middle Ages. Dante the Pilgrim reflects this tradition in his sad apostrophe to the individual who first would have introduced wealth to the Church and who, unknowingly, would be ultimately responsible for its present corruption.

And while I sang these very notes to him,
    his big flat feet kicked fiercely out of anger,
      —or perhaps it was his conscience gnawing him.   120

I think my master liked what I was saying,
    for all the while he smiled and was intent
      on hearing the ring of truly spoken words.   123

Then he took hold of me with both his arms,
    and when he had me firm against his breast,
      he climbed back up the path he had come down.   126

He did not tire of the weight clasped tight to him,
    but brought me to the top of the bridge's arch,
      the one that joins the fourth bank to the fifth.   129

And here he gently set his burden down
    gently, for the ridge, so steep and rugged,
      would have been hard even for goats to cross.   132

From there another valley opened to me.

Canto XXI

When the two reach the summit of the arch over the Fifth *Bolgia,* they see in the ditch below the bubbling of boiling pitch. Virgil's sudden warning of danger frightens the Pilgrim even before he sees a black devil rushing toward them, with a sinner slung over his shoulder. From the bridge the devil flings the sinner into the pitch, where he is poked at and tormented by the family of Malebranche devils. Virgil, advising his ward to hide behind a rock, crosses the bridge to face the devils alone. They threaten him with their pitchforks, but when he announces to their leader, Malacoda, that Heaven has willed that he lead another through Hell, the devil's arrogance collapses. Virgil calls the Pilgrim back to him. Scarmiglione, who tries to take a poke at him, is rebuked by his leader, who tells the travelers that the sixth arch is broken here but farther on they will find another bridge to cross. He chooses a squad of his devils to escort them there: Alichino, Calcabrina, Cagnazzo, Barbariccia, Libicocco, Draghignazzo, Ciriatto, Graffiacane, Farfarello, and Rubicante. The Pilgrim's suspicion about their unsavory escorts is brushed aside by his guide, and the squad starts off, giving an obscene salute to their captain, who returns their salute with a fart.

From this bridge to the next we walked and talked
    of things my Comedy does not care to tell;
      and when we reached the summit of the arch,   3

we stopped to see the next fosse of Malebolge
    and to hear more lamentation voiced in vain:
      I saw that it was very strangely dark!   6

In the vast and busy shipyard of the Venetians
   there boils all winter long a tough, thick pitch
   that is used to caulk the ribs of unsound ships.   9

Since winter will not let them sail, they toil:
   some build new ships, others repair the old ones,
   plugging the planks come loose from many sailings;   12

some hammer at the bow, some at the stern,
   one carves the oars while others twine the ropes,
   one mends the jib, one patches up the mainsail;   15

here, too, but heated by God's art, not fire,
   a sticky tar was boiling in the ditch
   that smeared the banks with viscous residue.   18

I saw it there, but I saw nothing in it,
   except the rising of the boiling bubbles
   breathing in air to burst and sink again.   21

I stood intently intently gazing there below,
   my guide, shouting to me: "Watch out, watch out!"
   took hold of me and drew me to his side.   24

I turned my head like one who can't resist
   looking to see what makes him run away
   (his body's strength draining with sudden fear),   27

but, looking back, does not delay his flight;
   and I saw coming right behind our backs,
   rushing along the ridge, a devil, black!   30

His face, his look, how frightening it was!
   With outstretched wings he skimmed along the rock,
   and every single move he made was cruel;   33

on one of his high-hunched and pointed shoulders
   he had a sinner slung by both his thighs,
   held tightly clawed at the tendons of his heels.   36

He shouted from our bridge: "Hey, Malebranche,
   here's one of Santa Zita's elders for you!
   You stick him under—I'll go back for more;   39

7–15. During the Middle Ages the shipyard at Venice, built in 1104, was one of the most active and productive in all Europe. The image of the busy shipyard with its activity revolving around a vat of viscous pitch establishes the tone for this canto (and the next) as one of tense and excited movement.

I've got that city stocked with the likes of him,
    they're all a bunch of grafters, save Bonturo!
    You can change a 'no' to 'yes' for cash in Lucca."   42

He flung him in, then from the flinty cliff
    sprang off. No hound unleashed to chase a thief
    could have taken off with greater speed than he.   45

That sinner plunged, then floated up stretched out,
    and the devils underneath the bridge all shouted:
    "You shouldn't imitate the Holy Face!   48

The swimming's different here from in the Serchio!
    We have our grappling-hooks along with us—
    don't show yourself above the pitch, or else!"   51

With a hundred prongs or more they pricked him, shrieking:
    "You've got to do your squirming under cover,
    try learning how to cheat beneath the surface."   54

They were like cooks who make their scullery boys
    poke down into the caldron with their forks
    to keep the meat from floating to the top.   57

My master said: "We'd best not let them know that
    you are here with me; crouch down behind
    some jutting rock so that they cannot see you;   60

whatever insults they may hurl at me,
    you must not fear, I know how things are run here;
    I have been caught in as bad a fix before."   63

He crossed the bridge and walked on past the end;
    as soon as he set foot on the sixth bank
    he forced himself to look as bold as possible.   66

With all the sound and fury that breaks loose
    when dogs rush out at some poor begging tramp,
    making him stop and beg from where he stands,   69

the ones who hid beneath the bridge sprang out
    and blocked him with a flourish of their pitchforks,
    but he shouted: "All of you behave yourselves!   72

46–51. The "Holy Face" was a wooden crucifix at Lucca. The sinner surfaces stretched out (46) on his back with arms flung wide like the figure on a crucifix—and this gives rise to the devil's remark that here in Hell one does not swim the same way as in the Serchio (a river near Lucca). In other words, in the Serchio people swim for pleasure, often floating on their backs (in the position of a crucifix).

Before you start to jab me with your forks,
 let one of you step forth to hear me out,
 and then decide if you still care to grapple."   75

They all cried out: "Let Malacoda go!"
 One stepped forward—the others stood their ground
 and moving, said, "What good will this do him?"   78

"Do you think, Malacoda," said my master,
 "that you would see me here, come all this way,
 against all opposition, and still safe,   81

without propitious fate and God's permission?
 Now let us pass, for it is willed in Heaven
 that I lead another by this savage path."   84

With this the devil's arrogance collapsed,
 his pitchfork, too, dropped right down to his feet,
 as he announced to all: "Don't touch this man!"   87

"You, hiding over there," my guide called me,
 "behind the bridge's rocks, curled up and quiet,
 come back to me, you may return in safety.   90

At his words I rose and then I ran to him
 and all the devils made a movement forward;
 I feared they would not really keep their pact.   93

(I remember seeing soldiers under truce,
 as they left the castle of Caprona, frightened
 to be passing in the midst of such an enemy.)   96

I drew up close to him, as close as possible,
 and did not take my eyes from all those faces
 that certainly had nothing good about them.   99

Their prongs were aimed at me, and one was saying:
 "Now do I let him have it in the rump?"
 They answered all for one: "Sure, stick him good!"   102

---

76. Malacoda is the leader of the devils in this *bolgia*. It is significant that a devil whose name means "evil tail" ends this canto with a fart (139).

94–96. Dante's personal recollection concerns the siege of Caprona (a fortress on the Arno River near Pisa) by Guelph troops from Lucca and Florence in 1289.

But the devil who had spoken with my guide
    was quick to spin around and scream an order:
      "At ease there, take it easy, Scarmiglione!" 105

Then he said to us: "You cannot travel straight
    across this string of bridges, for the sixth arch
      lies broken at the bottom of its ditch; 108

if you have made your mind up to proceed,
    you must continue on along this ridge;
      not far, you'll find a bridge that crosses it. 111

Five hours more and it will be one thousand,
    two hundred sixty-six years and a day
      since the bridge-way here fell crumbling to the ground. 114

I plan to send a squad of mine that way
    to see that no one airs himself down there;
      go along with them, they will not misbehave. 117

Front and center, Alichino, Calcabrina,"
    he shouted his commands, "you too, Cagnazzo;
      Barbariccia, you be captain of the squad. 120

Take Libicocco with you and Draghignazzo,
    toothy Ciriatto and Graffiacane,
      Farfarello and our crazy Rubicante. 123

Now tour the ditch, inspect the boiling tar;
    these two shall have safe passage to the bridge
      connecting den to den without a break." 126

"O master, I don't like the looks of this,"
    I said, "let's go, just you and me, no escort,
      you know the way. I want no part of them! 129

If you're observant, as you usually are,
    why is it you don't see them grind their teeth
      and wink at one another?—we're in danger!" 132

112–114. Christ's death on Good Friday, A.D. 34, would in five hours, according to Malacoda, have occurred 1266 years ago yesterday—"today" being the morning of Holy Saturday, 1300. Although the bridge across the next *bolgia* was shattered by the earthquake following Christ's crucifixion, Malacoda tells Virgil and the Pilgrim that there is another bridge that crosses this *bolgia*. This lie, carefully contrived by the spokesman for the devils, sets the trap for the overly confident, trusting Virgil and his wary charge.

And he to me: "I will not have you frightened;
    let them do all the grinding that they want,
    they do it for the boiling souls, not us."   135

Before they turned left-face along the bank
    each one gave their good captain a salute
    with farting tongue pressed tightly to his teeth,   138

and he blew back with his bugle of an ass-hole.

Circle IX (also known as Cocytus) is reserved for traitors. It has four subdivisions: Caina, which contains traitors against kin; Antenora, for those who betray their homeland; Ptolomea, where we find those who violate the bond between host and guest; and Judecca, the eternal home of those who betray their benefactors. It is here, at the very bottom of hell, that we come across Lucifer.

Canto XXXII

They descend farther down into the darkness of the immense plain of ice in which shades of Traitors are frozen. In the outer region of the ice-lake, Caïna, are those who betrayed their kin in murder; among them, locked in a frozen embrace, are Napoleone and Alessandro of Mangona, and others are Mordred, Focaccia, Sassol Mascheroni, and Camicion de'pazzi.

If I had words grating and crude enough
    that really could describe this horrid hole
    supporting the converging weight of Hell,   3

I could squeeze out the juice of my memories
    to the last drop. But I don't have these words,
    and so I am reluctant to begin.   6

To talk about the bottom of the universe
    the way it truly is, is no child's play,
    no task for tongues that gurgle baby-talk.   9

But may those heavenly ladies aid my verse
    who aided Amphion to wall-in Thebes,
    that my words may tell exactly what I saw.   12

O misbegotten rabble of all rabble,
    who crowd this realm, hard even to describe,
    it were better you had lived as sheep or goats!   15

When we reached a point of darkness in the well
   below the giant's feet, farther down the slope,
   and I was gazing still at the high wall,   18

I heard somebody say: "Watch where you step!
   Be careful that you do not kick the heads
   of this brotherhood of miserable souls."   21

At that I turned around and saw before me
   a lake of ice stretching beneath my feet,
   more like a sheet of glass than frozen water.   24

In the depths of Austria's wintertime, the Danube
   never in all its course showed ice so thick,
   nor did the Don beneath its frigid sky,   27

as this crust here; for if Mount Tambernic
   or Pietrapana would crash down upon it,
   not even at its edges would a crack creak.   30

The way the frogs (in the season when the harvest
   will often haunt the dreams of the peasant girl)
   sit croaking with their muzzles out of water,   33

so these frigid, livid shades were stuck in ice
   up to where a person's shame appears;
   their teeth clicked notes like storks' beaks snapping shut.   36

And each one kept his face bowed toward the ice:
   the mouth bore testimony to the cold,
   the eyes, to sadness welling in the heart.   39

I gazed around awhile and then looked down,
   and by my feet I saw two figures clasped
   so tight that one's hair could have been the other's.   42

"Tell me, you two, pressing your chests together,"
   I asked them, "who are you?" Both stretched their necks
   and when they had their faces raised toward me,   45

their eyes, which had before been only glazed,
   dripped tears down to their lips, and the cold froze
   the tears between them, locking the pair more tightly.   48

Wood to wood with iron was never clamped
   so firm! And the two of them like billy-goats
   were butting at each other, mad with anger.   51

Another one with both ears frozen off,
 and head still bowed over his icy mirror,
 cried out: "What makes you look at us so hard?   54

If you're interested to know who these two are:
 the valley where Bisenzio's waters flow
 belonged to them and to their father, Albert;   57

the same womb bore them both, and if you scour
 all of Caïna, you will not turn up one
 who's more deserving of this frozen aspic—   60

not him who had his breast and shadow pierced
 with one thrust of the lance from Arthur's hand;
 not Focaccia; not even this one here,   63

whose head gets in my way and blocks my view,
 known in the world as Sassol Mascheroni,
 and if you're Tuscan you must know who he was.   66

To save me from your asking for more news:
 I was Camicion de' Pazzi, and I await
 Carlin, whose guilt will make my own seem less."   69

Farther on I saw a thousand doglike faces,
 purple from the cold. That's why I shudder,
 and always will, when I see a frozen pond.   72

55–58. The two brothers were Napoleone and Alessandro, sons of Count Alberto of Mangona, who owned part of the valley of the Bisenzio near Florence. The two quarreled often and eventually killed each other in a fight concerning their inheritance.

59. The icy ring of Cocytus is named Caïna after Cain, who slew his brother Abel. Thus, in the first division of this, the Ninth Circle, are punished those treacherous shades who murderously violated family bonds.

61–62, Mordred, the wicked nephew of King Arthur, tried to kill the king and take his kingdom. But Arthur pierced him with such a mighty blow that when the lance was pulled from the dying traitor a ray of sunlight traversed his body and interrupted Mordred's shadow. The story is told in the Old French romance *Lancelot du Lac,* the book that Francesca claims led her astray with Paolo in Canto V, 127.

63. Focaccia was one of the Cancellieri family of Pistoia and a member of the White parry. His treacherous murder of his cousin, Detto de' Cancellieri (a Black), was possibly the act that led to the Florentine intervention in Pistoian affairs.

65. The early commentators say that Sassot Mascheroni was a member of the Toschi family in Florence who murdered his nephew in order to gain his inheritance.

68–69. Nothing is known of Camicion de' Pazzi except that he murdered one Umbertino, a relative. Another of Camicion's kin, Carlino de' Pazzi (69) from Valdarno, was still alive when the Pilgrim's conversation with Camicion was taking place. But Camicion already knew that Carlino, in July 1302, would accept a bribe to surrender the castle of Piantravigne to the Blacks of Florence.

Canto XXXIV

Far across the frozen ice can be seen the gigantic figure of Lucifer, who appears from this distance like a windmill seen through fog; and as the two travelers walk on toward that terrifying sight, they see the shades of sinners totally buried in the frozen water. At the center of the earth Lucifer stands frozen from the chest downward, and his horrible ugliness (he has three faces) is made more fearful by the fact that in each of his three mouths he chews on one of the three worst sinners of all mankind, the worst of those who betrayed their benefactors: Judas Iscariot, Brutus, and Cassius. Virgil, with the Pilgrim on his back, begins the descent down the shaggy body of Lucifer. They climb down through a crack in the ice, and when they reach the Evil One's thighs, Virgil turns and begins to struggle upward (because they have passed the center of the earth), still holding on to the hairy body of Lucifer, until they reach a cavern, where they stop for a short rest. Then a winding path brings them eventually to the earth's surface, where they see the stars.

"*Vexilla regis prodeunt Inferni,*"
    my master said, "closer to us, so now
    look ahead and see if you can make him out."   3

A far-off windmill turning its huge sails
    when a thick fog begins to settle in,
    or when the light of day begins to fade,   6

that is what I thought I saw appearing.
    And the gusts of wind it stirred made me shrink back
    behind my guide, my only means of cover.   9

Down here, I stood on souls fixed under ice
    (I tremble as I put this into verse);
    to me they looked like straws worked into glass.   12

Some lying flat, some perpendicular,
    either with their heads up or their feet,
    and some bent head to foot, shaped like a bow.   15

When we had moved far enough along the way
    that my master thought the time had come to show me
    the creature who was once so beautiful,   18

he stepped aside, and stopping is announced:
    "This is he, this is Dis; this is the place
    that calls for all the courage you have in you."   21

---

1. The opening lines of the hymn "*Vexilla regis prodeunt*"—"The banners of the King advance"—(written by Venantius Fortunatus, sixth-century bishop of Poitiers; this hymn belongs to the liturgy of the Church) are here parodied by the addition of the word *Inferni*, "of Hell," to the word *regis*, "of the King." Sung on Good Friday, the hymn anticipates the unveiling of the Cross; Dante, who began his journey on the evening of Good Friday, is prepared by Virgil's words for the sight of Lucifer, who will appear like a "windmill" in a "thick fog." The banners referred to are Lucifer's wings.

How chilled and nerveless, Reader, I felt then;
  do not ask me—I cannot write about it—
  there are no words to tell you how I felt.   24

I did not die—I was not living either!
  Try to imagine, if you can imagine,
  me there, deprived of life and death at once.   27

The king of the vast kingdom of all grief
  stuck out with half his chest above the ice;
  my height is closer to the height of giants   30

than theirs is to the length of his great arms;
  consider now how large all of him was:
  this body in proportion to his arms.   33

If once he was as fair as now he's foul
  and dared to raise his brows against his Maker,
  it is fitting that all grief should spring from him.   36

Oh, how amazed I was when I looked up
  and saw a head—one head wearing three faces!
  One was in front (and that was a bright red),   39

the other two attached themselves to this one
  just above the middle of each shoulder,
  and at the crown all three were joined in one: 42

The right face was a blend of white and yellow,
  the left the color of those people's skin
  who live along the river Nile's descent.   45

Beneath each face two mighty wings stretched out,
  the size you might expect of this huge bird
  (I never saw a ship with larger sails):   48

not feathered wings but rather like the ones
  a bat would have. He flapped them constantly,
  keeping three winds continuously in motion   51

to lock Cocytus eternally in ice.
  He wept from his six eyes, and down three chins
  were dripping tears all mixed with bloody slaver.   54

38–45. Dante presents Lucifer's head as a perverted parallel of the Trinity. The colors of the three single faces (red, yellow, black) are probably antithetically analogous to the qualities attributed to the Trinity (see Canto III, 5—6). Thereore, Highest Wisdom would be opposed by ignorance (black), Divine Omnipotence by impotence (yellow), Primal Love by hatred or envy (red).

In each of his three mouths he crunched a sinner,
    with teeth like those that rake the hemp and flax,
    keeping three sinners constantly in pain;   57

the one in front—the biting he endured
    was nothing like the clawing that he took:
    sometimes his back was raked clean of its skin.   60

"That soul up there who suffers most of all,"
    my guide explained, "is Judas Iscariot:
    the one with head inside and legs out kicking.   63

As for the other two whose heads stick out,
    the one who hangs from that black face is Brutus
    see how he squirms in silent desperation;   66

the other one is Cassius, he still looks sturdy.
    But soon it will be night. Now is the time
    to leave this place, for we have seen it all."   69

I held on to his neck, as he told me to,
    while he watched and waited for the time and place,
    and when the wings were stretched out just enough,   72

he grabbed on to the shaggy sides of Satan;
    then downward, tuft by tuft, he made his way
    between the tangled hair and frozen crust.   75

When we had reached the point exactly where
    the thigh begins, right at the haunch's curve,
    my guide, with strain and force of every muscle,   78

turned his head toward the shaggy shanks of Dis
    and grabbed the hair as if about to climb—
    I thought that we were heading back to Hell.   81

"Hold tight, there is no other way," he said,
    panting, exhausted, "only by these stairs
    can we leave behind the evil we have seen."   84

61–63. Having betrayed Christ for thirty pieces of silver, Judas endures greater punishment than the other two souls.

65. Marcus Brutus, who was deceitfully persuaded by Cassius (67) to join the conspiracy, aided in the assassination of Julius Caesar. It is fitting that in his final vision of the Inferno the Pilgrim should see those shades who committed treacherous acts against Divine and worldly authorities: the Church and the Roman Empire. This provides the culmination, at least in this canticle, of these basic themes: Church and Empire.

67. Caius Cassius Longinus was another member of the conspiracy against Caesar. By describing Cassius as "still look[ing] sturdy," Dante shows he has evidently confused him with Lucius Cassius, whom Cicero calls *adeps*, "corpulent."

When he had got me through the rocky crevice,
    he raised me to its edge and set me down,
    then carefully he climbed and joined me there.   87

I raised my eyes, expecting I would see
    the half of Lucifer I saw before.
    Instead I saw his two legs stretching upward.   90

If at that sight I found myself confused,
    so will those simple-minded folk who still
    don't see what point it was I must have passed.   93

"Get up," my master said, "get to your feet,
    the way is long, the road a rough climb up,
    already the sun approaches middle tierce!"   96

It was no palace promenade we came to,
    but rather like some dungeon Nature built:
    it was paved with broken stone and poorly lit.   99

"Before we start to struggle out of here,
    O master," I said when I was on my feet,
    "I wish you would explain some things to me.   102

Where is the ice? And how can he be lodged
    upside-down? And how, in so little time,
    could the sun go all the way from night to day?"   105

"You think you're still on the center's other side,"
    he said, "where I first grabbed the hairy worm
    of rottenness that pierces the earth's core;   108

and you were there as long as I moved downward
    but, when I turned myself, you passed the point
    to which all weight from every part is drawn.   111

Now you are standing beneath the hemisphere
    which is opposite the side covered by land,
    where at the central point was sacrificed   114

the Man whose birth and life were free of sin.
    You have both feet upon a little sphere
    whose other side Judecca occupies;   117

---

96. The time is approximately halfway between the canonical hours of Prime and Tierce, i.e., 7:30 A.M. The rapid change from night ("But soon it will be night," 68) to day (96) is the result of the travelers' having passed the earth's center, thus moving into the Southern Hemisphere, which is twelve hours ahead of the Northern.

when it is morning here, there it is evening.
    And he whose hairs were stairs for our descent
    has not changed his position since his fall.   120

When he fell from the heavens on this side,
    all of the land that once was spread out here,
    alarmed by his plunge, took cover beneath the sea   123

and moved to our hemisphere; with equal fear
    the mountain-land, piled up on this side, fled
    and made this cavern here when it rushed upward.   126

Below somewhere there is a space, as far
    from Beelzebub as the limit of his tomb,
    known not by sight but only by the sound   129

of a little stream that makes its way down here
    through the hollow of a rock that it has worn,
    gently winding in gradual descent."   132

My guide and I entered that hidden road
    to make our way back up to the bright world.
    We never thought of resting while we climbed.   135

We climbed, he first and I behind, until,
    through a small round opening ahead of us
    I saw the lovely things the heavens hold,   138

and we came out to see once more the stars.

127–132. Somewhere below the land that rushed upward to form the Mount of Purgatory "there is a space" (127) through which a stream runs, and it is through this space that Virgil and Dante will climb to reach the base of the Mount. The "space" is at the edge of the natural dungeon that constitutes Lucifer's "tomb," and serves as the entrance to the passage from the earth's center to its circumference, created by Lucifer in his fall from Heaven to Hell.

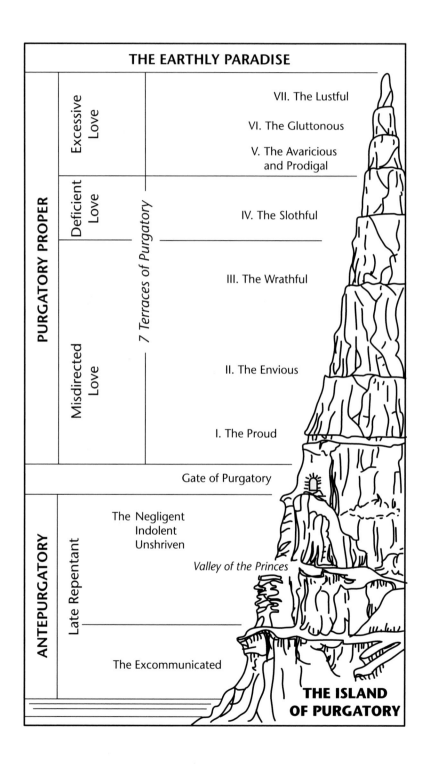

THE EARTHLY PARADISE

PURGATORY PROPER

Excessive Love
- VII. The Lustful
- VI. The Gluttonous
- V. The Avaricious and Prodigal

Deficient Love
- IV. The Slothful

7 Terraces of Purgatory

Misdirected Love
- III. The Wrathful
- II. The Envious
- I. The Proud

Gate of Purgatory

ANTEPURGATORY

Late Repentant

The Negligent
Indolent
Unshriven

Valley of the Princes

The Excommunicated

THE ISLAND OF PURGATORY

Purgatory

Purgatory is depicted by Dante as a mountain that one ascends by circling around, beginning from the plain at its base. The sins represented in *Purgatory* are not different from those we saw in *Inferno.* What distinguishes the punishment of sin in purgatory is that the sinners desire to change their ways and are now engaged in a process of purification and conversion. Once in purgatory there is no turning back; eventually they will be in paradise. However, as we see in Canto II below, those who are in the process of being saved do not necessarily realize how strenuous this process of conversion will be—they prefer to congregate at the foot of the mountain, catching up on the latest news from home and singing songs from the good old days. In order to get them to appreciate the seriousness of what lies ahead for them and to get them to begin to ascend the mountain, Dante employs the Roman statesman and philosopher, Cato, a figure noted for his integrity and no-nonsense ways.

Canto II

As the sun rises, Dante and Virgil are still standing at the water's edge and wondering which road to take in order to ascend the mountain of Purgatory, when the Pilgrim sees a reddish glow moving across the water. The light approaches at an incredible speed, and eventually they are able to discern the wings of an angel. The angel is the miraculous pilot of a ship containing souls of the Redeemed, who are singing the psalm *In exitu Israel de Aegypto.* At a sign from the angel boatsman, these souls disembark, only to roam about on the shore. Apparently, they are strangers, and, mistaking Virgil and Dante for familiars of the place, they ask them which road leads up the mountainside. Virgil answers that they, too, are pilgrims, only recently arrived. At this point some of the souls realize that the Pilgrim is still alive, and they stare at him in fascination. Recognizing a face that he knows in this crowd of souls, Dante tries three times in vain to embrace the shade of his old friend Casella, a musician; then he asks Casella for a song and, as he sings, all the souls are held spellbound. Suddenly the Just Old Man, Cato, appears to disperse the rapt crowd, sternly rebuking them for their negligence and exhorting them to run to the mountain to begin their ascent.

The sun was touching the horizon now,
    the highest point of whose meridian arc
    was just above Jerusalem; and Night,   3

revolving always opposite to him,
    rose from the Ganges with the Scales that fall
    out of her hand when she outweighs the day.   6

Thus, where we were, Aurora's lovely face
    with a vermilion flush on her white cheeks
    was aging in a glow of golden light.   9

1–6. At the time the canto opens, it is midnight at the Ganges, sunset at Jerusalem, noon at the Pillars of Hercules, and dawn at Purgatory.

We were still standing at the water's edge,
    wondering about the road ahead, like men
    whose thoughts go forward while their bodies stay,   12

when, suddenly, I saw, low in the west
    (like the red glow of Mars that burns at dawn
    through the thick haze that hovers on the sea),   15

a light—I hope to see it come again!—
    moving across the waters at a speed
    faster than any earthly flight could be.   18

I turned in wonder to my guide, and then,
    when I looked back at it again, the light
    was larger and more brilliant than before,   21

and there appeared, on both sides of this light,
    a whiteness indefinable, and then,
    another whiteness grew beneath the shape.   24

My guide was silent all the while, but when
    the first two whitenesses turned into wings,
    and he saw who the steersman was, he cried: 27

"Fall to your knees, fall to your knees! Behold
    the angel of the Lord! And fold your hands.
    Expect to see more ministers like him.   30

See how he scorns to use man's instruments;
    he needs no oars, no sails, only his wings
    to navigate between such distant shores.   33

See how he has them pointing up to Heaven:
    he fans the air with these immortal plumes
    that do not moult as mortal feathers do."   36

Closer and closer to our shore he came,
    brighter and brighter shone the bird of God,
    until I could no longer bear the light,   39

and bowed my head. He steered straight to the shore,
    his boat so swift and light upon the wave,
    it left no sign of truly sailing there;   42

---

42. The boat draws no water because the souls of the Saved have no weight.

and the celestial pilot stood astern
   with blessedness inscribed upon his face.
   More than a hundred souls were in his ship: 45

In exitu Israël de Aegypto,
   they all were singing with a single voice,
   chanting it verse by verse until the end.   48

The angel signed them with the holy cross,
   and they rushed from the ship onto the shore;
   he disappeared, swiftly, as he had come.   51

The souls left there seemed strangers to this place:
   they roamed about, while looking all around,
   endeavoring to understand new things.   54

The sun, which with its shafts of light had chased
   the Goat out of the heavens' highest field,
   was shooting rays of day throughout the sky,   57

when those new souls looked up to where we were,
   and called to us: "If you should know the road
   that leads up to the mountainside, show us."   60

And Virgil answered them: "You seem to think
   that we are souls familiar with this place,
   but we, like all of you, are pilgrims here;   63

we just arrived, not much ahead of you,
   but by a road which was so rough and hard
   to climb this mountain now will be like play."   66

Those souls who noticed that my body breathed,
   and realized that I was still alive,
   in their amazement turned a deathly pale.   69

Just as a crowd, greedy for news, surrounds
   the messenger who bears the olive branch,
   and none too shy to elbow-in his way,   72

---

46. "*In exitu Israël de Aegypto*"—"When Israel came out of Egypt" (Psalm 113)—is a song of thanksgiving to God for freeing the nation of Israel from the bondage of Egypt. For Christians the Exodus, or liberation of the Jews, prefigures Christ's Resurrection from the dead. In turn, his death and Resurrection served to free each individual Christian soul from the slavery of sin. Since at this point in the action of the poem it is Easter Sunday morning, the very day of the Resurrection, the singing of this psalm is particularly appropriate, and the connection between the Exodus and Resurrection is thus reinforced.

55–57. At dawn the constellation Capricorn lies on the meridian, ninety degrees from the horizon. Because of the sun's ever-increasing light, Capricorn is now invisible. In other words, the daylight is getting stronger.

so all the happy souls of these Redeemed
    stared at my face, forgetting, as it were,
    the way to go to make their beauty whole.   75

One of these souls pushed forward, arms outstretched,
    and he appeared so eager to embrace me
    that his affection moved me to show mine.   78

O empty shades, whose human forms seem real!
    Three times I clasped my hands around his form,
    as many times they came back to my breast.   81

I must have been the picture of surprise,
    for he was smiling as he drew away,
    and I plunged forward still in search of him.   84

Then, gently, he suggested I not try,
    and by his voice I knew who this shade was;
    I begged him stay and speak to me awhile.   87

"As once I loved you in my mortal flesh,
    without it now I love you still," he said.
    "Of course I'll stay. But tell me why you're here."   90

"I make this journey now, O my Casella,
    hoping one day to come back here again,"
    I said. "But how did you lose so much time?"   93

He answered: "I cannot complain if he
    who, as he pleases, picks his passengers,
    often refused to take me in his boat,   96

for that Just Will is always guiding his.
    But for the last three months, indulgently,
    he has been taking all who wish to cross;   99

so when I went to seek the shore again,
    where Tiber's waters turn to salty sea,
    benignly, he accepted me aboard.   102

Now, back again he flies to Tiber's mouth,
    which is the meeting place of all the dead,
    except for those who sink to Acheron's shore."   105

---

91. Casella, a musician and singer, was a friend of Dante's and very likely set to music Dante's *canzone* "Amor che ne la mente mi ragiona," if not others as well.

101. Ostia, where the Tiber River enters the sea, is the place where souls departing for Purgatory gather to await transport.

"If no new law prevents remembering
    or practicing those love songs that once brought
    peace to my restless longings in the world,"   108

I said, "pray sing, and give a little rest
    to my poor soul which, burdened by my flesh,
    has climbed this far and is exhausted now."   111

Amor che ne la mente mi ragiona.
    began the words of his sweet melody—
    their sweetness still is sounding in my soul.   114

My master and myself and all those souls
    that came with him were deeply lost in joy,
    as if that sound were all that did exist.   117

And while we stood enraptured by the sound
    of those sweet notes—a sudden cry: "What's this,
    you lazy souls?" It was the Just Old Man.   120

"What negligence to stand around like this!
    Run to the mountain, shed that slough which still
    does not let God be manifest to you!"   123

Just as a flock of pigeons in a field
    peacefully feeding on the grain and tares,
    no longer strutting proud of how they look,   126

immediately abandon all their food,
    flying away, seized by a greater need
    if something should occur that startles them—   129

so did that new-formed flock of souls give up
    their feast of song, and seek the mountainside,
    rushing to find a place they hoped was there.   132

And we were just as quick to take to flight.

---

112. *"Amor the ne la mente mi ragiona"* ("Love that speaks to me in my mind") is the first verse of the second *canzone*, which Dante comments on in the third book of his *Convivio*.

Having climbed the mountain of Purgatory, Dante and Virgil must pass through a purifying wall of flame before they can enter the earthly paradise, otherwise known as the Garden of Eden. Dante is fearful, but with Virgil's encouragement he proceeds through the flames. Standing within the Garden, Dante witnesses a heavenly procession leading the way toward Paradise. He desires nothing more than to ascend to the heavenly realm, but suddenly Beatrice appears and reminds him rather sternly that his conversion is not yet complete.

Canto XXVII

The sun is near setting when the poets leave the souls of the Lustful and encounter the angel of Chastity, singing the beatitude "Blessed are the Pure of Heart." The angel tells them that they can go no farther without passing through the flames, but, numbed with fear, the Pilgrim hesitates for a long time. Finally Virgil prevails upon him and they make the crossing through the excruciating heat. As they emerge on the other side, they hear the invitation "Come O ye blessed of my Father," and an angel exhorts them to climb as long as there is still daylight. But soon the sun sets and the poets are overcome by sleep. Toward morning the Pilgrim dreams of Leah and Rachel, who represent the active and contemplative lives, respectively. When he awakes, he is refreshed and eager and races up the remaining steps. In the last few lines Virgil describes the moral development achieved by the Pilgrim—such that he no longer needs his guidance. These are the last words that Virgil will speak in the poem.

It was the hour the sun's first rays shine down
    upon the land where its Creator shed
    his own life's blood, the hour the Ebro flows   3

beneath high Scales, and Ganges' waters boil
    in noonday heat: so day was fading, then,
    when God's angel of joy appeared to us.   6

Upon the bank beyond the fire's reach
    he stood, singing *Beati mundo corde!*
    The living beauty of his voice rang clear.   9

Then: "Holy souls, no farther can you go
    without first suffering fire. So, enter now,
    and be not deaf to what is sung beyond,"   12

he said to us as we came up to him.
    I, when I heard these words, felt like a man
    who is about to be entombed alive.   15

1–6. The hour is six o'clock in the morning at Jerusalem, midnight at Spain (where the Ebro River is located), noon at India (through which the Ganges flows), and six o'clock in the evening at Purgatory.

8. "*Beati mundo corde*" begins the last beatitude (Matthew 5:8), "Blessed are the pure of heart, for they shall see God."

Gripping my hands together, I leaned forward
    and, staring at the fire, I recalled
    what human bodies look like burned to death.   18

Both of my friendly guides turned toward me then,
    and Virgil said to me: "O my dear son,
    there may be pain here, but there is no death.   21

Remember all your memories! If I
    took care of you when we rode Geryon,
    shall I do less when we are nearer God?   24

Believe me when I say that if you spent
    a thousand years within the fire's heart,
    it would not singe a single hair of yours;   27

and if you still cannot believe my words,
    approach the fire and test it for yourself
    on your own robe: just touch it with the hem.   30

It's time, high time, to put away your fears;
    turn towards me, come, and enter without fear!"
    But I stood there, immobile—and ashamed.   33

He said, somewhat annoyed to see me fixed
    and stubborn there, "Now, don't you see, my son:
    only this wall keeps you from Beatrice."   36

As Pyramus, about to die, heard Thisbe
    utter her name, he raised his eyes and saw
    her there, the day mulberries turned blood red—   39

just so, my stubbornness melted away:
    hearing the name which blooms eternally
    within my mind, I turned to my wise guide.   42

He shook his head and smiled, as at a child
    won over by an apple, as he said:
    "Well, then, what are we doing on this side?"   45

"That precious fruit which all men eagerly
    go searching for on many different boughs
    will give, today, peace to your hungry soul."   117

---

115. The fruit, which grows on many different branches, is the ideal happiness that mankind seeks in various ways.

These were the words that Virgil spoke to me,
  and never was a more auspicious gift
  received, or given, with more joyfulness.   120

Growing desire, desire to be up there,
  was rising in me: with every step I took
  I felt my wings were growing for the flight.   123

Once the stairs, swiftly climbed, were all behind
  and we were standing on the topmost step,
  Virgil addressed me, fixing his eyes on mine: 126

You now have seen, my son, the temporal
  and the eternal fire, you've reached the place
  where my discernment now has reached its end.   129

I led you here with skill and intellect;
  from here on, let your pleasure be your guide:
  the narrow ways, the steep, are far below.   132

Behold the sun shining upon your brow,
  behold the tender grass, the flowers, the trees,
  which, here, the earth produces of itself.   135

Until those lovely eyes rejoicing come,
  which, tearful, once urged me to come to you,
  you may sit here, or wander, as you please.   138

Expect no longer words or signs from me.
  Now is your will upright, wholesome and free,
  and not to heed its pleasure would be wrong: 141

I crown and miter you lord of yourself!"

Canto XXX

One hundred singing angels appear in the sky overhead; they fill the air with a rain of flowers. Through the flowers, Beatrice appears. The Pilgrim turns to Virgil to confess his overpowering emotions, only to find that Virgil has disappeared! Beatrice speaks sternly to Dante, calling him by name and reprimanding him for having wasted his God-given talents, wandering from the path that leads to Truth. So hopeless, in fact, was his case, to such depths did he sink, that the journey to see the souls of the Damned in Hell was the only way left of setting him back on the road to salvation.

127–128. The temporal fire is the fire of Purgatory: the purifying punishments of the mountain, including the wall of fire on the Seventh Terrace, which will disappear on the Judgment Day. The eternal fire is the fire of Hell.

When the Septentrion of the First Heaven
   (which never sets nor rises nor has known
   any cloud other than the veil of sin), 3

which showed to everyone his duty there
   (just as our lower constellation guides
   the helmsman on his way to port on earth), 6

stopped short, that group of prophets of the truth
   who were between the griffin and those lights
   turned to the car as to their source of peace; 9

then, one of them, as sent from Heaven, sang
   Veni, sponsa, de Libano, three times,
   and all the other voices followed his. 12

As at the Final Summons all the blest
   will rise out of their graves, ready to raise
   new-bodied voices singing 'Hallelujah!' 15

just so rose up above the heavenly cart
   a hundred spirits *ad vocem tanti senis*,
   eternal heralds, ministers of God, 18

all shouting: *Benedictus qui venis!* then,
   tossing a rain of flowers in the air,
   Manibus, O, date lilia plenis! 21

Sometimes, as day approaches, I have seen
   all of the eastern sky a glow of rose,
   the rest of heaven beautifully clear, 24

---

1. The constellation sometimes called Septentrion is probably the Little Dipper (Ursa Minor), which contains seven stars, including the North Star. Thus the "Septentrion of the First Heaven" (the Empyrean) must be the seven blazing candlesticks that direct the procession.

11. "*Veni, sponsa, de Libano*" ("Come, bride, from Lebanon") is taken from the Song of Solomon (4:8), where the bride is interpreted as the soul wedded to Christ. Here the song has to do with the advent of Beatrice, one of whose allegorical meanings is Sapientia, or the wisdom of God.

17. "*Ad vocem tanti senis*" translates as "At the voice of so great an elder."

19. "*Benedictus qui venis*" ("Blessed are Thou that comest") is a slightly modified version of Matthew 21:9, *Benedictus qui venit* ("Blessed is He who cometh"). Note that while Dante felt free to shift from the third to the second person in quoting this line, he left intact *Benedictus*, with its masculine form. In this way the word, though applied to Beatrice, who is about to appear, retains its original reference to Christ.

21. "O give us lilies with full hands." This quotation from the *Aeneid* (VI, 883) is surely intended as high tribute to Virgil, the Pilgrim's guide, since his words are placed on the same level as verses from the Bible.

the sun's face rising in a misty veil
   of tempering vapors that allow the eye
   to look straight at it for a longer time: 27

even so, within a nebula of flowers
   that flowed upward from angels' hands and then
   poured down, covering all the chariot,   30

appeared a lady—over her white veil
   an olive crown and, under her green cloak,
   her gown, the color of eternal flame.   33

And instantly—though many years had passed
   since last I stood trembling before her eyes,
   captured by adoration, stunned by awe—   36

my soul, that could not see her perfectly,
   still felt, succumbing to her mystery
   and power, the strength of its enduring love.   39

No sooner were my eyes struck by the force
   of the high, piercing virtue I had known
   before I quit my boyhood years, than I   42

turned to the left—with all the confidence
   that makes a child run to its mother's arms,
   when he is frightened or needs comforting—   45

to say to Virgil: "Not one drop of blood
   is left inside my veins that does not throb:
   I recognize signs of the ancient flame."   48

But Virgil was not there. We found ourselves
   without Virgil, sweet father, Virgil to whom
   for my salvation I gave up my soul.   51

All the delights around me, which were lost
   by our first mother, could not keep my cheeks,
   once washed with dew, from being stained with tears.   54

"Dante, though Virgil leaves you, do not weep,
   not yet, that is, for you shall have to weep
   from yet another wound. Do not weep yet."   57

31–33. The lady is Beatrice, and the colors she wears are those of the three theological virtues: Faith, Hope, and Charity.

55. This is the first time that the Pilgrim hears his own name during his journey.

Just as an admiral, from bow or stern,
    watches his men at work on other ships,
    encouraging their earnest labors—so,   60

rising above the chariot's left rail
    (when I turned round, hearing my name called out,
    which of necessity I here record),   63

I saw the lady who had first appeared
    beneath the angelic festival of flowers
    gazing upon me from beyond the stream.   66

Although the veil that flowed down from her head,
    fixed by the crown made of Minerva's leaves,
    still kept me from a perfect view of her,   69

I sensed the regal sternness of her face,
    as she continued in the tone of one
    who saves the sharpest words until the end: 72

"Yes, look at me! Yes, I am Beatrice!
    So, you at last have deigned to climb the mount?
    You learned at last that here lies human bliss?"   78

I lowered my head and looked down at the stream,
    but, filled with shame at my reflection there,
    I quickly fixed my eyes upon the grass.   78

I was the guilty child facing his mother,
    abject before her harshness: harsh, indeed,
    is unripe pity not yet merciful.   81

As she stopped speaking, all the angels rushed
    into the psalm *In te, Domine, speravi,*
    but did not sing beyond *pedes meos.*   84

As snow upon the spine of Italy,
    frozen among the living rafters there,
    blown and packed hard by wintry northeast winds,   87

will then dissolve, dripping into itself,
    when, from the land that knows no noonday shade,
    there comes a wind like flame melting down wax;   90

83–84. The angels are singing the first part of the thirty-first psalm, which begins, "In Thee, O lord, have I put my trust." They continue through line 8 (*pedes meos*), "Thou hast set my feet in a spacious place"—which is precisely the place where the Pilgrim is standing at this moment.

89. The land is equatorial Africa, where the sun is often directly overhead, sending its rays straight down so that objects cast no shadow.

so tears and sighs were frozen hard in me,
  until I heard the song of those attuned
  forever to the music of the spheres;   93

but when I, sensed in their sweet notes the pity
  they felt for me (it was as if they said:
  "Lady, why do you shame him so?"), the bonds   96

of ice packed tight around my heart dissolved,
  becoming breath and water: from my breast,
  through mouth and eyes, anguish came pouring forth.   99

Still on the same side of the chariot
  she stood immobile; then she turned her words
  to that compassionate array of beings: 102

"With your eyes fixed on the eternal day,
  darkness of night or sleep cannot conceal
  from you a single act performed on earth;   105

and though I speak to you, my purpose is
  to make the one who weeps on that far bank
  perceive the truth and match his guilt with grief.   108

Not only through the working of the spheres,
  which brings each seed to its appropriate end
  according as the stars keep company,   111

but also through the bounty of God's grace,
  raining from vapors born so high above
  they cannot be discerned by human sight,   114

was this man so endowed, potentially,
  in early youth—had he allowed his gifts
  to bloom, he would have reaped abundantly.   117

But the more vigorous and rich the soil,
  the wilder and the weedier it grows
  when left untilled, its bad seeds flourishing.   120

There was a time my countenance sufficed,
  as I let him look into my young eyes
  for guidance on the straight path to his goal;   123

but when I passed into my second age
  and changed my life for Life, that man you see
  strayed after others and abandoned me;   126

when I had risen from the flesh to spirit,
    become more beautiful, more virtuous,
    he found less pleasure in me, loved me less,   129

and wandered from the path that leads to truth,
    pursuing simulacra of the good,
    which promise more than they can ever give.   132

I prayed that inspiration come to him
    through dreams and other means: in vain I tried
    to call him back, so little did he care.   135

To such depths did he sink that, finally,
    there was no other way to save his soul
    except to have him see the Damned in Hell.   138

That this might be, I visited the Dead,
    and offered my petition and my tears
    to him who until now has been his guide.   141

The highest laws of God would be annulled
    if he crossed Lethe, drinking its sweet flow,
    without having to pay at least some scot   144

of penitence poured forth in guilty tears."

Paradise

Having led Dante into Paradise, the guidance of Beatrice eventually yields to that of St. Bernard of Clairvaux (1090–1153). Bernard was one of the great monastic reformers of the Middle Ages, a driving force in the development and spread of the Cistercian order of monks. He was also a renowned theologian and a mystic. His appearance as the one who will lead Dante to his final vision of heaven is entirely appropriate. For Dante, Bernard would have represented an ideal of what leadership within the church is meant to be— leadership that he found so frequently lacking in the church authorities of his own time. Bernard combined spiritual depth, an impressive intellect, and great ability as an organizer. The combination of these qualities would have placed him high in Dante's esteem. *The Divine Comedy* concludes with Dante caught up within the celestial Rose, at one with those saints who line its interior, overcome with the love of God.

Canto XXXII

Rapt in love's Bliss, that contemplative soul
    generously assumed the role of guide
    as he began to speak these holy words: 3

"The wound which Mary was to close and heal
    she there, who sits so lovely at her feet,
    would open wider then and prick the flesh.   6

And sitting there directly under her
    among the thrones of the third tier is Rachel,
    and, there, see Beatrice by her side.   9

Sarah, Rebecca, Judith, and then she,
    who was the great-grandmother of the singer
    who cried for his sin: '*Miserere mei,*'   12

you see them all as I go down from tier
    to tier and name them in their order,
    petal by petal, downward through the Rose.   15

4–6. When Mary gave birth to Christ she provided the means of healing the wound of original sin. She "who sits so lovely at her feet" (5) is Eve, who disobeyed God and surrendered to the serpent.

10. Sarah was Abraham's wife and the mother of Isaac. Rebecca was the daughter of Bethuel and the sister of Laban. She was married to Isaac and bore Esau and Jacob. Judith was the daughter of Meraris. She murdered Holofernes (Nebuchadnezzar's general) while he slept and thus saved Bethulia, which was under siege by the Assyrians. After the Assyrians fled the city Judith was celebrated by the Jews as their deliverer.

11–12. Ruth was the wife of Boaz and great-grandmother of David (the "singer"), author of the psalm of penitence, the *Miserere mei* ("have mercy on me," Psalm 51).

Down from the seventh row, as up to it,
    was a descending line of Hebrew women
    that parted all the petals of the Rose;   18

according to the ways in which the faith
    viewed Christ, these women constitute the wall
    dividing these ranks down the sacred stairs.   21

On this side where the flower is full bloomed
    to its last petal, sit the souls of those
    who placed their faith upon Christ yet to come;   24

on that side where all of the semi-circles
    are broken by the empty seats, sit those
    who turned their face to Christ already come.   27

And just as on this side the glorious throne
    of Heaven's lady with the other seats
    below it form this great dividing wall,   30

so, facing her, the throne of the great John
    who, ever holy, suffered through the desert,
    and martyrdom, then Hell for two more years,   33

and under him, chosen to mark the line,
    Francis, Benedict, Augustine and others
    descend from round to round as far as here.   36

Now marvel at the greatness of God's plan:
    this garden shall be full in equal number
    of this and that aspect of the one faith.   39

And know that downward from the center row
    which cuts the two dividing walls midway,
    no soul through his own merit earned his seat,   42

but through another's, under fixed conditions,
    for all these spirits were absolved of sin
    before they reached the age to make free choice.   45

You need only to look upon their faces
    and listen to the young sound of their voices
    to see and hear this clearly for yourself.   48

But you have doubts, doubts you do not reveal,
    so now I will untie the tangled knot
    in which your searching thoughts have bound you tight. 51

Within the vastness of this great domain
   no particle of chance can find a place
   no more than sorrow, thirst, or hunger can—   54

for all that you see here has been ordained
   by the eternal law with such precision
   that ring and finger are a perfect fit.   57

And, therefore, all these souls of hurried comers
   to the true life are not ranked *sine causa*
   some high, some low, according to their merit.   60

The King, through whom this kingdom is at rest
   in so much love and in so much delight
   that no will dares to wish for any more,   63

creating all minds in His own mind's bliss,
   endows each with as much grace as He wishes,
   at His own pleasure—let this fact suffice.   66

And Holy Scriptures set this down for you
   clear and expressly, speaking of those twins
   whose anger flared while in their mother's womb;   69

so, it is fitting that God's lofty light
   crown them with grace, as much as each one merits,
   according to the color of their hair.   72

Thus, through no merit of their own good works
   are they ranked differently; the difference is
   only in God's gift of original grace.   75

During mankind's first centuries on earth
   for innocent children to achieve salvation,
   only the faith of parents was required;   78

but then, when man's first age came to an end,
   all males had to be circumcised to give
   innocent wings the strength to fly to Heaven;   81

but when the age of grace came down to man,
   then, without perfect baptism in Christ,
   such innocence to Limbo was confined.   84

---

59. *Sine causa* is a Latin legal expression meaning "without cause."

68–69. Jacob and Esau were the twin sons of Rebecca and Isaac (see Genesis 25:21–34). St. Bernard mentions them as an example of the mystery of Divine Grace.

79. Man's "first age" is from the time of Abraham until the birth of Christ.

Now look at that face which resembles Christ
    the most, for only in its radiance
    will you be made ready to look at Christ."   87

I saw such bliss rain down upon her face,
    bestowed on it by all those sacred minds
    created to fly through those holy heights,   90

that of all things I witnessed to this point
    nothing had held me more spellbound than this,
    nor shown a greater likeness unto God;   93

and that love which had once before descended
    now sang, *Ave, Maria, gratïa plena,*
    before her presence there with wings spread wide.   96

Response came to this holy prayer of praise
    from all directions of the Court of Bliss
    and every face grew brighter with that joy.   99

"O holy father, who for my sake deigns
    to stand down here, so far from the sweet throne
    destined for you throughout eternity,   102

who is that angel who so joyously
    looks straight into the eyes of Heaven's Queen,
    so much in love he seems to burn like fire?"   105

Thus, I turned for instruction once again
    to that one who in Mary's beauty glowed
    as does the morning star in fresh sunlight.   108

And he: "All loving pride and gracious joy,
    as much as soul or angel can possess,
    is all in him, and we would have it so,   111

for he it is who bore the palm below
    to Mary when the Son of God had willed
    to bear the weight of man's flesh on Himself.   114

Now let your eyes follow my words as I
    explain to you, and note the great patricians
    of this most just and pious of all realms.   117

---

108. Reference to the morning star, Venus, is made in the litany to the Blessed Virgin.

Those two who sit most blest in their high thrones
　　because they are the closest to the Empress
　　are, as it were, the two roots of our Rose:　　　　　　　　　120

he, sitting on her left side, is that father,
　　the one through whose presumptuous appetite
　　mankind still tastes the bitterness of shame;　　　　　　　123

and on her right, you see the venerable
　　Father of Holy Church to whom Christ gave
　　the keys to this beautiful Rose of joy.　　　　　　　　　126

And he who prophesied before he died
　　the sad days destined for the lovely Bride
　　whom Christ won for himself with lance and nails　　　129

sits at his side. Beside the other sits
　　the leader of those nurtured on God's manna,
　　who were a fickle, ingrate, stubborn lot.　　　　　　　132

Across from Peter, see there, Anna sits,
　　so happy to be looking at her daughter,
　　she does not move an eye singing Hosanna;　　　　　　135

facing the head of mankind's family
　　sits Lucy, who first sent your lady to you
　　when you were bent, headlong, on your own ruin.　　　138

But since the time left for your journey's vision
　　grows short, let us stop here—like the good tailor
　　who cuts the gown according to his cloth,　　　　　　141

and turn our eyes upon the Primal Love
　　so that, looking toward Him, you penetrate
　　His radiance as deep as possible.　　　　　　　　　　144

But lest you fall backwards beating your wings,
　　believing to ascend on your own power,
　　we must offer a prayer requesting grace,　　　　　　　147

---

120. Adam is one root of the Rose because from him sprung those who believed in Christ to come; St. Peter is the other because from him sprung those who believed in Christ who had already come.

127–130. St. John the Evangelist, author of the *Apocalypse,* foretold the adversity that would befall the Church. (Cf. *Purgatory* XXIX, 143–144.) The "lance and nails" (129) refers to the Crucifixion.

130. The "other" is Adam.

grace from the one who has power to help you.
    Now, follow me, with all of your devotion,
    and do not let your heart stray from my words."   150

And he began to say this holy prayer:

Canto XXXIII

"Oh Virgin Mother, daughter of your son,
    most humble, most exalted of all creatures
    chosen of God in His eternal plan,   3

you are the one who ennobled human nature
    to the extent that He did not disdain,
    Who was its Maker, to make Himself man.   6

Within your womb rekindled was the love
    that gave the warmth that did allow this flower
    to come to bloom within this timeless peace.   9

For all up here you are the noonday torch
    of charity, and down on earth, for men,
    the living spring of their eternal hope.   12

Lady, you are so great, so powerful,
    that who seeks grace without recourse to you
    would have his wish fly upward without wings.   15

Not only does your loving kindness rush
    to those who ask for it, but often times
    it flows spontaneously before the plea.   18

In you is tenderness, in you is pity,
    in you munificence—in you unites
    all that is good in God's created beings.   21

This is a man who from the deepest pit
    of all the universe up to this height
    has witnessed, one by one, the lives of souls,   24

who begs you that you grant him through your grace
    the power to raise his vision higher still
    to penetrate the final blessedness.   27

And I who never burned for my own vision
    more than I burn for his, with all my prayers
    I pray you—and I pray they are enough—   30

that you through your own prayers dispel the mist
    of his mortality, that he may have
    the Sum of Joy revealed before his eyes.   33

I pray you also, Queen who can achieve
    your every wish, keep his affections sound
    once he has had the vision and returns.   36

Protect him from the stirrings of the flesh:
    you see, with Beatrice, all the Blest,
    hands clasped in prayer, are praying for my prayer."   39

Those eyes so loved and reverenced by God,
    now fixed on him who prayed, made clear to us
    how precious true devotion is to her;   42

then she looked into the Eternal Light,
    into whose being, we must believe, no eyes
    of other creatures pierce with such insight.   45

And I who was approaching now the end
    of all man's yearning, strained with all the force
    in me to raise my burning longing high.   48

Bernard then gestured to me with a smile
    that I look up, but I already was
    instinctively what he would have me be: 51

for now my vision as it grew more clear
    was penetrating more and more the Ray
    of that exalted Light of Truth Itself.   54

And from then on my vision rose to heights
    higher than words, which fail before such sight,
    and memory fails, too, at such extremes.   57

As he who sees things in a dream and wakes to
    feel the passion of the dream still there
    although no part of it remains in mind,   60

just such am I: my vision fades and all
    but ceases, yet the sweetness born of it
    I still can feel distilling in my heart: 63

so imprints on the snow fade in the sun,
    and thus the Sibyl's oracle of leaves
    was swept away and lost into the wind.   66

O Light Supreme, so far beyond the reach
    of mortal understanding, to my mind
    relend now some small part of Your own Self,   69

and give to my tongue eloquence enough
    to capture just one spark of all Your glory
    that I may leave for future generations;   72

for, by returning briefly to my mind
    and sounding, even faintly, in my verse,
    more of Your might will be revealed to men.   75

If I had turned my eyes away, I think,
    from the sharp brilliance of the living Ray
    which they endured, I would have lost my senses.   78

And this, as I recall, gave me more strength
    to keep on gazing till I could unite
    my vision with the Infinite Worth I saw.   81

O grace abounding and allowing me to dare
    to fix my gaze on the Eternal Light,
    so deep my vision was consumed in It!   84

I saw how it contains within its depths
    all things bound in a single book by love
    of which creation is the scattered leaves: 87

how substance, accident, and their relation
    were fused in such a way that what I now
    describe is but a glimmer of that Light.   90

I know I saw the universal form,
    the fusion of all things, for I can feel,
    while speaking now, my heart leap up in joy.   93

One instant brings me more forgetfulness
    than five and twenty centuries brought the quest
    that stunned Neptune when he saw Argo's keel.   96

91–93. The conjoining of substance and accident in God and the union of the temporal and the eternal is what Dante saw at that moment.

And so my mind was totally entranced
   in gazing deeply, motionless, intent;
     the more it saw the more it burned to see.   99

And one is so transformed within that Light
   that it would be impossible to think
     of ever turning one's eyes from that sight,   102

because the good which is the goal of will
   is all collected there, and outside it
     all is defective that is perfect there.   105

Now, even in the things I do recall
   my words have no more strength than does a babe
     wetting its tongue, still at its mother's breast.   108

Not that within the Living Light there was
   more than a sole aspect of the Divine
     which always is what It has always been,   111

yet as I learned to see more, and the power
   of vision grew in me, that single aspect
     as I changed, seemed to me to change Itself.   114

Within Its depthless clarity of substance
   I saw the Great Light shine into three circles
     in three clear colors bound in one same space;   117

the first seemed to reflect the next like rainbow on rainbow,
   and the third was like a flame
     equally breathed forth by the other two.   120

How my weak words fall short of my conception,
   which is itself so far from what I saw
     that "weak" is much too weak a word to use!   123

O Light Eternal fixed in Self alone,
   known only to Yourself, and knowing Self,
     You love and glow, knowing and being known!   126

That circling which, as I conceived it, shone
   in You as Your own first reflected light
     when I had looked deep into It a while,   129

seemed in Itself and in Its own Self-color
   to be depicted with man's very image.
     My eyes were totally absorbed in It.   132

As the geometer who tries so hard
   to square the circle, but cannot discover,
   think as he may, the principle involved,   135

so did I strive with this new mystery:
   I yearned to know how could our image fit
   into that circle, how could it conform;   138

but my own wings could not take me so high—
   then a great flash of understanding struck
   my mind, and suddenly its wish was granted.   141

At this point power failed high fantasy
   but, like a wheel in perfect balance turning,
   I felt my will and my desire impelled   144

by the Love that moves the sun and the other stars.

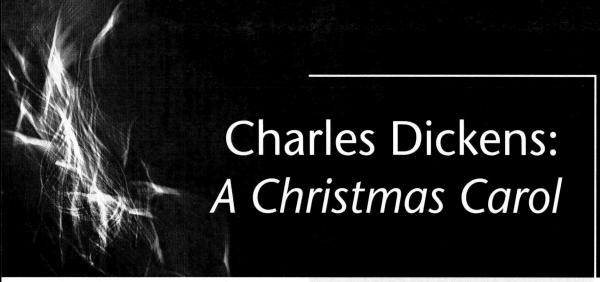

Charles Dickens: *A Christmas Carol*

Editors' Introduction

"A squeezing, wrenching, grasping, scraping, clutching, covetous old sinner" is how Dickens describes Ebenezer Scrooge, the most famous miser in western literature. *A Christmas Carol* tells the tale of Scrooge's transformation from a solitary misanthrope to a paradigm of what it means to embody the spirit of Christmas. The story is without question Dickens's most well-known work, not only in its written form, but in its many adaptions for theater and film.

Financial concerns were certainly on Dickens's mind when in 1843 he set out to write *A Christmas Carol.* Although he was already a famous and popular author, he was at the time a married man with an immediate and an extended family in need of support. In addition, his previous novel, *Martin Chuzzlewit,* had not been selling very well, and his publishers threatened to reduce his share of the proceeds of his future work. But Dickens's reasons for writing *A Christmas Carol* were not solely financial; he was also motivated by a sense of responsibility to address some of the pressing social issues of his day. These motivations can be explained to a significant degree by the shape of his life up to this point.

Born in 1812 in the English city of Portsmouth, Dickens moved to London with his family in 1815. London was the city in which he would spend most of his life, the city whose character and whose characters he would so vividly convey to his readers. His father John was a naval clerk, an amiable, irresponsible spendthrift whose free spending ways would eventually land him in debtors' prison in 1824. The Dickens family was forced to sell many of their prized possessions, including young Charles's beloved collection of books. But things would get worse. During this period families would sometimes move into the prison to be near their imprisoned relative, so with the exception of twelve-year-old Charles the rest of his family moved into the Marshalsea Prison to be with John Dickens. In the meantime, Charles was sent to work in Warren's Blacking Warehouse, a shoe polish factory that was dark, dingy, and rat-infested. He was seated next to a window that looked out onto the street, where passersby could look at him as he pasted labels on bottles of shoe polish. For a sensitive, intellectually precocious child who already viewed himself as belonging to a different class of people than those with whom he worked, this was a deeply humiliating and traumatic experience. Having been yanked out of school, here he was consigned to do mindless work, and the thought that this might be his fate for the rest of his life made him despair. When John Dickens inherited some money a few months later, he was released from prison, but John and his wife Elizabeth decided that Charles would continue to work in the factory, a decision that wounded him deeply. After a relatively short time, his father, seeing how damaging this experience was to Charles, insisted (against his wife's objections, who wanted Charles to remain at work) that his son leave the factory and resume his studies.

Dickens almost never spoke about this experience later in life—the thought of it filled him with a mixture of anger, fear, and shame. The experience left him with an abiding fear of poverty, which showed itself in his preoccupation with money and financial security. It also made him acutely sensitive to the ways in which the social, economic, and political system could oppress and destroy people. He would remain attuned to social problems and speak out against them for the rest of his life. Dickens died in 1870.

Debt, poverty, heartlessness, cold, dark, the lack of generosity, the withholding of love, fear, and a feeling of isolation—these experiences from Dickens's early life would make their appearance in *A Christmas Carol*. However, these evils do not have the final word in the story. Scrooge changes; he is able to confront his past, and under the guidance of the three spirits of Christmas, he becomes a kind and generous benefactor to all those with whom he comes in contact. Dickens would refer to the ideas reflected in the story as his "Carol philosophy," and while he gave expression to this philosophy throughout the tale, the words of Scrooge's nephew Fred sum it up well:

> "But I am sure I have always thought of Christmas time . . . as a good time; a kind, forgiving, charitable, pleasant time: the only time I know of, in the long calendar of the year, when men and women seem by one consent to open their shut-up hearts freely, and to think of people below them as if they really were fellow-passengers to the grave, and not another race of creatures bound on other journeys."

With regard to the social, economic, and political implications of this "Carol philosophy," it should be noted that while Dickens was a social reformer, he was no revolutionary. He saw his role as moving people to change by moving them by his words. Both in his fiction and in his many speeches and articles, he addressed issues of poverty, education, and institutional reform. Throughout his life he gave public readings from his works, and *A Christmas Carol* was one of the works he read most frequently, in an attempt to bring about in his listeners a greater sense of charity and solidarity with the unfortunate.

Although it is probably going too far to claim that Dickens was alone responsible for the way in which we understand and celebrate Christmas today—getting together with family and friends, sharing food and drink around a table with those we love, giving gifts, being friendly and charitable to strangers—Dickens certainly did much to foster this conception of the feast. This way of understanding Christmas has occasionally led some readers to the conclusion that Dickens contributed to the secularization of the holiday. Such a conclusion, however, is hard to sustain once we have a sense of the role religion played in Dickens's life. As an infant, he had been baptized into the Anglican Church, and apart from a three or four year period during which he was attracted to Unitarianism (mainly because he admired the minister), he remained at least nominally a member of the Church of England. He was an irregular churchgoer, but from what we know he seems to have accepted the fundamental doctrines of Christianity, and he was known to have prayed daily in the morning and the evening. More specifically, he was quite clear that the teaching of the New Testament was very important to him, both personally and as an essential part of his writing. When his youngest son was about to depart to work in Australia, Dickens had this to say among his parting words: "[The New Testament is] the best book that ever was or will be known in the world . . . I now most solemnly impress upon you the truth and beauty of the Christian religion as it came from Christ himself . . ." With reference to the influence of the New Testament on his work, he wrote that "one of my most constant and most earnest endeavors has been to exhibit in all my good people some faint reflections of the teachings of our great Master . . . All my strongest illustrations are derived from the New Testament; all my social abuses are shown as departures from its spirit." He further insisted that in his Christmas

Books (of which *A Christmas Carol* is the first) "there is an express text preached on, and that text is always taken from the lips of Christ."

Throughout his fiction Dickens can be scathing in his depictions of those he judges to be religious hypocrites, but this should not blind us to the ways in which a deep appreciation for the spirit of the New Testament animates his work. Dickens can at times be overly sentimental, but as far as his religious vision is concerned he is rarely heavy-handed or preachy. He prefers to allow his understanding of religion to emerge from the interactions among his characters. Because these characters are often so colorful and vivid, there can be a tendency to miss the psychological subtlety Dickens brings to his creations. This observation can be applied to his work as a whole and to *A Christmas Carol* in particular. In some ways, this story has become a victim of its own popularity, readily dismissed as "uplifting" or obvious. Scrooge's conversion is viewed by some as unconvincing and superficial. Readers will form their own judgments on these questions, but when read carefully, *A Christmas Carol* reveals Dickens as a writer who is not only entertaining, but profound, sensitive, and capable of deep insight into the human condition.

A Christmas Carol

STAVE 1: MARLEY'S GHOST

Marley was dead: to begin with. There is no doubt whatever about that. The register of his burial was signed by the clergyman, the clerk, the undertaker, and the chief mourner. Scrooge signed it. And Scrooge's name was good upon 'Change, for anything he chose to put his hand to.

Old Marley was as dead as a door-nail.

Mind! I don't mean to say that I know, of my own knowledge, what there is particularly dead about a door-nail. I might have been inclined, myself, to regard a coffin-nail as the deadest piece of ironmongery in the trade. But the wisdom of our ancestors is in the simile; and my unhallowed hands shall not disturb it, or the Country's done for. You will therefore permit me to repeat, emphatically, that Marley was as dead as a door-nail.

Scrooge knew he was dead? Of course he did. How could it be otherwise? Scrooge and he were partners for I don't know how many years. Scrooge was his sole executor, his sole administrator, his sole assign, his sole residuary legatee, his sole friend, and sole mourner. And even Scrooge was not so dreadfully cut up by the sad event, but that he was an excellent man of business on the very day of the funeral, and solemnised it with an undoubted bargain. The mention of Marley's funeral brings me back to the point I started from. There is no doubt that Marley was dead. This must be distinctly understood, or nothing wonderful can come of the story I am going to relate. If we were not perfectly convinced that Hamlet's Father died before the play began, there would be nothing more remarkable in his taking a stroll at night, in an easterly wind, upon his own ramparts, than there would be in any other middle-aged gentleman rashly turning out after dark in a breezy spot—say Saint Paul's Churchyard for instance—literally to astonish his son's weak mind.

Scrooge never painted out Old Marley's name. There it stood, years afterwards, above the warehouse door: Scrooge and Marley. The firm was known as Scrooge and Marley. Sometimes people new to the business called Scrooge Scrooge, and sometimes Marley, but he answered to both names. It was all the same to him.

Oh! But he was a tight-fisted hand at the grindstone, Scrooge! a squeezing, wrenching, grasping, scraping, clutching, covetous, old sinner! Hard and sharp as flint, from which no steel had ever struck out generous fire; secret, and self-contained, and solitary as an oyster. The cold within him froze his old features, nipped his pointed nose, shrivelled his cheek, stiffened his gait; made his eyes red, his thin lips blue; and spoke out shrewdly in his grating voice. A frosty rime was on his head, and on his eyebrows, and his wiry chin. He carried his own low temperature always about with him; he iced his office in the dogdays; and didn't thaw it one degree at Christmas.

External heat and cold had little influence on Scrooge. No warmth could warm, no wintry weather chill him. No wind that blew was bitterer than he, no falling snow was more intent upon its purpose, no pelting rain less open to entreaty. Foul weather didn't know where to have him. The heaviest rain, and snow, and hail, and sleet, could boast of the advantage over him in only one respect. They often 'came down' handsomely, and Scrooge never did.

Nobody ever stopped him in the street to say, with gladsome looks, 'My dear Scrooge, how are you? When will you come to see me?' No beggars implored him to bestow a trifle, no children asked him what it was o'clock, no man or woman ever once in all his life inquired the way to such and such a place, of Scrooge. Even the blind men's dogs appeared to know him; and when they saw him coming on, would tug their owners into doorways and up courts; and then would wag their tails as though they said, 'No eye at all is better than an evil eye, dark master!'

But what did Scrooge care! It was the very thing he liked. To edge his way along the crowded paths of life, warning all human sympathy to keep its distance, was what the knowing ones call 'nuts' to Scrooge.

Once upon a time—of all the good days in the year, on Christmas Eve—old Scrooge sat busy in his counting-house. It was cold, bleak, biting weather: foggy withal: and he could hear the people in the court outside, go wheezing up and down, beating their hands upon their breasts, and stamping their feet upon the pavement stones to warm them. The city clocks had only just gone three, but it was quite dark already—it had not been light all day—and candles were flaring in the windows of the neighbouring offices, like ruddy smears upon the palpable brown air. The fog came pouring in at every chink and keyhole, and was so dense without, that although the court was of the narrowest, the houses opposite were mere phantoms. To see the dingy cloud come drooping down, obscuring everything, one might have thought that Nature lived hard by, and was brewing on a large scale.

The door of Scrooge's counting-house was open that he might keep his eye upon his clerk, who in a dismal little cell beyond, a sort of tank, was copying letters. Scrooge had a very small fire, but the clerk's fire was so very much smaller that it looked like one coal. But he couldn't replenish it, for Scrooge kept the coal-box in his own room; and so surely as the clerk came in with the shovel, the master predicted that it would be necessary for them to part. Wherefore the clerk put on his white comforter, and tried to warm himself at the candle; in which effort, not being a man of a strong imagination, he failed.

'A merry Christmas, uncle! God save you!' cried a cheerful voice. It was the voice of Scrooge's nephew, who came upon him so quickly that this was the first intimation he had of his approach.

'Bah!' said Scrooge, 'Humbug!'

He had so heated himself with rapid walking in the fog and frost, this nephew of Scrooge's, that he was all in a glow; his face was ruddy and handsome; his eyes sparkled, and his breath smoked again. 'Christmas a humbug, uncle!' said Scrooge's nephew. 'You don't mean that, I am sure?'

'I do,' said Scrooge. 'Merry Christmas! What right have you to be merry? What reason have you to be merry? You're poor enough.'

'Come, then,' returned the nephew gaily. 'What right have you to be dismal? What reason have you to be morose? You're rich enough.'

Scrooge having no better answer ready on the spur of the moment, said 'Bah!' again; and followed it up with 'Humbug.'

'Don't be cross, uncle!' said the nephew.

'What else can I be,' returned the uncle, 'when I live in such a world of fools as this? Merry Christmas! Out upon merry Christmas! What's Christmas time to you but a time for paying bills without money; a time for finding yourself a year older, but not an hour richer; a time for balancing your books and having every item in 'em through a round dozen of months presented dead against you? If I could work my will,' said Scrooge indignantly, 'every idiot who goes about with "Merry Christmas" on his lips, should be boiled with his own pudding, and buried with a stake of holly through his heart. He should!'

'Uncle!' pleaded the nephew.

'Nephew!' returned the uncle sternly, 'keep Christmas in your own way, and let me keep it in mine.'

'Keep it!' repeated Scrooge's nephew. 'But you don't keep it.'

'Let me leave it alone, then,' said Scrooge. 'Much good may it do you! Much good it has ever done you!'

'There are many things from which I might have derived good, by which I have not profited, I dare say,' returned the nephew. 'Christmas among the rest. But I am sure I have always thought of Christmas time, when it has come round—apart from the veneration due to its sacred name and origin, if anything belonging to it can be apart from that—as a good time; a kind, forgiving, charitable, pleasant time: the only time I know of, in the long calendar of the year, when men and women seem by one consent to open their shut-up hearts freely, and to think of people below them as if they really were fellow-passengers to the grave, and not another race of creatures bound on other journeys. And therefore, uncle, though it has never put a scrap of gold or silver in my pocket, I believe that it has done me good, and will do me good; and I say, God bless it!'

The clerk in the tank involuntarily applauded. Becoming immediately sensible of the impropriety, he poked the fire, and extinguished the last frail spark for ever.

'Let me hear another sound from you,' said Scrooge, 'and you'll keep your Christmas by losing your situation! You're quite a powerful speaker, sir,' he added, turning to his nephew. 'I wonder you don't go into Parliament.'

'Don't be angry, uncle. Come! Dine with us tomorrow.'

Scrooge said that he would see him—yes, indeed he did. He went the whole length of the expression, and said that he would see him in that extremity first.

'But why?' cried Scrooge's nephew. 'Why?'

'Why did you get married?' said Scrooge.

'Because I fell in love.'

'Because you fell in love!' growled Scrooge, as if that were the only one thing in the world more ridiculous than a merry Christmas. 'Good afternoon!'

'Nay, uncle, but you never came to see me before that happened. Why give it as a reason for not coming now?'

'Good afternoon,' said Scrooge.

'I want nothing from you; I ask nothing of you; why cannot we be friends?'

'Good afternoon,' said Scrooge.

'I am sorry, with all my heart, to find you so resolute. We have never had any quarrel, to which I have been a party. But I have made the trial in homage to Christmas, and I'll keep my Christmas humour to the last. So A Merry Christmas, uncle!'

'Good afternoon,' said Scrooge.

'And A Happy New Year!'

'Good afternoon,' said Scrooge.

His nephew left the room without an angry word, notwithstanding. He stopped at the outer door to bestow the greetings of the season on the clerk, who cold as he was, was warmer than Scrooge; for he returned them cordially.

'There's another fellow,' muttered Scrooge; who overheard him: 'my clerk, with fifteen shillings a week, and a wife and family, talking about a merry Christmas. I'll retire to Bedlam.'

This lunatic, in letting Scrooge's nephew out, had let two other people in. They were portly gentlemen, pleasant to behold, and now stood, with their hats off, in Scrooge's office. They had books and papers in their hands, and bowed to him.

'Scrooge and Marley's, I believe,' said one of the gentlemen, referring to his list. 'Have I the pleasure of addressing Mr. Scrooge, or Mr. Marley?'

'Mr. Marley has been dead these seven years,' Scrooge replied. 'He died seven years ago, this very night.'

'We have no doubt his liberality is well represented by his surviving partner,' said the gentleman, presenting his credentials.

It certainly was; for they had been two kindred spirits. At the ominous word 'liberality,' Scrooge frowned, and shook his head, and handed the credentials back.

'At this festive season of the year, Mr. Scrooge,' said the gentleman, taking up a pen, 'it is more than usually desirable that we should make some slight provision for the Poor and Destitute, who suffer greatly at the present time. Many thousands are in want of common necessaries; hundreds of thousands are in want of common comforts, sir.'

'Are there no prisons?' asked Scrooge.

'Plenty of prisons,' said the gentleman, laying down the pen again.

'And the Union workhouses?' demanded Scrooge. 'Are they still in operation?'

'They are. Still,' returned the gentleman, 'I wish I could say they were not.'

'The Treadmill and the Poor Law are in full vigour, then?' said Scrooge.

'Both very busy, sir.'

'Oh! I was afraid, from what you said at first, that something had occurred to stop them in their useful course,' said Scrooge. 'I'm very glad to hear it.'

'Under the impression that they scarcely furnish Christian cheer of mind or body to the multitude,' returned the gentleman, 'a few of us are endeavouring to raise a fund to buy the Poor some meat and drink and means of warmth. We choose this time, because it is a time, of all others, when Want is keenly felt, and Abundance rejoices. What shall I put you down for?'

'Nothing!' Scrooge replied.

'You wish to be anonymous?'

'I wish to be left alone,' said Scrooge. 'Since you ask me what I wish, gentlemen, that is my answer. I don't make merry myself at Christmas and I can't afford to make idle people merry. I help to support the establishments I have mentioned—they cost enough; and those who are badly off must go there.'

'Many can't go there; and many would rather die.'

'If they would rather die,' said Scrooge, 'they had better do it, and decrease the surplus population. Besides—excuse me—I don't know that.'

'But you might know it,' observed the gentleman.

'It's not my business,' Scrooge returned. 'It's enough for a man to understand his own business, and not to interfere with other people's. Mine occupies me constantly. Good afternoon, gentlemen!'

Seeing clearly that it would be useless to pursue their point, the gentlemen withdrew. Scrooge returned his labours with an improved opinion of himself, and in a more facetious temper than was usual with him.

Meanwhile the fog and darkness thickened so, that people ran about with flaring links, proffering their services to go before horses in carriages, and conduct them on their way. The ancient tower of a church, whose gruff old bell was always peeping slily down at Scrooge out of a Gothic window in the wall, became invisible, and struck the hours and quarters in the clouds, with tremulous vibrations afterwards as if its teeth were chattering in its frozen head up there. The cold became intense. In the main street at

the corner of the court, some labourers were repairing the gas-pipes, and had lighted a great fire in a brazier, round which a party of ragged men and boys were gathered: warming their hands and winking their eyes before the blaze in rapture. The water-plug being left in solitude, its overflowing sullenly congealed, and turned to misanthropic ice. The brightness of the shops where holly sprigs and berries crackled in the lamp heat of the windows, made pale faces ruddy as they passed. Poulterers' and grocers' trades became a splendid joke; a glorious pageant, with which it was next to impossible to believe that such dull principles as bargain and sale had anything to do. The Lord Mayor, in the stronghold of the mighty Mansion House, gave orders to his fifty cooks and butlers to keep Christmas as a Lord Mayor's household should; and even the little tailor, whom he had fined five shillings on the previous Monday for being drunk and bloodthirsty in the streets, stirred up to-morrow's pudding in his garret, while his lean wife and the baby sallied out to buy the beef.

Foggier yet, and colder! Piercing, searching, biting cold. If the good Saint Dunstan had but nipped the Evil Spirit's nose with a touch of such weather as that, instead of using his familiar weapons, then indeed he would have roared to lusty purpose. The owner of one scant young nose, gnawed and mumbled by the hungry cold as bones are gnawed by dogs, stooped down at Scrooge's keyhole to regale him with a Christmas carol: but at the first sound of

'God bless you, merry gentleman! May nothing you dismay!'

Scrooge seized the ruler with such energy of action, that the singer fled in terror, leaving the keyhole to the fog and even more congenial frost.

At length the hour of shutting up the counting-house arrived. With an ill-will Scrooge dismounted from his stool, and tacitly admitted the fact to the expectant clerk in the Tank, who instantly snuffed his candle out, and put on his hat.

'You'll want all day to-morrow, I suppose?' said Scrooge.

'If quite convenient, sir.'

'It's not convenient,' said Scrooge, 'and it's not fair. If I was to stop half-a-crown for it, you'd think yourself ill-used, I'll be bound?'

The clerk smiled faintly.

'And yet,' said Scrooge, 'you don't think me ill-used, when I pay a day's wages for no work.'

The clerk observed that it was only once a year.

'A poor excuse for picking a man's pocket every twenty-fifth of December!' said Scrooge, buttoning his great-coat to the chin. 'But I suppose you must have the whole day. Be here all the earlier next morning.'

The clerk promised that he would; and Scrooge walked out with a growl. The office was closed in a twinkling, and the clerk, with the long ends of his white comforter dangling below his waist (for he boasted no great-coat), went down a slide on Cornhill, at the end of a lane of boys, twenty times, in honour of its being Christmas Eve, and then ran home to Camden Town as hard as he could pelt, to play at blindman's-buff.

Scrooge took his melancholy dinner in his usual melancholy tavern; and having read all the newspapers, and beguiled the rest of the evening with his banker's-book, went home to bed. He lived in chambers which had once belonged to his deceased partner. They were a gloomy suite of rooms, in a lowering pile of building up a yard, where it had so little business to be, that one could scarcely help fancying it must have run there when it was a young house, playing at hide-and-seek with other houses, and forgotten the way out again. It was old enough now, and dreary enough, for nobody lived in it but Scrooge, the other rooms being all let out as offices. The yard was so dark that even Scrooge, who knew its every stone, was fain to grope with his hands. The fog and frost so hung about the black old gateway of the house, that it seemed as if the Genius of the Weather sat in mournful meditation on the threshold.

Now, it is a fact, that there was nothing at all particular about the knocker on the door, except that it was very large. It is also a fact, that Scrooge had seen it, night and morning, during his whole residence in that place; also that Scrooge had as little of what is called fancy about him as any man in the city of London, even including—which is a bold word—the corporation, aldermen, and livery. Let it also be borne in mind that Scrooge had not bestowed one thought on Marley, since his last mention of his seven years' dead partner that afternoon. And then let any man explain to me, if he can, how it happened that Scrooge, having his key in the lock of the door, saw in the knocker, without its undergoing any intermediate process of change—not a knocker, but Marley's face.

Marley's face. It was not in impenetrable shadow as the other objects in the yard were, but had a dismal light about it, like a bad lobster in a dark cellar. It was not angry or ferocious, but looked at Scrooge as Marley used to look: with ghostly spectacles turned up on its ghostly forehead. The hair was curiously stirred, as if by breath or hot air; and, though the eyes were wide open, they were perfectly motionless. That, and its livid colour, made it horrible; but its horror seemed to be in spite of the face and beyond its control, rather than a part or its own expression.

As Scrooge looked fixedly at this phenomenon, it was a knocker again.

To say that he was not startled, or that his blood was not conscious of a terrible sensation to which it had been a stranger from infancy, would be untrue. But he put his hand upon the key he had relinquished, turned it sturdily, walked in, and lighted his candle.

He did pause, with a moment's irresolution, before he shut the door; and he did look cautiously behind it first, as if he half-expected to be terrified with the sight of Marley's pigtail sticking out into the hall. But there was nothing on the back of the door, except the screws and nuts that held the knocker on, so he said 'Pooh, pooh!' and closed it with a bang.

The sound resounded through the house like thunder. Every room above, and every cask in the wine-merchant's cellars below, appeared to have a separate peal of echoes of its own. Scrooge was not a man to be frightened by echoes. He fastened the door, and walked across the hall, and up the stairs; slowly too: trimming his candle as he went.

You may talk vaguely about driving a coach-and-six up a good old flight of stairs, or through a bad young Act of Parliament; but I mean to say you might have got a hearse up that staircase, and taken it broadwise, with the splinter-bar towards the wall and the door towards the balustrades: and done it easy. There was plenty of width for that, and room to spare; which is perhaps the reason why Scrooge thought he saw a locomotive hearse going on before him in the gloom. Half a dozen gas-lamps out of the street wouldn't have lighted the entry too well, so you may suppose that it was pretty dark with Scrooge's dip.

Up Scrooge went, not caring a button for that. Darkness is cheap, and Scrooge liked it. But before he shut his heavy door, he walked through his rooms to see that all was right. He had just enough recollection of the face to desire to do that.

Sitting-room, bedroom, lumber-room. All as they should be. Nobody under the table, nobody under the sofa; a small fire in the grate; spoon and basin ready; and the little saucepan of gruel (Scrooge had a cold in his head) upon the hob. Nobody under the bed; nobody in the closet; nobody in his dressing-gown, which was hanging up in a suspicious attitude against the wall. Lumber-room as usual. Old fire-guards, old shoes, two fish-baskets, washing-stand on three legs, and a poker.

Quite satisfied, he closed his door, and locked himself in; double-locked himself in, which was not his custom. Thus secured against surprise, he took off his cravat; put on his dressing-gown and slippers, and his nightcap; and sat down before the fire to take his gruel.

It was a very low fire indeed; nothing on such a bitter night. He was obliged to sit close to it, and brood over it, before he could extract the least sensation of warmth from such a handful of fuel. The fireplace was an old one, built by some Dutch merchant long ago, and paved all round with quaint Dutch tiles, designed to illustrate the Scriptures. There were Cains and Abels, Pharaohs' daughters; Queens of Sheba, Angelic messengers descending through the air on clouds like feather-beds, Abrahams, Belshazzars, Apostles putting off

to sea in butter-boats, hundreds of figures to attract his thoughts—and yet that face of Marley, seven years dead, came like the ancient Prophet's rod, and swallowed up the whole. If each smooth tile had been a blank at first, with power to shape some picture on its surface from the disjointed fragments of his thoughts, there would have been a copy of old Marley's head on every one.

'Humbug!' said Scrooge; and walked across the room.

After several turns, he sat down again. As he threw his head back in the chair, his glance happened to rest upon a bell, a disused bell, that hung in the room, and communicated for some purpose now forgotten with a chamber in the highest story of the building. It was with great astonishment, and with a strange, inexplicable dread, that as he looked, he saw this bell begin to swing. It swung so softly in the outset that it scarcely made a sound; but soon it rang out loudly, and so did every bell in the house.

This might have lasted half a minute, or a minute, but it seemed an hour. The bells ceased as they had begun, together. They were succeeded by a clanking noise, deep down below; as if some person were dragging a heavy chain over the casks in the wine merchant's cellar. Scrooge then remembered to have heard that ghosts in haunted houses were described as dragging chains.

The cellar-door flew open with a booming sound, and then he heard the noise much louder, on the floors below; then coming up the stairs; then coming straight towards his door.

'It's humbug still!' said Scrooge. 'I won't believe it.'

His colour changed though, when, without a pause, it came on through the heavy door, and passed into the room before his eyes. Upon its coming in, the dying flame leaped up, as though it cried 'I know him; Marley's Ghost!' and fell again.

The same face: the very same. Marley in his pigtail, usual waistcoat, tights and boots; the tassels on the latter bristling, like his pigtail, and his coat-skirts, and the hair upon his head. The chain he drew was clasped about his middle. It was long, and wound about him like a tail; and it was made (for Scrooge observed it closely) of cash-boxes, keys, padlocks, ledgers, deeds, and heavy purses wrought in steel. His body was transparent; so that Scrooge, observing him, and looking through his waistcoat, could see the two buttons on his coat behind.

Scrooge had often heard it said that Marley had no bowels, but he had never believed it until now.

No, nor did he believe it even now. Though he looked the phantom through and through, and saw it standing before him; though he felt the chilling influence of its death-cold eyes; and marked the very texture of the folded kerchief bound about its head and chin, which wrapper he had not observed before; he was still incredulous, and fought against his senses.

'How now!' said Scrooge, caustic and cold as ever. 'What do you want with me?'

'Much!'—Marley's voice, no doubt about it.

'Who are you?'

'Ask me who I was.'

'Who were you then?' said Scrooge, raising his voice. 'You're particular, for a shade.' He was going to say 'to a shade,' but substituted this, as more appropriate.

'In life I was your partner, Jacob Marley.'

'Can you—can you sit down?' asked Scrooge, looking doubtfully at him.

'I can.'

'Do it, then.'

Scrooge asked the question, because he didn't know whether a ghost so transparent might find himself in a condition to take a chair; and felt that in the event of its being impossible, it might involve the necessity of an embarrassing explanation. But the ghost sat down on the opposite side of the fireplace, as if he were quite used to it.

'You don't believe in me,' observed the Ghost.

'I don't,' said Scrooge.

'What evidence would you have of my reality beyond that of your senses?'

'I don't know,' said Scrooge.

'Why do you doubt your senses?'

'Because,' said Scrooge, 'a little thing affects them. A slight disorder of the stomach makes them cheats. You may be an undigested bit of beef, a blot of mustard, a crumb of cheese, a fragment of an underdone potato. There's more of gravy than of grave about you, whatever you are!'

Scrooge was not much in the habit of cracking jokes, nor did he feel, in his heart, by any means waggish then. The truth is, that he tried to be smart, as a means of distracting his own attention, and keeping down his terror; for the spectre's voice disturbed the very marrow in his bones.

To sit, staring at those fixed glazed eyes, in silence for a moment, would play, Scrooge felt, the very deuce with him. There was something very awful, too, in the spectre's being provided with an infernal atmosphere of its own. Scrooge could not feel it himself, but this was clearly the case; for though the Ghost sat perfectly motionless, its hair, and skirts, and tassels, were still agitated as by the hot vapour from an oven.

'You see this toothpick?' said Scrooge, returning quickly to the charge, for the reason just assigned; and wishing, though it were only for a second, to divert the vision's stony gaze from himself.

'I do,' replied the Ghost.

'You are not looking at it,' said Scrooge.

'But I see it,' said the Ghost, 'notwithstanding.'

'Well!' returned Scrooge, 'I have but to swallow this, and be for the rest of my days persecuted by a legion of goblins, all of my own creation. Humbug, I tell you! humbug!'

At this the spirit raised a frightful cry, and shook its chain with such a dismal and appalling noise, that Scrooge held on tight to his chair, to save himself from falling in a swoon. But how much greater was his horror, when the phantom taking off the bandage round its head, as if it were too warm to wear indoors, its lower jaw dropped down upon its breast!

Scrooge fell upon his knees, and clasped his hands before his face.

'Mercy!' he said. 'Dreadful apparition, why do you trouble me?'

'Man of the worldly mind!' replied the Ghost, 'do you believe in me or not?'

'I do,' said Scrooge. 'I must. But why do spirits walk the earth, and why do they come to me?'

'It is required of every man,' the Ghost returned, 'that the spirit within him should walk abroad among his fellowmen, and travel far and wide; and if that spirit goes not forth in life, it is condemned to do so after death. It is doomed to wander through the world—oh, woe is me!—and witness what it cannot share, but might have shared on earth, and turned to happiness!'

Again the spectre raised a cry, and shook its chain and wrung its shadowy hands.

'You are fettered,' said Scrooge, trembling. 'Tell me why?'

'I wear the chain I forged in life,' replied the Ghost. 'I made it link by link, and yard by yard; I girded it on of my own free will, and of my own free will I wore it. Is its pattern strange to you?'

Scrooge trembled more and more.

'Or would you know,' pursued the Ghost, 'the weight and length of the strong coil you bear yourself? It was full as heavy and as long as this, seven Christmas Eves ago. You have laboured on it, since. It is a ponderous chain!'

Scrooge glanced about him on the floor, in the expectation of finding himself surrounded by some fifty or sixty fathoms of iron cable: but he could see nothing.

'Jacob,' he said, imploringly. 'Old Jacob Marley, tell me more. Speak comfort to me, Jacob!'

'I have none to give,' the Ghost replied. 'It comes from other regions, Ebenezer Scrooge, and is conveyed by other ministers, to other kinds of men. Nor can I tell you what I would. A very little more, is all permitted to me. I cannot rest, I cannot stay, I cannot linger anywhere. My spirit never walked beyond our counting-house—mark me!—in life my spirit never roved beyond the narrow limits of our money-changing hole; and weary journeys lie before me!'

It was a habit with Scrooge, whenever he became thoughtful, to put his hands in his breeches pockets. Pondering on what the Ghost had said, he did so now, but without lifting up his eyes, or getting off his knees.

'You must have been very slow about it, Jacob,' Scrooge observed, in a business-like manner, though with humility and deference.

'Slow!' the Ghost repeated.

'Seven years dead,' mused Scrooge. 'And travelling all the time!'

'The whole time,' said the Ghost. 'No rest, no peace. Incessant torture of remorse.'

'You travel fast?' said Scrooge.

'On the wings of the wind,' replied the Ghost.

'You might have got over a great quantity of ground in seven years,' said Scrooge.

The Ghost, on hearing this, set up another cry, and clanked its chain so hideously in the dead silence of the night, that the Ward would have been justified in indicting it for a nuisance.

'Oh! captive, bound, and double-ironed,' cried the phantom, 'not to know, that ages of incessant labour, by immortal creatures, for this earth must pass into eternity before the good of which it is susceptible is all developed. Not to know that any Christian spirit working kindly in its little sphere, whatever it may be, will find its mortal life too short for its vast means of usefulness. Not to know that no space of regret can make amends for one life's opportunity misused! Yet such was I! Oh! such was I!'

'But you were always a good man of business, Jacob,' faltered Scrooge, who now began to apply this to himself.

'Business!' cried the Ghost, wringing its hands again. 'Mankind was my business. The common welfare was my business; charity, mercy, forbearance, and benevolence, were, all, my business. The dealings of my trade were but a drop of water in the comprehensive ocean of my business!'

It held up its chain at arm's length, as if that were the cause of all its unavailing grief, and flung it heavily upon the ground again.

'At this time of the rolling year,' the spectre said 'I suffer most. Why did I walk through crowds of fellow-beings with my eyes turned down, and never raise them to that blessed Star which led the Wise Men to a poor abode? Were there no poor homes to which its light would have conducted me!'

Scrooge was very much dismayed to hear the spectre going on at this rate, and began to quake exceedingly.

'Hear me!' cried the Ghost. 'My time is nearly gone.'

'I will,' said Scrooge. 'But don't be hard upon me! Don't be flowery, Jacob! Pray!'

'How it is that I appear before you in a shape that you can see, I may not tell. I have sat invisible beside you many and many a day.'

It was not an agreeable idea. Scrooge shivered, and wiped the perspiration from his brow.

'That is no light part of my penance,' pursued the Ghost. 'I am here to-night to warn you, that you have yet a chance and hope of escaping my fate. A chance and hope of my procuring, Ebenezer.'

'You were always a good friend to me,' said Scrooge. 'Thank 'ee!'

'You will be haunted,' resumed the Ghost, 'by Three Spirits.'

Scrooge's countenance fell almost as low as the Ghost's had done.

'Is that the chance and hope you mentioned, Jacob?' he demanded, in a faltering voice.

'It is.'

'I—I think I'd rather not,' said Scrooge.

'Without their visits,' said the Ghost, 'you cannot hope to shun the path I tread. Expect the first tomorrow, when the bell tolls One.'

'Couldn't I take 'em all at once, and have it over, Jacob?' hinted Scrooge.

'Expect the second on the next night at the same hour. The third upon the next night when the last stroke of Twelve has ceased to vibrate. Look to see me no more; and look that, for your own sake, you remember what has passed between us!'

When it had said these words, the spectre took its wrapper from the table, and bound it round its head, as before. Scrooge knew this, by the smart sound its teeth made, when the jaws were brought together by the bandage. He ventured to raise his eyes again, and found his supernatural visitor confronting him in an erect attitude, with its chain wound over and about its arm.

The apparition walked backward from him; and at every step it took, the window raised itself a little, so that when the spectre reached it, it was wide open. It beckoned Scrooge to approach, which he did. When they were within two paces of each other, Marley's Ghost held up its hand, warning him to come no nearer. Scrooge stopped.

Not so much in obedience, as in surprise and fear: for on the raising of the hand, he became sensible of confused noises in the air; incoherent sounds of lamentation and regret; wailings

inexpressibly sorrowful and self-accusatory. The spectre, after listening for a moment, joined in the mournful dirge; and floated out upon the bleak, dark night.

Scrooge followed to the window: desperate in his curiosity. He looked out.

The air was filled with phantoms, wandering hither and thither in restless haste, and moaning as they went. Every one of them wore chains like Marley's Ghost; some few (they might be guilty governments) were linked together; none were free. Many had been personally known to Scrooge in their lives. He had been quite familiar with one old ghost, in a white waistcoat, with a monstrous iron safe attached to its ankle, who cried piteously at being unable to assist a wretched woman with an infant, whom it saw below, upon a door-step. The misery with them all was, clearly, that they sought to interfere, for good, in human matters, and had lost the power for ever.

Whether these creatures faded into mist, or mist enshrouded them, he could not tell. But they and their spirit voices faded together; and the night became as it had been when he walked home.

Scrooge closed the window, and examined the door by which the Ghost had entered. It was double-locked, as he had locked it with his own hands, and the bolts were undisturbed. He tried to say 'Humbug!' but stopped at the first syllable. And being, from the emotion he had undergone, or the fatigues of the day, or his glimpse of the Invisible World, or the dull conversation of the Ghost, or the lateness of the hour, much in need of repose; went straight to bed, without undressing, and fell asleep upon the instant.

STAVE 2: THE FIRST OF THE THREE SPIRITS

When Scrooge awoke, it was so dark, that looking out of bed, he could scarcely distinguish the transparent window from the opaque walls of his chamber. He was endeavouring to pierce the darkness with his ferret eyes, when the chimes of a neighbouring church struck the four quarters. So he listened for the hour.

To his great astonishment the heavy bell went on from six to seven, and from seven to eight, and regularly up to twelve; then stopped. Twelve. It was past two when he went to bed. The clock was wrong. An icicle must have got into the works. Twelve.

He touched the spring of his repeater, to correct this most preposterous clock. Its rapid little pulse beat twelve: and stopped.

'Why, it isn't possible,' said Scrooge, 'that I can have slept through a whole day and far into another night. It isn't possible that anything has happened to the sun, and this is twelve at noon.'

The idea being an alarming one, he scrambled out of bed, and groped his way to the window. He was obliged to rub the frost off with the sleeve of his dressing-gown before he could see anything; and could see very little then. All he could make out was, that it was still very foggy and extremely cold, and that there was no noise of people running to and fro, and making a great stir, as there unquestionably would have been if night had beaten off bright day, and taken possession of the world. This was a great relief, because "Three days after sight of this First of Exchange pay to Mr. Ebenezer Scrooge on his order," and so forth, would have become a mere United States security if there were no days to count by.

Scrooge went to bed again, and thought, and thought, and thought it over and over, and could make nothing of it. The more he thought, the more perplexed he was; and, the more he endeavoured not to think, the more he thought.

Marley's Ghost bothered him exceedingly. Every time he resolved within himself, after mature inquiry that it was all a dream, his mind flew back again, like a strong spring released, to its first position, and presented the same problem to be worked all through, "Was it a dream or not?"

Scrooge lay in this state until the chime had gone three-quarters more, when he remembered, on a sudden, that the Ghost had warned him of a visitation when the bell tolled one. He resolved to lie awake until the hour was passed; and, considering that he could no more go to sleep than

go to heaven, this was, perhaps, the wisest resolution in his power.

The quarter was so long, that he was more than once convinced he must have sunk into a doze unconsciously, and missed the clock. At length it broke upon his listening ear.

"Ding, dong!"

"A quarter past," said Scrooge, counting.

"Ding, dong!"

"Half past," said Scrooge.

"Ding, dong!"

"A quarter to it," said Scrooge. "Ding, dong!"

"The hour itself," said Scrooge triumphantly, "and nothing else!"

He spoke before the hour bell sounded, which it now did with a deep, dull, hollow, melancholy ONE. Light flashed up in the room upon the instant, and the curtains of his bed were drawn.

The curtains of his bed were drawn aside, I tell you, by a hand. Not the curtains at his feet, nor the curtains at his back, but those to which his face was addressed. The curtains of his bed were drawn aside; and Scrooge, starting up into a half-recumbent attitude, found himself face to face with the unearthly visitor who drew them: as close to it as I am now to you, and I am standing in the spirit at your elbow.

It was a strange figure—like a child: yet not so like a child as like an old man, viewed through some supernatural medium, which gave him the appearance of having receded from the view, and being diminished to a child's proportions. Its hair, which hung about its neck and down its back, was white as if with age; and yet the face had not a wrinkle in it, and the tenderest bloom was on the skin. The arms were very long and muscular; the hands the same, as if its hold were of uncommon strength. Its legs and feet, most delicately formed, were, like those upper members, bare. It wore a tunic of the purest white, and round its waist was bound a lustrous belt, the sheen of which was beautiful. It held a branch of fresh green holly in its hand; and, in singular contradiction of that wintry emblem, had its dress trimmed with summer flowers. But the strangest thing about it was, that from the crown of its head there sprung a bright clear jet of light, by which all this was visible; and which was doubtless the occasion of its using, in its duller moments, a great extinguisher for a cap, which it now held under its arm.

Even this, though, when Scrooge looked at it with increasing steadiness, was not its strangest quality. For as its belt sparkled and glittered now in one part and now in another, and what was light one instant, at another time was dark, so the figure itself fluctuated in its distinctness: being now a thing with one arm, now with one leg, now with twenty legs, now a pair of legs without a head, now a head without a body: of which dissolving parts, no outline would be visible in the dense gloom wherein they melted away. And in the very wonder of this, it would be itself again; distinct and clear as ever.

'Are you the Spirit, sir, whose coming was foretold to me?' asked Scrooge.

'I am.'

The voice was soft and gentle. Singularly low, as if instead of being so close beside him, it were at a distance.

'Who, and what are you?' Scrooge demanded.

'I am the Ghost of Christmas Past.'

'Long Past.' inquired Scrooge: observant of its dwarfish stature.

'No. Your past.'

Perhaps, Scrooge could not have told anybody why, if anybody could have asked him; but he had a special desire to see the Spirit in his cap; and begged him to be covered.

'What!' exclaimed the Ghost, 'would you so soon put out, with worldly hands, the light I give? Is it not enough that you are one of those whose passions made this cap, and force me through whole trains of years to wear it low upon my brow!'

Scrooge reverently disclaimed all intention to offend or any knowledge of having wilfully bonneted the Spirit at any period of his life. He then made bold to inquire what business brought him there.

'Your welfare!' said the Ghost.

Scrooge expressed himself much obliged, but could not help thinking that a night of unbroken rest would have been more conducive to that end. The Spirit must have heard him thinking, for it said immediately:

'Your reclamation, then. Take heed!'

It put out its strong hand as it spoke, and clasped him gently by the arm.

'Rise! and walk with me!'

It would have been in vain for Scrooge to plead that the weather and the hour were not adapted to pedestrian purposes; that bed was warm, and the thermometer a long way below freezing; that he was clad but lightly in his slippers, dressing-gown, and nightcap; and that he had a cold upon him at that time. The grasp, though gentle as a woman's hand, was not to be resisted. He rose: but finding that the Spirit made towards the window, clasped his robe in supplication.

'I am mortal,' Scrooge remonstrated, 'and liable to fall.'

'Bear but a touch of my hand there,' said the Spirit, laying it upon his heart,' and you shall be upheld in more than this!'

As the words were spoken, they passed through the wall, and stood upon an open country road, with fields on either hand. The city had entirely vanished. Not a vestige of it was to be seen. The darkness and the mist had vanished with it, for it was a clear, cold, winter day, with snow upon the ground.

'Good Heaven!' said Scrooge, clasping his hands together, as he looked about him. 'I was bred in this place. I was a boy here!'

The Spirit gazed upon him mildly. Its gentle touch, though it had been light and instantaneous, appeared still present to the old man's sense of feeling. He was conscious of a thousand odours floating in the air, each one connected with a thousand thoughts, and hopes, and joys, and cares long, long, forgotten!

'Your lip is trembling,' said the Ghost. 'And what is that upon your cheek?'

Scrooge muttered, with an unusual catching in his voice, that it was a pimple; and begged the Ghost to lead him where he would.

'You recollect the way?' inquired the Spirit.

'Remember it!' cried Scrooge with fervour; 'I could walk it blindfold.'

'Strange to have forgotten it for so many years!' observed the Ghost. 'Let us go on.'

They walked along the road, Scrooge recognising every gate, and post, and tree; until a little market-town appeared in the distance, with its bridge, its church, and winding river. Some shaggy ponies now were seen trotting towards them with boys upon their backs, who called to other boys in country gigs and carts, driven by farmers. All these boys were in great spirits, and shouted to each other, until the broad fields were so full of merry music, that the crisp air laughed to hear it.

'These are but shadows of the things that have been,' said the Ghost. 'They have no consciousness of us.'

The jocund travellers came on; and as they came, Scrooge knew and named them every one. Why was he rejoiced beyond all bounds to see them! Why did his cold eye glisten, and his heart leap up as they went past! Why was he filled with gladness when he heard them give each other Merry Christmas, as they parted at cross-roads and bye-ways, for their several homes! What was merry Christmas to Scrooge? Out upon merry Christmas! What good had it ever done to him?

'The school is not quite deserted,' said the Ghost. 'A solitary child, neglected by his friends, is left there still.'

Scrooge said he knew it. And he sobbed.

They left the high-road, by a well-remembered lane, and soon approached a mansion of dull red brick, with a little weathercock-surmounted cupola, on the roof, and a bell hanging in it. It was a large house, but one of broken fortunes; for the spacious offices were little used, their walls were damp and mossy, their windows broken, and their gates decayed. Fowls clucked and strutted in the stables; and the coach-houses and sheds were over-run with grass. Nor was it more retentive of its ancient state, within; for entering the dreary hall, and glancing through the open doors of many rooms, they found them poorly furnished, cold, and vast. There was an earthy savour in the air, a chilly bareness in the place, which associated itself somehow with too much getting up by candle-light, and not too much to eat.

They went, the Ghost and Scrooge, across the hall, to a door at the back of the house. It opened before them, and disclosed a long, bare, melancholy room, made barer still by lines of plain deal forms and desks. At one of these a lonely boy was reading near a feeble fire; and Scrooge sat down upon a form, and wept to see his poor forgotten self as he used to be.

Not a latent echo in the house, not a squeak and scuffle from the mice behind the panelling, not a drip from the half-thawed water-spout in the dull yard behind, not a sigh among the leafless boughs of one despondent poplar, not the idle swinging of an empty store-house door, no, not a clicking in the fire, but fell upon the heart of Scrooge with a softening influence, and gave a freer passage to his tears.

The Spirit touched him on the arm, and pointed to his younger self, intent upon his reading. Suddenly a man, in foreign garments: wonderfully real and distinct to look at: stood outside the window, with an axe stuck in his belt, and leading by the bridle an ass laden with wood.

'Why, it's Ali Baba!' Scrooge exclaimed in ecstasy. 'It's dear old honest Ali Baba! Yes, yes, I know! One Christmas time, when yonder solitary child was left here all alone, he did come, for the first time, just like that. Poor boy! And Valentine,' said Scrooge,' and his wild brother, Orson; there they go! And what's his name, who was put down in his drawers, asleep, at the Gate of Damascus; don't you see him! And the Sultan's Groom turned upside down by the Genii; there he is upon his head! Serve him right. I'm glad of it. What business had he to be married to the Princess!'

To hear Scrooge expending all the earnestness of his nature on such subjects, in a most extraordinary voice between laughing and crying; and to see his heightened and excited face; would have been a surprise to his business friends in the city, indeed.

'There's the Parrot!' cried Scrooge. 'Green body and yellow tail, with a thing like a lettuce growing out of the top of his head; there he is! Poor Robin Crusoe, he called him, when he came home again after sailing round the island.

'Poor Robin Crusoe, where have you been, Robin Crusoe?' The man thought he was dreaming, but he wasn't. It was the Parrot, you know. There goes Friday, running for his life to the little creek! Halloa! Hoop! Hallo!'

Then, with a rapidity of transition very foreign to his usual character, he said, in pity for his former self, 'Poor boy!' and cried again.

'I wish,' Scrooge muttered, putting his hand in his pocket, and looking about him, after drying his eyes with his cuff: 'but it's too late now.'

'What is the matter?' asked the Spirit.

'Nothing,' said Scrooge. 'Nothing. There was a boy singing a Christmas Carol at my door last night. I should like to have given him something: that's all.'

The Ghost smiled thoughtfully, and waved its hand: saying as it did so, 'Let us see another Christmas!'

Scrooge's former self grew larger at the words, and the room became a little darker and more dirty. The panels shrunk, the windows cracked; fragments of plaster fell out of the ceiling, and the naked laths were shown instead; but how all this was brought about, Scrooge knew no more than you do. He only knew that it was quite correct; that everything had happened so; that there he was, alone again, when all the other boys had gone home for the jolly holidays.

He was not reading now, but walking up and down despairingly.

Scrooge looked at the Ghost, and with a mournful shaking of his head, glanced anxiously towards the door.

It opened; and a little girl, much younger than the boy, came darting in, and putting her arms about his neck, and often kissing him, addressed him as her 'Dear, dear brother.'

'I have come to bring you home, dear brother!' said the child, clapping her tiny hands, and bending down to laugh. 'To bring you home, home, home!'

'Home, little Fan?' returned the boy.

'Yes.' said the child, brimful of glee. 'Home, for good and all. Home, for ever and ever. Father is so much kinder than he used to be, that home's like Heaven. He spoke so gently to me one dear night when I was going to bed, that I was not afraid to ask him once more if you might come home; and he said Yes, you should; and sent me in a coach to bring you. And you're to be a man!' said the child, opening her eyes,' and are never to come back here; but first, we're to be together all the Christmas long, and have the merriest time in all the world.'

'You are quite a woman, little Fan!' exclaimed the boy.

She clapped her hands and laughed, and tried to touch his head; but being too little, laughed again, and stood on tiptoe to embrace him. Then she began to drag him, in her childish eagerness, towards the door; and he, nothing loth to go, accompanied her.

A terrible voice in the hall cried. 'Bring down Master Scrooge's box, there!' and in the hall appeared the schoolmaster himself, who glared on Master Scrooge with a ferocious condescension, and threw him into a dreadful state of mind by shaking hands with him. He then conveyed him and his sister into the veriest old well of a shivering best-parlour that ever was seen, where the maps upon the wall, and the celestial and terrestrial globes in the windows, were waxy with cold. Here he produced a decanter of curiously light wine, and a block of curiously heavy cake, and administered instalments of those dainties to the young people: at the same time, sending out a meagre servant to offer a glass of something to the postboy, who answered that he thanked the gentleman, but if it was the same tap as he had tasted before, he had rather not. Master Scrooge's trunk being by this time tied on to the top of the chaise, the children bade the schoolmaster goodbye right willingly; and getting into it, drove gaily down the garden-sweep: the quick wheels dashing the hoar-frost and snow from off the dark leaves of the evergreens like spray.

'Always a delicate creature, whom a breath might have withered,' said the Ghost. 'But she had a large heart!'

'So she had,' cried Scrooge. 'You're right. I will not gainsay it, Spirit. God forbid!'

'She died a woman,' said the Ghost, 'and had, as I think, children.'

'One child,' Scrooge returned.

'True,' said the Ghost. 'Your nephew.'

Scrooge seemed uneasy in his mind; and answered briefly, 'Yes.'

Although they had but that moment left the school behind them, they were now in the busy thoroughfares of a city, where shadowy passengers passed and repassed; where shadowy carts and coaches battle for the way, and all the strife and tumult of a real city were. It was made plain enough, by the dressing of the shops, that here too it was Christmas time again; but it was evening, and the streets were lighted up.

The Ghost stopped at a certain warehouse door, and asked Scrooge if he knew it.

'Know it!' said Scrooge. 'I was apprenticed here!'

They went in. At sight of an old gentleman in a Welsh wig, sitting behind such a high desk, that if he had been two inches taller he must have knocked his head against the ceiling, Scrooge cried in great excitement:

'Why, it's old Fezziwig! Bless his heart; it's Fezziwig alive again!'

Old Fezziwig laid down his pen, and looked up at the clock, which pointed to the hour of seven. He rubbed his hands; adjusted his capacious waistcoat; laughed all over himself, from his shows to his organ of benevolence; and called out in a comfortable, oily, rich, fat, jovial voice:

'Yo ho, there! Ebenezer! Dick!'

Scrooge's former self, now grown a young man, came briskly in, accompanied by his fellow-prentice.

'Dick Wilkins, to be sure!' said Scrooge to the Ghost. 'Bless me, yes. There he is. He was very much attached to me, was Dick. Poor Dick! Dear, dear!'

'Yo ho, my boys!' said Fezziwig. 'No more work to-night. Christmas Eve, Dick. Christmas, Ebenezer! Let's have the shutters up,' cried old Fezziwig, with a sharp clap of his hands,' before a man can say Jack Robinson!'

You wouldn't believe how those two fellows went at it! They charged into the street with the shutters—one, two, three—had them up in their places—four, five, six—barred them and pinned then—seven, eight, nine—and came back before you could have got to twelve, panting like race-horses.

'Hilli-ho!' cried old Fezziwig, skipping down from the high desk, with wonderful agility. 'Clear away, my lads, and let's have lots of room here! Hilli-ho, Dick! Chirrup, Ebenezer!'

Clear away. There was nothing they wouldn't have cleared away, or couldn't have cleared away, with old Fezziwig looking on. It was done in a minute. Every movable was packed off, as if it were dismissed from public life for evermore; the floor was swept and watered, the lamps were trimmed, fuel was heaped upon the fire; and the warehouse was as snug, and warm, and dry, and bright a ball-room, as you would desire to see upon a winter's night.

In came a fiddler with a music-book, and went up to the lofty desk, and made an orchestra of it, and tuned like fifty stomach-aches. In came Mrs Fezziwig, one vast substantial smile. In came the three Miss Fezziwigs, beaming and lovable. In came the six young followers whose hearts they broke. In came all the young men and women employed in the business. In came the housemaid, with her cousin, the baker. In came the cook, with her brother's particular friend, the milkman. In came the boy from over the way, who was suspected of not having board enough from his master; trying to hide himself behind the girl from next door but one, who was proved to have had her ears pulled by her mistress. In they all came, one after another; some shyly, some boldly, some gracefully, some awkwardly, some pushing, some pulling; in they all came, anyhow and everyhow. Away they all went, twenty couples at once; hands half round and back again the other way; down the middle and up again; round and round in various stages of affectionate grouping; old top couple always turning up in the wrong place; new top couple starting off again, as soon as they got there; all top couples at last, and not a bottom one to help them. When this result was brought about, old Fezziwig, clapping his hands to stop the dance, cried out,' Well done!' and the fiddler plunged his hot face into a pot of porter, especially provided for that purpose. But scorning rest, upon his re-appearance, he instantly began again, though there were no dancers yet, as if the other fiddler had been carried home, exhausted, on a shutter, and he were a bran-new man resolved to beat him out of sight, or perish.

There were more dances, and there were forfeits, and more dances, and there was cake, and there was negus, and there was a great piece of Cold Roast, and there was a great piece of Cold Boiled, and there were mince-pies, and plenty of beer. But the great effect of the evening came after the Roast and Boiled, when the fiddler (an artful dog, mind. The sort of man who knew his business better than you or I could have told it him.) struck up Sir Roger de Coverley.' Then old Fezziwig stood out to dance with Mrs Fezziwig. Top couple, too; with a good stiff piece of work cut out for them; three or four and twenty pair of partners; people who were not to be trifled with; people who would dance, and had no notion of walking.

But if they had been twice as many—ah, four times—old Fezziwig would have been a match for them, and so would Mrs Fezziwig. As to her, she was worthy to be his partner in every sense of the term. If that's not high praise, tell me higher, and I'll use it. A positive light appeared to issue from Fezziwig's calves. They shone in every part of the dance like moons. You couldn't have predicted, at any given time, what would have become of them next. And when old Fezziwig and Mrs Fezziwig had gone all through the dance; advance and retire, both hands to your partner, bow and curtsey, corkscrew, thread-the-needle, and back again to your place; Fezziwig cut—cut so deftly, that he appeared to wink with his legs, and came upon his feet again without a stagger.

When the clock struck eleven, this domestic ball broke up. Mr and Mrs Fezziwig took their stations, one on either side of the door, and shaking hands with every person individually as he or she went out, wished him or her a Merry Christmas. When everybody had retired but the two prentices, they did the same to them; and thus the cheerful voices died away, and the lads were left to their beds; which were under a counter in the back-shop.

During the whole of this time, Scrooge had acted like a man out of his wits. His heart and soul were in the scene, and with his former self. He corroborated everything, remembered everything, enjoyed everything, and underwent the strangest agitation. It was not until now, when the bright faces of his former self and Dick were turned from them, that he remembered the Ghost, and became conscious that it was looking full upon him, while the light upon its head burnt very clear.

'A small matter,' said the Ghost, 'to make these silly folks so full of gratitude.'

'Small!' echoed Scrooge.

The Spirit signed to him to listen to the two apprentices, who were pouring out their hearts in praise of Fezziwig: and when he had done so, said,

'Why! Is it not? He has spent but a few pounds of your mortal money: three or four perhaps. Is that so much that he deserves this praise?'

'It isn't that,' said Scrooge, heated by the remark, and speaking unconsciously like his former, not his latter, self. 'It isn't that, Spirit. He has the power to render us happy or unhappy; to make our service light or burdensome; a pleasure or a toil. Say that his power lies in words and looks; in things so slight and insignificant that it is impossible to add and count them up: what then? The happiness he gives, is quite as great as if it cost a fortune.'

He felt the Spirit's glance, and stopped.

'What is the matter?' asked the Ghost.

'Nothing in particular,' said Scrooge.

'Something, I think?' the Ghost insisted.

'No,' said Scrooge,' No. I should like to be able to say a word or two to my clerk just now! That's all.'

His former self turned down the lamps as he gave utterance to the wish; and Scrooge and the Ghost again stood side by side in the open air.

'My time grows short,' observed the Spirit. 'Quick!'

This was not addressed to Scrooge, or to any one whom he could see, but it produced an immediate effect. For again Scrooge saw himself. He was older now; a man in the prime of life. His face had not the harsh and rigid lines of later years; but it had begun to wear the signs of care and avarice. There was an eager, greedy, restless motion in the eye, which showed the passion that had taken root, and where the shadow of the growing tree would fall.

He was not alone, but sat by the side of a fair young girl in a mourning-dress: in whose eyes there were tears, which sparkled in the light that shone out of the Ghost of Christmas Past.

'It matters little,' she said, softly. 'To you, very little. Another idol has displaced me; and if it can cheer and comfort you in time to come, as I would have tried to do, I have no just cause to grieve.'

'What Idol has displaced you?' he rejoined.

'A golden one.'

'This is the even-handed dealing of the world!' he said. 'There is nothing on which it is so hard as poverty; and there is nothing it professes to condemn with such severity as the pursuit of wealth!'

'You fear the world too much,' she answered, gently. 'All your other hopes have merged into the hope of being beyond the chance of its sordid reproach. I have seen your nobler aspirations fall off one by one, until the master-passion, Gain, engrosses you. Have I not?'

'What then?' he retorted. 'Even if I have grown so much wiser, what then? I am not changed towards you.'

She shook her head.

'Am I?'

'Our contract is an old one. It was made when we were both poor and content to be so, until, in good season, we could improve our worldly fortune by our patient industry. You are changed. When it was made, you were another man.'

'I was a boy,' he said impatiently.

'Your own feeling tells you that you were not what you are,' she returned. 'I am. That which promised happiness when we were one in heart, is fraught with misery now that we are two. How often and how keenly I have thought of this, I will not say. It is enough that I have thought of it, and can release you.'

'Have I ever sought release?'

'In words. No. Never.'

'In what, then?'

'In a changed nature; in an altered spirit; in another atmosphere of life; another Hope as its great end. In everything that made my love of any worth or value in your sight. If this had never been between us,' said the girl, looking mildly, but with steadiness, upon him;' tell me, would you seek me out and try to win me now? Ah, no!'

He seemed to yield to the justice of this supposition, in spite of himself. But he said with a struggle,' You think not.'

'I would gladly think otherwise if I could,' she answered, 'Heaven knows! When I have learned a Truth like this, I know how strong and irresistible it must be. But if you were free to-day, to-morrow, yesterday, can even I believe that you would choose a dowerless girl—you who, in your very confidence with her, weigh everything by Gain: or, choosing her, if for a moment you were false enough to your one guiding principle to do so, do I not know that your repentance and regret would surely follow? I do; and I release you. With a full heart, for the love of him you once were.'

He was about to speak; but with her head turned from him, she resumed.

'You may—the memory of what is past half makes me hope you will—have pain in this. A very, very brief time, and you will dismiss the recollection of it, gladly, as an unprofitable dream, from which it happened well that you awoke. May you be happy in the life you have chosen.'

She left him, and they parted.

'Spirit!' said Scrooge,' show me no more! Conduct me home. Why do you delight to torture me?'

'One shadow more!' exclaimed the Ghost.

'No more!' cried Scrooge. 'No more, I don't wish to see it. Show me no more!'

But the relentless Ghost pinioned him in both his arms, and forced him to observe what happened next.

They were in another scene and place; a room, not very large or handsome, but full of comfort. Near to the winter fire sat a beautiful young girl, so like that last that Scrooge believed it was the same, until he saw her, now a comely matron, sitting opposite her daughter. The noise in this room was perfectly tumultuous, for there were more children there, than Scrooge in his agitated state of mind could count; and, unlike the celebrated herd in the poem, they were not forty children conducting themselves like one, but every child was conducting itself like forty. The consequences were uproarious beyond belief; but no one seemed to care; on the contrary, the mother and daughter laughed heartily, and enjoyed it very much; and the latter, soon beginning to mingle in the sports, got pillaged by the young brigands most ruthlessly. What would I not have given to be one of them! Though I never could have been so rude, no, no! I wouldn't for the wealth of all the world have crushed that braided hair, and torn it down; and for the precious little shoe, I wouldn't have plucked it off, God bless my soul! to save my life. As to measuring her waist in sport, as they did, bold young brood, I couldn't have done it; I should have expected my arm to have grown round it for a punishment, and never come straight again. And yet I should have dearly liked, I own, to have touched her lips; to have questioned her, that she might have opened them; to have looked upon the lashes of her downcast eyes, and never raised a blush; to have let loose waves of hair, an inch of which would be a keepsake beyond price: in short, I should have liked, I do confess, to have had the lightest licence of a child, and yet to have been man enough to know its value.

But now a knocking at the door was heard, and such a rush immediately ensued that she with laughing face and plundered dress was borne towards it the centre of a flushed and boisterous group, just in time to greet the father, who came home attended by a man laden with Christmas toys and presents. Then the shouting and the struggling, and the onslaught that was made on the defenceless porter. The scaling him, with chairs for ladders to dive into his pockets, despoil him of brown-paper parcels, hold on tight by his cravat, hug him round his neck, pommel his back, and kick his legs in irrepressible affection. The shouts of wonder and delight with which the development of every package was received! The terrible announcement that the baby had been taken in the act of putting a doll's frying-pan into his mouth, and was more than suspected of having swallowed a fictitious turkey, glued on a wooden platter! The immense

relief of finding this a false alarm! The joy, and gratitude, and ecstasy! They are all indescribable alike. It is enough that by degrees the children and their emotions got out of the parlour, and by one stair at a time, up to the top of the house; where they went to bed, and so subsided.

And now Scrooge looked on more attentively than ever, when the master of the house, having his daughter leaning fondly on him, sat down with her and her mother at his own fireside; and when he thought that such another creature, quite as graceful and as full of promise, might have called him father, and been a spring-time in the haggard winter of his life, his sight grew very dim indeed.

'Belle,' said the husband, turning to his wife with a smile,' I saw an old friend of yours this afternoon.'

'Who was it?'

'Guess!'

'How can I? Tut, don't I know.' she added in the same breath, laughing as he laughed. 'Mr Scrooge.'

'Mr Scrooge it was. I passed his office window; and as it was not shut up, and he had a candle inside, I could scarcely help seeing him. His partner lies upon the point of death, I hear; and there he sat alone. Quite alone in the world, I do believe.'

'Spirit!' said Scrooge in a broken voice,' remove me from this place.'

'I told you these were shadows of the things that have been,' said the Ghost. 'That they are what they are, do not blame me.'

'Remove me!' Scrooge exclaimed,' I cannot bear it!'

He turned upon the Ghost, and seeing that it looked upon him with a face, in which in some strange way there were fragments of all the faces it had shown him, wrestled with it.

'Leave me! Take me back. Haunt me no longer!'

In the struggle, if that can be called a struggle in which the Ghost with no visible resistance on its own part was undisturbed by any effort of its adversary, Scrooge observed that its light was burning high and bright; and dimly connecting that with its influence over him, he seized the extinguisher-cap, and by a sudden action pressed it down upon its head.

The Spirit dropped beneath it, so that the extinguisher covered its whole form; but though Scrooge pressed it down with all his force, he could not hide the light, which streamed from under it, in an unbroken flood upon the ground.

He was conscious of being exhausted, and overcome by an irresistible drowsiness; and, further, of being in his own bedroom. He gave the cap a parting squeeze, in which his hand relaxed; and had barely time to reel to bed, before he sank into a heavy sleep.

STAVE 3: THE SECOND OF THE THREE SPIRITS

Awaking in the middle of a prodigiously tough snore, and sitting up in bed to get his thoughts together, Scrooge had no occasion to be told that the bell was again upon the stroke of One. He felt that he was restored to consciousness in the right nick of time, for the especial purpose of holding a conference with the second messenger despatched to him through Jacob Marley's intervention. But, finding that he turned uncomfortably cold when he began to wonder which of his curtains this new spectre would draw back, he put them every one aside with his own hands, and lying down again, established a sharp look-out all round the bed. For, he wished to challenge the Spirit on the moment of its appearance, and did not wish to be taken by surprise, and made nervous.

Gentlemen of the free-and-easy sort, who plume themselves on being acquainted with a move or two, and being usually equal to the time-of-day, express the wide range of their capacity for adventure by observing that they are good for anything from pitch-and-toss to manslaughter; between which opposite extremes, no doubt, there lies a tolerably wide and comprehensive range of subjects. Without venturing for Scrooge quite as hardily as this, I don't mind calling on you to believe that he was ready for a good broad field of strange appearances, and that nothing between a baby and rhinoceros would have astonished him very much.

Now, being prepared for almost anything, he was not by any means prepared for nothing; and, consequently, when the bell struck One, and no shape appeared, he was taken with a violent fit of trembling. Five minutes, ten minutes, a quarter of an hour went by, yet nothing came. All this time, he lay upon his bed, the very core and centre of a blaze of ruddy light, which streamed upon it when the clock proclaimed the hour; and which, being only light, was more alarming than a dozen ghosts, as he was powerless to make out what it meant, or would be at; and was sometimes apprehensive that he might be at that very moment an interesting case of spontaneous combustion, without having the consolation of knowing it. At last, however, he began to think—as you or I would have thought at first; for it is always the person not in the predicament who knows what ought to have been done in it, and would unquestionably have done it too—at last, I say, he began to think that the source and secret of this ghostly light might be in the adjoining room, from whence, on further tracing it, it seemed to shine. This idea taking full possession of his mind, he got up softly and shuffled in his slippers to the door.

The moment Scrooge's hand was on the lock, a strange voice called him by his name, and bade him enter. He obeyed.

It was his own room. There was no doubt about that. But it had undergone a surprising transformation. The walls and ceiling were so hung with living green, that it looked a perfect grove; from every part of which, bright gleaming berries glistened. The crisp leaves of holly, mistletoe, and ivy reflected back the light, as if so many little mirrors had been scattered there; and such a mighty blaze went roaring up the chimney, as that dull petrification of a hearth had never known in Scrooge's time, or Marley's, or for many and many a winter season gone. Heaped up on the floor, to form a kind of throne, were turkeys, geese, game, poultry, brawn, great joints of meat, sucking-pigs, long wreaths of sausages, mince-pies, plum-puddings, barrels of oysters, red-hot chestnuts, cherry-cheeked apples, juicy oranges, luscious pears, immense twelfth-cakes, and seething bowls of punch, that made the chamber dim with their delicious steam. In easy state upon this couch, there sat a jolly Giant, glorious to see, who bore a glowing torch, in shape not unlike Plenty's horn, and held it up, high up, to shed its light on Scrooge, as he came peeping round the door.

'Come in!' exclaimed the Ghost. 'Come in, and know me better, man!'

Scrooge entered timidly, and hung his head before this Spirit. He was not the dogged Scrooge he had been; and though the Spirit's eyes were clear and kind, he did not like to meet them.

'I am the Ghost of Christmas Present,' said the Spirit. 'Look upon me!'

Scrooge reverently did so. It was clothed in one simple green robe, or mantle, bordered with white fur. This garment hung so loosely on the figure, that its capacious breast was bare, as if disdaining to be warded or concealed by any artifice. Its feet, observable beneath the ample folds of the garment, were also bare; and on its head it wore no other covering than a holly wreath, set here and there with shining icicles. Its dark brown curls were long and free; free as its genial face, its sparkling eye, its open hand, its cheery voice, its unconstrained demeanour, and its joyful air. Girded round its middle was an antique scabbard; but no sword was in it, and the ancient sheath was eaten up with rust.

'You have never seen the like of me before!' exclaimed the Spirit.

'Never,' Scrooge made answer to it.

'Have never walked forth with the younger members of my family; meaning (for I am very young) my elder brothers born in these later years?' pursued the Phantom.

'I don't think I have,' said Scrooge. 'I am afraid I have not. Have you had many brothers, Spirit?'

'More than eighteen hundred,' said the Ghost.

'A tremendous family to provide for!' muttered Scrooge.

The Ghost of Christmas Present rose.

'Spirit,' said Scrooge submissively,' conduct me where you will. I went forth last night on compulsion, and I learnt a lesson which is working now. To-night, if you have aught to teach me, let me profit by it.'

'Touch my robe!'

Scrooge did as he was told, and held it fast.

Holly, mistletoe, red berries, ivy, turkeys, geese, game, poultry, brawn, meat, pigs, sausages, oysters, pies, puddings, fruit, and punch, all vanished instantly. So did the room, the fire, the ruddy glow, the hour of night, and they stood in the city streets on Christmas morning, where (for the weather was severe) the people made a rough, but brisk and not unpleasant kind of music, in scraping the snow from the pavement in front of their dwellings, and from the tops of their houses, whence it was mad delight to the boys to see it come plumping down into the road below, and splitting into artificial little snow-storms.

The house fronts looked black enough, and the windows blacker, contrasting with the smooth white sheet of snow upon the roofs, and with the dirtier snow upon the ground; which last deposit had been ploughed up in deep furrows by the heavy wheels of carts and waggons; furrows that crossed and recrossed each other hundreds of times where the great streets branched off; and made intricate channels, hard to trace in the thick yellow mud and icy water. The sky was gloomy, and the shortest streets were choked up with a dingy mist, half thawed, half frozen, whose heavier particles descended in shower of sooty atoms, as if all the chimneys in Great Britain had, by one consent, caught fire, and were blazing away to their dear hearts' content. There was nothing very cheerful in the climate or the town, and yet was there an air of cheerfulness abroad that the clearest summer air and brightest summer sun might have endeavoured to diffuse in vain.

For, the people who were shovelling away on the housetops were jovial and full of glee; calling out to one another from the parapets, and now and then exchanging a facetious snowball—better-natured missile far than many a wordy jest—laughing heartily if it went right and not less heartily if it went wrong. The poulterers' shops were still half open, and the fruiterers' were radiant in their glory. There were great, round, pot-bellied baskets of chestnuts, shaped like the waistcoats of jolly old gentlemen, lolling at the doors, and tumbling out into the street in their apoplectic opulence. There were ruddy, brown-faced, broad-girthed Spanish onions, shining in the fatness of their growth like Spanish Friars, and winking from their shelves in wanton slyness at the girls as they went by, and glanced demurely at the hung-up mistletoe. There were pears and apples, clustered high in blooming pyramids; there were bunches of grapes, made, in the shop-keepers' benevolence to dangle from conspicuous hooks, that people's mouths might water gratis as they passed; there were piles of filberts, mossy and brown, recalling, in their fragrance, ancient walks among the woods, and pleasant shufflings ankle deep through withered leaves; there were Norfolk Biffins, squab and swarthy, setting off the yellow of the oranges and lemons, and, in the great compactness of their juicy persons, urgently entreating and beseeching to be carried home in paper bags and eaten after dinner. The very gold and silver fish, set forth among these choice fruits in a bowl, though members of a dull and stagnant-blooded race, appeared to know that there was something going on; and, to a fish, went gasping round and round their little world in slow and passionless excitement.

The Grocers'! oh the Grocers'! nearly closed, with perhaps two shutters down, or one; but through those gaps such glimpses! It was not alone that the scales descending on the counter made a merry sound, or that the twine and roller parted company so briskly, or that the canisters were rattled up and down like juggling tricks, or even that the blended scents of tea and coffee were so grateful to the nose, or even that the raisins were so plentiful and rare, the almonds so extremely white, the sticks of cinnamon so long and straight, the other spices so delicious, the candied fruits so caked and spotted with molten sugar as to make the coldest lookers-on feel faint and subsequently bilious. Nor was it that the figs were moist and pulpy, or that the French plums blushed in modest tartness from their highly-decorated boxes, or that everything was good to eat and in its Christmas dress; but the customers were all so hurried and so eager in the hopeful promise of the day, that they tumbled up against each other at the door, crashing their wicker baskets wildly, and left their purchases upon the counter, and came running back to fetch them, and committed hundreds of the like mistakes, in the best humour possible; while the Grocer and his people were so frank and fresh that the polished hearts with which they fastened their aprons behind might have been their own, worn outside for general inspection, and for Christmas daws to peck at if they chose.

But soon the steeples called good people all, to church and chapel, and away they came, flocking through the streets in their best clothes, and with their gayest faces. And at the same time there emerged from scores of bye-streets, lanes, and nameless turnings, innumerable people, carrying their dinners to the bakers' shops. The sight of these poor revellers appeared to interest the Spirit very much, for he stood with Scrooge beside him in a baker's doorway, and taking off the covers as their bearers passed, sprinkled incense on their dinners from his torch. And it was a very uncommon kind of torch, for once or twice when there were angry words between some dinner-carriers who had jostled each other, he shed a few drops of water on them from it, and their good humour was restored directly. For they said, it was a shame to quarrel upon Christmas Day. And so it was! God love it, so it was!

In time the bells ceased, and the bakers were shut up; and yet there was a genial shadowing forth of all these dinners and the progress of their cooking, in the thawed blotch of wet above each baker's oven; where the pavement smoked as if its stones were cooking too.

'Is there a peculiar flavour in what you sprinkle from your torch?' asked Scrooge.

'There is. My own.'

'Would it apply to any kind of dinner on this day?' asked Scrooge.

'To any kindly given. To a poor one most.'

'Why to a poor one most?' asked Scrooge.

'Because it needs it most.'

'Spirit,' said Scrooge, after a moment's thought,' I wonder you, of all the beings in the many worlds about us, should desire to cramp these people's opportunities of innocent enjoyment.'

'I!' cried the Spirit.

'You would deprive them of their means of dining every seventh day, often the only day on which they can be said to dine at all,' said Scrooge. 'Wouldn't you?'

'I!' cried the Spirit.

'You seek to close these places on the Seventh Day?' said Scrooge. 'And it comes to the same thing.'

'*I* seek!' exclaimed the Spirit.

'Forgive me if I am wrong. It has been done in your name, or at least in that of your family,' said Scrooge.

'There are some upon this earth of yours,' returned the Spirit,' who lay claim to know us, and who do their deeds of passion, pride, ill-will, hatred, envy, bigotry, and selfishness in our name, who are as strange to us and all our kith and kin, as if they had never lived. Remember that, and charge their doings on themselves, not us.'

Scrooge promised that he would; and they went on, invisible, as they had been before, into the suburbs of the town. It was a remarkable quality of the Ghost (which Scrooge had observed at the baker's), that notwithstanding his gigantic size, he could accommodate himself to any place with ease; and that he stood beneath a low roof quite as gracefully and like a supernatural creature, as it was possible he could have done in any lofty hall.

And perhaps it was the pleasure the good Spirit had in showing off this power of his, or else it was his own kind, generous, hearty nature, and his sympathy with all poor men, that led him straight to Scrooge's clerk's; for there he went, and took Scrooge with him, holding to his robe; and on the threshold of the door the Spirit smiled, and stopped to bless Bob Cratchit's dwelling with the sprinkling of his torch. Think of that! Bob had but fifteen bob a-week himself; he pocketed on Saturdays but fifteen copies of his Christian name; and yet the Ghost of Christmas Present blessed his four-roomed house!

Then up rose Mrs Cratchit, Cratchit's wife, dressed out but poorly in a twice-turned gown, but brave in ribbons, which are cheap and make a goodly show for sixpence; and she laid the cloth, assisted by Belinda Cratchit, second of her daughters, also brave in ribbons; while Master Peter Cratchit plunged a fork into the saucepan

of potatoes, and getting the corners of his monstrous shirt collar (Bob's private property, conferred upon his son and heir in honour of the day) into his mouth, rejoiced to find himself so gallantly attired, and yearned to show his linen in the fashionable Parks. And now two smaller Cratchits, boy and girl, came tearing in, screaming that outside the baker's they had smelt the goose, and known it for their own; and basking in luxurious thoughts of sage and onion, these young Cratchits danced about the table, and exalted Master Peter Cratchit to the skies, while he (not proud, although his collars nearly choked him) blew the fire, until the slow potatoes bubbling up, knocked loudly at the saucepan-lid to be let out and peeled.

'What has ever got your precious father then.' said Mrs Cratchit. 'And your brother, Tiny Tim! And Martha warn't as late last Christmas Day by half-an-hour!'

'Here's Martha, mother!' said a girl, appearing as she spoke.

'Here's Martha, mother!' cried the two young Cratchits. 'Hurrah! There's such a goose, Martha!'

'Why, bless your heart alive, my dear, how late you are!' said Mrs Cratchit, kissing her a dozen times, and taking off her shawl and bonnet for her with officious zeal.

'We'd a deal of work to finish up last night,' replied the girl,' and had to clear away this morning, mother!'

'Well. Never mind so long as you are come,' said Mrs Cratchit. 'Sit ye down before the fire, my dear, and have a warm, Lord bless ye!'

'No, no! There's father coming,' cried the two young Cratchits, who were everywhere at once. 'Hide, Martha, hide!'

So Martha hid herself, and in came little Bob, the father, with at least three feet of comforter exclusive of the fringe, hanging down before him; and his threadbare clothes darned up and brushed, to look seasonable; and Tiny Tim upon his shoulder. Alas for Tiny Tim, he bore a little crutch, and had his limbs supported by an iron frame.

'Why, where's our Martha?' cried Bob Cratchit, looking round.

'Not coming,' said Mrs Cratchit.

'Not coming!' said Bob, with a sudden declension in his high spirits; for he had been Tim's blood horse all the way from church, and had come home rampant. 'Not coming upon Christmas Day!'

Martha didn't like to see him disappointed, if it were only in joke; so she came out prematurely from behind the closet door, and ran into his arms, while the two young Cratchits hustled Tiny Tim, and bore him off into the wash-house, that he might hear the pudding singing in the copper.

'And how did little Tim behave?' asked Mrs Cratchit, when she had rallied Bob on his credulity, and Bob had hugged his daughter to his heart's content.

'As good as gold,' said Bob,' and better. Somehow he gets thoughtful, sitting by himself so much, and thinks the strangest things you ever heard. He told me, coming home, that he hoped the people saw him in the church, because he was a cripple, and it might be pleasant to them to remember upon Christmas Day, who made lame beggars walk, and blind men see.'

Bob's voice was tremulous when he told them this, and trembled more when he said that Tiny Tim was growing strong and hearty.

His active little crutch was heard upon the floor, and back came Tiny Tim before another word was spoken, escorted by his brother and sister to his stool before the fire; and while Bob, turning up his cuffs—as if, poor fellow, they were capable of being made more shabby—compounded some hot mixture in a jug with gin and lemons, and stirred it round and round and put it on the hob to simmer; Master Peter, and the two ubiquitous young Cratchits went to fetch the goose, with which they soon returned in high procession.

Such a bustle ensued that you might have thought a goose the rarest of all birds; a feathered phenomenon, to which a black swan was a matter of course—and in truth it was something very like it in that house. Mrs Cratchit made the gravy (ready beforehand in a little saucepan) hissing hot; Master Peter mashed the potatoes with incredible vigour; Miss Belinda sweetened up the apple-sauce; Martha dusted the hot plates; Bob took Tiny Tim beside him in a tiny corner at the table; the two young Cratchits set chairs for everybody, not forgetting themselves, and mounting guard upon their posts, crammed spoons into their mouths, lest they should shriek for goose before their turn came to be helped. At last the dishes were set on, and grace was said. It was succeeded by a breathless pause, as Mrs Cratchit, looking slowly all along the carving-knife, prepared to plunge it in the breast; but when she did, and when the long expected gush of stuffing issued forth, one murmur of delight arose all round the board, and even Tiny Tim, excited by the two young Cratchits, beat on the table with the handle of his knife, and feebly cried Hurrah!

There never was such a goose. Bob said he didn't believe there ever was such a goose cooked. Its tenderness and flavour, size and cheapness, were the themes of universal admiration. Eked out by apple-sauce and mashed potatoes, it was a sufficient dinner for the whole family; indeed, as Mrs Cratchit said with great delight (surveying one small atom of a bone upon the dish), they hadn't ate it all at last. Yet every one had had enough, and the youngest Cratchits in particular, were steeped in sage and onion to the eyebrows. But now, the plates being changed by Miss Belinda, Mrs Cratchit left the room alone—too nervous to bear witnesses—to take the pudding up and bring it in.

Suppose it should not be done enough! Suppose it should break in turning out! Suppose somebody should have got over the wall of the back-yard, and stolen it, while they were merry with the goose—a supposition at which the two young Cratchits became livid. All sorts of horrors were supposed.

Hallo! A great deal of steam! The pudding was out of the copper. A smell like a washing-day! That was the cloth. A smell like an eating-house and a pastrycook's next door to each other, with a laundress's next door to that! That was the pudding. In half a minute Mrs Cratchit entered—flushed, but smiling proudly—with the pudding, like a speckled cannon-ball, so hard and firm, blazing in half of half-a-quartern of ignited brandy, and bedight with Christmas holly stuck into the top.

Oh, a wonderful pudding! Bob Cratchit said, and calmly too, that he regarded it as the greatest success achieved by Mrs Cratchit since their marriage. Mrs Cratchit said that now the weight was off her mind, she would confess she had had her doubts about the quantity of flour. Everybody had something to say about it, but nobody said or thought it was at all a small pudding for a large family. It would have been flat heresy to do so. Any Cratchit would have blushed to hint at such a thing.

At last the dinner was all done, the cloth was cleared, the hearth swept, and the fire made up. The compound in the jug being tasted, and considered perfect, apples and oranges were put upon the table, and a shovel-full of chestnuts on the fire. Then all the Cratchit family drew round the hearth, in what Bob Cratchit called a circle, meaning half a one; and at Bob Cratchit's elbow stood the family display of glass. Two tumblers, and a custard-cup without a handle.

These held the hot stuff from the jug, however, as well as golden goblets would have done; and Bob served it out with beaming looks, while the chestnuts on the fire sputtered and cracked noisily. Then Bob proposed:

'A Merry Christmas to us all, my dears. God bless us!'

Which all the family re-echoed.

'God bless us every one!' said Tiny Tim, the last of all.

He sat very close to his father's side upon his little stool. Bob held his withered little hand in his, as if he loved the child, and wished to keep him by his side, and dreaded that he might be taken from him.

'Spirit,' said Scrooge, with an interest he had never felt before, 'tell me if Tiny Tim will live.'

'I see a vacant seat,' replied the Ghost, 'in the poor chimney-corner, and a crutch without an owner, carefully preserved. If these shadows remain unaltered by the Future, the child will die.'

'No, no,' said Scrooge. 'Oh, no, kind Spirit! say he will be spared.'

'If these shadows remain unaltered by the Future, none other of my race,' returned the Ghost, 'will find him here. What then? If he be like to die, he had better do it, and decrease the surplus population.'

Scrooge hung his head to hear his own words quoted by the Spirit, and was overcome with penitence and grief. 'Man,' said the Ghost, 'if man you be in heart, not adamant, forbear that wicked cant until you have discovered What the surplus is, and Where it is. Will you decide what men shall live, what men shall die? It may be, that in the sight of Heaven, you are more worthless and less fit to live than millions like this poor man's child. Oh God! to hear the Insect on the leaf pronouncing on the too much life among his hungry brothers in the dust!'

Scrooge bent before the Ghost's rebuke, and trembling cast his eyes upon the ground. But he raised them speedily, on hearing his own name.

'Mr. Scrooge!' said Bob; 'I'll give you Mr. Scrooge, the Founder of the Feast!'

'The Founder of the Feast indeed!' cried Mrs Cratchit, reddening. 'I wish I had him here. I'd give him a piece of my mind to feast upon, and I hope he'd have a good appetite for it.'

'My dear,' said Bob, 'the children. Christmas Day.'

'It should be Christmas Day, I am sure,' said she, 'on which one drinks the health of such an odious, stingy, hard, unfeeling man as Mr Scrooge. You know he is, Robert! Nobody knows it better than you do, poor fellow.'

'My dear,' was Bob's mild answer, 'Christmas Day.'

'I'll drink his health for your sake and the Day's,' said Mrs Cratchit, 'not for his. Long life to him! A merry Christmas and a happy new year! He'll be very merry and very happy, I have no doubt!'

The children drank the toast after her. It was the first of their proceedings which had no heartiness. Tiny Tim drank it last of all, but he didn't care twopence for it. Scrooge was the Ogre of the family. The mention of his name cast a dark shadow on the party, which was not dispelled for full five minutes.

After it had passed away, they were ten times merrier than before, from the mere relief of Scrooge the Baleful being done with. Bob

Cratchit told them how he had a situation in his eye for Master Peter, which would bring in, if obtained, full five-and-sixpence weekly. The two young Cratchits laughed tremendously at the idea of Peter's being a man of business; and Peter himself looked thoughtfully at the fire from between his collars, as if he were deliberating what particular investments he should favour when he came into the receipt of that bewildering income. Martha, who was a poor apprentice at a milliner's, then told them what kind of work she had to do, and how many hours she worked at a stretch, and how she meant to lie abed to-morrow morning for a good long rest; to-morrow being a holiday she passed at home. Also how she had seen a countess and a lord some days before, and how the lord was much about as tall as Peter; at which Peter pulled up his collars so high that you couldn't have seen his head if you had been there. All this time the chestnuts and the jug went round and round; and by-and-bye they had a song, about a lost child travelling in the snow, from Tiny Tim, who had a plaintive little voice, and sang it very well indeed.

There was nothing of high mark in this. They were not a handsome family; they were not well dressed; their shoes were far from being water-proof; their clothes were scanty; and Peter might have known, and very likely did, the inside of a pawnbroker's. But, they were happy, grateful, pleased with one another, and contented with the time; and when they faded, and looked happier yet in the bright sprinklings of the Spirit's torch at parting, Scrooge had his eye upon them, and especially on Tiny Tim, until the last.

By this time it was getting dark, and snowing pretty heavily; and as Scrooge and the Spirit went along the streets, the brightness of the roaring fires in kitchens, parlours, and all sorts of rooms, was wonderful. Here, the flickering of the blaze showed preparations for a cosy dinner, with hot plates baking through and through before the fire, and deep red curtains, ready to be drawn to shut out cold and darkness. There all the children of the house were running out into the snow to meet their married sisters, brothers, cousins, uncles, aunts, and be the first to greet them. Here, again, were shadows on the window-blind of guests assembling; and there a group of handsome girls, all hooded and fur-booted, and all chattering at once, tripped lightly off to some near neighbour's house; where, woe upon the single man who saw them enter—artful witches, well they knew it—in a glow!

But, if you had judged from the numbers of people on their way to friendly gatherings, you might have thought that no one was at home to give them welcome when they got there, instead of every house expecting company, and piling up its fires half-chimney high. Blessings on it, how the Ghost exulted! How it bared its breadth of breast, and opened its capacious palm, and floated on, outpouring, with a generous hand, its bright and harmless mirth on everything within its reach! The very lamplighter, who ran on before, dotting the dusky street with specks of light, and who was dressed to spend the evening somewhere, laughed out loudly as the Spirit passed, though little kenned the lamplighter that he had any company but Christmas!

And now, without a word of warning from the Ghost, they stood upon a bleak and desert moor, where monstrous masses of rude stone were cast about, as though it were the burial-place of giants; and water spread itself wheresoever it listed, or would have done so, but for the frost that held it prisoner; and nothing grew but moss and furze, and coarse rank grass. Down in the west the setting sun had left a streak of fiery red, which glared upon the desolation for an instant, like a sullen eye, and frowning lower, lower, lower yet, was lost in the thick gloom of darkest night.

'What place is this?' asked Scrooge.

'A place where Miners live, who labour in the bowels of the earth,' returned the Spirit. 'But they know me. See!'

A light shone from the window of a hut, and swiftly they advanced towards it. Passing through the wall of mud and stone, they found a cheerful company assembled round a glowing fire. An old, old man and woman, with their children and their children's children, and another generation beyond that, all decked out gaily in their holiday attire. The old man, in a voice that seldom rose above the howling of the wind upon the barren waste, was singing them a Christmas song—it had been a very old song when he was a boy—and from time to time they all joined in the chorus. So surely as they raised their voices, the old man got quite blithe and loud; and so surely as they stopped, his vigour sank again.

The Spirit did not tarry here, but bade Scrooge hold his robe, and passing on above the moor, sped—whither? Not to sea? To sea. To Scrooge's horror, looking back, he saw the last of the land, a frightful range of rocks, behind them; and his ears were deafened by the thundering of water, as it rolled and roared, and raged among the dreadful caverns it had worn, and fiercely tried to undermine the earth.

Built upon a dismal reef of sunken rocks, some league or so from shore, on which the waters chafed and dashed, the wild year through, there stood a solitary lighthouse. Great heaps of sea-weed clung to its base, and storm-birds—born of the wind one might suppose, as sea-weed of the water—rose and fell about it, like the waves they skimmed.

But even here, two men who watched the light had made a fire, that through the loophole in the thick stone wall shed out a ray of brightness on the awful sea. Joining their horny hands over the rough table at which they sat, they wished each other Merry Christmas in their can of grog; and one of them: the elder, too, with his face all damaged and scarred with hard weather, as the figure-head of an old ship might be: struck up a sturdy song that was like a Gale in itself.

Again the Ghost sped on, above the black and heaving sea—on, on—until, being far away, as he told Scrooge, from any shore, they lighted on a ship. They stood beside the helmsman at the wheel, the look-out in the bow, the officers who had the watch; dark, ghostly figures in their several stations; but every man among them hummed a Christmas tune, or had a Christmas thought, or spoke below his breath to his companion of some bygone Christmas Day, with homeward hopes belonging to it. And every man on board, waking or sleeping, good or bad, had had a kinder word for another on that day than on any day in the year; and had shared to some extent in its festivities; and had remembered those he cared for at a distance, and had known that they delighted to remember him.

It was a great surprise to Scrooge, while listening to the moaning of the wind, and thinking what a solemn thing it was to move on through the lonely darkness over an unknown abyss, whose depths were secrets as profound as Death: it was a great surprise to Scrooge, while thus engaged, to hear a hearty laugh. It was a much greater surprise to Scrooge to recognise it as his own nephew's and to find himself in a bright, dry, gleaming room, with the Spirit standing smiling by his side, and looking at that same nephew with approving affability!

'Ha, ha!' laughed Scrooge's nephew. 'Ha, ha, ha!'

If you should happen, by any unlikely chance, to know a man more blest in a laugh than Scrooge's nephew, all I can say is, I should like to know him too. Introduce him to me, and I'll cultivate his acquaintance.

It is a fair, even-handed, noble adjustment of things, that while there is infection in disease and sorrow, there is nothing in the world so irresistibly contagious as laughter and good-humour. When Scrooge's nephew laughed in this way: holding his sides, rolling his head, and twisting his face into the most extravagant contortions: Scrooge's niece, by marriage, laughed as heartily as he. And their assembled friends being not a bit behindhand, roared out lustily.

'Ha, ha! Ha, ha, ha, ha!'

'He said that Christmas was a humbug, as I live!' cried Scrooge's nephew. 'He believed it too!'

'More shame for him, Fred!' said Scrooge's niece, indignantly. Bless those women; they never do anything by halves. They are always in earnest.

She was very pretty: exceedingly pretty. With a dimpled, surprised-looking, capital face; a ripe little mouth, that seemed made to be kissed—as no doubt it was; all kinds of good little dots about her chin, that melted into one another when she laughed; and the sunniest pair of eyes you ever saw in any little creature's head. Altogether she was what you would have called provoking, you know; but satisfactory.

'He's a comical old fellow,' said Scrooge's nephew,' that's the truth: and not so pleasant as he might be. However, his offences carry their own punishment, and I have nothing to say against him.'

'I'm sure he is very rich, Fred,' hinted Scrooge's niece. 'At least you always tell me so.'

'What of that, my dear!' said Scrooge's nephew. 'His wealth is of no use to him. He don't do any good with it. He don't make himself comfortable with it. He hasn't the satisfaction of thinking—ha, ha, ha!—that he is ever going to benefit us with it.'

'I have no patience with him,' observed Scrooge's niece. Scrooge's niece's sisters, and all the other ladies, expressed the same opinion.

'Oh, I have!' said Scrooge's nephew. 'I am sorry for him; I couldn't be angry with him if I tried. Who suffers by his ill whims? Himself, always. Here, he takes it into his head to dislike us, and he won't come and dine with us. What's the consequence? He don't lose much of a dinner.'

'Indeed, I think he loses a very good dinner,' interrupted Scrooge's niece. Everybody else said the same, and they must be allowed to have been competent judges, because they had just had dinner; and, with the dessert upon the table, were clustered round the fire, by lamplight.

'Well. I'm very glad to hear it,' said Scrooge's nephew, 'because I haven't great faith in these young housekeepers. What do you say, Topper?'

Topper had clearly got his eye upon one of Scrooge's niece's sisters, for he answered that a bachelor was a wretched outcast, who had no right to express an opinion on the subject. Whereat Scrooge's niece's sister—the plump one with the lace tucker: not the one with the roses—blushed.

'Do go on, Fred,' said Scrooge's niece, clapping her hands. 'He never finishes what he begins to say! He is such a ridiculous fellow!'

Scrooge's nephew revelled in another laugh, and as it was impossible to keep the infection off; though the plump sister tried hard to do it with aromatic vinegar; his example was unanimously followed.

'I was only going to say,' said Scrooge's nephew,' that the consequence of his taking a dislike to us, and not making merry with us, is, as I think, that he loses some pleasant moments, which could do him no harm. I am sure he loses pleasanter companions than he can find in his own thoughts, either in his mouldy old office, or his dusty chambers. I mean to give him the same chance every year, whether he likes it or not, for I pity him. He may rail at Christmas till he dies, but he can't help thinking better of it—I defy him—if he finds me going there, in good temper, year after year, and saying Uncle Scrooge, how are you? If it only puts him in the vein to leave his poor clerk fifty pounds, that's something; and I think I shook him yesterday.'

It was their turn to laugh now at the notion of his shaking Scrooge. But being thoroughly good-natured, and not much caring what they laughed at, so that they laughed at any rate, he encouraged them in their merriment, and passed the bottle joyously.

After tea. they had some music. For they were a musical family, and knew what they were about, when they sung a Glee or Catch, I can assure you: especially Topper, who could growl away in the bass like a good one, and never swell the large veins in his forehead, or get red in the face over it. Scrooge's niece played well upon the harp; and played among other tunes a simple little air (a mere nothing: you might learn to whistle it in two minutes), which had been familiar to the child who fetched Scrooge from the boarding-school, as he had been reminded by the Ghost of Christmas Past. When this strain of music sounded, all the things that Ghost had shown him, came upon his mind; he softened more and more; and thought that if he could have listened to it often, years ago, he might have cultivated the kindnesses of life for his own happiness with his own hands, without resorting to the sexton's spade that buried Jacob Marley.

But they didn't devote the whole evening to music. After a while they played at forfeits; for it is good to be children sometimes, and never better than at Christmas, when its mighty Founder was a child himself. Stop! There was first a game at blind-man's buff. Of course there was. And I no more believe Topper was really blind than I believe he had eyes in his boots. My opinion is, that it was a done thing between him and Scrooge's nephew; and that the Ghost of Christmas Present knew it. The way he went after that plump sister in the lace tucker, was an outrage on the credulity of human nature. Knocking down the fire-irons, tumbling over the chairs, bumping against the piano, smothering himself among the curtains, wherever she went, there went he. He always knew where the plump sister was. He wouldn't catch anybody else. If you had fallen up against him (as some of them did), on purpose, he would have made a feint of endeavouring to seize you, which would have been an affront to your understanding, and would instantly have sidled off in the direction of the plump sister. She often cried out that it wasn't fair; and it really was not. But when at last, he caught her; when, in spite of all her silken rustlings, and her rapid flutterings past him, he got her into a corner whence there was no escape; then his conduct was the most execrable. For his pretending not to know her; his pretending that it was necessary to touch her head-dress, and further to assure himself of her identity by pressing a certain ring upon her finger, and a certain chain about her neck; was vile, monstrous! No doubt she told him her opinion of it, when, another blind-man being in office, they were so very confidential together, behind the curtains.

Scrooge's niece was not one of the blind-man's buff party, but was made comfortable with a large chair and a footstool, in a snug corner, where the Ghost and Scrooge were close behind her. But she joined in the forfeits, and loved her love to admiration with all the letters of the alphabet. Likewise at the game of How, When, and Where, she was very great, and to the secret joy of Scrooge's nephew, beat her sisters hollow: though they were sharp girls too, as Topper could have told you. There might have been twenty people there, young and old, but they all played, and so did Scrooge, for, wholly forgetting the interest he had in what was going on, that his voice made no sound in their ears, he sometimes came out with his guess quite loud, and very often guessed quite right, too; for

the sharpest needle, best Whitechapel, warranted not to cut in the eye, was not sharper than Scrooge; blunt as he took it in his head to be.

The Ghost was greatly pleased to find him in this mood, and looked upon him with such favour, that he begged like a boy to be allowed to stay until the guests departed. But this the Spirit said could not be done.

'Here is a new game,' said Scrooge. 'One half hour, Spirit, only one!'

It was a Game called Yes and No, where Scrooge's nephew had to think of something, and the rest must find out what; he only answering to their questions yes or no, as the case was. The brisk fire of questioning to which he was exposed, elicited from him that he was thinking of an animal, a live animal, rather a disagreeable animal, a savage animal, an animal that growled and grunted sometimes, and talked sometimes, and lived in London, and walked about the streets, and wasn't made a show of, and wasn't led by anybody, and didn't live in a menagerie, and was never killed in a market, and was not a horse, or an ass, or a cow, or a bull, or a tiger, or a dog, or a pig, or a cat, or a bear. At every fresh question that was put to him, this nephew burst into a fresh roar of laughter; and was so inexpressibly tickled, that he was obliged to get up off the sofa and stamp. At last the plump sister, falling into a similar state, cried out:

'I have found it out! I know what it is, Fred! I know what it is!'

'What is it?' cried Fred.

'It's your Uncle Scrooge!'

Which it certainly was. Admiration was the universal sentiment, though some objected that the reply to 'Is it a bear?' ought to have been 'Yes;' inasmuch as an answer in the negative was sufficient to have diverted their thoughts from Mr Scrooge, supposing they had ever had any tendency that way.

'He has given us plenty of merriment, I am sure,' said Fred,' and it would be ungrateful not to drink his health. Here is a glass of mulled wine ready to our hand at the moment; and I say, "Uncle Scrooge!"'

'Well! Uncle Scrooge!' they cried.

'A Merry Christmas and a Happy New Year to the old man, whatever he is!' said Scrooge's nephew. 'He wouldn't take it from me, but may he have it, nevertheless. Uncle Scrooge!'

Uncle Scrooge had imperceptibly become so gay and light of heart, that he would have pledged the unconscious company in return, and thanked them in an inaudible speech, if the Ghost had given him time. But the whole scene passed off in the breath of the last word spoken by his nephew; and he and the Spirit were again upon their travels.

Much they saw, and far they went, and many homes they visited, but always with a happy end. The Spirit stood beside sick beds, and they were cheerful; on foreign lands, and they were close at home; by struggling men, and they were patient in their greater hope; by poverty, and it was rich. In almshouse, hospital, and jail, in misery's every refuge, where vain man in his little brief authority had not made fast the door and barred the Spirit out, he left his blessing, and taught Scrooge his precepts.

It was a long night, if it were only a night; but Scrooge had his doubts of this, because the Christmas Holidays appeared to be condensed into the space of time they passed together. It was strange, too, that while Scrooge remained unaltered in his outward form, the Ghost grew older, clearly older. Scrooge had observed this change, but never spoke of it, until they left a children's Twelfth Night party, when, looking at the Spirit as they stood together in an open place, he noticed that its hair was grey.

'Are spirits' lives so short?' asked Scrooge.

'My life upon this globe, is very brief,' replied the Ghost. 'It ends to-night.'

'To-night!' cried Scrooge.

'To-night at midnight. Hark! The time is drawing near.'

The chimes were ringing the three quarters past eleven at that moment.

'Forgive me if I am not justified in what I ask,' said Scrooge, looking intently at the Spirit's robe,' but I see something strange, and not belonging to yourself, protruding from your skirts. Is it a foot or a claw?'

'It might be a claw, for the flesh there is upon it,' was the Spirit's sorrowful reply. 'Look here.'

From the foldings of its robe, it brought two children; wretched, abject, frightful, hideous, miserable. They knelt down at its feet, and clung upon the outside of its garment.

'Oh, Man! look here. Look, look, down here!' exclaimed the Ghost.

They were a boy and a girl. Yellow, meagre, ragged, scowling, wolfish; but prostrate, too, in their humility. Where graceful youth should have filled their features out, and touched them with its freshest tints, a stale and shrivelled hand, like that of age, had pinched, and twisted them, and pulled them into shreds. Where angels might have sat enthroned, devils lurked, and glared out menacing. No change, no degradation, no perversion of humanity, in any grade, through all the mysteries of wonderful creation, has monsters half so horrible and dread.

Scrooge started back, appalled. Having them shown to him in this way, he tried to say they were fine children, but the words choked themselves, rather than be parties to a lie of such enormous magnitude.

'Spirit! are they yours?' Scrooge could say no more.

'They are Man's,' said the Spirit, looking down upon them. 'And they cling to me, appealing from their fathers. This boy is Ignorance. This girl is Want. Beware them both, and all of their degree, but most of all beware this boy, for on his brow I see that written which is Doom, unless the writing be erased. Deny it!' cried the Spirit, stretching out its hand towards the city. 'Slander those who tell it ye! Admit it for your factious purposes, and make it worse! And abide the end!'

'Have they no refuge or resource?' cried Scrooge.

'Are there no prisons?' said the Spirit, turning on him for the last time with his own words. 'Are there no workhouses?' The bell struck twelve.

Scrooge looked about him for the Ghost, and saw it not. As the last stroke ceased to vibrate, he remembered the prediction of old Jacob Marley, and lifting up his eyes, beheld a solemn Phantom, draped and hooded, coming, like a mist along the ground, towards him.

STAVE 4: THE LAST OF THE SPIRITS

The Phantom slowly, gravely, silently approached. When it came, Scrooge bent down upon his knee; for in the very air through which this Spirit moved it seemed to scatter gloom and mystery.

It was shrouded in a deep black garment, which concealed its head, its face, its form, and left nothing of it visible save one outstretched hand. But for this it would have been difficult to detach its figure from the night, and separate it from the darkness by which it was surrounded.

He felt that it was tall and stately when it came beside him, and that its mysterious presence filled him with a solemn dread. He knew no more, for the Spirit neither spoke nor moved.

'I am in the presence of the Ghost of Christmas Yet To Come?' said Scrooge.

The Spirit answered not, but pointed onward with its hand.

'You are about to show me shadows of the things that have not happened, but will happen in the time before us,' Scrooge pursued. 'Is that so, Spirit?'

The upper portion of the garment was contracted for an instant in its folds, as if the Spirit had inclined its head. That was the only answer he received.

Although well used to ghostly company by this time, Scrooge feared the silent shape so much that his legs trembled beneath him, and he found that he could hardly stand when he prepared to follow it. The Spirit pauses a moment, as observing his condition, and giving him time to recover.

But Scrooge was all the worse for this. It thrilled him with a vague uncertain horror, to know that behind the dusky shroud, there were ghostly eyes intently fixed upon him, while he, though he stretched his own to the utmost, could see nothing but a spectral hand and one great heap of black.

'Ghost of the Future!' he exclaimed,' I fear you more than any spectre I have seen. But as I know your purpose is to do me good, and as I hope to live to be another man from what I was, I am prepared to bear you company, and do it with a thankful heart. Will you not speak to me?'

It gave him no reply. The hand was pointed straight before them.

'Lead on!' said Scrooge. 'Lead on! The night is waning fast, and it is precious time to me, I know. Lead on, Spirit!'

The Phantom moved away as it had come towards him. Scrooge followed in the shadow of its dress, which bore him up, he thought, and carried him along.

They scarcely seemed to enter the city; for the city rather seemed to spring up about them, and encompass them of its own act. But there they were, in the heart of it; on Change, amongst the merchants; who hurried up and down, and chinked the money in their pockets, and conversed in groups, and looked at their watches, and trifled thoughtfully with their great gold seals; and so forth, as Scrooge had seen them often.

The Spirit stopped beside one little knot of business men. Observing that the hand was pointed to them, Scrooge advanced to listen to their talk.

'No,' said a great fat man with a monstrous chin,' I don't know much about it, either way. I only know he's dead.'

'When did he die?' inquired another.

'Last night, I believe.'

'Why, what was the matter with him?' asked a third, taking a vast quantity of snuff out of a very large snuff-box. 'I thought he'd never die.'

'God knows,' said the first, with a yawn.

'What has he done with his money?' asked a red-faced gentleman with a pendulous excrescence on the end of his nose, that shook like the gills of a turkey-cock.

'I haven't heard,' said the man with the large chin, yawning again. 'Left it to his company, perhaps. He hasn't left it to me. That's all I know.'

This pleasantry was received with a general laugh.

'It's likely to be a very cheap funeral,' said the same speaker;' for upon my life I don't know of anybody to go to it. Suppose we make up a party and volunteer?'

'I don't mind going if a lunch is provided,' observed the gentleman with the excrescence on his nose. 'But I must be fed, if I make one.'

Another laugh.

'Well, I am the most disinterested among you, after all,' said the first speaker,' for I never wear black gloves, and I never eat lunch. But I'll offer to go, if anybody else will. When I come to think of it, I'm not at all sure that I wasn't his most particular friend; for we used to stop and speak whenever we met. Bye, bye!'

Speakers and listeners strolled away, and mixed with other groups. Scrooge knew the men, and looked towards the Spirit for an explanation.

The Phantom glided on into a street. Its finger pointed to two persons meeting. Scrooge listened again, thinking that the explanation might lie here.

He knew these men, also, perfectly. They were men of business: very wealthy, and of great importance. He had made a point always of standing well in their esteem: in a business point of view, that is; strictly in a business point of view.

'How are you?' said one.

'How are you?' returned the other.

'Well!' said the first. 'Old Scratch has got his own at last, hey?'

'So I am told,' returned the second. 'Cold, isn't it?'

'Seasonable for Christmas time. You're not a skater, I suppose?'

'No. No. Something else to think of. Good morning!'

Not another word. That was their meeting, their conversation, and their parting.

Scrooge was at first inclined to be surprised that the Spirit should attach importance to conversations apparently so trivial; but feeling assured that they must have some hidden purpose, he set himself to consider what it was likely to be. They could scarcely be supposed to have any bearing on the death of Jacob, his old partner, for that was Past, and this Ghost's province was the Future. Nor could he think of any one immediately connected with himself, to whom he could apply them. But nothing doubting that to whomsoever they applied they had some latent moral for his own improvement, he resolved to treasure up every word he heard, and everything he saw; and especially to observe the shadow of himself when it appeared. For he had an expectation that the conduct of his future self would give him the clue he missed, and would render the solution of these riddles easy.

He looked about in that very place for his own image; but another man stood in his accustomed corner, and though the clock pointed to his usual time of day for being there, he saw no likeness of himself among the multitudes that poured in through the Porch. It gave him little surprise, however; for he had been revolving in his mind a change of life, and thought and hoped he saw his new-born resolutions carried out in this.

Quiet and dark, beside him stood the Phantom, with its outstretched hand. When he roused himself from his thoughtful quest, he fancied from the turn of the hand, and its situation in reference to himself, that the Unseen Eyes were looking at him keenly. It made him shudder, and feel very cold.

They left the busy scene, and went into an obscure part of the town, where Scrooge had never penetrated before, although he recognised its situation, and its bad repute. The ways were foul and narrow; the shops and houses wretched; the people half-naked, drunken, slipshod, ugly. Alleys and archways, like so many cesspools, disgorged their offences of smell, and dirt, and life, upon the straggling streets; and the whole quarter reeked with crime, with filth, and misery.

Far in this den of infamous resort, there was a low-browed, beetling shop, below a pent-house roof, where iron, old rags, bottles, bones, and greasy offal, were bought. Upon the floor within, were piled up heaps of rusty keys, nails, chains, hinges, files, scales, weights, and refuse iron of all kinds. Secrets that few would like to scrutinise were bred and hidden in mountains of unseemly rags, masses of corrupted fat, and sepulchres of bones. Sitting in among the wares he dealt in, by a charcoal stove, made of old bricks, was a grey-haired rascal, nearly seventy years of age; who had screened himself from the cold air without, by a frousy curtaining of miscellaneous tatters, hung upon a line; and smoked his pipe in all the luxury of calm retirement.

Scrooge and the Phantom came into the presence of this man, just as a woman with a heavy bundle slunk into the shop. But she had scarcely entered, when another woman, similarly laden, came in too; and she was closely followed by a man in faded black, who was no less startled by the sight of them, than they had been upon the recognition of each other. After a short period of blank astonishment, in which the old man with the pipe had joined them, they all three burst into a laugh.

'Let the charwoman alone to be the first!' cried she who had entered first. 'Let the laundress alone to be the second; and let the undertaker's man alone to be the third. Look here, old Joe, here's a chance. If we haven't all three met here without meaning it!'

'You couldn't have met in a better place,' said old Joe, removing his pipe from his mouth. 'Come into the parlour. You were made free of it long ago, you know; and the other two an't strangers. Stop till I shut the door of the shop. Ah! How it skreeks! There an't such a rusty bit of metal in the place as its own hinges, I believe; and I'm sure there's no such old bones here, as mine. Ha, ha! We're all suitable to our calling, we're well matched. Come into the parlour. Come into the parlour.'

The parlour was the space behind the screen of rags. The old man raked the fire together with an old stair-rod, and having trimmed his smoky lamp (for it was night), with the stem of his pipe, put it in his mouth again.

While he did this, the woman who had already spoken threw her bundle on the floor, and sat down in a flaunting manner on a stool; crossing her elbows on her knees, and looking with a bold defiance at the other two.

'What odds then! What odds, Mrs Dilber?' said the woman. 'Every person has a right to take care of themselves. *He* always did!'

'That's true, indeed!' said the laundress. 'No man more so.'

'Why then, don't stand staring as if you was afraid, woman; who's the wiser? We're not going to pick holes in each other's coats, I suppose.'

'No, indeed!' said Mrs Dilber and the man together. 'We should hope not.'

'Very well, then!' cried the woman. 'That's enough. Who's the worse for the loss of a few things like these? Not a dead man, I suppose.'

'No, indeed!' said Mrs Dilber, laughing.

'If he wanted to keep them after he was dead, a wicked old screw,' pursued the woman,' why wasn't he natural in his lifetime? If he had been, he'd have had somebody to look after him when he was struck with Death, instead of lying gasping out his last there, alone by himself.'

'It's the truest word that ever was spoke,' said Mrs Dilber. 'It's a judgment on him.'

'I wish it was a little heavier judgment,' replied the woman;' and it should have been, you may depend upon it, if I could have laid my hands on anything else. Open that bundle, old Joe, and let me know the value of it. Speak out plain. I'm not afraid to be the first, nor afraid for them to see it. We know pretty well that we were helping ourselves, before we met here, I believe. It's no sin. Open the bundle, Joe.'

But the gallantry of her friends would not allow of this; and the man in faded black, mounting the breach first, produced his plunder. It was not extensive. A seal or two, a pencil-case, a pair of sleeve-buttons, and a brooch of no great value, were all. They were severally examined and appraised by old Joe, who chalked the sums he was disposed to give for each, upon the wall, and added them up into a total when he found there was nothing more to come.

'That's your account,' said Joe,' and I wouldn't give another sixpence, if I was to be boiled for not doing it. Who's next?'

Mrs Dilber was next. Sheets and towels, a little wearing apparel, two old-fashioned silver tea-spoons, a pair of sugar-tongs, and a few boots. Her account was stated on the wall in the same manner.

'I always give too much to ladies. It's a weakness of mine, and that's the way I ruin myself,' said old Joe. 'That's your account. If you asked me for another penny, and made it an open question, I'd repent of being so liberal and knock off half-a-crown.'

'And now undo my bundle, Joe,' said the first woman.

Joe went down on his knees for the greater convenience of opening it, and having unfastened a great many knots, dragged out a large and heavy roll of some dark stuff.

'What do you call this?' said Joe. 'Bed-curtains!'

'Ah!' returned the woman, laughing and leaning forward on her crossed arms. 'Bed-curtains!'

'You don't mean to say you took them down, rings and all, with him lying there?' said Joe.

'Yes I do,' replied the woman. 'Why not?'

'You were born to make your fortune,' said Joe,' and you'll certainly do it.'

'I certainly shan't hold my hand, when I can get anything in it by reaching it out, for the sake of such a man as he was, I promise you, Joe,' returned the woman coolly. 'Don't drop that oil upon the blankets, now.'

'His blankets?' asked Joe.

'Whose else's do you think?' replied the woman. 'He isn't likely to take cold without them, I dare say.'

'I hope he didn't die of any thing catching? Eh?' said old Joe, stopping in his work, and looking up.

'Don't you be afraid of that,' returned the woman. 'I an't so fond of his company that I'd loiter about him for such things, if he did. Ah! you may look through that shirt till your eyes ache; but you won't find a hole in it, nor a threadbare place. It's the best he had, and a fine one too. They'd have wasted it, if it hadn't been for me.'

'What do you call wasting of it?' asked old Joe.

'Putting it on him to be buried in, to be sure,' replied the woman with a laugh. 'Somebody was fool enough to do it, but I took it off again. If calico an't good enough for such a purpose, it isn't good enough for anything. It's quite as becoming to the body. He can't look uglier than he did in that one.'

Scrooge listened to this dialogue in horror. As they sat grouped about their spoil, in the scanty light afforded by the old man's lamp, he viewed them with a detestation and disgust, which could hardly have been greater, though they had been obscene demons, marketing the corpse itself.

'Ha, ha!' laughed the same woman, when old Joe, producing a flannel bag with money in it, told out their several gains upon the ground. 'This is the end of it, you see! He frightened every one away from him when he was alive, to profit us when he was dead! Ha, ha, ha!'

'Spirit!' said Scrooge, shuddering from head to foot. 'I see, I see. The case of this unhappy man might be my own. My life tends that way, now. Merciful Heaven, what is this!'

He recoiled in terror, for the scene had changed, and now he almost touched a bed: a bare, uncurtained bed: on which, beneath a ragged sheet, there lay a something covered up, which, though it was dumb, announced itself in awful language.

The room was very dark, too dark to be observed with any accuracy, though Scrooge glanced round it in obedience to a secret impulse, anxious to know what kind of room it was. A pale light, rising in the outer air, fell straight upon the bed; and on it, plundered and bereft, unwatched, unwept, uncared for, was the body of this man.

Scrooge glanced towards the Phantom. Its steady hand was pointed to the head. The cover was so carelessly adjusted that the slightest raising of it, the motion of a finger upon Scrooge's part, would have disclosed the face. He thought of it, felt how easy it would be to do, and longed to do it; but had no more power to withdraw the veil than to dismiss the spectre at his side.

Oh cold, cold, rigid, dreadful Death, set up thine altar here, and dress it with such terrors as thou hast at thy command: for this is thy dominion! But of the loved, revered, and honoured head, thou canst not turn one hair to thy dread purposes, or make one feature odious. It is not that the hand is heavy and will fall down when released; it is not that the heart and pulse are still; but that the hand was open, generous, and true; the heart brave, warm, and tender; and the pulse a man's. Strike, Shadow, strike! And see his good deeds springing from the wound, to sow the world with life immortal!

No voice pronounced these words in Scrooge's ears, and yet he heard them when he looked upon the bed. He thought, if this man could be raised up now, what would be his foremost thoughts. Avarice, hard-dealing, griping cares? They have brought him to a rich end, truly!

He lay, in the dark empty house, with not a man, a woman, or a child, to say that he was kind to me in this or that, and for the memory of one kind word I will be kind to him. A cat was tearing at the door, and there was a sound of gnawing rats beneath the hearth-stone. What they wanted in the room of death, and why they were so restless and disturbed, Scrooge did not dare to think.

'Spirit!' he said,' this is a fearful place. In leaving it, I shall not leave its lesson, trust me. Let us go!'

Still the Ghost pointed with an unmoved finger to the head.

'I understand you,' Scrooge returned,' and I would do it, if I could. But I have not the power, Spirit. I have not the power.'

Again it seemed to look upon him.

'If there is any person in the town, who feels emotion caused by this man's death,' said Scrooge quite agonised, 'show that person to me, Spirit, I beseech you!'

The Phantom spread its dark robe before him for a moment, like a wing; and withdrawing it, revealed a room by daylight, where a mother and her children were.

She was expecting some one, and with anxious eagerness; for she walked up and down the room; started at every sound; looked out from the window; glanced at the clock; tried, but in vain, to work with her needle; and could hardly bear the voices of the children in their play.

At length the long-expected knock was heard. She hurried to the door, and met her husband; a man whose face was careworn and depressed, though he was young. There was a remarkable expression in it now; a kind of serious delight of which he felt ashamed, and which he struggled to repress.

He sat down to the dinner that had been boarding for him by the fire; and when she asked him faintly what news (which was not until after a long silence), he appeared embarrassed how to answer.

'Is it good.' she said, 'or bad?'—to help him.

'Bad,' he answered.

'We are quite ruined?'

'No. There is hope yet, Caroline.'

'If he relents,' she said, amazed, 'there is! Nothing is past hope, if such a miracle has happened.'

'He is past relenting,' said her husband. 'He is dead.'

She was a mild and patient creature if her face spoke truth; but she was thankful in her soul to hear it, and she said so, with clasped hands. She prayed forgiveness the next moment, and was sorry; but the first was the emotion of her heart.

'What the half-drunken woman whom I told you of last night, said to me, when I tried to see him and obtain a week's delay; and what I thought was a mere excuse to avoid me; turns out to have been quite true. He was not only very ill, but dying, then.'

'To whom will our debt be transferred?'

'I don't know. But before that time we shall be ready with the money; and even though we were not, it would be a bad fortune indeed to find so merciless a creditor in his successor. We may sleep to-night with light hearts, Caroline!'

Yes. Soften it as they would, their hearts were lighter. The children's faces, hushed and clustered round to hear what they so little understood, were brighter; and it was a happier house for this man's death. The only emotion that the Ghost could show him, caused by the event, was one of pleasure.

'Let me see some tenderness connected with a death,' said Scrooge;' or that dark chamber, Spirit, which we left just now, will be for ever present to me.'

The Ghost conducted him through several streets familiar to his feet; and as they went along, Scrooge looked here and there to find himself, but nowhere was he to be seen. They entered poor Bob Cratchit's house; the dwelling he had visited before; and found the mother and the children seated round the fire.

Quiet. Very quiet. The noisy little Cratchits were as still as statues in one corner, and sat looking up at Peter, who had a book before him. The mother and her daughters were engaged in sewing. But surely they were very quiet.

'And he took a child, and set him in the midst of them.'

Where had Scrooge heard those words? He had not dreamed them. The boy must have read them out, as he and the Spirit crossed the threshold. Why did he not go on?

The mother laid her work upon the table, and put her hand up to her face.

'The colour hurts my eyes,' she said.

The colour? Ah, poor Tiny Tim!

'They're better now again,' said Cratchit's wife. 'It makes them weak by candle-light; and I wouldn't show weak eyes to your father when he comes home, for the world. It must be near his time.'

'Past it rather,' Peter answered, shutting up his book. 'But I think he has walked a little slower than he used, these few last evenings, mother.'

They were very quiet again. At last she said, and in a steady, cheerful voice, that only faltered once:

'I have known him walk with—I have known him walk with Tiny Tim upon his shoulder, very fast indeed.'

'And so have I,' cried Peter. 'Often.'

'And so have I!' exclaimed another. So had all.

'But he was very light to carry,' she resumed, intent upon her work,' and his father loved him so, that it was no trouble: no trouble. And there is your father at the door!'

She hurried out to meet him; and little Bob in his comforter—he had need of it, poor fellow—came in. His tea was ready for him on the hob, and they all tried who should help him to it most. Then the two young Cratchits got upon his knees and laid, each child a little cheek, against his face, as if they said,' Don't mind it, father. Don't be grieved!'

Bob was very cheerful with them, and spoke pleasantly to all the family. He looked at the work upon the table, and praised the industry and speed of Mrs Cratchit and the girls. They would be done long before Sunday, he said.

'Sunday! You went to-day, then, Robert?' said his wife.

'Yes, my dear,' returned Bob. 'I wish you could have gone. It would have done you good to see how green a place it is. But you'll see it often. I promised him that I would walk there on a Sunday. My little, little child!' cried Bob. 'My little child!'

He broke down all at once. He couldn't help it. If he could have helped it, he and his child would have been farther apart perhaps than they were.

He left the room, and went up-stairs into the room above, which was lighted cheerfully, and hung with Christmas. There was a chair set close beside the child, and there were signs of some one having been there, lately. Poor Bob sat down in it, and when he had thought a little and composed himself, he kissed the little face. He was reconciled to what had happened, and went down again quite happy.

They drew about the fire, and talked; the girls and mother working still. Bob told them of the extraordinary kindness of Mr Scrooge's nephew, whom he had scarcely seen but once, and who, meeting him in the street that day, and seeing that he looked a little—'just a little down you know,' said Bob, inquired what had happened to distress him. 'On which,' said Bob,' for he is the pleasantest-spoken gentleman you ever heard, I told him. 'I am heartily sorry for it, Mr Cratchit,' he said,' and heartily sorry for your good wife.' By the bye, how he ever knew that, I don't know.'

'Knew what, my dear?'

'Why, that you were a good wife,' replied Bob.

'Everybody knows that!' said Peter.

'Very well observed, my boy!' cried Bob. 'I hope they do. 'Heartily sorry,' he said,' for your good wife. If I can be of service to you in any way,' he said, giving me his card,' that's where I live. Pray come to me.' Now, it wasn't,' cried Bob,' for the sake of anything he might be able to do for us, so much as for his kind way, that this was quite delightful. It really seemed as if he had known our Tiny Tim, and felt with us.'

'I'm sure he's a good soul!' said Mrs Cratchit.

'You would be surer of it, my dear,' returned Bob,' if you saw and spoke to him. I shouldn't be at all surprised—mark what I say.—if he got Peter a better situation.'

'Only hear that, Peter,' said Mrs Cratchit.

'And then,' cried one of the girls,' Peter will be keeping company with some one, and setting up for himself.'

'Get along with you!' retorted Peter, grinning.

'It's just as likely as not,' said Bob,' one of these days; though there's plenty of time for that, my dear. But however and when ever we part from one another, I am sure we shall none of us forget poor Tiny Tim—shall we—or this first parting that there was among us?'

'Never, father!' cried they all.

'And I know,' said Bob,' I know, my dears, that when we recollect how patient and how mild he was; although he was a little, little child; we shall not quarrel easily among ourselves, and forget poor Tiny Tim in doing it.'

'No, never, father!' they all cried again.

'I am very happy,' said little Bob,' I am very happy!'

Mrs Cratchit kissed him, his daughters kissed him, the two young Cratchits kissed him, and Peter and himself shook hands. Spirit of Tiny Tim, thy childish essence was from God!

'Spectre,' said Scrooge,' something informs me that our parting moment is at hand. I know it, but I know not how. Tell me what man that was whom we saw lying dead.'

The Ghost of Christmas Yet To Come conveyed him, as before—though at a different time, he thought: indeed, there seemed no order in these latter visions, save that they were in the Future—into the resorts of business men, but showed him not himself. Indeed, the Spirit did not stay for anything, but went straight on, as to the end just now desired, until besought by Scrooge to tarry for a moment.

'This court,' said Scrooge,' through which we hurry now, is where my place of occupation is, and has been for a length of time. I see the house. Let me behold what I shall be, in days to come.'

The Spirit stopped; the hand was pointed elsewhere.

'The house is yonder,' Scrooge exclaimed. 'Why do you point away.'

The inexorable finger underwent no change.

Scrooge hastened to the window of his office, and looked in. It was an office still, but not his. The furniture was not the same, and the figure in the chair was not himself. The Phantom pointed as before.

He joined it once again, and wondering why and whither he had gone, accompanied it until they reached an iron gate. He paused to look round before entering.

A churchyard. Here, then, the wretched man whose name he had now to learn, lay underneath the ground. It was a worthy place. Walled in by houses; overrun by grass and weeds, the growth of vegetation's death, not life; choked up with too much burying; fat with repleted appetite. A worthy place!

The Spirit stood among the graves, and pointed down to One. He advanced towards it trembling. The Phantom was exactly as it had been, but he dreaded that he saw new meaning in its solemn shape.

'Before I draw nearer to that stone to which you point,' said Scrooge, 'answer me one question. Are these the shadows of the things that Will be, or are they shadows of things that May be, only?'

Still the Ghost pointed downward to the grave by which it stood.

'Men's courses will foreshadow certain ends, to which, if persevered in, they must lead,' said Scrooge. 'But if the courses be departed from, the ends will change. Say it is thus with what you show me!'

The Spirit was immovable as ever.

Scrooge crept towards it, trembling as he went; and following the finger, read upon the stone of the neglected grave his own name, EBENEZER SCROOGE.

'Am I that man who lay upon the bed?' he cried, upon his knees.

The finger pointed from the grave to him, and back again.

'No, Spirit! Oh no, no!'

The finger still was there.

'Spirit!' he cried, tight clutching at its robe,' hear me! I am not the man I was. I will not be the man I must have been but for this intercourse. Why show me this, if I am past all hope!'

For the first time the hand appeared to shake.

'Good Spirit,' he pursued, as down upon the ground he fell before it:' Your nature intercedes for me, and pities me. Assure me that I yet may change these shadows you have shown me, by an altered life!'

The kind hand trembled.

'I will honour Christmas in my heart, and try to keep it all the year. I will live in the Past, the Present, and the Future. The Spirits of all Three shall strive within me. I will not shut out the lessons that they teach. Oh, tell me I may sponge away the writing on this stone!'

In his agony, he caught the spectral hand. It sought to free itself, but he was strong in his entreaty, and detained it. The Spirit, stronger yet, repulsed him.

Holding up his hands in a last prayer to have his fate reversed, he saw an alteration in the Phantom's hood and dress. It shrunk, collapsed, and dwindled down into a bedpost.

STAVE 5: THE END OF IT

Yes! and the bedpost was his own. The bed was his own, the room was his own. Best and happiest of all, the Time before him was his own, to make amends in!

'I will live in the Past, the Present, and the Future!' Scrooge repeated, as he scrambled out of bed. 'The Spirits of all Three shall strive within me. Oh Jacob Marley! Heaven, and the Christmas Time be praised for this! I say it on my knees, old Jacob, on my knees!'

He was so fluttered and so glowing with his good intentions, that his broken voice would scarcely answer to his call. He had been sobbing violently in his conflict with the Spirit, and his face was wet with tears.

'They are not torn down.' cried Scrooge, folding one of his bed-curtains in his arms,' they are not torn down, rings and all. They are here—I am here—the shadows of the things that would

have been, may be dispelled. They will be. I know they will!'

His hands were busy with his garments all this time; turning them inside out, putting them on upside down, tearing them, mislaying them, making them parties to every kind of extravagance.

'I don't know what to do,' cried Scrooge, laughing and crying in the same breath; and making a perfect Laocoon of himself with his stockings. 'I am as light as a feather, I am as happy as an angel, I am as merry as a schoolboy. I am as giddy as a drunken man. A merry Christmas to everybody! A happy New Year to all the world. Hallo here! Whoop! Hallo!'

He had frisked into the sitting-room, and was now standing there: perfectly winded.

'There's the saucepan that the gruel was in!' cried Scrooge, starting off again, and going round the fireplace. 'There's the door, by which the Ghost of Jacob Marley entered! There's the corner where the Ghost of Christmas Present, sat! There's the window where I saw the wandering Spirits! It's all right, it's all true, it all happened. Ha ha ha!'

Really, for a man who had been out of practice for so many years, it was a splendid laugh, a most illustrious laugh. The father of a long, long line of brilliant laughs!

'I don't know what day of the month it is!' said Scrooge. 'I don't know how long I've been among the Spirits. I don't know anything. I'm quite a baby. Never mind. I don't care. I'd rather be a baby. Hallo! Whoop! Hallo here!'

He was checked in his transports by the churches ringing out the lustiest peals he had ever heard. Clash, clang, hammer; ding, dong, bell. Bell, dong, ding; hammer, clang, clash! Oh, glorious, glorious!

Running to the window, he opened it, and put out his head. No fog, no mist; clear, bright, jovial, stirring, cold; cold, piping for the blood to dance to; Golden sunlight; Heavenly sky; sweet fresh air; merry bells. Oh, glorious. Glorious!

'What's to-day?' cried Scrooge, calling downward to a boy in Sunday clothes, who perhaps had loitered in to look about him.

'Eh?' returned the boy, with all his might of wonder.

'What's to-day, my fine fellow?' said Scrooge.

'To-day!' replied the boy. 'Why, Christmas Day.'

'It's Christmas Day!' said Scrooge to himself. 'I haven't missed it. The Spirits have done it all in one night. They can do anything they like. Of course they can. Of course they can. Hallo, my fine fellow!'

'Hallo!' returned the boy.

'Do you know the Poulterer's, in the next street but one, at the corner?' Scrooge inquired.

'I should hope I did,' replied the lad.

'An intelligent boy!' said Scrooge. 'A remarkable boy! Do you know whether they've sold the prize Turkey that was hanging up there—Not the little prize Turkey: the big one?'

'What, the one as big as me?' returned the boy.

'What a delightful boy!' said Scrooge. 'It's a pleasure to talk to him. Yes, my buck!'

'It's hanging there now,' replied the boy.

'Is it?' said Scrooge. 'Go and buy it.'

'Walk-er!' exclaimed the boy.

'No, no,' said Scrooge, 'I am in earnest. Go and buy it, and tell them to bring it here, that I may give them the direction where to take it. Come back with the man, and I'll give you a shilling. Come back with him in less than five minutes and I'll give you half-a-crown!'

The boy was off like a shot. He must have had a steady hand at a trigger who could have got a shot off half so fast.

'I'll send it to Bob Cratchit's!' whispered Scrooge, rubbing his hands, and splitting with a laugh. 'He shan't know who sends it. It's twice the size of Tiny Tim. Joe Miller never made such a joke as sending it to Bob's will be!'

The hand in which he wrote the address was not a steady one, but write it he did, somehow, and went down-stairs to open the street door, ready for the coming of the poulterer's man. As he stood there, waiting his arrival, the knocker caught his eye.

'I shall love it, as long as I live!' cried Scrooge, patting it with his hand. 'I scarcely ever looked at it before. What an honest expression it has in its face! It's a wonderful knocker!—Here's the Turkey. Hallo! Whoop! How are you! Merry Christmas!'

It *was* a Turkey. He never could have stood upon his legs, that bird. He would have snapped them short off in a minute, like sticks of sealing-wax.

'Why, it's impossible to carry that to Camden Town,' said Scrooge. 'You must have a cab.'

The chuckle with which he said this, and the chuckle with which he paid for the Turkey, and the chuckle with which he paid for the cab, and the chuckle with which he recompensed the boy, were only to be exceeded by the chuckle with which he sat down breathless in his chair again, and chuckled till he cried.

Shaving was not an easy task, for his hand continued to shake very much; and shaving requires attention, even when you don't dance while you are at it. But if he had cut the end of his nose off, he would have put a piece of sticking-plaster over it, and been quite satisfied.

He dressed himself all in his best, and at last got out into the streets. The people were by this time pouring forth, as he had seen them with the Ghost of Christmas Present; and walking with his hands behind him, Scrooge regarded every one with a delighted smile. He looked so irresistibly pleasant, in a word, that three or four good-humoured fellows said,' Good morning, sir! A merry Christmas to you!' And Scrooge said often afterwards, that of all the blithe sounds he had ever heard, those were the blithest in his ears.

He had not gone far, when coming on towards him he beheld the portly gentleman, who had walked into his counting-house the day before, and said,' Scrooge and Marley's, I believe?' It sent a pang across his heart to think how this old gentleman would look upon him when they met; but he knew what path lay straight before him, and he took it.

'My dear sir,' said Scrooge, quickening his pace, and taking the old gentleman by both his hands. 'How do you do? I hope you succeeded yesterday. It was very kind of you. A merry Christmas to you, sir!'

'Mr Scrooge?'

'Yes,' said Scrooge. 'That is my name, and I fear it may not be pleasant to you. Allow me to ask your pardon. And will you have the good-ness'—here Scrooge whispered in his ear.

'Lord bless me!' cried the gentleman, as if his breath were taken away. 'My dear Mr Scrooge, are you serious?'

'If you please,' said Scrooge. 'Not a farthing less. A great many back-payments are included in it, I assure you. Will you do me that favour?'

'My dear sir,' said the other, shaking hands with him. 'I don't know what to say to such munificence.'

'Don't say anything please,' retorted Scrooge. 'Come and see me. Will you come and see me?'

'I will!' cried the old gentleman. And it was clear he meant to do it.

'Thank you,' said Scrooge. 'I am much obliged to you. I thank you fifty times. Bless you!'

He went to church, and walked about the streets, and watched the people hurrying to and fro, and patted children on the head, and questioned beggars, and looked down into the kitchens of houses, and up to the windows, and found that everything could yield him pleasure. He had never dreamed that any walk—that any-thing—could give him so much happiness. In the afternoon he turned his steps towards his nephew's house.

He passed the door a dozen times, before he had the courage to go up and knock. But he made a dash, and did it:

'Is your master at home, my dear?' said Scrooge to the girl. Nice girl! Very.

'Yes, sir.'

'Where is he, my love?' said Scrooge.

'He's in the dining-room, sir, along with mis-tress. I'll show you up-stairs, if you please.'

'Thank you. He knows me,' said Scrooge, with his hand already on the dining-room lock. 'I'll go in here, my dear.'

He turned it gently, and sidled his face in, round the door. They were looking at the table (which was spread out in great array); for these young housekeepers are always nervous on such points, and like to see that everything is right.

'Fred!' said Scrooge.

Dear heart alive, how his niece by marriage started! Scrooge had forgotten, for the moment,

about her sitting in the corner with the footstool, or he wouldn't have done it, on any account.

'Why bless my soul!' cried Fred,' who's that?'

'It's I. Your uncle Scrooge. I have come to din-ner. Will you let me in, Fred?'

Let him in! It is a mercy he didn't shake his arm off. He was at home in five minutes. Nothing could be heartier. His niece looked just the same. So did Topper when he came. So did the plump sister when she came. So did every one when they came. Wonderful party, wonderful games, wonderful unanimity, wonderful happiness!

But he was early at the office next morning. Oh, he was early there. If he could only be there first, and catch Bob Cratchit coming late. That was the thing he had set his heart upon.

And he did it; yes, he did! The clock struck nine. No Bob. A quarter past. No Bob. He was full eighteen minutes and a half behind his time. Scrooge sat with his door wide open, that he might see him come into the Tank.

His hat was off, before he opened the door; his comforter too. He was on his stool in a jiffy; driving away with his pen, as if he were trying to overtake nine o'clock.

'Hallo!' growled Scrooge, in his accustomed voice, as near as he could feign it. 'What do you mean by coming here at this time of day?'

'I am very sorry, sir,' said Bob. 'I am behind my time.'

'You are.' repeated Scrooge. 'Yes. I think you are. Step this way, sir, if you please.'

'It's only once a year, sir,' pleaded Bob, appear-ing from the Tank. 'It shall not be repeated. I was making rather merry yesterday, sir.'

'Now, I'll tell you what, my friend,' said Scrooge,' I am not going to stand this sort of thing any longer. And therefore,' he continued, leaping from his stool, and giving Bob such a dig in the waistcoat that he staggered back into the Tank again;' and therefore I am about to raise your salary!'

Bob trembled, and got a little nearer to the ruler. He had a momentary idea of knocking Scrooge down with it, holding him, and call-ing to the people in the court for help and a strait-waistcoat.

'A merry Christmas, Bob!' said Scrooge, with an earnestness that could not be mistaken, as he clapped him on the back. 'A merrier Christmas, Bob, my good fellow, than I have given you for many a year! I'll raise your salary, and endeavour to assist your struggling family, and we will discuss your affairs this very afternoon, over a Christmas bowl of smoking bishop, Bob! Make up the fires, and buy another coal-scuttle before you dot another i, Bob Cratchit!'

Scrooge was better than his word. He did it all, and infinitely more; and to Tiny Tim, who did not die, he was a second father. He became as good a friend, as good a master, and as good a man, as the good old city knew, or any other good old city, town, or borough, in the good old world. Some people laughed to see the alteration in him, but he let them laugh, and little heeded them; for he was wise enough to know that nothing ever happened on this globe, for good, at which some people did not have their fill of laughter in the outset; and knowing that such as these would be blind anyway, he thought it quite as well that they should wrinkle up their eyes in grins, as have the malady in less attractive forms. His own heart laughed: and that was quite enough for him.

He had no further intercourse with Spirits, but lived upon the Total Abstinence Principle, ever afterwards; and it was always said of him, that he knew how to keep Christmas well, if any man alive possessed the knowledge. May that be truly said of us, and all of us! And so, as Tiny Tim observed, God Bless Us, Every One!

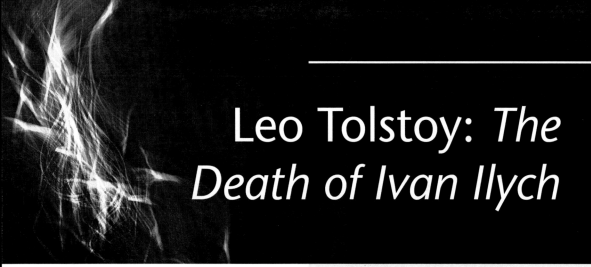

Leo Tolstoy: *The Death of Ivan Ilych*

Editors' Introduction

"Ivan Ilych's life had been most simple and most ordinary and therefore most terrible." This somber judgment expresses the central focus of Tolstoy's short novel. To understand the reason for this judgment is to gain an insight into some of Tolstoy's deepest convictions concerning the best way to live.

For most of his life (1828–1910) Lev Tolstoy was engaged in an unrelenting process of self-examination. In both his fiction and non-fiction he returns over and over again to questions about how we should live. Like many of the great novelists, his work reflects the struggles involved in his own ongoing conversion. Even when not explicitly so (as in St. Augustine's *Confessions*), Tolstoy's writings are fundamentally autobiographical.

Tolstoy came from an old, aristocratic, and wealthy Russian family (he was, in fact, referred to as Count Tolstoy). His parents died before he was ten years old, and he and his siblings were raised by a succession of female relatives. He attended Kazan University, but left without ever attaining his degree. He and his brother Nikolai also spent time in the army, serving in the Caucasus for several years (1851–56). In 1852 he published his first significant work, the novel *Childhood,* which brought him acclaim and instant recognition as one of Russia's most talented new writers. Tolstoy's diaries from this period in his life reveal a self-centered young man who is obsessed with schemes for self-improvement while simultaneously preoccupied with gambling, sex, and a desire for fame. But they also reveal someone who reflects frequently on spiritual and religious questions.

When Tolstoy turned twenty years of age he inherited his family's estate at Yasnaya Polyana ("Clear Glade" in English). For the rest of his life this would be his permanent home. Tolstoy was a person of many enthusiasms, and after returning to Yasnaya Polyana after his stint in the army he threw himself into the project of providing education for the children of the peasants on his estate. His interest in education led him to tour Europe for ten months in 1860–61. In 1862 he entered into the most important relationship of his life—his marriage to Sofia Andreevna Behrs. Entire books could be (and have been) written on the Tolstoys' marriage. Suffice it to say that theirs was an intense, close, complicated, and often tumultuous relationship, one that produced thirteen children.

After writing his two greatest novels, *War and Peace* (1869) and *Anna Karenina* (1877), Tolstoy entered into a period in which he began to question the meaning and purpose of life. His marriage had brought him stability and happiness well into the 1870s, but his restless search concerning the best way to live led him to become increasingly dissatisfied with the kind of life he was leading. He was already being acclaimed as Russia's greatest writer, his family life was generally good, and by the standards of his time (as well as ours) he had achieved great success. But the question "So what?" would give him no rest, and the crisis of meaning in which he was embroiled led him to even contemplate suicide. Tolstoy chronicled his struggle during these years in his *Confession* (1879). At first he tried to find meaning by throwing himself fully into the practices and beliefs of the Russian Orthodox faith in which he had been raised. However, he found himself increasingly questioning the doctrines of the Church, and he devoted several years to the study of Orthodox theology and the gospels. The result of these studies was that Tolstoy found it difficult to believe much of what he had been taught concerning religious doctrine. However, he also concluded that Christianity, pruned of the accretions that had been added to it by church authorities, did contain the answers he was seeking about the meaning of life. It can certainly be argued that for the rest of his life he devoted himself to working out the implications of his newly reformulated understanding of the Christian message, both in writing and in practice. He became convinced that the gospel teaching on love implied an uncompromising attitude of non-violence and pacifism. Consequently, he came to denounce war, capital punishment, and all other forms of coercion. He came to see all government as a form of violence, leading him to become an outspoken critic of the Russian authorities and their policies. Tolstoy's espousal of religious views contrary to Orthodox teaching and his public criticism of the Orthodox Church eventually led to him being excommunicated by the Holy Synod in 1901.

Tolstoy's attempts to put his newly found views into practice also led to increasing friction within his family. In particular, he experienced a good deal of resistance from his wife and from many of his children when he attempted to divest himself of his property and to renounce the copyright to many of his literary works. His friend and devoted disciple Vladimir Chertkov, encouraged (some would say manipulated) Tolstoy to take these dramatic actions, further exacerbating Tolstoy's increasingly strained relationship with his wife. Eventually his domestic situation reached a point that Tolstoy found intolerable, and in November 1910, without telling his wife, he left home (along with his youngest daughter Alexandra and his physician/friend Dushan Makovitsky), hoping to spend the rest of his days in quiet and contemplation. Shortly after leaving home he caught pneumonia and died at the train station in the village of Astapovo. In accordance with his wishes, he was buried on his estate without any religious ceremony. The Russian government tried to prevent people from attending the burial, but despite these attempts, thousands made their way to Yasnaya Polyana and lined the road as the funeral procession made its way.

The Death of Ivan Ilych was written in 1886. It is Tolstoy's first "post-conversion" work of fiction and is generally considered one of his best works. On one level the novel offers a scathing satire of the life of the professional classes in the Russia of the time. On a deeper level the story raises profound and disturbing questions about the purpose of life and the meaning of success. Unlike such novelists as Dickens and Dostoevsky, who excel at exaggerating certain features of their characters in order to convey their message, Tolstoy had a knack for disclosing just how spiritually empty and alienating are the lives that we take to be "normal" and successful. Nowhere is this ability displayed with greater power than in *The Death of Ivan Ilych*.

During the time in which the story was being written, Tolstoy was becoming increasingly dissatisfied with the life he and his family were leading. He was becoming more and more convinced that he and others of his class were parasites, living off the work of others. His attempts to convince his family to adopt his new view toward life met with incomprehension. A diary entry from 1884 reflects this situation:

"It's very depressing in the family. Depressing, because I can't sympathize with them. All their joys, the examination, social successes, music furniture, shopping—I consider them all a misfortune and an evil for them, and I can't tell them so. I can and do speak, but my words don't get through to anyone . . . I've been assigned the role of a querulous old man, and in their eyes I can't escape from it: if I take part in their life I renounce the truth, and they would be the first to cast this renunciation in my teeth. If I look sadly, as now, at their madness—I'm a querulous old man, like all old men."

A year later he writes in a similar vein:

"Thought about my unhappy family: my wife, sons and daughters who live side by side with me and deliberately put barriers between me and themselves in order not to see the truth and the good, which would expose the falseness of their lives, but would also save them from suffering . . . I thought further: to do the will of Him who sent me—that is my food. What simple and profound significance. You can only be at peace and always content when you take as your purpose not something external, but doing the will of Him who sent you."

These glimpses into Tolstoy's state of mind at the time of the writing of the novel offer important clues as to why he considered the life of Ivan Ilych to be most simple, most ordinary, and most terrible.

The Death of Ivan Ilych

I̅

During an interval in the Melvinski trial in the large building of the Law Courts the members and public prosecutor met in Ivan Egorovich Shebek's private room, where the conversation turned on the celebrated Krasovski case. Fedor Vasilievich warmly maintained that it was not subject to their jurisdiction, Ivan Egorovich maintained the contrary, while Peter Ivanovich, not having entered into the discussion at the start, took no part in it but looked through the *Gazette* which had just been handed in.

"Gentlemen," he said, "Ivan Ilych has died!"

"You don't say so!"

"Here, read it yourself," replied Peter Ivanovich, handing Fedor Vasilievich the paper still damp from the press. Surrounded by a black border were the words: "Praskovya Fedorovna Golovina, with profound sorrow, informs relatives and friends of the demise of her beloved husband Ivan Ilych Golovin, Member of the Court of Justice, which occurred on February the 4th of this year 1882. the funeral will take place on Friday at one o'clock in the afternoon."

Ivan Ilych had been a colleague of the gentlemen present and was liked by them all. He had been ill for some weeks with an illness said to be incurable. His post had been kept open for him, but there had been conjectures that in case of his death Alexeev might receive his appointment, and that either Vinnikov or Shtabel would succeed Alexeev. So on receiving the news of Ivan Ilych's death the first thought of each of the gentlemen in that private room was of the changes and promotions it might occasion among themselves or their acquaintances.

"I shall be sure to get Shtabel's place or Vinnikov's," thought Fedor Vasilievich. "I was promised that long ago, and the promotion means an extra eight hundred rubles a year for me besides the allowance."

"Now I must apply for my brother-in-law's transfer from Kaluga," thought Peter Ivanovich. "My wife will be very glad, and then she won't be able to say that I never do anything for her relations."

"I thought he would never leave his bed again," said Peter Ivanovich aloud. "It's very sad."

"But what really was the matter with him?"

"The doctors couldn't say—at least they could, but each of them said something different. When last I saw him I thought he was getting better."

"And I haven't been to see him since the holidays. I always meant to go."

"Had he any property?"

"I think his wife had a little—but something quite trifling."

"We shall have to go to see her, but they live so terribly far away."

"Far away from you, you mean. Everything's far away from your place."

"You see, he never can forgive my living on the other side of the river," said Peter Ivanovich, smiling at Shebek. Then, still talking of the distances between different parts of the city, they returned to the Court.

Besides considerations as to the possible transfers and promotions likely to result from Ivan Ilych's death, the mere fact of the death of a near acquaintance aroused, as usual, in all who heard of it the complacent feeling that, "it is he who is dead and not I."

Each one thought or felt, "Well, he's dead but I'm alive!" But the more intimate of Ivan Ilych's acquaintances, his so-called friends, could not help thinking also that they would now have to fulfil the very tiresome demands of propriety by attending the funeral service and paying a visit of condolence to the widow.

Fedor Vasilievich and Peter Ivanovich had been his nearest acquaintances. Peter Ivanovich had studied law with Ivan Ilych and had considered himself to be under obligations to him.

Having told his wife at dinner-time of Ivan Ilych's death, and of his conjecture that it might be possible to get her brother transferred to their circuit, Peter Ivanovich sacrificed his usual nap, put on his evening clothes and drove to Ivan Ilych's house.

At the entrance stood a carriage and two cabs. Leaning against the wall in the hall downstairs near the cloakstand was a coffin-lid covered with cloth of gold, ornamented with gold cord and tassels, that had been polished up with metal powder. Two ladies in black were taking off their fur cloaks. Peter Ivanovich recognized one of them as Ivan Ilych's sister, but the other was a stranger to him. His colleague Schwartz was just coming downstairs, but on seeing Peter Ivanovich enter he stopped and winked at him, as if to say: "Ivan Ilych has made a mess of things—not like you and me."

Schwartz's face with his Piccadilly whiskers, and his slim figure in evening dress, had as usual an air of elegant solemnity which contrasted with the playfulness of his character and had a special piquancy here, or so it seemed to Peter Ivanovich.

Peter Ivanovich allowed the ladies to precede him and slowly followed them upstairs. Schwartz did not come down but remained where he was, and Peter Ivanovich understood that he wanted to arrange where they should play bridge that evening. The ladies went upstairs to the widow's room, and Schwartz with seriously compressed lips but a playful looking his eyes, indicated by a twist of his eyebrows the room to the right where the body lay.

Peter Ivanovich, like everyone else on such occasions, entered feeling uncertain what he would have to do. All he knew was that at such times it is always safe to cross oneself. But he was not quite sure whether one should make obseisances while doing so. He therefore adopted a middle course. On entering the room he began crossing himself and made a slight movement resembling a bow. At the same time, as far as the motion of his head and arm allowed, he surveyed the room. Two young men—apparently nephews, one of whom was a high-school pupil—were leaving the room, crossing themselves as they did so. An old woman was standing motionless, and a lady with strangely arched eyebrows was saying something to her in a whisper. A vigorous, resolute Church Reader, in a frock- coat, was reading something in a loud voice with an expression that precluded any contradiction. The butler's assistant, Gerasim, stepping lightly in front of Peter Ivanovich, was strewing something on the floor. Noticing this, Peter Ivanovich was immediately aware of a faint odour of a decomposing body.

The last time he had called on Ivan Ilych, Peter Ivanovich had seen Gerasim in the study. Ivan Ilych had been particularly fond of him and he was performing the duty of a sick nurse.

Peter Ivanovich continued to make the sign of the cross slightly inclining his head in an intermediate direction between the coffin, the Reader, and the icons on the table in a corner of the room. Afterwards, when it seemed to him that this movement of his arm in crossing himself had gone on too long, he stopped and began to look at the corpse.

The dead man lay, as dead men always lie, in a specially heavy way, his rigid limbs sunk in the soft cushions of the coffin, with the head forever bowed on the pillow. His yellow waxen brow with bald patches over his sunken temples was thrust up in the way peculiar to the dead, the protruding nose seeming to press on the upper lip. He was much changed and grown even thinner since Peter Ivanovich had last seen him, but, as is always the case with the dead, his face was handsomer and above all more dignified than when he was alive. the expression on the face said that what was necessary had been accomplished, and accomplished rightly. Besides this there was in that expression a reproach and a warning to the living. This warning seemed to Peter Ivanovich out of place, or at least not applicable to him. He felt a certain discomfort and so he hurriedly crossed himself once more and turned and went out of the door—too hurriedly and too regardless of propriety, as he himself was aware.

Schwartz was waiting for him in the adjoining room with legs spread wide apart and both hands toying with his top-hat behind his back.

The mere sight of that playful, well-groomed, and elegant figure refreshed Peter Ivanovich. He felt that Schwartz was above all these happenings and would not surrender to any depressing influences. His very look said that this incident of a church service for Ivan Ilych could not be a sufficient reason for infringing the order of the session—in other words, that it would certainly not prevent his unwrapping a new pack of cards and shuffling them that evening while a footman placed fresh candles on the table: in fact, that there was no reason for supposing that this incident would hinder their spending the evening agreeably. Indeed he said this in a whisper as Peter Ivanovich passed him, proposing that they should meet for a game at Fedor Vasilievich's. But apparently Peter Ivanovich was not destined to play bridge that evening. Praskovya Fedorovna (a short, fat woman who despite all efforts to the contrary had continued to broaden steadily from her shoulders downwards and who had the same extraordinarily arched eyebrows as the lady who had been standing by the coffin), dressed all in black, her head covered with lace, came out of her own room with some other ladies, conducted them to the room where the dead body lay, and said: "The service will begin immediately. Please go in."

Schwartz, making an indefinite bow, stood still, evidently neither accepting nor declining this invitation. Praskovya Fedorovna recognizing Peter Ivanovich, sighed, went close up to him, took his hand, and said: "I know you were a true friend to Ivan Ilych . . ." and looked at him awaiting some suitable response. And Peter Ivanovich knew that, just as it had been the right thing to cross himself in that room, so what he had to do here was to press her hand, sigh, and say, "Believe me . . ." So he did all this and as he did it felt that the desired result had been achieved: that both he and she were touched.

"Come with me. I want to speak to you before it begins," said the widow. "Give me your arm."

Peter Ivanovich gave her his arm and they went to the inner rooms, passing Schwartz who winked at Peter Ivanovich compassionately.

"That does for our bridge! Don't object if we find another player. Perhaps you can cut in when you do escape," said his playful look.

Peter Ivanovich sighed still more deeply and despondently, and Praskovya Fedorovna pressed his arm gratefully. When they reached the drawing-room, upholstered in pink cretonne and lighted by a dim lamp, they sat down at the table—she on a sofa and Peter Ivanovich on a low pouffe, the springs of which yielded spasmodically under his weight. Praskovya Fedorovna had been on the point of warning him to take another seat, but felt that such a warning was out of keeping with her present condition and so changed her mind. As he sat down on the pouffe Peter Ivanovich recalled how Ivan Ilych had arranged this room and had consulted him regarding this pink cretonne with green leaves. The whole room was full of furniture and knick-knacks, and on her way to the sofa the lace of the widow's black shawl caught on the edge of the table. Peter Ivanovich rose to detach it, and the springs of the pouffe, relieved of his weight, rose also and gave him a push. The widow began detaching her shawl herself, and Peter Ivanovich again sat down, suppressing the rebellious springs of the pouffe under him. But the widow had not quite freed herself and Peter Ivanovich got up again, and again the pouffe rebelled and even creaked. When this was all over she took out a clean cambric handkerchief and began to weep. The episode with the shawl and the struggle with the pouffe had cooled Peter Ivanovich's emotions and he sat there with a sullen look on his face. This awkward situation was interrupted by Sokolov, Ivan Ilych's butler, who came to report that the plot in the cemetery that Praskovya Fedorovna had chosen would cost two hundred rubles. She stopped weeping and, looking at Peter Ivanovich with the air of a victim, remarked in French that it was very hard for her. Peter Ivanovich made a silent gesture signifying his full conviction that it must indeed be so.

"Please smoke," she said in a magnanimous yet crushed voice, and turned to discuss with Sokolov the price of the plot for the grave.

Peter Ivanovich while lighting his cigarette heard her inquiring very circumstantially into the prices of different plots in the cemetery and finally decide which she would take. when that was done she gave instructions about engaging the choir. Sokolov then left the room.

"I look after everything myself," she told Peter Ivanovich, shifting the albums that lay on the table; and noticing that the table was endangered by his cigarette-ash, she immediately passed him an ash-tray, saying as she did so: "I consider it an affectation to say that my grief prevents my attending to practical affairs. On the contrary, if anything can—I won't say console me, but—distract me, it is seeing to everything concerning him." She again took out her handkerchief as if preparing to cry, but suddenly, as if mastering her feeling, she shook herself and began to speak calmly. "But there is something I want to talk to you about."

Peter Ivanovich bowed, keeping control of the springs of the pouffe, which immediately began quivering under him.

"He suffered terribly the last few days."

"Did he?" said Peter Ivanovich.

"Oh, terribly! He screamed unceasingly, not for minutes but for hours. for the last three days he screamed incessantly. It was unendurable. I cannot understand how I bore it; you could hear him three rooms off. Oh, what I have suffered!"

"Is it possible that he was conscious all that time?" asked Peter Ivanovich.

"Yes," she whispered. "To the last moment. He took leave of us a quarter of an hour before he died, and asked us to take Volodya away."

The thought of the suffering of this man he had known so intimately, first as a merry little boy, then as a schoolmate, and later as a grown-up colleague, suddenly struck Peter Ivanovich with horror, despite an unpleasant consciousness of his own and this woman's dissimulation. He again saw that brow, and that nose pressing down on the lip, and felt afraid for himself.

"Three days of frightful suffering and the death! Why, that might suddenly, at any time, happen to me," he thought, and for a moment felt terrified. But—he did not himself know how—the customary reflection at once occurred to him that this had happened to Ivan Ilych and not to him, and that it should not and could not happen to him, and that to think that it could would be yielding to depression which he ought not to do, as Schwartz's expression plainly showed. After which reflection Peter Ivanovich felt reassured, and began to ask with interest about the details of Ivan Ilych's death, as though death was an accident natural to Ivan Ilych but certainly not to himself.

After many details of the really dreadful physical sufferings Ivan Ilych had endured (which details he learnt only from the effect those sufferings had produced on Praskovya Fedorovna's nerves) the widow apparently found it necessary to get to business.

"Oh, Peter Ivanovich, how hard it is! How terribly, terribly hard!" and she again began to weep.

Peter Ivanovich sighed and waited for her to finish blowing her nose. When she had done so he said, "Believe me . . ." and she again began talking and brought out what was evidently her chief concern with him—namely, to question him as to how she could obtain a grant of money from the government on the occasion of her husband's death. She made it appear that she was asking Peter Ivanovich's advice about her pension, but he soon saw that she already knew about that to the minutest detail, more even than he did himself. She knew how much could be got out of the government in consequence of her husband's death, but wanted to find out whether she could not possibly extract something more. Peter Ivanovich tried to think of some means of doing so, but after reflecting for a while and, out of propriety, condemning the government for its niggardliness, he said he thought that nothing more could be got. Then she sighed and evidently began to devise means of getting rid of her visitor. Noticing this, he put out his cigarette, rose, pressed her hand, and went out into the anteroom.

In the dining-room where the clock stood that Ivan Ilych had liked so much and had bought at an antique shop, Peter Ivanovich met a priest and a few acquaintances who had come to attend the service, and he recognized Ivan Ilych's daughter, a handsome young woman. She was in black and her slim figure appeared slimmer than ever. She had a gloomy, determined, almost angry expression, and bowed to Peter Ivanovich as though he were in some way to blame. Behind her, with the same offended look, stood a wealthy young man, and examining magistrate, whom Peter Ivanovich also knew and who was her fiance, as he had heard. He bowed mournfully to them and was about to pass into the death-chamber, when from under the stairs appeared the figure of Ivan Ilych's schoolboy son, who was extremely like his father. He seemed a little Ivan Ilych, such as Peter Ivanovich remembered when they studied law together. His tear-stained eyes had in them the look that is seen in the eyes of boys of thirteen or fourteen who are not pure-minded. When he saw Peter Ivanovich he scowled morosely and shamefacedly. Peter Ivanovich nodded to him and entered the death-chamber. The service began: candles, groans, incense, tears, and sobs. Peter Ivanovich stood looking gloomily down at his feet. He did not look once at the dead man, did not yield to any depressing influence, and was one of the first to leave the room. There was no one in the anteroom, but Gerasim darted out of the dead man's room, rummaged with his strong hands among the fur coats to find Peter Ivanovich's and helped him on with it.

"Well, friend Gerasim," said Peter Ivanovich, so as to say something. "It's a sad affair, isn't it?"

"It's God will. We shall all come to it some day," said Gerasim, displaying his teeth—the even white teeth of a healthy peasant—and, like a man in the thick of urgent work, he briskly opened the front door, called the coachman, helped Peter Ivanovich into the sledge, and sprang back to the porch as if in readiness for what he had to do next.

Peter Ivanovich found the fresh air particularly pleasant after the smell of incense, the dead body, and carbolic acid.

"Where to sir?" asked the coachman.

"It's not too late even now. . . . I'll call round on Fedor Vasilievich."

He accordingly drove there and found them just finishing the first rubber, so that it was quite convenient for him to cut in.

II

Ivan Ilych's life had been most simple and most ordinary and therefore most terrible.

He had been a member of the Court of Justice, and died at the age of forty-five. His father had been an official who after serving in various ministries and departments in Petersburg had made the sort of career which brings men to positions from which by reason of their long service they cannot be dismissed, though they are obviously unfit to hold any responsible position, and for whom therefore posts are specially created, which though fictitious carry salaries of from six to ten thousand rubles that are not fictitious, and in receipt of which they live on to a great age.

Such was the Privy Councillor and superfluous member of various superfluous institutions, Ilya Epimovich Golovin.

He had three sons, of whom Ivan Ilych was the second. The eldest son was following in his father's footsteps only in another department, and was already approaching that stage in the service at which a similar sinecure would be reached. The third son was a failure. He had ruined his prospects in a number of positions and was now serving in the railway department. His father and brothers, and still more their wives, not merely disliked meeting him, but avoided remembering his existence unless compelled to do so. His sister had married Baron Greff, a Petersburg official of her father's type. Ivan Ilych was *le phenix de la famille* as people said. He was neither as cold and formal as his elder brother nor as wild as the younger, but was a happy mean between them—an intelligent polished, lively and agreeable man. He had studied with his younger brother at the School of Law, but the latter had failed to complete the course and was expelled when he was in the fifth class. Ivan Ilych finished the course well. Even when he was at the School of Law he was just what he remained for the rest of his life: a capable, cheerful, good-natured, and sociable man, though strict in the fulfillment of what he considered to be his duty: and he considered his duty to be what was so considered by those in authority. Neither as a boy nor as a man was he a toady, but from early youth was by nature attracted to people of high station as a fly is drawn to the light, assimilating their ways and views of life and establishing friendly relations with them. All the enthusiasms of childhood and youth passed without leaving much trace on him; he succumbed to sensuality, to vanity, and latterly among the highest classes to liberalism, but always within limits which his instinct unfailingly indicated to him as correct.

At school he had done things which had formerly seemed to him very horrid and made him feel disgusted with himself when he did them; but when later on he saw that such actions were done by people of good position and that they did not regard them as wrong, he was able not exactly to regard them as right, but to forget about them entirely or not be at all troubled at remembering them.

Having graduated from the School of Law and qualified for the tenth rank of the civil service, and having received money from his father for his equipment, Ivan Ilych ordered himself clothes at Scharmer's, the fashionable tailor, hung a medallion inscribed *respice finem* on his watch-chain, took leave of his professor and the prince who was patron of the school, had a farewell dinner with his comrades at Donon's first-class restaurant, and with his new and fashionable portmanteau, linen, clothes, shaving and other toilet appliances, and a travelling rug, all purchased at the best shops, he set off for one of the provinces where through his father's influence, he had been attached to the governor as an official for special service.

In the province Ivan Ilych soon arranged as easy and agreeable a position for himself as he had had at the School of Law. He performed his official task, made his career, and at the same time amused himself pleasantly and decorously. Occasionally he paid official visits to country districts where

he behaved with dignity both to his superiors and inferiors, and performed the duties entrusted to him, which related chiefly to the sectarians, with an exactness and incorruptible honesty of which he could not but feel proud.

In official matters, despite his youth and taste for frivolous gaiety, he was exceedingly reserved, punctilious, and even severe; but in society he was often amusing and witty, and always good-natured, correct in his manner, and *bon enfant,* as the governor and his wife—with whom he was like one of the family—used to say of him.

In the province he had an affair with a lady who made advances to the elegant young lawyer, and there was also a milliner; and there were carousals with aides-de-camp who visited the district, and after-supper visits to a certain outlying street of doubtful reputation; and there was too some obsequiousness to his chief and even to his chief's wife, but all this was done with such a tone of good breeding that no hard names could be applied to it. It all came under the heading of the French saying: *"Il faut que jeunesse se passe."* It was all done with clean hands, in clean linen, with French phrases, and above all among people of the best society and consequently with the approval of people of rank.

So Ivan Ilych served for five years and then came a change in his official life. The new and reformed judicial institutions were introduced, and new men were needed. Ivan Ilych became such a new man. He was offered the post of examining magistrate, and he accepted it though the post was in another province and obliged him to give up the connexions he had formed and to make new ones. His friends met to give him a send-off; they had a group photograph taken and presented him with a silver cigarette-case, and he set off to his new post.

As examining magistrate Ivan Ilych was just as *comme il faut* and decorous a man, inspiring general respect and capable of separating his official duties from his private life, as he had been when acting as an official on special service. His duties now as examining magistrate were far more interesting and attractive than before. In his former position it had been pleasant to wear an undress uniform made by Scharmer, and to pass through the crowd of petitioners and officials who were timorously awaiting an audience with the governor, and who envied him as with free and easy gait he went straight into his chief's private room to have a cup of tea and a cigarette with him. But not many people had then been directly dependent on him—only police officials and the sectarians when he went on special missions—and he liked to treat them politely, almost as comrades, as if he were letting them feel that he who had the power to crush them was treating them in this simple, friendly way. There were then but few such people. But now, as an examining magistrate, Ivan Ilych felt that everyone without exception, even the most important and self-satisfied, was in his power, and that he need only write a few words on a sheet of paper with a certain heading, and this or that important, self-satisfied person would be brought before him in the role of an accused person or a witness, and if he did not choose to allow him to sit down, would have to stand before him and answer his questions. Ivan Ilych never abused his power; he tried on the contrary to soften its expression, but the consciousness of it and the possibility of softening its effect, supplied the chief interest and attraction of his office. In his work itself, especially in his examinations, he very soon acquired a method of eliminating all considerations irrelevant to the legal aspect of the case, and reducing even the most complicated case to a form in which it would be presented on paper only in its externals, completely excluding his personal opinion of the matter, while above all observing every prescribed formality. The work was new and Ivan Ilych was one of the first men to apply the new Code of 1864.

On taking up the post of examining magistrate in a new town, he made new acquaintances and connexions, placed himself on a new footing and assumed a somewhat different tone. He took up an attitude of rather dignified aloofness towards the provincial authorities, but picked out the best circle of legal gentlemen and wealthy gentry living in the town and assumed a tone of slight dissatisfaction with the government, of

moderate liberalism, and of enlightened citizenship. At the same time, without at all altering the elegance of his toilet, he ceased shaving his chin and allowed his beard to grow as it pleased.

Ivan Ilych settled down very pleasantly in this new town. The society there, which inclined towards opposition to the governor was friendly, his salary was larger, and he began to play *vint* [a form of bridge], which he found added not a little to the pleasure of life, for he had a capacity for cards, played good-humouredly, and calculated rapidly and astutely, so that he usually won.

After living there for two years he met his future wife, Praskovya Fedorovna Mikhel, who was the most attractive, clever, and brilliant girl of the set in which he moved, and among other amusements and relaxations from his labours as examining magistrate, Ivan Ilych established light and playful relations with her.

While he had been an official on special service he had been accustomed to dance, but now as an examining magistrate it was exceptional for him to do so. If he danced now, he did it as if to show that though he served under the reformed order of things, and had reached the fifth official rank, yet when it came to dancing he could do it better than most people. So at the end of an evening he sometimes danced with Praskovya Fedorovna, and it was chiefly during these dances that he captivated her. She fell in love with him. Ivan Ilych had at first no definite intention of marrying, but when the girl fell in love with him he said to himself: "Really, why shouldn't I marry?"

Praskovya Fedorovna came of a good family, was not bad looking, and had some little property. Ivan Ilych might have aspired to a more brilliant match, but even this was good. He had his salary, and she, he hoped, would have an equal income. She was well connected, and was a sweet, pretty, and thoroughly correct young woman. To say that Ivan Ilych married because he fell in love with Praskovya Fedorovna and found that she sympathized with his views of life would be as incorrect as to say that he married because his social circle approved of the match. He was swayed by both these considerations: the marriage gave him personal satisfaction, and at the same time it was considered the right thing by the most highly placed of his associates.

So Ivan Ilych got married.

The preparations for marriage and the beginning of married life, with its conjugal caresses, the new furniture, new crockery, and new linen, were very pleasant until his wife became pregnant—so that Ivan Ilych had begun to think that marriage would not impair the easy, agreeable, gay and always decorous character of his life, approved of by society and regarded by himself as natural, but would even improve it. But from the first months of his wife's pregnancy, something new, unpleasant, depressing, and unseemly, and from which there was no way of escape, unexpectedly showed itself.

His wife, without any reason—*de gaiete de coeur* as Ivan Ilych expressed it to himself—began to disturb the pleasure and propriety of their life. She began to be jealous without any cause, expected him to devote his whole attention to her, found fault with everything, and made coarse and ill-mannered scenes.

At first Ivan Ilych hoped to escape from the unpleasantness of this state of affairs by the same easy and decorous relation to life that had served him heretofore: he tried to ignore his wife's disagreeable moods, continued to live in his usual easy and pleasant way, invited friends to his house for a game of cards, and also tried going out to his club or spending his evenings with friends. But one day his wife began upbraiding him so vigorously, using such coarse words, and continued to abuse him every time he did not fulfil her demands, so resolutely and with such evident determination not to give way till he submitted—that is, till he stayed at home and was bored just as she was—that he became alarmed. He now realized that matrimony—at any rate with Praskovya Fedorovna—was not always conducive to the pleasures and amenities of life, but on the contrary often infringed both comfort and propriety, and that he must therefore entrench himself against such infringement. And Ivan Ilych began to seek for means of doing so. His official duties were the one thing that imposed upon Praskovya Fedorovna, and by means

of his official work and the duties attached to it he began struggling with his wife to secure his own independence.

With the birth of their child, the attempts to feed it and the various failures in doing so, and with the real and imaginary illnesses of mother and child, in which Ivan Ilych's sympathy was demanded but about which he understood nothing, the need of securing for himself an existence outside his family life became still more imperative.

As his wife grew more irritable and exacting and Ivan Ilych transferred the center of gravity of his life more and more to his official work, so did he grow to like his work better and became more ambitious than before.

Very soon, within a year of his wedding, Ivan Ilych had realized that marriage, though it may add some comforts to life, is in fact a very intricate and difficult affair towards which in order to perform one's duty, that is, to lead a decorous life approved of by society, one must adopt a definite attitude just as towards one's official duties.

And Ivan Ilych evolved such an attitude towards married life. He only required of it those conveniences—dinner at home, housewife, and bed—which it could give him, and above all that propriety of external forms required by public opinion. For the rest he looked for lighthearted pleasure and propriety, and was very thankful when he found them, but if he met with antagonism and querulousness he at once retired into his separate fenced-off world of official duties, where he found satisfaction.

Ivan Ilych was esteemed a good official, and after three years was made Assistant Public Prosecutor. His new duties, their importance, the possibility of indicting and imprisoning anyone he chose, the publicity his speeches received, and the success he had in all these things, made his work still more attractive.

More children came. His wife became more and more querulous and ill-tempered, but the attitude Ivan Ilych had adopted towards his home life rendered him almost impervious to her grumbling.

After seven years' service in that town he was transferred to another province as Public Prosecutor. They moved, but were short of money and his wife did not like the place they moved to. Though the salary was higher the cost of living was greater, besides which two of their children died and family life became still more unpleasant for him.

Praskovya Fedorovna blamed her husband for every inconvenience they encountered in their new home. Most of the conversations between husband and wife, especially as to the children's education, led to topics which recalled former disputes, and these disputes were apt to flare up again at any moment. There remained only those rare periods of amorousness which still came to them at times but did not last long. These were islets at which they anchored for a while and then again set out upon that ocean of veiled hostility which showed itself in their aloofness from one another. This aloofness might have grieved Ivan Ilych had he considered that it ought not to exist, but he now regarded the position as normal, and even made it the goal at which he aimed in family life. His aim was to free himself more and more from those unpleasantness and to give them a semblance of harmlessness and propriety. He attained this by spending less and less time with his family, and when obliged to be at home he tried to safeguard his position by the presence of outsiders. The chief thing however was that he had his official duties. The whole interest of his life now centered in the official world and that interest absorbed him. The consciousness of his power, being able to ruin anybody he wished to ruin, the importance, even the external dignity of his entry into court, or meetings with his subordinates, his success with superiors and inferiors, and above all his masterly handling of cases, of which he was conscious—all this gave him pleasure and filled his life, together with chats with his colleagues, dinners, and bridge. So that on the whole Ivan Ilych's life continued to flow as he considered it should do—pleasantly and properly.

So things continued for another seven years. His eldest daughter was already sixteen, another child had died, and only one son was left, a schoolboy and a subject of dissension. Ivan Ilych wanted to put him in the School of Law, but to spite him Praskovya Fedorovna entered him at the High School. The daughter had been educated at home and had turned out well: the boy did not learn badly either.

III

So Ivan Ilych lived for seventeen years after his marriage. He was already a Public Prosecutor of long standing, and had declined several proposed transfers while awaiting a more desirable post, when an unanticipated and unpleasant occurrence quite upset the peaceful course of his life. He was expecting to be offered the post of presiding judge in a University town, but Happe somehow came to the front and obtained the appointment instead. Ivan Ilych became irritable, reproached Happe, and quarrelled both with him and with his immediate superiors—who became colder to him and again passed him over when other appointments were made.

This was in 1880, the hardest year of Ivan Ilych's life. It was then that it became evident on the one hand that his salary was insufficient for them to live on, and on the other that he had been forgotten, and not only this, but that what was for him the greatest and most cruel injustice appeared to others a quite ordinary occurrence. Even his father did not consider it his duty to help him. Ivan Ilych felt himself abandoned by everyone, and that they regarded his position with a salary of 3,500 rubles as quite normal and even fortunate. He alone knew that with the consciousness of the injustices done him, with his wife's incessant nagging, and with the debts he had contracted by living beyond his means, his position was far from normal.

In order to save money that summer he obtained leave of absence and went with his wife to live in the country at her brother's place.

In the country, without his work, he experienced *ennui* for the first time in his life, and not only *ennui* but intolerable depression, and he decided that it was impossible to go on living like that, and that it was necessary to take energetic measures.

Having passed a sleepless night pacing up and down the veranda, he decided to go to Petersburg and bestir himself, in order to punish those who had failed to appreciate him and to get transferred to another ministry.

Next day, despite many protests from his wife and her brother, he started for Petersburg with the sole object of obtaining a post with a salary of five thousand rubles a year. He was no longer bent on any particular department, or tendency, or kind of activity. All he now wanted was an appointment to another post with a salary of five thousand rubles, either in the administration, in the banks, with the railways in one of the Empress Marya's Institutions, or even in the customs—but it had to carry with it a salary of five thousand rubles and be in a ministry other than that in which they had failed to appreciate him.

And this quest of Ivan Ilych's was crowned with remarkable and unexpected success. At Kursk an acquaintance of his, F. I. Ilyin, got into the first-class carriage, sat down beside Ivan Ilych, and told him of a telegram just received by the governor of Kursk announcing that a change was about to take place in the ministry: Peter Ivanovich was to be superseded by Ivan Semonovich.

The proposed change, apart from its significance for Russia, had a special significance for Ivan Ilych, because by bringing forward a new man, Peter Petrovich, and consequently his friend Zachar Ivanovich, it was highly favourable for Ivan Ilych, since Sachar Ivanovich was a friend and colleague of his.

In Moscow this news was confirmed, and on reaching Petersburg Ivan Ilych found Zachar Ivanovich and received a definite promise of an appointment in his former Department of Justice.

A week later he telegraphed to his wife: "Zachar in Miller's place. I shall receive appointment on presentation of report."

Thanks to this change of personnel, Ivan Ilych had unexpectedly obtained an appointment in his former ministry which placed him two states above his former colleagues besides giving him five thousand rubles salary and three thousand five hundred rubles for expenses connected with his removal. All his ill humour towards his former enemies and the whole department vanished, and Ivan Ilych was completely happy.

He returned to the country more cheerful and contented than he had been for a long time. Praskovya Fedorovna also cheered up and a truce was arranged between them. Ivan Ilych told of how he had been feted by everybody in Petersburg, how all those who had been his enemies were put to shame and now fawned on him, how envious they were of his appointment, and how much everybody in Petersburg had liked him.

Praskovya Fedorovna listened to all this and appeared to believe it. She did not contradict anything, but only made plans for their life in the town to which they were going. Ivan Ilych saw with delight that these plans were his plans, that he and his wife agreed, and that, after a stumble, his life was regaining its due and natural character of pleasant lightheartedness and decorum.

Ivan Ilych had come back for a short time only, for he had to take up his new duties on the 10th of September. Moreover, he needed time to settle into the new place, to move all his belongings from the province, and to buy and order many additional things: in a word, to make such arrangements as he had resolved on, which were almost exactly what Praskovya Fedorovna too had decided on.

Now that everything had happened so fortunately, and that he and his wife were at one in their aims and moreover saw so little of one another, they got on together better than they had done since the first years of marriage. Ivan Ilych had thought of taking his family away with him at once, but the insistence of his wife's brother and her sister-in-law, who had suddenly become particularly amiable and friendly to him and his family, induced him to depart alone.

So he departed, and the cheerful state of mind induced by his success and by the harmony between his wife and himself, the one intensifying the other, did not leave him. He found a delightful house, just the thing both he and his wife had dreamt of. Spacious, lofty reception rooms in the old style, a convenient and dignified study, rooms for his wife and daughter, a study for his son—it might have been specially built for them. Ivan

Ilych himself superintended the arrangements, chose the wallpapers, supplemented the furniture (preferably with antiques which he considered particularly *comme il faut*), and supervised the upholstering. Everything progressed and progressed and approached the ideal he had set himself: even when things were only half completed they exceeded his expectations. He saw what a refined and elegant character, free from vulgarity, it would all have when it was ready. On falling asleep he pictured to himself how the reception room would look. Looking at the yet unfinished drawing room he could see the fireplace, the screen, the what-not, the little chairs dotted here and there, the dishes and plates on the walls, and the bronzes, as they would be when everything was in place. He was pleased by the thought of how his wife and daughter, who shared his taste n this matter, would be impressed by it. They were certainly not expecting as much. He had been particularly successful in finding, and buying cheaply, antiques which gave a particularly aristocratic character to the whole place. But in his letters he intentionally understated everything in order to be able to surprise them. All this so absorbed him that his new duties—though he liked his official work—interested him less than he had expected. Sometimes he even had moments of absent-mindedness during the court sessions and would consider whether he should have straight or curved cornices for his curtains. He was so interested in it all that he often did things himself, rearranging the furniture, or rehanging the curtains. Once when mounting a step- ladder to show the upholsterer, who did not understand, how he wanted the hangings draped, he made a false step and slipped, but being a strong and agile man he clung on and only knocked his side against the knob of the window frame. The bruised place was painful but the pain soon passed, and he felt particularly bright and well just then. He wrote: "I feel fifteen years younger." He thought he would have everything ready by September, but it dragged on till mid-October. But the result was charming not only in his eyes but to everyone who saw it.

In reality it was just what is usually seen in the houses of people of moderate means who want to appear rich, and therefore succeed only in resembling others like themselves: there are damasks, dark wood, plants, rugs, and dull and polished bronzes—all the things people of a certain class have in order to resemble other people of that class. His house was so like the others that it would never have been noticed, but to him it all seemed to be quite exceptional. He was very happy when he met his family at the station and brought them to the newly furnished house all lit up, where a footman in a white tie opened the door into the hall decorated with plants, and when they went on into the drawing-room and the study uttering exclamations of delight. He conducted them everywhere, drank in their praises eagerly, and beamed with pleasure. At tea that evening, when Praskovya Fedorovna among others things asked him about his fall, he laughed, and showed them how he had gone flying and had frightened the upholsterer.

"It's a good thing I'm a bit of an athlete. Another man might have been killed, but I merely knocked myself, just here; it hurts when it's touched, but it's passing off already—it's only a bruise."

So they began living in their new home—in which, as always happens, when they got thoroughly settled in they found they were just one room short—and with the increased income, which as always was just a little (some five hundred rubles) too little, but it was all very nice.

Things went particularly well at first, before everything was finally arranged and while something had still to be done: this thing bought, that thing ordered, another thing moved, and something else adjusted. Though there were some disputes between husband and wife, they were both so well satisfied and had so much to do that it all passed off without any serious quarrels. When nothing was left to arrange it became rather dull and something seemed to be lacking, but they were then making acquaintances, forming habits, and life was growing fuller.

Ivan Ilych spent his mornings at the law court and came home to diner, and at first he was generally in a good humour, though he occasionally became irritable just on account of his house. (Every spot on the tablecloth or the upholstery, and every broken window- blind string, irritated him. He had devoted so much trouble to arranging it all that every disturbance of it distressed him.) But on the whole his life ran its course as he believed life should do: easily, pleasantly, and decorously.

He got up at nine, drank his coffee, read the paper, and then put on his undress uniform and went to the law courts. there the harness in which he worked had already been stretched to fit him and he donned it without a hitch: petitioners, inquiries at the chancery, the chancery itself, and the sittings public and administrative. In all this the thing was to exclude everything fresh and vital, which always disturbs the regular course of official business, and to admit only official relations with people, and then only on official grounds. A man would come, for instance, wanting some information. Ivan Ilych, as one in whose sphere the matter did not lie, would have nothing to do with him: but if the man had some business with him in his official capacity, something that could be expressed on officially stamped paper, he would do everything, positively everything he could within the limits of such relations, and in doing so would maintain the semblance of friendly human relations, that is, would observe the courtesies of life. As soon as the official relations ended, so did everything else. Ivan Ilych possessed this capacity to separate his real life from the official side of affairs and not mix the two, in the highest degree, and by long practice and natural aptitude had brought it to such a pitch that sometimes, in the manner of a virtuoso, he would even allow himself to let the human and official relations mingle. He let himself do this just because he felt that he could at any time he chose resume the strictly official attitude again and drop the human relation. and he did it all easily, pleasantly, correctly, and even artistically. In the intervals between the sessions he smoked, drank tea, chatted a little about politics, a little about general topics, a little about cards, but most of all about official appointments. Tired, but with the feelings of a virtuoso—one of the first violins who has played his part in an orchestra with precision—he would return home to find that his wife and daughter had been out paying calls, or had

a visitor, and that his son had been to school, had done his homework with his tutor, and was surely learning what is taught at High Schools. Everything was as it should be. After dinner, if they had no visitors, Ivan Ilych sometimes read a book that was being much discussed at the time, and in the evening settled down to work, that is, read official papers, compared the depositions of witnesses, and noted paragraphs of the Code applying to them. This was neither dull nor amusing. It was dull when he might have been playing bridge, but if no bridge was available it was at any rate better than doing nothing or sitting with his wife. Ivan Ilych's chief pleasure was giving little dinners to which he invited men and women of good social position, and just as his drawing-room resembled all other drawing-rooms so did his enjoyable little parties resemble all other such parties.

Once they even gave a dance. Ivan Ilych enjoyed it and everything went off well, except that it led to a violent quarrel with his wife about the cakes and sweets. Praskovya Fedorovna had made her own plans, but Ivan Ilych insisted on getting everything from an expensive confectioner and ordered too many cakes, and the quarrel occurred because some of those cakes were left over and the confectioner's bill came to forty-five rubles. It was a great and disagreeable quarrel. Praskovya Fedorovna called him "a fool and an imbecile," and he clutched at his head and made angry allusions to divorce.

But the dance itself had been enjoyable. The best people were there, and Ivan Ilych had danced with Princess Trufonova, a sister of the distinguished founder of the Society "Bear My Burden."

The pleasures connected with his work were pleasures of ambition; his social pleasures were those of vanity; but Ivan Ilych's greatest pleasure was playing bridge. He acknowledged that whatever disagreeable incident happened in his life, the pleasure that beamed like a ray of light above everything else was to sit down to bridge with good players, not noisy partners, and of course to four-handed bridge (with five players it was annoying to have to stand out, though one pretended not to mind), to play a clever and serious game (when the cards allowed it) and then to have supper and drink a glass of wine. After a game of bridge, especially if he had won a little (to win a large sum was unpleasant), Ivan Ilych went to bed in a specially good humour.

So they lived. They formed a circle of acquaintances among the best people and were visited by people of importance and by young folk. In their views as to their acquaintances, husband, wife and daughter were entirely agreed, and tacitly and unanimously kept at arm's length and shook off the various shabby friends and relations who, with much show of affection, gushed into the drawing-room with its Japanese plates on the walls. Soon these shabby friends ceased to obtrude themselves and only the best people remained in the Golovins' set.

Young men made up to Lisa, and Petrishchev, an examining magistrate and Dmitri Ivanovich Petrishchev's son and sole heir, began to be so attentive to her that Ivan Ilych had already spoken to Praskovya Fedorovna about it, and considered whether they should not arrange a party for them, or get up some private theatricals.

So they lived, and all went well, without change, and life flowed pleasantly.

IV

They were all in good health. It could not be called ill health if Ivan Ilych sometimes said that he had a queer taste in his mouth and felt some discomfort in his left side.

But this discomfort increased and, though not exactly painful, grew into a sense of pressure in his side accompanied by ill humour. And his irritability became worse and worse and began to mar the agreeable, easy, and correct life that had established itself in the Golovin family. Quarrels between husband and wife became more and more frequent, and soon the ease and amenity disappeared and even the decorum was barely maintained. Scenes again became frequent, and very few of those islets remained on which husband and wife could meet without an explosion. Praskovya Fedorovna now had good reason to

say that her husband's temper was trying. With characteristic exaggeration she said he had always had a dreadful temper, and that it had needed all her good nature to put up with it for twenty years. It was true that now the quarrels were started by him. His bursts of temper always came just before dinner, often just as he began to eat his soup. Sometimes he noticed that a plate or dish was chipped, or the food was not right, or his son put his elbow on the table, or his daughter's hair was not done as he liked it, and for all this he blamed Praskovya Fedorovna. At first she retorted and said disagreeable things to him, but once or twice he fell into such a rage at the beginning of dinner that she realized it was due to some physical derangement brought on by taking food, and so she restrained herself and did not answer, but only hurried to get the dinner over. She regarded this self-restraint as highly praiseworthy. Having come to the conclusion that her husband had a dreadful temper and made her life miserable, she began to feel sorry for herself, and the more she pitied herself the more she hated her husband. She began to wish he would die; yet she did not want him to die because then his salary would cease. And this irritated her against him still more. She considered herself dreadfully unhappy just because not even his death could save her, and though she concealed her exasperation, that hidden exasperation of hers increased his irritation also.

After one scene in which Ivan Ilych had been particularly unfair and after which he had said in explanation that he certainly was irritable but that it was due to his not being well, she said that he was ill it should be attended to, and insisted on his going to see a celebrated doctor.

He went. Everything took place as he had expected and as it always does. There was the usual waiting and the important air assumed by the doctor, with which he was so familiar (resembling that which he himself assumed in court), and the sounding and listening, and the questions which called for answers that were foregone conclusions and were evidently unnecessary, and the look of importance which implied that "if only you put yourself in our hands we will arrange everything—we know indubitably how it has to be done, always in the same way for everybody alike." It was all just as it was in the law courts. The doctor put on just the same air towards him as he himself put on towards an accused person.

The doctor said that so-and-so indicated that there was so-and-so inside the patient, but if the investigation of so-and-so did not confirm this, then he must assume that and that. If he assumed that and that, then . . . and so on. To Ivan Ilych only one question was important: was his case serious or not? But the doctor ignored that inappropriate question. From his point of view it was not the one under consideration, the real question was to decide between a floating kidney, chronic catarrh, or appendicitis. It was not a question the doctor solved brilliantly, as it seemed to Ivan Ilych, in favour of the appendix, with the reservation that should an examination of the urine give fresh indications the matter would be reconsidered. All this was just what Ivan Ilych had himself brilliantly accomplished a thousand times in dealing with men on trial. The doctor summed up just as brilliantly, looking over his spectacles triumphantly and even gaily at the accused. From the doctor's summing up Ivan Ilych concluded that things were bad, but that for the doctor, and perhaps for everybody else, it was a matter of indifference, though for him it was bad. And this conclusion struck him painfully, arousing in him a great feeling of pity for himself and of bitterness towards the doctor's indifference to a matter of such importance.

He said nothing of this, but rose, placed the doctor's fee on the table, and remarked with a sigh: "We sick people probably often put inappropriate questions. But tell me, in general, is this complaint dangerous, or not? . . ."

The doctor looked at him sternly over his spectacles with one eye, as if to say: "Prisoner, if you will not keep to the questions put to you, I shall be obliged to have you removed from the court."

"I have already told you what I consider necessary and proper. The analysis may show something more." And the doctor bowed.

Ivan Ilych went out slowly, seated himself disconsolately in his sledge, and drove home. All the way home he was going over what the doctor had said, trying to translate those complicated, obscure, scientific phrases into plain language and find in them an answer to the question: "Is my condition bad? Is it very bad? Or is there as yet nothing much wrong?" And it seemed to him that the meaning of what the doctor had said was that it was very bad. Everything in the streets seemed depressing. The cabmen, the houses, the passers-by, and the shops, were dismal. His ache, this dull gnawing ache that never ceased for a moment, seemed to have acquired a new and more serious significance from the doctor's dubious remarks. Ivan Ilych now watched it with a new and oppressive feeling.

He reached home and began to tell his wife about it. She listened, but in the middle of his account his daughter came in with her hat on, ready to go out with her mother. She sat down reluctantly to listen to this tedious story, but could not stand it long, and her mother too did not hear him to the end.

"Well, I am very glad," she said. "Mind now to take your medicine regularly. Give me the prescription and I'll send Gerasim to the chemist's." And she went to get ready to go out.

While she was in the room Ivan Ilych had hardly taken time to breathe, but he sighed deeply when she left it.

"Well," he thought, "perhaps it isn't so bad after all."

He began taking his medicine and following the doctor's directions, which had been altered after the examination of the urine. but then it happened that there was a contradiction between the indications drawn from the examination of the urine and the symptoms that showed themselves. It turned out that what was happening differed from what the doctor had told him, and that he had either forgotten or blundered, or hidden something from him. He could not, however, be blamed for that, and Ivan Ilych still obeyed his orders implicitly and at first derived some comfort from doing so.

From the time of his visit to the doctor, Ivan Ilych's chief occupation was the exact fulfillment of the doctor's instructions regarding hygiene and the taking of medicine, and the observation of his pain and his excretions. His chief interest came to be people's ailments and people's health. When sickness, deaths, or recoveries were mentioned in his presence, especially when the illness resembled his own, he listened with agitation which he tried to hide, asked questions, and applied what he heard to his own case.

The pain did not grow less, but Ivan Ilych made efforts to force himself to think that he was better. And he could do this so long as nothing agitated him. But as soon as he had any unpleasantness with his wife, any lack of success in his official work, or held bad cards at bridge, he was at once acutely sensible of his disease. He had formerly borne such mischances, hoping soon to adjust what was wrong, to master it and attain success, or make a grand slam. But now every mischance upset him and plunged him into despair. He would say to himself: "there now, just as I was beginning to get better and the medicine had begun to take effect, comes this accursed misfortune, or unpleasantness . . ." And he was furious with the mishap, or with the people who were causing the unpleasantness and killing him, for he felt that this fury was killing him but he could not restrain it. One would have thought that it should have been clear to him that this exasperation with circumstances and people aggravated his illness, and that he ought therefore to ignore unpleasant occurrences. But he drew the very opposite conclusion: he said that he needed peace, and he watched for everything that might disturb it and became irritable at the slightest infringement of it. His condition was rendered worse by the fact that he read medical books and consulted doctors. The progress of his disease was so gradual that he could deceive himself when comparing one day with another—the difference was so slight. But when he consulted the doctors it seemed to him that he was getting worse, and even very rapidly. Yet despite this he was continually consulting them.

That month he went to see another celebrity, who told him almost the same as the first had done but put his questions rather differently, and the interview with this celebrity only increased Ivan Ilych's doubts and fears. A friend of a friend of his, a very good doctor, diagnosed his illness again quite differently from the others, and though he predicted recovery, his questions and suppositions bewildered Ivan Ilych still more and increased his doubts. A homeopathist diagnosed the disease in yet another way, and prescribed medicine which Ivan Ilych took secretly for a week. But after a week, not feeling any improvement and having lost confidence both in the former doctor's treatment and in this one's, he became still more despondent. One day a lady acquaintance mentioned a cure effected by a wonder-working icon. Ivan Ilych caught himself listening attentively and beginning to believe that it had occurred. This incident alarmed him. "Has my mind really weakened to such an extent?" he asked himself. "Nonsense! It's all rubbish. I mustn't give way to nervous fears but having chosen a doctor must keep strictly to his treatment. That is what I will do. Now it's all settled. I won't think about it, but will follow the treatment seriously till summer, and then we shall see. From now there must be no more of this wavering!" This was easy to say but impossible to carry out. The pain in his side oppressed him and seemed to grow worse and more incessant, while the taste in his mouth grew stranger and stranger. It seemed to him that his breath had a disgusting smell, and he was conscious of a loss of appetite and strength. There was no deceiving himself: something terrible, new, and more important than anything before in his life, was taking place within him of which he alone was aware. Those about him did not understand or would not understand it, but thought everything in the world was going on as usual. That tormented Ivan Ilych more than anything. He saw that his household, especially his wife and daughter who were in a perfect whirl of visiting, did not understand anything of it and were annoyed that he was so depressed and so exacting, as if he were to blame for it. Though they tried to disguise it he saw that he was an obstacle in their path, and that his wife had adopted a definite line in regard to his illness and kept to it regardless of anything he said or did. Her attitude was this: "You know," she would say to her friends, "Ivan Ilych can't do as other people do, and keep to the treatment prescribed for him. One day he'll take his drops and keep strictly to his diet and go to bed in good time, but the next day unless I watch him he'll suddenly forget his medicine, eat sturgeon—which is forbidden—and sit up playing cards till one o'clock in the morning."

"Oh, come, when was that?" Ivan Ilych would ask in vexation. "Only once at Peter Ivanovich's."

"And yesterday with Shebek."

"Well, even if I hadn't stayed up, this pain would have kept me awake."

"Be that as it may you'll never get well like that, but will always make us wretched."

Praskovya Fedorovna's attitude to Ivan Ilych's illness, as she expressed it both to others and to him, was that it was his own fault and was another of the annoyances he caused her. Ivan Ilych felt that this opinion escaped her involuntarily—but that did not make it easier for him.

At the law courts too, Ivan Ilych noticed, or thought he noticed, a strange attitude towards himself. It sometimes seemed to him that people were watching him inquisitively as a man whose place might soon be vacant. Then again, his friends would suddenly begin to chaff him in a friendly way about his low spirits, as if the awful, horrible, and unheard-of thing that was going on within him, incessantly gnawing at him and irresistibly drawing him away, was a very agreeable subject for jests. Schwartz in particular irritated him by his jocularity, vivacity, and *savoir-faire,* which reminded him of what he himself had been ten years ago.

Friends came to make up a set and they sat down to cards. They dealt, bending the new cards to soften them, and he sorted the diamonds in his hand and found he had seven. His partner said "No trumps" and supported him with two diamonds. What more could be wished for? It ought to be jolly and lively. They would make a grand slam. But suddenly Ivan Ilych was conscious of that gnawing pain, that taste in his mouth, and it seemed ridiculous that in such circumstances he should be pleased to make a grand slam.

He looked at his partner Mikhail Mikhaylovich, who rapped the table with his strong hand and instead of snatching up the tricks pushed the cards courteously and indulgently towards Ivan Ilych that he might have the pleasure of gathering them up without the trouble of stretching out his hand for them. "Does he think I am too weak to stretch out my arm?" thought Ivan Ilych, and forgetting what he was doing he overtrumped his partner, missing the grand slam by three tricks. And what was most awful of all was that he saw how upset Mikhail Mikhaylovich was about it but did not himself care. And it was dreadful to realize why he did not care.

They all saw that he was suffering, and said: "We can stop if you are tired. Take a rest." Lie down? No, he was not at all tired, and he finished the rubber. All were gloomy and silent. Ivan Ilych felt that he had diffused this gloom over them and could not dispel it. They had supper and went away, and Ivan Ilych was left alone with the consciousness that his life was poisoned and was poisoning the lives of others, and that this poison did not weaken but penetrated more and more deeply into his whole being.

With this consciousness, and with physical pain besides the terror, he must go to bed, often to lie awake the greater part of the night. Next morning he had to get up again, dress, go to the law courts, speak, and write; or if he did not go out, spend at home those twenty-four hours a day each of which was a torture. And he had to live thus all alone on the brink of an abyss, with no one who understood or pitied him.

##

So one month passed and then another. Just before the New Year his brother-in-law came to town and stayed at their house. Ivan Ilych was at the law courts and Praskovya Fedorovna had gone shopping. When Ivan Ilych came home and entered his study he found his brother-in-law there—a healthy, florid man—unpacking his portmanteau himself. He raised his head on hearing Ivan Ilych's footsteps and looked up at him for a moment without a word. That stare told Ivan Ilych everything. His brother-in-law opened his mouth to utter an exclamation of surprise but checked himself, and that action confirmed it all.

"I have changed, eh?"

"Yes, there is a change."

And after that, try as he would to get his brother-in-law to return to the subject of his looks, the latter would say nothing about it. Praskovya Fedorovna came home and her brother went out to her. Ivan Ilych locked to door and began to examine himself in the glass, first full face, then in profile. He took up a portrait of himself taken with his wife, and compared it with what he saw in the glass. The change in him was immense. Then he bared his arms to the elbow, looked at them, drew the sleeves down again, sat down on an ottoman, and grew blacker than night.

"No, no, this won't do!" he said to himself, and jumped up, went to the table, took up some law papers and began to read them, but could not continue. He unlocked the door and went into the reception-room. The door leading to the drawing-room was shut. He approached it on tiptoe and listened.

"No, you are exaggerating!" Praskovya Fedorovna was saying.

"Exaggerating! Don't you see it? Why, he's a dead man! Look at his eyes—there's no life in them. But what is it that is wrong with him?"

"No one knows. Nikolaevich [that was another doctor] said something, but I don't know what. And Seshchetitsky [this was the celebrated specialist] said quite the contrary . . ."

Ivan Ilych walked away, went to his own room, lay down, and began musing; "The kidney, a floating kidney." He recalled all the doctors had told him of how it detached itself and swayed about. And by an effort of imagination he tried to catch that kidney and arrest it and support it. So little was needed for this, it seemed to him. "No, I'll go to see Peter Ivanovich again." [That was the friend whose friend was a doctor.] He rang, ordered the carriage, and got ready to go.

"Where are you going, Jean?" asked his wife with a specially sad and exceptionally kind look.

This exceptionally kind look irritated him. He looked morosely at her.

"I must go to see Peter Ivanovich."

He went to see Peter Ivanovich, and together they went to see his friend, the doctor. He was in, and Ivan Ilych had a long talk with him.

Reviewing the anatomical and physiological details of what in the doctor's opinion was going on inside him, he understood it all.

There was something, a small thing, in the vermiform appendix. It might all come right. Only stimulate the energy of one organ and check the activity of another, then absorption would take place and everything would come right. He got home rather late for dinner, ate his dinner, and conversed cheerfully, but could not for a long time bring himself to go back to work in his room. At last, however, he went to his study and did what was necessary, but the consciousness that he had put something aside—an important, intimate matter which he would revert to when his work was done—never left him. When he had finished his work he remembered that this intimate matter was the thought of his vermiform appendix. But he did not give himself up to it, and went to the drawing-room for tea. There were callers there, including the examining magistrate who was a desirable match for his daughter, and they were conversing, playing the piano, and singing. Ivan Ilych, as Praskovya Fedorovna remarked, spent that evening more cheerfully than usual, but he never for a moment forgot that he had postponed the important matter of the appendix. At eleven o'clock he said goodnight and went to his bedroom. Since his illness he had slept alone in a small room next to his study. He undressed and took up a novel by Zola, but instead of reading it he fell into thought, and in his imagination that desired improvement in the vermiform appendix occurred. There was the absorption and evacuation and the re-establishment of normal activity. "Yes, that's it!" he said to himself. "One need only assist nature, that's all." He remembered his medicine, rose, took it, and lay down on his back watching for the beneficent action of the medicine and for it to lessen the pain. "I need only take it regularly and avoid all injurious influences. I am already feeling better, much better." He began touching his side: it was not painful to the touch. "There, I really don't feel it. It's much better already." He put out the light and turned on his side . . . "The appendix is getting better, absorption is occurring." Suddenly he felt the old, familiar, dull, gnawing pain, stubborn and serious. There was the same familiar loathsome taste in his mouth. His heart sank and he felt dazed. "My God! My God!" he muttered. "Again, again! And it will never cease." And suddenly the matter presented itself in a quite different aspect. "Vermiform appendix! Kidney!" he said to himself. "It's not a question of appendix or kidney, but of life and . . . death. Yes, life was there and now it is going, going and I cannot stop it. Yes. Why deceive myself? Isn't it obvious to everyone but me that I'm dying, and that it's only a question of weeks, days . . . it may happen this moment. There was light and now there is darkness. I was here and now I'm going there! Where?" A chill came over him, his breathing ceased, and he felt only the throbbing of his heart.

"When I am not, what will there be? There will be nothing. Then where shall I be when I am no more? Can this be dying? No, I don't want to!" He jumped up and tried to light the candle, felt for it with trembling hands, dropped candle and candlestick on the floor, and fell back on his pillow.

"What's the use? It makes no difference," he said to himself, staring with wide-open eyes into the darkness. "Death. Yes, death. And none of them knows or wishes to know it, and they have no pity for me. Now they are playing." (He heard through the door the distant sound of a song and its accompaniment.) "It's all the same to them, but they will die too! Fools! I first, and they later, but it will be the same for them. And now they are merry . . . the beasts!"

Anger choked him and he was agonizingly, unbearably miserable. "It is impossible that all men have been doomed to suffer this awful horror!" He raised himself.

"Something must be wrong. I must calm myself—must think it all over from the beginning." And he again began thinking. "Yes, the beginning of my illness: I knocked my side, but I was still quite well that day and the next. It hurt a little, then rather more. I saw the doctors, then followed despondency and anguish, more doctors, and I drew nearer to the abyss. My strength grew less and I kept coming nearer and nearer, and now I have wasted away and there is no light in my eyes. I think of the appendix—but this is death! I think of mending the appendix, and all the while here is death! Can it really be death?" Again terror seized him and he gasped for breath. He leant down and began feeling for the matches, pressing with his elbow on the stand beside the bed. It was in his way and hurt him, he grew furious with it, pressed on it still harder, and upset it. Breathless and in despair he fell on his back, expecting death to come immediately.

Meanwhile the visitors were leaving. Praskovya Fedorovna was seeing them off. She heard something fall and came in.

"What has happened?"

"Nothing. I knocked it over accidentally."

She went out and returned with a candle. He lay there panting heavily, like a man who has run a thousand yards, and stared upwards at her with a fixed look.

"What is it, Jean?"

"No . . . o . . . thing. I upset it." ("Why speak of it? She won't understand," he thought.)

And in truth she did not understand. She picked up the stand, lit his candle, and hurried away to see another visitor off. When she came back he still lay on his back, looking upwards.

"What is it? Do you feel worse?"

"Yes."

She shook her head and sat down.

"Do you know, Jean, I think we must ask Leshchetitsky to come and see you here."

This meant calling in the famous specialist, regardless of expense. He smiled malignantly and said "No." She remained a little longer and then went up to him and kissed his forehead.

While she was kissing him he hated her from the bottom of his soul and with difficulty refrained from pushing her away.

"Good night. Please God you'll sleep."

"Yes."

VI

Ivan Ilych saw that he was dying, and he was in continual despair.

In the depth of his heart he knew he was dying, but not only was he not accustomed to the thought, he simply did not and could not grasp it.

The syllogism he had learnt from Kiesewetter's Logic: "Caius is a man, men are mortal, therefore Caius is mortal," had always seemed to him correct as applied to Caius, but certainly not as applied to himself. That Caius—man in the abstract—was mortal, was perfectly correct, but he was not Caius, not an abstract man, but a creature quite, quite separate from all others. He had been little Vanya, with a mamma and a papa, with Mitya and Volodya, with the toys, a coachman and a nurse, afterwards with Katenka and will all the joys, griefs, and delights of childhood, boyhood, and youth. What did Caius know of the smell of that striped leather ball Vanya had been so fond of? Had Caius kissed his mother's hand like that, and did the silk of her dress rustle so for Caius? Had he rioted like that at school when the pastry was bad? Had Caius been in love like that? Could Caius preside at a session as he did? "Caius really was mortal, and it was right for him to die; but for me, little Vanya, Ivan Ilych, with all my thoughts and emotions, it's altogether a different matter. It cannot be that I ought to die. That would be too terrible."

Such was his feeling.

"If I had to die like Caius I would have known it was so. An inner voice would have told me so, but there was nothing of the sort in me and I and all my friends felt that our case was quite different from that of Caius. and now here it is!" he said to himself. "It can't be. It's impossible! But here it is. How is this? How is one to understand it?"

He could not understand it, and tried to drive this false, incorrect, morbid thought away and to replace it by other proper and healthy thoughts. But that thought, and not the thought only but the reality itself, seemed to come and confront him.

And to replace that thought he called up a succession of others, hoping to find in them some support. He tried to get back into the former current of thoughts that had once screened the thought of death from him. But strange to say, all that had formerly shut off, hidden, and destroyed his consciousness of death, no longer had that effect. Ivan Ilych now spent most of his time in attempting to re-establish that old current. He would say to himself: "I will take up my duties again—after all I used to live by them." And banishing all doubts he would go to the law courts, enter into conversation with his colleagues, and sit carelessly as was his wont, scanning the crowd with a thoughtful look and leaning both his emaciated arms on the arms of his oak chair; bending over as usual to a colleague and drawing his papers nearer he would interchange whispers with him, and then suddenly raising his eyes and sitting erect would pronounce certain words and open the proceedings. But suddenly in the midst of those proceedings the pain in his side, regardless of the stage the proceedings had reached, would begin its own gnawing work. Ivan Ilych would turn his attention to it and try to drive the thought of it away, but without success. *It* would come and stand before him and look at him, and he would be petrified and the light would die out of his eyes, and he would again begin asking himself whether *It* alone was true. And his colleagues and subordinates would see with surprise and distress that he, the brilliant and subtle judge, was becoming confused and making mistakes. He would shake himself, try to pull himself together, manage somehow to bring the sitting to a close, and return home with the sorrowful consciousness that his judicial labours could not as formerly hide from him what he wanted them to hide, and could not deliver him from *It*. And what was worst of all was that *It* drew his attention to itself not in order to make him take some action but only that he should look at *It*, look it straight in the face: look at it and without doing anything, suffer inexpressibly.

And to save himself from this condition Ivan Ilych looked for consolations—new screens—and new screens were found and for a while seemed to save him, but then they immediately fell to pieces or rather became transparent, as if *It* penetrated them and nothing could veil *It*.

In these latter days he would go into the drawing-room he had arranged—that drawing-room where he had fallen and for the sake of which (how bitterly ridiculous it seemed) he had sacrificed his life—for he knew that his illness originated with that knock. He would enter and see that something had scratched the polished table. He would look for the cause of this and find that it was the bronze ornamentation of an album, that had got bent. He would take up the expensive album which he had lovingly arranged, and feel vexed with his daughter and her friends for their untidiness—for the album was torn here and there and some of the photographs turned upside down. He would put it carefully in order and bend the ornamentation back into position. Then it would occur to him to place all those things in another corner of the room, near the plants. He would call the footman, but his daughter or wife would come to help him. They would not agree, and his wife would contradict him, and he would dispute and grow angry. But that was all right, for then he did not think about *It*. *It* was invisible.

But then, when he was moving something himself, his wife would say: "Let the servants do it. You will hurt yourself again." And suddenly *It* would flash through the screen and he would see it. It was just a flash, and he hoped it would disappear, but he would involuntarily pay attention to his side. "It sits there as before, gnawing just the same!" And he could no longer forget *It*, but could distinctly see it looking at him from behind the flowers. "What is it all for?"

"It really is so! I lost my life over that curtain as I might have done when storming a fort. Is that possible? How terrible and how stupid. It can't be true! It can't, but it is."

He would go to his study, lie down, and again be alone with *It*: face to face with *It*. And nothing could be done with *It* except to look at it and shudder.

VII

How it happened it is impossible to say because it came about step by step, unnoticed, but in the third month of Ivan Ilych's illness, his wife, his daughter, his son, his acquaintances, the doctors, the servants, and above all he himself, were aware that the whole interest he had for other people was whether he would soon vacate his place, and at last release the living from the discomfort caused by his presence and be himself released from his sufferings.

He slept less and less. He was given opium and hypodermic injections of morphine, but this did not relieve him. The dull depression he experienced in a somnolent condition at first gave him a little relief, but only as something new, afterwards it became as distressing as the pain itself or even more so.

Special foods were prepared for him by the doctors' orders, but all those foods became increasingly distasteful and disgusting to him.

For his excretions also special arrangements had to be made, and this was a torment to him every time—a torment from the uncleanliness, the unseemliness, and the smell, and from knowing that another person had to take part in it.

But just through this most unpleasant matter, Ivan Ilych obtained comfort. Gerasim, the butler's young assistant, always came in to carry the things out. Gerasim was a clean, fresh peasant lad, grown stout on town food and always cheerful and bright. At first the sight of him, in his clean Russian peasant costume, engaged on that disgusting task embarrassed Ivan Ilych.

Once when he got up from the commode to weak to draw up his trousers, he dropped into a soft armchair and looked with horror at his bare, enfeebled thighs with the muscles so sharply marked on them.

Gerasim with a firm light tread, his heavy boots emitting a pleasant smell of tar and fresh winter air, came in wearing a clean Hessian apron, the sleeves of his print shirt tucked up over his strong bare young arms; and refraining from looking at his sick master out of consideration for his feelings, and restraining the joy of life that beamed from his face, he went up to the commode.

"Gerasim!" said Ivan Ilych in a weak voice.

"Gerasim started, evidently afraid he might have committed some blunder, and with a rapid movement turned his fresh, kind, simple young face which just showed the first downy signs of a beard.

"Yes, sir?"

"That must be very unpleasant for you. You must forgive me. I am helpless."

"Oh, why, sir," and Gerasim's eyes beamed and he showed his glistening white teeth, "what's a little trouble? It's a case of illness with you, sir."

And his deft strong hands did their accustomed task, and he went out of the room stepping lightly. Five minutes later he as lightly returned.

Ivan Ilych was still sitting in the same position in the armchair.

"Gerasim," he said when the latter had replaced the freshly- washed utensil. "Please come here and help me." Gerasim went up to him. "Lift me up. It is hard for me to get up, and I have sent Dmitri away."

Gerasim went up to him, grasped his master with his strong arms deftly but gently, in the same way that he stepped—lifted him, supported him with one hand, and with the other drew up his trousers and would have set him down again, but Ivan Ilych asked to be led to the sofa. Gerasim, without an effort and without apparent pressure, led him, almost lifting him, to the sofa and placed him on it.

"Thank you. How easily and well you do it all!"

Gerasim smiled again and turned to leave the room. But Ivan Ilych felt his presence such a comfort that he did not want to let him go.

"One thing more, please move up that chair. No, the other one—under my feet. It is easier for me when my feet are raised."

Gerasim brought the chair, set it down gently in place, and raised Ivan Ilych's legs on it. It seemed to Ivan Ilych that he felt better while Gerasim was holding up his legs.

"It's better when my legs are higher," he said. "Place that cushion under them."

Gerasim did so. He again lifted the legs and placed them, and again Ivan Ilych felt better while Gerasim held his legs. When he set them down Ivan Ilych fancied he felt worse.

"Gerasim," he said. "Are you busy now?"

"Not at all, sir," said Gerasim, who had learnt from the townsfolk how to speak to gentlefolk.

"What have you still to do?"

"What have I to do? I've done everything except chopping the logs for tomorrow."

"Then hold my legs up a bit higher, can you?"

"Of course I can. Why not?" and Gerasim raised his master's legs higher and Ivan Ilych thought that in that position he did not feel any pain at all.

"And how about the logs?"

"Don't trouble about that, sir. There's plenty of time."

Ivan Ilych told Gerasim to sit down and hold his legs, and began to talk to him. And strange to say it seemed to him that he felt better while Gerasim held his legs up.

After that Ivan Ilych would sometimes call Gerasim and get him to hold his legs on his shoulders, and he liked talking to him. Gerasim did it all easily, willingly, simply, and with a good nature that touched Ivan Ilych. Health, strength, and vitality in other people were offensive to him, but Gerasim's strength and vitality did not mortify but soothed him.

What tormented Ivan Ilych most was the deception, the lie, which for some reason they all accepted, that he was not dying but was simply ill, and he only need keep quiet and undergo a treatment and then something very good would result. He however knew that do what they would nothing would come of it, only still more agonizing suffering and death. This deception tortured him—their not wishing to admit what they all knew and what he knew, but wanting to lie to him concerning his terrible condition, and wishing and forcing him to participate in that lie. Those lies—lies enacted over him on the eve of his death and destined to degrade this awful, solemn act to the level of their visitings, their curtains, their sturgeon for dinner—were a terrible agony for Ivan Ilych. And strangely enough, many times when they were going through their antics over him he had been within a hairbreadth of calling out to them: "Stop lying! You know and I know that I am dying. Then at least stop lying about it!" But he had never had the spirit to do it. The awful, terrible act of his dying was, he could see, reduced by those about him to the level of a casual, unpleasant, and almost indecorous incident (as if someone entered a drawing room defusing an unpleasant odour) and this was done by that very decorum which he had served all his life long. He saw that no one felt for him, because no one even wished to grasp his position. Only Gerasim recognized it and pitied him. And so Ivan Ilych felt at ease only with him. He felt comforted when Gerasim supported his legs (sometimes all night long) and refused to go to bed, saying: "Don't you worry, Ivan Ilych. I'll get sleep enough later on," or when he suddenly became familiar and exclaimed: "If you weren't sick it would be another matter, but as it is, why should I grudge a little trouble?" Gerasim alone did not lie; everything showed that he alone understood the facts of the case and did not consider it necessary to disguise them, but simply felt sorry for his emaciated and enfeebled master. Once when Ivan Ilych was sending him away he even said straight out: "We shall all of us die, so why should I grudge a little trouble?"—expressing the fact that he did not think his work burdensome, because he was doing it for a dying man and hoped someone would do the same for him when his time came.

Apart from this lying, or because of it, what most tormented Ivan Ilych was that no one pitied him as he wished to be pitied. At certain moments after prolonged suffering he wished most of all (though he would have been ashamed to confess it) for someone to pity him as a sick child is pitied. He longed to be petted and comforted. he knew he was an important functionary, that

he had a beard turning grey, and that therefore what he longed for was impossible, but still he longed for it. and in Gerasim's attitude towards him there was something akin to what he wished for, and so that attitude comforted him. Ivan Ilych wanted to weep, wanted to be petted and cried over, and then his colleague Shebek would come, and instead of weeping and being petted, Ivan Ilych would assume a serious, severe, and profound air, and by force of habit would express his opinion on a decision of the Court of Cassation and would stubbornly insist on that view. This falsity around him and within him did more than anything else to poison his last days.

VIII

It was morning. He knew it was morning because Gerasim had gone, and Peter the footman had come and put out the candles, drawn back one of the curtains, and begun quietly to tidy up. Whether it was morning or evening, Friday or Sunday, made no difference, it was all just the same: the gnawing, unmitigated, agonizing pain, never ceasing for an instant, the consciousness of life inexorably waning but not yet extinguished, the approach of that ever dreaded and hateful Death which was the only reality, and always the same falsity. What were days, weeks, hours, in such a case?

"Will you have some tea, sir?"

"He wants things to be regular, and wishes the gentlefolk to drink tea in the morning," thought Ivan Ilych, and only said "No."

"Wouldn't you like to move onto the sofa, sir?"

"He wants to tidy up the room, and I'm in the way. I am uncleanliness and disorder," he thought, and said only:

"No, leave me alone."

The man went on bustling about. Ivan Ilych stretched out his hand. Peter came up, ready to help.

"What is it, sir?"

"My watch."

Peter took the watch which was close at hand and gave it to his master.

"Half-past eight. Are they up?"

"No sir, except Vladimir Ivanovich" (the son) "who has gone to school. Praskovya Fedorovna ordered me to wake her if you asked for her. Shall I do so?"

"No, there's no need to." "Perhaps I'd better have some tea," he thought, and added aloud: "Yes, bring me some tea."

Peter went to the door, but Ivan Ilych dreaded being left alone. "How can I keep him here? Oh yes, my medicine." "Peter, give me my medicine." "Why not? Perhaps it may still do some good." He took a spoonful and swallowed it. "No, it won't help. It's all tomfoolery, all deception," he decided as soon as he became aware of the familiar, sickly, hopeless taste. "No, I can't believe in it any longer. But the pain, why this pain? If it would only cease just for a moment!" And he moaned. Peter turned towards him. "It's all right. Go and fetch me some tea."

Peter went out. Left alone Ivan Ilych groaned not so much with pain, terrible though that was, as from mental anguish. Always and for ever the same, always these endless days and nights. If only it would come quicker! If only *what* would come quicker? Death, darkness? . . . No, no! anything rather than death!

When Peter returned with the tea on a tray, Ivan Ilych stared at him for a time in perplexity, not realizing who and what he was. Peter was disconcerted by that look and his embarrassment brought Ivan Ilych to himself.

"Oh, tea! All right, put it down. Only help me to wash and put on a clean shirt."

And Ivan Ilych began to wash. With pauses for rest, he washed his hands and then his face, cleaned his teeth, brushed his hair, looked in the glass. He was terrified by what he saw, especially by the limp way in which his hair clung to his pallid forehead.

While his shirt was being changed he knew that he would be still more frightened at the sight of his body, so he avoided looking at it. Finally he was ready. He drew on a dressing-gown, wrapped himself in a plaid, and sat down

in the armchair to take his tea. For a moment he felt refreshed, but as soon as he began to drink the tea he was again aware of the same taste, and the pain also returned. He finished it with an effort, and then lay down stretching out his legs, and dismissed Peter.

Always the same. Now a spark of hope flashes up, then a sea of despair rages, and always pain; always pain, always despair, and always the same. When alone he had a dreadful and distressing desire to call someone, but he knew beforehand that with others present it would be still worse. "Another dose of morphine--to lose consciousness. I will tell him, the doctor, that he must think of something else. It's impossible, impossible, to go on like this."

An hour and another pass like that. But now there is a ring at the door bell. Perhaps it's the doctor? It is. He comes in fresh, hearty, plump, and cheerful, with that look on his face that seems to say: "There now, you're in a panic about something, but we'll arrange it all for you directly!" The doctor knows this expression is out of place here, but he has put it on once for all and can't take it off—like a man who has put on a frock-coat in the morning to pay a round of calls.

The doctor rubs his hands vigorously and reassuringly.

"Brr! How cold it is! There's such a sharp frost; just let me warm myself!" he says, as if it were only a matter of waiting till he was warm, and then he would put everything right.

"Well now, how are you?"

Ivan Ilych feels that the doctor would like to say: "Well, how are our affairs?" but that even he feels that this would not do, and says instead: "What sort of a night have you had?"

Ivan Ilych looks at him as much as to say: "Are you really never ashamed of lying?" But the doctor does not wish to understand this question, and Ivan Ilych says: "Just as terrible as ever. The pain never leaves me and never subsides. If only something . . ."

"Yes, you sick people are always like that. . . . There, now I think I am warm enough. Even Praskovya Fedorovna, who is so particular, could find no fault with my temperature. Well, now I can say good-morning," and the doctor presses his patient's hand.

Then dropping his former playfulness, he begins with a most serious face to examine the patient, feeling his pulse and taking his temperature, and then begins the sounding and auscultation.

Ivan Ilych knows quite well and definitely that all this is nonsense and pure deception, but when the doctor, getting down on his knee, leans over him, putting his ear first higher then lower, and performs various gymnastic movements over him with a significant expression on his face, Ivan Ilych submits to it all as he used to submit to the speeches of the lawyers, though he knew very well that they were all lying and why they were lying.

The doctor, kneeling on the sofa, is still sounding him when Praskovya Fedorovna's silk dress rustles at the door and she is heard scolding Peter for not having let her know of the doctor's arrival.

She comes in, kisses her husband, and at once proceeds to prove that she has been up a long time already, and only owing to a misunderstanding failed to be there when the doctor arrived.

Ivan Ilych looks at her, scans her all over, sets against her the whiteness and plumpness and cleanness of her hands and neck, the gloss of her hair, and the sparkle of her vivacious eyes. He hates her with his whole soul. And the thrill of hatred he feels for her makes him suffer from her touch.

Her attitude towards him and his disease is still the same. Just as the doctor had adopted a certain relation to his patient which he could not abandon, so had she formed one towards him—that he was not doing something he ought to do and was himself to blame, and that she reproached him lovingly for this—and she could not now change that attitude.

"You see he doesn't listen to me and doesn't take his medicine at the proper time. And above all he lies in a position that is no doubt bad for him—with his legs up."

She described how he made Gerasim hold his legs up.

The doctor smiled with a contemptuous affability that said: "What's to be done? These sick people do have foolish fancies of that kind, but we must forgive them."

When the examination was over the doctor looked at his watch, and then Praskovya Fedorovna announced to Ivan Ilych that it was of course as he pleased, but she had sent today for a celebrated specialist who would examine him and have a consultation with Michael Danilovich (their regular doctor).

"Please don't raise any objections. I am doing this for my own sake," she said ironically, letting it be felt that she was doing it all for his sake and only said this to leave him no right to refuse. He remained silent, knitting his brows. He felt that he was surrounded and involved in a mesh of falsity that it was hard to unravel anything.

Everything she did for him was entirely for her own sake, and she told him she was doing for herself what she actually was doing for herself, as if that was so incredible that he must understand the opposite.

At half-past eleven the celebrated specialist arrived. Again the sounding began and the significant conversations in his presence and in another room, about the kidneys and the appendix, and the questions and answers, with such an air of importance that again, instead of the real question of life and death which now alone confronted him, the question arose of the kidney and appendix which were not behaving as they ought to and would now be attached by Michael Danilovich and the specialist and forced to amend their ways.

The celebrated specialist took leave of him with a serious though not hopeless look, and in reply to the timid question Ivan Ilych, with eyes glistening with fear and hope, put to him as to whether there was a chance of recovery, said that he could not vouch for it but there was a possibility. The look of hope with which Ivan Ilych watched the doctor out was so pathetic that Praskovya Fedorovna, seeing it, even wept as she left the room to hand the doctor his fee.

The gleam of hope kindled by the doctor's encouragement did not last long. The same room, the same pictures, curtains, wall-paper, medicine bottles, were all there, and the same aching suffering body, and Ivan Ilych began to moan. They gave him a subcutaneous injection and he sank into oblivion.

It was twilight when he came to. They brought him his dinner and he swallowed some beef tea with difficulty, and then everything was the same again and night was coming on.

After dinner, at seven o'clock, Praskovya Fedorovna came into the room in evening dress, her full bosom pushed up by her corset, and with traces of powder on her face. She had reminded him in the morning that they were going to the theatre. Sarah Bernhardt was visiting the town and they had a box, which he had insisted on their taking. Now he had forgotten about it and her toilet offended him, but he concealed his vexation when he remembered that he had himself insisted on their securing a box and going because it would be an instructive and aesthetic pleasure for the children.

Praskovya Fedorovna came in, self-satisfied but yet with a rather guilty air. She sat down and asked how he was, but, as he saw, only for the sake of asking and not in order to learn about it, knowing that there was nothing to learn—and then went on to what she really wanted to say: that she would not on any account have gone but that the box had been taken and Helen and their daughter were going, as well as Petrishchev (the examining magistrate, their daughter's fiance) and that it was out of the question to let them go alone; but that she would have much preferred to sit with him for a while; and he must be sure to follow the doctor's orders while she was away.

"Oh, and Fedor Petrovich" (the fiance) "would like to come in. May he? And Lisa?"

"All right."

Their daughter came in in full evening dress, her fresh young flesh exposed (making a show of that very flesh which in his own case caused so much suffering), strong, healthy, evidently in love, and impatient with illness, suffering, and death, because they interfered with her happiness.

Fedor Petrovich came in too, in evening dress, his hair curled *a la Capoul,* a tight stiff collar round his long sinewy neck, an enormous white shirt-front and narrow black trousers tightly stretched over his strong thighs. He had one white glove tightly drawn on, and was holding his opera hat in his hand.

Following him the schoolboy crept in unnoticed, in a new uniform, poor little fellow, and wearing gloves. Terribly dark shadows showed under his eyes, the meaning of which Ivan Ilych knew well.

His son had always seemed pathetic to him, and now it was dreadful to see the boy's frightened look of pity. It seemed to Ivan Ilych that Vasya was the only one besides Gerasim who understood and pitied him.

They all sat down and again asked how he was. A silence followed. Lisa asked her mother about the opera glasses, and there was an altercation between mother and daughter as to who had taken them and where they had been put. This occasioned some unpleasantness.

Fedor Petrovich inquired of Ivan Ilych whether he had ever seen Sarah Bernhardt. Ivan Ilych did not at first catch the question, but then replied: "No, have you seen her before?"

"Yes, in *Adrienne Lecouvreur.*"

Praskovya Fedorovna mentioned some roles in which Sarah Bernhardt was particularly good. Her daughter disagreed. Conversation sprang up as to the elegance and realism of her acting—the sort of conversation that is always repeated and is always the same.

In the midst of the conversation Fedor Petrovich glanced at Ivan Ilych and became silent. The others also looked at him and grew silent. Ivan Ilych was staring with glittering eyes straight before him, evidently indignant with them. This had to be rectified, but it was impossible to do so. The silence had to be broken, but for a time no one dared to break it and they all became afraid that the conventional deception would suddenly become obvious and the truth become plain to all. Lisa was the first to pluck up courage and break that silence, but by trying to hide what everybody was feeling, she betrayed it.

"Well, if we are going it's time to start," she said, looking at her watch, a present from her father, and with a faint and significant smile at Fedor Petrovich relating to something known only to them. She got up with a rustle of her dress.

They all rose, said good-night, and went away.

When they had gone it seemed to Ivan Ilych that he felt better; the falsity had gone with them. But the pain remained—that same pain and that same fear that made everything monotonously alike, nothing harder and nothing easier. Everything was worse.

Again minute followed minute and hour followed hour. Everything remained the same and there was no cessation. And the inevitable end of it all became more and more terrible.

"Yes, send Gerasim here," he replied to a question Peter asked.

IX

His wife returned late at night. She came in on tiptoe, but he heard her, opened his eyes, and made haste to close them again. She wished to send Gerasim away and to sit with him herself, but he opened his eyes and said: "No, go away."

"Are you in great pain?"

"Always the same."

"Take some opium."

He agreed and took some. She went away.

Till about three in the morning he was in a state of stupefied misery. It seemed to him that he and his pain were being thrust into a narrow, deep black sack, but though they were pushed further and further in they could not be pushed to the bottom. And this, terrible enough in itself, was accompanied by suffering. He was frightened yet wanted to fall through the sack, he struggled but yet co-operated. And suddenly he broke through, fell, and regained consciousness. Gerasim was sitting at the foot of the bed dozing quietly and patiently, while he himself lay with his emaciated stockinged legs resting on Gerasim's shoulders; the same shaded candle was there and the same unceasing pain.

"Go away, Gerasim," he whispered.

"It's all right, sir. I'll stay a while."

"No. Go away."

He removed his legs from Gerasim's shoulders, turned sideways onto his arm, and felt sorry for himself. He only waited till Gerasim had gone into the next room and then restrained himself no longer but wept like a child. He wept on account of his helplessness, his terrible loneliness, the cruelty of man, the cruelty of God, and the absence of God.

"Why hast Thou done all this? Why hast Thou brought me here? Why, why dost Thou torment me so terribly?"

He did not expect an answer and yet wept because there was no answer and could be none. The pain again grew more acute, but he did not stir and did not call. He said to himself: "Go on! Strike me! But what is it for? What have I done to Thee? What is it for?"

Then he grew quiet and not only ceased weeping but even held his breath and became all attention. It was as though he were listening not to an audible voice but to the voice of his soul, to the current of thoughts arising within him.

"What is it you want?" was the first clear conception capable of expression in words, that he heard.

"What do you want? What do you want?" he repeated to himself.

"What do I want? To live and not to suffer," he answered.

And again he listened with such concentrated attention that even his pain did not distract him.

"To live? How?" asked his inner voice.

"Why, to live as I used to—well and pleasantly."

"As you lived before, well and pleasantly?" the voice repeated.

And in imagination he began to recall the best moments of his pleasant life. But strange to say none of those best moments of his pleasant life now seemed at all what they had then seemed—none of them except the first recollections of childhood. There, in childhood, there had been something really pleasant with which it would be possible to live if it could return. But the child who had experienced that happiness existed no longer, it was like a reminiscence of somebody else.

As soon as the period began which had produced the present Ivan Ilych, all that had then seemed joys now melted before his sight and turned into something trivial and often nasty.

And the further he departed from childhood and the nearer he came to the present the more worthless and doubtful were the joys. This began with the School of Law. A little that was really good was still found there—there was light-heartedness, friendship, and hope. But in the upper classes there had already been fewer of such good moments. Then during the first years of his official career, when he was in the service of the governor, some pleasant moments again occurred: they were the memories of love for a woman. Then all became confused and there was still less of what was good; later on again there was still less that was good, and the further he went the less there was. His marriage, a mere accident, then the disenchantment that followed it, his wife's bad breath and the sensuality and hypocrisy: then that deadly official life and those preoccupations about money, a year of it, and two, and ten, and twenty, and always the same thing. And the longer it lasted the more deadly it became. "It is as if I had been going downhill while I imagined I was going up. And that is really what it was. I was going up in public opinion, but to the same extent life was ebbing away from me. And now it is all done and there is only death.

"Then what does it mean? Why? It can't be that life is so senseless and horrible. But if it really has been so horrible and senseless, why must I die and die in agony? There is something wrong!

"Maybe I did not live as I ought to have done," it suddenly occurred to him. "But how could that be, when I did everything properly?" he replied, and immediately dismissed from his mind this, the sole solution of all the riddles of life and death, as something quite impossible.

"Then what do you want now? To live? Live how? Live as you lived in the law courts when the usher proclaimed 'The judge is coming!' The judge is coming, the judge!" he repeated to himself. "Here he is, the judge. But I am not guilty!" he exclaimed angrily. "What is it for?" And he ceased crying, but turning his face to the wall continued to ponder on the same question: Why, and for what purpose, is there all this horror? But however much he pondered he found no answer. And whenever the thought occurred to him, as it often did, that it all resulted from his not having lived as he ought to have done, he at once recalled the correctness of his whole life and dismissed so strange an idea.

$\overline{\text{X}}$

Another fortnight passed. Ivan Ilych now no longer left his sofa. He would not lie in bed but lay on the sofa, facing the wall nearly all the time. He suffered ever the same unceasing agonies and in his loneliness pondered always on the same insoluble question: "What is this? Can it be that it is Death?" And the inner voice answered: "Yes, it is Death."

"Why these sufferings?" And the voice answered, "For no reason—they just are so." Beyond and besides this there was nothing.

From the very beginning of his illness, ever since he had first been to see the doctor, Ivan Ilych's life had been divided between two contrary and alternating moods: now it was despair and the expectation of this uncomprehended and terrible death, and now hope and an intently interested observation of the functioning of his organs. Now before his eyes there was only a kidney or an intestine that temporarily evaded its duty, and now only that incomprehensible and dreadful death from which it was impossible to escape.

These two states of mind had alternated from the very beginning of his illness, but the further it progressed the more doubtful and fantastic became the conception of the kidney, and the more real the sense of impending death.

He had but to call to mind what he had been three months before and what he was now, to call to mind with what regularity he had been going downhill, for every possibility of hope to be shattered.

Latterly during the loneliness in which he found himself as he lay facing the back of the sofa, a loneliness in the midst of a populous town and surrounded by numerous acquaintances and relations but that yet could not have been more complete anywhere—either at the bottom of the sea or under the earth—during that terrible loneliness Ivan Ilych had lived only in memories of the past. Pictures of his past rose before him one after another. They always began with what was nearest in time and then went back to what was most remote—to his childhood—and rested there. If he thought of the stewed prunes that had been offered him that day, his mind went back to the raw shrivelled French plums of his childhood, their peculiar flavour and the flow of saliva when he sucked their stones, and along with the memory of that taste came a whole series of memories of those days: his nurse, his brother, and their toys. "No, I mustn't think of that. . . . It is too painful," Ivan Ilych said to himself, and brought himself back to the present—to the button on the back of the sofa and the creases in its morocco. "Morocco is expensive, but it does not wear well: there had been a quarrel about it. It was a different kind of quarrel and a different kind of morocco that time when we tore father's portfolio and were punished, and mamma brought us some tarts. . . ." And again his thoughts dwelt on his childhood, and again it was painful and he tried to banish them and fix his mind on something else.

Then again together with that chain of memories another series passed through his mind—of how his illness had progressed and grown worse. There also the further back he looked the more life there had been. There had been more of what was good in life and more of life itself. The two merged together. "Just as the pain went on getting worse and worse, so my life grew worse and worse," he thought. "There is one bright spot there at the back, at the beginning of life, and afterwards all becomes blacker and blacker and proceeds more and more rapidly—in inverse ratio to the square of the distance from death," thought Ivan Ilych. And the example of a stone falling downwards with increasing velocity entered his mind. Life, a series of increasing sufferings, flies further and further towards its end—the most terrible suffering. "I am flying. . . ." He shuddered, shifted himself, and tried to resist, but was already aware that resistance was impossible, and again with eyes weary of gazing but unable to cease seeing what was before them, he stared at the back of the sofa and waited—awaiting that dreadful fall and shock and destruction.

"Resistance is impossible!" he said to himself. "If I could only understand what it is all for! But that too is impossible. An explanation would be possible if it could be said that I have not lived as I ought to. But it is impossible to say that," and he remembered all the legality, correctitude, and propriety of his life. "That at any rate can certainly not be admitted," he thought, and his lips smiled ironically as if someone could see that smile and be taken in by it. "There is no explanation! Agony, death. . . . What for?"

XI

Another two weeks went by in this way and during that fortnight an even occurred that Ivan Ilych and his wife had desired. Petrishchev formally proposed. It happened in the evening. The next day Praskovya Fedorovna came into her husband's room considering how best to inform him of it, but that very night there had been a fresh change for the worse in his condition. She found him still lying on the sofa but in a different position. He lay on his back, groaning and staring fixedly straight in front of him.

She began to remind him of his medicines, but he turned his eyes towards her with such a look that she did not finish what she was saying; so great an animosity, to her in particular, did that look express.

"For Christ's sake let me die in peace!" he said.

She would have gone away, but just then their daughter came in and went up to say good morning. He looked at her as he had done at his wife, and in reply to her inquiry about his health said dryly that he would soon free them all of himself. They were both silent and after sitting with him for a while went away.

"Is it our fault?" Lisa said to her mother. "It's as if we were to blame! I am sorry for papa, but why should we be tortured?"

The doctor came at his usual time. Ivan Ilych answered "Yes" and "No," never taking his angry eyes from him, and at last said: "You know you can do nothing for me, so leave me alone."

"We can ease your sufferings."

"You can't even do that. Let me be."

The doctor went into the drawing room and told Praskovya Fedorovna that the case was very serious and that the only resource left was opium to allay her husband's sufferings, which must be terrible.

It was true, as the doctor said, that Ivan Ilych's physical sufferings were terrible, but worse than the physical sufferings were his mental sufferings which were his chief torture.

His mental sufferings were due to the fact that that night, as he looked at Gerasim's sleepy, good-natured face with it prominent cheek-bones, the question suddenly occurred to him: "What if my whole life has been wrong?"

It occurred to him that what had appeared perfectly impossible before, namely that he had not spent his life as he should have done, might after all be true. It occurred to him that his scarcely perceptible attempts to struggle against what was considered good by the most highly placed people, those scarcely noticeable impulses which he had immediately suppressed, might have been the real thing, and all the rest false. And his professional duties and the whole arrangement of his life and of his family, and all his social and official interests, might all have been false. He tried to defend all those things to himself and suddenly felt the weakness of what he was defending. There was nothing to defend.

"But if that is so," he said to himself, "and I am leaving this life with the consciousness that I have lost all that was given me and it is impossible to rectify it—what then?"

He lay on his back and began to pass his life in review in quite a new way. In the morning when he saw first his footman, then his wife, then his daughter, and then the doctor, their every word and movement confirmed to him the awful truth that had been revealed to him during the night. In them he saw himself—all that for which he had lived—and saw clearly that it was not real at all, but a terrible and huge deception which had hidden both life and death. This consciousness intensified his physical suffering tenfold. He groaned and tossed about, and pulled at his clothing which choked and stifled him. And he hated them on that account.

He was given a large dose of opium and became unconscious, but at noon his sufferings began again. He drove everybody away and tossed from side to side.

His wife came to him and said:

"Jean, my dear, do this for me. It can't do any harm and often helps. Healthy people often do it."

He opened his eyes wide.

"What? Take communion? Why? It's unnecessary! However . . ."

She began to cry.

"Yes, do, my dear. I'll send for our priest. He is such a nice man."

"All right. Very well," he muttered.

When the priest came and heard his confession, Ivan Ilych was softened and seemed to feel a relief from his doubts and consequently from his sufferings, and for a moment there came a ray of hope. He again began to think of the vermiform appendix and the possibility of correcting it. He received the sacrament with tears in his eyes.

When they laid him down again afterwards he felt a moment's ease, and the hope that he might live awoke in him again. He began to think of the operation that had been suggested to him. "To live! I want to live!" he said to himself.

His wife came in to congratulate him after his communion, and when uttering the usual conventional words she added:

"You feel better, don't you?"

Without looking at her he said "Yes."

Her dress, her figure, the expression of her face, the tone of her voice, all revealed the same thing. "This is wrong, it is not as it should be. All you have lived for and still live for is falsehood and deception, hiding life and death from you." And as soon as he admitted that thought, his hatred and his agonizing physical suffering again sprang up, and with that suffering a consciousness of the unavoidable, approaching end. And to this was added a new sensation of grinding shooting pain and a feeling of suffocation.

The expression of his face when he uttered that "Yes" was dreadful. Having uttered it, he looked her straight in the eyes, turned on his face with a rapidity extraordinary in his weak state and shouted:

"Go away! Go away and leave me alone!"

XII

From that moment the screaming began that continued for three days, and was so terrible that one could not hear it through two closed doors without horror. At the moment he answered his wife realized that he was lost, that there was no return, that the end had come, the very end, and his doubts were still unsolved and remained doubts.

"Oh! Oh! Oh!" he cried in various intonations. He had begun by screaming "I won't!" and continued screaming on the letter "O".

For three whole days, during which time did not exist for him, he struggled in that black sack into which he was being thrust by an invisible, resistless force. He struggled as a man condemned to death struggles in the hands of the executioner, knowing that he cannot save himself. And every moment he felt that despite all his efforts he was drawing nearer and nearer to what terrified him. He felt that his agony was due to his being thrust into that black hole and still more to his not being able to get right into it. He was hindered from getting into it by his conviction that his life had been a good one. That very justification of his life held him fast and prevented his moving forward, and it caused him most torment of all.

Suddenly some force struck him in the chest and side, making it still harder to breathe, and he fell through the hole and there at the bottom was a light. What had happened to him was like the sensation one sometimes experiences in a railway carriage when one thinks one is going backwards while one is really going forwards and suddenly becomes aware of the real direction.

"Yes, it was not the right thing," he said to himself, "but that's no matter. It can be done. But what *is* the right thing? he asked himself, and suddenly grew quiet.

This occurred at the end of the third day, two hours before his death. Just then his schoolboy son had crept softly in and gone up to the bedside. The dying man was still screaming desperately and waving his arms. His hand fell on the boy's head, and the boy caught it, pressed it to his lips, and began to cry.

At that very moment Ivan Ilych fell through and caught sight of the light, and it was revealed to him that though his life had not been what it should have been, this could still be rectified. He asked himself, "What *is* the right thing?" and grew still, listening. Then he felt that someone was kissing his hand. He opened his eyes, looked at his son, and felt sorry for him. His wife came up to him and he glanced at her. She was gazing at him open-mouthed, with undried tears on her nose and cheek and a despairing look on her face. He felt sorry for her too.

"Yes, I am making them wretched," he thought. "They are sorry, but it will be better for them when I die." He wished to say this but had not the strength to utter it. "Besides, why speak? I must act," he thought. With a look at his wife he indicated his son and said: "Take him away . . . sorry for him . . . sorry for you too. . . ." He tried to add, "Forgive me," but said "Forego" and waved his hand, knowing that He whose understanding mattered would understand.

And suddenly it grew clear to him that what had been oppressing him and would not leave him was all dropping away at once from two sides, from ten sides, and from all sides. He was sorry for them, he must act so as not to hurt them: release them and free himself from these sufferings. "How good and how simple!" he thought. "And the pain?" he asked himself. "What has become of it? Where are you, pain?"

He turned his attention to it.

"Yes, here it is. Well, what of it? Let the pain be."

"And death . . . where is it?"

He sought his former accustomed fear of death and did not find it. "Where is it? What death?" There was no fear because there was no death.

In place of death there was light.

"So that's what it is!" he suddenly exclaimed aloud. "What joy!"

To him all this happened in a single instant, and the meaning of that instant did not change.

For those present his agony continued for another two hours. Something rattled in his throat, his emaciated body twitched, then the gasping and rattle became less and less frequent.

"It is finished!" said someone near him.

He heard these words and repeated them in his soul.

"Death is finished," he said to himself. "It is no more!"

He drew in a breath, stopped in the midst of a sigh, stretched out, and died.

Pope Benedict XVI:
God Is Love
(Deus Caritas Est)

Editors' Introduction

Cardinal Joseph Ratzinger was elected pope on April 19, 2005, taking the name Benedict. Born in the southern German state of Bavaria in 1927, Ratzinger came to the papacy having served in the Vatican since 1981 as prefect (director) of the Vatican Congregation for the Doctrine of the Faith. As is evident from the title of the Congregation, this is the body within the Vatican that oversees Catholic doctrine. Cardinal Ratzinger came to this position as a well-known and respected theologian. During the Second Vatican Council (see the introduction to *Nostra Aetate*), Ratzinger had a reputation as one of the leading reformers among the theologians involved in the Council's deliberations. Some commentators have come to the conclusion that over the years Ratzinger's thought has taken a more conservative turn. He, however, has always maintained that his theological views, while they developed over time, have remained consistent, and that there has been no break with his earlier writings. The question as to just what constitutes "liberal/reformer" and "conservative/traditional," and whether these terms are at all useful in describing the work of a nuanced thinker like Joseph Ratzinger, needs to be understood within the wider context of the ongoing debate concerning the meaning and proper interpretation of the Second Vatican Council.

"God Is Love" is the first encyclical of Benedict XVI. An encyclical was originally understood as a letter from a bishop that was circulated within a particular territory. In Roman Catholicism the term has come to mean a letter from the pope (who is the bishop of Rome). Usually, the title of the encyclical is taken from its first few words. Sometimes an encyclical is addressed to the pope's fellow bishops, but it can also be directed to the entire church (as is the case with "God Is Love"). Encyclicals vary in terms of content; some might deal with particular issues involving social justice, sexual morality, liturgical matters, etc., while others take up and explore theological themes. In some cases (such as "God Is Love"), an encyclical will combine both themes. In the Roman Catholic tradition, a papal encyclical is taken very seriously, since it is an expression of the pope's thinking on a particular theme or issue.

If, as some believe, the first encyclical of a pope gives some indication of the themes or concerns that will animate his papacy, then it is noteworthy that Benedict's first offering in this genre focuses on love. The title of the encyclical is inspired by the affirmation that God is love found in the New Testament in the First Letter of John (1 John 4:16). Beginning with this text, Benedict offers an extended reflection on the nature of love as understood within the Christian tradition. True to his philosophical and theological background, he interweaves these reflections with other views of love taken largely from the traditions of classical Greek culture. In particular, Benedict explores the relationship between the notion of love (*agape* in Greek) emphasized in the New Testament and the Greek idea of love as *eros*. This theological exploration of the nature of love constitutes the first part of the encyclical. In the second part, Benedict moves from a primarily theoretical perspective to an application of the Christian understanding of love to the life of the Church and society.

God Is Love (Deus Caritas Est)

INTRODUCTION

1. "God is love, and he who abides in love abides in God, and God abides in him" (*1 Jn* 4:16). These words from the *First Letter of John* express with remarkable clarity the heart of the Christian faith: the Christian image of God and the resulting image of mankind and its destiny. In the same verse, Saint John also offers a kind of summary of the Christian life: "We have come to know and to believe in the love God has for us".

We have come to believe in God's love: in these words the Christian can express the fundamental decision of his life. Being Christian is not the result of an ethical choice or a lofty idea, but the encounter with an event, a person, which gives life a new horizon and a decisive direction. Saint John's Gospel describes that event in these words: "God so loved the world that he gave his only Son, that whoever believes in him should . . . have eternal life" (3:16). In acknowledging the centrality of love, Christian faith has retained the core of Israel's faith, while at the same time giving it new depth and breadth. The pious Jew prayed daily the words of the *Book of Deuteronomy* which expressed the heart of his existence: "Hear, O Israel: the Lord our God is one Lord, and you shall love the Lord your God with all your heart, and with all your soul and with all your might" (6:4-5). Jesus united into a single precept this commandment of love for God and the commandment of love for neighbour found in the *Book of Leviticus:* "You shall love your neighbour as yourself" (19:18; cf. *Mk* 12:29-31). Since God has first loved us (cf. *1 Jn* 4:10), love is now no longer a mere "command"; it is the response to the gift of love with which God draws near to us.

In a world where the name of God is sometimes associated with vengeance or even a duty of hatred and violence, this message is both timely and significant. For this reason, I wish in my first Encyclical to speak of the love which God lavishes upon us and which we in turn must share with others. That, in essence, is what the two main parts of this Letter are about, and they are profoundly interconnected. The first part is more speculative, since I wanted here—at the beginning of my Pontificate—to clarify some essential facts concerning the love which God mysteriously and gratuitously offers to man, together with the intrinsic link between that Love and the reality of human love. The second part is more concrete, since it treats the ecclesial exercise of the commandment of love of neighbour. The argument has vast implications, but a lengthy treatment would go beyond the scope of the present Encyclical. I wish to emphasize some basic elements, so as to call forth in the world renewed energy and commitment in the human response to God's love.

PART I

THE UNITY OF LOVE IN CREATION AND IN SALVATION HISTORY

A Problem of Language

2. God's love for us is fundamental for our lives, and it raises important questions about who God is and who we are. In considering this, we immediately find ourselves hampered by a problem of language. Today, the term "love" has become one of the most frequently used and misused of words, a word to which we attach quite different meanings. Even though this Encyclical will deal primarily with the understanding and practice of love in sacred Scripture and in the Church's Tradition, we cannot simply prescind from the meaning of the word in the different cultures and in present-day usage.

Let us first of all bring to mind the vast semantic range of the word "love": we speak of love of country, love of one's profession, love between friends, love of work, love between parents and children, love between family members, love of neighbour and love of God. Amid this multiplicity of meanings, however, one in particular stands out: love between man and woman, where body and soul are inseparably joined and human beings glimpse an apparently irresistible promise of happiness. This would seem to be the very epitome of love; all other kinds of love immediately seem to fade in comparison. So we need to ask: are all these forms of love basically one, so that love, in its many and varied manifestations, is ultimately a single reality, or are we merely using the same word to designate totally different realities?

"Eros" and "Agape"— ## Difference and Unity

3. That love between man and woman which is neither planned nor willed, but somehow imposes itself upon human beings, was called eros by the ancient Greeks. Let us note straight away that the Greek Old Testament uses the word eros only twice, while the New Testament does not use it at all: of the three Greek words for love, *eros, philia* (the love of friendship) and *agape,* New Testament writers prefer the last, which occurs rather infrequently in Greek usage. As for the term *philia,* the love of friendship, it is used with added depth of meaning in Saint John's Gospel in order to express the relationship between Jesus and his disciples. The tendency to avoid the word *eros,* together with the new vision of love expressed through the word *agape,* clearly point to something new and distinct about the Christian understanding of love. In the critique of Christianity which began with the Enlightenment and grew progressively more radical, this new element was seen as something thoroughly negative. According to Friedrich Nietzsche, Christianity had poisoned eros, which for its part, while not completely succumbing, gradually degenerated into vice. Here the German philosopher was expressing a widely-held perception: doesn't the Church, with all her commandments and prohibitions, turn to bitterness the most precious thing in life? Doesn't she

blow the whistle just when the joy which is the Creator's gift offers us a happiness which is itself a certain foretaste of the Divine?

4. But is this the case? Did Christianity really destroy *eros?* Let us take a look at the pre- Christian world. The Greeks—not unlike other cultures—considered *eros* principally as a kind of intoxication, the overpowering of reason by a "divine madness" which tears man away from his finite existence and enables him, in the very process of being overwhelmed by divine power, to experience supreme happiness. All other powers in heaven and on earth thus appear secondary: *"Omnia vincit amor"* says Virgil in the *Bucolics*— love conquers all—and he adds: *"et nos cedamus amori"*—let us, too, yield to love. In the religions, this attitude found expression in fertility cults, part of which was the "sacred" prostitution which flourished in many temples. *Eros* was thus celebrated as divine power, as fellowship with the Divine.

The Old Testament firmly opposed this form of religion, which represents a powerful temptation against monotheistic faith, combating it as a perversion of religiosity. But it in no way rejected *eros* as such; rather, it declared war on a warped and destructive form of it, because this counterfeit divinization of eros actually strips it of its dignity and dehumanizes it. Indeed, the prostitutes in the temple, who had to bestow this divine intoxication, were not treated as human beings and persons, but simply used as a means of arousing "divine madness": far from being goddesses, they were human persons being exploited. An intoxicated and undisciplined *eros,* then, is not an ascent in "ecstasy" towards the Divine, but a fall, a degradation of man. Evidently, *eros* needs to be disciplined and purified if it is to provide not just fleeting pleasure, but a certain foretaste of the pinnacle of our existence, of that beatitude for which our whole being yearns.

5. Two things emerge clearly from this rapid overview of the concept of eros past and present. First, there is a certain relationship between love and the Divine: love promises infinity, eternity— a reality far greater and totally other than our everyday existence. Yet we have also seen that the

way to attain this goal is not simply by submitting to instinct. Purification and growth in maturity are called for; and these also pass through the path of renunciation. Far from rejecting or "poisoning" *eros,* they heal it and restore its true grandeur.

This is due first and foremost to the fact that man is a being made up of body and soul. Man is truly himself when his body and soul are intimately united; the challenge of *eros* can be said to be truly overcome when this unification is achieved. Should he aspire to be pure spirit and to reject the flesh as pertaining to his animal nature alone, then spirit and body would both lose their dignity. On the other hand, should he deny the spirit and consider matter, the body, as the only reality, he would likewise lose his greatness. The epicure Gassendi used to offer Descartes the humorous greeting: "O Soul!" And Descartes would reply: "O Flesh!". Yet it is neither the spirit alone nor the body alone that loves: it is man, the person, a unified creature composed of body and soul, who loves. Only when both dimensions are truly united, does man attain his full stature. Only thus is love —*eros*—able to mature and attain its authentic grandeur.

Nowadays Christianity of the past is often criticized as having been opposed to the body; and it is quite true that tendencies of this sort have always existed. Yet the contemporary way of exalting the body is deceptive. *Eros,* reduced to pure "sex", has become a commodity, a mere "thing" to be bought and sold, or rather, man himself becomes a commodity. This is hardly man's great "yes" to the body. On the contrary, he now considers his body and his sexuality as the purely material part of himself, to be used and exploited at will. Nor does he see it as an arena for the exercise of his freedom, but as a mere object that he attempts, as he pleases, to make both enjoyable and harmless. Here we are actually dealing with a debasement of the human body: no longer is it integrated into our overall existential freedom; no longer is it a vital expression of our whole being, but it is more or less relegated to the purely biological sphere. The apparent exaltation of the body can quickly turn into a hatred of bodiliness.

Christian faith, on the other hand, has always considered man a unity in duality, a reality in which spirit and matter compenetrate, and in which each is brought to a new nobility. True, *eros* tends to rise "in ecstasy" towards the Divine, to lead us beyond ourselves; yet for this very reason it calls for a path of ascent, renunciation, purification and healing.

6. Concretely, what does this path of ascent and purification entail? How might love be experienced so that it can fully realize its human and divine promise? Here we can find a first, important indication in the *Song of Songs,* an Old Testament book well known to the mystics. According to the interpretation generally held today, the poems contained in this book were originally love-songs, perhaps intended for a Jewish wedding feast and meant to exalt conjugal love. In this context it is highly instructive to note that in the course of the book two different Hebrew words are used to indicate "love". First there is the word *dodim,* a plural form suggesting a love that is still insecure, indeterminate and searching. This comes to be replaced by the word *ahabà,* which the Greek version of the Old Testament translates with the similar-sounding *agape,* which, as we have seen, becomes the typical expression for the biblical notion of love. By contrast with an indeterminate, "searching" love, this word expresses the experience of a love which involves a real discovery of the other, moving beyond the selfish character that prevailed earlier. Love now becomes concern and care for the other. No longer is it self-seeking, a sinking in the intoxication of happiness; instead it seeks the good of the beloved: it becomes renunciation and it is ready, and even willing, for sacrifice.

It is part of love's growth towards higher levels and inward purification that it now seeks to become definitive, and it does so in a twofold sense: both in the sense of exclusivity (this particular person alone) and in the sense of being "for ever". Love embraces the whole of existence in each of its dimensions, including the dimension of time. It could hardly be otherwise, since its promise looks towards its definitive goal: love looks to the eternal. Love is indeed "ecstasy", not in the sense of a moment of intoxication, but rather as a journey, an ongoing exodus out of the closed inward-looking self towards its liberation through self-giving, and thus towards authentic self-discovery and indeed the discovery of God: "Whoever seeks to gain his life will lose it, but whoever loses his life will preserve it" (*Lk* 17:33), as Jesus says throughout the Gospels (cf. *Mt* 10:39; 16:25; *Mk* 8:35; *Lk* 9:24; *Jn* 12:25). In these words, Jesus portrays his own path, which leads through the Cross to the Resurrection: the path of the grain of wheat that falls to the ground and dies, and in this way bears much fruit. Starting from the depths of his own sacrifice and of the love that reaches fulfilment therein, he also portrays in these words the essence of love and indeed of human life itself.

7. By their own inner logic, these initial, somewhat philosophical reflections on the essence of love have now brought us to the threshold of biblical faith. We began by asking whether the different, or even opposed, meanings of the word "love" point to some profound underlying unity, or whether on the contrary they must remain unconnected, one alongside the other. More significantly, though, we questioned whether the message of love proclaimed to us by the Bible and the Church's Tradition has some points of contact with the common human experience of love, or whether it is opposed to that experience. This in turn led us to consider two fundamental words: *eros,* as a term to indicate "worldly" love and *agape,* referring to love grounded in and shaped by faith. The two notions are often contrasted as "ascending" love and "descending" love. There are other, similar classifications, such as the distinction between possessive love and oblative love (*amor concupiscentiae—amor benevolentiae*), to which is sometimes also added love that seeks its own advantage.

In philosophical and theological debate, these distinctions have often been radicalized to the point of establishing a clear antithesis between them: descending, oblative love—*agape*—would be typically Christian, while on the other hand ascending, possessive or covetous love—*eros*—would be typical of non-Christian, and particularly

Greek culture. Were this antithesis to be taken to extremes, the essence of Christianity would be detached from the vital relations fundamental to human existence, and would become a world apart, admirable perhaps, but decisively cut off from the complex fabric of human life. Yet *eros* and *agape*—ascending love and descending love—can never be completely separated. The more the two, in their different aspects, find a proper unity in the one reality of love, the more the true nature of love in general is realized. Even if *eros* is at first mainly covetous and ascending, a fascination for the great promise of happiness, in drawing near to the other, it is less and less concerned with itself, increasingly seeks the happiness of the other, is concerned more and more with the beloved, bestows itself and wants to "be there for" the other. The element of *agape* thus enters into this love, for otherwise *eros* is impoverished and even loses its own nature. On the other hand, man cannot live by oblative, descending love alone. He cannot always give, he must also receive. Anyone who wishes to give love must also receive love as a gift. Certainly, as the Lord tells us, one can become a source from which rivers of living water flow (cf. *Jn* 7:37-38). Yet to become such a source, one must constantly drink anew from the original source, which is Jesus Christ, from whose pierced heart flows the love of God (cf. *Jn* 19:34).

In the account of Jacob's ladder, the Fathers of the Church saw this inseparable connection between ascending and descending love, between *eros* which seeks God and *agape* which passes on the gift received, symbolized in various ways. In that biblical passage we read how the Patriarch Jacob saw in a dream, above the stone which was his pillow, a ladder reaching up to heaven, on which the angels of God were ascending and descending (cf. *Gen* 28:12; *Jn* 1:51). A particularly striking interpretation of this vision is presented by Pope Gregory the Great in his *Pastoral Rule.* He tells us that the good pastor must be rooted in contemplation. Only in this way will he be able to take upon himself the needs of others and make them his own: "*per pietatis viscera in se infirmitatem caeterorum transferat*". Saint Gregory speaks in this context of Saint Paul, who was borne aloft to the most exalted mysteries of God, and hence, having descended once more, he was able to become all things to all men (cf. *2 Cor* 12:2-4; *1 Cor* 9:22). He also points to the example of Moses, who entered the tabernacle time and again, remaining in dialogue with God, so that when he emerged he could be at the service of his people. "Within [the tent] he is borne aloft through contemplation, while without he is completely engaged in helping those who suffer: *intus in contemplationem rapitur, foris infirmantium negotiis urgetur.*"

8. We have thus come to an initial, albeit still somewhat generic response to the two questions raised earlier. Fundamentally, "love" is a single reality, but with different dimensions; at different times, one or other dimension may emerge more clearly. Yet when the two dimensions are totally cut off from one another, the result is a caricature or at least an impoverished form of love. And we have also seen, synthetically, that biblical faith does not set up a parallel universe, or one opposed to that primordial human phenomenon which is love, but rather accepts the whole man; it intervenes in his search for love in order to purify it and to reveal new dimensions of it. This newness of biblical faith is shown chiefly in two elements which deserve to be highlighted: the image of God and the image of man.

The Newness of Biblical Faith

9. First, the world of the Bible presents us with a new image of God. In surrounding cultures, the image of God and of the gods ultimately remained unclear and contradictory. In the development of biblical faith, however, the content of the prayer fundamental to Israel, the *Shema,* became increasingly clear and unequivocal: "Hear, O Israel, the Lord our God is one Lord" (*Dt* 6:4). There is only one God, the Creator of heaven and earth, who is thus the God of all. Two facts are significant about this statement: all other gods are not God, and the universe in which we live has its source in God and was created by him. Certainly, the notion of creation is found elsewhere, yet only here does it become absolutely clear that it is not one god among many, but the one true God himself who is the source of all that exists; the whole world comes into existence by the power of his creative Word. Consequently, his creation is dear to him, for it was willed by him and "made" by him. The second important element now emerges: this God loves man. The divine power that Aristotle at the height of Greek philosophy sought to grasp through reflection, is indeed for every being an object of desire and of love—and as the object of love this divinity moves the world—but in itself it lacks nothing and does not love: it is solely the object of love. The one God in whom Israel believes, on the other hand, loves with a personal love. His love, moreover, is an elective love: among all the nations he chooses Israel and loves her—but he does so precisely with a view to healing the whole human race. God loves, and his love may certainly be called *eros,* yet it is also totally *agape.*

The Prophets, particularly Hosea and Ezekiel, described God's passion for his people using boldly erotic images. God's relationship with Israel is described using the metaphors of betrothal and marriage; idolatry is thus adultery and prostitution. Here we find a specific reference—as we have seen—to the fertility cults and their abuse of *eros,* but also a description of the relationship of fidelity between Israel and her God. The history of the love-relationship between God and Israel consists, at the deepest level, in the fact that he gives her the *Torah,* thereby opening Israel's eyes to man's true nature and showing her the path leading to true humanism. It consists in the fact that man, through a life of fidelity to the one God, comes to experience himself as loved by God, and discovers joy in truth and in righteousness—a joy in God which becomes his essential happiness: "Whom do I have in heaven but you? And there is nothing upon earth that I desire besides you . . . for me it is good to be near God" (*Ps* 73 [72]:25, 28).

10. We have seen that God's *eros* for man is also totally *agape.* This is not only because it is bestowed in a completely gratuitous manner, without any previous merit, but also because it is love which forgives. Hosea above all shows us that

this *agape* dimension of God's love for man goes far beyond the aspect of gratuity. Israel has committed "adultery" and has broken the covenant; God should judge and repudiate her. It is precisely at this point that God is revealed to be God and not man: "How can I give you up, O Ephraim! How can I hand you over, O Israel! . . . My heart recoils within me, my compassion grows warm and tender. I will not execute my fierce anger, I will not again destroy Ephraim; for I am God and not man, the Holy One in your midst" (*Hos* 11:8-9). God's passionate love for his people—for humanity—is at the same time a forgiving love. It is so great that it turns God against himself, his love against his justice. Here Christians can see a dim prefiguration of the mystery of the Cross: so great is God's love for man that by becoming man he follows him even into death, and so reconciles justice and love.

The philosophical dimension to be noted in this biblical vision, and its importance from the standpoint of the history of religions, lies in the fact that on the one hand we find ourselves before a strictly metaphysical image of God: God is the absolute and ultimate source of all being; but this universal principle of creation—the *Logos,* primordial reason—is at the same time a lover with all the passion of a true love. *Eros* is thus supremely ennobled, yet at the same time it is so purified as to become one with *agape.* We can thus see how the reception of the *Song of Songs* in the canon of sacred Scripture was soon explained by the idea that these love songs ultimately describe God's relation to man and man's relation to God. Thus the *Song of Songs* became, both in Christian and Jewish literature, a source of mystical knowledge and experience, an expression of the essence of biblical faith: that man can indeed enter into union with God—his primordial aspiration. But this union is no mere fusion, a sinking in the nameless ocean of the Divine; it is a unity which creates love, a unity in which both God and man remain themselves and yet become fully one. As Saint Paul says: "He who is united to the Lord becomes one spirit with him" (*1 Cor* 6:17).

11. The first novelty of biblical faith consists, as we have seen, in its image of God. The second, essentially connected to this, is found in the image of man. The biblical account of creation speaks of the solitude of Adam, the first man, and God's decision to give him a helper. Of all other creatures, not one is capable of being the helper that man needs, even though he has assigned a name to all the wild beasts and birds and thus made them fully a part of his life. So God forms woman from the rib of man. Now Adam finds the helper that he needed: "This at last is bone of my bones and flesh of my flesh" (*Gen* 2:23). Here one might detect hints of ideas that are also found, for example, in the myth mentioned by Plato, according to which man was originally spherical, because he was complete in himself and self-sufficient. But as a punishment for pride, he was split in two by Zeus, so that now he longs for his other half, striving with all his being to possess it and thus regain his integrity. While the biblical narrative does not speak of punishment, the idea is certainly present that man is somehow incomplete, driven by nature to seek in another the part that can make him whole, the idea that only in communion with the opposite sex can he become "complete". The biblical account thus concludes with a prophecy about Adam: "Therefore a man leaves his father and his mother and cleaves to his wife and they become one flesh" (*Gen* 2:24).

Two aspects of this are important. First, *eros* is somehow rooted in man's very nature; Adam is a seeker, who "abandons his mother and father" in order to find woman; only together do the two represent complete humanity and become "one flesh". The second aspect is equally important. From the standpoint of creation, *eros* directs man towards marriage, to a bond which is unique and definitive; thus, and only thus, does it fulfil its deepest purpose. Corresponding to the image of a monotheistic God is monogamous marriage. Marriage based on exclusive and definitive love becomes the icon of the relationship between God and his people and vice versa. God's way of loving becomes the measure of human love. This close connection between *eros* and marriage in the Bible has practically no equivalent in extra-biblical literature.

Jesus Christ—The Incarnate Love of God

12. Though up to now we have been speaking mainly of the Old Testament, nevertheless the profound compenetration of the two Testaments as the one Scripture of the Christian faith has already become evident. The real novelty of the New Testament lies not so much in new ideas as in the figure of Christ himself, who gives flesh and blood to those concepts—an unprecedented realism. In the Old Testament, the novelty of the Bible did not consist merely in abstract notions but in God's unpredictable and in some sense unprecedented activity. This divine activity now takes on dramatic form when, in Jesus Christ, it is God himself who goes in search of the "stray sheep", a suffering and lost humanity. When Jesus speaks in his parables of the shepherd who goes after the lost sheep, of the woman who looks for the lost coin, of the father who goes to meet and embrace his prodigal son, these are no mere words: they constitute an explanation of his very being and activity. His death on the Cross is the culmination of that turning of God against himself in which he gives himself in order to raise man up and save him. This is love in its most radical form. By contemplating the pierced side of Christ (cf. 19:37), we can understand the starting-point of this Encyclical Letter: "God is love" (*1 Jn* 4:8). It is there that this truth can be contemplated. It is from there that our definition of love must begin. In this contemplation the Christian discovers the path along which his life and love must move.

13. Jesus gave this act of oblation an enduring presence through his institution of the Eucharist at the Last Supper. He anticipated his death and resurrection by giving his disciples, in the bread and wine, his very self, his body and blood as the new manna (cf. *Jn* 6:31-33). The ancient world had dimly perceived that man's real food—what truly nourishes him as man—is ultimately the *Logos*, eternal wisdom: this same *Logos* now truly becomes food for us—as love. The Eucharist draws us into Jesus' act of self-oblation. More than just statically receiving the incarnate *Logos*, we enter into the very dynamic of his self-giving. The imagery of marriage between God and Israel is now realized in a way previously inconceivable: it had meant standing in God's presence, but now it becomes union with God through sharing in Jesus' self-gift, sharing in his body and blood. The sacramental "mysticism", grounded in God's condescension towards us, operates at a radically different level and lifts us to far greater heights than anything that any human mystical elevation could ever accomplish.

14. Here we need to consider yet another aspect: this sacramental "mysticism" is social in character, for in sacramental communion I become one with the Lord, like all the other communicants. As Saint Paul says, "Because there is one bread, we who are many are one body, for we all partake of the one bread" (*1 Cor* 10:17). Union with Christ is also union with all those to whom he gives himself. I cannot possess Christ just for myself; I can belong to him only in union with all those who have become, or who will become, his own. Communion draws me out of myself towards him, and thus also towards unity with all Christians. We become "one body", completely joined in a single existence. Love of God and love of neighbour are now truly united: God incarnate draws us all to himself. We can thus understand how *agape* also became a term for the Eucharist: there God's own *agape* comes to us bodily, in order to continue his work in us and through us. Only by keeping in mind this Christological and sacramental basis can we correctly understand Jesus' teaching on love. The transition which he makes from the Law and the Prophets to the two-fold commandment of love of God and of neighbour, and his grounding the whole life of faith on this central precept, is not simply a matter of morality—something that could exist apart from and alongside faith in Christ and its sacramental re-actualization. Faith, worship and *ethos* are interwoven as a single reality which takes shape in our encounter with God's *agape*. Here the usual

contraposition between worship and ethics simply falls apart. "Worship" itself, Eucharistic communion, includes the reality both of being loved and of loving others in turn. A Eucharist which does not pass over into the concrete practice of love is intrinsically fragmented. Conversely, as we shall have to consider in greater detail below, the "commandment" of love is only possible because it is more than a requirement. Love can be "commanded" because it has first been given.

15. This principle is the starting-point for understanding the great parables of Jesus. The rich man (cf. *Lk* 16:19-31) begs from his place of torment that his brothers be informed about what happens to those who simply ignore the poor man in need. Jesus takes up this cry for help as a warning to help us return to the right path. The parable of the Good Samaritan (cf. *Lk* 10:25-37) offers two particularly important clarifications. Until that time, the concept of "neighbour" was understood as referring essentially to one's countrymen and to foreigners who had settled in the land of Israel; in other words, to the closely-knit community of a single country or people. This limit is now abolished. Anyone who needs me, and whom I can help, is my neighbour. The concept of "neighbour" is now universalized, yet it remains concrete. Despite being extended to all mankind, it is not reduced to a generic, abstract and undemanding expression of love, but calls for my own practical commitment here and now. The Church has the duty to interpret ever anew this relationship between near and far with regard to the actual daily life of her members. Lastly, we should especially mention the great parable of the Last Judgement (cf. *Mt* 25:31-46), in which love becomes the criterion for the definitive decision about a human life's worth or lack thereof. Jesus identifies himself with those in need, with the hungry, the thirsty, the stranger, the naked, the sick and those in prison. "As you did it to one of the least of these my brethren, you did it to me" (*Mt* 25:40). Love of God and love of neighbour have become one: in the least of the brethren we find Jesus himself, and in Jesus we find God.

Love of God and Love of Neighbour

16. Having reflected on the nature of love and its meaning in biblical faith, we are left with two questions concerning our own attitude: can we love God without seeing him? And can love be commanded? Against the double commandment of love these questions raise a double objection. No one has ever seen God, so how could we love him? Moreover, love cannot be commanded; it is ultimately a feeling that is either there or not, nor can it be produced by the will. Scripture seems to reinforce the first objection when it states: "If anyone says, 'I love God,' and hates his brother, he is a liar; for he who does not love his brother whom he has seen, cannot love God whom he has not seen" (1 *Jn* 4:20). But this text hardly excludes the love of God as something impossible. On the contrary, the whole context of the passage quoted from the *First Letter of John* shows that such love is explicitly demanded. The unbreakable bond between love of God and love of neighbour is emphasized. One is so closely connected to the other that to say that we love God becomes a lie if we are closed to our neighbour or hate him altogether. Saint John's words should rather be interpreted to mean that love of neighbour is a path that leads to the encounter with God, and that closing our eyes to our neighbour also blinds us to God.

17. True, no one has ever seen God as he is. And yet God is not totally invisible to us; he does not remain completely inaccessible. God loved us first, says the *Letter of John* quoted above (cf. 4:10), and this love of God has appeared in our midst. He has become visible in as much as he "has sent his only Son into the world, so that we might live through him" (1 *Jn* 4:9). God has made himself visible: in Jesus we are able to see the Father (cf. *Jn* 14:9). Indeed, God is visible in a number of ways. In the love-story recounted by the Bible, he comes towards us, he seeks to win our hearts, all the way to the Last Supper, to the piercing of his heart on the Cross, to his appearances after the Resurrection and to the great deeds by which, through the activity of the Apostles, he guided the nascent Church along its path. Nor has the

Lord been absent from subsequent Church history: he encounters us ever anew, in the men and women who reflect his presence, in his word, in the sacraments, and especially in the Eucharist. In the Church's Liturgy, in her prayer, in the living community of believers, we experience the love of God, we perceive his presence and we thus learn to recognize that presence in our daily lives. He has loved us first and he continues to do so; we too, then, can respond with love. God does not demand of us a feeling which we ourselves are incapable of producing. He loves us, he makes us see and experience his love, and since he has "loved us first", love can also blossom as a response within us.

In the gradual unfolding of this encounter, it is clearly revealed that love is not merely a sentiment. Sentiments come and go. A sentiment can be a marvellous first spark, but it is not the fullness of love. Earlier we spoke of the process of purification and maturation by which *eros* comes fully into its own, becomes love in the full meaning of the word. It is characteristic of mature love that it calls into play all man's potentialities; it engages the whole man, so to speak. Contact with the visible manifestations of God's love can awaken within us a feeling of joy born of the experience of being loved. But this encounter also engages our will and our intellect. Acknowledgment of the living God is one path towards love, and the "yes" of our will to his will unites our intellect, will and sentiments in the all- embracing act of love. But this process is always open-ended; love is never "finished" and complete; throughout life, it changes and matures, and thus remains faithful to itself. *Idem velle atque idem nolle*—to want the same thing, and to reject the same thing—was recognized by antiquity as the authentic content of love: the one becomes similar to the other, and this leads to a community of will and thought. The love-story between God and man consists in the very fact that this communion of will increases in a communion of thought and sentiment, and thus our will and God's will increasingly coincide: God's will is no longer for me an alien will, something imposed on me from without by the commandments, but it is now my own will, based on the realization that God is in fact more deeply present to me than I am to myself. Then self- abandonment to God increases and God becomes our joy (cf. *Ps* 73 [72]:23-28).

18. Love of neighbour is thus shown to be possible in the way proclaimed by the Bible, by Jesus. It consists in the very fact that, in God and with God, I love even the person whom I do not like or even know. This can only take place on the basis of an intimate encounter with God, an encounter which has become a communion of will, even affecting my feelings. Then I learn to look on this other person not simply with my eyes and my feelings, but from the perspective of Jesus Christ. His friend is my friend. Going beyond exterior appearances, I perceive in others an interior desire for a sign of love, of concern. This I can offer them not only through the organizations intended for such purposes, accepting it perhaps as a political necessity. Seeing with the eyes of Christ, I can give to others much more than their outward necessities; I can give them the look of love which they crave. Here we see the necessary interplay between love of God and love of neighbour which the *First Letter of John* speaks of with such insistence. If I have no contact whatsoever with God in my life, then I cannot see in the other anything more than the other, and I am incapable of seeing in him the image of God. But if in my life I fail completely to heed others, solely out of a desire to be "devout" and to perform my "religious duties", then my relationship with God will also grow arid. It becomes merely "proper", but loveless. Only my readiness to encounter my neighbour and to show him love makes me sensitive to God as well. Only if I serve my neighbour can my eyes be opened to what God does for me and how much he loves me. The saints—consider the example of Blessed Teresa of Calcutta—constantly renewed their capacity for love of neighbour from their encounter with the Eucharistic Lord, and conversely this encounter acquired its realism and depth in their service to others. Love of God

and love of neighbour are thus inseparable, they form a single commandment. But both live from the love of God who has loved us first. No longer is it a question, then, of a "commandment" imposed from without and calling for the impossible, but rather of a freely-bestowed experience of love from within, a love which by its very nature must then be shared with others. Love grows through love. Love is "divine" because it comes from God and unites us to God; through this unifying process it makes us a "we" which transcends our divisions and makes us one, until in the end God is "all in all" (*1 Cor* 15:28).

PART II

CARITAS

THE PRACTICE OF LOVE BY THE CHURCH AS A "COMMUNITY OF LOVE"

The Church's Charitable Activity as a Manifestation of Trinitarian Love

19. "If you see charity, you see the Trinity", wrote Saint Augustine. In the foregoing reflections, we have been able to focus our attention on the Pierced one (cf. *Jn* 19:37, *Zech* 12:10), recognizing the plan of the Father who, moved by love (cf. *Jn* 3:16), sent his only-begotten Son into the world to redeem man. By dying on the Cross— as Saint John tells us—Jesus "gave up his Spirit" (*Jn* 19:30), anticipating the gift of the Holy Spirit that he would make after his Resurrection (cf. *Jn* 20:22). This was to fulfil the promise of "rivers of living water" that would flow out of the hearts of believers, through the outpouring of the Spirit (cf. *Jn* 7:38-39). The Spirit, in fact, is that interior power which harmonizes their hearts with Christ's heart and moves them to love their brethren as Christ loved them, when he bent down to wash the feet of the disciples (cf. *Jn*

13:1-13) and above all when he gave his life for us (cf. *Jn* 13:1, 15:13).

The Spirit is also the energy which transforms the heart of the ecclesial community, so that it becomes a witness before the world to the love of the Father, who wishes to make humanity a single family in his Son. The entire activity of the Church is an expression of a love that seeks the integral good of man: it seeks his evangelization through Word and Sacrament, an undertaking that is often heroic in the way it is acted out in history; and it seeks to promote man in the various arenas of life and human activity. Love is therefore the service that the Church carries out in order to attend constantly to man's sufferings and his needs, including material needs. And this is the aspect, this *service of charity*, on which I want to focus in the second part of the Encyclical.

Charity as a Responsibility of the Church

20. Love of neighbour, grounded in the love of God, is first and foremost a responsibility for each individual member of the faithful, but it is also a responsibility for the entire ecclesial community at every level: from the local community to the particular Church and to the Church universal in its entirety. As a community, the Church must practise love. Love thus needs to be organized if it is to be an ordered service to the community. The awareness of this responsibility has had a constitutive relevance in the Church from the beginning: "All who believed were together and had all things in common; and they sold their possessions and goods and distributed them to all, as any had need" (*Acts* 2:44-5). In these words, Saint Luke provides a kind of definition of the Church, whose constitutive elements include fidelity to the "teaching of the Apostles", "communion" (*koinonia*), "the breaking of the bread" and "prayer" (cf. *Acts* 2:42). The element of "communion" (*koinonia*) is not initially defined, but appears concretely in the verses quoted above: it consists in the fact that believers hold all things in common and that among them, there is no longer any distinction between rich and poor (cf. also *Acts* 4:32-37). As the Church grew, this radical form of material communion

could not in fact be preserved. But its essential core remained: within the community of believers there can never be room for a poverty that denies anyone what is needed for a dignified life.

21. A decisive step in the difficult search for ways of putting this fundamental ecclesial principle into practice is illustrated in the choice of the seven, which marked the origin of the diaconal office (cf. *Acts* 6:5-6). In the early Church, in fact, with regard to the daily distribution to widows, a disparity had arisen between Hebrew speakers and Greek speakers. The Apostles, who had been entrusted primarily with "prayer" (the Eucharist and the liturgy) and the "ministry of the word", felt over-burdened by "serving tables", so they decided to reserve to themselves the principal duty and to designate for the other task, also necessary in the Church, a group of seven persons. Nor was this group to carry out a purely mechanical work of distribution: they were to be men "full of the Spirit and of wisdom" (cf. *Acts* 6:1-6). In other words, the social service which they were meant to provide was absolutely concrete, yet at the same time it was also a spiritual service; theirs was a truly spiritual office which carried out an essential responsibility of the Church, namely a well-ordered love of neighbour. With the formation of this group of seven, "*diaconia*"—the ministry of charity exercised in a communitarian, orderly way—became part of the fundamental structure of the Church.

22. As the years went by and the Church spread further afield, the exercise of charity became established as one of her essential activities, along with the administration of the sacraments and the proclamation of the word: love for widows and orphans, prisoners, and the sick and needy of every kind, is as essential to her as the ministry of the sacraments and preaching of the Gospel. The Church cannot neglect the service of charity any more than she can neglect the Sacraments and the Word. A few references will suffice to demonstrate this. Justin Martyr († *c.* 155) in speaking of the Christians' celebration of Sunday, also mentions their charitable activity, linked with the Eucharist as such. Those who are able make offerings in accordance with their means, each as he or she wishes; the Bishop in turn makes use of these to support orphans, widows, the sick and those who for other reasons find themselves in need, such as prisoners and foreigners. The great Christian writer Tertullian († after 220) relates how the pagans were struck by the Christians' concern for the needy of every sort. And when Ignatius of Antioch († *c.* 117) described the Church of Rome as "presiding in charity (*agape*)", we may assume that with this definition he also intended in some sense to express her concrete charitable activity.

23. Here it might be helpful to allude to the earliest legal structures associated with the service of charity in the Church. Towards the middle of the fourth century we see the development in Egypt of the "*diaconia*": the institution within each monastery responsible for all works of relief, that is to say, for the service of charity. By the sixth century this institution had evolved into a corporation with full juridical standing, which the civil authorities themselves entrusted with part of the grain for public distribution. In Egypt not only each monastery, but each individual Diocese eventually had its own *diaconia;* this institution then developed in both East and West. Pope Gregory the Great († 604) mentions the *diaconia* of Naples, while in Rome the *diaconiae* are documented from the seventh and eighth centuries. But charitable activity on behalf of the poor and suffering was naturally an essential part of the Church of Rome from the very beginning, based on the principles of Christian life given in the *Acts of the Apostles.* It found a vivid expression in the case of the deacon Lawrence († 258). The dramatic description of Lawrence's martyrdom was known to Saint Ambrose († 397) and it provides a fundamentally authentic picture of the saint. As the one responsible for the care of the poor in Rome, Lawrence had been given a period of time, after the capture of the Pope and of Lawrence's fellow deacons, to collect the treasures of the Church and hand them over to the civil authorities. He distributed to the poor whatever funds were available and then presented to the authorities the poor themselves as the real treasure of the Church. Whatever historical reliability one

attributes to these details, Lawrence has always remained present in the Church's memory as a great exponent of ecclesial charity.

24. A mention of the emperor Julian the Apostate († 363) can also show how essential the early Church considered the organized practice of charity. As a child of six years, Julian witnessed the assassination of his father, brother and other family members by the guards of the imperial palace; rightly or wrongly, he blamed this brutal act on the Emperor Constantius, who passed himself off as an outstanding Christian. The Christian faith was thus definitively discredited in his eyes. Upon becoming emperor, Julian decided to restore paganism, the ancient Roman religion, while reforming it in the hope of making it the driving force behind the empire. In this project he was amply inspired by Christianity. He established a hierarchy of metropolitans and priests who were to foster love of God and neighbour. In one of his letters, he wrote that the sole aspect of Christianity which had impressed him was the Church's charitable activity. He thus considered it essential for his new pagan religion that, alongside the system of the Church's charity, an equivalent activity of its own be established. According to him, this was the reason for the popularity of the "Galileans". They needed now to be imitated and outdone. In this way, then, the Emperor confirmed that charity was a decisive feature of the Christian community, the Church.

25. Thus far, two essential facts have emerged from our reflections:

a) The Church's deepest nature is expressed in her three-fold responsibility: of proclaiming the word of God (*kerygma-martyria*), celebrating the sacraments (*leitourgia*), and exercising the ministry of charity (*diakonia*). These duties presuppose each other and are inseparable. For the Church, charity is not a kind of welfare activity which could equally well be left to others, but is a part of her nature, an indispensable expression of her very being.

b) The Church is God's family in the world. In this family no one ought to go without the necessities of life. Yet at the same time *caritas-agape* extends beyond the frontiers of the Church. The parable of the Good Samaritan remains as a standard which imposes universal love towards the needy whom we encounter "by chance" (cf. *Lk* 10:31), whoever they may be. Without in any way detracting from this commandment of universal love, the Church also has a specific responsibility: within the ecclesial family no member should suffer through being in need. The teaching of the *Letter to the Galatians* is emphatic: "So then, as we have opportunity, let us do good to all, and especially to those who are of the household of faith" (6:10).

Justice and Charity

26. Since the nineteenth century, an objection has been raised to the Church's charitable activity, subsequently developed with particular insistence by Marxism: the poor, it is claimed, do not need charity but justice. Works of charity—almsgiving—are in effect a way for the rich to shirk their obligation to work for justice and a means of soothing their consciences, while preserving their own status and robbing the poor of their rights. Instead of contributing through individual works of charity to maintaining the *status quo*, we need to build a just social order in which all receive their share of the world's goods and no longer have to depend on charity. There is admittedly some truth to this argument, but also much that is mistaken. It is true that the pursuit of justice must be a fundamental norm of the State and that the aim of a just social order is to guarantee to each person, according to the principle of subsidiarity, his share of the community's goods. This has always been emphasized by Christian teaching on the State and by the Church's social doctrine. Historically, the issue of the just ordering of the collectivity had taken a new dimension with the industrialization of society in the nineteenth century. The rise of modern industry caused the old social structures to collapse, while the growth of a class of salaried workers provoked radical changes in the fabric of society. The relationship between capital and labour now became the decisive issue—an issue

which in that form was previously unknown. Capital and the means of production were now the new source of power which, concentrated in the hands of a few, led to the suppression of the rights of the working classes, against which they had to rebel.

27. It must be admitted that the Church's leadership was slow to realize that the issue of the just structuring of society needed to be approached in a new way. There were some pioneers, such as Bishop Ketteler of Mainz († 1877), and concrete needs were met by a growing number of groups, associations, leagues, federations and, in particular, by the new religious orders founded in the nineteenth century to combat poverty, disease and the need for better education. In 1891, the papal magisterium intervened with the Encyclical *Rerum Novarum* of Leo XIII. This was followed in 1931 by Pius XI's Encyclical *Quadragesimo Anno.* In 1961 Blessed John XXIII published the Encyclical *Mater et Magistra,* while Paul VI, in the Encyclical *Populorum Progressio* (1967) and in the Apostolic Letter *Octogesima Adveniens* (1971), insistently addressed the social problem, which had meanwhile become especially acute in Latin America. My great predecessor John Paul II left us a trilogy of social Encyclicals: *Laborem Exercens* (1981), *Sollicitudo Rei Socialis* (1987) and finally *Centesimus Annus* (1991). Faced with new situations and issues, Catholic social teaching thus gradually developed, and has now found a comprehensive presentation in the *Compendium of the Social Doctrine of the Church* published in 2004 by the Pontifical Council *Iustitia et Pax.* Marxism had seen world revolution and its preliminaries as the panacea for the social problem: revolution and the subsequent collectivization of the means of production, so it was claimed, would immediately change things for the better. This illusion has vanished. In today's complex situation, not least because of the growth of a globalized economy, the Church's social doctrine has become a set of fundamental guidelines offering approaches that are valid even beyond the confines of the Church: in the face of ongoing development these guidelines need to be addressed in the context of dialogue with all those seriously concerned for humanity and for the world in which we live.

28. In order to define more accurately the relationship between the necessary commitment to justice and the ministry of charity, two fundamental situations need to be considered:

a) The just ordering of society and the State is a central responsibility of politics. As Augustine once said, a State which is not governed according to justice would be just a bunch of thieves: *"Remota itaque iustitia quid sunt regna nisi magna latrocinia?"*. Fundamental to Christianity is the distinction between what belongs to Caesar and what belongs to God (cf. *Mt* 22:21), in other words, the distinction between Church and State, or, as the Second Vatican Council puts it, the autonomy of the temporal sphere. The State may not impose religion, yet it must guarantee religious freedom and harmony between the followers of different religions. For her part, the Church, as the social expression of Christian faith, has a proper independence and is structured on the basis of her faith as a community which the State must recognize. The two spheres are distinct, yet always interrelated.

Justice is both the aim and the intrinsic criterion of all politics. Politics is more than a mere mechanism for defining the rules of public life: its origin and its goal are found in justice, which by its very nature has to do with ethics. The State must inevitably face the question of how justice can be achieved here and now. But this presupposes an even more radical question: what is justice? The problem is one of practical reason; but if reason is to be exercised properly, it must undergo constant purification, since it can never be completely free of the danger of a certain ethical blindness caused by the dazzling effect of power and special interests.

Here politics and faith meet. Faith by its specific nature is an encounter with the living God—an encounter opening up new horizons extending beyond the sphere of reason. But it is also a purifying force for reason itself. From

God's standpoint, faith liberates reason from its blind spots and therefore helps it to be ever more fully itself. Faith enables reason to do its work more effectively and to see its proper object more clearly. This is where Catholic social doctrine has its place: it has no intention of giving the Church power over the State. Even less is it an attempt to impose on those who do not share the faith ways of thinking and modes of conduct proper to faith. Its aim is simply to help purify reason and to contribute, here and now, to the acknowledgment and attainment of what is just.

The Church's social teaching argues on the basis of reason and natural law, namely, on the basis of what is in accord with the nature of every human being. It recognizes that it is not the Church's responsibility to make this teaching prevail in political life. Rather, the Church wishes to help form consciences in political life and to stimulate greater insight into the authentic requirements of justice as well as greater readiness to act accordingly, even when this might involve conflict with situations of personal interest. Building a just social and civil order, wherein each person receives what is his or her due, is an essential task which every generation must take up anew. As a political task, this cannot be the Church's immediate responsibility. Yet, since it is also a most important human responsibility, the Church is duty-bound to offer, through the purification of reason and through ethical formation, her own specific contribution towards understanding the requirements of justice and achieving them politically.

The Church cannot and must not take upon herself the political battle to bring about the most just society possible. She cannot and must not replace the State. Yet at the same time she cannot and must not remain on the sidelines in the fight for justice. She has to play her part through rational argument and she has to reawaken the spiritual energy without which justice, which always demands sacrifice, cannot prevail and prosper. A just society must be the achievement of politics, not of the Church. Yet the promotion of justice through efforts to bring about openness of mind and will to the demands of the common good is something which concerns the Church deeply.

b) Love—*caritas*—will always prove necessary, even in the most just society. There is no ordering of the State so just that it can eliminate the need for a service of love. Whoever wants to eliminate love is preparing to eliminate man as such. There will always be suffering which cries out for consolation and help. There will always be loneliness. There will always be situations of material need where help in the form of concrete love of neighbour is indispensable. The State which would provide everything, absorbing everything into itself, would ultimately become a mere bureaucracy incapable of guaranteeing the very thing which the suffering person—every person—needs: namely, loving personal concern. We do not need a State which regulates and controls everything, but a State which, in accordance with the principle of subsidiarity, generously acknowledges and supports initiatives arising from the different social forces and combines spontaneity with closeness to those in need. The Church is one of those living forces: she is alive with the love enkindled by the Spirit of Christ. This love does not simply offer people material help, but refreshment and care for their souls, something which often is even more necessary than material support. In the end, the claim that just social structures would make works of charity superfluous masks a materialist conception of man: the mistaken notion that man can live "by bread alone" (*Mt* 4:4; cf. *Dt* 8:3)—a conviction that demeans man and ultimately disregards all that is specifically human.

29. We can now determine more precisely, in the life of the Church, the relationship between commitment to the just ordering of the State and society on the one hand, and organized charitable activity on the other. We have seen that the formation of just structures is not directly

the duty of the Church, but belongs to the world of politics, the sphere of the autonomous use of reason. The Church has an indirect duty here, in that she is called to contribute to the purification of reason and to the reawakening of those moral forces without which just structures are neither established nor prove effective in the long run.

The direct duty to work for a just ordering of society, on the other hand, is proper to the lay faithful. As citizens of the State, they are called to take part in public life in a personal capacity. So they cannot relinquish their participation "in the many different economic, social, legislative, administrative and cultural areas, which are intended to promote organically and institutionally the *common good*." The mission of the lay faithful is therefore to configure social life correctly, respecting its legitimate autonomy and cooperating with other citizens according to their respective competences and fulfilling their own responsibility. Even if the specific expressions of ecclesial charity can never be confused with the activity of the State, it still remains true that charity must animate the entire lives of the lay faithful and therefore also their political activity, lived as "social charity".

The Church's charitable organizations, on the other hand, constitute an *opus proprium,* a task agreeable to her, in which she does not cooperate collaterally, but acts as a subject with direct responsibility, doing what corresponds to her nature. The Church can never be exempted from practising charity as an organized activity of believers, and on the other hand, there will never be a situation where the charity of each individual Christian is unnecessary, because in addition to justice man needs, and will always need, love.

Thomas Merton: "Learning to Live"

Editors' Introduction

In an age where higher learning and the university system have come more to resemble a technical school preparing worker drones to occupy cubicles in multinational corporations than a place of profound thought and deep intellectual and spiritual reflection upon the meaning of life and the formation of the soul, Thomas Merton's essay "Learning to Live" may come as both a shock and a challenge to how you approach your education here at Seton Hall. In one of the oft quoted lines from this incredible essay, Merton exhorts his readers, "If I had a message to my contemporaries, I said, it is surely this: Be anything you like, be madmen, drunks and bastards of every shape and form, but at all costs avoid one thing: success."

Merton spent most of his adult life as a Roman Catholic Cistercian monk (more commonly called Trappists) and a priest. He found great similarity between his education at Columbia University, where he was trained to think and reflect through a core of courses not unlike the "Journey of Transformation" and its sequel, "Christianity and Culture in Dialogue," and his life as a cloistered contemplative monk. Eventually, toward the end of his life (he died suddenly in 1968 while on a trip to Asia), Merton lived as a hermit, separated from the rest of his fellow monks. Merton spent most of his day in prayer, study, and labor (the three pillars of all Christian monks) in a small cabin deep in the woods on the land owned by the monastery to which he was attached, The Abbey of Our Lady Gethsemane, in Trappist, Kentucky. It is about an hour's drive from nearby Louisville.

If there was ever a poster child for the journey of transformation, Merton is it. In many ways, his life story parallels the *Confessions* of St. Augustine. Merton's most famous book, *The Seven Storey Mountain* (an autobiography), is his personal version of Augustine's *Confessions*. In *The Seven Storey Mountain* Merton details how he went from living the life of a Bohemian, hedonistic, nonconformist, journalist, poet and novelist to the Christian hermit who practiced Zen Buddhist meditation. Merton studied the religions of the world with as much depth and determination as he did the Roman Catholic faith into which he was baptized (as a convert in his adult life) in November 1938. As a result of a life of prayer, study, and work, eventually Merton became one of the most powerful voices of conscience of the twentieth century, widely read by Catholics, Protestants, Jews, Buddhists, and atheists. Particularly through his social writings, Merton challenged the Catholic Church and modern society in general in relation to issues such as war (Merton was a pacifist), the use of technology (of which Merton was highly suspicious and worried about the negative and the numbing effects technology would have on the human spirit), on civil rights for African Americans and, ultimately, for the liberation of oppressed persons the world over. Merton was also one of the pioneers of what is now referred to as "interreligiosity." While there are some in the Catholic Church who would disagree with this claim,

Merton did indeed figure out how to be Christian (and thus Roman Catholic) "interreligiously." In his numerous correspondence, Merton refers to himself as a Catholic, a Quaker, a Buddhist, and a Sufi.

In the essay you are about to read, Merton sees the university as a place that provides many opportunities to plumb the depths of our being through the subject matter of the courses taught as part of the university curriculum. Merton writes that , in taking various courses, students can create for themselves the soul that will be their guiding light for the rest of their lives. Monks, Merton claims, are engaged in a similar process. He wrote, "A university, like a monastery, (and here I have medievalists to back me up, but presume that footnotes are not needed), is at once a microcosm and a paradise. Both monastery and university came into being in a civilization open to the sacred, that is to say in a civilization which paid a great deal of attention to what it considered to be its own primordial roots in a mythical and archetypal holy ground, a spiritual creation." In fact, monasteries have often been referred to as universities of the soul in the manuals that serve as the rule for living by which Christian monks of the Western and the Eastern Church guide and pattern their lives either in community or as solitary seekers after Truth and in pursuit of union with the Divine Presence.

Merton fully understood that when it comes to the journey of transformation that is the life of the intellect as much as it is the life of the soul, one simply does not know where the journey will or could end. Merton's journey of transformation ended tragically (but also joyfully in a strange sort of way), when on December 10, 1968, suddenly and somewhat providentially (for Merton had many premonitions that his death was near), he was accidentally electrocuted by the faulty wiring in a fan he touched as he was getting out of the shower while attending a conference for Asian, American, and European monks and nuns in Bangkok, Thailand. As you read through this, one of the best and most challenging of Merton's essays, please keep in mind what Merton writes within its pages: "The whole of life is learning to ignite without dependence on any specific external means, whether cloistered, Zenist, Tantric, psychedelic or what have you." The essay provides a good opportunity for you to ponder more deeply why you enrolled in a university, why Seton Hall in particular, and for what purpose you might use your education: To become a "successful" corporate drone in a cubical or in order to create the soul Merton references above and provide you with the deep values that will be your guide through the course of your life with all its joys and sufferings.

"Learning to Live"

• • •

Life consists in learning to live on one's own, spontaneous, freewheeling: to do this one must recognize what is one's own—be familiar and at home with oneself. This means basically learning who one is, and learning what one has to offer to the contemporary world, and then learning how to make that offering valid.

The purpose of education is to show a person how to define himself authentically and spontaneously in relation to his world—not to impose a prefabricated definition of the world, still less an arbitrary definition of the individual himself. The world is made up of the people who are fully alive in it: that is, of the people who can be themselves in it and can enter into a living and fruitful relationship with each other in it. The world is, therefore, more real in proportion as the people in it are able to be more fully and more humanly alive: that is to say, better able to make a lucid and conscious use of their freedom. Basically, this freedom must consist first of all in the capacity to choose their own lives, to find themselves on the deepest possible level. A superficial freedom to wander aimlessly here or there, to taste this or that, to make a choice of distractions (in Pascal's sense) is simply a sham. It claims to he a freedom of "choice" when it has evaded the basic task of discovering who it is that chooses. It is not free because it is unwilling to face the risk of self-discovery.

The function of a university is, then, first of all to help the student to discover himself: to recognize himself, and to identify who it is that chooses.

This description will be recognized at once as unconventional and, in fact, monastic. To put it in even more outrageous terms, the function of the university is to help men and women save their souls and, in so doing, to save their society: from what? From the hell of meaninglessness, of obsession, of complex artifice, of systematic lying, of criminal evasions and neglects, of self-destructive futilities.

It will be evident from my context that the business of saving one's soul means more than taking an imaginary object, "a soul," and entrusting it to some institutional bank for deposit until it is recovered with interest in heaven.

Speaking as a Christian existentialist, I mean by "soul" not simply the Aristotelian essential form but the mature personal identity, the creative fruit of an authentic and lucid search, the "self" that is found after other partial and exterior selves have been discarded as masks.

This metaphor must not mislead: this inner identity is not "found" as an object, but is the very self that finds. It is lost when it forgets to find, when it does not know how to seek, or when it seeks itself as an object. (Such a search is futile and self-contradictory.) Hence the paradox that it finds best when it stops seeking: and the graduate level of learning is when one learns to sit still and be what one has become, which is what one does not know and does not need to know. In the language of Sufism, the end of the ascetic life is *Rida,* satisfaction. Debts are paid (and they were largely imaginary). One no longer seeks something else. One no longer seeks to be told by another who one is. One no longer demands reassurance. But there is the whole infinite depth of *what is* remaining to be revealed. And it is not revealed to those who seek it from others.

Education in this sense means more than learning; and for such education, one is awarded no degree. One graduates by rising from the dead. Learning to be oneself means, therefore, learning to die in order to live. It means discovering in the ground of one's being a "self" which is ultimate and indestructible, which not only survives the destruction of all other more superficial selves but finds its identity affirmed and clarified by their destruction.

The inmost self is naked. Nakedness is not socially acceptable except in certain crude forms which can be commercialized without any effort of imagination (topless waitresses). Curiously, this cult of bodily nakedness is a veil and a distraction, a communion in futility, where all identities get lost in their nerve endings. Everybody claims to like it. Yet no one is really happy with it. It makes money.

Spiritual nakedness, on the other hand, is far too stark to be useful. It strips life down to the root where life and death are equal, and this is what nobody likes to look at. But it is where freedom really begins: the freedom that cannot be guaranteed by the death of somebody else. The point where you become free not to kill, not to exploit, not to destroy, not to compete, because you are no longer afraid of death or the devil or poverty or failure. If you discover this nakedness, you'd better keep it private. People don't like it. But can you keep it private? Once you are exposed . . . Society continues to do you the service of keeping you in disguises, not for your comfort, but for its own. It is quite willing to strip you of this or that outer skin (a stripping which is a normal ritual and which everybody enjoys). The final metaphysical stripping goes too far, unless you happen to be in Auschwitz.

If I say this description is "monastic," I do not necessarily mean "theological." The terms in which it has been stated here are open to interpretation on several levels: theologically, ascetically, liturgically, psychologically. Let's assume that this last is the more acceptable level for most readers. And let's assume that I am simply speaking from experience as one who, from a French lycée and an English public school, has traveled through various places of "learning" and has, in these, learned one thing above all: to keep on going. I have described the itinerary elsewhere, but perhaps a few new ideas may be added here. The journey went from Europe to America, from Cambridge to Columbia. At Columbia, having got the necessary degrees, I crossed the boundary that separates those who learn as students from those who learn as teachers. Then I went to teach English at a Catholic college (St. Bonaventure).* After which I went to be a novice in a Trappist monastery, where I also "learned" just enough

theology to renounce all desire to be a theologian. Here also (for I am still in Kentucky) I learned by teaching: not theology as such, but the more hazardous and less charted business of monastic education, which deals with the whole person in a situation of considerable ambiguity and hazard: the novice, the young monk who wants to become a contemplative and who is (you sooner or later discover) trapped both by the institution and by his own character in a situation where what he desperately wants beyond all else on earth will probably turn out to be impossible. Perhaps I would have been safer back at Columbia teaching elementary English composition. Fortunately, I am no longer teaching anybody anything.

On the basis of this experience, I can, anyhow, take up an ancient position that views monastery and university as having the same kind of function. After all, that is natural enough to one who could walk about Cambridge saying to himself, "Here were the Franciscans at one time, here the Dominicans, here—at my own college—Chaucer was perhaps a clerk."

A university, like a monastery (and here I have medievalists to back me up, but presume that footnotes are not needed), is at once a microcosm and a paradise. Both monastery and university came into being in a civilization open to the sacred, that is to say, in a civilization which paid a great deal of attention to what it considered to be its own primordial roots in a mythical and archetypal holy ground, a spiritual creation. Thus the *Logos or Ratio*** of both monastery and university is pretty much the same. Both are "schools," and they teach not so much by imparting information as by bringing the clerk (in the university) or the monk (in the monastery) to direct contact with "the beginning," the archetypal paradise world. This was often stated symbolically by treating the various disciplines of university and monastic life, respectively, as the "four rivers of paradise." At the same time, university and monastery tended sometimes to

---

* Now St Bonaventure University.
**[Purpose.]

be in very heated conflict, for though they both aimed at "participation" in and "experience" of the hidden and sacred values implanted in the "ground" and the "beginning," they arrived there by different means: the university by *scientia,* intellectual knowledge, and the monastery by *sapientia,* or mystical contemplation. (Of course, the monastery itself easily tended to concentrate on *scientia*—the science of the Scriptures—and in the university there could be mystics like Aquinas, Scotus, and Eckhart. So that in the end, in spite of all the fulminations of the Cistercian St. Bernard, a deeper *sapientia* came sometimes from schools than from monasteries.)

The point I am making here is this: far from suggesting that Columbia ought to return to the ideal of Chartres and concentrate on the trivium and quadrivium, I am insinuating that this archetypal approach, this "microcosm-paradise" type of sacred humanism, is basically personalistic.

I admit that all through the Middle Ages men were actively curious about the exact location of the earthly paradise. This curiosity was not absent from the mind of Columbus. The Pilgrim Fathers purified it a little, spiritualized it a little, but New England to them was a kind of paradise: and to make sure of a paradisic institution they created, of all things, Harvard. But the monks of the Middle Ages, and the clerks too, believed that the inner paradise was the ultimate ground of freedom in man's heart. To find it one had to travel, as Augustine had said, not with steps, but with yearnings. The journey was from man's "fallen" condition, in which he was not free not to be untrue to himself, to that original freedom in which, made in the image and likeness of God, he was no longer able to be untrue to himself. Hence, he recovered that nakedness of Adam which needed no fig leaves of law, of explanation, of justification, and no social garments of skins (Gregory of Nyssa). Paradise is simply the person, the self, but the radical self in its uninhibited feedom. The self no longer clothed with an ego.

One must not forget the dimension of relatedness to others. True freedom is openness, availability, the capacity for gift. But we must also remember that the difficult dialectic of fidelity to others in fidelity to oneself requires one to break through the veils of infidelity which, as individual egoists or as a selfish community, we set up to prevent ourselves from living in the truth.

This sacred humanism was, of course, abused and perverted by the sacred institution, and in the end monasticism, by a curious reversal that is so usual in the evolution of societies, identified the fig leaf with the paradise condition and insisted on the monk having at least enough of a self to serve the organization itself pressed into the service of more mundane interests. Freedom, then, consisted in blind obedience, and contemplation consisted in renouncing nakedness in favor of elaborate and ritual vestments. The "person" was only what he was in the eyes of the institution because the institution was, for all intents and purposes, Paradise, the domain of God, and indeed God himself. To be in Paradise, then, consisted in being defined by the paradisic community—or by Academe. Hence, the dogmatic absolutism for which the late Middle Ages are all too well known—and for which they are by no means uniquely responsible.

The original and authentic "paradise" idea, both in the monastery (*paradisus claustralis*)* and in the university, implied not simply a celestial store of theoretic ideas to which the Magistri and Doctores held the key, but the inner self of the student who, in discovering the ground of his own personality as it opened out into the center of all created being, found in himself the light and the wisdom of his Creator, a light and wisdom in which everything comprehensible could be comprehended and what was not comprehensible could nevertheless be grasped in the darkness of contemplation by a direct and existential contact.

Thus, the fruit of education, whether in the university (as for Eckhart) or in the monastery (as for Ruysbroeck) was the activation of that inmost center, that *scintilla animae,* that "apex" or "spark" which is a freedom beyond freedom, an identity beyond essence, a self beyond all ego, a

---

*[Cloistered paradise.]

being beyond the created realm, and a conscious-ness that transcends all division, all separation. To activate this spark is not to be, like Plotinus, "alone with the Alone," but to recognize the Alone which is by itself in everything because there is nothing that can be apart from It and yet nothing that can be with It, and nothing that can realize It. It can only realize itself. The "spark" which is my true self is the flash of the Absolute recognizing itself in me.

This realization at the apex is a coincidence of all opposites (as Nicholas of Cusa might say), a fusion of freedom and unfreedom, being and unbeing, life and death, self and nonself, man and God. The "spark" is not so much a stable entity which one finds but an event, an explo-sion which happens as all opposites clash with-in oneself. Then it is seen that the ego is not. It vanishes in its non-seeing when the flash of the spark alone is. When all things are reduced to the spark, who sees it? Who knows it? If you say "God," you are destroyed; and if you say no one, you will plunge into hell; and if you say I, you prove you are not even in the ballgame.

The purpose of all learning is to dispose man for this kind of event.

The purpose of various disciplines is to pro-vide ways or paths which lead to this capacity for ignition.

Obviously it would be a grave mistake to do, as some have done and still do, and declare that the only way is to be found in a cloister and the only discipline is asceticism or Zen sitting or, for that matter, turning on with a new drug. The whole of life is learning to ignite without depen-dence on any specific external means, whether cloistered, Zenist Tantric, psychedelic, or what have you. It is learning that the spark, being a flash at the apex and explosion of all freedoms, can never be subject to control or to enlighten-ment, can never be got by pressing buttons. A spark that goes off when you swallow something or stick yourself with something may be a fair-ly passable imitation of the real thing, but it is not the real thing. (I will not argue that it can-not teach you a great deal about the real thing.) In the same way a cloistered complacency—a

"peace" that is guaranteed only by getting out of the traffic, turning off the radio, and forgetting the world—is not by itself the real thing either.

The danger of education, I have found, is that it so easily confuses means with ends. Worse than that, it quite easily forgets both and devotes itself merely to the mass production of uneducated graduates—people literally unfit for anything ex-cept to take part in an elaborate and completely artificial charade which they and their contem-poraries have conspired to call "life."

A few years ago a man who was compiling a book entitled *Success* wrote and asked me to con-tribute a statement on how I got to be a success. I replied indignantly that I was not able to con-sider myself a success in any terms that had a meaning to me. I swore I had spent my life stren-uously avoiding success. If it so happened that I had once written a best seller, this was a pure accident, due to inattention and naïveté, and I would take very good care never to do the same again. If I had a message to my contemporaries, I said, it was surely this: Be anything you like, be madmen, drunks, and bastards of every shape and form, but at all costs avoid one thing: suc-cess. I heard no more from him and I am not aware that my reply was published with the oth-er testimonials.

Thus, I have undercut all hope of claiming that Columbia made me a success. On the con-trary, I believe I can thank Columbia, among so many other things, for having helped me learn the value of unsuccess. Columbia was for me a microcosm, a little world, where I exhausted my-self in time. Had I waited until after graduation, it would have been too late. During the few years in which I was there, I managed to do so many wrong things that I was ready to blow my mind. But fortunately I learned, in so doing, that this was good. I might have ended up on Madison Avenue if I hadn't. Instead of preparing me for one of those splendid jobs, Columbia cured me forever of wanting one. Instead of adapting me to the world downtown, Columbia did me the fa-vor of lobbing me half conscious into the Village, where I occasionally came to my senses and

where I continued to learn. I think I have sufficiently explained, elsewhere, how much I owed,
in this regard, to people like Mark Van Doren
(who lived around the corner from me in the
Village) and Joseph Wood Krutch (who became,
as I have become, a hermit). Such people taught
me to imitate not Rockefeller but Thoreau. Of
course, I am not trying to say that one has to be
Thoreau rather than Rockefeller, nor am I slyly
intimating that I have discovered a superior form
of resentment, an off-beat way of scoring on everybody by refusing to keep score.

What I am saying is this: the score is not
what matters. Life does not have to be regarded
as a game in which scores are kept and somebody wins. If you are too intent on winning,
will never enjoy playing. If you are too obsessed
with success, you will forget to live. If you have
learned only how to be a success, your life has
probably been wasted. If a university concentrates on producing successful people, it is lam-
entably failing in its obligation to society and to
the students themselves.

Now I know that even in the thirties, at
Columbia, the business of wanting to be a success was very much in the air. There was, in fact,
a scandal about the yearbook senior poll. The
man who was voted "most likely to succeed" was
accused of having doctored the results in his own
favor after a surreptitious deal with a yearbook
staff member who was voted "best dressed."
Incidentally, I was voted best writer. I was not accused of trickery, but everyone understood that
the vote, which had been between me and Hank
Liebermann, had been decided by my fraternity
brothers. (Incidentally, whatever became of the
man "most likely to succeed"?)

In any case, no one really cared. Since that
time many of my classmates have attained to
eminence with all its joys and all its sorrows, and
the ones I have seen since then are marked by
the signature of anguish. So am I. I do not claim
exemption. Yet I never had the feeling that our
alma mater just wanted us to become well-paid
operators, or to break our necks to keep on the
front pages of the *Times*. On the contrary—maybe this is a delusion, but if it is a delusion it is a

salutary one—I always felt at Columbia that people around me, half amused and perhaps at times
half incredulous, were happy to let me be myself.
(I add that I seldom felt this way at Cambridge.)
The thing I always liked best about Columbia was
the sense that the university was on the whole
glad to turn me loose in its library, its classrooms,
and among its distinguished faculty, and let me
make what I liked out of it all. I did. And I ended
up by being turned on like a pinball machine
by Blake, Thomas Aquinas, Augustine, Eckhart,
Coomaraswamy, Traherne, Hopkins, Maritain,
and the sacraments of the Catholic Church. After
which I came to the monastery in which (this
is public knowledge) I have continued to be the
same kind of maverick and have, in fact, ended
as a hermit who is also fully identified with the
peace movement, with Zen, with a group of Latin
American hippie poets, etc., etc.

The least of the work of learning is done in
classrooms. I can remember scores of incidents,
remarks, happenings, encounters that took place
all over the campus and sometimes far from
the campus: small bursts of light that pointed
out my way in the dark of my own identity. For
instance, Mark Van Doren saying to me as we
crossed Amsterdam Avenue: "Well, if you have a
vocation to the monastic life, it will not be possible for you to decide not to enter" (or words to
that effect). I grasped at once the existential truth
of this statement.

One other scene, much later on. A room in
Butler Hall, over-looking some campus buildings.
Daisetz Suzuki, with his great bushy eyebrows
and the hearing aid that aids nothing. Mihoko,
his beautiful secretary, has to repeat everything.
She is making tea. Tea ceremony, but a most unconventional one, for there are no rites and no
rules. I drink my tea as reverently and attentively
as I can. She goes into the other room. Suzuki, as
if waiting for her to go, hastily picks up his cup
and drains it.

It was at once as if nothing at all had happened and as if the roof had flown off the building. But in reality nothing had happened. A very
very old deaf Zen man with bushy eyebrows had
drunk a cup of tea, as though with the complete

wakefulness of a child and as though at the same time declaring with utter finality: "This is not important!"

The function of a university is to teach a man how to drink tea, not because anything is important, but because it is usual to drink tea, or, for that matter, anything else under the sun. And whatever you do, every act, however small, can teach you everything—provided you see who it is that is acting.